HANDBOOKS IN OPERATIONS RESEARCH
AND MANAGEMENT SCIENCE
VOLUME 3

Handbooks in Operations Research and Management Science

Editors

G.L. Nemhauser
Georgia Institute of Technology

A.H.G. Rinnooy Kan
Erasmus University Rotterdam

Volume 3

NORTH-HOLLAND
AMSTERDAM · LONDON · NEW YORK · TOKYO

Computing

Edited by

E.G. Coffman, Jr.
AT&T Bell Laboratories

J.K. Lenstra
Eindhoven University of Technology
CWI, Amsterdam

A.H.G. Rinnooy Kan
Erasmus University Rotterdam

1992
NORTH-HOLLAND
AMSTERDAM·LONDON·NEW YORK·TOKYO

ELSEVIER SCIENCE PUBLISHERS B.V.

P.O. Box 211, 1000 AE Amsterdam, The Netherlands

Library of Congress Cataloging-in-Publication Data

Computing / edited by E.G. Coffman, Jr., J.K. Lenstra, A.H.G. Rinnooy
Kan.
    p.   cm. -- (Handbooks in operations research and management
science ; v. 3)
  Includes bibliographical references and index.
  ISBN 0-444-88097-6 (alk. paper)
  1. Computer science. 2. Operations research.   I. Coffman, E. G.
(Edward Grady), 1934-   . II. Lenstra, J. K. III. Rinnooy Kan, A.
H. G., 1949-   . IV. Series.
QA76.C5822 1992
003'.3--dc20   92-16696
                                                             CIP

ISBN: 0 444 88097 6

Transferred to digital print, 2008
Printed and bound by CPI Antony Rowe, Eastbourne

Preface

The origins of computing and operations research as modern scientific disciplines can both be traced back some 45 years. This is not entirely coincidental, since both may be looked upon as outcomes of the technological advances of the second world war. In spite of several notable exceptions, these disciplines developed largely along separate lines in the first 25 years of growth. To be sure, operations research has always been a principal computer user, but in this respect it differed little from other scientific disciplines and broad application areas in business and industry. It has only been in the last 20 years that the two disciplines have grown hand in hand, creating a permanent bond in academia and industry. Students in these fields soon learn, in overlapping courses of study, that many of the leading contributors in one field are equally well known for major contributions in the other.

Nowhere is the symbiotic relationship between operations research and computer science more evident than in the design and analysis of algorithms, often called algorithmics, which lies at the heart of both disciplines. Classical problems in operations research formed the basis of many of the fundamental algorithms used as prototypes in the theory of algorithms and complexity. The platform for this theory also consisted of mathematical tools in applied probability and combinatorics that were supplied by operations researchers. In their turn, computer scientists have discovered more efficient algorithms for operations research problems, quite often by introducing novel techniques for structuring information. Of equal importance to operations research has been the general methodology developed by computer scientists for the design and analysis of numerical and combinatorial algorithms, and for identifying the inherent complexity of computational problems. As a result, the study of algorithmics in this volume has become an essential part of optimization, the subject of Volume 1 of this series, and of the computations that accompany stochastic modeling, the subject of Volume 2 of this series.

The chapters in this volume can be grouped into three parts. We have already commented on the material of Part II, which covers algorithmics. Chapters 6–9 break this subject down into matrix computations, fundamental algorithms and data structures, design and analysis of efficient algorithms, and computational complexity.

The study of algorithmics is preceded in Part I by an introductory course in the design and operation of computers and computer systems. Chapters 1–5 comprise a standard decomposition into computer hardware, programming languages, operating systems, databases, and software engineering. The reader might argue that much of this material is not essential to the computer user, any more than an understanding of internal combustion engines is needed by drivers of automobiles. Yet a knowledge of basic principles can prove very useful in appreciating the potential and limitations of computer systems, and in coping with unusual problems that arise in applications. Conveying this knowledge along with perspectives on the history and future of computers is the burden of Part I.

Part III brings out the relation between computer systems and operations research applications. Chapter 10 reviews the use of stochastic models in computer system performance evaluation. In representing computer systems as case studies in operations research, it forms another link with Volume 2. Chapters 11 and 12 investigate the computer's role in the problem-solving process. Chapter 11 concerns one of the central methodologies of operations research: mathematical programming. During four decades of development, mathematical programming systems have matured greatly, thereby providing an active meeting ground for computer science and operations research. Chapter 12 studies user interfaces, i.e., the hardware, languages, and software packages designed to facilitate the interactive use of computers. The chapter discusses techniques for enhancing expressiveness in user–computer communication and for designing systems that help the user acquire insights into problem structures.

This volume was designed and written for use in the operations research and management science community. Apart from the background provided by Chapters 1–5, the emphasis is on the computational tools, algorithms, languages, and systems that assist the problem solver. This objective explains the selection of material and, in particular, the omission of material on the mathematical foundations of computing, e.g., the theories of automata, recursive functions, and formal languages. There are several other topics in computer science that have been omitted, either because they were not yet in vogue or because their impact on operations research was not yet significant when the book was designed. The most prominent example is the area of artificial intelligence, knowledge-based systems and computational learning. Another example is computational geometry; however, a chapter on this subject will be included in Volume 5 of this series.

We are pleased to express our gratitude to everyone who contributed to the realization of this volume. Many thanks are due to the authors, most of whom are willing to contribute to a handbook series which is only peripheral to their own area of interest. We are also grateful to Jan van Leeuwen, George Nemhauser and David Shmoys for their help and suggestions throughout the project, and to a number of other colleagues, who reviewed individual chapters and have to remain unnamed.

E.G. Coffman, Jr.
J.K. Lenstra
A.H.G. Rinnooy Kan

Contents

E.G. Coffman et al., Eds., *Handbooks in OR & MS, Vol. 3*

Chapter 1

Computer Systems – Past, Present & Future

Henk J. Sips

Department of Applied Physics, Delft University of Technology, Lorentzweg 1,
2628 CJ Delft, The Netherlands

1. Introduction

Historically, there has been a wide variation in the improvements introduced by new devices for helping humans perform basic tasks. For example, with walking speed as a basis of comparison, the approximate 200-fold increase in transportation speed brought about by airplanes is far more impressive than the five-fold increase created by bicycles. In these terms, computers outrival most other devices. For instance, consider the multiplication of two nine digit numbers. By hand, this takes about 10 minutes of time by an average person (try it!). Current, fast computers can perform such a multiplication in 100 nanoseconds (10^{-9} seconds). This implies a speed improvement of 10 orders of magnitude, an increase so large that it revolutionizes the applications in which calculations and, in a more general sense, data processing tasks, play an important role. The most astonishing fact is that this improvement in technology required a time span of only 40 years.

However, the past few decades have been no more than an acceleration of a development that began centuries ago. This chapter traces the history of computer systems from its origins to the current state of the art, and concludes with a perspective on future computer systems. Computer systems are regarded here as a composite of central processing units, storage devices, peripheral equipment, and basic system software. The relationships among these components are discussed as well as the factors that have influenced their design.

2. A bit of history

The modern computer was not a single invention. Rather it has resulted from the spread of ideas across the disciplinary boundaries of mathematics, physics, mechanical engineering, and electrical engineering. Below, some of the more important developments leading to the current state of computer technology are sketched. As will be seen, the implementation of well understood principles of operation has occasionally had to wait many years for the required technological breakthroughs to materialize.

2.1. Prelude

The only technology available before the 19th century was the mechanical one. The first calculating aids were the counting frame (abacus) and counting tables [Husky & Husky, 1976], dating as far back as 500 BC. The development of modern calculating machines only started in the 17th century. Two well-known scientists of that time were involved, Pascal and Leibnitz. Pascal developed a two-operations (addition and subtraction) machine in 1642 and Leibnitz a four-operations machine in 1671 that included multiplication and division. These machines were true mechanical calculators. The technology of these machines eventually led to the class of mechanical desk calculators, in use until a few decades ago, when they were replaced by electromechanical calculators and, from 1975 onwards, by all-electronic calculators (such as the common pocket calculator).

Early calculators could perform only a single operation at a time, but not a programmable sequence of operations. However, at that time machines also existed, made for completely different purposes than calculating, for which sequences of actions could be set up in advance. These sequences can be considered as a program, which controlled those machines automatically, i.e., without human intervention.

Two developments are worth mentioning, as they form the prelude of the stored program concept to be discussed later on. The first is that of mechanical musical instruments or automatophones. The first historically documented automatophone dates back to the 9th century in Baghdad, where three brothers constructed an automatophone whose 'brain' was a revolving cylinder with pegs [Sadie, 1984]. This technique of revolving cylinders was also applied in the 16th and 17th centuries to carillons placed in clock towers and to the first barrel organs in the 18th century. The second development is the use of punched cards in 18th century weaving machines that produced fabrics with complicated patterns. The punched cards defined the patterns and could be connected to each other to form a chain of varying patterns.

The Jacquard punched-card controlling mechanism inspired Charles Babbage in 1833 in the design of the Analytical Engine [Goldstine, 1972; Wilkes, 1956]. Although the Analytical Engine was never completed, its design is of importance because it introduced the concept of a stored program for controlling a calculating engine.

Another important development was the use of punched cards to store and automatically process the enormous amounts of data involved in the 1890 census in the USA. Herman Hollerith developed a system in which information such as age, sex, etc. could be stored on a punched card. After all the cards had been gathered, an automatic electromechanical machine was used to tabulate the appropriate data. This tabulating machine became a great success.

In fact, the development was the birth of what we now call the data processing field. Hollerith set up his own company, the Tabulating Machine Company, in 1889. After consolidation with two other companies this company became what is now known as the IBM (International Business Machines) corporation.

Besides technological advancements, there was the progress in mathematics needed to provide the proper foundations of computing systems. The early work of George Boole [1854] showed that logic could be reduced to a simple algebraic system (Boolean algebra). His work remained a curiosity until Whitehead and Russell's *Principia Mathematica* in 1910–13. Later, formal logic resulted in the revolutionary results of Gödel and provided the basis for the work of Turing and many others. In 1936 Turing published a paper [Turing, 1936] that forms a theoretical basis for computing machines. He stated that for every effectively computable problem it is possible to construct a machine to solve that problem. He described this machine, later called the Turing machine, in mechanical terms. This work did not immediately result in an actual machine, but has influenced our perception of the essentials of computing systems. For a more detailed discussion on this subject the reader is referred to Harel [1991].

2.2. Analog computers

An important distinction in computer systems is the difference between *analog* and *digital* computing. The use of analog computers predated the use of digital computers. In an analog computer, the dependent variables are represented by physical quantities such as current, voltage, number of rotations per second, and appear in continuous form. The history of analog computing devices started with the invention of the slide rule, in which the scale length is the physical analog of numbers to a logarithmic base [Husky & Husky, 1976]. At the beginning of the 19th century the planimeter, a form of mechanical integrator, was developed. The concept of a differential analyzer was originated by W. Thomson (later Lord Kelvin), who described a harmonic analyzer that used an improved mechanical integrator, to solve a system of differential equations [Thomson, 1876].

The first successful mechanical differential analyzer was constructed by Vannevar Bush [1931]. In fact, analog computers were the first tools in history to make a considerable reduction of problem calculation times possible. These mechanical differential analyzers improved calculation speeds by a factor of 50 as compared to a skilled mathematician [Goldstine, 1972]. However, the mechanical nature of those differential analyzers made them very inflexible, leading to large problem set-up times. After World War II all mechanical components were gradually replaced by electronic components.

Later, it was recognized that analog and digital computers each had their specific advantages. To see this, one must realize that in order to compute it is necessary for a machine to provide components that can perform the basic operations of mathematics. These basic operations are usually understood to be the four operations: addition, subtraction, multiplication, and division. Now, addition and subtraction are easily implemented in analog computers, but multiplication and division are much more cumbersome. On the other hand, the analog computer has an unusual basic operation: integration. Solutions to problems that involve integration can be easily implemented on analog computers, while in digital computers integration must be approximated by numerical methods. To have the advantages of both worlds, the analog and digital computer were combined in a hybrid computer, yielding a very powerful simulation for dynamical systems [Bekey & Karplus, 1968].

In the 1970s the digital computer took over, except for special cases where high speed is mandatory. Nowadays some interest in analog computers as special-purpose computers has returned (see Section 5.5.3 on neural networks).

2.3. Digital computers

In 1944 Howard Aiken completed an automatic calculating machine at Harvard University, called the 'Automatic Sequence Controlled Calculator', or Mark I, based on the principles developed by Hollerith and co-workers. It was to be the first fully implemented general-purpose automatic digital calculator. When designing the machine, Aiken estimated that it could perform a multiplication 100 times faster than a mechanical calculator. Eventually, it turned out that the machine was only three to five times faster than a mechanical calculator. The main reason for this was the relatively slow electromechanical nature of the machine's components (relays).

In 1943 John Mauchly and J. Presper Eckert started work on the first completely electronic computer. This machine, called the ENIAC (Electronic Numerical Integrator and Calculator), was completed in 1946. The U.S. Defense Department funded this project, because they needed a device that could speed up the process of calculating the trajectories of shells and bombs. The multiplication operation largely determined the total time to produce such tables. For a typical projectile trajectory 750 multiplications were required [Goldstine, 1972]. A cannon needed about 2000–4000 trajectories to be calculated, which took 30 days with an analog computer and 180 days on the ASCC Mark I. This clearly was too long. The ENIAC proved to be 500 times faster than the ASCC Mark I, a major improvement.

During the construction of the ENIAC, John von Neumann joined the project. Although the ENIAC was a major step forward, the design had many shortcomings. It lacked a large storage capacity, and programming was implemented by means of plugged wires that connected the machine components. During the discussions on improved designs, John von Neumann prepared a manuscript called 'First draft of a report on the EDVAC' [Stern, 1981; Goldstine, 1972], in which the concepts of the new machine were laid down. The report was never completed, but it soon became widely known. The concepts put forward in the draft strongly influenced the development of the computers that followed and formed the basis of modern digital computers.

Because of its unfinished status, the draft created disputes about who was to receive credit for what. Still, von Neumann's name has been definitively attached to current computer architectures.

The main contribution of the EDVAC design proposal was that a computer could be thought of as consisting of five parts: a central arithmetic unit, a central control unit, memory, and input and output units. The last two units were for transferring information to and from outside recording media. A second important observation was that 'Conceptually we have. . . two different forms of memory: storage of numbers and storage of orders. If, however, the orders to the machine are reduced to a numerical code and if the machine can in some fashion distinguish a number from an order, the memory organ can be used to store both numbers and orders' [Burks, Goldstine & von Neumann, 1946]. The central-memory concept by which storage addresses refer to both *instructions* (orders) and *operands* (numbers) was thus defined.

The value of von Neumann's contribution is confirmed by the fact that the large majority of computer systems today can still be modeled according to the same basic principles.

2.4. *Programming digital computers*

So far nothing has been said about programming computer systems. The reason is simple. In the early days, very little was known about general concepts of programming digital computers. The ENIAC program consists of a set of plugwires to connect the machine components, which is a very error prone and inflexible way to program a computer. The ASCC had a punched-tape sequence as its program. It soon became clear that a more structured way of thinking about programs was needed. The first observation was that it was wasteful to duplicate pieces of the program that performed identical, frequently used functions. Eckert and Mauchly envisioned in 1945 some sort of 'subsidiary routines' later called "subroutines" in a progress report on the EDVAC. In the same year Turing also posed the need of some "sort of library". The first actual subroutine library appeared on an English machine (the EDSAC) in 1949.

The first *assembler*-like systems emerged at the beginning of the 1950s. Assemblers use mnemonic codes in a symbolic representation of operations and operand addresses. Assembler programming languages relieved some of the burdens of programming computers, but they were still a long way from achieving a machine-independent language similar to those with which humans were accustomed to describe algorithms. In 1954 Backus and Herrick posed a 'vital question': 'Can a machine translate a sufficiently rich mathematical language into a sufficiently economical machine program at sufficiently low cost to make the whole affair feasible?' [Bashe, Johnson, Palmer & Pugh, 1986]. The FORTRAN programming language was an initial response to this question. The basic features of this language (such as the 'DO' concept) were established by John Backus and his colleagues in a preliminary report for the IBM 704 project. The first compiler was shipped in 1957. FORTRAN was intended for scientific applications and lacked a number of features needed for business applications. This need was fulfilled by the COBOL language, the specifications of which were established in 1960.

Many, more elegant languages and programming paradigms have followed FORTRAN and COBOL. In fact, it is currently a fruitful area of research in the computer science community. Applied to modern computer architectures (see Section 5), the original question of Backus and Herwick remains to be fully answered. However, the importance of the first step from an assembler to a high-level language can be measured by the observation that FORTRAN (in an upgraded form) is still a frequently used language.

3. The basic computer structure

3.1. Building blocks

Although the structure of computer systems can be defined in terms of von Neumann's basic units, this structure does not give an explicit answer to the question: what sort of building blocks (circuits) and how many of them do we need to build a computer? Let us explore this a little further. A computer must be able to compute functions, either logical or arithmetical ones. Recall that these functions can be described by expressions in Boolean algebra, and are thus independent of any implementation.

All functions in the Boolean algebra can be expressed in terms of only two extremely simple logical operators: the AND operator and the NOT operator (or the OR and the NOT operators), also present in any standard programming language. If we can make two hardware components that can perform these operations, then all we need are a sufficient number of these components and the wires to interconnect them. In practice, the realization of such components is indeed very simple; a circuit with a few transistors can perform the task.

From the basic components building blocks can be constructed that can compute the required functions and can transform a set of input values to a set of output values. To control the proper order of the computations, the input and output values need to be captured during a certain time interval by memory elements. The contents of all the memory elements in the system constitute the *state* of the system. The state of the system changes every time computed values are stored in memory elements. Unfortunately, functions dependent on time cannot be properly described in Boolean algebra. A formulation of the system dynamics is required, one that can define the ordering of operations in the system.

Fortunately, we can enforce a total time ordering on the system, such that the state of the system changes only at certain events in time. This assumption does not impose serious restrictions on the model of the machine. In fact, almost all computing systems have this mode of operation. The device that generates the sequence of timing signals is usually called the *clock* of the system.

There is, however, another point to decide on, namely what should be implemented in hardware and what in the program (software) controlling that hardware. For a number of operations there is a possibility of exchanging the hardware for the software, leading to the question of the types and multiplicity of building blocks needed to build a computing system. We shall try to reason about this with a model of a computing machine for performing multiplication. Multiplication can be performed by first forming partial products followed by a summation of these partial products, e.g., $58 \times 63 = (58 \times 3) + (58 \times 60) = 174 + 3480 = 3654$. Suppose our machine has hardware building blocks available that can add two numbers. One way to solve this problem is to take one such building block and use it in a repetitive way to obtain the result of the summation (Figure 1a). At each clock cycle, a new number is entered into the addition component and added to the previously calculated result. Clearly, the total summation will take N steps. Another way to solve this problem is to take multiple-addition building blocks and interconnect them as shown in Figure 1b. We then need $N - 1$ building blocks and the summation is performed in $\log_2 N$ steps. From this example, it can be deduced that in implementing certain arithmetic or logic functions, we can have different choices with respect to space (number of building blocks) and to time (number of steps).

How should we decide on the available alternatives? In fact, this strongly depends on our objectives and relates to the cost of constructing a system. This cost can be evaluated if we have an applicable cost function. This cost function is not only dependent on the technology of the components constituting the building blocks, but also on the characteristics of the algorithm.

If we had only a single basic operation, such as summation, to deal with, decisions would be easy. Unfortunately, a typical computer system has a mix of basic algorithms and functions, which sometimes share building blocks. Also, weighting component cost and execution times is a subjective matter, reflecting what a designer of a computing system considers important. Although subjective, in actual designs this trade-off is being made, sometimes based on explicit cost criteria, but very often also in an implicit way through a mix of design constraints and marketing considerations.

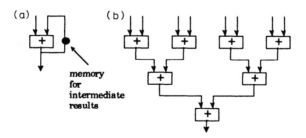

Fig. 1. Implementation alternatives for summation.

In general, these design trade-offs have the following consequences: if we have an expensive technology, we choose few components and many time steps, whereas if we have a cheap technology, we choose many components and few steps. This change in technology is perfectly reflected by the various ways of implementing the multiplication operation; early computers were built with expensive components and serialized the operation, while modern computers have increased speed through parallelization of the operation.

The complexity, in terms of cost functions, of hardware implementations that fit on a single chip is currently a popular research subject among theoretical computer scientists. One tries to find a lower bound on a space (area)/time cost function for a given computation and to find algorithms whose cost function approximates this bound [Ullman, 1984]. Thus far, this work has not had a serious impact on computer design, but it has been valuable in revealing some of the limitations in the hardware implementations of functions.

3.2. Basic units

Although computers come in an endless variety and complexity, if enough abstraction is taken, the basic components and their methods of operation are still essentially the same as in the days of von Neumann's EDVAC proposal. Conceptually, we have four components (see Figure 2): a *main memory*, a *control unit*, an *arithmetic/logic* unit, and an *input/output* (I/O) unit. Input and output are combined, for they exhibit a similar type of behavior. The combination of arithmetic/logic and control unit is often referred to as the *Central Processing Unit* (CPU).

The units are interconnected by means of a so-called *datapath* (sometimes called a *bus*), which is nothing more than a bunch of wires to transfer data from one unit to the other. Not every computer system contains a single datapath. There might be many such datapaths to speed up the transfer of data.

The *instructions* and *operands* (data to be operated upon) of a program reside in *main memory*. The main memory of a computer is commonly organized as a matrix of one-bit storage places. A *row* in this matrix is called a *word*, or alternatively a *storage location*. Usually, all bits in a row can be

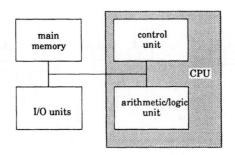

Fig. 2. Basic computer structure.

accessed simultaneously, by providing a row address or a *memory address*. The set of row addresses is called the *memory address space*. Often in actual machines, instruction and operand lengths match the number of bits in a memory location, or a small multiple of them.

Instructions are fetched and decoded by the *control unit* and the appropriate actions on the specified operands are effected. The action repertoire of a computer system is defined by the *instruction set* of that computer. An instruction usually consists of two fields: an *operation specification* field and an *operand specification* field, each occupying a number of bit positions in an instruction. The operation specification field specifies the type of action to be performed by the arithmetic/logic unit or control unit. Typical actions are the transfer of data between computer components or operations on certain operands (e.g., add, multiply). Each action is given a specific bit pattern and this bit pattern is used by the control unit to determine the required action. The operand specification part tells the control unit where to get the input operand(s) and where to store the result. Operands can be obtained from the main memory, but also from other available memory locations or *registers* residing in the arithmetic/logic unit. The same holds for the results. The reason for having memory locations available outside the main memory unit is motivated by efficiency. Access to a nearby register is faster than access to main memory. Repetitive computations can be performed faster by storing intermediate results in registers (see also the example in Figure 1a).

Operands themselves are operated upon according to prescribed formats. Most computers have fixed formats for data types like *integers* and *floating point* numbers. We call these data types *built-in data types*. If other formats are required in programs, operations on these data formats must be emulated by software. The price paid is inevitably a slowdown in execution speed.

Although built-in data types have a fixed format within a machine, in the past manufacturers have chosen different standards for their machines. This can cause portability problems of programs; that is problems in modifying programs working on one machine so that they can be made to work on another. To solve this problem, the IEEE (Institute of Electrical and Electronics Engineers) has proposed a standard for floating-point numbers [IEEE, 1985], which has been adopted by most microprocessor manufacturers. However, some major manufacturers still have their own standard.

In addition to the specifications of operation and operand, a third specification is necessary, namely of where to locate the next instruction. Most programs are written as a linear sequence of instructions. Therefore, most machines implicitly assume that the next instruction to be executed in a program resides in the next memory location. In these cases, the address of the next instruction is obtained by adding one to the *program counter*, which contains the address of the current instruction. In other cases, when it is desirable to break the linear flow of instructions, *branching* instructions are used. In these instructions the operand specification field specifies the next instruction address, which is to be placed into the program counter.

It is convenient to divide the instructions into classes that describe their generic behaviour. A common classification is

- data processing instructions,
- data movement instructions,
- control flow instructions.

Data processing instructions perform arithmetic or logic operations on operands. Data movement instructions merely move data around, e.g., between memory and the CPU or to and from external devices. Control instructions offer, among other things, the conditional possibility to deviate from the default next instruction fetch path. As an example, the next instruction to be executed can be made to depend on whether the number in some operand register is positive, negative, or zero.

In addition to the above categories, most computer systems have some additional instructions for various purposes. These instructions are not directly used by application programs, but are used by system programs such as parts of the operating system (see Chapter 3 of this volume).

3.3. Computer architecture and organization

The instruction set of a computer is one of the most important architectural features of a computer system. Computer manufacturers have their proprietary instruction sets for their range of machines. They can find a way in the architectural features of their systems to be different from the competition and to protect their investment. In reality, however, instruction sets are not that different, since many machines share equal to almost equal types of instructions. Still, there is no trend or pressure to obtain uniformity for the larger systems. On the other hand, in personal computers we can observe a certain forced uniformity. Since only a few manufacturers of personal computers can afford to design and build their own microprocessor, most of them adopt one from an independent manufacturer.

An useful distinction is that between *computer architecture* and *computer organization* [Stallings, 1990]. The architecture of a computer system comprises those attributes of the system that can be reached and used by a program (either application or system programs). The organization of a computer system refers to the actual configuration of the system, e.g. the type of operational units, their multiplicity, and their interconnections.

The main architectural specifications are the instruction set, the built-in data type representations, the memory organization, and the I/O system organization. For example, a multiplication instruction in the instruction set is an architectural feature. However, the way the multiplication is performed is an organizational issue.

3.4. Computer families

There is an important trend towards *computer families*. A family of computers can be defined as a series of computer systems with identical architectures
but different organizations. A user can start with a simple computer configuration and expand or upgrade the system as demand grows. There is no need to
adapt the application software. This concept was first introduced in the IBM
360 series of computers [Blaauw & Brooks, 1964] and caused a true revolution
in the computer industry. The family concept protects the investment of the
user in the application software and provides a path for future growth. Most
current manufacturers of large systems offer one or more families of computer
systems.

Migration problems are determined by the operating system as well as by the
computer architecture. One of the important functions of an operating system
is to provide an interface between the applications and the computer hardware
resources. To acquire computer resources, the application interacts with the
operating system. This causes a dependency, in the sense that the execution
under a different operating system can take place only after a sometimes
considerable conversion effort.

Therefore, for an application the combination of the operating system and
the architecture of a (family of) computer system(s) can be regarded as the
working environment. Migration within a specific working environment is
relatively easy; migration to a different working environment can pose serious
conversion problems. An example of such a working environment is the
MS-DOS operating system, combined with the processor family of the Intel
8086/8088/80186 series of microprocessors [Milenkovic, 1987].

Migration to a working environment with the same operating system but a
different computer architecture always requires recompilation of the program.
Although this is in principle simple, problems can occur with respect to
differences in the memory required by the compiled program, differences in
implementation of basic data types (e.g., floating-point formats), etc. [Tanen-
baum, Klint & Bohm, 1978].

Migration to a working environment with the same architecture but a
different operating system usually introduces more problems. In performing
I/O or in calling other application programs, programs use services offered by
the operating system. These 'calls' to the operating system have to be adopted
to the call formats of the operating system to which the program migrates.
Since there is no standardization at this level, this process might involve costly
changes in the program.

4. The influence of advances in technology

4.1. Technological developments

The organizational and architectural structuring of computer systems has
always been strongly oriented towards the existing technology. It is very

difficult to envision systems that cannot be realized in an existing technology. Therefore, technological developments have a large impact on the pace of development of the dependent software technologies, such as the design of programs and applications.

The size of computer components in the early computers was rather bulky compared to what we are now accustomed to. The number of basic components we can pack per unit space has increased greatly and is still increasing. The size of the components has been reduced from the vacuum tube to the transistor on a chip, occupying only a few square micrometers in space. A simple comparison illustrates this advance in technology. The ENIAC computer occupied 144 square meters of floor space [Stern, 1981]. If we assume a height of three meters, the system volume is 432 cubic meters. Today's personal computers have a volume of approximately 0.064 cubic meters. This implies a volume reduction by a factor of 6750. The ENIAC had some 17 000 tubes, while the current personal computer (inclusive of memory) has a few million transistors. A figure of 5 million gives an increase by a factor of around 300. From these figures it can easily be derived that the volume per component has decreased by six orders of magnitude. If we can further improve on the screen and disk technologies, more can be gained, since these components currently account for about 80% of the total volume of most personal computers.

Besides improving on the existing technology, in the sense of scaling down component sizes, research is also done on devices with faster switching speeds. Within the electrical domain, the search is for materials in which electrons have a higher mobility [Mead & Conway, 1980], resulting in a higher switching speed. Another approach is the application of optical technologies in processing components. Optical components use light as the information carrier instead of electrons. Light travels faster than electrons, so by using light we can expect to construct faster computers. General-purpose optical computers are still far from the market place, and it is not clear if they will ever be practical [Hecht, 1987]. The use of optical communications is closer to implementation, and the use of optics in memory technology is also promising.

How have all these improvements and extra computational power been used? Have they changed the fundamentals of computer architecture or have they merely changed computer organization? We shall discuss some aspects of this issue in the following sections.

4.2. Memory organization

In early computer systems, memory was a very scarce resource, requiring ingenious assembler language programming for some programming tasks to be achieved. Later on, there was some improvement, but programmers still faced a memory limitation in the sense that programs were not allowed to grow beyond the size of the physical memory. This limitation had the effect that software applications developers had to take great care that their code stayed within the boundaries of the physical memory. Another side effect was that, because of this limitation, migration of the application code within a computer family could be restricted. Only after the introduction of virtual-memory techniques [Milenkovic, 1987], was real freedom in program size achieved.

4.2.1. Virtual memory

The concept of *virtual memory* is a solution to the discrepancy between the *logical* memory address space and the *physical* memory address space. The logical memory address space is determined by the number of bits reserved for the operand address specification. For instance, if the address field is 32 bits long, we can address $2^{32} = 4\,294\,967\,296$ memory locations. Current physical address spaces are usually much smaller.

Virtual memory solves this problem by subdividing both the logical and physical address space into *pages*. Each page consists of an equal number of memory locations. In virtual-memory systems, only a few pages of a program's logical address space reside in the physical (also called the *real*) memory. The rationale of this approach is that in practice the address patterns generated by a program in execution, exhibit some *locality*. Hence, it suffices to have a limited part of the total memory space of the program 'nearby' in real memory. When the program generates an address not present in the pages residing in the real memory, intricate hardware and software schemes acquire the correct page(s) from a secondary storage (disk) and replace some of the current available pages. This whole process is 'invisible' to the end user, freeing application programmers from having to worry about memory limitations.

However, there is a price to pay for these advantages. Virtual memory requires a fast disk as secondary storage and is in general slower because of swapping pages between the main memory and the disk. In addition the page-swap mechanism needs hardware support, to determine quickly whether or not an address resides in real memory and if not, which page(s) are to be replaced by new ones. The result is that a fraction of the potential speed of the CPU is absorbed in facilitating a better organization of memory. Virtual memory is still a virtue of large systems, many personal computers still lack this feature; however, it is only a matter of time before this shortcoming is rectified (for more on virtual-memory techniques see Silberschatz & Peterson [1988]).

Virtual-memory techniques do not obviate the need for large real memories. Improved execution speed is the major reason for incorporating increasingly larger main memories into computer systems. The increase in main memory space largely follows the developments in memory-chip technology. As long as memory-chip densities continue growing, so will the main memories.

4.2.2. Caches

Another observation is that the *access time* of these large main memories has not decreased with their growth rate and this is not expected to change very much. On the other hand, CPUs become faster and consequently a mismatch occurs between the main memory speed and the CPU speed. To give an idea of the numbers involved: memory access times of 100–200 nanoseconds per word, against CPU calculation times of 25 nanoseconds for modern microprocessors, like the Intel i860 (one CPU cycle may produce up to three results in this system). If nothing is done, the advantage of having a fast CPU may be completely lost.

A method for removing this mismatch is to place a *cache* memory between the CPU and the main memory. A cache memory is faster than the main memory, but is much smaller in size, and is to be regarded as an intermediate store for frequently used instructions and data. Typical cache sizes are in the kiloword range (e.g., the aforementioned i860 system has a 4-kilobyte instruction and a 8-kilobyte data cache).

Caches are completely transparent to the program. Again the locality concept forms the rationale for incorporating caches into computer systems. Measurements on typical programs have shown, that with a limited cache size, 'hit' rates of 90% can be achieved. Therefore, average access time will be shorter than main memory access time. For instance, if the access times of a cache and a main memory are 25 nanoseconds and 100 nanoseconds, respectively, the average access time with a cache is 32.5 nanoseconds (with a hit-rate probability of 0.9).

4.2.3. Future trends

Besides a better memory organization by applying virtual memory and protection techniques, from the programmers point of view the main memory can still be seen as a random addressable, linear data space. In this sense nothing has changed, although research is performed on different computer architectures having a memory structure that is better suited for certain domains of application (e.g., artificial intelligence problems). Whether this approach will be commercially successful is still an open question.

Because the structure of the main memory is linear and very simple, it is easily extendible. Therefore, many improvements in technology have been developed for the extension of the size of the main memories. This will continue until improvements in technology come to a halt when theoretical or practical barriers are reached.

4.3. CPU organization

Within the CPU a number of operations and functions have had to be implemented partially in the software, because of the limitations on the number of hardware components. Improvements in technology have primarily been used to implement these basic functions in hardware. Every operation that was serialized is now parallelized. An example is the multiplication operation already discussed.

A second way to exploit the extra possibilities allowed by new technologies is to incorporate more and more complex instructions. The idea behind this is that high-level languages could be better supported by incorporating more powerful instructions. We shall come to this issue latter on.

Another, rather simple, extension is the incorporation of more registers within the CPU. More registers enlarge the capacity for keeping data local within the CPU whenever possible, without going back all the way to main memory, thus improving on execution speed.

This also supports modern programming practice; modular programming techniques yield many procedure invocations per time unit, requiring many context switchings within the CPU. Large register sets increase the speed for the switching of context considerably, because less information has to be saved in the main memory.

4.3.1. Pipelining

Further improvements in speed can be obtained by using the concept of *pipelining*. The idea behind pipelining is quite simple; one breaks down a complex operation into more simple suboperations, such that each suboperation is executed in an equal amount of time. If we separate the suboperations by storage elements (*pipeline registers*), a number of equal and mutually independent calculations can be executed in an *overlapped* manner. The principle is shown in Figure 3. Here, an operation S is subdivided in three operations S_1, S_2, and S_3. The time diagram shows that, as soon as S_1 has been finished for the first calculation, S_1 can be performed for the second calculation, etc.

So in principle, with an *n*-stage pipeline, an execution speed *n* times greater than the non-pipelined case can be obtained. In practice, the yield is a little less, due among other factors to the time overhead caused by the pipeline registers. Several types of operations in computer systems can be pipelined. Examples are arithmetic operations, such as floating-point addition (possible suboperations: exponent comparison, mantissa alignment, mantissa addition) and instructions (possible suboperations: fetch, decode, execute).

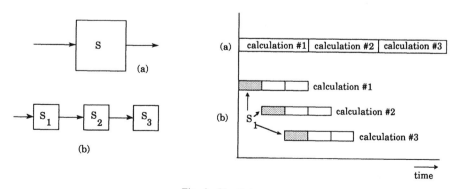

Fig. 3. Pipelining.

4.4. Peripheral equipment

All the improvements in the architecture and organization of the main memory and the CPU would have been virtually useless, if the peripheral equipment, such as the disk and tape units, had not been improved on the same scale. Early disks had only a few kilowords of storage capacity, but current magnetic disk capacities range from 20–1000 gigabits of storage capacity and are substantially smaller [Voelcker, 1987]. Optical storage even promises a much larger storage capacity in the near future. Some authors even claim that with the storage capacities that will become available, erasing of files will become obsolete, giving the ultimate in version management and backup [Gait, 1988]. For instance, with one terabyte (8×10^{12} bits) of write-once optical memory, the disk will become full only after 31 years if 5 pages a second of 1000 bits each are written on it during normal working hours.

4.5. The trend downwards

Until about 1980, the need for computer power was mainly satisfied by general-purpose computers (large mini frame and mainframe computers). This has led to computer configurations within organizations consisting of a few large computers and many terminals connected to those computers, directly or by means of some switching system.

Such a centralized approach has the following advantages: the user is confronted with a single working environment, software support and maintenance are relatively easy to organize, and highly trained support personnel can assist in solving the user's problems. However, many disadvantages also became apparent. Due to the increasing complexity and computational intensiveness of many application programs, large turn-around times became normal practice. However, users want to communicate interactively with their computer system and their particular applications. The only way to make this possible is to *distribute* the computing power. As a consequence, this software/mainframe tradition is rapidly changing, among others due to modern very large scale integration (VLSI) technology.

An important step in the distribution of the computing power is the shift from general-purpose mainframes to intelligent workstations or personal computers, interconnected by a computer network. With the distribution of computer power to personalized workstations, many of the flaws of centralized systems have disappeared. However, what is omitted is the single working environment in which all computer users operate and can exchange applications and data. Along with the decentralization process, the number of vendors of computing equipment has also grown. This makes the integration process much more difficult. The ensemble of all computer systems in an organization, or even beyond, can be viewed as a large distributed system where all the parts are in some way interconnected by means of a networking system. The creation of a single working environment of such a large *distributed system* will be a great challenge in the coming decades.

4.6. The computer pyramid

The need for personalized computing does not imply that all large systems will disappear from the computer spectrum. There will always be a need for very powerful computers for number crunching or large commercial data processing applications. These so-called *supercomputers* are intended for solving problems that cannot be solved by 'normal' computing systems. 'Cannot be solved' is here to be interpreted as 'not in a reasonable time'. Examples of such problems are weather forecasting, aerodynamical calculations, etc. Supercomputers were popularized by the appearance of the CRAY-1 supercomputer in 1977 [Cray, 1977]. Since then a few hundred supercomputers have been installed worldwide.

Supercomputers can be characterized as consisting of highly-engineered processors using the fastest and, consequently, the most expensive component technologies. They strive for the fastest clock cycle times (currently, a few nanoseconds) and make great use of pipelining techniques throughout the CPU. Because of the pipelining of operations, supercomputers can perform *vectorial operations* very quickly; hence also the name *vector processors* for these types of machines.

Between the low-end personal computer systems and the most advanced computer systems a large price/performance gap exists. This gap is being filled with cheaper systems, the so-called near-supercomputers, which are not as powerful as the top-of-the-line supercomputers, but have a better price/performance ratio. The resulting spectrum of computer systems is shaped like a pyramid, with relatively few computers at the top and very many computers on the bottom.

4.7. Performance measures

When new and improved systems are being brought onto the market we would like to have some indication of their performance. What we want to know is: how must faster can my application be processed by this new machine? In general, this question is very difficult to answer for various reasons. Gathering statistics from a production application is almost impossible, since it requires the new computer to be completely installed in that production environment. Secondly, many computer systems have a mix of applications, making the judgements even more complicated.

4.7.1. MIPS and MFLOPS

However, measures of performance are still very much wanted by users and vendors to have some means of comparing systems. The simplest performance indicators are the average instruction execution rate, in units of *million instructions per second* (MIPS), and the average operation execution rate, in units of *million floating-point operations per second* (MFLOPS). As a measure, the number of MIPS is not a very accurate one, since instruction sets can differ quite profoundly. Some computers can perform a certain operation with a single instruction, while others need several instructions to perform the same job. In order to compare average instruction execution times, we also have to give a weight to the number of times those instructions are used in typical programs. Still, the MIPS unit is a frequently used, and misused, measure in comparisons between different computer systems.

Within computer families comparisons between different models in the family are a little easier, since they all share the same type of architecture. In this case, comparisons can be made relative to some model in the series. For estimating the CPU power this can be done quite well. However, different models may have different types of computer organization. This can have serious effects on, for example, the I/O performance of the system. If an application is I/O bound, that is if the transfer of data between the CPU and the disk dominates the total processing time of an application, putting more MIPS into the CPU has minor effects on the systems performance, while improving the I/O bandwidth would help quite a lot. A difficulty in this case is that the I/O performance is dependent on many factors in the computer organization. Therefore, defining measures that can be used for the comparison between the I/O performance of systems is not a simple task, not even within a family.

4.7.2. Synthetic benchmarks

To obtain more accurate estimates of the real performance of a computer system, several measures have been developed, based on so-called synthetic benchmark tests. A *benchmark suite* is a relatively small collection of programs, of which the behavior approximates the behavior of a class of applications. The most well known benchmark suites are the Whetstone and the Dhrystone [Serlin, 1986] benchmarks. The Whetstone is the oldest one and is biased towards numerical types of programs, while the Dhrystone puts more emphasis on operations occurring in system programs. But even benchmark suites have serious flaws as indicators of performance. Because benchmark suites are programs, the way they are compiled can have a large influence on the final result. So not only the system's efficiency is measured, but also the efficiency of the compiler. Other environmental parameters might also influence the results of the test. So great care has to be taken in interpreting data obtained from executing benchmark suites.

5. Current and future developments

5.1. Changes in instruction sets: The RISC/CISC war

The instruction set determines the power and flexibility of a computer system from the programmer's point of view. The computer architect designs the instruction set as a compromise between what is thought of as being useful to programmers and compiler writers and what is technologically possible. The advances in technology have been used to enhance instruction sets with more powerful and elaborate instructions and more complicated addressing schemes. For a long time there had been no validation of whether or not the instructions are actually useful, in the sense that they are frequently executed by average programs.

When people started measuring and gathering statistics about instruction usage frequencies, they found out that some instructions were actually never used and some other instructions were used very frequently. It even turned out that some instruction sequences appeared very often, while there was no appropriate instruction available to perform that operation in a single step. This happened, for instance, in the case of subroutine or procedure calls. If a program wants to execute a subroutine, it needs to save a lot of context information (register contents, program counter, etc.). When the calling program is to resume execution, this context information has to be restored. Current programming practice tends to use subroutines much more frequently then a decade ago, amongst other reasons because of the popularity of the modular programming paradigm. Furthermore, it turned out that compiler writers did not use the complex instructions available to speed up the execution of high-level language (HLL) programs, while the computer architect had included those instructions for exactly this propose!

Another consequence of more complex instruction sets is that the decoding of the instruction takes more time and leads to a more complex decoding circuitry. This also slows down the instruction execution speed, but this was thought to be compensated for by more processing work done per instruction.

To overcome the above-mentioned problems, a number of computer architects started to design so-called *reduced instruction set computers* (RISC) as opposed to the *complex instruction set computers* (CISC) [Stallings, 1990]. Their recipe is: reduce the number of instructions by deleting all instructions that are not frequently used, simplify the remaining instructions as much as possible to ease the instruction-decoding process, and enlarge the number of registers to accommodate procedure calls and compiler optimizations. A faster computer system will then result. This approach has been adopted by some computer manufacturers, who now offer systems which are claimed to have been developed according to this concept.

The debate on which concept is superior, RISC or CISC, is still going on. Part of the difficulties in resolving this issue is: what do we mean by computer performance and how do we measure it, a problem already discussed in the previous section. Instruction execution is clearly faster on a RISC machine than on a CISC machine, leading to larger MIPS values. However, instruction sets are hard to compare between RISC and CISC. Most RISC architectures make a fresh start in instruction set and technology. Many CISC architectures had to be upwards compatible with previously developed architectures, making the design more complicated and slowing down the execution speed. There are also some indications that compiled code for a RISC machine takes more memory than compiled code for a CISC machine.

More generally, one could say that a machine performs well for the type of problems it has been optimized for. This also holds for RISC machines. If we execute programs with characteristics that are not compatible with the execution model of the target machine, performance problems can be expected. Stated in a more elaborate way: a program might perform badly if a semantic gap exists between the model of computation of the coded algorithm and the model of computation of the target machine. By a semantic gap we mean that some basic operation in a programming language is executed by the target machine by a much more complicated series of basic machine operations. Such a phenomenon can be observed, when executing, e.g., functional types of languages, like LISP, on conventional machines. In LISP, operations on list structures are easy to define. However, on a traditional computer manipulating list structures is not directly supported by the instruction set. To overcome these problems, special architectures have been developed to speed up the execution [Pleszkun & Thatzhuthaveetil, 1987] of these types of languages.

5.2. Multiprocessing

In principle, only a single CPU is needed within a computer system to perform all the tasks required. In practice, however, this has the effect of a single resource that is to be shared by many tasks. Of course, all these tasks are related in some sense, but if we put a more narrow time window on them to look at their behavior, they usually proceed independently. Therefore, sharing the CPU resource among many tasks requires a lot of switching among tasks, which slows down the computation. Because some of the tasks are largely independent of each other and only interact occasionally, a distribution of the CPU resource is attractive.

The first form of the distribution of computing power is *functional distribution*. Certain functions that are frequently performed by the CPU are transferred to smaller or more specialized processors. Such is the case in many of the more advanced I/O systems, where special I/O processors perform the data transfer functions and the associated book-keeping overhead. Other examples are intelligent terminal controllers.

So in fact a computer system becomes an ensemble of *cooperating processors*. However, the actual processing task of a user is still performed by a single CPU. To obtain more computing power, a second form of distribution can be applied, namely the incorporation of multiple CPUs within a single computer system. Non-related tasks, such as different users or different jobs for a single user can be assigned to different CPUs according to some scheduling scheme. These systems are called multiprocessors. In this way the total throughput of the computer system can be enlarged. More and more systems with multiprocessor capabilities are becoming available.

The multiprocessor method of distribution does enlarge the systems throughput, but often not the elapsed time of a single program or application. If a single program is to be speeded up, we have to distribute parts of that program over a number of processors and let them interact in such a way that the program results remain the same. This third form of distribution is also called *parallel processing*, because we execute several parts of our problem in parallel. We shall explore this subject further in the following sections.

5.3. The limit in speed

The present improvement in the speed of the computer cannot go on forever. There are a number of limiting factors that will inhibit further improvements from being made, and the ultimate speed will be not very far from where we are now. There are two main causes for this. The first is the limitations imposed upon us by the fundamental laws of nature. These are the strictest ones: with our current knowledge they form the bottom line. The second is related to the way we design and implement computing devices. Design decisions influence computing speed. Usually, design trade-offs have to be made in constructing computer systems. Some estimates for the attainable computing speed can be made by a brief consideration of these factors.

In the von Neumann type of machine the memory plays a crucial role in the performance of the system. Instructions are retrieved from the memory one after the other. The output of the memory, when viewed against time, shows the different bit patterns of the instructions. So an individual bit position at the memory output has to frequently 'switch' from one state (either 0 or 1) to the other state. This switching is achieved by some hardware component and takes time. The speed in which this component can make a state transition is a measure of the maximum attainable computing speed. This switching speed is dependent on the applied technology, but switching speeds of the order of picoseconds (10^{-12} sec) are attainable with superconducting devices or optical switching elements [Mead & Conway, 1980; West, 1987]. This optimistically suggests that execution rates of 1000 GIPS (giga instructions per second = 10^9 instructions per second) can be obtained.

However, something has to be done with an instruction, i.e., a number of operations have to be performed on the instruction bit pattern. This can be translated as a series of basic components (or 'gates') which have to be passed, each component operating with the switching speed mentioned above. The actual number of components to be passed depends on the operation to be performed and the choices made by the computer designer and varies between 10 and 40. This number can be made smaller by applying pipelining techniques, as discussed in Section 4.3. For instance, if instruction pipelining is applied, the next instruction can then be fed into the system without the first one being completed.

The number of components to be passed before the (possibly transformed) information is stored in a memory, determines the clock speed of the system. Taking the above considerations into account, the attainable instruction execution speed is reduced to 25–100 GIPS.

Another factor influencing the computer speed is the rate at which instructions can be retrieved from the main memory. Of course the switching speed of components provides an upper limit, but the organization of the memory imposes some extra constraints. In current memory designs the next instruction can only be retrieved if the current one has physically left the memory. The travel time of a bit from its storage location to the output of the memory determines the actual attainable instruction fetch rate. Suppose we have a square memory chip with a size of $0.25 \, cm^2$. The time it takes for a signal to cross 0.5 cm with the speed of light is 16.66 picoseconds. Hence, the equivalent instruction rate yields 60 GIPS. This would make a nice match with the previously estimated instruction rate. However, the speed of electrical signals in silicon is a factor of ten slower than the speed of light, resulting in 6 GIPS. A faster rate can only be obtained by diminishing the memory size or completely reorganizing the memory structure. Diminishing the memory size is contrary to the trend of making larger memories. In executing programs, large memories are required to keep frequently needed code and data in the main memory. A different memory organization imposes technical problems which are not discussed here.

The overall conclusion is, that the maximal speed of (sequential) computer systems, as we know them today, will be limited to a few GIPS. Considering the fact that the most powerful computers available already have instruction rates of a few hundred MIPS, it must be concluded that the conventional sequential digital computer is approaching its ultimate in speed.

5.4. Going parallel

To obtain orders of magnitude improvement in speed in the future, radically different computer architectures are needed. In general, we use the following simple idea: we take a multiplicity of computers, say N, interconnect them in some way, and solve the problem N times more quickly. The computers within such a *parallel-computer* architecture are often referred to as *Processing Elements* (PEs). For instance, with 1000 PEs we can obtain a three orders of magnitude improvement in processing speed.

For years parallel processing was largely an academic curiosity, but now the advances in technology and economics of computing has brought it to the forefront of commercial innovation. Although its impact on the supercomputing market is already secure, its use in cheaper machines will have a much more extensive effect on the computer industry. In these cases, the motivation will not be absolute performance, but a much better price/performance ratio. Instead of a small number of highly-engineered processors using the fastest and most expensive component technologies, these parallel machines will have a larger . number of processing elements based on low-cost, mass-produced, industry standard microprocessors.

However, there are disadvantages. To obtain maximal performance out of a parallel processor is not an easy task. We shall review some of the problems encountered. The actual performance of a computing system is dependent on the efficient use of its resources. In the early days, the programmer had full control over the resources by means of an assembly language, which reflected the internal architecture of the computer. Nowadays, this has been replaced by the compiler of a high-level language and the operating system.

Although high-level programming languages free the programmer from any knowledge about the underlying machine architecture, many of the current popular languages (e.g., FORTRAN, C, Pascal) implicitly reflect the model of computation of the traditional sequential computer.

5.4.1. Characteristics of parallel processors

Parallel processors are used to obtain a significant increase in speed over the use of a single processor to solve a problem. So the efficiency considerations mentioned above also hold in this case. However, a few extra characteristics of parallel processors do make the efficiency issue much more complicated.

In the first place, the model of computation used in parallel processors has more degrees of freedom than the model of computation used in a sequential processor. A model of computation defines the functionality of a processor based upon the available resources of the machine and the set of allowable operations on those resources. The extra elements in the model of computation for parallel processors are the *processor–memory* pairing, the *control structure*, and the *interconnection topology*.

The processor–memory pairing is the relation between the memory space and the processing elements of the parallel processor. For instance, one can have parallel processors in which all processing elements share a single memory (*shared-memory* systems), or systems where each processor has its own local memory (*distributed-memory* systems).

The control structure of a parallel processor determines to what extent the processing elements can be programmed individually. This can vary from systems where all the processing elements operate in a lock step mode; that is, the processing elements compute the same function, but on different data sets, to systems where all processing elements can be programmed individually. According to Flynn's taxonomy [Flynn, 1972], the first method of operation is called *single instruction stream, multiple data stream* (SIMD) processing, while the second method of operation is called *multiple instruction stream, multiple data stream* (MIMD) processing.

5.4.2. Interconnection topologies

The interconnection topology is the way in which the processing elements (and memories, if applicable) are connected. Many interconnection schemes exist, all with different characteristics for the network complexity, maximal delay, and scalability [Feng, 1981].

In reality, we would like to have a direct path from each processor to every other processor (see Figure 4a). However, it is clear that the number of interconnections grows quadratically with the number of processors in the system. From a technological viewpoint this is impractical. Therefore, other

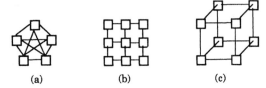

Fig. 4. Some interconnection schemes: (a) full interconnection, (b) mesh, (c) hypercube ($k = 3$).

interconnection schemes such as the *mesh* and the *hypercube* are more popular. In a mesh (Figure 4b), each processor is only connected to its nearest neighbors, giving a constant number of interconnection channels per processor. However, the communication time is bounded by O(N). The mesh has the advantage that it can be easily mapped on a two-dimensional surface.

A hypercube interconnection scheme (Figure 4c) can be regarded as an attractive compromise between a full interconnection and a mesh. In a hypercure, $N = 2^k$ processors form a k-dimensional hypercube. Hence, each processor has $\Theta(\log_2 N)$ communication channels attached. The communication time between any two processors is bounded by O($\log_2 N$).

5.4.3. Problem partitioning

On a parallel computer a program has to be partitioned and the partitions have to be assigned for execution to the available processing elements. The partitioning can be done manually by the application developer, automatically by the appropriate programming means, or by a combination of both. Partitioning of a problem is not a trivial task and if done manually, it is rather laborious, requiring detailed information about the application and the architecture of the target parallel processor. Therefore, much research is currently being performed on the software support for this task. One approach is directed towards the extraction of parallelism from procedural languages like FORTRAN [Allen & Kennedy, 1985; Padua & Wolfe, 1986]. Other approaches are the inclusion of the notion of communication in programming languages, such as in Occam [May, 1986], facilitating the construction of parallel programs. In addition to programming support, scheduling techniques for mapping programs onto processing elements also play an important role [Lawler, Lenstra, Rinnooy Kan & Shmoys, 1992].

5.4.4. Amdahl's law

An important limitation to increases in speed is governed by Amdahl's law [Amdahl, 1967]. Originally posed for the relation between the vector and scalar performances of a computer, it is equally valid for every other form of speed-up by means of parallel processors. In general, an application run can be considered as consisting of an intrinsically sequential part and a part that can be speeded up by means of some parallel architecture. For parallel processors,

Amdahl's law can be stated as

$$S = \frac{1}{(1-f) + f/N} \, ,$$

where f is the fraction of the application run that can be parallelized, N is the number of processors, and S is the effective speed-up of the total run. In Figure 5 the behavior of the performance for a hypothetical application run is shown for $N = 20$. It shows, that good values of speed-up can only be obtained in this case at the high end of the curve. From this it follows that a satisfactory speed-up can be obtained only if the sequential part is sufficiently small.

The time length of the sequential (or non-parallelizable) part is determined among other factors by the sequential part of the applied algorithm(s) and the time needed to access data (usually from the main memory or disk). For a specific application these factors have to be properly analyzed before the merits of a parallel architecture for that application can be given.

5.5. More exotic solutions

In the previous section, it has been assumed that the processing elements of a parallel processor are fairly standard processors as we know them today. In research, other directions are also being explored, often leading to radically different models of computation.

5.5.1. Data flow computing
One such direction is *data flow* computing [Sharp, 1985]. Unlike conventional control flow computing, a program in a data flow computer is described by the flow of operands through the network of operations. Operations are 'fired' to processing elements if all the input operands are available. Think of the process as firing a multiplication, if the multiplier and multiplicand have

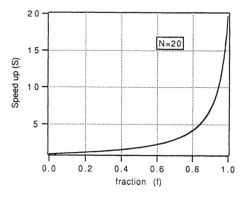

Fig. 5. Amdahl's law: speed-up as a function of parallelization ($N = 20$).

arrived. Operations that are mutually independent can be fired at the same time, provided that a free processing element is available.

The processing elements in data flow computers have no private memory. In fact, there is no memory in the classical sense. Instead, there is a so-called *matching store*, where the results are 'matched' against operations that require them as input values. The availability of data (=results) determines the order of execution, instead of an imposed order, as in conventional machines. Hence, the name data flow. Apart from their different architecture and organization, data flow computers are general-purpose computers, which are not restricted to a specific task.

A number of experimental data flow computers have been built, but a major breakthrough of this concept has not (yet) occurred. There are other developments, such as the use of parallel processors in functional language execution [Hudak, 1988], but their discussion is beyond the scope of this chapter.

5.5.2. Systolic arrays

Another direction in computer architecture research is to tailor the architecture of a computer to the algorithm(s) to be solved. In this way problems can be solved faster than by the use of a general-purpose architecture. This approach can be advantageous if the algorithm to be executed is computationally intensive and has to be executed many times. The algorithm must also be stable, in the sense that it is not likely to be replaced by a different and better algorithm in the near future. We can then exploit the specific properties of the algorithm in designing a so-called *special-purpose* architecture.

An important class of special-purpose architectures are the *systolic array* architectures [Kung & Leiserson, 1979; Fortes & Way, 1987]. Systolic architectures have emerged from the specific opportunities offered by VLSI technology. In this technology, complete systems can be placed on a single piece of silicon. In order to profit from this, designs must have relatively simple structures, regular interconnection patterns, and they must be scalable; that is, it should be easy to expand the design when more space becomes available. As an example of such systems let us look at the way in which the multiplication of two square matrices is performed systolically. As a basis, we have a mesh of processing elements, without a private memory, the size of the mesh being equal to the dimensions of the matrices. This is shown in Figure 6 for matrices A and B, both of size 3×3. The elements of the matrices to be multiplied are, so to speak, pumped through the array; the elements of B from top to bottom and the elements of A from left to right. As is shown, the elements of A and B are skewed in time, in order to let them arrive at the correct time in the correct processing elements. Each processing element performs the operation $a * b + c$ in every cycle, where a and b are the incoming elements of A and B, respectively, and c is the result of the computation in the previous cycle in that processing element. After processing, the elements of the result matrix reside in the respective processing elements; that is, the uppermost processor on the left-hand side contains an element r_{11} of the results matrix R, etc.

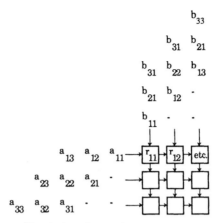

Fig. 6. Systolic matrix multiplication.

5.5.3. Neural networks

A step further is to consider a completely different mathematical model for solving problems. This approach is taken in *neural computing*, an area currently of great interest in computer research. The fact that the human brain can be considered as a gigantic computing system has intrigued many researchers. The key computing element is the *neuron* and the understanding of its behaviour is paramount in order to understand the model of computation of the brain. There are approximately 10^{11} neurons in the human brain, interconnected in a complex way, and more knowledge about their behavior can be used to obtain more insight into the functioning of the brain (such as in learning, pattern recognition, etc.). On the other hand, knowledge of this kind can also be used by applying this model of computation to solve computational problems for which conventional computer systems are not very well equipped. These computing systems are referred to as *artificial neural systems* [Hopfield & Tank, 1986; Shriver, 1988]. The problems for which these systems are suited include tasks as vision, speech, and pattern recognition.

In artificial neural systems, a model of a neuron must be chosen. The first neural models were simple on–off models, following the early work of McCulloch & Pitts [1943]. Neurons modeled in this way could only be in two states, either 'on' or 'off'. When organized in a network, simple Boolean functions can be computed. More recent studies have used continuous dynamical models of neurons. A set of cooperating neurons can be modeled as a set of nonlinear differential equations. The use of differential models for neurons also results in renewed attention for analog computing, for analog devices are capable of solving differential models quickly. For adequate implementation, neural computers depend heavily on the application of massive parallelism; although the basic processing element can be kept relatively simple.

Artificial neural systems will not replace the mainstream of current computer systems, but they provide an alternate way of solving problems, for which the model of computation of current digital computers is not very suitable.

6. Further reading

There are numerous good text books about basic computer architecture of which Stallings [1990], Tanenbaum [1984], and Kuck [1978] are good examples. Fundamental papers in the field can be found in several of the transactions of the ACM and the IEEE (for instance, the *IEEE Transactions on Computers* and the *ACM Transaction on Computer Systems*). Collections of important research papers on specific subjects are published regularly by the IEEE Press. For survey-like articles, magazines like *Computer* and *Software* from the IEEE Press are an excellent place to look.

References

Allen, J.R., K. Kennedy (1985). A parallel programming environment. *IEEE Software* 2(4), 21–30.
Amdahl, G. (1967). The validity of the single processor approach to achieving large scale computing capabilities. *AFIPS* 30, 483–485.
Bashe, C.J., L.R. Johnson, J.H. Palmer, E.W. Pugh (1986). *IBM's early computers*, MIT Press, Cambridge, MA.
Bekey, G.A., W.A. Karplus (1968). *Hybrid Computation*, Wiley, New York.
Blauw, G.A., F.P. Brooks (1964). The structure of the system/360, Part I – Outline of the logical structure. *IBM Syst. J.* 3(2), 119–135.
Boole, G. (1954). *An Investigation of the Laws of Thought on which are founded the Mathematical Theories of Logic and Probabilities*, Walton and Meberley, London.
Burks, A., H. Goldstine, J. von Neumann (1946). Preliminary discussion of the logical design of an electronic computing instrument: A reprint can be found in: *Computer structures: Readings and Examples*, Bell, C.G., A. Newell (1971). McGraw-Hill, New York.
Bush, V. (1931) The differential analyzer. A new machine for solving differential equations. *J. Franklin Institute* 212, 447–488.
Cray (1977). *Cray-1 Computer System, Reference Manual*, Cray Research Inc.
Feng, T.Y. (1981) A survey of interconnection networks. *IEEE Computer* 14(12), 12–27.
Flynn, M.J. (1972). Some computer organizations and their effectiveness. *IEEE Trans. Comput.* C-21, 948–960.
Fortes, J.A.B., B. Way (1987). Systolic arrays – from conception to implementation. *IEEE Computer* 20(7), 12–17.
Gait, J. (1988). The optical file cabinet: A random-access file system for write-once optical disks. *IEEE Computer* 21, 11–22.
Goldstine, H.H. (1972). *The computer from Pascal to von Neumann*, Princeton University Press, 1972. Princeton, NJ.
Harel, D. (1991). *Algorithms, the Spirit of Computing, 2nd edition*, Addison-Wesley, Reading, MA.
Hecht J. (1987). Optical Computers. *High Technology*, February, 44–65.
Hopfield, J.J., D.W. Tank (1986). Computing with neural circuits: A model. *Science* 233, 625–633.
Hudak, P. (1988). Exploring parafunctional programming: Separating the What from the How. *IEEE Software*, January, 54–62.
Husky, H.D., V.R. Husky (1976). Chronology of computing devices. *IEEE Trans. Comput.* C-25(12), 1190–1199.
IEEE (1985). IEEE standard for binary floating-point arithmetic, ANSI/IEEE std 754–1985.
Kuck, D.J. (1978). *The Structure of Computers and Computations*, Wiley, New York.

Kung, H.T., C.E. Leiserson (1979). Systolic arrays (for VLSI), *Proceedings Sparse Matrix Computation 1978*, Academic Press, Orlando, FL.

Lawler, E.L., J.K. Lenstra, A.H.G. Rinnooy Kan, D.B. Shmoys (1992). Sequencing and scheduling: Algorithms and complexity, in: S.C. Graves, A.H.G. Rinnooy Kan, P. Zipkin (eds.), *Handbooks in Operations Research and Management Science, Vol. 4: Logistics of Production and Inventory*, North-Holland, Amsterdam.

McCulloch, W.S., W. Pitts (1943). A logical calculus of the ideas immanent in nervous activity. *Bull. Math. Biophys.* 5, 115–133.

Mead, C., L. Conway (1980). *Introduction to VLSI systems*, Addison-Wesley, Reading, MA.

Milenkovic, M. (1987). *Operating Systems*, MacGraw-Hill, New York.

Padua, D.A., M.J. Wolfe (1986). Advanced compiler optimizations for supercomputers. *Commun. ACM* 29(12), 1184–1201.

Pleszkun, A.R., M.T. Thatzhuthaveetil (1987). The Architecture of Lisp machines. *IEEE Computer* 20(3), 35–44.

Sadie, S. (1984). *The New Grove Dictionary of Musical Instruments*, MacMillan, New York.

Serlin, O. (1986). MIPS, Drystones and other tales. *Datamation*, June.

Sharp, J.A. (1985). *Data Flow Computing*, Ellis Horwood, Chichester.

Shriver, B.D. (ed.) (1988). Artificial neural systems. *IEEE Comput* (3), special issue.

Silberschatz, A., J.L. Peterson (1988). *Operating System Concepts*, Addison-Wesley, Reading, MA.

Stallings, W. (ed.) (1986). *Tutorial on Reduced Instruction Set Computers*, IEEE Computer Soc. Press, Washington, DC.

Stallings, W. (1990). *Computer Organization and Architecture*, MacMillan, New York.

Stern, N. (1981). *From ENIAC to UNIVAC*, Digital Press, Belford, MA.

Tanenbaum, A.S. (1984). *Structured Computer Organization*, Prentice-Hall, Englewood Cliffs, NJ.

Tanenbaum, A.S., P. Klint, W. Bohm (1978). Guidelines for software portability. *Software – Pract. Exper.*, August, 681–689.

Thomson, W. (1876). Mechanical integration of linear differential equations of the second order with variable coefficients. *Proc. R. Soc. London* 24, 230–265.

Turing, A.M. (1936). On computable numbers with an application to the entscheidungsproblem, *Proc. London Math. Soc. (2)* 42, 230–265.

Ullman, J.D. (1984). *Computational aspects of VLSI*, Computer Science Press, Rockville, MD.

Voelcker, J. (1987). Winchester disks reach for a gigabyte. *IEEE Spectrum* 24, 16–25.

West, L.C. (1987). Picosecond integrated optical logic. *IEEE Computer* 20, 34–48.

Wilkes, M.V. (1956). *Automatic Digital Computers*, Mathuen, London.

E.G. Coffman et al., Eds., *Handbooks in OR & MS, Vol. 3*

Chapter 2

Programming Languages

Henri E. Bal and Dick Grune

Department of Mathematics and Computer Science, Vrije Universiteit De Boelelaan 1081a, 1081 HV Amsterdam, The Netherlands

1. Introduction

One of the jokes computer scientists like to tell each other is the following: 'What happens if you have a problem and ask a computer scientist to write a program to solve it? The answer: he will come back a year later, presenting you with a brand new programming language ideally suited for solving your problem.'

Although intended as a joke, it shows the strong involvement that researchers have in programming languages. The number of programming languages in use in the world is estimated to lie between 2000 and 3000. Over a decade ago, the US Department of Defense decided to standardize on a single (new!) programming language. At that time, people were writing military applications in about 300 different languages and dialects. This was not a joke.

This chapter will first examine some general issues in programming languages; then, in Sections 2 through 7, we will survey the algorithmic (imperative), object-oriented, functional, logic, parallel and real-time languages, respectively. For each of these classes of languages, we will treat the principles and concepts, and give some examples. Section 8 provides some literature pointers.

A few programming languages are treated in some detail, but many more are mentioned only in passing. For the former, literature references are given in Section 8, but for the latter we refer the interested reader to the general books on programming languages in Section 8, primarily to Ghezzi & Jazayeri [1987].

1.1. Why programming languages?

The primary purpose of a programming language is to enable the user to enlist the help of a computer in solving problems in the domain he or she is interested in. This places the problem at one end and the machine at the other.

The user would probably like to be isolated completely from the influence of the machine, but this, if at all possible, can only be done at great expense; it is a secondary purpose of a programming language to allow the gap between machine and problem domain to be bridged.

To understand better some of the features found in programming languages, and some of the issues in programming language design, it is useful to know a little about the machine. In very broad outline, a computer consists of a memory which includes registers, main memory (RAM) and file system, a central processing unit (CPU) that can inspect and modify the memory, and peripheral equipment, which may include display, keyboard, mouse, and printer. The memory contains the machine instructions, i.e., the program, and the data, both represented as sequences of *bits*, generally grouped into *bytes* of 8 bits each. At any point in time, the computer is in a certain *state*, determined by the contents of its memory and the state of the peripherals. A central item in the state is the *instruction pointer*, which points to the next instruction in memory to be executed. The series of successive values of the instruction pointer is called the *flow of control*; manipulating it is a main issue of many programming languages.

The fundamentals of a computer have not changed since its inception in the early 1940s. A program running on a computer was and is a sequence of machine instructions, and thus a sequence of bits. Programming the computer by writing this sequence of bits by hand was necessary in the very early days, but was abandoned as soon as possible, for obvious reasons. Soon a notation was invented that was more palatable to humans: *assembler language*, in which names were given to machine instructions, data, and positions in the program. Still, the written text was completely machine-specific, and a more *machine-independent* notation was desired. This coincided with an increased demand for a more problem-oriented notation and resulted in the *high(er)-level languages* (HLLs).

As an example we show here a short program fragment, which counts from 1 to 10, in machine code in hexadecimal and in assembler language, both for the Motorola MC 68000 series, and in the high-level language C.

```
Machine code (hex):              Assembler:
23fc  0000  0001  0000  0040       movl #1,n
                                 compare:
0cb9  0000  000a  0000  0040       cmpl #10,n
6e0c                               bgt end_of_loop
06b9  0000  0001  0000  0040       addl #1,n
60e8                               bra compare
                                 end_of_loop:
              C code:
              for (n=1; n<=10; n++) {
              }
```

1.2. Some history

Just as fashions and life-styles can be labeled by decades, the history of programming languages can be divided in a series of decades, each with a more or less clear theme.

The late 1940s can be characterized as the *pre-lingual stage*: programs for the very early computers looked roughly like pages from a railroad schedule. A very notable exception was the work of Zuse [1976] who, in 1944 in exile in Switzerland, designed his Plankalkül, which is definitely a programming language by any definition. Historical events prevented it from becoming known to the rest of the world until the early 1970s, or present day programming languages would have looked quite different.

The 1950s were concerned with *exploiting machine power*. Most, uniquely-built, computers were programmed in assembler language. FORTRAN emerged as the first higher-level language.

During the 1960s, *increasing the expressive power* was given much attention, resulting in a plethora of languages: COBOL, Lisp, ALGOL60, BASIC, PL/I, to name a few. Often these languages were considered luxuries, though; most 'serious' programming was still done in assembler languages.

Reducing machine dependency was the main theme of the 1970s, with the keyword 'portability'. Languages like Pascal, ALGOL68 and C, aided by the decreasing variety of the hardware, achieved a considerable measure of portability; but assemblers lived quietly on.

During the 1980s the emphasis was on *reducing the complexity*, both of the programming task and of the program management task. Traditionally-styled new languages like Ada [DoD, 1983] and Modula-2 [Wirth, 1985] were supplemented by program management systems like make [Feldman, 1979] and APSE (Ada programming support environment) [IEEE, 1985] while other languages were designed to be directly integrated with the programming environment, an approach of which Smalltalk and Miranda are examples. Assemblers were not forgotten, though: most of the code inside the Giotto probe that scouted Halley's comet on March 14, 1986 was written in assembler language.

Turning to our crystal ball, we suggest that the 1990s will be the decade of *exploiting parallel and distributed hardware*. Emerging languages are Linda, Orca, and Concurrent Prolog. Such languages allow problems to be solved efficiently, by splitting them up into subproblems that can be worked on in parallel, by different machines. It is widely believed that the speed of sequential computers will eventually reach a limit, and that parallelism is required to obtain performance beyond this limit.

1.3. Lexical and syntactic structure

Just as the building blocks of a natural language are lexical items called words, the building blocks of a programming language are lexical items called *tokens*. The lexical structure of different programming languages is reasonably uniform. The lexical items of almost all programming languages can be classified as keywords, identifiers, operators, separators, literals and comment. *Keywords* are fixed words in the language that help determining the syntactical structure; examples are begin, if, else and procedure. *Identifiers* are names, chosen by the programmer to identify objects of interest; examples are x_prime, number_of_employees, and FFT. Sometimes keywords and identifiers are distinguishable, e.g., by using upper case letters for the former and lower case for the latter, sometimes they are not; in the latter case the keywords are also *reserved words*. *Operators* serve to identify actions on *operands*; examples are +, − and ÷. *Separators*, like keywords, support the syntactic structure, but do not look like identifiers; examples are ,, :, ;, (and). Both operators and separators may be composite: +=, << and ;;. *Literals* denote values directly. Examples are 1, 3.14 and 'a'; the latter represents the character a, as opposed to the identifier a. A *comment* embeds some explanatory text in a program, but is otherwise ignored; it starts with a keyword, e.g., comment, or a separator, e.g., /* or −−, and ends with a separator, e.g., ; or */, or at the end of the line on which it started.

The syntactical structure of a programming language is often described precisely by a grammar, often in Backus Naur form (BNF) or extended BNF. Using a grammar rather than English has a dual purpose; it facilitates answering detailed questions about the language ('Can I have a declaration that declares no identifiers?') and it serves as a basis to derive language processors, e.g., compilers, interpreters, editors, etc., semi-automatically. The syntactic structures of different programming languages differ greatly; no general classification like the one above can be made.

1.4. The programming language as a communication medium

Like a natural language, a programming language can be viewed as a means of communication. The most common mode of communication is that from human to machine, but other modes are not unusual: from human to human, where text in a programming language serves to convey an algorithm, approach or technique, or from machine to machine, in the not at all uncommon situation in which a program generates a second program, thus achieving results often hard to obtain by other means.

Although the code in most programming languages communicates a set of instructions, this is not invariably true. Some programming languages, notably the *logic* programming languages, communicate relations between objects, and others, the *functional* programming languages, communicate definitions of objects in terms of other objects. Those languages that concentrate on sets of instructions are called *imperative* or *algorithmic* languages.

Each form of communication has a speaker and a listener, a writer and a reader. In the early days of programming it was already difficult enough to express one's wishes in a computer-acceptable form, and writeability, often called 'ease of use', had a high priority in the design of programming languages. Writeability reached its peak with languages like APL. As the art of programming matured, designers realized that, since any serious program is read many more times during its life-time than it is written, readability is the more important aspect. Languages like Modula-2 and Ada reflect this attitude. It should be noted, though, that the designers of COBOL emphasized readability already in 1959.

There is one fundamental difference between natural-language communication and human–machine communication: the lack of feed-back in the latter. Humans, if of good will, are very fault-tolerant in their communications, whereas the computer requires every detail to be spelled out without any room for error. This makes human–machine communication unexpectedly more complicated and taxing than human–human communication, a phenomenon that was not recognized in the 1950s and 1960s and that was at least partially responsible for the software crisis in the 1970s.

Providing support for managing and reducing the unexpected and unfamiliar complexity of ultra-precise communication is *the* challenge of present-day programming language design. Many techniques and devices have been proposed, in equally many programming languages, and most of them have been found wanting. Among the few survivors are procedures, modules and abstract data types in various guises.

Some modern programming languages provide advanced programming support at the expense of a considerable loss in efficiency; examples are SETL [Schwartz, Dewar, Dubinsky & Schonberg, 1986] and ABC [Geurts, Meertens & Pemberton 1990]. Such languages are very suitable for prototyping, since they allow complex processes to be specified relatively simply and reliably, but the loss of efficiency precludes wider usage. Some designers try to improve programming by removing those features that are found to be most dangerous in the face of complexity; a well-known slogan of this approach is 'feature X considered harmful'. This may result in a loss of expressivity, and may even reduce it to a level that the programmer finds unacceptable; some argue that functional languages come in this category, notably Backus' FP. The successful exorcism of the goto-statement has shown, however, that a restriction that is unacceptable to one generation of programmers may very well go unnoticed by the next generation.

In summary, it is the task of a modern programming language to assist the user in managing and reducing the complexity of the programming task, without unduly restricting the expressivity, and without undue loss in efficiency.

1.5. Managing and reducing complexity

It seems that all known techniques for successfully handling complex problems fall into one of three classes: subdividing the problem (decomposition), ignoring irrelevant detail in a safe way (abstraction), and having an independent agent check the internal consistency (strong checking). The first two provide guidelines for solving the problem, the third serves to provide early warnings. A good programming language should support all three.

Note that, in this chapter as elsewhere in computer science, the phrase 'to abstract from X' is used in the sense of 'to ignore X judiciously as being irrelevant to the present level of discussion' rather than in the possibly more common sense of 'to excerpt'.

Various collections of complexity-reducing techniques have been called *structured programming* over the years, but the term has been abused so often that it is virtually meaningless now.

1.5.1. Problem decomposition

The technique of decomposing a problem into two or more smaller problems that are hoped to be easier to solve was already known in antiquity: 'divide et impera'. It is variously known as 'divide and conquer', 'separation of concerns', etc. Some of the subproblems may be the same as the original problem, in which case the problem decomposition leads us to a recursive solution. This recursive solution is viable provided each of the subproblems is in some sense smaller than the original problem.

The traditional example of a problem that yields easily and in many ways to decomposition is that of sorting the items in a list. If we call the list L and the number of items in it N, the following technique will sort the list:

sort (L, N):
  case 1: $N < 2$: do nothing
        (a list of fewer than two items is always sorted)
  case 2: $N \geqslant 2$:
        □ split the list in two sublists, L_1 with length N_1 and L_2
           with length N_2, such that $N_1 > 0$ and $N_2 > 0$
           (this can always be done since there are at least two items)
        □ sort(L_1, N_1) and sort(L_2, N_2)
           (both problems are guaranteed to be smaller than the
           original since $N_1 < N$ and $N_2 < N$)
        □ merge L_1 and L_2, preserving the sorted order.

This example shows several features of problem decomposition. First, there must always be at least one alternative that does not define the problem in terms of itself: the escape hatch; it is often the trivial case, as it is in the above example. Second, one has to be careful to assure that the subproblems are indeed smaller; if one of them is not, subdivision continues but no real progress is made. Third, the details of the subdivision can be decided independently, yielding different algorithms for different decisions. If N_1 is always 1, the above example describes a variant of insertion sort; if N_1 and N_2 are chosen as close together as possible, sort-merge results; and if L_1 is chosen to contain all items below a certain threshold and L_2 the rest, a variant of quick-sort results.

Problem decomposition hinges on procedures, recursion and parameter passing, and can be applied in almost all high-level programming languages and in assembler languages.

1.5.2. Abstraction

The desire to 'ignore irrelevant detail in a safe way' immediately raises two questions: what is 'irrelevant detail', and what is 'in a safe way'. Irrelevant detail is detail that should be of no concern to the user in solving his problem. It should be of no concern to the user of complex numbers, whether these numbers are represented in Cartesian or polar coordinates internally, as long as his operations on them work properly. Note that this introduces a 'user' and consequently a 'used', the set of complex numbers implemented in a particular way. The user can apply a number of operations on the 'used' and expect them to work properly; the user is not supposed to look into the used object to see, let alone modify, its internal structure. Such a stylized access to an object, with the user on one side and the object on the other, is called an *interface*. The interface to complex numbers may include such operations as: create a complex number variable, add two complex numbers and yield the result, and yield the real part, imaginary part, absolute value or phase of a complex number. Each of these operations can be implemented using the Cartesian or the polar representation, although the efficiency may differ; yielding the absolute value is trivial in the polar representation and requires some calculation in the Cartesian representation.

An interface allows the user of a feature to abstract from the internal details of that feature and it allows the implementer of that feature to change those details of the implementation that do not affect the interface, without having to bother or even notify the user. The interface hides the secret of the implementation.

Such interfaces can exist entirely in the mind of the user: he restricts himself, through disciplined programming, to the 'published' facilities the implementation supplies and through sheer willpower resists the temptation to go around the interface and gain efficiency. Since no compiler support is required, interfaces can be used in any language.

'Ignoring irrelevant details *in a safe way*' implies that the secret hidden by the interface must be, indeed, an impenetrable secret. The user should not be so much *allowed* to abstract from the underlying implementation, he should have *no choice* but to abstract from it; only then can the implementer of the feature be sure that the user cannot, by accident or by intent, use code that is dependent on implementation details. Such interfaces do not exist exclusively in the mind of the user, they show in the program code, and are known to the compiler and to other program-processing programs.

Safe abstraction by information hiding requires the support of the programming environment, most often the compiler/linker. Such an abstraction then takes the form of a *package* or *module*, i.e., an encapsulated implementation of a data type, encapsulated in that it allows the user only a restricted number of well-defined actions on the internal data; all the rest is inaccessible. The technique the compiler uses to guard the secret is very simple: since all directly accessible objects are made so by names that are bound to them, the compiler just makes sure that names that are bound to secret objects on the implementer's side of the interface are not bound, or bound to some other object, on the user's side of the interface. Information hiding is done entirely by clever name manipulation.

Packages and modules, as they are called in Ada and Modula-2, respectively, can be seen as implementations of the concept of *abstract data type*. For a somewhat different approach, see the section on object-oriented programming, Section 3. For an example, see Section 2.2.4.3.

1.5.3. Semantic checking

Text, both in natural languages and in programming languages, can suffer from syntactic or semantic errors. Syntax errors will faze neither human nor machine: 'Him of quickly five' will be rejected as readily as 'begin (end', but semantic errors are different. Children can be confused by questions like: 'What color are elephant's eggs?' and even adults can have trouble answering intelligently to the rather more vicious, and famous, variant: 'When did you stop beating your wife?' Given the total lack of understanding on the part of the computer, it is not amazing that computers are even more susceptible to semantic errors than humans, and it would be nice to have reliable formal methods for checking semantic errors that possess the same power as those we have for syntax checking. Unfortunately, only a few, very simple semantic checks can be done properly; most of the more comprehensive semantic correctness tests have been proved to be recursively unsolvable. So we shall have to do with less.

The simple semantic checks routinely done by a compiler include such things as checking for undeclared identifiers and checking the number of parameters in procedure calls. At the other end of the spectrum, recursively unsolvable semantic checks include those for termination, dynamic reachability of code, and many others. Only one advanced semantic check has proved its value through the years: strong type checking. Furthermore, there are a number of heuristic checks.

The instructions on data in an imperative programming language fall under one of two categories: built-in actions and programmer-defined actions. The built-in actions generally require the values of their operands to belong to certain domains; for example, an if-statement requires the conditions to be a value from the domain {true, false} and the plus operator may require both operands to be a value in the range {−32768..32767}. Many programming languages require the programmer to specify the domains of the operands of the actions he defines. If this is done properly, the compiler can, from a static analysis of the program, check whether any action can ever be presented with a value that is not in the expected domain. The domains are generally called *types*; if the domain consistency checking will signal *all* domain inconsistencies, it is called *strong type checking*, otherwise it is called *weak type checking*.

Strong type checking is useful in that it provides the programmer with early warnings about possible semantic errors in his program. This protection is, however, partial: a type-consistent program can still be semantically incorrect, e.g., the second operand of a division operation may be of the correct type integer, but the actual value may be zero at run time, and a type-inconsistent program need not always come to harm when run, since the offending code may never be reached. Still, the general experience with strong type checking is very favorable, and modern imperative programming languages like Ada and Modula-2 support it.

In an attempt to supply even more semantic checking, some compilers perform *heuristic checks* on the program. A good heuristic check has the property that if it identifies an error, the error is certain to occur at run time, provided the pertaining code is executed at all; if the heuristic check does not find the error, the error may still be there, though. An example could be the test whether a recursive routine has an escape hatch (see Section 1.5.1): if each invocation of a routine will inevitably result in another invocation of that same routine, the program is certainly erroneous.

We are now reaching the outskirts of programming methodology, however, and shall not pursue the subject any further.

1.6. Program processing

Writing a program is not enough, the program must also be run on a computer. The hardware of the computer is unable to execute, say, Ada commands directly, but it can execute machine instructions directly. There are basically two ways to run a program in a high-level language, called the *source program*, on a computer: interpretation and compilation.

1.6.1. Interpretation and compilation

In the first method, we have a special program, consisting of machine instructions and running directly on the hardware, that is capable of reading, analyzing and executing, e.g., Ada commands. Such a program is called an *interpreter*, in this case an Ada-interpreter. To run the program using an interpreter, we call the interpreter and give it the name of our source program; it then reads and analyzes our program, may give warnings or error messages, and starts executing our program. The interpreter has access to our complete source program text while it is running; this allows the interpreter to formulate possible error messages or statistics in terms of the source program.

In the second method, we have a different special program, also consisting of machine instructions and running directly on the hardware, that is also capable of reading and analyzing commands in a high-level language, but that translates them to machine instructions rather than executing them. Such a program is called a *compiler*. To run the program using a compiler, we call the compiler and give it the name of our source program. From it, the compiler produces an *object program*, which consists mainly of machine instructions and some administration; in a sense, the source and object programs are semantically equivalent. Contrary to expectations, the object program cannot be run directly; we first have to call a second special program, called a *linker*, which adds to the object program some run-time library routines; this results in an *executable binary program*, also called *binary*, for short, which is indeed, as the name says, executable on the hardware. To actually run our program, we call the binary program; we can, of course, repeat the last step as often as we want, without having to repeat the first two steps.

This two-stage compile-and-link scenario allows programmers to split their programs into manageable chunks, compile them separately and combine them using the linker. Also, complicated source code commands, e.g., the Pascal `write` command or the Ada tasking commands, are often not translated to the full required sets of machine instructions but rather to references to such sets. The linker then resolves these references, allowing the programmer to specify the desired libraries from which to resolve them.

The advantage of compilation is that execution of a binary program can easily be a factor of a hundred faster than execution through an interpreter. A disadvantage is that in most compilers, most of the original source code structure is lost in the binary, so run-time error messages can be given only in terms of the machine code instructions, and are often next to meaningless to the user.

In the beginning of this section we have claimed for simplicity that both the interpreter and the compiler consist of machine instructions, that is, result from compilation. In fact, both could again be interpreted, but it will be clear that this stacking of interpreters must end somewhere in an interpreter consisting of machine instructions.

1.6.2. Debugging tools

The indigestibility of run-time error messages given by compiled programs has led to the development of a number of debugging tools. The simplest of these read the machine error message, which often takes the form of a core dump, and try to display information and answer questions about it; they make a mediocre job of it at best, but are better than nothing. Much of today's debugging is still done at stone-age level. Modern systems keep the entire source code in the binary and use it to display the information in a form relevant to the user. The best allow the user to navigate through various states of the running program. These debuggers approach, and sometimes surpass, the reporting capabilities of interpreting systems.

1.6.3. Programming environments

In practice, compiling a program is often more complicated than described above, especially during the development phase. In a well-organized program, the program text is spread out over many files, many of which each implement a single abstract data type. Each file can be compiled separately to produce the corresponding object file. The linker gathers all these object files and composes one executable binary from it, the runnable program. When a program under development is run, more often than not an error shows up, the correction of which necessitates the modification of one or more of the program files, followed by recompilation. It would be foolish and wasteful to recompile all program files; recreating only the object files that are affected by the modifications suffices. The linker then constructs a new executable binary and the development cycle continues.

Keeping track of which files have been modified and finding out which object files and/or executable binaries should be reconstructed can be a major effort in a fair-sized project, but fortunately the activity can be automated to a large extent. Such *program management systems* come in two varieties: general and integrated.

A general program management system is an independent program or set of programs that can in principle manage programs in any language, including natural language. It can, in some way, be parametrized with knowledge about the programs it should manage, available compilers, program dependencies, user wishes, etc. Examples are the UNIX program make or the VMS program MMS.

An integrated program management system is built in or around a programming language. Often the language cannot be used outside the program management system: the programs are not available as separate files to the user and all code is under control of the program management system. In exchange, the system can give much relevant support. Program management systems are appreciated differently by different people; some like them for the support they give, some hate them for the freedom they take away. An example of a partially integrated program management system is APSE, the Ada programming support environment. The algorithmic language ABC supplies a largely integrated programming environment; the functional language Miranda and the object-oriented programming language Smalltalk come as fully integrated program management systems.

2. Algorithmic languages

In the early years, programming languages were designed by abstracting more and more from the hardware; in a sense virtual hardware was created of a higher level. Then the emphasis shifted to the algorithmic, the recipe-like nature of a program; this resulted among other things in a better understanding of data types and flow of control and allowed the level of the virtual hardware to be raised even more, thus creating the algorithmic languages.

In reaction to these automaton-flavored if not machine-oriented languages, some designers set out from the other end, based their design on different abstract paradigms such as mathematical functions, predicate calculus or lambda calculus, and left it to the compiler writer community to reach the hardware level from there. Such classes of languages will be treated in Sections 4 and 5.

These developments did not mark the end of the algorithmic paradigm. On the contrary, algorithmic languages have continued to grow and to be used. The reason for this may be twofold. First, on present-day hardware, algorithmic languages will often be ten or a hundred times faster than the other types of languages, and they are certainly not ten or a hundred times more difficult to use. Second, the algorithmic paradigm is fairly congenial to the present-day western mind, often more so than the other paradigms. Both effects may change, though, as hardware develops and culture changes.

Almost all serious programming today is done in an algorithmic language; attempts to change this by using a variant of Prolog in the Japanese fifth generation computer system project have not met with the success some had hoped for. The most prominent algorithmic languages at the moment are Ada, C, ANSI C, Pascal and Modula-2, although FORTRAN and COBOL may still be more widely used.

2.1. Principles

The basis of the algorithmic paradigm is the fully specified and fully controlled manipulation of named data in a step-wise fashion. This paradigm fits comfortably in the human mind, which is already used to cooking from recipes or to following instructions for changing brake linings on a car. It also fits in well with the hardware, which already manipulates data in a step-wise fashion; all we have to do in an algorithmic program is to specify the data and the manipulations, and to control the stepping.

Since algorithmic languages have a 'do this, then do that' structure, they are also called *imperative*, or, since they are the oldest type of languages around, *classical*. Assembler is the archetypal imperative language.

2.2. Concepts

Specifying the named data is done through data declarations (Section 2.2.1), data manipulation is done through statements (Section 2.2.2) and controlling the stepping is called flow of control (Section 2.2.3).

The language constructs will be illustrated with examples from ANSI C [Kernighan & Ritchie, 1988] in the left column, and Ada [DoD, 1983] in the right column. Case differences are significant in C and are ignored in Ada. Both languages use small letters for the keywords; identifiers are in small letters in C but traditionally in capitals in Ada. To avoid duplication, we shall use small letters in the running text, thus: 'the variable i' where the C text has i and the Ada text has I.

2.2.1. Data

A data item in memory has the form of a number of bits, without any hints as to what these bits represent. In order to manipulate the data item meaningfully, structure has to be imposed on it and for many purposes it has to be given a name. A *data declaration* does both; it binds a name to the data item and to a structure. The imposed structure is specified as a *type* and the name is an identifier. The bit pattern combined with the imposed structure determines the *value* of the data item. Since the hardware allows the bit pattern to be modified or replaced under control of machine instructions, the value of the data item can be changed; hence it is called a *variable*. Note that the data item exists in the machine, while its structure and its name exist only in the program.

Data declarations look slightly different in C and in Ada:

```
int i, j;                    I, J: INTEGER;
```

Both declare two data items, named i and j, respectively, both represented by bit patterns that are to be interpreted as integers. Note that the type is also indicate by a name: `int` / `INTEGER`.

Some languages allow the data items to be *initialized* upon declaration:

```
int i = 3, j = 5;            I, J: INTEGER := 5;
```

Unlike Ada, C allows each identifier in a declaration to be initialized to a different value.

Some languages allow *constant* declarations: the bit pattern cannot be modified after initialization:

```
const int i = 3, j = 5;      I, J: constant INTEGER := 5;
```

Note that this is software protection: the compiler will not translate any code that can modify i or j, but the hardware locations of i and j remain as modifiable as ever.

2.2.1.1. Types. From a hardware point of view, a type is a method for interpreting data bits in a computer; from a programming language point of view, it is a set of values and a set of operations defined on those values. It is the task of the compiler writer to find the most appropriate hardware type for a given programming language type. Generally the hardware supplies *characters*, which are actually integers in the range $\{0..255\}$, *integer numbers* of various sizes, . among which the ranges $\{-32768..+32767\}$, $\{0..65535\}$, and $\{-2147483648..+2147483647\}$ are common, and *real numbers* of various sizes and precisions.

These form the basic types in many programming languages. Some declarations are:

```
                        type UNSIGNED_INT is
                          range 0 . . 65535;
char c;                 C: CHAR;
int i;                  I: INTEGER;
unsigned int ui;        UI: UNSIGNED_INT;
float d;                D: REAL;
```

Values of these types can be obtained by writing them down literally in a program. Examples of common notations are `'g'` for the character *g*, `-123` for the integer -123 and `3.14` or `6.02e23` for the real numbers 3.14 and $6.02*10^{23}$. Characters can be arrayed together into *strings*, with a usual notation `"Operations Research"` for a string consisting of 19 characters, including the space. Notations that carry their values directly are called *literals*.

It will be clear that infinite-sized integers or infinite-precision real numbers cannot be stored in a finite computer. The mathematical objects $\mathbb{N}$ and $\mathbb{R}$ cannot be faithfully modeled on a computer, common intuition notwithstanding.

Since a type is, among other things, a set of values, the empty set also corresponds to a type; it corresponds to zero bits in memory and is known as *void* in some languages, but is conspicuously absent from many others.

The above types and their names are generally built into the language. The programmer can extend the set of available types in the program by using *type constructors*, which construct new types out of zero or more old types. Some languages allow the thus constructed types to be used directly and anonymously in a declaration:

```
int ia[10];             IA: array (INTEGER range 1 . . 10)
                                of INTEGER;
```

while others require the constructed type to be bound to a name first, in a type definition:

```
                        type INT10_ARRAY is
                            array (INTEGER range 1 . . 10)
                                of INTEGER;
                        IA: INT10_ARRAY;
```

The latter method is probably to be preferred.

2.2.1.2. Type constructors. The following description of type constructors is highly simplified; most type constructors have strange quirks and unexpected limitations in practice, generally for implementation reasons.

The simplest type constructor is the *enumeration*; it does not build upon other types, but rather defines a set of names to be the values of the new data type: the type definition

```
typedef enum {                 type TRAFFIC_LIGHT_COLOR is
    red, amber, green              (RED, AMBER, GREEN);
} traffic_light_color;
```

defines a new type `traffic_light_color` with only three values: `red`, `amber` and `green`. We can use the type in defining the lights on a crossing:

```
traffic_light_color            N, E, S, W:
    n, e, s, w;                    TRAFFIC_LIGHT_COLOR;
```

One would expect the only operations allowed on values of an enumeration type to be copying and comparison for equality, but most programming languages also allow ordering (comparison for greater/smaller) or even incrementing (taking the next one).

The simplest type constructor that builds on another type is the *array*. An array is a series of a known number of items, all of the same type. An item in the array, called an *element*, can be reached by specifying its ordinal number, called its *index*, through the indexing operation [ ]. There is generally an operator to determine the number of elements in the array. Given the array variable declaration

```
int ia[10];                    IA: array (INTEGER range 1 .. 10)
                                   of INTEGER;
```

the first element can be accessed as

```
ia[0]                          IA(1)
```

In Ada, the index of the first element is defined by the programmer; in C this index is always zero.

The above are one-dimensional arrays; one can also have multi-dimensional arrays and some languages allow arrays of arrays. Trying to access a non-existing element, e.g., `ia[11]` is erroneous and the attempt may or may not be caught in an actual system.

A second type constructor that builds from only one type is the *sequence* or *list*. A sequence is a series of an unknown number of elements, all of the same type; elements in a sequence cannot be reached by indexing. The first element can be accessed through the `head` operator, the rest of the sequence through the `tail` operator, both of which may legally fail if the sequence is empty. There is definitely no operator to determine the size of the sequence. Given the implementation problems of dealing with an unknown number of items, hardly any algorithmic language supports the sequence as a type constructor, although a sequential file may be seen as an example.

Sequences and arrays are often confused and although strings are generally used as sequences, most languages model them as arrays, at the expense of much messy programming.

A third type constructor that builds from one type only is the *powerset*. A powerset over a type T with a set of values V is a type the values of which are sets of the elements of V. Neither C nor Ada feature powersets; the Modula-2 code

```
TYPE CharSetType = SET OF CHAR;
VAR ChSet: CharSetType;
```

defines a powerset type `CharSetType` over the characters and a variable `ChSet` of that type. The language features a set constructor, { }, and a checking operator in:

```
ChSet := { 'q', 'w', 'e' };
IF 'z' IN ChSet THEN . . .
```

Often the need arises to group together a fixed number of data items of differing types into one data item. The type of this item can be constructed as a *record*, also called *struct*. Provided a type `brand_type` has been defined before, the following record definition describes some aspects of a car:

```
typedef struct {              type CAR_TYPE is record
    brand_type brand;             BRAND: BRAND_TYPE;
    int number_of_doors;          NUMBER_OF_DOORS: INTEGER;
    unsigned int price;           PRICE: UNSIGNED_INT;
} car_type;                   end record;
```

The items in a record are called *fields*; they can be accessed by using their names, which in this case are called *selectors*: given a variable `new_car` of type `car_type`, its brand can be accessed as

```
new_car.brand                 NEW_CAR.BRAND
```

The dot . for selecting from a record serves a purpose similar to the brackets [ ] for indexing an array.

Unlike the basic and constructed types treated earlier, records can be recursive: a record can, in a sense, contain an item of the same type. This is highly convenient in programming; a binary tree of type `bin_tree_type` could be described effectively as a collection of nodes of the type

```
typedef struct {            type BIN_TREE_TYPE is record
    bin_tree_type               LEFT, RIGHT:
        left, right;                BIN_TREE_TYPE;
    item_type value;            VALUE: ITEM_TYPE;
} bin_tree_type;            end record;
```

but it is immediately clear that this has a problem: a data item of say *N* bytes cannot contain 2*N*-plus bytes, and the above two declarations are in effect incorrect. The problem is solved by storing the internal nodes left and right elsewhere as independent nodes and replace them inside the record by the machine addresses of the nodes placed elsewhere. The machine addresses have a fixed size, regardless of the size of the item they address, and thus the size of a node is kept finite. This trick also supplies the escape hatch needed in any form of recursion: if the left or right node is absent, the corresponding machine address is a special value which does not, actually or by convention, address any node.

As an accidental result of historical development, the administrative task of declaring, manipulating and checking these machine addresses is put on the programmer's shoulders, even in high-level languages. The machine addresses are known as *pointers*, which are said to *point to* or to *refer to* the addressed item; the special value indicating the absence of an item is called a *null pointer*, since its bit pattern is often zero.

Consequently, the above record declarations for bin_tree_type are incorrect; both require the insertion of a pointer, indicated in C by a * and in Ada by access. Note that both languages employ some mechanism to deal with the mutual dependency of the names:

```
                            type BIN_TREE_TYPE;
                            type BIN_TREE_ACCESS_TYPE is
                                access BIN_TREE_TYPE;
typedef
struct _bin_tree_type {     type BIN_TREE_TYPE is record
    struct _bin_tree_type       LEFT, RIGHT:
        *left, *right;              BIN_TREE_ACCESS_TYPE;
    item_type value;            VALUE: ITEM_TYPE;
} bin_tree_type;            end record;
```

A value having a given pointer type can be obtained by using an *allocator*; the forms

```
(bin_tree_type *)           new BIN_TREE_TYPE
    malloc(sizeof
        (bin_tree_type))
```

allocate memory for one record of type bin_tree_type and yield a pointer to it. The item referred to by a pointer `bin_tree_pointer` can be accessed as:

```
*bin_tree_pointer                    BIN_TREE_POINTER.all
```

Pointers are also used to make data manipulation more efficient; copying a pointer to an item is generally much more efficient than copying the item.

Pointers are a constant source of programming errors. They have to be checked before nearly each use, to avoid following a null pointer. The memory allocated to the item may be reclaimed for further use, but a pointer to it may continue to exist and in the end be used; such a pointer is termed a *dangling pointer*. They are not valid across networks (see Section 6); etc. Yet the efficiency and convenience of their use are so high that hardly any algorithmic language has dared to abolish the pointer, although most take some measures to tame it. Examples of algorithmic languages without pointers are ABC and SETL, whereas Orca features a fully tamed pointer.

A record of a type with *N* fields contains field 1 *and* field 2 *and* . . . *and* field *N*. Sometimes, though rarely, it is useful to specify a data type of which the values are either a field 1 *or* field 2 *or* . . . *or* field *N*. Such a type is called a *union*. To model a garage that can contain either one car or a number of bicycles we can write:

```
                              type CONTENTS is
                                 (HAS_CAR, HAS_BICYCLES);
typedef union {               type GARAGE (DISCR: CONTENTS) is
                              record
                                 case DISCR is
                                    when HAS_CAR =>
     car_type car;                    CAR: CAR_TYPE;
                                    when HAS_BICYCLES =>
     int number_of_bicycles;             NUMBER_OF_BICYCLES:
                                             INTEGER;
                                 end case;
} garage;                     end record;
```

In C, the burden of remembering which of the fields of the union is present rests on the programmer; the union is *undiscriminated*. In Ada, there is a special field in the record (DISCR in this example) that records the nature of the active field: the union is *discriminated*. In this case Ada requires much more code from the programmer, but gives much more support than C does.

A few languages allow procedures and functions to be manipulated and used as ordinary values, though often with restrictions of some sort. This feature is useful for many purposes; for one thing it allows us to declare arrays of functions, thus modeling vectors of functions. Many designers, however, feel that having functions as values constitutes an undesirable mixing of data and flow of control. C has pointers to functions as data, Ada does not allow any data involving functions.

In principle, all of the above type constructors can be combined, i.e., applied successively; we can have arrays of records, records containing arrays, or powersets of powersets of pointers to unions, to give a few examples. In practice, though, each language has its own set of restrictions, mostly dictated by implementation considerations. For instance, most languages which have powersets at all, allow them only for enumeration types.

2.2.2. Statements

The main activity of a program in an algorithmic language is changing the internal state of the machine as represented by the values of its variables, and the external state as stored in its input/output devices. The state of some output devices can be observed, e.g., as print-out on paper, and is called the *result* of the program.

Through a historical accident, commands in a programming language have come to be called *statements*.

The value of a variable can be modified by executing an *assignment* statement:

```
i=(x+y) / 2;                    I := (X+Y) / 2;
```

will calculate the value of the *expression* $(x+y)/2$ and assign the result as the new value to i. Note that the assignment differs fundamentally from the equality in mathematics in that it does not set up a permanent relation: i will keep its new value only until the next assignment to it. This makes assignments like i = i + 1; legal and meaningful.

The external state can be changed with an *output* statement:

```
printf("%d", (x+y)/2);          PUT((X+Y)/2);
```

will evaluate the expression and display its result in readable form on some output device.

In both cases, the value assigned or displayed is the result of evaluating an expression. Expressions have a form similar to those in mathematics, linearized and extended with notations for access to elements of constructed types. The type of the resulting value can normally be derived from the expression alone, without having to run the program: the type is known statically. Examples are:

```
i * j + 3                       I * J + 3
```

which yields an integer;

```
car.number_of_doors == 4        CAR.NUMBER_OF_DOORS=4
```

which yields a boolean value; and

(ia[0] + ia[1]) / 2   (IA(1) + IA(2)) / 2

which yields the average of the first two elements of ia.

Note that the assignment is not performed until the expression has been evaluated completely:

i = i + 1;   I := I + 1;

will increase the value of i by one. Contrast this to the expression

i == i + 1   I = I + 1

which will yield false, regardless of the value of i.

The above examples show that there is a certain confusion in notation between assignment and test for equality: C uses = for assignment and == for test for equality, Ada and most other languages use := and =, respectively.

2.2.3. Flow-of-control

Algorithmic languages allow the programmer extensive control over the order in which the statements in the program are executed or skipped: the *flow of control*. The usual mechanisms are sequencing, selection, delegation and repetition, in various varieties.

2.2.3.1. Sequencing. A *sequencer* tells explicitly which statement must be executed next. The usual sequencer is the semicolon, as in

i = i + 1; j = j + 1;   I := I + 1; J := J + 1;

which tells that the next statement to be executed is the textually following one. Explicit deviation from the in-line sequence can be achieved by the *goto* statement, which specifies a *label* which must label a statement elsewhere in the program; the flow of control then jumps to there:

```
        goto bad_case;                    goto BAD_CASE;
          . . .                             . . .
          . . .                             . . .
bad_case: . . .                   ≪ BAD _CASE ≫ . . .
```

The goto-statement has had much deserved bad publicity and has disappeared almost completely from the programming scene, with the GOTO in BASIC being the notable exception. It should be pointed out, though, that the actual culprit is the label. To understand an algorithmic program, the reader must at all times know what the state of the machine means. Arriving at a label, however, he can no longer know this, unless he checks the meaning of the state of the machine at all places from which flow of control can reach the label; and that is an unattractive and error-prone task.

Some modern algorithmic languages, e.g., Modula-2 or Orca, have abandoned the goto-statement, while others, e.g., C or Ada, retain it, often mainly to cater for computer-generated programs.

2.2.3.2. Selection. In its simplest form, the *if* statement allows one of two pieces of code to be selected for execution, depending on the value of a boolean expression; the if-statement

```
if (x < 0) {              if X < 0 then
     y = -x;                   Y := -X;
} else {                  else
     y=x;                     Y := X;
}                         end if;
```

will set y to the absolute value of x. Many languages, but not C, also have an if...then...elsif...then...elsif...then... construction.

Selection among a number of pieces of code, based on an integer or enumeration value, can be expressed by a *case* statement:

```
switch (n) {              case N is
case 0:                       when 0 =>
    printf("empty set");          PUT("empty set");
    break;
case 1:                       when 1 =>
    printf("singleton");          PUT("singleton");
    break;
default:                      when others =>
    printf("multiple");           PUT("multiple");
    break;
}                         end case;
```

For the bizarre syntax of the C switch-statement, see any book on C.

2.2.3.3. Delegation. When the same sequence of statements has to be performed in a number of different places in the program, it is convenient to encapsulate the sequence in a named procedure (see Section 2.2.4.2) and to replace it by a *procedure call* in the places in which it needs to be performed. The procedure call names the procedure; its execution transfers the flow of control to the beginning of the procedure, but, unlike the goto, it guarantees that the flow of control will eventually return here, i.e., just after the procedure call. Example:

```
read_next_line( );                    READ_NEXT_LINE;
```

which delegates the work of reading the next line, presumably into a variable with a known name, to the procedure read_next_line.

2.2.3.4. Repetition. A sequence of statements can be repeated a precalculated number of times by using a *for-statement*. The for-statement also features a *controlled variable*, which serves as a repetition counter and which is available to the sequence of statements to be repeated. Example: the statements

```
sum = 0;                         SUM := 0;
   for ( i = 0; i < 10; i++) {   for I in 1 .. 10 loop
   sum += a[i];                     SUM := SUM + A( I );
}                                end loop;
```

will sum the values of the elements of the 10-element array a into the variable sum; i is the controlled variable. The C syntax is again bizarre: i = 0; initializes the control variable, the check i < 10 is performed before each repetition and the increment operation i++ is performed after each repetition; the ++ is a built-in operator in C, which increments its left hand operand; the operator += adds the value of its right operand to its left operand.

A sequence of statements can be repeated an indeterminate number of times by using a *while-statement*: repetition continues as long as a given condition remains fulfilled. Example:

```
n=1;                             N := 1;
sum = 0.0;                       SUM := 0.0;
while (1.0/(n*n) > 1e-11) {      while (1.0/N*N) > 1E-11 loop
    sum += 1.0/(n*n);                SUM := SUM + 1.0/(N*N);
    n++;                             N := N + 1;
}                                end loop;
```

is a, numerically naive, way of calculating $\sum_{n=1}^{\infty} 1/n^2$ to a certain accuracy.

Many languages feature, in addition to the while-statement, a *repeat-until-statement*, which continues to repeat the enclosed sequence of statements until a given condition is met. Example:

```
do {
    read_next_line( );
    process_line( );
} while (!end_of_file( ));
```

reads and processes lines from a file until the file is exhausted. The ! is the negation operator in C.

The repeat-until-statement is to be avoided, since it embodies the idea that a set or sequence cannot be empty: the above code crashes abysmally when presented with an empty input file. Ada has no repeat-until-statement.

2.2.4. *Program composition*

To be effective, the above statements must somehow be grouped into complete programs. Four levels of hierarchy can be distinguished here: blocks, procedures/functions, modules/packages and programs. Another important ingredient of program composition, abstract data types, is treated here as a special case of modules/packages.

2.2.4.1. Blocks. A *block* is the smallest grouping of statements; it is generally delimited by keywords like begin and end or { and } and is itself again a statement. Syntactically, it allows a set of statements in a context where one statement is expected. Semantically, its main feature is that it defines a local *scope*, a set of names that are known only within the block; these names originate in local declarations and generally refer to temporary (auxiliary) variables. The following block swaps the values of the non-local integer variables x and y, using a temporary variable t:

```
                          declare
{                             T: INTEGER;
  int t;                  begin
  t = x; x = y; y = t;        T := X; X := Y; Y := T;
}                         end;
```

The flow of control enters the block at the top and leaves it at the bottom. Entities declared in the block can no longer be accessed after the flow of control has left the block and can then be removed by the system.

A direct consequence of the fact that a block is composed of statements and is itself a statement is the possibility of having nested blocks; each such block defines its own local scope. The rules that determine which names from surrounding blocks are accessible in a given block are known as the *scope rules*; they differ from language to language, but never allow an outer block to access names from an inner block.

Most programming languages have an outermost level of declarations, the *global scope*. Variables declared on this level remain in existence and accessible throughout the entire program run.

2.2.4.2. Procedures and functions. A *procedure* is a named and parametrized block; the block is called the *body* of the procedure. It originates from a procedure declaration, the execution of which does *not* activate the code in the body. A procedure is activated by a procedure call, which names the procedure and supplies information about the parameters. The procedure call starts by identifying the procedure, transfers parameter information to the procedure, causes the flow of control to enter the top of the body of the procedure, waits until the body has finished and then leads the flow of control back to the statement after the call.

In its simplest form, the parameter information is a value passed from the call, where it is known as the *actual parameter*; it then serves as the initial value of the *formal parameter* in the procedure. This input parameter semantics is called *call by value*. Most languages, but not C, allow some form of output parameters: the procedure can change the values of some of its actual parameters by assigning to the corresponding formal parameter. The change is then effected immediately or upon return from the call; the former mechanism is called *call by reference* and the latter *call by result*. There are many other parameter passing mechanisms of varying degrees of sophistication, but reliance on clever parameter mechanisms has waned over the last decade.

A procedure without output parameters is useful only if it changes some state outside itself; the following procedure pr_sq prints the square of its parameter:

```
                              procedure PR_SQ(N: INTEGER) is
pr_sq(int n) {                begin
    printf("%d", n*n);            PUT(N*N);
}                             end PR_SQ;
```

Note that the formal parameter n is declared *with* its type, but in a manner different from a local variable declaration. Calls can be pr_sq(-1); and pr_sq(i+j);.

An example of the use of an output parameter is the Ada call GET(I), which will read an integer value from the standard input and assign it to the variable I. The corresponding procedure definition is:

```
                    procedure GET(I: out INTEGER);
```

In C, an output variable can be simulated by passing a pointer to it as an input parameter. Rather than assigning to the parameter, the called procedure assigns to the item the pointer refers to.

A *function* differs from a procedure in that it returns a value; its call must be used in an expression rather than as a statement. To specify and return the value, the function body must execute a *return-statement* in most algorithmic languages. The following function sq returns the square of its parameter:

```
                              function SQ(N: INTEGER)
                                  return INTEGER is
int sq(int n) {               begin
    return n*n;                   return N*N;
}                             end SQ;
```

Examples of calls are n = sq(n);, which squares n, or p = sq(sq(n));, which sets p to the fourth power of n.

In some languages, e.g., Pascal, the function value is returned by assigning it to the function identifer and then returning from the function in the normal fashion, i.e., by reaching its textual end.

Both procedure and function bodies can contain direct or indirect calls to themselves, and are then *recursive*. Recursive procedures and functions are treated in Section 4.2.1.

2.2.4.3. Modules and packages. A number of related declarations of types, variables, procedures, etc., can be grouped together in a *module*, also called a *package*. If this grouping is done correctly, the module implements a data type or provides a service through a simple interface. A module consists of a *specification* or *definition* part, which contains a description of the interface which the module implements, and an *implementation* part, which contains the code that implements the interface. Module boundaries are explicit in Ada using the keyword package, and coincide with file boundaries in C. Since even a very small module is often already tens of lines long, we give here an incomplete example, concerning the implementation of complex numbers; rather than printing the programs in the usual two columns, we give them one after the other.

The C version consists of two files, complex.h and complex.c; we assume that the function sqrt () has been defined elsewhere. The file complex.h contains:

```
typedef struct {
     double re, im;
} complex;
extern double c_abs(complex);
```

The file complex.c contains:

```
static double sq(double x) {
     return x*x;
}
double c_abs(complex x) {
     return sqrt(sq(x.re) + sq(x.im));
}
```

The Ada version consists of two compilation units, the package specification and the package body. The package specification is:

```
package COMPLEX is
     type COMPLEX is record
          RE, IM: REAL;
     end record;

     function ABS(X: COMPLEX) return REAL;
end COMPLEX;
```

The package body is:

```
package body COMPLEX is
      function SQ(X: REAL) return REAL is
      begin
            return X*X;
      end SQ;

      function ABS(X: COMPLEX) return REAL is
      begin
            return SQRT(SQ(X.RE)+SQ(X.IM));
      end ABS;
end COMPLEX;
```

In C, the definition module is traditionally a so-called *header* file; it is the file complex.h in our example. Any interpretation as a definition module is convention rather than being enforced by the compiler. In Ada, the definition and implementation modules are identified syntactically.

The names in the implementation module come in two classes, public and private. The public names are available to the user through the interface, the private ones are local to the module. Languages vary widely in the means by which the difference is indicated. C uses extern for public and static for private names supplemented by some trickery not explained here, Ada relies on not mentioning the private names in the package specification, some languages use *export-* and *import-statements*, and other schemes can be found.

The user of a module is concerned with the interface definition or package specification only. User programs that use the service supplied by a module must refer to the interface definition, in C through an *include-statement* and in Ada through a *with-clause*. This reference then introduces the names with their proper types, values, etc., through which the service can be accessed. A small procedure is given below, which declares one complex number variable, gives it a value and prints its absolute value. The style in which it is programmed has suffered by our wish to keep it short and to keep the two versions as similar as possible.

In C we have:

```
#include "complex.h"

test(){
    complex c;

    c.re=3.0;
    c.im=5.0;
    printf("%f", c_abs(c));
}
```

In Ada we have:

```
with COMPLEX;
procedure TEST is
    C: COMPLEX;
begin
    C.RE := 3.0;
    C.IM := 5.0;
    PUT (COMPLEX.ABS(C));
end TEST;
```

2.2.4.4. Abstract data types. A data type is a set of values, often available as literals, together with a set of procedures and functions for manipulating the values. An *abstract data type* is a named data type defined solely through functions and procedures for creating and manipulating values of that data type; if literals are available, they are known by name only. All internal structure is hidden from the user.

Strange as it may seem, many present-day programming languages do not have special language constructs for dealing with abstract data types. The reason is that modules/packages are eminently suitable for the implementation of abstract data types: they provide just the right amount of abstraction and information hiding. If one considers the present module structure to be derived from the Simula 67 class concept, one can see the module structure as *the* special language construct for abstract data types.

Object-oriented languages have far heavier support for abstract data types, but most designers of algorithmic languages feel that the ensuing complexity and inefficiency are not justified in an algorithmic language. Notable exceptions are Eiffel [Meyer, 1988] and, to a certain extent, Oberon.

2.2.4.5. Program construction. Whereas linguistic support for blocks and procedures is strong in almost all languages, and support for modules is often reasonable, linguistic support for program construction is non-existent in most languages. As a result of historical development, the assembly of program parts, e.g., modules, into a complete program is considered a task of the operating system rather than of the language processor. The final result of processing a module is an object file, and there the responsibility of the language processor ends. The operating system has a special facility, called a *linker*, which blindly connects the various object files it is offered into a program file, and a second facility, called the *loader*, which loads the contents of the program file into memory and starts its execution. In some operating systems, these facilities are not well separated.

A major consequence of all this is that there is no software protection against combining the wrong object files into a program: an object file using one version of, say, `complex.h` may very well be combined with an object file using another version, with predictably disastrous results.

Sometimes facilities are present to mitigate the bad effects; for example, the consistency of a set of C modules can be subjected to the heuristic checking program `lint`; also, a measure of support can be given by the program `make`. Some modern languages come with their own linker, while some advanced operating systems may allow private, nonsystem, loaders.

2.3. Examples

Many examples of algorithmic languages have already been shown, the most prominent ones being C, ANSI C, Ada, Pascal and Modula-2. It is not difficult to extend this list with names like Algol 60, PL/I, Coral 66, Algol 68, Simula, and, of late, Turing and Oberon. Because of the similarity between these languages, they are called *Algol-like*. Algol 68 deserves special mention, since it has had great influence on language designers, if not always on language design. Many programming language concepts (coercions, dereferencing and void, to name a few) were formulated clearly and concisely for the first time in Algol 68.

Examples of non-Algol-like algorithmic languages are COBOL, FORTRAN, Lisp and BASIC. More modern, very different, examples are ABC and SETL.

3. Object-oriented languages

Unlike the other paradigms we discuss, the object-oriented paradigm is not just a programming method but also a method for building systems. Object-oriented design typically deals with the problem of building large, complex systems that are subject to change. In building such a system, programming the individual modules is often the least difficult problem. It is much harder to integrate the modules, make the system manageable and understandable, and facilitate changes. Object-oriented design tries to give a solution to these problems. Still, since we are discussing programming languages rather than design methods here, we will focus on the language aspects of the object-oriented paradigm.

3.1. Principles

In an object-oriented language, the state of a problem is encapsulated in so-called *objects*. An object contains data and provides operations for accessing these data. The key idea is that the data of an object can only be accessed through these operations. In other words, the variables of an object are not visible outside the object.

This principle of *data encapsulation* is essential to the object-oriented paradigm. It establishes a firewall between the user of an object and the code implementing it. In particular, the user does not know or care how the data of an object are represented. As an example, consider a stack object with operations for pushing and popping elements. The stack could be represented as an array, a list, or whatever. Since the representation of a stack object is unknown outside the object, it can be changed without affecting the users.

In a pure object-oriented language, all entities are objects. An expression such as '5 − 3' is interpreted as applying the operation 'subtract 3 and return result' to the integer object '5'. The computational model consists of objects that invoke each other's operations.

Of course, data encapsulation is also provided by abstract data types (see Section 2.2.4.4). A distinguishing feature of object-oriented languages, however, is *inheritance*. Roughly speaking, inheritance allows object kinds to be built hierarchically, with the most general one at the top and more specific ones at the bottom of the hierarchy. Each object kind now inherits the operations from the higher levels of the hierarchy. So, an object does not have to implement all the operations itself; rather, it can reuse some operations from object kinds higher in the hierarchy.

As an example, we can have a hierarchy of vehicles, as shown below:

Object kind	Operations
Vehicles	weight
Motorized	maximumSpeed, horsePower
Car	numberOfDoors
Bus	numberOfSeats
NotMotorized	
Bike	numberOfGears
HorseSleigh	numberOfHorses

Consider one of the leaf nodes of the hierarchy, a car. A car supports the operation `numberOfDoors`. Since a car is a motorized vehicle, it also supports the inherited operations `maximumSpeed` and `horsePower`. Finally, since a car is a vehicle, it also inherits the operation weight.

So, using inheritance it is possible to implement objects that are extensions of existing objects. In other words, to build a new kind of object, one does not have to start from scratch; one can often use an object kind that already exists. We will later discuss how inheritance is expressed in an object-oriented language.

Besides inheritance, another key difference between algorithmic and object-oriented languages is the binding time of operations [Cox, 1986]. In Pascal, if a user calls a procedure `f`, it is determined during compile time which code will be invoked. In contrast, in an object-oriented language a procedure (operation) will always be executed by some object and it is this object that decides which code will be executed. Since, in general, the object executing the operation is determined at run-time, the choice of which code to execute is made dynamically.

As an example, reconsider the hierarchy of vehicles. Suppose we want each vehicle to support an operation `draw` that draws a picture of it. Since all pictures will be different, each object type needs to implement a different `draw` operation, so we have four different operations for a car, bus, bike, and horsesleigh. If we apply the `draw` operation to a specific vehicle X, the run time system will automatically choose the right operation, based on the kind of X. This approach is called *late binding*.

Now think of a Pascal implementation of the same operation. A vehicle would probably be defined as a record with variants. The `draw` procedure would take such a record as a parameter and would test what kind of vehicle it has to draw and then choose the right code to execute:

```
case X.kind of
     car:          draw_car(X);
     bus:          draw_bus(X);
     bike:         draw_bike(X);
     horsesleigh: draw_horsesleigh(X)
end
```

This approach has many disadvantages. Each time a new kind of vehicle is added, the case statement has to be modified. In an object-oriented language, only a new object kind has to be implemented. The code above is specialized for a single application, in which we need precisely the four types of vehicles mentioned in the case statement. It is hard to imagine reusing this code for another application.

In summary, the key principles of object-oriented languages are data encapsulation, inheritance, and late binding. As we will see later, however, not all languages that claim to be object-oriented support all three features.

3.2. Concepts

In this subsection we will discuss the most important concepts used in object-oriented languages. We will look at classes, objects, methods, messages, and inheritance.

The concept of a *class* is fundamental to object-oriented programming. A class gives a description of an object kind. In the vehicles example, we would have seven classes: Vehicles, Motorized, NotMotorized, Car, Bus, Bike, and HorseSleigh. A class description contains:

(1) A description of the local variables of instances of the class.

(2) The operations that can be applied to instances of the class.

In addition, a class description can specify a parent class (or *superclass*) from which operations are to be inherited. For example, the class `Motorized` would specify `Vehicles` as superclass, and `Bike` would specify `NotMotorized`. A class inherits all variables and operations from its superclass, and, by applying this rule recursively, from all other ancestors in the class hierarchy.

An *object* is nothing but an instance of a class. An object is created dynamically, using a **new** construct, which specifies its class. For example

> myCar ← **new** car

creates a new car object. A pointer to the object is stored in the variable myCar. The **new** construct automatically allocates space for the local variables of the car object, for example for the variables containing the number of doors, the maximum speed, the number of horsepowers, and weight.

Once an object has been created, it is willing to execute the operations that are defined for it. In object-oriented jargon, the object implements some *methods* (operations); to execute a method, a *message* must be sent to the object. The receiving object will accept the message, execute the method – possibly modifying its local state – and return a result. As an example of sending a message to an object, consider:

> nDoors ← myCar numberOfDoors

which sends a numberOfDoors message to the object pointed at by the variable myCar and stores the result in the variable nDoors.

We are now able to describe in greater detail what inheritance means. If an object receives a message for a method m, it will (at least conceptually) look in its class description to see if the method is defined there. If so, it executes the method and returns the result. If not, it will look at the description of its superclass, to see if method m is implemented there. If so, it will execute that method, else it will examine the superclass of its superclass. This search continues until either the method is found or the top of the hierarchy is reached. In the latter case, the object does not know how to implement method m, so it gives an error message, probably causing the program to abort.

The search procedure described above is carried out dynamically. For example, suppose the variable myCar is assigned a new object of an entirely different class that also supports the method numberOfDoors (say a class House). If the statement

> nDoors ← myCar numberOfDoors

is executed again, a different method will be found and executed.

This dynamic approach makes object-oriented languages highly flexible, but it also renders impossible compile-time checking. If a wrong message is sent to an object, the user will be told during run time that the object does not know what to do with the message. In Pascal, on the other hand, if the user applies an illegal operation to an operand, such as negating a string, the compiler will tell that *it* does not know what to do with the operation. So with object-oriented languages, one looses the benefit of an early warning.

3.3. Examples

Many languages are sometimes claimed to be object-oriented, e.g., Ada, Simula 67, CLU, Smalltalk-80 (trademark of ParcPlace systems), C++, Objective-C, Eiffel, Flavors, and Loops. What is frequently meant by this is that the language can be used in combination with the object-oriented design method. A more restrictive definition is that the language must regard all entities in the system as objects and that it must support inheritance. If the latter condition is dropped, the language is called *object-based*. Many so-called object-oriented languages merely support abstract data types, and, by the above definitions, should not even be called object-based. Ada, for example, belongs to this category. Simula 67 was the first language to use a class concept. CLU uses abstract data types and objects, but not inheritance. Below, we will look at Smalltalk-80, the first pure object-oriented language.

3.3.1. Smalltalk-80

Smalltalk-80 was developed at Xerox PARC. It is not just a programming language, but also a programming environment. The environment integrates many tools, so, e.g., the editor and the command line interpreter use similar syntax as the language itself. The Smalltalk environment also promotes the use of bitmap graphics, windows, and pointing devices (e.g., a mouse). The environment is open to the user; users have all Smalltalk-80 source code on-line and can change everything, including the operating system.

The Smalltalk-80 language supports all the concepts described above: classes, objects, methods, messages, and inheritance. The language is untyped, so the same variable can point to different kinds of objects at different times. Objects are allocated through a **new** construct (as explained above) and are deallocated automatically, using garbage collection.

A message in Smalltalk can be either a *unary* or a *keyword* message. A unary message does not have arguments; it merely specifies the message name. For example, numberOfDoors used above is a unary message. A keyword message contains one or more keywords, one for each argument. Keywords and arguments are separated by a colon. For example:

```
flightReservations reserveOnFlight:'KL641'
                    date:'25dec91' seats:2 inClass:'E'
```

sends a message with four arguments to the object flightReservations.

Keyword messages are also used for implementing control structures. For example, the predefined class Boolean implements a message ifTrue that takes a pieces of code as parameter, and only executes it if the Boolean object to which the message is sent contains the value True. The following code illustrates this idea.

```
flightReservations isEmpty:'KL641'
  ifTrue: [flightReservations cancelFlight:'KL641']
```

This code first sends an isEmpty message to object flightReservations, passing a flight number as argument. The result returned by this object will be a Boolean object. This Boolean object is sent the message ifTrue, with a so-called *block* of code as argument. It is essential here that the block of code is not yet evaluated, but passed literally to the Boolean object. Only if this object is true, it will execute the code block, so it will send a cancelFlight message to object flightReservations.

So, Smalltalk-80 is a pure object-oriented language. It treats all entities as objects and supports classes and inheritance. Even control structures are expressed through message passing between objects.

4. Functional languages

Algorithmic languages allow programmers to express algorithms, which are accurate descriptions of *how* to solve given problems. The underlying computational model uses an implicit state, consisting of the variables manipulated by the program. This state is repeatedly modified, e.g., through assignment statements. After termination, the final state defines the program's outcome. This model can be implemented by storing the state in the main memory and by translating the operations on the state into machine instructions. All in all, the model fairly closely resembles the underlying computer.

This resemblance is a strength as well as a weakness. On the one hand, algorithmic languages can be implemented efficiently, just because the mapping to the hardware is straightforward. On the other hand, programmers have to think in terms of state variables that get changed, instead of in higher-level terms. They have to specify in detail how the machine should solve their problems.

The latter observation has motivated some researches to develop alternative models which do not reflect the hardware, but are easier to use for programmers. The ideal is to have the programmer merely specify *what* has to be computed, rather than *how*. Languages that try to meet this goal are called *declarative* languages, while algorithmic languages are said to be *imperative*. The primary representatives of declarative languages are functional languages (discussed here) and logic languages (discussed in the next section), although object-oriented languages sometimes also are claimed to be declarative.

Of course, the difference between 'how' and 'what' is not always crystal clear, and neither is the difference between imperative and declarative languages. A point at issue that is less vague is performance. Declarative languages usually are much harder to implement efficiently. Naive implementations may easily be orders of magnitude slower than those for algorithmic languages. Even without an efficient implementation, however, declarative languages can still be useful, for instance for rapid prototyping.

4.1. Principles

To appreciate the principles of functional languages, one first has to understand the objections that advocates of this paradigm have against algorithmic languages. As said before, algorithmic languages use an implicit state that is repeatedly modified. The statements in the language are typically executed for their side-effects on the state. Procedure calls, e.g., may change global variables. Of course, a programmer is not forced to use global variables, but nearly all programmers using algorithmic languages do. Moreover, nothing in the language prevents programmers from using global variables.

The defenders of functional languages think that this model of statements modifying global state has a lot of disadvantages. Since different parts (e.g., procedures) of a program interact indirectly through variables, programs become hard to understand. It cannot be determined what the true consequences of a call to procedure P are without considering how the variables changed by P are used in other parts of the program. In addition, the presence of side-effects is a major obstacle for correctness proofs, optimization, and automatic parallelization of programs. (These and other arguments against algorithmic languages are perhaps best described in Backus' classical Turing award paper [Backus, 1978], which also introduces the now famous terms *word-at-a-time programming* and *Von Neumann bottleneck*.)

A functional (or *applicative*) language is based on the evaluation of expressions built out of function calls (applications). A function is like a pure mathematical function: it maps values taken from one domain onto values of another (co)domain. Put in other words, a function computes a certain value, based on its input parameters and nothing else. An infix expression like '2 + 3' is also treated as a function application: it applies the function ' + ' to the arguments 2 and 3.

The key issue here is that there is *no implicit state*, so functions cannot have side effects. At first sight, it may seem impossible to solve any nontrivial problem without using a modifiable state. Yet, functional programs do have a state, and it can be modified, but the state is made explicit rather than implicit. Also, the state is modified by manipulating the names rather than the values. More concretely, the state is carried around in the arguments of the functions.

As a simple but illustrative example, consider a procedure P that uses a local variable X. In a procedural language, P could modify X by assigning a new value to it. In a functional language, P – now a function – would be passed X as input parameter and the effect of writing X is obtained by calling P itself recursively with the new value of X, as in:

```
function P (X: integer) → SomeType;
    . . .
    return P (3*X+1)      % simulate X := 3*X+1
end
```

A similar technique can be used for global variables. To obtain the effect of an assignment to a global variable X, P returns the new value of X and the caller of P uses this new value.

So, at least in theory, the functional approach seems viable, although not everyone will immediately like the idea of having to pass all modifiable variables around as arguments. But what exactly have we gained by eliminating implicit state and side effects? The answer is *referential transparency*, which probably is the most important term in functional programming. It means that the result of a function application does not depend on *when* the function is called but only on how it is called (i.e., with which arguments). In an algorithmic language, the result of

$$f(x) + f(x)$$

need not be the same as that of

$$2 * f(x)$$

because the first call to f may change x or any other variable accessed by f. In a functional language, the two expressions always are equal.

Advocates of functional programming claim that, since the behavior of functions no longer depends on global variables, functional programs will be easier to understand than programs written in an algorithmic language. This statement applies both to a human reader as well as a machine. For example, suppose an optimizing compiler considers optimizing $f(x) + f(x)$ into $2 * f(x)$. A compiler for a functional language is always allowed to do this transformation, because of the referential transparency. A compiler for, say, Pascal, on the other hand would first have to prove that the result of the second call does not depend on variables that are changed during the first call. Likewise, a parallelizing compiler will encounter exactly the same problem if it wants to run function calls in parallel.

Besides these advantages, functional programming also has its disadvantages. A well-known problem is modifying a complex data structure. Changing, say, the rightmost leaf node of a tree is a simple matter in a low-level language like C: just follow the right pointers and modify the leaf. In a functional language, the tree cannot be modified. Instead, code must be written to copy the whole tree, except for its rightmost leaf, and substitute a new value for this leaf. This approach is more complicated and, at least potentially, far less efficient that just manipulating pointers.

In summary, functional languages are based on the evaluation of expressions, which consist of function applications. Global state variables and assignment are eliminated, so the value computed by a function application depends only on the arguments. State information is manipulated explicitly, through function parameters.

4.2. Concepts

Functional languages use a wide variety of concepts. Here, we will describe only those concepts that are used by a wide range of functional languages. We will look at recursion, data structures, higher-order functions, and lazy evaluation. The latter two concepts give functional programming its power and are also very important for building modular functional programs [Hughes, 1989]. For a discussion of other concepts (e.g., polymorphism, pattern matching, parallelism, nondeterminism) as well as the mathematical theory underlying functional languages (lambda calculus) we refer the reader to the survey paper by Hudak [1989] and to the book by Field & Harrison [1988].

4.2.1. Recursion

Recursive functions are allowed in most languages, whether functional or not. In functional languages, however, recursion plays a key role. It is used for replacing iteration and, as described above, for carrying around state information. The classical example, used in most introductory texts, is computing a factorial. We will comply with this tradition and show how a factorial can be computed in an algorithmic way and in a functional way.

A simple algorithm for computing the factorial of n is shown below.

```
var r: integer; % r will contain the result
r := 1;
% compute n * (n-1) * (n-2) * . . . * 1;
for i := n downto 1 do
    r := r * i;
return r;
```

Note that the algorithm uses a state variable (r) that is modified repeatedly inside the for loop. In a functional language (and in algorithmic languages allowing recursion), a factorial can be computed as follows.

```
function fac(n: integer) → integer;
    return (if n = 0 then 1 else n * fac (n-1))
```

Instead of a for loop, this program uses a recursive function call. Each call to fac corresponds with one iteration of the for loop. The recursive call is the last action of the function fac; this form of recursion is usually called *tail-*

recursion. Thus the factorial example illustrates how functional languages can use tail-recursion instead of iteration.

4.2.2. Data structures

In most algorithmic languages, the array is the primary data structure. For functional languages, lists usually take over this key role. This is partly because lists better fit the recursive programming style of functional languages, and partly because lists are better suited than arrays for symbolic applications, which probably are the most important applications for functional languages.

In Ada and C, a list can be built out of dynamically allocated chunks of memory that are tied together through pointers, as discussed in Section 2.2.1.2. The operations on lists are implemented through low-level pointer manipulations. Allocation and deallocation of memory blocks is the responsibility of the programmer.

Functional languages have a higher-level view of lists. Pointers are completely hidden from the programmer. Lists can be created out of individual elements, and they can be concatenated, split, and traversed. Most importantly, the management of the memory for list cells is done by the language run-time system (RTS). The RTS allocates memory whenever needed. To concatenate two lists, e.g., it allocates enough cells to contain the elements of both lists. The RTS automatically detects if a certain block of memory is no longer in use and then deallocates it. This is usually implemented with a technique called *automatic garbage collection*, which periodically scans the memory and looks for cells that are inaccessible. Having the language RTS handle memory (de)allocation eliminates an important source of programming errors and is a major benefit.

4.2.3. Higher-order functions

Many algorithmic languages treat variables and functions differently. Variables can be manipulated (read, written, passed around) while functions can only be invoked. Functional languages usually treat functions as first-class objects, which can be passed as arguments, returned as function results, and stored in data structures. A function that takes another function as argument is called a higher-order function. Besides their conceptual elegance, higher-order functions also offer practical advantages. For example, it now becomes possible to write a function, `map`, that applies a given function to all elements of a given list:

```
function map(f: integer→ integer; L: list of integer)
                                    → list of integer;
% apply f to all elements of L and return resulting list
```

In languages that do not allow functions as arguments, it would not be possible to write a map function, since it requires an argument that is itself a function. Most functional languages also provide a notation for function values. In the language Hope, e.g., the notation lambda x => x + 1 is a value of a function type. It denotes a function that returns its first argument incremented by one. So, the value of the expression

    map(lambda x => x + 1, (1, 5, 7))

would be the list

    (2, 6, 8)

4.2.4. *Lazy evaluation*

The simplest way of evaluating a function call is to first evaluate the arguments and then to invoke the function. For example, in

    f(g(3), h(4))

the function applications g(3) and h(4) would be done first, in whatever order; after these values have been computed, f is applied to them.

Although this evaluation order seems obvious, it does have disadvantages. Suppose we want to implement a function cond that takes a boolean value B as first argument and that returns its second argument if B is true and its third if B is false. If all three arguments of cond are evaluated before this function is executed, there are two problems:

(1) One of the arguments of cond will be evaluated needlessly, thus wasting compute cycles.

(2) If the argument expression that is evaluated needlessly does not terminate, the whole expression will loop forever.

As an example of the latter case, suppose we use this function to sum all integers from 0 to n, as follows:

```
function sum(n: integer) → integer
    return (cond(n=0, 0, n + sum(n-1)))
end
```

If the third argument is always evaluated, the function sum will never terminate.

These problems have led to the concept of *lazy evaluation*. The idea of lazy evaluation is to evaluate the arguments of a function only when their values are needed. So, the arguments are not evaluated before the call takes place, but only when their values are actually needed.

Lazy evaluation solves the problems described earlier. In the example above, the third argument of cond will not be evaluated if n equals zero, since in this case the argument is not needed. Lazy evaluation has another important advantage: it allows one to define data structures that are conceptually infinite. For instance, it is possible to define the list of all natural numbers. The implementation of the language will only build the finite part of the list that is actually needed.

Unfortunately, lazy evaluation is also costly to implement, just as call-by-name parameters in Algol 60. Clearly, evaluating the arguments before the call is much easier than postponing their execution, so there is a nontrivial overhead in lazy evaluation. Only recently have optimizations been developed for decreasing this overhead. Therefore, not all functional languages provide lazy evaluation. Languages that do not support this feature for user-defined functions typically have a cond function with lazy semantics built in.

4.3. Examples

Below we will look at two important functional languages: Lisp and Miranda (trademark of Research Software Ltd.). Other functional languages include Iswim, FP, Lucid, Hope, Standard ML, and Haskell [Hudak, 1989].

4.3.1. Lisp

Many concepts of functional programming have been introduced in John McCarthy's language Lisp, which was designed in 1958. Modern Lisp is not a pure functional language, since it supports variables and assignment statements. However, it was the first language to support the functional programming style. Lisp supports recursion and higher-order functions. Lists are the primary data structure. Memory allocation and deallocation are done automatically, using garbage collection.

Lisp was mainly designed for symbolic applications, such as artificial intelligence programs. For numerical computations, the early Lisp implementations were much too slow. Another often-heard criticism on the language is its hard-to-read syntax, which is dominated by parentheses. The syntax is very uniform, however, making it easy to store and manipulate Lisp programs as normal data. The feature is useful for writing debuggers and other tools in the language itself.

Another problem with Lisp is its lack of a type system. A list, e.g., can contain elements of different types. Although this freedom can be used to advantage in some cases, it also makes it impossible to detect type-system errors during compile time.

Lisp is the direct ancestor of many other languages (e.g., Scheme) and has influenced the design of all other functional languages. The successors of Lisp usually do have a type system, and frequently support features like lazy evaluation and pattern matching.

4.3.2. Miranda

Miranda is a modern, commercially marketed, functional language, developed by David Turner. Like Lisp, it supports lists and higher-order functions. Unlike Lisp, Miranda is strongly typed and uses lazy evaluation.

Although Miranda is strongly typed, type information does not have to be provided by the user (as in Ada), but can be derived automatically by the system. Functions can be polymorphic, meaning that they can take arguments of arbitrary types. As an example, reconsider the function map. The function as defined earlier works only for lists of integers. Using polymorphism, it is possible to implement a map function that works for lists of any type. Despite polymorphism, the language is still strongly typed, so the system checks if the functions and arguments are used in a consistent way.

The semantics of Miranda are based on lazy evaluation. As one of the advantages, programmers can use infinite data structures. For example, the following notation

```
[1 .. ]
```

denotes the list of all positive integers. The language run time system will only build that part of the list that is needed.

Another important feature of Miranda and some other functional languages is _currying_, which is also called _partial parameterization_. Consider, e.g., the function mult, defined as

```
mult a b=a * b
```

If mult is applied to two arguments, it will compute their product. Miranda also allows mult to be applied to one argument. In this case, the result will be another function, with one argument, so

```
mult 2
```

gives a function that doubles its argument.

5. Logic languages

The idea of letting the programmer specify what his problem is rather than how the computer is supposed to solve it is taken one step further by logic languages. A logic program consists of a list of facts and properties of a problem and it is up to the system to find the solution. Although this idea sounds simple, realizing it is hard. As every programmer knows, computers are bad at inventing solutions of their own. They work best when told explicitly how to solve a problem.

The success of logic programming is due to a formalism called _Horn logic_ that can be used for specifying problems, but, at the same time, can also be executed automatically. Horn logic does not achieve the ultimate goal of declarative languages (i.e., getting rid of programming altogether), but it is at least a step in this direction. Horn logic is the basis of Prolog, which is by far the most important logic programming language.

5.1. Principles

The key principle underlying logic programming is Horn clause logic, which is a subset of predicate logic. A Horn clause is a rule of the following form:

    G0 ← G1, G2, . . . , Gn.

which means that G0 is true if G1 until Gn are all true. The left-hand side of the rule is called the *head*; the right-hand side is called the *body*. G0 until Gn are called *goals*; goals in the body are also referred to as subgoals. The commas in the body should be read as logical **and** symbols. Beware that the body implies the head, but not the other way around. The '←' symbol should be interpreted as *if* and not as *if-and-only-if*.

A special case is where n is zero, so the body is empty. In this case, G0 is always true; such a rule is called a *fact*. Note that the head of a rule contains only a single goal. Predicate logic allows multiple goals here.

Each goal consists of a *predicate* name and zero or more arguments. The exact meaning of the arguments will be explained later, but for the time being just assume that they are either variables or constants. Variables begin with an upper case letter. With this information, we can write down examples of Horn clauses:

    queen(beatrix) ←.   (1)

    son(beatrix, alexander) ←.   (2)

    prince(P) ← son(Q, P), queen (Q).   (3)

This fragment contains two facts: beatrix is a queen (1) and alexander is the son of beatrix (2). The third line is a more general Horn clause. It uses two variables, P and Q, which begin with a capital letter. The rule says that if P is the son of Q and Q is a queen, then P is a prince. Note that the first two rules are statements about specific persons (constants), while the third one is a more general statement about any two persons.

Above, we claimed that specifications using Horn clauses can be executed automatically. Here, we will outline how this is done. A program is started by giving it an initial goal to prove. For example, if given the goal

    ?- prince(alexander).

the system will try to prove that alexander is a prince. (We use the Prolog convention here of putting a '? − ' before the initial goal.) The initial goal may also contain variables, as in

    ?- prince(P).

in which case the system will try to find any prince (i.e., prove that a prince exists) and, if it finds one, it will assign this prince to the variable P.

In general, there may be several different rules for solving the initial goal. Suppose the initial goal is g0, and the following rules for g0 exist:

g0 ← g1, g2, g3, g4.
g0 ← g5.
g0 ← g6, g7.

The key idea is that the system simply tries all possibilities, until one of them succeeds. So, it will first try to prove g1, g2, g3, and g4. If it succeeds in proving all of those four subgoals, it has succeeded in proving g0. If not, it continues with the next rule, and tries to prove g5, and so on. To prove a subgoal, such as g1, it applies this strategy recursively. In summary, the system just tries all possible ways of proving the initial goal. If a solution (proof) exists, the system will find one; this property is called *completeness of search*. Things get a bit more complicated if the goals have arguments, but the same basic search strategy can be used.

If the system fails to find a proof, it will return the answer 'no', which means that, as far as the system can tell, the given goal is not true. It assumes that goals that can be proven are true and goals that cannot be proven are false, which is the *closed-world assumption*.

Executing Horn clauses is somewhat similar to procedure calling in conventional languages. There are two important differences, however. The first difference is the back-tracking behavior of the system: if it chose the wrong alternative, it will automatically try the next one. A second difference is the way parameters are passed. This issue is discussed in the next subsection.

5.2. Concepts

The most important concept in logic languages is the *logical variable*. Logical variables are used for storing state information and for passing arguments between goals. A logical variable does not contain a value initially; it is said to be *unbound*. The variable may be assigned a value (i.e., it may become *bound*) if it is matched against a value or another bound variable. From then on, the value cannot be changed again, so logical variables have the *single-assignment* property.

As a concrete example, reconsider clause (3) from our earlier example:

$$\text{prince}(P) \leftarrow \text{son}(Q, P), \text{queen}(Q). \tag{3}$$

The clause contains two logical variables, P and Q. Suppose the user enters the initial goal

?- prince(alexander).

The system will try to prove this goal using the facts and rules defined above. It will first try to find a rule whose head has the same predicate name (prince) and uses a single argument. Clause (3) is such a rule. The goal in the head of clause (3) is matched against the initial goal. The matching process will try to make the two goals equal. Whenever necessary, it will bind some logical variables. The two goals prince(P) and prince(alexander) can be made equal by binding P to alexander. In this way, the logical variable P is assigned a value, which remains fixed for the rest of the clause.

Since P will not change any more, we can replace all its occurrences in clause (3) by its value, so the clause becomes:

$$prince(alexander) \leftarrow son(Q, alexander), queen(Q).$$

(3a)

The system will now proceed by trying to prove the two subgoals in the body. To prove the first subgoal, son(Q, alexander), this goal is matched against the head of clause (2), which is son(beatrix, alexander). To make these two goals equal, the logical variable Q is bound to the value beatrix. As before, all occurrences of Q in clause (3a) can be replaced by the new value, resulting in

$$prince(alexander) \leftarrow$$
$$son(beatrix, alexander), queen (beatrix).$$ (3b)

Finally, the system will try to prove the second subgoal, queen(beatrix). This goal was given as a fact above, so it is always true. In conclusion, the system has proved the initial goal that alexander is a prince.

So far, binding of logical variables does not look very exciting. An actual value is supplied in a goal and is used as a constant in the rule body. This use of logic variables is very similar to call-by-value parameter passing in algorithmic languages. One key issue is still missing from our examples, however. In matching a goal with the body of a rule, the system will make any binding necessary to make the two equal. So, it can also bind a variable in the goal, rather than in the head. For example, suppose we enter the initial goal

$$?- son(X, alexander).$$

to ask for a parent of alexander. This time, the system will match this goal with the head of rule (2), which is son(beatrix, alexander). To make the two equal, the variable X in the goal is bound to the value beatrix. Note that the information now flows the other way around, namely from the rule to the goal. This type of matching is roughly similar to call-by-result parameter passing.

These examples show that logical variables can be used both as input and output arguments, without having to specify in advance which argument is input and which is output. In fact, some Prolog programs can run forwards and backwards with equal ease. In contrast, Pascal requires the programmer to specify in the procedure header how each parameter is used. Therefore, it is not possible to write a two-way function son in Pascal that can be called with a value as first parameter and a variable as second parameter, as well as the other way around.

In essence, the Horn clause for son does not define a function but a *relation*. A function maps input arguments onto output arguments, e.g.: compute the son of X or compute the parent of Y. A Horn clause, on the other hand, specifies a relation that holds between different arguments, e.g.: X is the son of Y. This is an important difference between logic languages and functional or algorithmic languages.

The logical variables are even more general than we described above. A logical variable need not be bound to a constant (such as beatrix), but can also be bound to a structure or a list. Just to give a flavor of what this means, consider the following clause

$$h([3, X]) \leftarrow g(X).$$

and the initial goal

$$?- h([Y, 4]).$$

The predicate h has a single argument, which is a list. The list in the head of the goal contains two elements: the constant 3 and the logical variable X, which is also used in the body of the clause. The list in the initial goal also contains two elements, a variable and a constant. To solve the initial goal, the system will try to make the arguments in the head and in the initial goal equal. To this purpose, it will bind X (in the head of the clause) to the value 4, and Y (in the initial goal) to the value 3. Subsequently, it will try to prove g(4). As a net result, information is passed in both directions (from the head of the clause to the goal and vice versa) through a single argument.

This example should give some idea of the generality of logical variables and of the binding rules. The exact binding rules are based on a principle called *unification*, which was proposed by Robinson [1965].

5.3. Examples

Below we will discuss the most important logic language, Prolog. We will also give some programming examples. Entire textbooks exist giving numerous examples of logic programs solving realworld problems [Clocksin & Mellish, 1981; Sterling & Shapiro, 1986]. Here, we will just use two simple examples, to give the reader some idea of how Horn logic can be applied to real problems.

5.3.1. Prolog

Prolog was developed by Colmerauer and colleagues at the University of Marseilles. Although Prolog has been around since the mid-seventies, it has only become popular since 1982, when the Japanese fifth generation computer project adopted logic programming.

Prolog is based on Horn clause logic. It uses a fixed order of searching: alternative clauses for the same goal are searched in textual order, from top to bottom. Within the body of a goal, the subgoals are worked on from left to right. Unfortunately, this approach implies that Prolog will not guarantee always to find a solution if one exists. The following clauses:

```
x(1) ← x(1).
x(2).
```

will loop forever on the initial goal

```
x(N).
```

because the second clause will never be tried. So, Prolog does not have the completeness of search property.

Prolog has several arithmetic operations built-in. Of special importance is the is infix operator, which is used as in

```
X is 3 + 4.
```

If forces the evaluation of the expression on the right and matches the result with its left operand. Usually, the left operand is an unbound variable; is will then bind the value to this variable. The right operand must only contain bound variables or values.

We will use this operator in our first example, which adds all integers from 1 to N. We use the relation sum(N, S) to mean that the sum of the integers 1 until N equals S. This relation can be defined using two clauses:

```
sum(1, 1).
sum(N, S) ← N2 is N - 1, sum(N2, S0), S is S0 + N.
```

The first clause specifies that the sum of all integers from 1 until 1 equals 1, which is trivially true. The second one specifies that the sum from 1 to N equals the sum from 1 to N − 1 plus N. This clause uses the predicate sum recursively and binds the result to S0. It uses the is operator for computing N−1 as well as S0 + N.

If the predicate is used as follows

```
?- sum(2, S).
```

the system will first try to match sum(1, 1) with sum(2, S). This will fail, because the first argument does not match. Next, it will try the second clause, causing N to be bound to 2, and resulting in a recursive call sum(1, S0). This recursive call will match the first clause, sum(1, 1), and binds S0 to 1. Subsequently, the final result of the initial goal will be S = 1 + 1 = 2.

As a disadvantage of using the is operator, the predicate sum thus defined does not work in the opposite direction. If the predicate is used as:

```
?- sum(N, 6).
```

one might expect it to succeed and bind N to 3, since $1 + 2 + 3 = 6$. However, the subgoal N2 is N − 1 will fail, because N is not bound. So, sum as implemented above is not really a true relation.

As a more complicated example, consider sorting a list of numbers. This problem can be specified with Horn logic as follows:

```
sort(List, SortedList) ←
    permutation(List, SortedList), ordered(SortedList).
```

which says that SortedList is the result of sorting List if SortedList is a permutation of List and the elements of SortedList are ordered. Of course, we would also have to write clauses for the permutation and ordered clauses. The resulting program would correctly sort the initial list, but it would also be extremely slow. The reason is, the number of permutations of a list grows exponentially with the length of the list. As the program generates permutations more or less at random, it would require exponential time to execute, which is impractical for long lists.

This example is not to say that efficient sorting algorithms cannot be expressed in Prolog. In fact, a wide range of sorting algorithms can be written in Prolog, as shown by Clocksin [1981]. However, the example does show that merely specifying a problem is not always enough. Programmers sometimes still have to think about algorithms that instruct the computer how to solve the problem efficiently.

6. Parallel and distributed languages

In Sections 2 to 5 we discussed various models for general-purpose languages. We will now turn our attention to languages designed for solving specific types of problems. We will look at languages for parallel and distributed programming in this section and at languages for real-time programming in the next section.

6.1. Principles

Parallel and distributed languages differ from the languages described earlier in that they contain explicit constructs for running different pieces of a program in parallel. The languages discussed so far could perhaps be implemented using parallelism, but they do not make parallelism available to the programmer.

There are various reasons why one might need language constructs for parallelism. First, some problems exhibit inherent parallelism and are therefore easier to solve using parallelism. As an example, consider a discrete event simulator. This program deals with multiple active entities, such as clients, servers, and so on. A convenient approach for writing a simulator might be to use one piece of code for each active entity, and have all these pieces run in parallel.

Note that the simulator program is intended for single processors, rather than multiple processors. It is just simpler to implement it with parallelism than without. Since there is only one processor, the different parts of the program do not really execute at the same time; they run in *pseudo-parallel*. They all compete for the single CPU, and are all allocated some part of the CPU cycles.

Besides convenience, a second reason for using parallelism is to exploit the performance potential of parallel hardware systems. If the different parts of a parallel program are indeed executed by different processors, the program may take less time to finish. For example, when multiplying two matrices, one could use one processor for each of the elements of the result matrix, resulting in much higher performance.

In this case, of course, one needs parallel hardware. Many different parallel architectures exist. We will only consider parallel machines in the so-called MIMD (multiple instruction multiple data) class, which means that each processor executes its own instruction stream. This class includes shared-memory multiprocessors and distributed-memory multi-computers.

A third reason why one might need parallelism is for the construction of programs that run on multiple autonomous machines connected through a network, the so-called *distributed systems*. One example concerns multiple workstations connected by Ethernet. The user on one workstation may want to send electronic mail to users on other workstations. The e-mail program is a distributed application that runs on multiple machines. Other examples include applications on geographically distributed systems, such as banking or airline reservation.

We will treat languages for parallel and distributed programming in the same section, because they both need support for parallelism and communication. There is some confusion, however, about the difference between parallel and distributed systems and languages [Bal, Steiner & Tanenbaum, 1989]. For instance, distributed systems can also be used for running parallel applications [Bal, 1990].

Both parallel and distributed languages support parallelism. The parallel parts will have to cooperate in solving an overall task, so they must be able to communicate with each other. The languages therefore also support communication. (Some languages, in particular distributed languages, also give support for fault-tolerance; we will not look at this issue here, however.)

The way communication is expressed depends on the hardware being used, especially on the presence or absence of shared memory. Note that distributed systems do not have shared memory, while some parallel systems (multiprocessors) do and others (multicomputers) do not.

6.2. Concepts

Below we will look at various language constructs for parallelism and for communication on either shared-memory or distributed-memory machines. For a more detailed discussion of parallel hardware and software, we refer to the book by Almasi & Gottlieb [1989]. The issue of parallel programming is covered in depth in the book of Andrews [1991].

6.2.1. Parallelism

A simple language construct for expressing parallelism is the *coroutine*. Coroutines are routines that are executed in an interleaved fashion. At any point during its execution, a coroutine may save its state and resume another coroutine. If a coroutine is resumed, its state is restored, and it continues at the point it was before the switch took place. Coroutines can only be used for expressing pseudo-parallelism, since only one routine at a time is active. They are not useful for programming systems with multiple processors.

Another way of expressing parallelism is through parallel statements. Two examples are the **parbegin**, which executes a given list of statements in parallel, and the **parfor**, which runs multiple iterations of a loop in parallel:

```
parbegin                    parfor i := 1 to 10 do
    Statement 1                 Statements(i)
    Statement 2             od
    Statement 3
parend
```

Parallel statements can be used for true parallelism. However, they provide little support for structuring parallel programs, and are not as general as other constructs. They are used in only a few languages.

By far the most common way of expressing parallelism is through *processes*. A process is an abstraction for a physical processor. It executes code sequentially and it has its own state and data. Parallelism is obtained by creating multiple processes, possibly running on different machines.

In most languages, the number of processes that can be created is variable. Typically, one first defines a process type, much like a procedure, which describes the code to be executed by processes of this type. Next, any number of processes of this type can be created using a construct such as

fork `process-type(parameters);`

Forking a new process is similar to calling a procedure. The crucial difference is that, with procedures, the calling procedure waits until the called procedure has finished. With process creation, both the invoking parent process and the newly created child process continue in parallel. This immediately raises the question of how these processes recombine, both halfway (communication) and at the end (fork/wait). Several solutions have been proposed.

6.2.2. Communication

We will now address the second issue that parallel and distributed languages have to deal with: communication between the parallel processes (or whatever other unit of parallelism is used). Communication primitives fall into two classes: *shared variables* and *message passing*.

A shared variable is a variable that is known by name to more than one process and can be used as a normal variable by these processes. A shared variable abstracts from the fact that it may reside on a different machine than the processes using it. On a multiprocessor, shared variables are stored in the shared memory. Shared variables can be used for transfering information between processes, since data stored in the variable by one process can be read by all other processes. Shared variables are used mainly to program uni-processors and shared-memory multiprocessors.

The main problem with shared variables is synchronizing access to them. Consider the code shown below. Two processes, P1 and P2, share an integer variable X. Both processes try to increment the variable by first reading the current value and writing back the new, incremented, value.

```
X: integer := 0;          % variable shared by P1 and P2
process P1:                   process P2:
   Tmp1: integer;               Tmp2: integer; % local
   Tmp1 := X;                   Tmp2 := X;
   X := Tmp1 + 1;               X := Tmp2 + 1;
```

Now suppose that both processes simultaneously read the initial value of X, so the local variables Tmp1 and Tmp2 are both zero; subsequently, they both try to increment X by writing back the values of Tmp1 + 1 and Tmp2 + 1. As a result, X will be assigned the value 1 twice. Obviously, this is not what was intended. The value of X should have been 2 rather than 1. This value would have been obtained if one of the processes had executed before the other. Such an undesirable situation, where the result of a program depends on the exact timing of process execution, is called a *race condition*. The problem is how to prevent race conditions.

Race conditions occur if multiple processes simultaneously execute regions of code in which they access shared variables. Such regions are called *critical sections*. Race conditions can be avoided by allowing only a single process at a

time to enter a critical section. To implement this idea, many different
constructs have been proposed [Andrews & Schneider, 1983; Tanenbaum,
1987], such as semaphores, sleep/wakeup, and monitors.

The second class of communication primitives is message passing. With
message passing, each process has its own variables, which cannot be accessed
by other processes. Instead, processes communicate by sending messages to
each other. A message contains data that are transferred from the sender to
the receiver. With message passing, there is no risk of simultaneous updates of
the same variable, since each variable can only be accessed by a single process.

Many different forms of message passing exist. Here, we will only look at the
most important alternatives. We will consider synchronous/asynchronous message passing, direct/indirect naming, and one-way/two-way communication.

The most controversial issue in message passing is that between synchronous
and asynchronous messages. With both forms, the sender S sends a message to
a receiver R:

> S: **send** msg(data) **to** R

and the receiver accepts the message by executing the statement:

> R: **receive** msg(data) **from** S **do**
>   process the message
>   **od**

The question is whether or not the sender blocks while the message is being
processed. With synchronous message passing, the sender waits until the
receiver has finished executing the **receive** statement. At that time, the message
has been delivered at the receiving processor (possibly by transferring it across
the network), the receiver has executed its **receive** statement, and an acknowl-
edgment has been sent back. If the sender continues, it knows for sure that the
message has been processed.

With asynchronous message passing, the sender continues immediately after
issuing the **send** statement. Processing of the message will be done in the
background, while the sender continues its execution.

There are important differences between the two models. Synchronous
message passing is simpler to use, because, if the sender continues, it knows
the message has been processed. On the other hand, synchronous message
passing also is more restrictive, because the sender is forced to wait. For
parallel applications especially, this limitation may be too severe.

Another issue in message passing is how the sender and receiver should
address each other. In the simplest case, which we used above, both the sender
and the receiver explicitly name each other. This form, called symmetric direct
naming, is used in Hoare's CSP [Hoare, 1978].

Requiring the receiver to specify the sender of the message is rather
inflexible. For instance, it rules out the possibility of writing a generic server

(e.g., a file server) that accepts requests from any client. A better solution is to let the receiver accept messages sent by any process:

> R: **receive** msg(data) **do** . . . **od**

This is called asymmetric direct naming, since the sender specifies the receiver but not vice versa.

Yet another option is to use an intermediate object, usually called a *port*, rather than process names. In this case, both the sender and receiver specify a port:

> P: port-name
> S: **send** msg(data) **to** P
> R: **receive** msg(data) **from** P **do** . . . **od**

This form is most flexible, since neither party needs to know the identity of the other.

The **send** and **receive** primitives used above transfer information in one direction, from the sender to the receiver. In many cases, the receiver will want to return a reply to the sender. For example, if a file server receives a read request for a file, it should return (part of) the contents of the file. With send/receive, two messages would be needed, one in each direction, and the receiver would have to know the identity of the sender.

An attractive alternative is to use a single message-passing construct that transfers data in both directions. One such construct is the remote procedure call (RPC) [Birrell & Nelson, 1984], which is similar to a normal procedure call, except that the sender and receiver may be on different machines. RPC is a form of synchronous communication. The sender sends a message to a receiver and waits for a reply; the receiver accepts the message, processes it, and returns the reply message:

> S: output-data := **call** R.msg(input-data)
> R: **receive** msg(input-data) **do**
>   process message
>   **reply** output-data
>   **od**

Ada's rendezvous is a similar construct that also provides two-way communication.

Many other issues exist in message passing, besides the ones discussed above. For surveys of message passing primitives, we refer the reader to Andrews & Schneider [1983] and Bal, Steiner & Tanenbaum [1989].

The two classes of communication primitives, shared variables and message passing, differ in various ways. In general, shared variables are easier to program, especially if the application requires processes to share global state information. Also, a shared variable can be used for communication between any number of processes, whereas a message transfers data between two processes. On the other hand, message passing also has advantages. It does not require shared memory and it avoids problems with critical sections.

Bal & Tanenbaum [1991] give a more detailed comparison between shared variables and message passing. They note that the two classes should be regarded as the extremes of a spectrum of alternatives. They describe several primitives that fall in between these two extremes, such as Linda's Tuple Space and Orca's shared data-objects.

6.3. Examples

Many languages for parallel and distributed programming have been proposed. For distributed programming alone, there are more than 100 languages [Bal, Steiner & Tanenbaum, 1989]. Below we will look at three representative languages: Algol 68 is based on shared variables; Synchronizing Resources is based on message passing; and Linda is based on a communication model called Tuple Space.

6.3.1. Algol 68

Algol 68 [Van Wijngaarden, Mailloux, Peck, Koster, Sintzoff, Lindsey, Meertens & Fisker, 1975] handles parallelism in a regular and orthogonal way. Two items separated by semicolon are evaluated or carried out sequentially. The keywords **begin** and **end**, or, alternatively, parentheses can be used to group statements into blocks. A block prefixed with the keyword **par** is a parallel statement. The items of a parallel statement are separated by a comma and are carried out in parallel. Thus, e.g., the statement

$$(\textbf{par}(a, (\textbf{par}(b, c); d), (e; f)); g)$$

specifies that three actions (statements, procedure calls, etc.) are to take place in parallel: 'a', '(**par** (b, c); d)', and '(e; f)'. When the outer block starts, a, b, c, and e can all be started off in parallel. When b and c have both finished, d may begin. When e has finished, f may begin. When a through f have all completed, g may begin. By judicious placement of **par**s and commas, the programmer can specify in detail which activities may occur in parallel.

Since Algol 68 is a block-structured language, blocks and procedures may be lexically nested. Parallel activities may communicate by reading and writing all variables declared in outer blocks and procedures. This is the simplest form of communication using shared variables: unrestricted access to all visible variables.

Algol 68 also provides a mechanism for synchronizing parallel activities: semaphores. A semaphore is a shared integer variable with indivisible operations to increment and decrement it. The decrement operation blocks while the variable is zero, thus allowing parallel computations to synchronize.

Semaphores are a basic data type in Algol 68, and can be declared in any block or procedure. Two parallel processes can synchronize by using any semaphore visible to both of them.

6.3.2. Synchronizing Resources (SR)

SR is one of the many languages based on sequential processes and message passing [Andrews, Olsson, Coffin, Elshoff, Nilsen, Purdin & Townsend, 1988]. The philosophy behind SR is that none of the message passing alternatives is ideally suited for all applications. Therefore, SR provides many different forms of message passing. It supports synchronous and asynchronous messages, RPC, rendezvous, and more.

SR lets the programmer decide how a message is sent as well as how it is received. When sending a message, the options are synchronous (blocking) and asynchronous (non-blocking), which have been discussed above. The receiver has the choice between *explicit* receipt through a **receive** statement (discussed above) and *implicit* receipt. With implicit receipt, the receiving process creates a new process for each message that arrives. The new process handles the message and then terminates. It executes in pseudo-parallel with the main process and communicates with it through shared variables.

As a potential advantage of implicit receipt, messages are serviced immediately. With explicit receipt, messages are not accepted until the receiver executes a **receive** statement. Explicit receipt, on the other hand, gives the programmer more control over which messages to accept and in which order. In SR, the receiver can, e.g., order the messages based on their arrival time or their contents.

These two ways of sending and receiving messages can be combined in all four ways, yielding four different communication primitives. This orthogonal design keeps the language reasonably simple.

6.3.3. Linda

Linda is a set of primitives rather than a single language [Ahuja, Carriero & Gelernter, 1989]. The Linda primitives can be embedded in an existing host language, resulting in a parallel language, e.g., C/Linda or Fortran/Linda. Linda provides a new communication model, *Tuple Space*. Conceptually, Tuble Space is a globally shared memory consisting of tuples (records) that are addressed associatively (by contents). The implementation of Tuple Space, however, does not require physical shared memory. So, the model is based on logically shared data, but it can be used for shared-memory as well as distributed-memory systems.

Three atomic operations are defined on the Tuple Space: **out** adds a new tuple, **read** reads an existing tuple, and **in** reads and deletes a tuple. Tuples are addressed by specifying the values or types of the fields. For example,

```
x: integer;
read("abc", 3.1, ? &x);
```

tries to find a tuple with three fields: the string constant "abc", the real constant 3.1, and any integer. If it finds such a tuple, it assigns the contents of the third field to the variable x. If no matching tuple exists, the operation blocks until some other process adds a matching tuple, using **out**; if multiple tuples exist, one is chosen arbitrarily.

Tuple Space can be used to simulate other communication primitives, such as shared variables and message passing. It also leads to novel parallel programming styles [Carriero, Gelernter, 1988]. For example, the Tuple Space operations can be used for building distributed data structures, which can be accessed simultaneously by multiple processes.

Tuple Space can be implemented with reasonable efficiency on distributed systems by careful allocation of tuples to processors. The best distribution strategy, such as replication or partitioning of Tuple Space, depends on the underlying network topology. The overhead of associative addressing is reduced through global compiler optimizations.

Because of its portability and easy integration with existing languages, Linda is becoming one of the most popular parallel languages. Linda has influenced the design of another language, Orca [Bal, 1990], which also supports distributed data structures. Orca, however, allows users to define their own operations, whereas Linda has a fixed number of built-in operations. Also. Orca does not use associative addressing. A comparison between SR, Linda, Orca, and other languages is given by Bal [1991].

7. Real-time languages

The languages described in the previous section are designed especially for parallel and distributed applications. We will now consider another important class of languages intended for a specific application area, real-time languages. The differences between conventional and real-time applications will be explained first.

The correctness of a conventional program is determined only by its logical results. The correctness of a real-time program, however, also depends on *when* the results are produced. In general, a real-time program is restricted in when to respond to its inputs. It should not produce its outputs too soon or too late. Real-time programs are frequently used as part of a large system, such as an airplane or a missile. Such systems are called *embedded systems*.

7.1. Principles

Real-time applications need programming support in several areas [Burns & Wellings, 1990]. We will look at three of the most important issues: timing (performance), reliability, and low-level programming. Real-time programs frequently use parallelism to increase performance or reliability, or to control multiple hardware devices simultaneously. Parallelism has been addressed in Section 6.

Above all, a real-time program needs to deal with *time*. At the very least, it must be able to obtain the current time. Probably the most important issue in real-time programming, however, is how to meet *deadlines*. The designer of a real-time system should be able to specify that a certain output must be generated in a given time interval. Unfortunately, only very few languages give programming support for deadlines, due to lack of a sound underlying theory. The usual practice is to first write a program that is logically correct (i.e., produces the right outputs, but probably not at the right times), and then tune the program if it does not meet its timing specifications. Tuning may involve rewriting parts of the program is assembly code, or running different parts of a program in parallel.

Parallel programs can be tuned by assigning priorities to computations, so the system can give more CPU cycles to time-critical computations. If a computation has a tight deadline, it can be given a high priority, increasing the chance of meeting the deadline. Priorities are supported by several languages, but they do not give absolute guarantees that deadlines will be met.

The second issue to be addressed by a real-time language is reliability. A real-time program controlling, say, an aircraft should continue functioning no matter what happens. Ideally, it must survive malfunctionings in the devices it controls, crashes of CPUs it runs on, and even errors in its own software. In general, such problems must be addressed during the design of the system. A language, however, must allow exceptional situations to be detected, so the appropriate software can be run to solve the problem.

The third issue is support for low-level programming. A real-time program that controls hardware devices must be able to send data to the device interface, receive data from it, and respond to interrupts generated by the device. With memory-mapped devices, e.g., the program has to write bits or bytes to fixed hardware addresses. The language therefore must allow programmers to get around the typing mechanism and write arbitrary data to arbitrary locations.

7.2. Concepts

We will now look at some language concepts that have been proposed for dealing with time, reliability, and low-level programming. Our discussion primarily concerns reliability, since the other issues are usually addressed by ad hoc language constructs.

7.2.1. Timing

The notion of time can be dealt with in a simple way, e.g., through a library routine that returns the current value of a real-time clock. In addition, a construct for delaying a process for a certain time may be supported.

As stated before, many languages also allow priorities to be associated with computations, to facilitate meeting deadlines. A priority is usually a number that can be assigned to a process dynamically. The scheduler will always pick the process with the highest priority and run it. To prevent other processes from starving, the priority of the currently running process may be decreased periodically, so that eventually some other process will have the highest priority.

7.2.2. Reliability

Several language constructs exist for detecting errors during run time. The mechanism most frequently used is *exception handling*. An exception is an unexpected hardware or software error, such as a processor crash or a division by zero. An exception handler is a routine that is invoked automatically when an exception occurs. A handler is similar to a conventional procedure, except that it is not called explicitly from the program, but implicitly from the language run time system.

The idea is for the exception handler to start a software module that solves the problem causing the exception. Usually, the designer of the real-time system must have decided beforehand how to react to the problem, once it occurs.

In some languages, the program can resume from the point it was at when the exception occurred. A disadvantage of this approach is that the exception handler code may be invoked implicitly anywhere in the program, thus making static analysis of the program for correctness proofs or compile-time optimization close to impossible. Other languages force the current procedure to be abandoned, and continue execution at the caller of this procedure. This approach has the disadvantage that the cause of the exception may be lost when returning to the caller.

7.2.3. Low-level programming

The third issue, low-level programming, is dealt with in various ad hoc ways. One approach is to have a loophole in the typing system, allowing, say, integer constants to be used in place of variables names. Ada uses a somewhat cleaner approach, as we will see below.

7.3. Examples

Examples of languages for real-time programming include Ada, Occam, Conic, Pearl, and Real-Time Euclid [Burns, 1990]. Below, we will look at Ada.

7.3.1. Ada

The Ada language was designed on behalf of the US Department of Defense for embedded military applications. Ada is a procedural language containing features for programming-in-the-large, multi-tasking, and real-time programming.

Parallelism is expressed in Ada through *tasks* (processes). Tasks communicate through a form of synchronous, two-way message passing called *rendezvous*. A task can have *entries*, which are similar to procedures, except that they can be called by other, possibly remote, tasks. An invocation of an entry is serviced explicitly by the receiving task through an *accept statement*. An entry call transfers data from the sender to the receiver and back, and also synchronizes the two tasks.

A task can read the current time by calling the function CLOCK in the standard package CALENDAR. A task can delay itself for at least T seconds by executing the statement

delay T;

Tasks can have priorities, but they are assigned statically to task *types*. So, all tasks of the same type have the same priority, which is fixed during compile time. In practice, this scheme frequently is too inflexible, and it is one of the many points on which the language design has been criticized [Burns, Lister & Wellings 1987].

Ada addresses reliability through an exception handling mechanism. Exception handlers can be associated with each procedure (or other executable unit); different handlers can be defined for different types of exceptions. If an exception occurs, the run-time system tries to find a handler for it. If a handler is defined in the current procedure, it is executed and the procedure is then aborted; execution proceeds at the caller of this procedure. If no handler is defined in the current procedure, the procedure is aborted and the exception is raised again in the calling procedure, and so on, until a handler is found. If no exception handler is present anywhere in the dynamic calling sequence, the program or task will be aborted.

All in all, the exception handling mechanism of Ada is rather complicated, especially since exceptions can occur during inter-task communication. In this case, both tasks may become involved in handling the exception.

Ada supports low-level programming in the form of *representation specifications*. Such a specification may, e.g., specify the memory address of a variable. So, a device register of an interface can be treated much like a normal variable, except that its address is given by the programmer. As another example, interrupts can be associated with task entries, so a device interrupt will be treated like an entry call.

8. Literature

There are many good books on programming languages and their principles and it is impossible to mention them all. The reader could start by making a choice from the books by Ghezzi & Jazayeri [1987], Sethi [1989], Sebesta [1989], and Wilson & Clark [1988]. For the more philosophically inclined reader we recommend the book by Abelson, Sussman & Sussman [1985]. The early history of programming languages (1944–1976) has been described concisely but thoroughly by Wegner [1976].

Important research journals on the subject of programming languages are

ACM Transactions on Programming Languages and Systems (TOPLAS), *Computer Languages*, and *ACM SIGPLAN Notices*.

Acknowledgements

This chapter has greatly benefited from the careful reading by and the critical comments of Erik Baalbergen, Arnold Geels, Ceriel Jacobs, Andy Tanenbaum, Cees Visser, and the editors; we thank them for their efforts. We also thank Lily Ossendrijver for watching over our English.

References

Abelson, H., G.J. Sussman, J. Sussman (1985). *Structure and Interpretation of Computer Programs*, MIT Press, Cambridge, MA., p. 542.

Ahuja, S., N. Carriero, D. Gelernter (1986). Linda and friends. *IEEE Computer* 19(8), 26–34.

Almasi, G.S., A. Gottlieb (1989). *Highly Parallel Computing*, Benjamin/Cummings, Menlo Park, CA.

Andrews, G.R. (1991). *Concurrent Programming – Principles and Practice*, Benjamin/Cummings, Menlo Park, CA.

Andrews, G.R., R.A. Olsson, M. Coffin, I. Elshoff, K. Nilsen, T. Purdin, G. Townsend (1988). An overview of the SR language and implementation. *ACM Trans. Program. Lang. Syst.* 10(1), 51–86.

Andrews, G.R., F.B. Schneider (1983). Concepts and notations for concurrent programming. *ACM Comput. Surveys* 15(1), 3–43.

Backus, J. (1978). Can programming be liberated from the von Neumann style? A functional style and its algebra of programs. *Commun. ACM* 21(8), 613–641.

Bal, H.E. (1990). *Programming Distributed Systems*, Silicon Press, Summit, NJ.

Bal, H.E. (1991). A Comparative Study of Five Parallel Programming Languages, *European Spring 1991 Conference on Distributed Open Systems in Perspective*, Tromso (May 1991), pp. 209–228.

Bal, H.E., J.G. Steiner, A.S. Tanenbaum (1989). Programming languages for distributed computing systems. *ACM Comput. Surveys* 21(3), 261–322.

Bal, H.E., A.S. Tanenbaum (1991). Distributed programming with shared data. *Comput. Lang.* 16(2), 129–146.

Birrell, A.D., B.J. Nelson (1984). Implementing remote procedure calls. *ACM Trans. Comp. Syst.* 2(1), 39–59.

Burns, A., A.M. Lister, A.J. Wellings (1987). A Review of Ada Tasking, in: *Lecture Notes in Computer Science 262*, Springer, Berlin.

Burns, A., A.J. Wellings (1990). *Real-Time Systems and their Programming Languages*, Addison-Wesley, Wokingham, UK.

Carriero, N., D. Gelernter (1988). *How to Write Parallel Programs – A Guide to the Perplexed*, RR-628, Yale University Press, New Haven, CT.

Clocksin, W.F., C.S. Mellish (1981). *Programming in Prolog*, Springer, Berlin.

Cox, B.J. (1986). *Object Oriented Programming – An Evolutionary Approach*, Addison-Wesley, Reading, MA.

DoD (1983). Ada Programming Language, *ANSI/MIL-STD-1815A*, Washington, American National Standards Institute (22 January 1983).

Feldman, S.I. (1979). Make – A program for maintaining computer programs. *Software – Pract. Exper.* 9(4), 255–266.

Field, A.J., P.G. Harrison (1988). *Functional Programming*, Addison-Wesley, Reading, MA.

Geurts, L., L. Meertens, S. Pemberton (1990). *The ABC Programmer's Handbook*, Prentice-Hall, Englewood Cliffs, NJ.

Ghezzi, C., M. Jazayeri (1987). *Programming Language Concepts, 2nd edition*, Wiley, New York, p. 428.

Hoare, C.A.R. (1978). Communicating sequential processes. *Commun. ACM* 21(8), 666–677.

Hudak, P. (1989). Conception, evolution, and application of functional programming languages. *ACM Comput. Surveys* 21(3), 359–411.

Hughes, J. (1989). Why functional programming matters. *Comput. J.* 32(2), 98–107.

IEEE (1985). Special issue on Ada environments and tools. *IEEE Software* 2(2).

Kernighan, B.W., D.M. Ritchie (1988). *The C Programming Language, 2nd edition*, Prentice-Hall, Englewood Cliffs, NJ.

Meyer B. (1988). *Object-oriented Software Construction*, Prentice-Hall, Englewood Cliffs, NJ, p. 534.

Robinson, J.A. (1965). A machine oriented logic based on the resolution principle. *J. ACM*, 23–41.

Schwartz, J.T., R.B.K. Dewar, E. Dubinsky, E. Schonberg (1986). *Programming with Sets – An Introduction to SETL*, Springer, New York, p. 493.

Sebesta, R.W. (1989). *Concepts of Programming Languages*, Benjamin/Cummings, Menlo Park, CA, p. 497.

Sethi, R. (1989). *Programming Languages, Concepts & Constructs*, Addison-Wesley, Reading, MA, p. 478.

Sterling, L.S., E. Shapiro (1986). *The Art of Prolog*, MIT Press, Cambridge, MA.

Tanenbaum, A.S. (1987). *Operating Systems: Design and Implementation*, Prentice-Hall, Englewood Cliffs, NJ.

Van Wijngaarden, A., B.J. Mailloux, J.E.L. Peck, C.H.A. Koster, M. Sintzoff, C.H. Lindsey, L.G.L.T. Meertens, R.G. Fisker (1975). Revised report on the algorithmic language Algol 68. *Acta Inform.* 5, 1–236.

Wegner, P. (1976). Programming languages – The first 25 years. *IEEE Trans. Comput.* 25, 1207–1225.

Wilson, L.B., R.G. Clark (1988). *Comparative Programming Languages*, Addison-Wesley, Reading, MA, p. 379.

Wirth, N. (1985). *Programming in Modula-2 – Third, corrected edition*, Springer, Berlin, p. 202.

Zuse, K. (1976). *The Plankalkül*, BMFT-GMD-106, GMD, Bonn.

E.G. Coffman et al., Eds., *Handbooks in OR & MS, Vol. 3*

Chapter 3

Operating Systems – The State of the Art

Andrew S. Tanenbaum

Department of Mathematics and Computer Science, Vrije Universiteit De Boelelaan 1081a, 1081 HV Amsterdam, The Netherlands

An operating system is a program that controls the resources of a computer and provides the users with an interface that is more attractive than the bare machine. The first operating systems date from the early 1950s. This chapter traces the evolution of operating systems from their inception to the late 1980s and describes the various types. It also discusses one particularly significant system, UNIX®, in some detail. Finally, it concludes with a discussion of current work in network and distributed operating systems.

1. What is an operating system?

Most computer users have had some experience with an operating system, but it is difficult to pin down precisely what an operating system is. Part of the problem is that operating systems perform two basically unrelated functions, and depending on who is doing the talking, you hear mostly about one function or the other. Let us now look at both.

1.1. The operating system as an extended machine

The actual hardware of a modern computer, especially the I/O (Input/Output) hardware, is extremely complex. Consider for a moment the floppy disk on an IBM PC, which is a very unsophisticated device. To program it at the hardware level, the user must be aware of the 16 commands that it accepts. Each of these commands needs parameters. The READ command, for example, requires 13 parameters packed into 9 bytes, which must be passed to the disk at the proper rate, not too fast and not too slow. When the READ is completed, the disk returns 23 different status and error fields packed into 7 bytes.

Without going into the *real* details, it should be clear that the average programmer probably does not want to get too intimately involved with the programming of floppy disks (or any other disks). Instead, what the programmer wants is a simple, high-level abstraction to deal with. In the case of disks, a typical abstraction would be that the disk contains a collection of named files. Each file can be opened, read or written, and then finally closed. Details such as whether or not recording should use modified frequency modulation and what the current state of the motor is should not appear in the abstraction presented to the user.

The program that hides the truth about the hardware from the programmer and presents a nice, simple view of names files that can be read and written is, of course, the operating system. Just as the operating system shields the programmer from the disk hardware and presents a simple file-oriented interface, it also conceals a lot of unpleasant business concerning interrupts, timers, memory management, and other low-level features. In each case, the abstraction presented to the user of the operating system is simpler and easier to use than the underlying hardware.

In this view, the function of the operating system is to present the user with the equivalent of an *extended machine* or *virtual machine* that is easier to program than the underlying hardware.

1.2. The operating system as a resource manager

The concept of the operating system as primarily providing its users with a convenient interface is a top-down view. An alternative, bottom-up, view holds that the operating system is there to manage all the pieces of a complex system. Modern computers consist of processors, memories, timers, disks, terminals, magnetic tape drives, network interfaces, laser printers, and a wide variety of other devices. In this alternative view, the job of the operating system is to provide for an orderly and controlled allocation of the processors, memories, and I/O devices among the various programs competing for them.

Imagine what would happen if three programs running on some computer all tried to print their output simultaneously on the same printer. The first few lines of printout might be from program 1, the next few from program 2, then some from program 3, and so forth. The result would be chaos. The operating system can bring order to the potential chaos by buffering all the output destined for the printer on the disk. When one program is finished, the operating system can then copy its output from the disk file where it has been stored to the printer, while at the same time the order program can continue generating more output, oblivious to the fact that the output is not really going to the printer (yet).

When a computer has multiple users, the need for managing and protecting the memory, I/O devices, and other resources is even more apparent. This need arises because it is frequently necessary for users to share expensive resources such as tape drives and phototypesetters. Economic issues aside, it is also often necessary for users who are working together to share information. In short, this view of the operating system holds that its primary task is to keep track of who is using which resource, to grant resource requests, to account for usage, and to mediate conflicting requests from different programs and users.

2. A brief history of operating systems

Operating systems have been evolving through the years. Since operating systems have historically been closely tied to the architecture of the computers on which they run, we will look at successive generations of computers to see what their operating systems were like.

The first true digital computer was designed by the English mathematician Charles Babbage (1792–1871). Although Babbage spent most of his life and fortune trying to built his *analytical engine*, he never got it working properly because it was a purely mechanical design, and the technology of his day could not produce the wheels, gears, cogs and other mechanical parts to the high precision that he needed. Needless to say, the analytical engine did not have an operating system.

2.1. The first generation (1945–1955): Vacuum tubes and plugboards

After Babbage's unsuccessful efforts, little progress was made in constructing digital computers until World War II. Around the mid-1940s, Howard Aiken at Harvard, John von Neumann at the Institute for Advanced Study in Princeton, J. Presper Eckert and William Mauchley at the University of Pennsylvania, and Konrad Zuse in Germany, among others, all succeeded in building calculating engine using vacuum tubes. These machines were enormous, filling up entire rooms with tens of thousands of vacuum tubes, but were much slower than even the cheapest home computer available today. Since a failure in any one of the thousands of tubes could bring the machine to a grinding halt, these machines were not very reliable. They were exclusively used for numerical calculations, were programmed in (binary) machine language, and had no operating systems.

2.2. The second generation (1955–1965): Transistors and batch systems

The introduction of the transistor in the mid-1950s changed the picture radically. Computers became reliable enough that they could be manufactured and sold to paying customers with the expectation that they would continue to function long enough to get some useful work done. The normal way of programming these machines was for the programmer to first write the program on paper (in FORTRAN or assembly language), then punch it on cards. He would then bring the card deck down to the input room and hand it to one of the operators.

When the computer finished whatever job it was currently running, an operator would take one of the card decks that had been brought from the input room and read it in. If the FORTRAN compiler was needed, the operator would have to get it from a file cabinet and read it in. Much computer time was wasted while operators were walking around the machine room.

Given the high cost of the equipment, it is not surprising that people quickly looked for ways to reduce the wasted time. The solution generally adopted was the *batch system*. The idea behind it was to collect a tray full of jobs in the input room, and then read them onto a magnetic tape using a small, inexpensive computer, such as the IBM 1401.

After about an hour of collecting a batch of jobs, the tape was rewound and brought into the machine room, where it was mounted on a tape drive. The operator then loaded a special program (the ancestor of today's operating system), which read the first job from tape and ran it. The output was written onto a second tape, instead of being printed. After each job finished, the operating system automatically read the next job from the tape and began running it. When the whole batch was done, the operator removed the input and output tapes, replaced the input tape with the next batch, and took the output tape offline for printing.

2.3. The third generation (1965–1980): ICs and multiprogramming

Third generation computers introduced a major advance in their operating systems: *multiprogramming*. On the second generation machines, when the current job paused to wait for a tape or other I/O operation to complete, the CPU simply sat idle until the I/O finished. With heavily CPU-bound scientific calculations, I/O is infrequent, so this wasted time is not significant. With commercial data processing the I/O wait time can often be 80 or 90 percent of the total time, so something had to be done about it.

The solution that evolved was to partition memory into several pieces, with a different job in each partition. While one job was waiting for I/O to complete, another job could be using the CPU. If enough jobs could be held in main memory at once, the CPU could be kept busy nearly 100 percent of the time. Having multiple jobs in memory at once requires special hardware to protect each job against snooping and mischief by the other ones, so third generation systems were equipped with this hardware.

Another major feature present in third-generation operating systems was the ability to read jobs from cards onto the disk as soon as they were brought to the computer room. Then, whenever a running job finished, the operating system could load a new job from the disk into the now-empty part of memory and run it. This technique is called *spooling* (from Simultaneous Peripheral Operation On Line) and was also used for output. With spooling, the 1401s were no longer needed, and much carrying of tapes disappeared.

Although third-generation operating systems were well-suited for big scientific calculations and massive commercial data processing runs, they were still basically batch systems. Many programmers pined for the first generation days when they had the machine all to themselves for a few hours, so they could debug their programs quickly. With third generation systems, the time between submitting a job and getting back the output was often several hours, so a single misplaced comma could cause a compilation to fail, and the programmer to waste half a day.

This desire for quick response time paved the way for *time-sharing*, a variant of multiprogramming, in which each user has an on-line terminal. In a time-sharing system, if 20 users are logged in and 17 of them are thinking or talking or drinking coffee, the CPU can be allocated in turn to the three jobs that want service. Since people debugging programs usually issue short commands (e.g., compile a five-page program) rather than long ones (e.g., sort a million-record tape), the computer can provide fast, interactive service to a number of users and perhaps also work on big batch jobs in the background when the CPU is otherwise idle. The first serious time-sharing system (CTSS) was developed at MIT on a specially modified IBM 7094 [Corbato, Merwin-Dagget & Daley, 1962].

After the success of the CTSS system, MIT, Bell Labs, and General Electric (then a major computer manufacturer) decided to embark on the development of a 'computer utility', a machine that would support hundreds of simultaneous time-sharing users. Their model was the electricity distribution system – when you need electric power, you just stick a plug in the wall, and within reason, as much power as you need will be there. The designers of this system, known as *MULTICS* (MULTiplexed Information and Computing Service), envisioned one huge machine providing computing power for everyone in Boston. The idea that machines as powerful as their GE-645 would be sold as personal computers for a few thousand dollars only 20 years later was pure science fiction at the time.

To make a long story short, MULTICS introduced many seminal ideas into the computer literature, but building it was a lot harder than anyone had expected. Bell Labs dropped out of the project, and General Electric quit the computer business altogether. Eventually, MULTICS ran well enough to be used in a production environment at MIT and a few dozen sites elsewhere, but the concept of a computer utility fizzled out. Still, MULTICS had an enormous influence on subsequent systems. It is described by Corbato & Vyssotsky [1965], Daley & Dennis [1968], Organick [1972] and Saltzer [1974].

Another major development during the third generation was the phenomenal growth of minicomputers, starting with the DEC PDP-1 in 1961. The PDP-1 had only 4K of 18-bit words, but at 120 000 dollars per machine (less than 5 percent of the price of a 7094), they sold like hotcakes. For certain kinds of non-numerical work, it was almost as fast as the 7094, and gave birth to a whole new industry. It was quickly followed by a series of other PDPs (unlike IBM's family, all incompatible) culminating in the PDP-11.

One of the computer scientists at Bell Labs who had worked on the MULTICS project, Ken Thompson, subsequently found a small PDP-7 that no one was using and set out to write a stripped-down, one-user version of MULTICS. Brian Kernighan somewhat jokingly dubbed this system UNICS (UNiplexed Information and Computing Service), but the spelling was later changed to UNIX. It was later moved to a small PDP-11/20, where it worked well enough to convince Bell Labs' management to invest in a larger PDP-11/45 to continue the work.

Another Bell Labs computer scientist, Dennis Ritchie, then teamed up with

Thompson to rewrite the system in a high-level language called C, designed and implemented by Ritchie. Bell Labs licensed UNIX to universities almost for free, and within a few years hundreds of them were using it. It soon spread to the Interdata 7/32, VAX, Motorola 68000, and many other computers. UNIX has been moved ('ported') to more CPU types than any other operating system in history, and its use is still rapidly increasing.

2.4. The fourth generation (1980–1990): Personal computers

With the development of LSI (Large Scale Integration) circuits, chips containing thousands of transistors on a square centimeter of silicon, the age of the personal computer dawned. In terms of architecture, personal computers were not that different from minicomputers of the PDP-11 class, but in terms of price they certainly were different. Where the minicomputer made it possible for a department in a company or university to have its own computer, the microprocessor chip made it possible for a single individual to have his or her own personal computer.

The widespread availability of computing power, especially highly interactive computing power usually with excellent graphics, led to the growth of a major industry producing software for personal computers. Much of this software was *user-friendly*, meaning that it was intended for users who did not know anything about computers, and furthermore had absolutely no intention what-soever of learning. This was certainly a major change from OS/360, whose job control language, JCL, was so arcane that entire books have been written about it [e.g., Cadow, 1970].

Two operating systems have dominated the personal computer scene: MS-DOS, written by Microsoft, Inc. for the IBM PC and other machines using the Intel 8088 CPU and its successors, and UNIX, which is dominant on the larger personal computers using the Motorola 68000 CPU family. It is perhaps ironic that the direct descendant of MULTICS, designed for a gigantic computer utility, has become so popular on personal computers, but mostly it shows how well thought out the basic ideas in MULTICS and UNIX were. Although the initial version of MS-DOS was relatively primitive, subsequent versions have included more and more features from UNIX, which is not entirely surprising given that Microsoft was a major UNIX supplier, using the trade name of XENIX®.

An interesting development that began taking place during the mid-1980s is the growth of networks of personal computers running *network operating systems* and *distributed operating systems*. In a network operating system, the users are aware of the existence of multiple computers, and can log in to remote machines and copy files from one machine to another. Each machine runs its own local operating system and has its own user (or users).

A distributed operating system, in contrast, is one that appears to its users as a traditional uniprocessor system, even though it is actually composed of multiple processors. In a true distributed system, users should not be aware of where their programs are being run or where their files are located; that should all be handled automatically and efficiently by the operating system.

Network operating systems are not fundamentally different from single-processor operating systems. They obviously need a network interface controller and some low-level software to drive it, as well as programs to achieve remote login and remote file access, but these additions do not change the essential structure of the operating system.

True distributed operating systems require more than just adding a little code to a uniprocessor operating system, because distributed and centralized systems differ in critical ways. Distributed systems, for example, often allow programs to run on several processors at the same time, thus requiring more complex processor scheduling algorithms in order to optimize the amount of parallelism achieved.

Communication delays within the network often mean that these (and other) algorithms must run with incomplete, outdated, or even incorrect information. This situation is radically different from a single-processor system in which the operating system has complete information about the system state.

Fault-tolerance is another area in which distributed systems are different. It is common for a distributed system to be designed with the expectation that it will continue running, even if part of the hardware is currently broken. Needless to say, such an additional design requirement has enormous implications for the operating system.

3. An example operating system – UNIX

In this section we will discuss one operating system, as an example of the current state-of-the-art. The system we have chosen is the UNIX operating system [Ritchie & Thompson, 1974; Kernighan & Mashey, 1979]. The UNIX system was developed by Ken Thompson and Dennis Ritchie at AT & T Bell Laboratories in the 1970s and has since been developed further and has spread to a tremendous number of computers ranging from personal computers (e.g., IBM PC) to supercomputers (Cray-2) as mentioned above. It is the de facto standard on scientific workstations and in nearly all university computer science departments, and is making inroads in the microcomputer world.

3.1. The UNIX user interface

To the user at a terminal, the two primary aspects of UNIX are the file system and the shell. We will now look at each of these in turn. Information in UNIX is stored in *files*. Each file consists of a sequence of bytes, from 0 up to the last byte. Files can be of any length of the size of the device. The operating system does not distinguish between different kinds of files such as Pascal programs, binary programs, English text, and so on. As far as it is concerned, a file is just a sequence of bytes.

Much of the power of UNIX comes from this model of a file. Users do not have to think in terms of cylinders and heads or other physical device characteristics. There are no physical or logical records, and no blocking factors. No distinction is made between sequential files, random access files, or files with various access methods. There are no file types. Finally, there are no buffers or other file-related data structures in user programs. All of these points may seem obvious, but UNIX is almost the only operating system around that does not burden the user with any of these items.

Files can be grouped into *directories*. Each directory can hold as many or as few files as needed, and may also contain subdirectories, which themselves may also contain files and subdirectories. Thus the file system as a whole takes the form of a tree, with the *root directory* at the top. By convention, the root directory contains subdirectories

bin – for binary (executable) programs
lib – for libraries
dev – for special files (see below)
tmp – for temporary (scratch) files
usr – for user directories

Within the *usr* directory, there is one subdirectory for each user, known as the user's *home directory*. Users often have subdirectories for various projects in their home directory. File names can be specified by giving their *absolute path name*. For example, the path */usr/jim/research/report.4* references a file *report.4* in a directory *research* which is itself in a directory *jim*, which is located in the top-level directory *usr*. The initial / indicates that the path is absolute (i.e., starting in the root directory).

It is possible for a user to issue a command to designate a given directory as the *working directory*. Path names that do not begin with a / are relative to the working directory. Thus if */user/jim/research* is the working directory, the path *report.4* is equivalent to */user/jim/research/report.4*. In practice, it is common to go to a working directory at the start of a login session, and stay there for a substantial period, so most path names can be short relative names, rather than long absolute names.

UNIX allows both files and directories to be protected. A user can set the protection for a file or directory so that only the owner can read and/or write it, so that members of the owner's group (e.g., project team or department, depending on the installation) can read and/or write it, or so that everyone on the system has access. For example, it is easy to the protect a file so that the owner can both read and write (i.e., modify) it, members of the owner's group can read it but not write it, and no one else has any access at all.

In addition to the regular files described above, UNIX also supports *special files*. These files can be used to access I/O devices. For example, there may be a file */dev/disk* that represents the disk, and another file */dev/tty* that represents the terminal. Assuming the protection system allows it, these files can be used to real and write raw disk blocks and the terminal, respectively. Allowing I/O devices to be accessed the same way as files makes it easy to implement real-time and other applications that need direct access to I/O devices.

The other key feature of the user interface is the command interpreter, called the *shell*. Command lines typed by the user on the terminal are analyzed and executed by the shell. Some commands give output, and others do their work quietly. For example, the command

      date

might result in

      Fri Sep 4 17:16:09 EDT 1988

On the other hand, the command

      cp file1 file2

just copies *file1* to *file2* (i.e., it creates a new file called *file2* and gives it the same contents as *file1*).

Some commands require multiple file names, such as *cp* above. The shell permits certain kinds of abbreviations to reduce the amount of typing needed. For example, it is customary to have files that contain C programs have the suffix *.c* as in *prog1.c* and *prog2.c*. To get a listing of all the C programs in the current directory, one can type

      ls *.c

The * matches all strings, and thus lists all files ending in *.c*. What actually happens here is that the shell reads the working directory before calling the *ls* program, finds all the file names ending in *.c* and expands the *.c in the command line. The command that actually gets executed might be something like

      ls prog1.c prog2.c

The * is not the only 'magic' character. The ? character matches any single character, and [b-h] matches any character between 'b' and 'h' inclusive. Other abbreviations of this type are available, and are commonly used.

The standard output of most programs is written to the terminal. However, in some cases, the user would like to put it on a file, to be saved for later use. This can easily be done by *redirecting standard output*. The command

      ls >files

runs the command *ls*, and puts the output, the list of all files in the working directory, in the file *files* where it can be examined later, printed, edited, and so on. Similarly, commands that normally take their input from the terminal can also have that redirected. For example, the editor, *ed*, normally takes its commands from the terminal, but the command

     ed <script

causes it to read from the file *script* instead. This feature, known as *redirecting standard input* might be useful when a series of files has to be edited using the same editor commands.

The ability to redirect standard input and standard output can be utilized to connect programs together. Consider, for example, the program *prep* that reads a document and outputs each word on a separate line, eliminating all punctuation. To get an alphabetical list of all the words in the document, one could type:

     prep <document >temp
     sort <temp >output
     rm temp

which first runs *prep*, putting the output on a temporary file, then runs *sort* to sort the words and write the output on a file *output*. Finally, the temporary file is removed. Alternatively we could type:

     prep <document | sort >output

The '|' symbol, called a *pipe*, arranges for the output of the first program to be fed into the second one without using a temporary file. If we now wanted to remove duplicates from the list, we could use the program *uniq*:

     prep <document | sort | uniq >output

Programs that take their input from standard input and write their output on standard output are called *filters*. By combining filters with pipes, it is often possible to get a job done without having to write a program. Numerous filters that can be used as building blocks are part of UNIX.

Normally, when a command is given from the terminal, the user has to wait until it completes before proceeding. However, it is also possible to start a job up in the background by typing an ampersand (&) after the command. For example,

     pc prog.p &

starts up the Pascal compiler as a background job. The user can continue issuing normal commands from the terminal. The only effect of the background job will be some loss of performance due to the CPU cycles used by the compiler.

Another interesting feature of the shell is its ability to take commands from a file instead of a terminal. In fact, the shell is actually a small programming language. For example, consider a file, *words*, containing one line:

```
prep <$1 | sort | uniq >output
```

When the user types:

```
words doc3
```

the shell substitutes *doc3* for the first (and in this case, only) formal parameter, $1, and carries out the command:

```
prep <doc3 | sort | uniq >output
```

Files containing shell programs are called *shell scripts*. A more complex example is the shell script

```
for i in $*
do
   echo Results of $i
   prep <$i | sort | uniq
done
```

in which $* is replaced by all the parameters and the variable *i* iterates through them, one per iteration. The command *echo* just outputs its parameters to standard output. Thus if the above shell script were called *multiwords*, the command

```
multiwords doc1 doc2 doc3
```

would be equivalent to typing

```
echo Results of doc1
prep <doc1 | sort | uniq
echo Results of doc2
prep <doc2 | sort | uniq
echo Results of doc3
prep <doc3 | sort | uniq
```

The output of *multiwords* can, of course, also be redirected or used as input to a pipe. The shell also has variables, *while* loops and many other features that make it extremely powerful and easy to use. It is frequently possible to put together a little shell script to get a job done instead of spending a lot of time writing a program.

3.2. The UNIX implementation

Let us now turn from the user interface to take a quick look at how UNIX is implemented internally. Associated with each file is a small data structure called an *i-node*. The i-node tells who owns the file, how big it is, who may access it, and gives a list of the disk blocks that contain the data. All the i-nodes for all the files on a disk are located in consecutive blocks at the start of the disk. They are numbered from 1 up to some maximum. Given an i-node number, the system can find all the information about the file, both the administrative information and the data themselves.

Another key data structure is the *directory*. A directory is just a file containing (name, i-node number)-pairs. The system keeps track of the working directory by remembering its i-node number. When a user wants to read a file 'data', for example, the system locates the working directory using its i-node number, finds the blocks, and begins reading the entries until it finds one would name is 'data'. At that point it has the i-node number and can read in the i-node, to see if the user is permitted to access the file, where the blocks are, and so on. This scheme makes it possible for two or more users working together to share a file: they just make sure that each one has a (name, i-node number)-entry in one of their directories. Although there may be multiple directory entries for a file, there is always only one copy of the file itself.

The second major concept in the UNIX implementation is that of a *process*. A process is a program in execution. When the user types in a command, the shell (which is itself a process), creates a new process, and loads the program to be executed in the process. Normally, the shell waits until this new process finishes before reading the next command line from the terminal. However, if the previous command contained the ampersand symbol, the shell does not wait for termination. It reads and handles the next command immediately. This is how background jobs are implemented.

When a command line with multiple pipes is typed, the shell creates a separate process for each program to be executed. It then arranges for the standard output of the first one to refer to a kind of dummy file, and the standard input of the second one to refer to the same dummy file, and so on. These dummy files are handled internally in a more efficient way than ordinary scratch files.

The shell is not the only process that creates other processes. Any process that wants to can create new processes. In fact, when the system is brought up, a program called *init* is started. This program looks at a configuration file to see how many terminals the system has, and creates one process for each terminal. This process initially runs the *login* program, which asks for a name and password, and if successful, starts up a shell for that terminal. Thus all the processes in the whole system form a single tree, with the *init* process at the root.

3.3. *Virtual memory*

Many operating systems, including most versions of UNIX that run on minicomputers and mainframes have a feature called *virtual memory*, that allows users to execute programs larger than the amount of memory the computer actually has. The basic idea behind virtual memory is that each program has a certain amount of address space that it can reference. On a computer with 32-bit addresses, this address space would normally be 32-bits wide, allowing for over 4 billion addresses. Programs can use this address space for program text or data.

Of course a problem exists if the physical memory is much smaller than the allowed address space. The problem is typically solved by a technique called *paging*. Both the address space and the physical memory are broken up into fixed-size chunks called *pages*. Page sizes are always powers of two, typically 1K, 2K, 4K, or 8K bytes.

The computer's hardware maintains a mapping between address space pages and memory pages, but the mapping is not 1-to-1. For example, the first 4 pages of the address space might be mapped onto physical memory pages 7, 19, 2, and 5, respectively. With 1K pages, all memory references to addresses between 0K and 1K would automatically be mapped onto addresses between 7K and 8K. Similarly, references to addresses between 1K and 2K would be mapped onto 19K to 20K. Some address space pages are not mapped at all onto physical memory (because there are not enough physical memory pages). When an address on one of these pages is used (e.g., a jump is made to program text on it, or an attempt is made to read data on it), the hardware causes a trap to the operating system. The operating system then removes some other page from memory, brings in the needed page, changes the hardware page map, and restarts the instruction that failed.

A considerable amount of research has gone into discovering efficient algorithms for managing virtual memory systems, especially finding algorithms for choosing the page to remove [Denning, 1970]. An obvious (but unimplementable) strategy is to evict the page that will be referenced farthest in the future of all the pages currently in memory. Many algorithms have been devised that attempt to approximate this strategy. For example, one popular algorithm evicts the page least recently used, on the grounds that if it has not been used in a long time, it probably will not be used for a long time in the future, if ever again. Another one chooses the page that was loaded into memory before any of the other pages, on the grounds that it has been around long enough and it is time to give some other page a change. Many more complex algorithms have also been discussed in the literature. See any of the books cited in Section 6 for a fuller discussion of virtual memory.

4. Network operating systems

We have now finished our discussion of the UNIX system. As technology has progressed and computers have gotten cheaper, many organizations have become interested in connecting multiple computers together using local-area or wide-area networks. There are several reasons why this trend has occurred. In the first place, the price/performance ratio of smaller machines is much better than larger ones. Thus hooking up a number of smaller computers into one large system often given a more cost effective system. In the second place, a system with multiple processors is more redundant. If one of them fails, the others can continue. In the third place, many applications are inherently distributed and fit well with the model of multiple processors.

We can distinguish two kinds of operating systems for these multiple computer systems: *network operating systems* and *distributed operating systems*. In the former case, the systems are weakly coupled. Each machine retains its own identity and users. Each user logs into one specific machine, and to run programs or access files on another one requires explicitly accessing the other machine. In the latter case, all the computing resources act like a big pool. Users are generally not aware of where their computations or files are located. Decisions about where to put what are made by the operating system. In this section we will discuss network operating systems, quite a few of which are currently in operation. In the next section we will look at research into distributed operating systems.

The key feature that distinguishes a network operating system from a distributed operating system is the transparency – to what extent are the users aware that multiple machines are involved. If the users are clearly aware of the existence of multiple machines, and have to do remote login, file transfer, etc. by themselves, it is a network operating system. If these things all happen automatically, it is a distributed operating system. The visibility occurs in three primary areas: the file system, protection, and execution location. We will now look at each of these issues in turn.

4.1. File system

When connecting two or more distinct systems together, the first issue that must be faced is how to merge the file systems. Three approaches have been tried. The first approach is not to merge them at all. Going this route means that a program on machine A cannot access files on machine B by making system calls. Instead, the user must run a special file transfer program that copies the needed remote files to the local machine, where they can then be accessed normally. Sometimes remote printing and mail is also handled this way. One of the best-known examples of networks that primarily support file transfer and mail via special programs, and not system call access to remote files is the UNIX 'uucp' program, and its network, UUCPNET.

The next step upward in the direction of a distributed file system is to have *adjoining file systems*. In this approach, programs on one machine can open files on another machine by providing a path name telling where the file is located. For example, one could say

open("/machine1/pathname",READ_ONLY);
open("machine1!pathname",READ_ONLY); or
open("/../machine1/pathname",READ_ONLY)

The latter naming scheme is used in the Newcastle Connection [Brownbridge, Marshall & Randell, 1992] and Netix [Wambecq, 1983] and is derived from the creation of a virtual 'superdirectory' above the root directories of all the connected machines. Thus '/..' means start at the local root directory and go upwards one level (to the superdirectory), and then down to the root directory of *machine*. To access file *x* on machine *C*, one might say

open("/../C/x", READ_ONLY)

In the Newcastle system, the naming tree is actually more general, since 'machine1' may really be any directory, so one can attach a machine as a leaf anywhere in the hierarchy, not just at the top.

The third approach is the way it is done in distributed operating systems, namely to have a single global file system visible from all machines. When this method is used, there is one 'bin' directory for binary programs, one password file, and so on. When a program wants to read the password file it does something like

open("/etc/passwd",READ_ONLY)

without reference to where the file is. It is up to the operating system to locate the file and arrange for transport of data as it is needed. LOCUS is an example of a system using this approach [Popek, Walker, Chow, Edwards, Kline, Rudisin & Thiel, 1981; Walker Popek, English, Kline & Thiel, 1983; Weinstein, Page, Livesey & Popek, 1985].

The convenience of having a single global name space is obvious. In addition, this approach means that the operating system is free to move files around between machines to keep all the disks equally full and busy, and that the system can maintain replicated copies of files if it so chooses. When the user or program must specify the machine name, the system cannot decide on its own to move a file to a new machine because that would change the (user visible) name used to access the file. Thus in a network operating system, control over file placement must be done manually by the users, whereas in a distributed operating system it can be done automatically, by the system itself.

4.2. Protection

Closely related to the transparency of the file system is the issue of protection. UNIX, and many other operating systems, assign a unique internal identifier to each user. Each file in the file system has a little table associated with it (the i-node in UNIX), telling who the owner is, where the disk blocks are located, etc. If two previously independent machines are now connected, it may turn out that some internal User IDentifier (UID), e.g., number 12, has been assigned to a different user on each machine. Consequently, when user 12 tries to access a remote file, the remote file system cannot see whether the access is permitted, since two different users have the same UID.

One solution to this problem is to require all remote users wanting to access files on machine *C* to first log onto *C* using a user name that is local to *C*. When used this way, the network is just being used as a fancy switch to allow users at any terminal to log onto any computer, just as a telephone company switching center allows any subscriber to call any other subscriber.

This solution is usually inconvenient for people and impractical for programs, so something better is needed. The next step up is to allow any user to access files on any machine without having to log in, but to have the remote user appear to have the UID corresponding to 'GUEST' or 'DEMO' or some other publicly known login name. Generally such names have little authority, and can only access files that have been designated as readable or writable by all users.

A better approach is to have the operating system provide a mapping between UIDs, so when a user with UID 12 on his home machine accesses a remote machine on which his UID is 15, the remote machine treats all accesses as though they were done by user 15. This approach implies that sufficient tables are provided to map each user from his home (machine, UID)-pair to the appropriate UID for any other machine (and that messages cannot be tampered with).

In a true distributed system, there should be a unique UID for every user, and that UID should be valid on all machines without any mapping. In this way no protection problems arise on remote accesses to files; as far as protection goes, a remote access can be treated like a local access with the same UID. The protection issue makes the difference between a network operating system and a distributed one clear: in one case there are various machines, each with its own user-to-UID mapping, and in the other there is a single, system-wide mapping that is valid everywhere.

4.3. Execution location

Program execution is the third area in which machine boundaries are visible in network operating systems. When a user or a running program wants to create a new process, where is the process created? At least four schemes have been used so far. The first of these is that the user simply says 'CREATE PROCESS' in one way or another, and specifies nothing about where. Depending on the implementation, this can be the best way or the worst way to do it. In the most distributed case, the system chooses a CPU by looking at the load, location of files to be used, etc. In the least distributed case, the system always runs the process on one specific machine (usually the machine on which the user is logged in).

The second approach to process location is to allow users to run jobs on any machine by first logging in there. In this model, processes on different machines cannot communicate or exchange data, but a simple manual load balancing is possible.

The third approach is to use a special command that the user types at a terminal to cause a program to be executed on a specific machine. A typical command might be

> remote vax4 who

to run the *who* program on machine *vax4*. In this arrangement, the environment of the new process is the remote machine. In other words, if that process tries to read or write files from its current working directory, it will discover that its working directory is on the remote machine, and files that were in the parent process' directory are no longer present. Similarly, files written in the working directory will appear on the remote machine, not the local one.

The fourth approach is to provide the 'CREATE PROCESS' system call with a parameter specifying where to run the new process, possibly with a new system call for specifying the default site. As with the previous method, the environment will generally be the remote machine. In many cases, signals and other forms of interprocess communication between processes do not work properly between processes on different machines.

4.4. The OSI model

Network operating systems communicate by sending messages over a network. The content, format, and rules by which these messages are sent is called the network *protocol*. When computer networks were first established, each manufacturer had its own protocols, with the result that machines from one company could not talk to those of another. To alleviate this situation, a model was developed in which international standards could take the place of proprietary standards. In this section we will give a brief overview of this model.

The model was developed by ISO and is known as *OSI*, for *Open Systems Interconnection*. It consists of 7 layers (layer 7 on top, layer 1 on the bottom):

7. Application layer
6. Presentation layer
5. Session Layer
4. Transport Layer
3. Network Layer
2. Data Link Layer
1. Physical Layer

Each layer has a well-defined function and its own protocols. The idea is to start with the base network, and enhance its services by adding the physical layer to it. Then the data link layer is added, to enhance the services more, and so on. In the following paragraphs we will briefly summarize the function of each layer.

The *physical layer* is concerned with transmitting raw bits over a communication channel. The design issues have to do with making such that when one side sends a 1 bit, it is received by the other side as a 1 bit, not as a 0 bit. Typical questions here are how many volts should be used to represent a 1 and how many for a 0, how many microseconds a bit occupies, whether transmission may proceed simultaneously in both directions, how the initial connection is established and how it is torn down when both sides are finished, how many pins the network connector has and what each pin is used for. In some cases a transmission facility consists of multiple physical channels, in which case the physical layer can make them look like a single channel, although higher layers can also perform this function. The design issues here largely deal with mechanical, electrical, and procedural interfacing to the subnet.

The task of the *data link layer* is to take a raw transmission facility and transform it into a line that appears free of transmission errors to the network layer. It accomplishes this task done by breaking the input data up into *data frames*, transmitting the frames sequentially, and processing the *acknowledgement frames* sent back by the receiver. Since layer 1 merely accepts and transmits a stream of bits without any regard to meaning or structure, it is up to the data link layer to create and recognize frame boundaries. This can be accomplished by attaching special bit patterns to the beginning and end of the frame. These bit patterns can accidentally occur in the data, so special care must be taken to avoid confusion.

A noise burst on the line can destroy a frame completely. In this case, the layer 2 software on the source machine must retransmit the frame. However, multiple transmissions of the same frame introduce the possibility of duplicate frames. A duplicate frame could be sent, for example, if the acknowledgement frame from the receiver back to the sender was destroyed. It is up to this layer to solve the problems caused by damaged, lost, and duplicate frames, so that layer 3 can assume it is working with an error-free (virtual) line. Layer 2 may offer several different services classes to layer 3, each of a different quality and with a different price.

Another issue that arises at layer 2 (and at most of the higher layers as well) is how to keep a fast transmitter from drowning a slow receiver in data. Some mechanism must be employed to let the transmitter know how much buffer space the receiver has at the moment. Typically, this mechanism and the error handling are integrated together.

The *network layer* is concerned with controlling the operation of the network. A key design issue is how packet routes are determined. Routes could be based on static tables that are 'wired into' the network and rarely changed. They could also be determined at the start of each conversation, for example, a terminal session. Finally, they could be highly dynamic, being determined anew for each packet, to reflect the current network load.

If too many packets are present in the network at the same time, they will get in each others' way, forming bottlenecks. The control of such congestion also belongs to layer 3.

Since the operators of the network may well expect remuneration for their efforts, there is often some accounting function built into layer 3. At the very least, the software must count how many packets or characters or bits are sent by each customer, to produce billing information. When a packet crosses a national border, with different rates on each side, the accounting can become complicated.

When a packet has to travel from one network to another to get to its destination, many problems can arise. The addressing used by the second network may be different from the first one. The second one may not accept the packet at all because it is too large. The protocols may differ, and so on. It is up to the network layer to overcome all these problems to allow heterogeneous networks to be connected together.

The basic function of the *transport layer*, is to accept data from the session layer, split it up into smaller units if need be, pass these to the network layer, and ensure that the pieces all arrive correctly at the other end. Furthermore, all this must be done in the most efficient possible way, and in a way that isolates the session layer from the inevitable changes in the hardware technology.

Under normal conditions, the transport layer creates a distinct network (i.e., layer 3) connection for each transport (i.e., layer 4) connection required by the session layer. However, if the transport connection requires a high throughput, the transport layer might create multiple network connections, dividing the data among the network connections to improve throughput. On the other hand, if creating or maintaining a network connection is expensive, the transport layer might multiplex several transport connections onto the same network connection, to reduce the cost. In all cases, the transport layer is required to make the multiplexing transparent to the session layer.

The transport layer also determines what type of service to provide the session layer, and ultimately, the users of the network. The most popular type of transport connection is an error-free (virtual) point-to-point channel that delivers messages in the order in which they were sent. However, other possible kinds of transport service are transport of isolated messages with no guarantee about the order of delivery, and broadcasting of messages to multiple destinations. The type of service is determined when the connection is established.

The *session layer* allows users on different machines to establish *sessions* between them. A session allows ordinary data transport, as does the transport layer, but it also provides some enhanced services useful in a few applications. A session might be used to allow a user to log into a remote time-sharing system or to transfer a file between two machines.

One of the services of the session layer is to manage dialog control. Sessions can allow traffic to go in both directions at the same time, or in only one direction at a time. If traffic can only go one way at a time (analogous to a single railroad track), the session layer can help keep track of whose turn it is.

A related session service is *token management*. For certain protocols, it is essential that both sides do not attempt the same operation at the same time. To manage these activities, the session layer provides tokens that can be exchanged. Only the side holding the token may perform the critical operation.

Another session service is *synchronization*. Consider the problems that might occur when trying to do a 4 hour file transfer between two machines on a network with a 1 hour mean time between crashes. After each transfer was aborted, the whole transfer would have to start over again, and would probably fail again when the network next crashed. To eliminate this problem, the session layer can built in checkpoints, so that after a crash, only the data after the last checkpoint has to be repeated.

Another service is *quarantine service*, which has to do with telling the session layer on the receiving side not to deliver any data to the user process until all of it has arrived. The feature is useful to make sure that no work is started until it is known for sure that all the data has already arrived safely.

The *presentation layer* performs certain functions that are requested sufficiently often to warrant finding a general solution for them, rather than letting each user solve the problems. In particular, unlike all the lower layers, which are just interested in moving bits reliably from here to there, the presentation layer is concerned with the syntax and semantics of the information transmitted. These functions can often be performed by library routines called by the user.

A typical example of a presentation service is encoding data in a standard way that all machines can understand. Most user programs do not exchange random binary bit strings. They exchange things such as people's names, dates, amounts of money, and invoices. These items are represented as character strings, integers, floating point numbers, and structured values composed of several simpler items. Different computers have different codes for representing character strings (e.g., ASCII and EBCDIC), different systems for representing integers (e.g., one's complement and two's complement), and so on. In order to make it possible for computers with different representations to communicate, various conversions must take place. These conversions are done in the presentation layer.

The *application layer* contains a variety of protocols that are commonly needed. For example, there are hundreds of incompatible terminal types in the world. Consider the plight of a full screen editor that is supposed to work with many different terminal types, each with different screen layouts, escape sequences for inserting and deleting text, moving the cursor, and so on.

One way to solve this problem is to have a standard *network virtual terminal* that editors and other programs can be written to deal with. To attach a real terminal to the network, a piece of software must be written to map the functions of the network virtual terminal onto the real terminal. For example, when the editor moves the virtual terminal's cursor to the upper left-hand corner of the screen, this software must issue the proper command sequence to the real terminal to get its cursor there too. All the virtual terminal software is in the application layer.

Another application layer function is file transfer. Different file systems have different file naming conventions, different ways of representing text lines, and so on. Transferring a file between two different systems requires handling these and other incompatibilities. This work, too, belongs to the application layer, as do remote job entry and various other general-purpose and special-purpose facilities.

5. Distributed operating systems

Network operating systems are a step forward from single user systems. They allow users to harness the power of multiple machines instead of just one. However, they have the disadvantage of burdening the users with knowing about the details of what is located where. It would be far better to have the entire collection of machines act to the users as if it was a single machine, a *virtual uniprocessor*.

Needless to say, arranging for the illusion that there is really only one computer, when in fact there are many, is not easy. This difficult task is the job of the distributed operating system. A great deal of research in this area is presently in progress. In this section we will look at some of the principal design issues involved in the design of distributed operating systems. In this section we will look at five issues that distributed systems' designers are faced with:
– communication primitives,
– naming and protection,
– resource management,
– fault tolerance,
– services to provide.
While no list could possibly be exhaustive at this early stage of development, these topics should provide a reasonable impression of the areas in which current research is proceeding.

5.1. Communication primitives

The computers forming a distributed system normally do not share primary memory, so communication via shared memory techniques such as semaphores and monitors are generally not applicable. Instead, message passing in one form or another is used. One widely discussed framework for message-passing systems is the OSI reference model, discussed above. Unfortunately, the overhead created by all these layers is substantial. In a distributed systems consisting primarily of huge mainframes from different manufacturers, connected by slow leased lines (say, 56 kbps), the overhead might be tolerable.

Plenty of computing capacity would be available for running complex protocols, and the narrow bandwidth means that close coupling between the systems would be impossible anyway. On the other hand, in a distributed system consisting of identical microcomputers connected by a 10 Mbps or faster local network, the price of the OSI model is generally too high. Nearly all the experimental distributed systems discussed in the literature so far have opted for a different, much simpler model, so we will not mention the OSI model further in this paper.

5.1.1. Message passing

The model that is favored by researchers in this area is the *client-server model*, in which a client process wanting some service (e.g., reading some data from a file) sends a message to the server and then waits for a reply message. In the most naked form, the system just provides two primitives: SEND and RECEIVE. The SEND primitive specifies the destination and provides a message; the RECEIVE primitive tells from whom a message is desired (including 'anyone') and provides a buffer where the incoming message is to be stored. No initial setup is required, and no connection is established, hence no teardown is required.

Precisely what semantics these primitives ought to have has been a subject of much controversy among researchers. Two of the fundamental decision that must be made are unreliable vs. reliable and nonblocking vs. blocking primitives. At one extreme, SEND can put a message out onto the network and wish it good luck. No guarantee of delivery is provided, and no automatic retransmission is attempted by the system if the message is lost. At the other extreme, SEND can handle lost messages, retransmissions, and acknowledgements internally, so that when SEND terminates, the program is sure that the message has been received and acknowledged.

Blocking vs. nonblocking primitives. The other choice is between nonblocking and blocking primitives. With nonblocking primitives, SEND returns control to the user program as soon as the message has been queued for subsequent transmission (or a copy made). If no copy is made, any changes the program makes to the data before or (heaven forbid) *while* it is being sent, are made at the program's peril. When the message has been transmitted (or copied to a safe place for subsequent transmission), the program is interrupted to inform it that the buffer may be reused. The corresponding RECEIVE primitive signals a willingness to receive a message, and provides a buffer for it to be put into. When a message has arrived, the program is informed by interrupt or it can poll for status continuously, or go to sleep until the interrupt arrives. The advantage of these nonblocking primitives is that they provide the maximum flexibility: programs can compute and perform message I/O in parallel any way they want to.

Nonblocking primitives also have a disadvantage: they make programming tricky and difficult. Irreproducible, timing-dependent programs are painful to write and awful to debug. Consequently, many people advocate sacrificing some flexibility and efficiency by using blocking primitives. A blocking SEND does not return control to the user until the message has been sent (unreliable blocking primitive) or until the message has been sent and an acknowledgement received (reliable blocking primitive). Either way, the program may immediately modify the buffer without danger. A blocking RECEIVE does not return control until a message has been placed in the buffer. Reliable and unreliable RECEIVEs differ in that the former automatically acknowledges receipt of message, whereas the latter does not. It is not reasonable to combine a reliable SEND with an unreliable RECEIVE or vice versa, so the system designers must make a choice and provide one set or the other. Blocking and nonblocking primitives do not conflict, so there is no harm done if the sender uses one and the receiver the other.

Buffered vs. unbuffered primitives. Another design decision that must be made is whether or not to buffer messages. The simplest strategy is not to buffer. When a sender has a message for a receiver that has not (yet) executed a RECEIVE primitive, the sender is blocked until a RECEIVE has been done, at which time the message is copied from sender to receiver. This strategy is sometimes referred to as a *rendezvous*.

A slight variation on this theme is to copy the message to an internal buffer on the sender's machine, thus providing for a nonblocking version of the same scheme. As long as the sender does not do any more SENDs before the RECEIVE occurs, no problem occurs.

A more general solution is to have a buffering mechanism, usually in the operating system kernel, which allows senders to have multiple SENDs outstanding even without any interest on the part of the receiver. Although buffered message passing can be implemented in many ways, a typical approach is to provide users with a system call CREATEBUF, which creates a kernel buffer, sometimes called a *mail-box*, of a user-specified size. To communicate, a sender can now send messages to the receiver's mailbox, where they will be buffered until requested by the receiver. Buffering is not only more complex (creating, destroying, and generally managing the mailboxes), but also raises issues of protection, the need for special high-priority interrupt messages, what to do with mailboxes owned by processes that have been killed or died of natural cases, and more.

A more structured form of communication is achieved by distinguishing requests from replies. With this approach, one typically has three primitives: SEND_GET, GET_REQUEST, and SEND_REPLY. SEND_GET is used by clients to send requests and get replies. It combines a SEND to a server with a RECEIVE to get the server's reply. GET_REQUEST is done by servers to acquire messages containing work for them to do. When a server has carried out the work, it sends a reply with SEND_REPLY. By thus restricting the message traffic, and by using reliable, blocking primitives, one can create some order in the chaos.

5.1.2. Remote procedure call

The next step forward in message-passing systems is the realization that the model of 'client sends request and blocks until server sends reply' looks very similar to a traditional procedure call from the client to the server. This model has become known in the literature as *remote procedure call* and has been widely discussed [Birrell & Nelson, 1984; Nelson, 1981; Spector, 1982]. The idea is to make the semantics of intermachine communication as similar as possible to normal procedure calls because the latter is familiar, well understood, and has proved its worth over the years as a tool for dealing with abstraction. It can be viewed as a refinement of the reliable, blocking SEND_GET, GET_REQUEST SEND_REPLY primitives, with a more user-friendly syntax.

The remote procedure call can be organized as follows. The client (calling program) makes a normal procedure call, say $p(x, y)$, on its machine, with the intention of invoking the remote procedure p on some other machine. A dummy or *stub* procedure p must be included in the caller's address space, or at least be dynamically linked to it upon call. This procedure, which may be automatically generated by the compiler, collects the parameters and packs them into a message in a standard format. It then sends the message to the remote machine (using SEND_GET) and blocks, waiting for an answer.

At the remote machine, another stub procedure should be waiting for a message using GET_REQUEST. When a message comes in, the parameters are unpacked by an input handling procedure, which then makes the local call $p(x, y)$. The remote procedure p is thus called locally, so its normal assumptions about where to find parameters, the state of the stack, etc., are identical to the case of a purely local call. The only procedures that know that the call is remote are the stubs, which build and send the message on the client side and disassemble and make the call on the server size. The result of the procedure call follows an analogous path in the reverse direction.

5.1.3. Error handling

In error handling, the communication primitives of distributed systems differ radically from those of centralized systems. In a centralized system, a system crash means that the client, server, and communication channel are all completely destroyed, and no attempt is made to revive them. In a distributed system, matters are more complex. If a client has initiated a remote procedure call with a server that has crashed, the client may just be left hanging forever unless a timeout is built in. However, such a timeout introduces race conditions in the form of clients that time out too quickly, thinking that the server is down, when in fact, it is merely very slow.

Client crashes can also cause trouble for servers. Consider for example, the case of processes A and B communicating via the UNIX pipe model $A \mid B$ with A the server and B the client. B asks A for data and gets a reply, but unless that reply is acknowledged somehow, A does not know when it can safely discard data that it may not be able to reproduce. If *B* crashes, how long should *A* hold onto the data? (Hint: if the answer is less than infinity, problems will be introduced whenever *B* is slow in sending an acknowledgement.)

Closely related to this is the problem of what happens if a client cannot tell when a server has crashed. Simply waiting until the server is rebooted and trying again sometimes works and sometimes does not. A case where it works: client asks to read block 7 of some file. A case where it does not work: client says transfer a million dollars from one bank account to another. In the former case, it does not matter whether or not the server carried out the request before crashing; carrying it out a second time does no harm. In the latter case, one would definitely prefer the call to be carried out exactly once, no more and no less. Calls that may be repeated without harm (like the first example) are said to be *idempotent*. Unfortunately, it is not always possible to arrange for all calls to have this property. Any call that causes action to occur in the outside world, such as transferring money, printing lines, or opening a valve in an automated chocolate factory just long enough to fill exactly one vat, is likely to cause trouble if performed twice.

Spector [1982] and Nelson [1981] have looked at the problem of trying to make sure remote procedure calls are executed exactly once, and have developed taxonomies for classifying the semantics of different systems. These vary from systems that offer no guarantee at all (zero or more executions), to those that guarantee at most one execution (zero or one), to those that guarantee at least one execution (one or more).

Getting it right (exactly one) is probably impossible, because even if the remote execution can be reduced to one instruction (e.g., setting a bit in a device register that opens the chocolate valve), one can never be sure after a crash if the system went down a microsecond before, or a microsecond after, the one critical instruction. Sometimes one can make a guess based on observing external events (e.g., looking to see if the factory floor is covered with a sticky, brown material), but in general there is no way of knowing. Note that the problem of creating stable storage [Lampson, 1981] is fundamentally different, since remote procedure calls to the stable storage server in that model never causes events external to the computer.

5.2. Naming and protection

All operating systems objects such as files, directories, segments, mailboxes, processes, services, servers, nodes, and I/O devices. When a process wants to access one of these objects, it must present some kind of name to the operating system to specify which object it wants to access. In some instances these names are ASCII strings designed for human use, in others they are binary numbers used only internally. In all cases they have to be managed and protected from misuse.

5.2.1. Name servers

In centralized systems, the problem of naming can be effectively handled in a straightforward way. The system maintains a table or data base providing the necessary name-to-object mappings. The most straightforward generalization of this approach to distributed systems is the single name server model. In this model, a server accepts names in one domain and maps them onto names in another domain. For example, to locate services in some distributed systems, one sends the service name in ASCII to the name server, and it replies with the node number where that service can be found, or with the process name of the server process, or perhaps with the name of a mailbox to which requests for service can be sent. The name server's data base is built up by registering services, processes, etc., that want to be publicly known. File directories can be regarded as a special case of name service.

Although this model is often acceptable in a small distributed system located at a single site, in a large system it is undesirable to have a single centralized component (the name server) whose demise can bring the whole system to a grinding halt. In addition, if it becomes overloaded, performance will degrade. Furthermore, in a geographically distributed system that may have nodes in different cities or even countries, having a single name server will be inefficient due to the long delays in accessing it.

The next approach is to partition the system into domains, each with its own name server. If the system is composed of multiple local networks connected by gateways and bridges, it seems natural to have one name server per local network. One way to organize such a system is to have a global naming tree, with files and other objects having names of the form: /country/city/network/ pathname. When such a name is presented to any name server, it can immediately route the request to some name server in the designated country, which then sends it to a name server in the designated city, and so on until it reaches the name server in the network where the object is located, where the mapping can be done. Telephone numbers use such a hierarchy, composed of country code, area code, exchange code (first 3 digits of telephone number in North America), and subscriber line number.

Having multiple name servers does not necessarily require having a single, global naming hierarchy. Another way to organize the name servers is to have each one effectively maintain a table of, for example, (ASCII string, pointer)-pairs, where the pointer is really a kind of capability for any object or domain in the system. When a name, say $a/b/c$, is looked up by the local name server, it may well yield a pointer to another domain (name server), to which the rest of the name, b/c, is sent for further processing. This facility can be used to provide links (in the UNIX sense) to files or objects whose precise whereabouts is managed by a remote name server. Thus if a file *foobar* is located in another local network, n, with name server $n.s$, one can make an entry in the local name server's table for the pair $(x, n.s)$ and then access $x/foobar$ as though it were a local object. Any appropriately authorized user or process knowing the name $x/foobar$ could make its own synonym s and then perform accesses using *s/x/foobar.* Each name server parsing a name that involves multiple name servers just strips off the first component and passes the rest of the name to the name server found by looking up the first component locally.

A more extreme way of distributing the name server is to have each machine manage its own names. To look up a name, one broadcasts it on the network. At each machine, the incoming request is passed to the local name server, which replies only if it finds a match. Although broadcasting is easiest over a local network such as a ring net or CSMA net (e.g., Ethernet), it is also possible over store-and-forward packet switching networks such as the ARPAnet [Dalal, 1977].

Although the normal use of a name server is to map an ASCII string onto a binary number used internally to the system, such as a process identifier or machine number, once in a while the inverse mapping is also useful. For example, if a machine crashes, upon rebooting it could present its (hardwired) node number to the name server to ask what it was doing before the crash, i.e., ask for the ASCII string corresponding to the service it is supposed to be offering so it can figure out what program to reboot.

5.3. Resource management

Resource management in a distributed system differs from that in a centralized system in a fundamental way. Centralized systems always have tables that give complete and up-to-date status information about all the resources being managed; distributed systems do not. For example, the process manager in a traditional centralized operating system normally uses a 'process table' with one entry per potential process. When a new process has to be started, it is simple enough to scan the whole table to see if a slot is free. A distributed operating system, on the other hand, has a much harder job of finding out if a processor is free, especially if the system designers have rejected the idea of having any central tables at all, for reasons of reliability. Furthermore, even if there is a central table, recent events on outlying processors may have made some table entries obsolete without the table manager knowing it.

The problem of managing resources without having accurate global state information is very difficult. Relatively little work has been done in this area. In the following sections we will look at some work that has been done, including distributed process management and scheduling.

5.3.1. Scheduling

The hierarchical model provides a general model for resource control, but does not provide any specific guidance on how to do scheduling. If each process uses an entire processor (i.e., no multiprogramming), and each process is independent of all the others, any process can be assigned to any processor at random. However, if it is common that several processes are working together and must communicate frequently with each other, as in UNIX pipelines or in cascaded (nested) remote procedure calls, then it is desirable to make sure the whole group runs at once. In this section we will address that issue.

Let us assume that each processor can handle up to N processes. If there are plenty of machines and N is reasonably large, the problem is not finding a free machine (i.e., a free slot in some process table), but something more subtle. The basic difficulty can be illustrated by an example in which processes A and B run on one machine and processes C and D run on another. Each machine is time-shared in, say, 100 msec time slices, with A and C running in the even slices, and B and D running in the odd ones. Suppose that A sends many messages or makes many remote procedure calls of D. During time slice 0, A starts up and immediately calls D, which unfortunately is not running because it is now C's turn. After 100 msec, process switching takes place, and D gets A's message, carries out the work, and quickly replies. Because B is now running, it will be another 100 msec before A gets the reply and can proceed. The net result is one message exchange every 200 msec. What is needed is a way to ensure that processes that communicate frequently run simultaneously.

Although it is difficult to dynamically determine the interprocess communication patterns, in many cases, a group of related processes will be started off together. For example, it is usually a good bet that the filters in a UNIX pipeline will communicate with each other more than they will with other, previously started processes. Let us assume that processes are created in groups, and that intragroup communication is much more prevalent than intergroup communication. Let us further assume that a sufficiently large number of machines is available to handle the largest group, and that each machine is multiprogrammed with N process slots (N-way multiprogramming).

Ousterhout [1982] has proposed several algorithms based on the concept of *co-scheduling*, which takes interprocess communication patterns into account while scheduling to ensure that all members of a group run at the same time. The first algorithm uses a conceptual matrix in which each column is the process table for one machine. Thus, column 4 consists of all the processes that run on machine 4. Row 3 is the collection of all processes that are in slot 3 of some machine, starting with the process in slot 3 of machine 0, then the process in slot 3 of machine 1, and so on. The gist of his idea is to have each processor use a round robin scheduling algorithm with all processors first running the process in slot 0 for a fixed period, then all processors running the process in slot 1 for a fixed period, etc. A broadcast message could be used to tell each processor when to do process switching, to keep the time slices synchronized.

By putting all the members of a process group in the same slot number, but on different machines, one has the advantage of N-fold parallelism, with a guarantee that all the processes will be run at the same time, to maximize communication throughput. Thus the four processes that must communicate should be put into slot 3, on machines 1, 2, 3, and 4 for optimum performance.

5.3.2. Load balancing

The goal of Ousterhout's work is to place processes that work together on different processors, so that they can all run in parallel. Other researchers have tried to do precisely the opposite, namely, to find subsets of all the processes in the system that are working together, so closely related groups of processes can be placed on the same machine to reduce interprocess communication costs [Chu, Holloway, Min-Tsung & Efe, 1980; Chow & Abraham, 1982; Gylys & Edwards, 1976; Stone, 1977, 1978; Stone & Bokhari, 1978; Lo, 1984]. Yet other researches have been concerned primarily with load balancing, to prevent a situation in which some processors are overloaded while others are empty [Barak & Shiloh, 1985; Efe, 1982; Krueger & Finkel, 1983; Stankovic & Sidhu, 1984]. Of course, the goals of maximizing throughput, minimizing response time, and keeping the load uniform, are to some extent in conflict, so many of the researchers try to evaluate different compromises and tradeoffs.

Each of these different approaches to scheduling makes different assumptions about what is known and what is most important. The people trying to cluster processes to minimize communication costs, for example, assume that any process can run on any machine, that the computing needs of each process are known in advance, and that the interprocess communication traffic between each pair of processes is also known in advance. The people doing load balancing typically make the realistic assumption that nothing about the future behavior of a process is known. The minimizers are generally theorists, whereas the load balancers tend to be people making real systems who care less about optimality than devising algorithms that can actually be used. Let us now briefly look at each of these approaches.

Graph theoretic models. If the system consists of a fixed number of processes, each with known CPU and memory requirements, and a known matrix giving the average amount of traffic between each pair of processes, scheduling can be attacked as a graph-theoretic problem. The system can be represented as a graph, with each process a node, and each pair of communicating processes connected by an arc labeled with the data rate between them.

The problem of allocating all the processes to k processors then reduces to the problem of partitioning the graph into k disjoint subgraphs, such that each subgraph meets certain constraints (e.g., total CPU and memory requirements below some limit). Arcs that are entirely within one subgraph represent internal communication within a single processor (= fast), whereas arcs that cut across subgraph boundaries represent communication between two processors (= slow). The idea is to find a partitioning of the graph that meets the constraints and minimizes the network traffic, or some variation of this idea. Many papers have been written on this subject, for example, Chow & Abraham [1982], Stone [1977, 1978], Stone and Bokhari [1978], Lo [1984]. The results are somewhat academic, since in real systems virtually none of the assumptions (fixed number of processes with static requirements, known traffic matrix, error-free processors and communication) are ever met.

Heuristic load balancing. When the goal of the scheduling algorithm is dynamic, heuristic, load balancing, rather than finding related clusters, a different approach is taken. Here the idea is for each processor to continually estimate its own load, for processors to exchange load information, and for process creation and migration to utilize this information.

Various methods of load estimation are possible. One way is just to measure the number of runnable processes on each CPU periodically, and take the average of the last n measurements as the load. Another way [Bryant & Finkel, 1981] is to estimate the residual running times of all the processes and define the load on a processor as the number of CPU seconds all its processes will need to finish. The residual time can be estimated mostly simply by assuming it is equal to the CPU time already consumed. Bryant and Finkel also discuss other estimation techniques in which both the number of processes and length of remaining time are important. When round robin scheduling is used, it is better to be competing against one process that needs 100 sec than against 100 processes that each need 1 sec.

Once each processor has computed its load, a way is needed for each processor to find out how everyone else is doing. One way is for each processor to just broadcast its load periodically. After receiving a broadcast from a lightly loaded machine, a processor should shed some of its load by giving it to the lightly loaded processor. This algorithm has several problems. First, it requires a broadcast facility, which may not be available. Second, it consumes considerable bandwidth for all the 'Here is my load' messages. Third, there is a great danger that many processors will try to shed load to the same (previously) lightly loaded processor at once.

A different strategy [Smith, 1979; Barak & Shiloh, 1985] if for each processor to periodically pick another processor (possibly a neighbor, possibly at random), and exchange load information with it. After the exchange, the more heavily loaded processor can send processes to the other one until they are equally loaded. In this model, if 100 processes are suddenly created in an otherwise empty system, after one exchange we will have two machines with 50 processes, and after two exchanges most probably four machines with 25 processes. Processes diffuse around the network like a cloud of gas.

Actually migrating running processes is trivial in theory but close to impossible in practice. The hard part is not moving the code, data, and registers, but moving the environment, such as the current position within all the open files, the current values of any running timers, pointers or file descriptors for communicating with tape drives or other I/O devices, etc. All of these problems relate to moving variables and data structures related to the process that are scattered about inside the operating system. What is feasible in practice is to use the load information to create new processes on lightly loaded machines, rather than trying to move running processes.

If one has adopted the idea of creating new processes only on lightly loaded machines, another approach, called bidding, is possible [Faber & Larson, 1972; Stankovic & Sidhu, 1984]. When a process wants some work done, it broadcasts a request for bids, telling what it needs (e.g., a 68000 CPU 512 K memory, floating point, and a tape drive).

Other processors can then bid for the work, telling what their workload is, how much memory they have available, etc. The process making the request then chooses the most suitable machine and creates the process there. If multiple request-for-bid messages are outstanding at the same time, a processor accepting a bid may discover that the workload on the bidding machine is not what is expected because that processor has bid for and won other work in the meantime.

5.4. Fault tolerance

Proponents of distributed systems often claim that such systems can be more reliable than centralized systems. Actually, there are at least two issues involved here: reliability and availability. Reliability has to do with the system not corrupting or losing your data. Availability has to do with the system being up when you need it. A system could be highly reliable in the sense that it never loses data, but at the same time be down most of the time and hence hardly usable. However, many people use the term 'reliability' to cover availability as well, and we will not make the distinction either in the rest of the paper.

The reason why distributed systems are potentially more reliable than a centralized system is that if a system only has one instance of some critical component, such as a CPU, disk, or network interface, and that component fails, the system will go down. When there are multiple instances, the system may be able to continue in spite of occasional failures. In addition to hardware failures, one can also consider software failures. These are of two types: the software failed to meet the formal specification (implementation error), or the specification does not correctly model what the customer wanted (specification error). All work on program verification is aimed at the former, but the latter is also an issue. Distributed systems allow both hardware and software errors to be dealt with, albeit in somewhat different ways.

An important distinction should be made between systems that are fault tolerant and those that are fault intolerant. A fault tolerant system is one that can continue functioning (perhaps in a degraded form) even if something goes wrong. A fault intolerant system collapses as soon as any error occurs. Biological systems are highly fault tolerant; if you cut your finger, you probably will not die. If a memory failure garbles 1/10 of 1 percent of the program code or stack of a running program, the program will almost certainly crash instantly upon encountering the error.

It is sometimes useful to distinguish between expected faults and unexpected faults. When the ARPAnet was designed, people expected to lose packets from time to time. This particular error was expected and precautions were taken to deal with it. On the other hand, no one expected a memory error in one of the packet switching machines to cause that machine to tell the world that it had a delay time of zero to every machine in the network, which resulted in all network traffic being rerouted to the broken machine.

One of the key advantages of distributed systems is that there are enough resources to achieve fault tolerance, at least with respect to expected errors. The system can be made to tolerate both hardware and software errors, although it should be emphasized that in both cases it is the software, not the hardware, that cleans up the mess when an error occurs. In the past few years, two approaches to making distributed systems fault tolerant have emerged. They differ radically in orientation, goals, and attitude toward the theologically sensitive issue of the perfectability of mankind (programmers in particular). One approach is based on redundancy and the other is based on the notion of an atomic transaction. Both are described briefly below.

5.4.1. Redundancy techniques

All the redundancy techniques that have emerged take advantage of the existence of multiple processors by duplicating critical processes on two or more machines. A particularly simple, but effective, technique is to provide every process with a backup process on a different processor. All processes communicate by message passing. Whenever anyone sends a message to a process, it also sends the same message to the backup process. The system ensures that neither the primary nor the backup can continue running until it has been verified that both have correctly received the message.

Thus, if one process crashes due to any hardware fault, the other one can continue. Furthermore, the remaining process can then clone itself, making a new backup to maintain the fault tolerance in the future. Borg, Baumbach & Glazer [1983] have described a system using these principles.

One disadvantage of duplicating every process is the extra processors required, but another, more subtle problem, is that if processes exchange messages at a high rate, a considerable amount of CPU time may go into keeping the processes synchronized at each message exchange. Powell & Presotto [1983] have described a redundant system that puts almost no additional load on the processes being backed up. In their system, all messages sent on the network are recorded by a special 'recorder' process. From time to time, each process checkpoints itself onto a remote disk.

If a process crashes, recovery is done by sending the most recent checkpoint to an idle processor and telling it to start running. The recorder process then spoon-feeds it all the messages that the original process received between the checkpoint and the crash. Messages sent by the newly restarted process are discarded. Once the new process has worked its way up to the point of crash, it begins sending and receiving messages normally, without help from the recording process.

The beauty of this scheme is that the only additional work a process must do to become immortal is to checkpoint itself from time to time. In theory, even the checkpoints can be disposed with, if the recorder process has enough disk space to store all the messages sent by all the currently running processes. If no checkpoints are made, when a process crashes, the recorder will have to replay the process's whole history.

Both of the above techniques only apply to tolerance of hardware errors.

However, it is also possible to use redundancy in distributed systems to make systems tolerant of software errors. One approach is to structure each program as a collection of modules, each one with a well-defined function and a precisely specified interface to the other modules. Instead of writing a module only once, *N* programmers are asked to program it, yielding *N* functionally identical modules.

During execution, the program runs on *N* machines in parallel. After each module finishes, the machines compare their results and vote on the answer. If a majority of the machines say that the answer is *X*, then all of them use *X* as the answer, and all continue in parallel with the next module. In this manner, the effects of an occasional software bug can be voted down. If formal specifications for any of the modules are available, the answers can also be checked against the specifications to guard against the possibility of accepting an answer that is clearly wrong.

A variation of this idea can be used to improve system performance. Instead of always waiting for all the processes to finish, as soon as *k* of them agree on an answer, those that have not yet finished are told to drop what they are doing, accept the value found by the *k* processes, and continue with the next module. Some work in this area is discussed by Avizienis & Chen [1977], Avizienis & Kelly [1984], and Anderson & Lee [1981].

5.4.2. Atomic transactions

When multiple users on several machines are concurrently updating a distributed data base and one or more machines crash, the potential for chaos is truly impressive. In a certain sense, the current situation is a step backward from the technology of the 1950s, when the normal way of updating a data base was to have one magnetic tape, called the 'master file', and one or more tapes with updates (e.g., daily sales reports from all of a company's stores). The master tape and updates were brought to the computer center, which then mounted the master tape and one update tape, and ran the update program to produce a new master tape. This new tape was then used as the 'master' for use with the next update tape.

This scheme had the very real advantage that if the update program crashed, one could always fall back on the previous master tape and the update tapes. In other words, an update run could be viewed as either running correctly to completion (and producing a new master tape), or having no effect at all (crash part way through, new tape discarded). Furthermore, update jobs from different sources always ran in some (undefined) sequential order. It never happened that two users would concurrently read a field in a record (e.g., 6), each add 1 to the value, and each store a 7 in that field, instead of the first one storing a 7 and the second storing an 8.

The property of run-to-completion or do-nothing is called an *atomic update*. The property of not interleaving two jobs is called *serializability*. The goal of people working on the atomic transaction approach to fault tolerance has been to regain the advantages of the old tape system without giving up the convenience of data bases on disk that can be modified in place, and to be able to do everything in a distributed way.

Lampson [1981] has described a way of achieving atomic transactions by building up a hierarchy of abstractions. We will summarize his model below. Real disks can crash during READ and WRITE operations in unpredictable ways. Furthermore, even if a disk block is correctly written, there is a small (but nonzero) probability of it subsequently being corrupted by a newly developed bad spot on the disk surface. The model assumes that spontaneous block corruptions are sufficiently infrequent that the probability of *two* such events happening within some predetermined time, T, is negligible. To deal with real disks, the system software must be able to tell if a block is valid or not, for example, by using a checksum.

The first layer of abstraction on top of the real disk is the 'careful disk', in which every CAREFUL-WRITE is read back immediately to verify that it is correct. If the CAREFUL-WRITE persistently fails, the system marks the block as "bad" and then intentionally crashes. Since CAREFUL-WRITEs are verified, CAREFUL-READs will always be good, unless a block has gone bad after being written and verified.

The next layer of abstraction is *stable storage*. A stable storage block consists of an ordered pair of careful blocks, which are typically corresponding careful blocks on different drives, to minimize the chance of both being damaged by a hardware failure. The stable storage algorithm guarantees that at least one of the blocks is always valid. The STABLE-WRITE primitive first does a CAREFUL-WRITE on one block of the pair, and then the other. If the first one fails, a crash is forced, as mentioned above, and the second one is left untouched.

After every crash, and at least once every time period T, a special cleanup process is run to examine each stable block. If both blocks are 'good' and identical, nothing has to be done. If one is 'good' and one is 'bad' (failure during a CAREFUL-WRITE), the 'bad' one is replaced by the 'good' one. If both are 'good' but different (crash between two CAREFUL-WRITEs), the second one is replaced by a copy of the first one. This algorithm allows individual disk blocks to be updated atomically and survive infrequent crashes.

Stable storage can be used to create 'stable processors' [Lampson, 1981]. To make itself crashproof, a CPU must checkpoint itself on stable storage periodically. If it subsequently crashes, it can always restart itself from the last checkpoint. Stable storage can also be used to create stable monitors, in order to ensure that two concurrent processes never enter the same critical region at the same time, even if they are running on different machines.

Given a way to implement crashproof processors (stable processors) and crashproof disks (stable storage), it is possible to implement multicomputer atomic transactions. Before updating any part of the data in place, a stable processor first writes an intentions list to stable storage, providing the new value for each datum to be changed. Then it sets a commit flag to indicate that the intentions list is complete. The commit flag is set by atomically updating a special block on stable storage. Finally it begins making all the changes called for in the intentions list. Crashes during this phase have no serious consequences because the intentions list is stored in stable storage. Furthermore, the actual making of the changes is idempotent, so repeated crashes and restarts during this phase are not harmful.

Atomic actions have been implemented in a number of systems [see, e.g., Fridrich & Older, 1981; Mitchell & Dion, 1982; Brown, Kolling & Taft, 1985; Popek, Walker, Chow, Edwards, Kline, Rudisin & Thiel, 1981; Reed & Svobodova, 1981].

5.5. Services

In a distributed system, it is natural to provide functions by user-level server processes that have traditionally been provided by the operating system. This approach leads to a smaller (hence more reliable) kernel and makes it easier to provide, modify, and test new services. In the following sections, we will look at some of these services, but first we look at how services and servers can be structured.

5.5.1. File service

There is little doubt that the most important service in any distributed system is the file service. Many file services and file servers have been designed and implemented, so a certain amount of experience is available [e.g., Birrell & Needham, 1980; Dellar, 1982; Dion, 1980; Fridrich & Older, 1981; 1984; Mitchell & Dion, 1982; Mullender & Tanenbaum, 1985; Reed & Svobodova, 1981; Satyanarayanan, Howard, Nichols, Sidebotham, Spector & West, 1985; Schroeder, Gifford & Needham, 1985; Sturgis, Mitchell & Israel, 1980; Svobodova, 1981; Swinehart, McDaniel & Boggs, 1979]. A survey about file servers can be found in Svobodova [1984].

File services can be roughly classified into two kinds, 'traditional' and 'robust'. Traditional file service is offered by nearly all centralized operating systems (e.g., the UNIX file system). Files can be opened, read, and rewritten in place. In particular, a program can open a file, seek to the middle of the file, and update blocks of data within the file. The file server implements these updates by simply overwriting the relevant disk blocks. Concurrency control, if there is any, usually involves locking entire files before updating them.

Robust file service, on the other hand, is aimed at those applications that require extremely high reliability and whose users are prepared to pay a significant penalty in performance to achieve it. These file services generally offer atomic updates and similar features lacking in the traditional file service.

In the following paragraphs, we discuss some of the issues relating to traditional file service (and file servers) and then look at those issues that specifically relate to robust file service and servers. Since robust file service normally includes traditional file service as a subset, the issues covered in the first part also apply.

Conceptually, there are three components that a traditional file service normally has:
– disk service,
– flat file service,
– directory service.

The disk service is concerned with reading and writing raw disk blocks, without regard to how they are organized. A typical command to the disk service is to allocate and write a disk block, and return a capability or address (suitably protected) so the block can be read later.

The flat file service is concerned with providing its clients with an abstraction consisting of files, each of which is a linear sequence of records, possibly 1-byte records (as in UNIX) or client-defined records. The operations are reading and writing records, starting at some particular place in the file. The client need not be concerned with how or where the data in the file are stored.

The directory service provides a mechanism for naming and protecting files, so they can be accessed conveniently and safely. The directory service typically provides objects called directories that map ASCII names onto the internal identification used by the file service.

5.5.2. Print service

Compared to file service, on which a great deal of time and energy has been expended by a large number of people, the other services seem rather meager. Still, it is worth saying at least a little bit about a few of the more interesting ones.

Nearly all distributed systems have some kind of print service, to which clients can send files or file names or capabilities for files with instructions to print them on one of the available printers, possibly with some text justification or other formatting beforehand. In some cases, the whole file is sent to the print server in advance, and the server must buffer it. In other cases, only the file name or capability is sent, and the print server reads the file block by block as needed. The latter strategy eliminates the need for buffering (read: a disk) on the server side, but can cause problems if the file is modified after the print command is given but prior to the actual printing. Users generally prefer 'call by value' rather than 'call by reference' semantics for printers.

One way to achieve the 'call by value' semantics is to have a printer spooler server. To print a file, the client process sends the file to the spooler. When the file has been copied to the spooler's directory, an acknowledgement is sent back to the client.

The actual print server is then implemented as a print client. Whenever the print client has nothing to print, it requests another file or block of a file from the print spooler, prints it, and then requests the next one. In this way the print spooler is a server to both the client and the printing device.

Printer service is discussed by Needham & Herbert [1982].

5.5.3. Process service

Every distributed operating system needs some mechanism for creating new processes. At the lowest level, deep inside the system kernel, there must be a way of creating a new process from scratch. One way is to have a FORK call, as UNIX does, but other approaches are also possible. For example, in Amoeba, it is possible to ask the kernel to allocate chunks of memory of given sizes. The caller can then read and write these chunks, loading them with the text, data, and stack segments for a new process. Finally, the caller can give the filled-in segments back to the kernel and ask for a new process built up from these pieces. This scheme allows processes to be created remotely or locally, as desired.

At a higher level, it is frequently useful to have a process server that one can ask whether there is a Pascal, troff, or some other service, in the system. If there is, the request is forwarded to the relevant server. If not, it is the job of the process server to build a process somewhere and give it the request. After, say, a VLSI design rule checking server has been created and has done its work, it may or may not be a good idea to keep it is the machine where it was created, depending on how much work (e.g., network traffic) is required to load it, and how often it is called. The process server could easily manage a server cache on a least recently used basis, so that servers for common applications are usually preloaded and ready to go. As special-purpose VLSI processors become available for compilers and other applications, the process server should be given the job of managing them in a way that is transparent to the system's users.

5.5.4. Terminal service

How the terminals are tied to the system obviously depends to a large extent on the system architecture. If the system consists of a small number of minicomputers, each with a well-defined and stable user population, then each terminal can be hardwired to the computer its user normally logs on to. If, however, the system consists entirely of a pool of processors that are dynamically allocated as needed, it is better to connect all the terminals to one or more terminal servers that serve as concentrators.

The terminal servers can also provide such features as local echoing, intraline editing, and window management, if desired. Furthermore, the terminal server can also hide the idiosyncracies of the various terminals in use by mapping them all onto a standard virtual terminal. In this way, the rest of the software deals only with the virtual terminal characteristics and the terminal server takes care of the mappings to and from all the real terminals. The terminal server can also be used to support multiple windows per terminal, with each window acting as a virtual terminal.

5.5.5. Mail service

Electronic mail is a popular application of computers these days. Practically every university computer science department in the Western world is on at least one international network for sending and receiving electronic mail. When a site consists of only one computer, keeping track of the mail is easy. However, when a site has dozens of computers spread over multiple local networks, users often want to be able to read their mail on any machine they happen to be logged on to. This desire gives rise to the need for a machine-independent mail service, rather like a print service that can be accessed system wide. Almes, Black, Lazowska & Noe [1985] discuss how mail is handled in the Eden system.

5.5.6. Time service

There are two ways to organize a time service. In the simplest way, clients can just ask the service what time it is. In the other way, the time service can broadcast the correct time periodically, to keep all the clocks on the other machines in sync. The time server can be equipped with a radio receiver tuned to WWV or some other transmitter that provides the exact time down to the microsecond.

Even with these two mechanisms, it is impossible to have all processes exactly synchronized. Consider what happens when a process requests the time-of-day from the time server. The request message comes in to the server, and a reply is sent back immediately. That reply must propagate back to the requesting process, cause an interrupt on its machine, have the kernel started up, and finally have the time recorded somewhere. Each of these steps introduces an unknown, variable delay.

On an Ethernet, for example, the amount of time required for the time server to put the reply message onto the network is nondeterministic and depends on the number of machines contending for access at that instant. If a large distributed system has only one time server, messages to and from it may have to travel a long distance and pass over store-and-forward gateways with variable queueing delays. If there are multiple time servers, they may get out of synchronization because their crystals run at slightly different rates. Einstein's special theory of relativity also puts constraints on synchronizing remote clocks.

The result of all these problems is that having a single, global time is impossible. Distributed algorithms that depend on being able to find a unique global ordering of widely separated events may not work as expected. A number of researchers have tried to find solutions to the various problems caused by the lack of global time. [See, e.g., Jefferson, 1985; Lamport, 1984, 1978; Marzullo & Owicki, 1985; Reed, 1983; Reif & Spirakis, 1984].

5.5.7. Boot service

The boot service has two functions: bringing up the system from scratch when the power is turned on, and helping important services survive crashes. In both cases, it is helpful if the boot server has a hardware mechanism for forcing a recalcitrant machine to jump to a program in its own ROM, in order to reset it. The ROM program could simply sit in a loop waiting for a message from the boot service. The message would then be loaded into that machine's memory and executed as a program.

The second function alluded to above is the 'immortality service'. An important service could register with the boot service, which would then poll it periodically to see if it were still functioning. If not, the boot service could initiate measures to patch things up, for example, forcibly reboot it or allocate another processor to take over its work. To provide high reliability, the boot service should itself consist of multiple processors, each of which keeps checking that the other ones are still working properly.

6. Suggested readings

This chapter has only scratched the surface of the operating systems literature. For more complete introductions, a number of textbooks are available, including Bach [1986], Deitel [1983], Finkel [1986], Peterson & Silberschatz [1985], and Tanenbaum [1987, 1992]. Recent papers can often be found in the journal *ACM Transactions on Computer Systems*. There are two conferences that also have many papers on operating systems: *ACM Symposium on Operating Systems Principles* (held biannually in odd-numbered years), and IEEE's *Distributed Computer Systems* (held every year).

References

Almes, G.T., A.P. Black, E.D. Lazowska, J.D. Noe (1985). The Eden system: A technical review. *IEEE Trans. Software Engrg.* SE-11, 43–59.

Anderson, T., P.A. Lee (1981). *Fault Tolerance, Principles and Practice*, Prentice-Hall, Int'l, London.

Avizienis, A., L. Chen (1977). On the implementation of N-version programming for software fault-tolerance during execution, *Proc. COMPSAC*, IEEE, pp. 149–155.

Avizienis A., J. Kelly (1984). Fault tolerance by design diversity. *Computer* 17, 66–80.

Bach, M. (1986). *The Design of the UNIX Operating System*, Prentice-Hall, Englewood Cliffs, NJ.

Barak, A., A. Shiloh (1985). A distributed load-balancing policy for a multicomputer. *Software – Practice & Experience* 15, 901–913.

Birell, A.D., R.M. Needham (1980). A universal file server. *IEEE Trans. Software Engrg.* SE-6, 450–453.

Birell, A.D., B.J. Nelson (1984). Implementing remote procedure calls, *ACM Trans. Comput. Systems* 2, 39–59.

Borg, A., J. Baumbach, S. Glazer (1983). A message system supporting fault tolerance, *Proc. Ninth Symp. Operating Syst. Prin.*, ACM, pp. 90–99.

Brown, M.R., K.N. Kolling, E.A. Taft (1985). The Alpine file system. *ACM Trans. Comput. Syst.* 3, 261–293.

Brownbridge, D.R., L.F. Marshall, B. Randell (1982). The newcastle connection- or UNIXES or the World Unite! *Software – Practice & Experience* 12, 1147–1162.

Bryant, R.M., R.A. Finkel (1981). A stable distributed scheduling algorithm, *Proc. 2nd Int'l Conf. on Distributed Comput. Syst.*, IEEE, pp. 314–323.

Cadow, H. (1970). *OS/360 Job Control Language*, Prentice-Hall, Englewood Cliffs, NJ.

Chow, T.C.K., J.A. Abraham (1982). Load balancing in distributed systems, *IEEE Trans. Software Engrg.* SE-8, 401–412.

Chu, W.W., L.J. Holloway, L. Min-Tsung, K. Efe (1980). Task allocation in distributed data processing. *Computer* 13, 57–69.

Corbato, F.J., M. Merwin-Dagett, R.C. Daley (1962). An experimental time-sharing system, *Proc. AFIPS Fall Joint Computer Conf.*, 335–344.

Corbato, F.J., V.A. Vyssotsky (1965). Introduction and overview of the MULTICS system, *Proc. AFIPS Fall Joint Computer Conf.*, 185–196.

Dalal, Y.K. (1977). Broadcast protocols in packet switched computer networks, Ph.D. Thesis, Stanford Univ.

Daley, R.C., J.B. Dennis (1968). Virtual memory, process, and sharing in MULTICS. *Commun. of the ACM* 11, 306–312.

Deitel, H.M. (1983). *An Introduction to Operating Systems*, Addison-Wesley, Reading, MA.

Dellar, C. (1982). A file servers for a network of low-cost personal microcomputers. *Software – Practice & Experience* 12, 1051–1068.

Denning, P.J. (1970). Virtual memory. *Comput. Surveys* 2, 153–189.

Dion, J. (1980). The Cambridge file server. *Operating Syst. Rev.* 14, 41–49.

Efe, K. (1982). Heuristic models of task assignment scheduling in distributed systems, *Computer* 15, 50–56.

Farber, D.J., K.C. Larson (1972). The system architecture of the distributed computer system – The communications system, *Symp. Computer Netw.*, Polytechnic Institute of Brooklyn.

Finkel, R.A. (1986). *An Operating Systems Vade Mecum*, Prentice-Hall, Englewood Cliffs, NJ.

Fridrich, M., W. Older (1981). The Felix file server, *Proc. Eighth Symp. Operating Syst. Prin.*, ACM, pp. 37–44.

Fridrich, M., W. Older (1984). HELIX: The architecture of a distributed file system, *Proc. Fourth Int'l. Conf. on Distributed Comput. Syst.*, IEEE, pp. 422–431.

Gylys, V.B., J.A. Edwards (1976). Optimal partitioning of workload for distributed systems. *COMP-CON*, pp. 353–357.

Jefferson, D.R. (1985). Virtual time. *ACM Trans. Program. Lang. Syst.* 7, 404–425.

Kernighan, B.W., J.R. Mashey (1979). The UNIX programming environment. *Software – Practice & Experience* 9, 1–16.

Krueger, P., R.A. Finkel (1983). An adaptive load balancing algorithm for a multicomputer, Computer Science Dept., Univ. of Wisconsin.

Lamport, L. (1978). Time, clocks and the ordering of events in a distributed system. *Commun. ACM* 21, 558–565.

Lamport, L. (1984). Using time instead of timeout for fault-tolerant distributed systems. *ACM Trans. Program. Lang. Syst.* 6, 254–280.

Lampson, B.W. (1981). Atomic transactions, in: *Distributed Systems – Architecture and Implementation*, Springer-Verlag, Berlin, pp. 246–265.

Lo, V.M. (1984). Heuristic algorithms for task assignment in distributed systems, *Proc. Fourth Int'l Conf. on Distributed Comput. Syst.*, IEEE, pp. 30–39.

Marzullo, K., S. Owicki (1985). Maintaining the time in a distributed system. *Operating Syst. Rev.* 19, 44–54.

Mitchell, J.G., J. Dion (1982). A comparison of two network-based file servers. *Commun. ACM* 25, 233–245.

Mullender, S.J., A.S. Tanenbaum (1985). A distributed file service based on optimistic concurrency control, *Proc. Tenth Symp. Operating Syst. Prin.*, ACM, pp. 51–62.

Needham, R.M., A.J. Herbert (1982). *The Cambridge Distributed Computing System*, Addison-Wesley, Reading, MA.

Nelson, B.J. (1981). Remote procedure call, Techn. Rep. CSL-81-9, Xerox PARC.

Organick, E.I. (1972). *The Multics System*, M.I.T. Press, Cambridge, MA.

Ousterhout, J.K. (1982). Scheduling techniques for concurrent systems, *Proc. 3rd Int'l Conf. on Distributed Comput. Syst.*, IEEE, pp. 22–30.

Peterson, J.L., A. Silberschatz (1985). *Operating Systems Concepts, 2nd edition*, Addison-Wesley, Reading, MA.

Popek, G., B. Walker, J. Chow, D. Edwards, C. Kline, G. Rudisin, G. Thiel (1981). LOCUS: A network transparent, high reliability distributed system, *Proc. Eighth Symp. Operating Syst. Prin.*, ACM, pp. 160–168.

Powell, M.L., D.L. Presotto (1983). Publishing – A reliable broadcast communication mechanism, *Proc. Ninth Symp. Operating Syst. Prin.*, ACM, pp. 100–109.

Reed, D.P. (1983). Implementing atomic actions on decentralized data. *ACM Trans. Comput. Syst.* 1, 3–23.

Reed, D.P., L. Svobodova (1981). SWALLOW: A distributed data storage system for a local network, in: A. West, P. Janson (eds.), *Local Networks for Computer Communications*, North-Holland, Amsterdam, pp. 355–373.

Reif, J.H., P.G. Spirakis (1984). Real-time synchronization of interprocess communications, *ACM Trans. Program. Lang. Syst.* 6, 215–238.

Ritchie, D.M., K. Thompson (1974). The UNIX time-sharing system. *Commun. ACM* 17, 365–375.

Saltzer, J.H. (1974). Protection and control of information sharing in MULTICS. *Commun. ACM* 17, 388–402.

Satyanarayanan, M., J. Howard, D. Nichols, R. Sidebotham, A. Spector, M. West (1985). The ITC distributed file system: Principles and design, *Proc. Tenth Symp. Operating Syst. Prin.*, ACM, pp. 35–50.

Schroeder, M., D. Gifford, R. Needham (1985). A caching file system for a programmer's workstation, *Proc. Tenth Symp. Operating Syst. Prin.*, ACM, pp. 25–34.

Smith, R. (1979). The contract net protocol: High-level communication and control in a distributed problem solver, *Proc. 1st Int'l Conf. Distributed Comput. Syst.*, IEEE, pp. 185–192.

Spector, A.Z. (1982). Performing remote operations efficiently on a local computer network. *Commun. ACM* 25, 246–260.

Stankovic, J.A., I.S. Sidhu (1984). An adaptive bidding algorithm for processes, clusters, and distributed ups, *Proc. Fourth Int'l Conf. on Distributed Comput. Syst.*, IEEE, pp. 49–59.

Stone, H.S. (1977). Multiprocessor scheduling with the aid of network flow algorithms. *IEEE Trans. Software Engineering* SE-3, 88–93.

Stone, H.S. (1978). Critical load factors in distributed computer systems. *IEEE Trans. Software Engrg.* SE-4, 254–258.

Stone, H.S., S.H. Bokhari (1978). Control of distributed processes. *Computer* 11, 97–106.

Sturgis, H.E., J.G. Mitchell, J. Israel (1980). Issues in the design and use of a distributed file system. *Operating Systems Rev.* 14, 55–69.

Svobodova, L. (1981). A reliable object-oriented data repository for a distributed computer system, *Proc. Eight Symp. Operating Syst. Prin.*, ACM, pp. 47–58.

Svobodova, L. (1984). File servers for network-based distributed systems. *Comput. Surveys* 16, 353–398.

Swinehart, D., G. McDaniel, D. Boggs (1979). WFS: A simple shared file system for a distributed environment, *Proc. Seventh Symp. Operating Syst. Prin.*, ACM, pp. 9–17.

Tanenbaum, A.S. (1987). *Operating Systems: Design and Implementation*, Prentice-Hall, Englewood Cliffs, NJ.

Tanenbanm, A.S. (1992). *Modern Operating Systems*, Prentice-Hall, Englewood Cliffs, NJ.

Walker, B., G. Popek, R. English, C. Kline, G. Thiel (1983). The LOCUS distributed operating system, *Proc. Ninth Symp. Operating Syst. Prin.*, ACM, pp. 49–70.

Wambecq, A. (1983). NETIX: A network-using operating system, based on UNIX software, Proc. NFWO-ENRS Contact Group, Leuven, Belgium.

Weinstein, M.J., T.W. Page, Jr., B.K. Livesey, G.J. Popek (1985). Transactions and synchronization in a distributed operating system, *Proc. 10th Symp. Oper. Syst. Prin.*, pp. 115–125.

E.G. Coffman et al., Eds., *Handbooks in OR & MS, Vol. 3*

Chapter 4

Databases and Database Management

Gottfried Vossen

*Fachbereich Mathematik, Arbeitsgruppe Informatik, Justus-Liebig-Universität Giessen,
Arndtstrasse 2, W-6300 Giessen, Germany*

1. Introduction

The goal of this chapter is to provide a tutorial overview of the field of database and database management, to give an introduction to the practical aspects of databases as well as to a number of theoretical issues that are prominent in database research, to outline its historical development, to sketch its state-of-the-art, and to set a variety of pointers to relevant literature. Section 1 surveys the field from an evolutionary perspective and summarizes the central functionality of a database system both from a users' as well as from a systems' point of view. It also sketches where we stand today in terms of both theoretical and practical achievements, and motivates areas of ongoing research and development. Section 2 discusses relational databases primarily as seen by a user, in particular the language of the relational model, design issues, query languages, important facets of relational database theory, and implications of giving up one of the most basic assumptions in this model (first normal form). Section 3 takes a more system-oriented perspective and gives an introduction to the area of transaction management, in particular concurrency control and recovery. It starts from classical approaches, outlines their prominent incarnations, and discusses their limitations in unconventional environments as well as possible ways to overcome these limitations. Finally, Section 4 outlines a number of directions in which database research and development is currently being done.

1.1. The why and what

The practical need for efficient organization, creation, manipulation and maintenance of large collections of information, together with the recognition that data about the real world, which is manipulated by application programs, should be treated as an integrated resource independently of these programs, has led to the development of database management, an area of computer science that is roughly 30 years old. In brief, a *database system* (DBS) consists

133

of a piece of software, the *database management system* (DBMS), and some number of *databases*. The DBMS basically is a special-purpose program which is stored in a computer's main memory and executed under the control of the operating system. A database is a collection of data which represents information about a specific application from the real world. As such, the data in a database is strongly related from a logical point of view, and due to its size it is commonly stored in secondary memory. The DBMS then acts as an interface between users and a database: it ensures that users can access their data adequately, efficiently and under centralized control, and that the data itself is resilient against hardware crashes and software errors, and persists over long periods of time independent of programs that access it. Technically, a DBMS is a reentrant program shared by multiple activities (the database 'transactions') that especially when running on a general purpose computer is interfaced with the *communication subsystem* and the *operating system* as shown in Figure 1. The former, which contains, for example, the terminal monitor, permits communication with database applications, while the latter interfaces the DBMS with the hardware resources of the computer.

From a user's perspective, it is common to view a database at three levels of abstraction, at which different types of data are identified. This is part of the

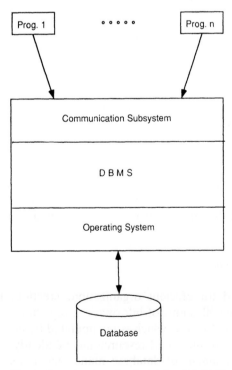

Fig. 1. Generic view of a (centralized) DBMS.

result of work by the American National Standards Institute (ANSI) Standards Planning and Requirements Committee (SPARC), which proposed an architectural framework (the *ANSI/SPARC architecture*) for DBMSs based on data organization. In this framework, the three abstraction levels, aimed at (physical and logical) *data independence*, are as follows: the lowest level, the *internal level*, deals with the physical definition and organization of data, i.e., the location of data on different storage devices and the mechanisms available for accessing and manipulating data. At the next higher level, the *conceptual level*, the time-invariant global structure of a database is described in the conceptual *schema* and in the language of a chosen data model which in particular abstracts from the details of physical storage. The conceptual schema represents the 'real world' view on data and the relationships among the data of the enterprise or application under consideration. At the highest level, the *external level*, individual users or user groups can have portions of the conceptual schema configured into an external *schema* (*view*), which reflects the way in which they want or are allowed to use the data.

Associated with these levels are various *languages* provided by a DBMS: conceptual and external schemata are created using a *data definition* language, while users work with the database by employing a high-level *data manipulation* language; for the internal level, a *data administration* language is available. The three levels and their associated languages are summarized in Figure 2. The ANSI/SPARC architecture actually describes a lot more than just the three distinct views on the data as explained; the interested reader is referred to Clemons [1985] and in particular Tsichritzis & Klug [1978].

From an implementor's perspective, a DBMS has to provide a variety of capabilities, some of which follow directly from the above exposition of how a database is seen by its users. In principle, we can view the functionality of a DBMS as being organized in four different layers as shown in Figure 3: the

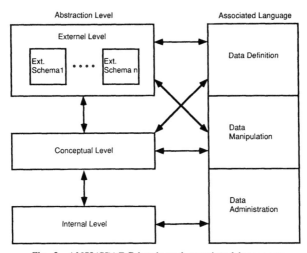

Fig. 2. ANSI/SPARC levels and associated languages.

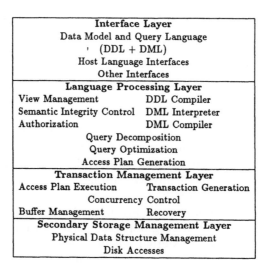

Fig. 3. Functional DBMS layers.

interface layer manages the interfaces to the various classes of users, including the database administrator, casual users and application programmers. These interfaces may be menu-based, graphical, language- or forms-based and provide DDL and DML as stand-alone languages or ones that are embedded into host languages. The *language processing layer* has to process the various forms of requests that can be directed against a database. To this end, views used in a query need to be resolved (replaced by their definition), semantic integrity predicates are added if applicable, and authorization is checked. Ad-hoc queries are processed by an interpreter, while queries embedded into a host language program are compiled. Next, a query is decomposed into elementary database operations; the resulting sequence is then subject to optimization with the goal of avoiding executions with poor performance. An executable query or program is passed to the *transaction management layer*, which is in charge of controlling concurrent accesses to a shared database ('concurrency control') and at the same time makes the system resilient against possible failures (through main-memory buffer management and through logging and recovery). Finally, the *secondary storage management layer* takes care of the physical data structures (files, pages, indexes) and performs disk accesses. Secondary storage is in this context not only used for holding the database itself,. but also for keeping *logs* that allow to restore a consistent state after a crash, and for keeping the *data dictionary* in which the information associated with the ANSI levels is collected.

1.2. A historical perspective

The historical development of database systems can be divided into three generations, of which we currently experience the transition from the second to the third and therefore delay an outline of the third to Section 1.4. There has also been a precursor generation consisting of file systems, which were available in the 1950s already, when computers were primarily used to *process* data under the control of a program (as opposed to *managing* data), and data was stored on tape. Sequential access to tape files was replaced by random access to disk files during the early 1960s, but what remained was the strong dependence of the data on the individual programs operating on it. It was soon recognized that this approach to data organization had a number of drawbacks for applications like banking, travel reservation, insurance companies, public administration and others: for example [see Date, 1990], redundancy between files due to the frequent replication of information in different places without an integrated control, inconsistencies in data collections due to insufficient or incomplete propagation of updates between files, or inflexibility against changes in the application. Database systems grew out of the idea to cope with these problems, by treating data, as was mentioned above, as a resource that is independent of its application programs.

1.2.1. Hierarchical and network databases

The first DBS generation roughly coincides with the 1970s and is characterized by the introduction of a preliminary distinction between *logical* and *physical* information. Data models were used for the first time to describe physical structures from a logical point of view. In particular, the *hierarchical model* and the *network model* [Elmasri & Navathe, 1989] evolved, among other things, from *Bachman diagrams* [Bachman, 1973] as the basis of *prerelational* systems. In these models, data is conceptually described in terms of trees or graphs, respectively, whose nodes represent record types, and whose edges represent (binary) relationships between them.

For example, Figure 4 shows a logical network for a sample library application, in which the two *record types* shown represent books and readers, respectively, and the edge represents a *set type* standing for the check-out relationship between readers and books. Each book is characterized by the attributes *callnumber, first author, additional authors, title, publisher, location, edition, year, return date* and *lend to*; each reader is characterized by *reader number, name* and *address*.

Physically, a database in both models is a collection of files (now under central DBMS control) with links between them. To work with a hierarchical

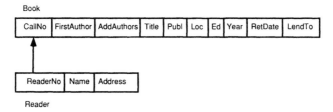

Fig. 4. A logical network.

or a network database, users have to employ a language that allows them to *navigate* within the records of one type or from the records of one type to those of another. Thus, application programmers are required to write quite complex programs, which even need to be rewritten whenever the underlying database structure changes. The reader is referred to Elmasri & Navathe [1989], Ullman [1988] or Vossen [1991a] for more detailed assessments of these data models and their languages. A survey of early hierarchical systems is Tsichritzis & Lochovsky [1976], one of early network systems Taylor & Frank [1976].

1.2.2. Relational databases

The second DBS generation, which reached the marketplace in the early 1980s and which is now subsumed under the term 'relational systems', was based on a fundamentally different approach to data organization which offered a much clearer distinction between a physical and a logical data model. In particular, relational systems provide a high degree of *physical data independence*, are based on a simple conceptual model (relations) and have more powerful languages available. The first aspect means that physical storage of data is transparent (invisible) to users, and that in principle both the physical and the logical side may be changed without the other side being affected. The latter aspect primarily results from a transition from *record-oriented* to *set-oriented* management and processing of the data in a database and yields nonprocedural or *declarative* languages. In a relational database, a user sees the data as tables. For example, Figure 5 shows a sample relational database for library application from Figure 4.

The tables of a relational database are accessed and manipulated via operators that process them as a whole, without the need to iterate through a relation on a record-by-record basis. Since relations are a well-known mathematical concept, it is not surprising that this DBS generation saw an enormous penetration from a theoretical point of view, which started in the early 1970s shortly after the model had been proposed by Codd [1970] (see Section 2). On

Book	CallNo	FirstAuthor	AddAuthors	Title	...
	123	Date	n	Intro DBS	
	234	Jones	y	Algorithms	
	345	King	n	Operating Syst.	

Reader	ReaderNo	Name	...
	225	Peter	
	347	Laura	

CheckOut	CallNo	ReaderNo	RetDate
	123	225	04-22-91
	234	347	07-31-91

Fig. 5. A sample relational database.

the other hand, relational *systems* rapidly acquired their position in the software market (Papazoglou & Valder [1989] is an introduction to implementing such systems), and still continue to do so today; see Schmidt & Brodie [1983] for an early account and Valduriez & Gardarin [1989] for a more recent one. Relational systems are now available on virtually any hardware platform, and are likely to become standard software on all new computers in the 1990s. Codd received the ACM Turing Award in 1982 for his pioneering work [Codd, 1982], and has designed a set of rules a truly relational system has to satisfy [Codd, 1986].

1.3. Where we stand today

At present, the database field has matured with respect to many issues, and at the same time is in transition with respect to many others. We briefly mention some of the former in this section, and some of the latter in more detail in subsequent sections.

1.3.1. Applications of database systems

Database systems, especially relational ones, are the state-of-the-art in present-day commercial or business applications, including (see above) automated banking, public administration, reservation systems, and many others. The reason why database systems could be successful in these areas is that they have many common characteristics, and requirements that are met by prerelational and relational technology. Among the characteristics is the fact that *record-based* data models are, in a sense, sufficient, i.e., the information arising in these applications can be cast into fixed-format records. Furthermore, simple data *types* like integers, strings or date and time values are enough for basically all attributes through which data in these applications can be characterized. End users in these applications are to a great extent *parametric* in the sense that they use standard types of queries and updates (*canned transactions*) that have been carefully programmed and tested, and that have been assigned a simple transaction code to ease calling upon their execution. Updates are made in place, meaning that old values can be overwritten as soon as new ones become valid. Transactions are short, but need to be executed at very high rates ('1000 transactions per second').

As will be argued in Section 1.4, the picture is vastly different in scientific and technical applications that have more recently begun to ask for database support.

1.3.2. Distributed DBMS

As was recognized some 10 years ago, organizations are frequently decentralized and hence require databases at multiple sites. For example, a nationwide bank has its branches all over its country and wants to keep its customer data at local sites, so that the data is available where it is actually used. In addition, decentralization increases the availability of a system in the presence of failures. As a result, *distributed database systems* began to emerge during the 1980s, and all major DBMS vendors are now commercializing distributed technology. In brief, a *distributed database* is a collection of multiple, logically interrelated databases distributed over a computer network as illustrated in Figure 6. A *distributed DBMS* is the software that permits the management of a distributed database and makes the data distribution transparent to its users. The latter means that a distributed system should look to its users as if it was nondistributed. This objective has a number of consequences and creates many new challenges for implementors, which will not be discussed in detail here. Among the core requirements to a distributed DBMS are the following: each site in the system should be locally autonomous, and should not be depending on a central master site. Users do not need to know at which site data is physically stored (*location transparency*), how data sets are internally fragmented (*fragmentation transparency*) or replicated at distinct sites (*replication transparency*), or how queries or transactions that access data at multiple sites are executed.

In the following, our discussion will focus on nondistributed systems; the reader is referred to Date [1990], Elmasri & Navathe [1989], and Özsu & Valduriez [1991a,b] for more information on distributed DBMSs, their problems and solutions.

1.3.3. Database design

The *database design problem* can briefly be stated as follows [Elmasri & Navathe, 1989]: design the logical and physical structure of a database to

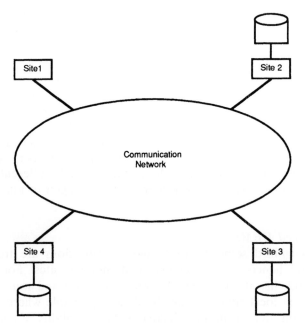

Fig. 6. Distributed DBMS environment.

accommodate the information needs of the users in an organization for some given set of applications. Obviously, this problem has to be solved *before* a database can be created and used. Indeed, Elmasri & Navathe [1989] place database design in the broader context of the 'database application system life cycle,' which consists of the consecutive phases shown in Figure 7. Also obvious is that database design is a nontrivial problem, as a variety of goals have to be met: to satisfy the information content requirements of prospective users and applications, to provide adequate information structuring, and to support given processing requirements and performance objectives.

In order to cope with the complexity of this problem, it is common to break it down into a number of phases as shown in Figure 8; for a detailed discussion of these, the reader should consult Elmasri & Navathe [1989]. Especially for

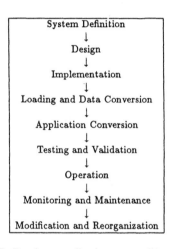

Fig. 7. Database application system life cycle.

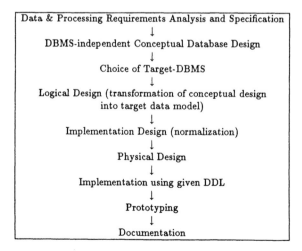

Fig. 8. Phases of the database design process.

the second phase of *conceptual database design*, it has turned out to be fruitful to use a high-level data model which is independent of (and hence abstracts from) the particular DBMS that has to be employed and its data model. A prominent example is the *entity-relationship model* (ER model) from Chen [1976, 1985], which is based on the perception that 'real worlds' are composed of *entities*, i.e., 'things' that have an independent (physical or conceptual) existence, and their *relationships*. For example, Figure 9 shows an ER *diagram* for the library database we have shown in Figures 4 and 5. In this figure, rectangles represent entity types, circles denote attributes, the diamond stands for a relationship between the two entity types, and the labels attached to relationship edges additionally state that the relationship is of complexity *many-one* (meaning in this case that a book can be checked out by at most one reader at a time, but conversely a reader can check out several books).

The use of a high-level model in the conceptual design phase, preferably one that even supports graphical representations like the ER model, is desirable for several reasons: abstraction from implementation details, ease of understanding, communication with nontechnical users, detection of incompleteness or conflicts. In the past, this has had at least two implications. First, a variety of

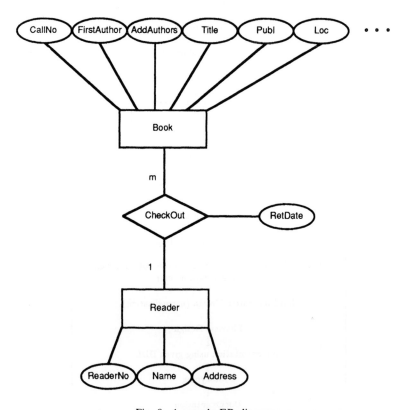

Fig. 9. A sample ER diagram.

alternatives to the ER model have been proposed; they all strive for capturing more meaning or semantic information about a given application than do data models that force designers to think in terms of records, and also for more natural and adequate structural representations. The various proposals are subsumed under the term *semantic data models* and surveyed by King & McLeod [1985], Hull & King [1987], or Peckham & Maryanski [1988]. Second, although the ER and other semantic models provide various sets of concepts for describing the structure and semantics of data, they are useless without a *methodology* which guides a designer in applying these concepts. To this end, a number of automated tools for database design have been developed and are commercially available, see Yao [1985], Teorey, Yang & Fry [1986], Elmasri & Navathe [1989], Teorey [1990], Batini, Ceri & Navathe [1992] and Reiner [1992]. Some of these concentrate on supporting conceptual design only, while others also support additional design phases.

1.3.4. Standardization efforts

In a field like database management, where a complex software system should on the one hand be made available for a variety of hardware platforms, and should on the other be interfaceable with other software already present on these platforms, the need for standardization is evident. So it does not come as a surprise that efforts in this direction have some tradition in the field; these efforts broadly fall into three categories: language standardization, development of a reference model for DBMS implementation and uniform performance evaluation. We consider each of these in turn.

Language standardization. Work leading towards database language standards began in the Conference on Data Systems Languages (CODASYL) Data Base Task Group (DBTG) in the 1960s, which developed specifications for network database systems [CODASYL, 1971, 1978]. This work continued in ANSI in the 1970s, and was in the early 1980s taken up by the International Standards Organization (ISO) and various national participating organizations. These efforts have resulted in two standards for database languages: NDL for network databases (which has not been implemented), and SQL for relational databases [Yannakoudakis & Cheng, 1988]. Since SQL is now available in some form or another in every relational DBMS and, unlike NDL, will continue to evolve, a few words on its history are apt.

The language SQL was originally developed by IBM for their first relational prototype System/R [Astrahan, Blasgen, Chamberlin et al., 1976; Blasgen, Astrahan, Chamberlin et al., 1981] (and then used to be an acronym for *Structured English Query Language* or *Sequel* for short). After IBM has released their first relational product SQL/Data System in 1981, an ANSI study group recommended to start working on a standard for relational databases, and a decision was made to base this work on SQL. In 1982, a database languages group was formed in ISO, originally intended to provide input to the ANSI developments; both streams of efforts resulted in the publication of a first standard in 1986, now referred to as SQL86 (with SQL now being an acronym for *Standard Query Language*). This standard contained only basic facilities for defining and manipulating relational databases, which at that time were already widely implemented, but nothing for declaring integrity relationships between relations. This gap was closed in a revision now called SQL89 ('Addendum 1'), which came with the 'integrity enhancement feature'. Currently, a revision of SQL89 is under development under the name SQL2 with further extensions; it is expected to be published in 1992. Already in the planning stage is the next revision, SQL3, expected to be published in the mid-1990s. This history of language standards is described in more detail by Shaw [1990]; a description of SQL89 is Date [1989].

Reference models. As we mentioned above, already in the 1970s a first standard for the architecture of a DBMS emerged in the form of the ANSI/SPARC framework. While this proposal is based on *data*, it is clear that a true reference model for DBMS implementation needs to take further aspects into account. To this end, the Database Architecture Framework Task Group (DAFTG) of ANSI defines a reference model as 'a conceptual framework whose purpose is to divide standardization work into manageable pieces and to show at a general level how these pieces are related with each other' [DAFTG, 1986] and proposes to additionally consider the *functions* as well as the *components* of such a system. In particular, the proposed reference model comprises a *Data Mapping Control System* (DMCS) which retrieves and stores application data, application schemas, and data dictionary schemas. The DMCS is bounded by two interfaces, the *Data Language* (DL) interface which defines the services offered by the DMCS to various *Data Management Tools*, and the *internal Data Language* (i-DL) interface which defines the services required by the DMCS from the host operating system. The cited report suggests the DL and the i-DL as candidates for standardization.

An additional reference model, this time for the user facility portion of a DBMS, was proposed in UFTG [1988]. This model serves as a front-end to the DAFTG reference model, and together with it can form a functionally compatible means to describe the interaction between a user and a database system.

Benchmarks. A *benchmark* is a standard program used to quantify, evaluate and compare the performance of a wide range of systems. As such it can be run on a variety of different systems in order to measure and record the performance ('work per second') and price of each and hence the price/performance ratio. Benchmarks have a long history in computer hardware development, especially for measuring system performance on numeric computations. However, database systems need different means for evaluation, since the goal now is to measure the performance of software algorithms rather than hardware speed. In addition, the performance of these systems can vary considerably from one application domain to another, so that *domain-specific* benchmarks are needed which specify a synthetic workload characterizing typical tasks in that domain. Various groups have started to define standard domain-specific DBMS benchmarks, standard price metrics, and standard ways of measuring and reporting results. An early effort resulted in the *Wisconsin benchmark* [Bitton, DeWitt & Turbyfill, 1983]; another relevant group is the *Transaction Processing Performance Council* (TPC), a consortium of 34 software and hardware vendors, which was founded in 1988 with the goal to define adequate benchmarks for transaction-processing and database systems. Its work has so far resulted in two benchmarks, TPC-A and TPC-B. Vendors now frequently quote the tps (transactions per second) ratings of their systems in terms of these benchmarks, and customers are beginning to request TPC ratings from vendors. A description of these and other benchmarks that have been developed especially for the database domain can be found in Gray [1991].

1.4. Next-generation systems

As was mentioned already, the database field is currently in transition from the second to the third generation of systems. In this section we briefly characterize the DBMS requirements from new applications and survey additional aspects that will drive future developments; specific directions will be looked into in Section 4.

1.4.1. New applications for DBS

While database systems are nowadays a well-integrated tool in many commercial and business applications, for a variety of scientific, engineering and other applications in which large collections of data arise, it was started to discover in the early 1980s that treating data as an integrated resource independent of application programs is an idea that might be beneficial for them also. As a result, they started to investigate whether the use of a database system in their specific domain was feasible, and soon recognized that this was not even the case for relational systems. Although such systems *are* in use in nonbusiness applications, it has become clear that new solutions are needed for a number of database issues, in order to make such a merger of a new domain with database technology adequate.

These new ('nonstandard') application domains for database systems include, among many others:

• spatial data processing, typically in geographical applications, in which data is used to encode the information found on maps;

• computer-aided design (CAD), where software systems (CAD packages) are employed by engineers for designing artifacts like VLSI circuits, automobiles or planes; these design objects typically have a complex structure, have to be maintained in a variety of descriptions, and exist in different versions during the design process;

• computer-integrated manufacturing (CIM), where data on all phases of plant operation, e.g., code for machine tools, test results or production schedules, needs to be managed;

• computer-aided software engineering (CASE), where relevant information concerns the various phases of a software life cycle, in particular the design, coding, documentation, etc. of programs.

The important point that makes the direct applicability of current database technology in any of these domains questionable is that they have requirements which vastly differ from those arising in business applications. The most important ones, which can be identified in virtually every domain mentioned above, are:

(1) The information arising in these applications can no longer be cast uniformly into fixed-format records, but consists of large and internally *complex objects*. For example, a VLSI chip has a hierarchical structure that is difficult to map onto flat relations or a network structure; images in a geographical application or protein structures in a chemical one are not suited for relational representations either.

(2) For abstraction purposes and ease of use, it seems appropriate to have higher data types available, like 'picture' or 'bitmap' or even 'bulk types' (for very long unstructured byte sequences), together with appropriate operations to handle data over these types (and appropriate data structures to store them). Thus, the *type systems* available in present-day systems are no longer sufficient; a general agreement is that a future system should allow a user to define his or her own types, i.e., have type systems that are *extensible*.

(3) In order to facilitate collaborative access to data especially in design environments, new approaches to transaction management are needed. In particular, it is no longer reasonable to assume that transactions are short, since design sessions might last days or weeks, or that updates are made in-place, since design objects typically exist in multiple versions simultaneously.

So, it can be expected that the third, postrelational, DBMS generation will go beyond current systems in many respects. The reader is referred to Cattell [1991], Elmasri & Navathe [1989], and Vossen [1991a] for more information on the requirements from new application domains, to Lockemann, Kemper & Moerkotte [1990] for an account of additional driving forces for next-generation systems, to Batory & Kim [1985], and Katz [1985, 1990] for CAD, and to The Committee for Advanced DBMS Function [1990], Laguna [1989], and Silberschatz, Stonebraker & Ullman [1990] for recent position papers on future DBMS development.

1.4.2. Evolution of data models

The requirement from new application domains that has attracted most of the attention in theoretical developments during the past decade is that of advanced data models. Work in this direction, in particular the question of how to overcome representational shortcomings of the relational model, goes back to Makinouchi [1977] or Kent [1979], who questioned the expressibility of structural and semantic information in this model. Makinouchi was even the first to suggest the use of 'nested' relations instead of flat ones (see Section 2.7). This together with the work of Chen [1976] or Smith & Smith [1977a,b] opened the door for the development of the above-mentioned semantic models as more powerful paradigms for high-level, target-model and target-system independent data modeling, to which Codd also made his contributions [Codd, 1979, 1990]. However, while originally the idea was to use those models for database design and to finally map a design result to the relational model, it became clear through the arrival of the new applications that also more powerful target models are needed. As a result, *complex object* models emerged as new data models on which to build systems [Abiteboul, Fischer & Schek, 1989; Vossen & Witt, 1991], and more recently *object-orientation*, a powerful and popular paradigm from the world of programming languages, began to penetrate the database field. Currently, *object-oriented databases* are one of the central research and development topics, and it is safe to expect the next DBMS generation (and SQL3) to include a number of object-oriented features; in Section 4 we will try to explain why. Figure 10 summarizes the evolution of data models [Schek & Scholl, 1990].

1.4.3. Cooperation and heterogeneous systems

We explained above that a distributed database system is *homogeneous* in the sense that all physical components of the system run the *same* distributed DBMS and keep portions of the *same* logical database; queries on this database are automatically translated into queries against the various sites. Some 10 years ago this was considered the ultimate goal for distributed database systems; the term 'distributed DBMS' became associated with transparency and integration. More recently, researchers in the area began to agree that transparency and integration may be incompatible with requirements for autonomy and diversity of implementations, which paved the way for *heteroge-*

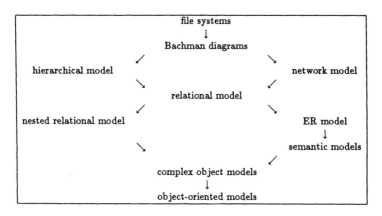

Fig. 10. Evolution of data models.

neous database systems, i.e., distributed systems that include *different* logical components. In other words, a heterogeneous or *federated* database system is a collection of cooperating, but autonomous component database systems, each of which has its own data model and query language. A close integration of these systems is usually neither necessary nor desirable. On the other hand. it *is* desirable that *interoperability* of these systems is possible. For example, a car company may wish to allow its suppliers to access new car designs that are under development, so that they can provide early feedback on component costs. This will allow more cost-effective car design and manufacturing, but requires a logical integration of databases from multiple organizations into a seemingly single database.

Heterogeneous distributed database systems are considered one of the most challenging research topics for the next couple of years by many people [Elmagarmid & Pu, 1990; Reiner, 1990; Silberschatz, Stonebraker & Ullman, 1990].

2. Relational databases

We now survey the relational data model [Codd, 1970] and outline a number of aspects centering around this model. More specifically, we introduce the modeling language of relations and its operational counterpart, consider the design of relational database schemata, query languages for relational databases, and selected issues in relational theory. Finally, we touch upon deductive databases and the implications of allowing relations to be nested within other relations. Most of the material touched upon in this section can be found in more elaborate form in a variety of textbooks on databases, including Korth & Silberschatz [1991], Maier [1983], Paredaens, De Bra, Gyssens & van Gucht [1989], Vossen [1991a] or Yang [1986].

2.1. The relational data model

The relational model was proposed by Codd [1970] as an elegant, well-motivated and appropriately restricted computational paradigm for database management. It underlies relational database *theory* as well as numerous current *system* implementations. The model is based on the mathematical notion of a *relation* and organizes data in the form of *tables*. A table has *attributes* describing properties of data objects (as headline) and *tuples* holding data values (as other rows) as was indicated in Figure 5. In essence, a table is hence a *set of tuples*, where tuple components can be identified by their associated attributes. This is restricted at least from a point of view of *types* in programming languages, since it only allows the application of a tuple *constructor* to attributes and given base domains, followed by the application of a set constructor (see Section 2.7). On the other hand, the simplicity of the relational model allows an elegant and in-depth formal treatment, sketches of which are given below using formal notation only as far as necessary.

Let $X = \{A_1, \ldots, A_m\}$ be a set of *attributes*, and let each attribute $A \in X$ have a nonempty, finite domain dom(A) of atomic values (integers, strings, etc.). Let $\bigcup_{A \in X} \text{dom}(A) =: \text{dom}(X)$. A *tuple* over X is an injective mapping $\mu : X \to \text{dom}(X)$ satisfying $\mu(A) \in \text{dom}(A)$ for each $A \in X$. For given X, let Tup(X) denote the set of all tuples over X. A *relation* r over X is a finite set of tuples over X, i.e., $r \subseteq \text{Tup}(X)$; the set of all relations over X is denoted by Rel(X).

An (intrarelational) *integrity constraint* ('data dependency') over X restricts a given state space Rel(X) to relations which are *meaningful* with respect to the underlying application. For example, a library database will only be considered a valid image of the real world if for each book on which data is stored the callnumber is unique. An important example of intrarelational constraints are functional dependencies: let X be a set of attributes, and let $Y, Z \subseteq X$. A *functional dependency* (FD) $Y \to Z$ is *valid* in $r \in \text{Rel}(X)$ (or r *satisfies* $Y \to Z$) if any two tuples from r which agree on Y also agree on Z. An important special case of FDs are *key dependencies*: for given X, $K \subseteq X$ is a *key* for X if $K \to X$ holds, and no proper subset of K also has this property (if the latter is violated, K is called a *candidate key*).

As an abstract example, let $X = ABCDE$, and let $r \in \text{Rel}(X)$ be as follows:

	A	B	C	D	E
	1	1	1	1	1
r:	1	0	1	1	1
	2	2	0	0	1
	2	3	2	0	1

It is easily verified that r satisfies the FD $AB \to C$, since any two tuples from r are distinct on AB. In addition, r satisfies $A \to D$ and $D \to E$ and hence the set $F = \{AB \to C, A \to D, D \to E\}$ of FDs.

A *relation schema* has the form $R = (X, F)$; it consists of a name (R), a set of attributes X and a set F of functional dependencies. It serves as a time-invariant description of the set Sat(R) of all relations over X that satisfy F. It is said to be in *first normal form* (1NF) if all domains contain atomic values only. We mention that FDs are not the only type of dependencies that can state meaningful relationships between the attributes of a relation (see Section 2.5.1). For simplicity, we restrict our discussion to FDs here.

As a concrete example, a relation scheme for the books of a library (see Section 1) could be named *Book*, have attributes *CallNo*, *FirstAuthor*, *AddAuthors*, *Title*, *Publ*, *Loc*, *Ed*, *Year*, and *CallNo* as key. Similarly, readership information could be described in a relation schema *Reader* with attributes *ReaderNo*, *Name*, *Address* with key *ReaderNo*; finally, checkout information would be captured in a schema *CheckOut* with attributes *CallNo* (identifying a book), *ReaderNo* (identifying the reader who has currently checked out that book), and *RetDate* and key *CallNo*.

Let $\mathbf{R} = \{R_1, \ldots, R_k\}$ be a (finite) set of relation schemas (in 1NF), where

$R_i = (X_i, F_i)$, $1 \le i \le k$, and $X_i \ne X_j$ for $i \ne j$. A (relational) *database d* (over R) is a set of (base) relations, $d = \{r_1, \ldots, r_k\}$, such that $r_i \in \mathrm{Sat}(R_i)$ for $1 \le i \le k$. Let $\mathrm{Dat}(R)$ denote the set of all databases over R.

In real-world applications, the various relations of a database are often connected via interrelational constraints such as *inclusion dependencies* which state that certain values in one relation have to form a subset of values in another. For example, in the library database it makes sense to require that only books can be checked out which are indeed available in the library, i.e., that the set of callnumbers appearing in the *CheckOut* relation always is a subset of the callnumbers appearing in the *Book* relation. More formally, let R be a set of relation schemas, R_i, $R_j \in R$, $R_i \ne R_j$, $R_i = (X_i, F_i)$, $R_j = (X_j, F_j)$. In addition, let V [W] be a sequence of distinct attributes from X_i [X_j], respectively. An *inclusion dependency* (IND) $R_i[V] \subseteq R_j[W]$ is *valid* in $d \in \mathrm{Dat}(R)$ (or *satisfied* by d) if

$$\{\mu[V] \mid \mu \in r_i\} \subseteq \{\mu[W] \mid \mu \in r_j\}.$$

Thus, the above-mentioned constraint for the library would be written as *CheckOut[CallNo]* $\subseteq$ *Book[CallNo]*. Another reasonable constraint would be *CheckOut[ReaderNo]* $\subseteq$ *Reader[ReaderNo]*. Here, the *ReaderNo* from *Check-Out* is called a *foreign key*, since this attribute also appears as key in another relation.

Now let R be a set of relation schemas, and Δ_R be a set of inclusion dependencies. A (relational) *database schema* is a named pair $D = (R, \Delta_R)$. It represents a time-invariant (conceptual) description of the set of all *consistent* databases over R satisfying all intra- and interrelational dependencies. Again, other types of interrelational dependencies can be thought of, but will not be discussed here.

2.2. Operations on relations

In general, a data model has a *specification component* that allows to describe structural aspects of an application and their semantics, and an *operational component* that allows manipulation of these structures. We now introduce the operational part of the relational model, namely the *algebraic operations* on relations as defined by Codd [1970]. These operations directly provide a formal semantics of a relational DML known as *relational algebra*, which will be described in Section 2.4. Their common features include that they all yield new (derived) relations from given ones, and that they can be computed efficiently. We formally define five fundamental algebraic operations on relations: projection, selection, union, difference, natural join. The first two of these are unary, while the others are binary operations. A number of additional operations like intersection, semijoin and division can be defined in terms of these. We also illustrate these operations by examples, and summarize some of their properties.

The two unary operations can be used to cut a table in vertical (projection) or horizontal (selection) direction. Let $R = (X, \cdot)$ be a relation schema, $r \in \mathrm{Rel}(X)$, and $Y \subseteq X$:

(i) *Projection* of r onto Y:

$$\pi_Y(r) := \{\mu[Y] \mid \mu \in r\}$$

($\mu[Y]$ denotes the restriction of μ onto Y);

(ii) *Selection* of r with respect to condition C:

$$\sigma_C(r) := \{\mu \in r \mid \mu \text{ satisfies } C\} .$$

Conditions may either be a term of the form '$A \Theta a$' or '$A \Theta B$', where $A, B \in X$, $a \in \mathrm{dom}(A)$, $\Theta \in \{<, \leq, >, \geq, =, \neq\}$, or several such terms connected by logical $\wedge$, $\vee$, and $\neg$.

As an example, consider the following relation $r \in \mathrm{Rel}(ABC)$:

	A	B	C
	1	2	1
r:	1	1	1
	2	2	2

Then the following holds:

	A	C
$\pi_{AC}(r)$:	1	1
	2	2

	A	B	C
$\sigma_{C>1}(r)$:	2	2	2

The following simple laws apply to selection and projection. Let $r \in \mathrm{Rel}(X)$:

(1) $Z \subseteq Y \subseteq X \Rightarrow \pi_Z(\pi_Y(r)) = \pi_Z(r)$;

(2) $Z, Y \subseteq X \Rightarrow \pi_Z(\pi_Y(r)) = \pi_{Z \cap Y}(r)$;

(3) $\sigma_{C_1}(\sigma_{C_2}(r)) = \sigma_{C_2}(\sigma_{C_1}(r))$;

(4) $A \in Y \subseteq X \Rightarrow \pi_Y(\sigma_{A\Theta a}(r)) = \sigma_{A\Theta a}(\pi_Y(r))$.

The three binary operations we introduce are as follows. Let $r, t \in \mathrm{Rel}(X)$, $s \in \mathrm{Rel}(Y)$:

(i) *Union*: $r \cup t := \{\mu \in \mathrm{Tup}(X) \mid \mu \in r \vee \mu \in t\}$;

(ii) *Difference*: $r - t := \{\mu \in r \mid \mu \notin t\}$;

(iii) *Natural Join*: $r \bowtie s := \{\mu \in \mathrm{Tup}(X \cup Y) \mid \mu[X] \in r \wedge \mu[Y] \in s\}$.

Note that the two set operations require operations which are compatible, i.e., over the same schema. As an example of the join operation, consider the following three relations:

	A	B	C		A	D		C	D	E
	1	1	1		1	1		1	1	0
r_1:	1	2	2	r_2:	0	1	r_3:	0	1	1
	2	0	2		2	0		2	1	0
								2	2	1

Then the following holds:

	A	B	C	D
	1	1	1	1
$r_1 \bowtie r_2$:	1	2	2	1
	2	0	2	0

	A	B	C	D	E
$(r_1 \bowtie r_2) \bowtie r_3$:	1	1	1	1	0
	1	2	2	1	0

Thus, a tuple in the result of a natural join is derived from those tuples in the operands that have *equal* value on *common* attributes. Natural join is easily generalized to more than two operands: let $X_1, \ldots, X_n$ be sets of attributes, and let $r_i \in \mathrm{Rel}(X_i)$ for $1 \leq i \leq n$:

$$\bowtie_{i=1}^{n} r_i := \{ \mu \in \mathrm{Tup}(\bigcup_{i=1}^{n} X_i) \mid (\forall i, 1 \leq i \leq n)\ \mu[X_i] \in r_i \}.$$

It is easily seen that natural join is commutative and associative; it degenerates to a Cartesian product [intersection] if the sets of attributes of the operands are disjoint [identical], respectively. It might be suspected that join and projection are in a sense inverses of each other; we indicate that this is not the case: let $X = \bigcup_{i=1}^{n} X_i$, $r \in \mathrm{Rel}(X)$, $r_i \in \mathrm{Rel}(X_i)$ for $1 \leq i \leq n$. Then the following hold:
 (1) $r \subseteq \bowtie_{i=1}^{n} (\pi_{X_i}(r))$;
 (2) $(\forall j, 1 \leq j \leq n)\ \pi_{X_j}(\bowtie_{i=1}^{n} r_i) \subseteq r_j$.
These inclusions are sometimes strict [Vossen, 1991a]. If equality holds in the first, the 'decomposition' of $r \in \mathrm{Rel}(X)$ onto the sets X_i of attributes is called *lossless*, since a join of all projections of r restores the original *exactly*. Otherwise, the join is called *lossy*, which basically means that the join yields *more* tuples (in the result) than were originally present in r.

Additional rules for the algebraic operations (see, e.g., Maier [1983] or Vossen [1991a]) state under which conditions selection and projection distribute over join, union and difference, or other forms of rewriting. Our five basic algebraic operations have the following time complexities: for given input relations of cardinality n, a selection can be performed in time $O(n)$; all other operations, which eventually involve sorting, can be performed in time $O(n \log n)$. Thus, they all can be computed in time polynomial in the cardinality of their input, independent of how this input is stored internally.

2.3. Design of relational schemata

We now sketch important approaches to the design of relational database schemata. On the basis of the general outline of the design process in Section 1.3.3, this concerns the two phases of logical and implementation design and, more specifically, the transformation of some conceptual design into the relational model and some kind of 'postprocessing' of the relational schemata that are obtained.

2.3.1. ER-based design

For the phase of logical design, we follow common practice in assuming that the result of the conceptual design phase is available in the form of an ER diagram as shown in Figure 9. What is needed now are *transformation rules* which tell us how to derive relational schemata from the entity and relationship types present in such a diagram. To this end, a basic observation is that the relational model, being confined to tables as the only structuring mechanism, must represent both ER constructs in tabular form, with dependencies stating which table contents are meaningful, and how the content of one table will relate to that of others. A straightforward way of transforming ER diagrams to relational schemata, as exemplified for example by Ullman [1988] or Vossen [1991a], is to provide one table for each entity or relationship type. For the former the resulting relation schema has all attributes of the corresponding entity type plus an appropriately chosen key. For the latter the resulting schema has the key attributes of the entity types participating in the relationship type in question, which together form the key, plus the additional attributes characterizing that relationship. An example for following this approach was presented in Section 1 already: A transformation of the ER diagram from Figure 9 yields the relational structure shown in Figure 5. The schemata for these relations would additionally have the functional and inclusion dependencies mentioned in Section 2.1. The fact that the relationship in this example is 'many-one' further simplifies the *CheckOut* schema: since books can be given to one reader at a time only, attribute *CallNo* suffices as key.

This latter remark indicates that the straightforward approach sketched above can be refined; indeed, this can be done in many ways, depending on how much information is captured in a given ER representation; Batini, Ceri & Navathe [1992], Elmasri & Navathe [1989] or Teorey [1990] describe more sophisticated transformation procedures that take a number of additional semantic aspects into account.

2.3.2. Algorithmic design

It can be argued that the result of a logical design phase as described above is intuitively appealing, but formal measures are missing for the 'quality' of the resulting schemata. Indeed, a designer might proceed to fully apply the relational tools to those schemata for analyzing them in more depth. For example, a closer look at the *Book* schema might reveal that not only every attribute in this schema is functionally dependent on *CallNo*, since the latter was chosen as the key, but there also exists the FD *Publ* → *Loc* (assuming that *Loc* values represent a publisher's main office). Thus, there is a transitive dependence of *Loc* on *CallNo*, which might have the following undesired effect: if a *Book* table has many entries of books from one publisher, the corresponding location information gets redundantly repeated for each. This redundancy can be avoided if attribute *Loc* is dropped from *Book*, and another schema is created with attributes *Publ* (as key) and *Loc*, which would now contain the location information for each publisher exactly once.

The quality measure of reducing or even eliminating redundancy in tuple values of a relation is just one among several others. In order to meet them, researchers have begun even prior to the arrival of the ER model to develop a theory of relational database design. In this theory properties that a 'good' relational schema has to have can be formalized, and algorithms are available which can be proved to achieve these properties subject to a number of general requirements [Beeri & Bernstein, 1979; Rissanen, 1977, 1978]. These properties center around various *normal forms* [Beeri, Bernstein & Goodman, 1978; Kent, 1983] (like *third* normal form which avoids transitivities between certain functionally related attributes). The algorithms hence are mostly *normalization procedures* [Bernstein, 1976; Fagin, 1977; Lien, 1985], which transform arbitrary relation schemas into normalized ones, e.g., by a *decomposition* in such a way that a join of the result relations losslessly restores the original (see the previous subsection) [Aho, Beeri & Ullman, 1979; Biskup, Dayal & Bernstein, 1979].

2.4. Query languages

In this section we discuss two distinct approaches to devising a query language for relational databases: relational algebra and relational calculus. The algebra is directly based on the operations introduced in Section 2.2, while the calculus is a declarative counterpart.

2.4.1. Relational algebra

We return to the operational part of the relational model and now define a language through which users can retrieve information from a relational database. This language is known as *relational algebra* (RA); its syntax can be described as follows: let $D = (R, \cdot)$ be a database schema, where $R = \{R_1, \ldots, R_k\}$. RA (more precisely: RA_D) is the following recursively defined set of expressions:

(1) $R_i \in$ RA for all $R_i \in R$;

(2) if $E_1 \in$ RA, $E_2 \in$ RA, C is a selection condition, and $X \subseteq \bigcup_{i=1}^k X_i$, then $\sigma_C(E_1)$, $\pi_X(E_1)$, $E_1 \bowtie E_2$, $E_1 \cup E_2$, $E_1 - E_2 \in$ RA;

(3) only those expressions that can be derived by a repeated application of (1) and (2) belong to RA.

Clearly, an RA expression can be represented as a tree, the *parse tree* of its generation, in which each internal node is labeled by an operator and each leaf by the name of a relation schema. The *semantics* (evaluation) of an expression $E \in$ RA can be defined as a function v_E from $\text{Dat}(R)$ to relations over the 'schema' of E (easily determined from E), which can be computed via a bottom-up evaluation of the parse tree of E: for input $d = \{r_1, \ldots, r_k\}$ associate with each leaf labeled R_i relation $r_i \in d$, and with each other node the result of its label operation applied to the relations associated with its child nodes.

For example, the following algebraic expression E over the library database schema is supposed to return the callnumber and title of each book checked out by Laura:

$$\pi_{CallNo,Title}(\sigma_{Name = 'Laura'}(Reader \bowtie CheckOut \bowtie Book))$$

The result is a relation with attributes *CallNo* and *Title*; when evaluated against the database shown in Figure 5, it only contains the tuple (234, Algorithms).

RA is a *procedural* language because the user is expected to specify *how* the result is to be obtained. In addition, RA is *closed* since its operators take one or more relations as operands and produce a result relation that may in turn be an operand to another operator. Finally, RA expressions can be evaluated efficiently, since all allowed operations have polynomial time complexity.

2.4.2. Query optimization

Before we turn to RA alternatives, let us take a brief detour motivated by the observation that the query shown at the end of the last subsection can alternatively be formulated as the following expression E':

$$\pi_{CallNo,Title}(\pi_{CallNo,Title}(Book) \bowtie CheckOut \bowtie \sigma_{Name = 'Laura'}(Reader))$$

This RA expression, when evaluated over the same database as the above, would yield the same result. In other words, the expressions E and E' are *equivalent*, commonly written $E \approx E'$, in the following sense: for each database d, $v_E(d) = v_{E'}(d)$. One way to prove equivalence is by just referring to the laws of relational algebra and to schema information. For example, if $R_1 = (AB, \cdot)$, $R_2 = (CD, \cdot)$, then

$$E = \pi_{AB}(\sigma_{A=5}(R_1 \bowtie R_2)) \approx E' = \sigma_{A=5}(R_1);$$

so the number of join operations could be reduced. In the first example, a projection and a selection could be moved towards the operands in order to perform them earlier. The latter is reasonable since selections and projections generally reduce (intermediate) results (with respect to the number of tuples or the number of attributes).

The aspect illustrated in these examples is one facet of *query optimization*, which when performed at the schema level attempts to cut the evaluation or response time down *without* knowing the internal data structures of the relations involved. In terms of parse trees, the above observations can be cast into *transformation rules* stating, e.g., under which conditions projections and selections may be pushed towards the leaves. Clearly, another such facet is *implementation-dependent* query optimization, which is at least equally important for system implementations. Again, the goal is to avoid bad execution times, now by characterizing them via *cost functions* based on the 'selectivity' of operations, the availability of indexes, or the implementations chosen for the operations. The interested reader should consult Yao [1979] or Kim, Reiner & Batory [1985].

2.4.3. Relational calculus

While relational algebra is procedural, it was observed by Codd [1970] already that there exists a *declarative* counterpart, *relational calculus* (RC). This observation was based on the insight that a relation schema R with n attributes and a relation symbol R in logic with arity n are similar concepts. Thus, a set of relation schemata $\{R_1, \ldots, R_k\}$ occurring in a database schema can be considered as a vocabulary of relation symbols; additionally, *variables* are needed which can range over tuples (*tuple calculus*, RTC) or, alternatively, domain elements (*domain calculus*, RDC).

Both RC languages have a solid theoretical foundation since they are based on first-order predicate logic. Semantics is given to formulas by interpreting them as assertions on a given database. For example, an RTC expression for projecting a relation whose schema R has attributes A, B, C, and D onto the first two would be written as

$$\{t \mid (\exists u)(R(u) \wedge t[A] = u[A] \wedge t[B] = u[B])\}$$

and read as 'find all tuples t for which there exists a tuple u in the relation over R agreeing with t on A and B'. Similarly, an RDC expression for the same query would be written as

$$\{ab \mid (\exists c)(\exists d) R(a, b, c, d)\}$$

We are not presenting the formal details of the RC languages here; these can be found, e.g., in Codd [1970], Maier [1983], Paredaens, De Bra, Gyssens & van Gucht [1989] or the theory survey by Kanellakis [1990]. Instead, we only mention some important results in this context.

Theorem 1 (Codd [1970]). *Every RA expression can be translated in time polynomial in its size into an equivalent RC expression and vice versa.*

The proof of this theorem, known as *Codd's Theorem*, can be found in Maier [1983], Paredaens, De Bra, Gyssens & van Gucht [1989] or Yang [1986]; it needs several technical prerequisites such as a *renaming* operation in RA, or a *safety condition* (assuring finite results) in RC. Its importance lies in that it shows that the procedural and the declarative approaches coincide. This has at least two immediate consequences. First, a measure of completeness for relational query languages is available. Indeed, RA, RDC and RTC are frequently called *Codd-complete*, and other languages are termed 'complete' if their expressive power coincides with that of, say, RA. Second, the efficiency of RA expression evaluation carries over to the other languages, since each expression transformation also takes at most polynomial time.

We finally mention that neither RA nor RC has been implemented in pure form in a relational DBMS; however, several language implementations have directly been based on them, such as QUEL [Stonebraker, 1986] and the already mentioned standard relational language SQL. In order to give the reader a flavor of the latter, we formulate the above query to the library database as an SQL expression:

```
Select CallNo, Title
From Book, CheckOut, Reader
Where Name='Laura'
      and Book.CallNo=CheckOut.CallNo
      and Reader.ReaderNo=CheckOut.ReaderNo
```

For a number of additional examples, see Vossen [1991a]. SQL is actually not just a query language, but also includes data definition and update features. This together with the fact that its query part even includes functions (e.g., for sorting relations or computing averages or sums) makes SQL more than complete. On the other hand, for suitable restrictions its equivalence to RA or RC can be proved formally [Paredaens, De Bra, Gyssens & van Gucht, 1989; Ceri & Gottlob, 1985].

2.5. Facets of relational theory

Several formal aspects of relational databases were already mentioned above; we now sketch a number of others that have attracted numerous researchers over the past twenty years and are interesting in their own right.

2.5.1. Dependency theory
The *theory of data dependencies* is one important topic in relational theory; for the purposes of this survey, we use FDs for presenting its fundamentals,

since they are the most practically relevant dependencies, and several basic concepts can nicely be illustrated on them.

Consider a relation schema $R = (X, F)$ with attribute set X and FD set F, and let $\mathrm{Sat}(F)$ denote the set of all relations over X satisfying F. From a design point of view, FDs are semantic specifications. From an operational point of view, they are integrity constraints which the DBMS has to maintain, especially if the database undergoes updates. Thus, it seems desirable to have small FD sets available, so that satisfaction can be tested efficiently. The following notion is intended to capture this intuition.

Let F and G be two sets of FDs over an attribute set X. F and G are *equivalent*, written $F \approx G$, if $\mathrm{Sat}(F) = \mathrm{Sat}(G)$. In other words, two sets F and G are equivalent if they are identical as semantic specifications. This notion can be reduced to a more basic one: let F be as above, and let f be an FD with attributes from X. F *implies* f, abbreviated $F \models f$, if $\mathrm{Sat}(F) \subseteq \mathrm{Sat}(\{f\})$ holds, i.e., every relation satisfying F also satisfies f. Then it is clear that $F \approx G$ iff $(\forall f \in F)\ G \models f$ and $(\forall g \in G)\ F \models g$. It is thus sufficient to take a closer look at implication. Since its definition does not suggest an efficient way of testing it, we ask whether there is something better in that respect. To this end, let $F^+ := \{f \mid F \models f\}$ denote the *closure* of a given set F of FDs. Then testing implication means to decide, for given F and f, whether $f \in F^+$ holds, which is called the *membership problem* for functional dependencies.

In an analogy to mathematical logic, a key point here is that the semantic notion of implication can be replaced by a syntactic notion of 'derivation'. To this end, a sound and complete axiomatization is needed, which can be based on *Armstrong's axioms*:

(A1) $Y \subseteq Z \;\Rightarrow\; Z \to Y$,
(A2) $Z \to Y \wedge Y \to V \;\Rightarrow\; Z \to V$,
(A3) $V \to Y \wedge Z \subseteq W \;\Rightarrow\; VW \to YZ$.

It is easily verified that these axioms are *sound*, i.e., every FD obtained through an application of them is indeed implied by the given ones. Formally, derivation can be defined as follows: let F be a set of FDs (over X), and let $Y \to Z$ be an FD such that $YZ \subseteq X$. $Y \to Z$ is *derivable* from F, denoted $F \vdash f$, if there exists a sequence $f_1, \ldots, f_n$ of FDs with the following properties: (i) f_n is of the form $Y \to Z$; (ii) for each $i, 1 \leq i \leq n$, either $f_i \in F$ holds, or f_i can be generated from $\{f_1, \ldots, f_{i-1}\}$ using (A1)–(A3).

The important point now is that the axioms are also *complete*, i.e., every FD implied by some F is also derivable from F.

Theorem 2 (Armstrong [1974]). *Let F be a set of FDs and f be a single FD. Then $F \models f$ iff $F \vdash f$.*

Thus, to show an implication it is sufficient to state a derivation. Derivations can even be performed in a 'normalized' manner if slightly different axioms are used [Maier, 1983]; to perform them efficiently, it is useful to employ the following: for $Y \subseteq X$ and a set F of FDs (over X),

$$cl_F(Y) := \{ A \in X \mid Y \rightarrow A \in F^+ \}$$

is called the *closure* of Y (under F). It is easily proved that $Y \rightarrow Z \in F^+$ iff $Z \subseteq cl_F(Y)$. By this characterization of membership, efficient algorithmic solutions are now obvious; for example, to compute $cl_F(Y)$ do the following:

$$Z := Y; \text{ while } (\exists S \rightarrow T \in F) \ S \subseteq Z \wedge T \not\subseteq Z \text{ do } Z := Z \cup T$$

This can straightforwardly be completed to a membership test. Careful design of the necessary data structures for this algorithm reveals that the membership problem for functional dependencies can be solved in time linear in the length of the representation of the input for the closure algorithm [Beeri & Bernstein, 1979]. Two immediate applications of the membership algorithm are computing keys and testing equivalence. While computing an *arbitrary* key for a relation schema is easy, it may happen that several keys exist for a given schema and the interest is in one with minimal cardinality. To this end, the following can be shown.

Theorem 3 (Lipski [1977]). *Let F be a set of FDs over X, and let k be a positive integer. The problem to decide whether there exists a key $K \subseteq X$ such that $|K| \leq k$ is NP-complete.*

This result is just one of the many NP-completeness results known in relational theory [Maier, 1983; Vossen, 1991a]. We conclude this brief discussion of dependencies by mentioning a generalization: *multivalued* dependencies (MVDs) intuitively state that in a relation with attribute set $X = U \cup V \cup W$ (where U, V and W are disjoint), each U value determines a *set* of V values, and does so independent of W values. For example, an employee may have several children, independent of his or her skills. For MVDs, the same program can be gone through as for FDs: devise of a notion of implication, an equivalent notion of derivation via a sound and complete axiomatization, and an efficient solution to the membership problem; in addition, it can be investigated how FDs and MVDs interact [Beeri, Fagin & Howard, 1977]. A study of this kind can be repeated for other types of dependencies and their combinations; for example, Casanova, Fagin & Papadimitriou [1984], Casanova, Tucherman, Furtado & Braga [1989], and Mitchell [1983] do so for FDs and INDs, now even with some negative results (regarding the axiomatizability of INDs). More promising seems the development of a general theory of dependencies, or to find general formalisms in which various types of dependencies can be uniformly stated. To this end, it was discovered, e.g., by Sagiv, Delobel, Parker & Fagin [1981], that there is a connection between database dependencies and first-order logic. This has resulted in several very general frameworks, which subsume FDs, MVDs and others as special cases; surveys are provided by Fagin & Vardi [1984], Vardi [1988] and Kanellakis [1990].

2.5.2. Theory of queries

We saw above that RA and RC have polynomial complexities; Vardi [1982] even shows that they have *low* polynomial complexities. However, the price to pay for this is a limited expressive power. To this end, consider a relation r over $X = AB$. The *transitive closure* of r, denoted r^+, is defined as follows:

$$r^+ := \{ \mu \in \text{Tup}(X) \mid (\exists \mu_1, \ldots, \mu_n \in r, n \geqslant 1)\ \mu(A) = \mu_1(A)$$
$$\wedge\ (\forall i, 1 \leqslant i \leqslant n - 1)\ \mu_i(B) = \mu_{i+1}(A)$$
$$\wedge\ \mu_n(B) = \mu(B)\}$$

Theorem 4 (Aho & Ullman [1979]). *Let R^+ denote the expression yielding r^+ when evaluated with respect to a database d such that $r \in d$. There exists no expression $E \in \text{RA}$ such that $E \approx R^+$, i.e., $(\forall d)\ v_E(d) = r^+$.*

Computing transitive closures is not an exotic task (think, e.g., of a parent/child relationship and a query that asks for ancestors). So the question arises of how RA can be extended so that more database queries can be formulated. One approach, often taken in DBMS implementations, is to interface a given database language with a host language, i.e., a general-purpose programming language. While this will obviously work, since programming languages allow to compute everything that is computable, it is unsatisfactory from a theoretical point of view, since the level of abstraction provided by RA (to consider sets of tuples independent of their internal representation) is generally lost (see also Section 4.1.6). Another, more appealing approach therefore is to extend the relational language itself with constructs (like one for computing transitive closures) that yield additional power. Clearly, the question remains whether some such constructs, and if so which ones, are sufficient to express *all* queries.

An upper bound in the respect was established by Chandra & Harel [1980, 1982], who introduced the notion of a *computable* query. A computable query is a partial recursive function, which given a database as input produces as output a relation over the domain of the database and satisfies a *consistency criterion* basically saying that the query output should be independent of the internal representation of the database.

It is easy to see that RA queries belong to the class of all computable queries, but form a strict subset of them because transitive closure also is a computable query. This observation raises the question of how a language must look like which can express all computable queries. One such language is described by Chandra & Harel [1980]; the basic idea is to generalize relational algebra into a programming language by introducing variables (that take relations as values), assignment statements and control structures (if-then-else, while-do). A new problem then is that the complexity of query evaluation may increase considerably. For obvious practical reasons, the interest is in languages whose queries can be computed efficiently, i.e., in time polynomial in the size of the underlying database. In other words, the problem (or goal) of language design is to find a good balance between expressiveness and complexity. With respect to the latter, it is obvious that queries should be polynomial-time computable, so that language design boils down to finding something intermediate between RA and polynomially computable queries [Immermann, 1986]. Various proposals in this direction have been made over the years, including the above-mentioned RA extension, an RC extension by a fixpoint operator [Chandra & Harel, 1982], and logic programming, which will be considered in Section 2.6. Surveys are provided by Abiteboul & Vianu [1992], Chandra [1988], Kanellakis [1990], and Vossen [1991a].

2.5.3. Universal relation data models

We next take a brief look at another direction in relational language design, which in contrast to RA extensions tries to cut RA down, in particular to get rid of the join operation. The motivation here is that relational databases were originally introduced to free programmers from the need to navigate when accessing data (see Section 1.2.1). Although this has been achieved with respect to *physical* navigation (i.e., access paths to data structures), the relational model fails to avoid *logical* navigation. For example, for posing the algebraic or SQL queries to the library database presented in Section 2.4, a user must be aware of the database structure in order to employ joins appropriately. *Universal relation data models* emerged as an answer to the question of how to simplify logical navigation.

The idea underlying these models in the following: suppose that in the context of a given application each attribute name completely expresses the meaning of this attribute, so that attribute names are globally unique. We can then imagine that the entire information about the application is stored in one big relation (the *universal* relation), so that users can state their queries in terms of selections and projections applied to it, but there is no more need for using a join. Clearly, it is unreasonable to assume that a universal relation is actually stored, so that it merely provides a global view on the underlying base relations. What is needed then is an evaluation strategy for queries directed against this view, or a transformation yielding, say, an RA expression from a universal relation query. The input to such a transformation consists of a set X of attributes (onto which the universal relation is to be projected, eventually subject to selection conditions) and a database d over the underlying schema; the final output will be a relation over X.

A variety of such transformations, commonly known as *window functions*, have been proposed in the literature. These differ considerably in their evaluation strategies (classified as bottom-up vs. top-down by Vossen [1991a]) as well as in the assumptions they impose on the underlying database (like the *strong* [Rissanen, 1978] or the *weak* [Sagiv, 1983] *universal instance assump-*

tion, or structural requirements like the unique derivability of attributes in the presence of FDs [Sagiv, 1983]). An interesting formal tool for describing and analyzing these strategies are *hypergraphs*, whose structural properties, in particular various degrees of acyclicity [Fagin, 1983], can have relevant impacts [Goodman, Shmueli & Tay, 1984; Vossen, 1991a]. More detailed surveys of this subject are provided by Maier, Ullman & Vardi [1984], Kanellakis [1990] and Ullman [1983].

2.5.4. Database updates

We mentioned in Section 2.4.3 that commercial relational languages like SQL are more than complete with respect to RA and RC, among other things because they include primitives for updating relations. Updating a relational database means inserting new tuples, deleting or modifying existing tuples in its relations, which can formally be described as mappings from the set of all databases over a given schema to itself. Language constructs for expressing such mappings are proposed by Abiteboul & Vianu [1988]; more general database transformations encompassing both updates *and* queries are studied by Abiteboul & Vianu [1990]. A good survey of this subject is Abiteboul [1988].

View updates. A specific update problem that combines issues in incomplete information [Paredaens, De Bra, Gyssens & van Gucht, 1989] with those of database updates is *view updating*. A view is a facility that allows users to deal only with parts of the information in a database (an external schema, see Section 1.1). If this facility is provided, users would like to query and update views and ignore the underlying database. However, while interpreting queries involving views is easy (it basically consists of replacing each view name by its definition), interpreting updates is nontrivial. The following example indicates some of the difficulties.

Consider an employee relation *EMP* with attributes *Emp#*, *Name*, *Branch*, where the company is assumed to have two branches, one in San Diego and one in Los Angeles. In addition, the company has a football team, and attribute *FB* contains information on whether an employee is a member of the football team or not. Let two views be declared over this relation, one for the manager of the LA branch ($V_1 := \sigma_{Branch=LA}(EMP)$), one for the coach of the football team ($V_2 := \sigma_{FB=Y}(EMP)$). If the manager of the LA branch wants to delete the employee with *Emp#*25 from V_1, a reasonable execution consists of a deletion of this employee from *EMP*. However, if the coach of the football team wants to perform the same deletion, now applied to V_2, it is unrealistic to delete the employee with number 25 from *EMP* as well, unless the coach is allowed to fire employees. Instead, it seems reasonable in this case to modify the *FB* value of the corresponding tuple. Thus, while the view deletion is executed as a deletion in the first case, in the second it results in a replacement.

A formalization of the view update problem is as follows. Let *V* denote a view definition, given, say, as an RA expression over database schema **D**. A view state, i.e., the result of an evaluation of V with respect to a database d over D, is denoted $V(d)$. A database update is a mapping t on d with result d', i.e., $t(d) = d'$. A view update u is specified by the user with respect to $V(d)$. It has to be translated into some database update t_u such that the new view state $V(d')$, which the user has specified by $u(V(d))$, can be derived from the new database state $d' = t_u(d)$. More formally, the diagram shown in Figure 11 shall commute; in other words, a database update t_u is a *translation* of the view update u if $u(V(d)) = V(t_u(d))$. As the examples indicate, in general there exist *several* translations for a given view update. In this case, a *translator* associates a particular translation t_u with a given view update u. The *view update problem* can hence be considered as the task of finding a translator for a given set of view updates. A survey of proposed translators is given by Langerak [1990].

2.6. Database logic programs

We now return to the issue of language design we discussed in Section 2.5.2 and present another way of extending first-order or algebraic languages. We do this in a separate section for two reasons. First, the approach we are about to sketch is one of the most active research topics in database theory these days. Second, the approach is already having a great impact on system implementations; in fact, the relevant terms of *deductive databases* or *knowledge bases* are frequently used in connection with DBMS that support this approach.

An important programming paradigm that emerged in the 1970s is *logic programming* [Apt & van Emden, 1982; Lloyd, 1987; van Emden & Kowalski, 1976]. It was heavily influenced by work in the areas of artificial intelligence and automated theorem proving, and somewhat culminated in the language *Prolog* that emphasizes a declarative style of programming. The confluence of logic programming and the area of databases has been driven by the identification of several common features. First, logic programming systems manage small 'databases' which are single-user, kept in main memory and consist of fact information and deduction rules. Database systems on the other hand deal with large, shared data collections kept in secondary memory, and support efficient update and retrieval, reliability and persistence. Second, a 'query' ('goal') in logic programming is answered through a chain of deductions built to prove or disprove some initial statement. A database query is processed by devising an efficient execution plan for extracting the desired information from the database. Third, dependencies specify which database states are considered correct, and a DBMS is expected to enforce them. In logic programming, constraints are rules that are activated whenever the 'database' is modified.

$$V(d) \xrightarrow{\ u\ } u(V(d)) \overset{!}{=} V(t_u(d))$$
$$V\uparrow \qquad \Downarrow \qquad \uparrow V$$
$$d \xrightarrow{\ t_u\ } t_u(d)$$

Fig. 11. Formalization of the view update problem.

Considering these commonalities, it seems reasonable and promising to combine the paradigm of logic programming with database technology. The result, a *logic-oriented database*, is capable of describing facts, rules, queries and constraints uniformly as sets of formulas in first-order logic, so that the notion of *logical implication* can be used as a basis for defining the semantics of a declarative language.

The most prominent example for the use of logic programming in the context of databases is *Datalog* [Maier & Warren, 1988; Ceri, Gottlob & Tanca, 1989, 1990; Ullman, 1988] (a number of earlier approaches are collected by Minker [1988]). This language has a syntax similar to that of (pure) Prolog, but, unlike Prolog, is set-oriented, insensitive to orderings of retrieval predicates or of the data, and has neither function symbols nor special-purpose predicates (for controlling the execution of a program). The basic idea behind Datalog and its application of expressing queries to a relational database is to define a new (derived or *intensional*) relation in terms of the (*extensional*) relations in a given database *and* the new relation itself, and to do so by providing a set of Horn clauses.

An *atom* in Datalog is an expression of the form $P(x_1, \ldots, x_n)$, where predicate P denotes a (base or derived) relation, and the x_i symbols are variables or constants. A *literal* is either an atom (*positive* literal) or a negated atom (*negative* literal); a *clause* is a disjunction of literals. A *Horn clause* (named after the German mathematician Alfred Horn) is a clause with at most one positive literal, and a Datalog *program* is a finite set of Horn clauses.

As an example, consider predicates T and R denoting binary relations. Then $\neg R(x, y) \vee T(x, y)$ and $\neg R(x, z) \vee \neg T(z, y) \vee T(x, y)$ are Horn clauses which are written in Datalog format as

$$T(x, y) :\text{-} R(x, y) .$$
$$T(x, y) :\text{-} R(x, z), T(z, y) .$$

The argument is that this program is to be interpreted as the query that computes (in T) the transitive closure (of R). To this end, the following informal semantics is given to each Horn clause of the form '$A :\text{-} B_1, \ldots, B_n.$': 'For each assignment of each variable, if B_1 is true and B_2 is true and ... and B_n is true, then A is true.' Hence, the first clause informally says that 'for every choice of x and y, if (x, y) is a tuple in (the instance of) R, then include it in (the result relation over) T'. Similarly, the second clause can be interpreted as 'for every choice of x, y and z, if (x, z) is in R and (z, y) is in T, then (x, y) is also in T'.

The following terms are common in this context: if $B :\text{-} A_1, A_2, \ldots, A_n$, is a clause occurring in a program, then B is the *head* of the clause, and $A_1, \ldots, A_n$ form its *body*. According to the definition of a Horn clause, three special cases can occur. (1) The clause consists of exactly one positive literal, and nothing else; then it is called a *fact*. Facts are used to describe the contents of a database in a Datalog program. (2) The clause has no positive literal; then it is an *integrity constraint*. (3) The clause is a *rule*, i.e., it consists of one positive literal and one or more negative ones.

Syntactically, a Datalog program is a set C of Horn clauses, which needs to be given a semantics. A possible approach is to give such a program an interpretation like the following: if R is a predicate occurring in C, a *relation r* for R is a set of *ground* atoms, i.e., atoms without variables (but constants only). The *input* to C consists of a relation for each predicate that does not appear in the head of any rule. The *output* computed by C basically consists of a relation for each predicate that occurs in the head of some rule; this computation proceeds as follows: the contents of a database is specified as ground atoms (facts) in C. A rule states that if certain facts are known others can be deduced from them. Newly deduced facts become ground atoms in the output and are at the same time considered to become available as (further) input, so that the rules can be applied again to deduce additional new facts. More precisely, a rule is used to deduce a new fact by *instantiating* its variables with constants, i.e., substituting a constant for each occurrence of a variable. If, under such an instantiation, each atom in the body of the rule in question becomes a ground atom, the instantiated head of the rule is added to the output.

It can be shown [Ceri, Gottlob & Tanca, 1990; Ullman, 1988] that the procedure sketched above describes a *least fixpoint* computation, whose result (for Datalog programs without negation in rule bodies) alternatively is the (uniquely determined) *minimal model* of the program in a *model-theoretic* sense, or the set of all facts deducible from the given database in a *proof-theoretic* sense. Furthermore, there is a way to describe it as a (view-defining) *equation* of relational algebra which for transitive closure has the form

$$T(x, y) = R(x, y) \cup \pi_{x,y}(R(x, z) \bowtie T(z, y))$$

Note that, due to the recursion involved, the meaning of this expression is not obtainable by an ordinary RA expression.

With respect to the expressive power of Datalog as a relational query language, Figure 12 describes its relationship to RA. The two languages are incomparable with respect to set inclusion: (1) they have a nonempty intersection, consisting of nonrecursive Datalog programs or, equivalently, relational algebra without the difference operator; (2) recursive queries like transitive

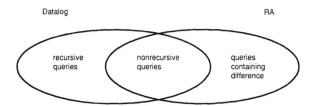

Fig. 12. Relationship between Datalog and RA.

closure are not RA expressible; (3) RA expressions involving difference are not Datalog expressible. This is due to the fact that Datalog programs are *monotone*, i.e., enlarging the input d to a Datalog program cannot yield a smaller result than on d itself, but difference is not a monotone operation.

So far we have excluded negation in rule bodies of Datalog programs; clearly, an extension in that direction increases the expressive power of the language. However, rule evaluation now becomes nondeterministic in general. One way around this problem is to control the use of negation by *stratification*. Informally, a Datalog program is *stratified* if the following holds: if a negative literal $\neg P$ is used in the body of a rule, then P must have been computed completely at this point. In other words, the program can be divided into *strata* (layers) which are evaluated sequentially. An example is the *complement* of transitive closure, which cannot be computed by an ordinary Datalog program; however, the following Datalog program does it:

$$T(x, y) :\text{-} R(x, y) .$$
$$T(x, y) :\text{-} R(x, z), T(z, y) .$$
$$C(x, y) :\text{-} \neg T(x, y) .$$

The first two lines represent Layer 1 of the stratification and compute the transitive closure (of R in T) as before. The third line, Layer 2, uses this result for computing the complement. The idea henceforth is to have Layer 1 processed completely before Layer 2 is entered (and to continue in the same way in the presence of more than two layers). More information on this and other extensions of Datalog can be found in Abiteboul & Vianu [1991], Bidoit [1991], Chandra [1988], Ceri, Gottlob & Tanca [1989, 1990], Chimenti, Gamboa, Krishnamurthy, Naqvi, Tsur & Zaniolo [1990], Gardarin & Valduriez [1989], Kanellakis [1990], Naqvi & Tsur [1989].

Datalog has been sketched here as a paradigm for defining intensional relations as a whole. Users of a database will often only be interested in a subset of such relations, which can be captured by introducing *goals* into Datalog programs. A goal might be written as '?-literal' and expresses an ad-hoc query against a view defined in the program. For both the evaluation of goals and the computation of intensional relations, a variety of methods are described in the literature which exhibit various degrees of efficiency [Bancilhon & Ramakrishnan, 1986; Bry, 1990; Ceri, Gottlob & Tanca, 1990; Ullman, 1989].

2.7. Nested relations and beyond

An important aspect of the relational data model is its simplicity, which is largely due to the basic assumption that data is represented as flat tables (in 1NF, see Section 2.1). Our price to pay for this is the inability of the model to directly represent hierarchical structures. To see that these are sometimes more adequate than flat ones, we briefly reconsider the library example and note that a book can have a *set* of authors, or that a publisher can have offices in several locations. This suggests a representation of book information as shown in Figure 13. (We do not claim that this is most adequate, since the publisher information would here be redundantly repeated for each book from the same publisher.)

The first proposal to generalize the relational model beyond 1NF tables was made by Makinouchi [1977]. The idea is to allow relations as values for attributes, so that relations may get *nested* into each other. For example, the nested relation shown in Figure 14 has two tuples, some components of which are themselves relations.

Many researchers have investigated the nested relational model, in particular issues like algebras [Schek & Scholl, 1986; Thomas & Fischer, 1986], calculi [Roth, Korth & Batory, 1987; Roth, Korth & Silberschatz, 1988], language completeness [Abiteboul, Fischer & Schek, 1989] or schema design [Özsoyoglu & Yuan, 1987]. Of particular relevance to algebraic languages are the two operations *nest* and *unnest* proposed by Jäschke & Schek [1982], or the introduction of a *powerset* operator [Gyssens & van Gucht, 1988, 1991]. Surveys of this model are provided by Paredaens De Bra, Gyssens & van Gucht [1989] or Vossen [1991a].

It has also been recognized (see, e.g., the survey by Hull [1987]) that what is really needed for coping with the modeling requirements of new applications are data models that are less restrictive with respect to the representation of complex objects. To this end, an important observation is that the *flat* relational model uses a tuple and a set *constructor* and allows their application

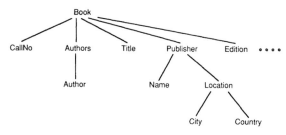

Fig. 13. Hierarchical view of books in a library.

| Book | CallNo | Authors | Title | Publisher | | ... |
| | | Author | | Name | Location | |
					City	Country
	234	Jones	Algorithms	Add-Wes	Bonn	Germ
		Clark			Reading	MA
	456	Smith	Computing	Prentice	Englewood	NJ
		Theo			Norwood	CA
		Wilkins				

Fig. 14. Book information gathered in a nested relation.

once and in that order (a flat relation is a *set of tuples*), whereas the *nested* relational model uses the same constructors, but these can now be applied several times in a strictly alternating fashion (a nested relation is a *set of tuples*, values of which may in turn be *sets of tuples* and so on). Thus, an immediate generalization is to give up this strict sequencing of constructor application, or making the constructors *orthogonal* to the given base data types. Obviously, another is to allow additional constructors (like 'list' for representing order). The result is a complex-object data model allowing the definition of a large repertoire of data types [Vossen & Witt, 1991]. Instances of these types are manipulated using languages that are extensions of RA or RC. An important distinction, besides the expressive power of such languages, is whether such languages are *statically type-checked* or not; an instance of the former appears in Abiteboul & Grumbach [1991], one of the latter in Bancilhon & Khoshafian [1989].

3. Transaction management

We now switch to a completely different database issue, in which once again lots of theoretical investigations have been undertaken with many fruitful results for practical implementations. As was mentioned in Section 1, a core DBMS functionality is to allow users shared access to a common database, and simultaneously to provide a certain degree of fault tolerance. For both purposes, a DBMS knows the concept of a *transaction* [Gray 1978, 1981]. The basic idea is to consider a given program that wants to operate on a database as a logical unit, and to process it as if the database was at its exclusive disposal. In this section, we first survey conventional approaches to making this idea work. In particular, we sketch the basic concepts of concurrency control and recovery that are employed in modern DBMS. After that, we indicate that especially new areas of DBMS application tend to require unconventional solutions to transaction management and what these might look like.

3.1. The ACID principle

If a DBMS allows multiple users shared access to a database, various conflicting goals have to be met: good throughput, shielding one user program against the others, avoidance of data losses or corruption, etc. To meet these goals, each individual user program, which might, for example, be a single SQL statement directed against a relational database, or an application program extracting data from a database for further processing, is treated by the DBMS as a transaction and processed such that the following properties are fulfilled:

• *Atomicity*. To the issuing user, it always appears that his transaction is executed *either completely or not at all*. Thus, effects which the transaction has on the database become visible to other transactions only if it can terminate successfully, and no errors have occurred in the meantime.

• *Consistency*. All integrity constraints of the database are maintained by each transaction, i.e., a transaction always maps a consistent database state to another such state.

• *Isolation*. Each individual transaction runs isolated from all others; thus, each transaction is guaranteed to see only consistent data from the database.

• *Durability*. If a transaction has terminated normally, its effects on the database are guaranteed to survive subsequent failures.

These properties are collectively called the *ACID principle*. In order to achieve them, the transaction manager of a DBMS has a *concurrency control* as well as a *recovery* component. In brief, the goal of the former is to synchronize concurrent accesses to a shared database, while that of the latter is to restore a consistent state after a failure, and to take provisions so it can guarantee that transaction results are durable.

To design concurrency control and recovery mechanisms, it is necessary to come up with a suitable *model* of transactions and their *executions*, to establish a notion of *correctness* of executions, and to devise *protocols* which achieve that. While the basic problem is not new for computer systems in general, the database context has its special requirements in that respect, namely to preserve the consistency of a given state, and to provide each database program with a consistent view of the data even in the presence of failures, so that specific solutions are needed. One general paradigm here is *serializability theory*, which is based on a computational model in which (at least) the following 'system components' are represented:

(1) A *database*, i.e., a set of objects on which certain operations can be executed,

(2) *transactions*, considered as programs under execution and described as (finite) sequences of operations,

(3) *schedules* for describing interleaved executions of distinct programs that operate on the same database,

(4) A notion of *conflict* for operations from distinct transactions occurring in a schedule.

In what follows we will first make this program more precise in terms of the *read–write model* of (*flat*) *transactions*. As will then be indicated, various approaches to realizing that program follow the same methodology that is used here. However, a number of issues will not be taken into account by that model, which motivates the search for others that at least for certain database applications seem more appropriate.

3.2. Concurrency control and recovery for read–write transactions

Synchronization of transactions on a shared database in the presence of failures is accomplished in commercial database systems by perceiving transactions as straight-line programs consisting of simple disk-based operations. In this section we describe the theory underlying this approach and its realizations.

3.2.1. The model

The most prominent transaction model (for centralized systems) considers transactions as *sequences of read and write operations*, thereby abstracting from all kinds of computations that a user program might execute in main memory or in its buffer. The computation model used is the following.

(1) The underlying database is considered as a countably infinite set $D = \{x, y, z, \ldots\}$ of objects, which can be assumed to be pages that can be read or written in one step, and that can atomically be transferred back and forth between primary and secondary memory.

(2) A *transaction* has the form $t = a_1 \cdots a_n$, where each a_i is of the form $r(x)$ ('read x') or $w(x)$ ('write x') for some $x \in D$.

(3) A *complete schedule* for transactions $t_1, \ldots, t_n$ is an ordering of all operations of these transactions, which respects the order of operations specified by the transactions and additionally contains a pseudo-step for each transaction following its last operation that states whether this transaction finally *commits* (i.e., ends successfully) or *aborts* (i.e., is canceled prior to successful termination). If t_i appears in the schedule, a commit [abort] is indicated by c_i [a_i], respectively. A *schedule* is a prefix of a complete schedule. A complete schedule is *serial* if for any two transactions t_i, t_j appearing in it either all of t_i precedes all of t_j or vice versa.

(4) Two steps from distinct transactions are *in conflict* in a given schedule, if they operate on the same database object and at least one of them is a write operation.

Common additional assumptions made in the model are, for example, that each transaction reads or writes every database object it operates upon at most once, or that reading of an object is done before writing in case both operations are desired.

The following is an example of a complete schedule for four transactions, in which t_0, t_2 and t_3 are committed and t_1 is aborted:

$$s_1 = w_0(x)r_1(x)w_0(z)r_1(z)r_2(x)w_0(y)c_0r_3(z)w_3(z)w_2(y)c_2w_1(x)w_3(y)a_1c_3$$

If T is a subset of the set of all transactions occurring in a schedule s, the *projection* of s onto T is obtained by erasing from s all steps from transactions not in T. For example, the projection of s_1 onto its committed transactions is the schedule

$$w_0(x)w_0(z)r_2(x)w_0(y)c_0r_3(z)w_3(z)w_2(y)c_2w_3(y)c_3$$

A serial schedule for the original four transactions would be $s_2 = t_0t_2t_1t_3$. Notice that in general there always exist $n!$ serial schedules for n transactions.

An important observation is that so far transactions and schedules are *purely syntactic* objects, describing only the sequencing of data accesses performed by a database program, how these are interleaved and what eventually happens to each transaction. A common assumption in traditional concurrency control theory is that the *semantics* of transactions are not known. On the other hand, a *pseudo-semantics* can be associated with a given transaction as follows. It is assumed that the (new) value of an object x written by some step $w(x)$ of a given transaction t depends on *all* values of objects that were previously read by t. The value of x read by some step $r(x)$ of t depends on the last $w(x)$ that occurred before $r(x)$ in t, or on the 'initial' value of x if no such $w(x)$ exists. This can be extended to schedules in the obvious way, with the additional condition that transactions which are aborted in the schedule are ignored. For example, in the schedule s_1 above, t_1 reads x and z from t_0, but the value produced by $w_1(x)$ will not appear in the database. A formalization of this intuition is given by Hadzilacos [1988].

The distinction between a complete schedule and a schedule captures a dynamic situation, in which transactions arrive at a scheduling device step by step, and the device has to decide on the spot whether or not to execute a given step. For various reasons it might happen that the device at some point discovers that a transaction cannot be completed successfully, so that it has to output an abort operation for this transaction. We do not consider yet how aborts (and also commits) are processed internally, but turn to the issue of schedule *correctness* next.

3.2.2. Serializability

Since a serial schedule is always (complete and) correct in the sense that it preserves the consistency of the underlying database (assuming that the transactions it contains are consistency preserving), it makes sense to establish a correctness criterion for nonserial schedules on the basis of a relationship to serial ones. The common way to achieve this is by first introducing an appropriate notion of *equivalence* for schedules and then defining *serializability* via equivalence to a serial schedule. All notions of serializability described in the literature are obtained in this way, including *final-state* as well as *view serializability* [Papadimitriou, 1979; Yannakakis, 1984; Vidyasankar, 1987, 1991]. We here restrict the attention to a notion of serializability which, although restricted, enjoys a number of interesting properties: unlike final-state or view serializability, which have an NP-complete decision problem, it can be tested in time linear in the number of given transactions. It enjoys closure properties that are relevant for correctness in a dynamic setting, and it allows to design simple protocols that can be implemented economically.

The *conflict relation* conf(s) of a schedule s consists of all pairs of steps (a, b) from distinct, unaborted transactions which are in conflict in s, and for which a occurs before b. If s and s' are two schedules for the same set of transactions, s and s' are *conflict equivalent*, denoted $s \approx_c s'$, if conf(s) = conf(s'). Finally, a complete schedule s is *conflict serializable* if there exists a serial schedule s' for the same set of transactions such that $s \approx_c s'$. Let CSR denote the class of all (complete and) conflict serializable schedules.

For example, it is easily verified for the schedule s_1 above that $\mathrm{conf}(s_1) = \mathrm{conf}(t_0 t_2 t_3)$. Since the latter schedule, which ignores the aborted t_1, is serial, $s_1 \in \mathrm{CSR}$. Another easy test whether a complete schedule s is in CSR is the following. First, construct the *conflict graph* $G(s) = (V, E)$ of s, whose set V of nodes consists of those transactions from s which are not aborted, and which contains an edge of the form (t_i, t_j) in E if some step from t_i is in conflict with a subsequent step from t_j. Second, test this graph for acyclicity:

Theorem 5 (Eswaran, Gray, Lorie & Traiger [1976]). *For every schedule s, $s \in \mathrm{CSR}$ iff $G(s)$ is acyclic.*

3.2.3. Commit-serializability and recoverability

As was discovered by Hadzilacos [1988] and other work, serializability alone is not sufficient as a correctness criterion for schedules if transactions or the system may fail. There are two basic reasons for that. First, since an uncommitted transactions may abort or a system failure may cause all of them to abort, a correctness criterion must concern the committed ones only. Second, since a system failure may occur at any time during a transaction execution, if a schedule is correct so must be each of its prefixes. Hadzilacos [1988] formalizes these intuitions as *closure properties* of schedule properties, in particular closure under commit operations and under taking prefixes, and proves the following.

Theorem 6 (Hadzilacos [1988]). *Membership in the class* CSR *is a prefix commit-closed* (pcc) *property, i.e., for each schedule $s \in$ CSR, the projection of any prefix of s onto the transaction committed therein is also in* CSR.

A schedule is *commit serializable* if the committed projection of any of its prefixes is serializable, i.e., in a correct schedule the committed transactions have been executed in a serializable fashion at any time. Hence a schedule must be commit serializable to ensure that the concurrent execution of transactions will not cause inconsistencies. A consequence of the last theorem is that CSR equals the class of all complete and commit conflict-serializable schedules. To ensure that a failure of transactions cannot cause the semantics of committed transactions to change, a schedule must additionally be *recoverable* in the following sense: if, in a schedule s, transaction t_i reads a value written by t_j and t_i is committed in s, then t_j is also committed and does so prior to t_i. In other words, at no time has a committed transaction read a value written by an uncommitted one. Ultimately, a *correct* schedule is one that is both commit serializable *and* recoverable. The latter, which is another pcc property, can be restricted in various ways, for example so that *cascading aborts* are avoided (where the abort of one transaction causes others to abort as well); details are in Hadzilacos [1988].

3.2.4. *Concurrency control protocols*

Concurrency control protocols developed for system implementations can generally be divided into two major classes:

(1) *Pessimistic protocols.* These are based on the assumption that conflicts between concurrent transactions are likely, so that provisions need to be taken to handle them. Known protocols in this class include *two-phase locking*, *timestamping* and *serialization graph testing*.

(2) *Optimistic protocols.* These are based on the opposite assumption that conflicts are rare. As a consequence, it is possible to schedule operations vastly arbitrarily, and just make sure from time to time that the schedule generated was correct. Protocols based on this idea are known as *validation protocols*.

Detailed descriptions of the protocols just mentioned and of many of their variations can be found in Bernstein, Hadzilacos & Goodman [1987] as well as in Papadimitriou [1986]. We here sketch the idea behind locking schedulers only, since these are most widely used in commercial systems, and also allow a theory that is interesting in its own right.

The basic idea underlying any locking scheduler is to require that accesses to database objects by distinct transactions are executed in a mutually exclusive way. In particular, a transaction cannot modify (write) an object as long as another transaction is still operating on it (reading or writing it). The central paradigm to implement this idea is the use of *locks*, which are set by the scheduler on behalf of a transaction before the latter reads or writes, and which are removed after the access has been executed. For read and write operations, two types of lock operations are basically sufficient: if a transaction wants to read [write] an object, it requests a read lock [write lock] (or locks the object in *shared* [*exclusive*] mode), respectively. A read lock indicates to other transactions which want to write that the object in question is currently available for reading only; a write lock indicates that the object is currently not available.

Two locks from distinct transactions are in *conflict* if both refer to the same object and (at least) one of them is exclusive. In this case, only one of the requests can be granted since the requests are *incompatible*. A scheduler operates according to a *locking protocol* if in every schedule generated by it all simultaneously held locks are compatible; it operates according to a *two-phase protocol* (2PL) if additionally no transaction sets a new lock after it has released one. The most popular variant of 2PL is to hold all locks of a transaction until this transaction terminates (*strict* 2PL). A straightforward motivation for its use is that a point in time at which a scheduler can be sure that a transaction will not request any further locks is the end of the transaction.

It is easy to verify that 2PL is a *safe* protocol, i.e., that every schedule generated by 2PL is conflict serializable. In addition, its strict variant even generates a subset of the recoverable schedules. Although this protocol is easy to implement, outperforms other protocols [Carey & Stonebraker, 1984] and can easily be generalized to distributed systems, it also has its shortcomings. For example, it is not free of *deadlocks*, so that additional means need to be taken to discover and resolve these. Other protocols avoid deadlocks, but do so at the expense of other restrictions [Bernstein, Hadzilacos & Goodman, 1987].

From a theoretical point of view, an interesting observation is that 2PL is unable to generate *every* schedule in the class CSR. This raises the question of characterizing the exact power of locking. For this and related questions a *geometrical interpretation* for locked transactions was introduced by Papadimitriou [1982, 1983], which for the case of two transactions roughly is as follows. For each transaction, its sequence of steps is represented as a sequence of equidistant integer points on one of the axes spanning the Euclidean plane. Thus, the two transactions define a rectangular *grid* in the plane. Grid points representing a pair of conflicting steps from the two transactions are *conflict points*, which fall into a *forbidden region* of the plane (when locking is used for synchronization) that is defined by the corresponding lock and unlock steps (points). A *schedule* becomes a monotone *curve* through the grid starting at point $(0, 0)$. *Legal* schedules are the ones that avoid forbidden regions, since any point within such a region represents a state in which the two transactions hold conflicting locks on the same object. However, legal schedules may not be serializable, but a legal schedule is serializable iff its curve does not *separate* two forbidden regions.

3.2.5. Recovery

Above we talked about abort operations and the need for recovery without specifying by what this might be caused or how to react to these causes. It is common to distinguish three classes of failures. *Transaction failures* occur when a transaction does not terminate normally, because inconsistencies in the database were detected while it was running, or the transaction became involved in a deadlock and was chosen as the victim. *System failures* are error situations in which the contents of main memory gets corrupted, e.g., due to bugs in the DBMS or operating system code or hardware failures in the CPU. Finally, *media failures* occur when parts of secondary memory are lost, e.g., because of a headcrash on a disk or a bug in an operating-system routine that writes to a disk.

In what follows we restrict our attention to system failures, since these are most frequent, subsume transaction failures, and their repair uses techniques that can easily be generalized to media failures. To understand the implications of such failures, it is safe to assume that a read operation causes an object transfer from disk to a *buffer* (in main memory), where further processing can be done. A write operation, on the other hand, causes an object transfer from the buffer back to disk. The basic scenario after a system failure then is that the buffer is corrupted, and that the transactions which already wrote into it can be distinguished by whether or not they were committed before the crash.

If they were, they must be *redone* in case the updates they produced had not yet been written back to the database; otherwise, the appropriate reaction is to *undo* (or *rollback*) them (and repeat them at a later time), in particular if some or all of the updates they produced have been written into the database already.

The basic paradigm for handling failures is to introduce some kind of redundancy called the *log*, in which the various actions performed by different transactions get protocoled (in a safe place like a disk) according to the following idea. If transaction *t* wants to update database object *x*, a *before-image* of *x* is written into the log first; similarly, the new value of *x* is recorded as an *after-image*. A redo [undo] of *t* can then be performed by processing the log entries for *t* and by restoring the after [before] image for each object which *t* accessed, respectively.

The log is under the control of a *recovery manager*, a device that takes three kinds of input. First, it receives the reads and writes from transactions as output by the scheduler. Second, it receives the commit and abort operations that are eventually generated by the scheduler. Finally, it must be able to handle a restart request from the operating system after a system failure. For simplicity, we assume that the buffer is ultimately under operating system control and managed according to some paging scheme, so that in particular a *page replacement* becomes necessary whenever a new page needs to be written into a full buffer. For recovery purposes, it is now important at what points in time updated pages get propagated from the buffer into the database: if a recovery manager executes the writes of a transaction by just writing into the buffer and keeps the updates in the buffer beyond the commit of this transaction, redo will be required if a crash occurs before the necessary propagation could be executed. Conversely, if updates made by a transaction are propagated to the database before the transaction commits, undo will be required in case the transaction aborts. As a result, four classes of recovery algorithms can be distinguished, based on whether (1) redo *and* undo are required, (2) *no* redo, but undo is required, (3) redo, but *no* undo is required, and (4) *neither* redo *nor* undo is required.

Independent of what strategy is chosen, each has to observe the following general rules: (i) In order to ensure that any committed transaction survives a subsequent crash, i.e., can be redone if necessary, the after-images produced by a transaction must be written to the database or the log *before* that transaction commits ('commit rule'). (ii) In order to guarantee that an active transaction can be properly undone after a crash if necessary, the before-image of an object must be written into the log *before* the after-image of this object is transferred into the database, in case the latter takes place before the transaction commits ('write-ahead-log protocol'). If the recovery manager does itself not control the writing of buffer pages to the database, a *write* operation is executed by reading the object in question into the buffer if it is not there already, writing a corresponding entry into the log, and finally overwriting the old value of the object in the buffer. If the corresponding page *p* is afterwards replaced (written into the database since it contains a new value) and the transaction t which wrote p aborts, an undo of t becomes necessary. If t commits and a crash destroys p before it has been replaced, it will be necessary to redo t. A recovery algorithm which does not require redo must make sure that *all* after-images produced by a transaction must be written into the *database* before (or when) the transaction commits. Similarly, a recovery algorithm which does not require undo must make sure that *no* after-image produced by a transaction is written into the database (but only into the log) before the transaction commits. Consequently, a recovery algorithm requires neither redo nor undo if after-images get propagated into the database exactly at commit time of each transaction. These strategies and their implementation techniques are discussed in detail by Bernstein, Goodman & Hadzilacos [1983], Bernstein, Hadzilacos & Goodman [1987] or Härder & Reuter [1983].

3.3. Generalizations of serializability theory

We now sketch various approaches to generalizing the theory of concurrency control based on serializability which have been discussed in the literature in recent years. These cover a wide spectrum, including

(1) allowing multiple versions of data objects to be present in a database simultaneously [Bernstein & Goodman, 1983; Hadzilacos & Papadimitriou, 1986; Papadimitriou & Kanellakis, 1984],

(2) extensions of the read–write model by new types of operations, for which a notion of conflict can be investigated vastly along the lines of the traditional approach,

(3) using information on the data structures used to represent the underlying database in secondary memory [Shasha & Goodman, 1988],

(4) using information on database states for synchronization purposes,

(5) introducing new correctness criteria beyond conflict serializability.

We consider some of these in turn.

3.3.1. Generalized communtativity

As a motivating example, consider two numerical database objects x and y representing *counters* which can be either incremented or decremented, and let transactions t_1 and t_2 both increment both counters in different order. The two transactions can hence be written as $t_1 = \mathrm{incr}(x)\,\mathrm{incr}(y)$ and $t_2 = \mathrm{incr}(y)\,\mathrm{incr}(x)$. Now assume that an action $\mathrm{incr}(z)$ is executed as $r(z)w(z)$, and consider the following schedule:

$$s = r_1(x)r_2(y)w_1(x)w_2(y)r_1(y)w_1(y)c_1r_2(x)w_2(x)c_2$$

Since $G(s)$ is cyclic, $s \notin \mathrm{CSR}$. However, from a semantic point of view s represents the sequence

$$\text{incr}_1(x)\,\text{incr}_2(y)\,\text{incr}_1(y)\,\text{incr}_2(x)$$

of actions. Thus, although $G(s)$ is cyclic, s seems acceptable since the increment operations commute.

In general, two operations (from distinct transactions) which access the same database object *commute* if the order in which they are executed is immaterial, i.e., for any given initial state (value) of the object the final states (values) produced by ordering the operations either way are equal. (In the read–write model of transactions, noncommutation coincides with being in conflict.)

An early proposal in this direction, subsuming the one sketched above, is Bernstein, Goodman & Lai [1983], which considers an extended model including increments and decrements on numerical objects (in addition to ordinary reads and writes on arbitrary objects). For such a model, it is even easy to extend, for example, the 2PL protocol to take into account these new operations. An important application of this approach is the handling of *hot spot* data, which is data that is accessed by write operations at a very high rate (so that the use of exclusive locks is prohibitive with respect to performance); see Gawlick [1985] or Härder [1988] for corresponding techniques.

Vianu & Vossen [1988] describe an approach which is based on update operations as they appear at the conceptual level of a relational database, and a concurrency control theory is developed for this semantically richer model. Yet another transaction model based on abstract data types is considered by Schwarz & Spector [1984]. ADTs have been used to enrich the transaction concept with additional operations (and to make it usable even beyond the context of database management), and to take information on the *state* of the underlying database into account. The properties of ADTs make them particularly interesting for the area of object-oriented database systems which will be discussed in Section 4.

3.3.2. Alternative correctness criteria

Although serializability, i.e., equivalence to seriality, has a solid motivation in transaction processing and proved to be a reasonable concept, many researchers have asked whether alternatives to it might be feasible under certain circumstances, and which ones. An early proposal in the direction by Garcia-Molina [1983], which is based on the assumption that a schedule is correct as long as it preserves database consistency; in other words, a schedule is acceptable as long as a user does not see inconsistent data. To this end, Garcia-Molina [1983] suggests that users classify their transactions into groups of 'compatible' ones, and that a scheduler takes that knowledge into account during operation. A generalization of this approach is *multilevel atomicity* as first defined by Lynch [1983]. An orthogonal suggestion is made by Vianu & Vossen [1989]; here, transactions are equipped with 'goals', and concurrent execution of transactions whose goals conflict is forbidden.

While most proposals of correctness criteria that depart from serializability rely on a transaction model other than the read-write one, even in this model

various alternatives can be stated. For example, Korth & Speegle [1988]
propose *predicatewise serializability* (PWSR), whose idea is that if the database
consistency constraint is in conjunctive normal form, it can be maintained by
enforcing serializability only with respect to data items which share a disjunc-
tive clause. For example, in a database with two objects x and y, consistency
might be defined by two conjuncts one of which is over x, the other over y.
Now consider the following schedule:

$$s = r_1(x)w_1(x)r_2(x)r_2(y)w_2(y)r_1(y)w_1(y)c_1c_2$$

Obviously, $s \notin CSR$, but s is PWSR because it can be decomposed into the two
schedules $s_1 = r_1(x)w_1(x)c_1r_2(x)c_2$ and $s_2 = r_2(y)w_2(y)c_2r_1(y)w_1(y)c_1$, each of
which is even serial. The PWSR notion is actually more general and can be
applied in a variety of nonstandard contexts. A final alternative we mention is
quasi-serializability as defined by Du & Elmagarmid [1989], a notion that
seems particularly suited for heterogeneous databases.

3.4. Beyond ACID transactions

We conclude this section by taking a short look at more recent developments
in transaction management. These are motivated by a number of observations
made in both conventional and unconventional database environments [Gray,
1981]. With respect to the former, it has become common to organize a DBMS
as a hierarchy of functional layers and/or layers of abstraction as described in
Section 1. A natural question then to be asked is why not make a transaction
concept available at distinct layers of this hierarchy instead of just at the lowest
one; this concurs with recent developments in operating systems. Another
observation is that sometimes complex activities cannot be modeled adequately
with standard ACID transactions. For example, consider a travel reservation
activity consisting of flight reservations, car rentals, and hotel bookings.
Although the trip can safely be made only if all reservations have been made
successfully, there is no reason why they cannot be made in parallel, and it
even makes sense to consider each as a subtransaction of the entire transaction.
This renders it possible to abort individual ones, for example, if a flight is fully
booked and a switch to another needs to be made. With respect to unconventional database environments, we mentioned in Section 1 that transactions
might now be long-lived activities (such as a design session in a CAD
database), for which the requirements of atomicity and isolation immediately
create problems. The support of cooperation between distinct user groups or
between autonomous subsystems in a federated system is also not realistic with
standard transactions.

As a result, recent proposals in the area of transaction management center
around the idea of giving up the ACID principle in its traditional strict form
[Elmagarmid, 1991]. We consider two important developments in this direction
next.

3.4.1. Nested transactions

A more flexible interaction with a database is achievable if *flat* transactions are replaced by *nested* ones. The basic idea is to allow transactions to contain other transactions as *subtransactions*, thereby giving transactions a tree structure whose leaves are elementary operations, but whose other nodes all represent transactions. Even if the ACID principle is iteratively applied to subtransactions, this yields additional flexibility. For example, if a subtransaction appears atomic to its parent, it can be reset without causing the parent to abort too. Furthermore, if subtransactions are isolated from each other, they can execute in parallel. Two prominent special cases of nested transactions are *closed* ones, in which subtransactions have to delay their commit until the end of their root transaction, and *open* ones in which subtransactions are allowed to commit autonomously. If all leaves in a transaction tree are of the same height, *multilevel* transactions result, in which the generation of subtransactions can be driven by the functional layers of the underlying system. The theory of nested transactions has been developed in a number of recent papers, including Beeri, Schek & Weikum [1988], Beeri, Bernstein & Goodman [1989], Moss [1985], Lynch & Merritt [1988], Fekete, Lynch, Merritt & Weihl [1990], Weikum [1991].

3.4.2. Application-dependent execution control

Another idea of getting rid of a strict enforcement of the ACID properties is to allow users to switch them off if desired. For example, if a transaction contains alternative actions not all of which are executed (e.g., booking a flight on Lufthansa *or* KLM), atomicity should be given up. If transactions are allowed to view the results of others prior to their commit, isolation is no longer feasible. We mention two concrete proposals in that direction. *Sagas* are introduced by Garcia-Molina & Salem [1987] as (two-level) chains of atomic subtransactions in which an abort of a subtransaction results in its rollback, but for which an abort of the entire transaction results in a rollback of active subtransactions and a *compensation* of already committed ones. *ConTracts* [Reuter & Wächter, 1991] are fault-tolerant executions of sequences of predefined steps according to an explicitly given control flow description.

4. Current directions

In Section 1.4 we mentioned several new application domains for database management and argued that these come with a number of specific requirements. In Section 2.7 we indicated in what way especially their data modeling requirements might be met. In Section 3.4 we pointed out that, on the other hand, even in traditional application domains some issues might need additional attention beyond what has been achieved so far. In general, the requirements to database support that come from nonstandard applications differ from one domain to the next, and also differ from most of the issues considered unresolved in traditional applications. Therefore, it is not surprising that much research activity in recent years has considered individual aspects in the first place, some important ones of which will be sketched in this section. However, it also became clear that future database systems will need a functionality that can handle a variety of such issues, so that appropriate combinations are apt. While research and development has also investigated this, the big question behind it is whether there is a unifying paradigm upon which next-generation systems can be built. We conclude this chapter by describing the currently most prominent such paradigm, which consists of integrating object-orientation into database management.

4.1. Specific research issues

In this section we survey several features that next-generation database systems are likely to support; some of these are domain-specific, while others arise in one form or another in or are relevant to various domains.

4.1.1. Time in databases

A feature of current database systems that has been criticized early on is that information becomes effective the moment it is recorded in the database. In other words, databases represent the state of an enterprise at a single moment of time. For example, if a university administration keeps an employee database, it is easy to record the fact, say, that Peter is an assistant professor; if he gets promoted to the associated level, the former entry is updated. As a consequence, the information that Peter once *was* an assistant professor is no longer available. Also, updating Peter's record prior to his new appointment (thereby recording that he *will be* an associate professor from a certain date on) would result in an incorrect image of the underlying world. Thus, standard databases view updates as modifications of the state of the underlying application and cannot distinguish between the *registration time* at which certain data is entered into the database, and the *logical time* period for which the given data values are (or were) valid. *Temporal* databases are an attempt to overcome these limitations by supporting *transaction time* as well as *valid time*, where the former is used for recording the history of updates and the latter for recording a history of the real world. They can record, for example, retroactive changes, where a new value became valid in the real world before it was recorded in the database, or proactive ones, where a new value will become valid in the real world after it has been entered into the database. Applications of. temporal databases include payroll and accounting systems or medical information systems (where a patient's medical history is important). The issues investigated in this area include the formulation of a semantics of time at the conceptual database level, the development of a data model capturing temporal aspects (with appropriate operations), and the design and implementation of temporal query languages. Snodgrass [1990] is a recent survey of the field.

4.1.2. Spatial data

In brief, a *spatial* database contains multi-dimensional data with explicit knowledge about data objects, their extent and position in space. Spatial data arises in mechanical CAD, VLSI CAD, cartography and other domains, including robotics, visual perception, autonomous navigation or medical imaging. For example, in CAD the objects are three-dimensional, in cartography they are typically two-dimensional. What these applications have in common is their need to manage geometrical data, i.e., data for which a geometric component is characteristic. For example, a VLSI chip with multiple layers can be described in terms of rectangles positioned parallel to the axes of the Euclidean plane; in cartography, polygons delimiting areas are used to describe how a large area is composed of smaller ones. Geometrical objects are typically complex with respect to their geometry, which requires specific operations like computing the intersection of two polygons, and with respect to their representation, e.g., a polygon with many edges. Geometric operations refer to the positioning of objects in space and frequently also to distances. For example, a *range query* asks for all objects having a nonempty intersection with a given region; a *nearest-neighbor query* asks for the object that is closest to a given point. Spatial *data structures* support queries to geometric objects by providing efficient access to them; spatial *query languages* allow an easy formulation of such queries. An important point is that the specific application domains have distinct requirements to spatial data management, so that many techniques developed for data representation, storage and access or for language support are case-specific. A survey of the field is Günther & Buchmann [1990].

4.1.3. Scientific data

Natural sciences like physics or biology are another domain of forthcoming database support. What is needed here are *scientific* databases, i.e., databases containing data that represents structural or functional models or results from experiments, like measurements of physical phenomena, and simulations. In addition, they contain data describing the configuration or instrumentation of an experiment, and data derived from the results of an experiment or simulation. Typically, all this data is subject to further analysis, and the nature of such an analysis determines which representation of the data is appropriate. Also, the data is usually huge in volume; for example, in a database containing human genome information describing DNA structures base data volume is in the order 10^9 nucleotides (letters from the alphabet $\{A, C, T, G\}$). Finally, the data might be imprecise, so that uncertainty must be taken into account when the data is evaluated. An introduction to this field is Shoshani, Olken & Wong [1984].

4.1.4. Realtime and activeness in databases

A realtime system roughly consists of a controlled process, i.e., the underlying application, and a controller which monitors the status of the process and supplies it with appropriate driving signals. The important aspect is that the supported application has stringent timing constraints, i.e., when the process reaches a certain state some actions are required instantaneously. The controller must thus be capable of responding to state changes within very short periods of time.

A *realtime* database incorporates timing constraints into a database. In particular, transactions executing on the database are not only required to perform correctly, but they must additionally complete their execution within a specified deadline. For example, a computer-controlled stock market is a process whose state is partially captured by variables such as current stock prices, changes in stock prices, volume of trading, trends and composite indexes. These variables can be stored in a database, in which one type of process then continuously senses the market and updates the database as new information becomes available. Another type of process might analyze the information in the database in order to respond to a user query, e.g., a query asking for a current bid or the price of a particular stock, or to initiate a trade in the stock market. It is clear that both types of processes must meet realtime constraints. Another application of realtime databases is threat analysis, where the system consists of a radar to track objects and a computer to perform image processing and control. A radar signature is collected and compared against a database of signatures of known objects, which must be done in realtime.

The issues to be investigated for realtime database systems involve the search for an appropriate data model, the design of languages for specifying realtime constraints, and of methods for describing and evaluating triggers, i.e., events or conditions in the database that cause certain actions to occur. A primary design objective for such a system is to attain extremely fast response for updates and queries. Since database operations are mostly I/O bound, one approach here is the elimination of disk accesses, i.e., storing the entire database in main memory. See Son [1988] for a survey of the field.

The issue of triggers also relates to the fact that conventional databases are *passive* data repositories, i.e., to determine whether a change to data in the database has made a condition become true, an external query has to be issued. If the answer to this query must be available within a predefined short time interval, one solution is to poll the database on a regular basis. *Active* database systems are intended to provide the basic mechanisms for reducing the waste of time typically incurred by polling. Conditions can be defined on database states, and events and corresponding actions can be defined as part of the database. A survey is Dayal [1988].

4.1.5. Extensibility

We have mentioned several times in this exposition that the need of advanced data models is crucial in new applications, and the discussion in Section 2.7 indicated that straightforward extensions of the relational model might not be good enough. What people have tried then is to do something that is common in programming languages, namely to allow users to define 'arbitrary' data types using some given base types plus constructors that are orthogonal to the base types. In Section 2.7, we showed how this idea can lead to complex-object models. The key system functionality that supports this is *extensibility*, i.e., the ability of a system to accept new type definitions as well as operations on these types from users at any time, and to support them in the same way as the built-in types and operations are supported. Clearly, this only covers the logical side of a database, and the question arises whether this is all that extensibility should mean in a system context. To this end, several proposals have been made; ultimately, the idea is to *configure* logically *and physically* extensible systems from certain kernel facilities along a given architectural framework. Building a complete system then requires the use of a *generator* which derives the system from these so that it is customized for a specific application domain. Thus, a DBMS generator contains tools to (at least partially) automate the generation of a full DBMS, and typically also libraries of software components that are useful for various application domains. One such toolbox is Exodus [Carey & DeWitt, 1987; Richardson & Carey, 1987], another Genesis [Batory, Barnett, Garza, Smith, Tsukuda, Twichell & Wise, 1988; Batory, Leung & Wise, 1988].

4.1.6. Database programming languages

We mentioned in Section 2.5.2 that one way to cope with the limited expressive power of relational algebra is to *embed* it in a host programming language. The obvious problem with this approach is a loss of the relational abstraction concept, which is available in the algebra, but not in a programming language.

In general, a programming language differs from a database language in that it considers data and programs as integrated, and optimization is concerned with program execution. Also, there is only one level of abstraction: an external level is unknown, and the conceptual and the physical levels are not clearly separated. In addition, the computational paradigm is often imperative, but almost never declarative. Finally, the atomic unit of work is one record at a time, and persistence can only be achieved by *explicit* reads and writes to secondary storage. However, programming languages are computationally ('Turing') complete and therefore attractive for many database system developers to gain the expressive power needed for their domains of application. As a result, many efforts are currently underway towards integrating database and programming languages into *database programming languages* (DBPLs).

Clearly, simple host language embeddings need to use *cursors* on relations for processing one tuple at a time, procedure calls in a program to access the database or a mapping between the two distinct underlying name spaces. These problems, subsumed under the term *impedance mismatch*, have serious implications. At development time, a programmer has to convert data back and forth, know two languages and their underlying paradigms, decide where processing should take place, etc. At execution time, a user has to pay the cost of communication between two processes. The impedance mismatch problem is partially due to a lack of extensibility as discussed in Section 4.1.5. In addition, it results in a limited support for interoperability (as discussed in Section 1.4.3) provided by current database languages. Indeed, even for coupling a database language with a customized user interface or for enabling data exchange with standard software, only ad-hoc solutions are yet available, which fall short of providing a single and truly integrated linguistic framework.

Various attempts are currently being made at solving the impedance mismatch problem for database application programming, among them object-oriented database systems as sketched in the next subsection and DBPLs. Surveys of this latter field are given by Atkinson [1990], Atkinson & Buneman [1987], Bancilhon & Buneman [1990], and Schmidt & Matthes [1990].

4.2. Object-orientation in databases

In this final subsection we describe a paradigm that has attracted the attention of lots of database researchers over the past ten years, *object-orientation*, in some detail. We mention that this is not the only paradigm that people have recognized as a possible framework in which a number of requirements to future database systems can be treated in a uniform manner. Indeed, another such paradigm is logic orientation, for which we discussed some basics in Section 2.6 since it directly grew out of a logical interpretation of the relational model. Recent surveys of the area of deductive databases are provided by Zaniolo [1990] and Tsur [1991]; we concentrate here on object-orientation since this has not yet been discussed in this chapter.

Object-orientation has been recognized as an important new paradigm in the area of programming languages ever since the arrival of the language *Simula*. It is roughly based on five fundamental principles [Bertino & Martino, 1991; Khoshafian & Abnous, 1990; Stein & Maier, 1988]:

(1) Each entity of the real world is modeled as an *object* which has an existence of its own, manifested in terms of a unique *identifier* (distinct from its value).

(2) Each object has *encapsulated* into it a *structure* and a *behavior*. The former is described in terms of attributes (*instance variables*), where attribute values, which together represent the state of the object, can be other objects so that complex objects can be defined via aggregation. The latter consists of a set of *methods*, i.e., procedures that can be executed on the object.

(3) The state of an object can be accessed or modified exclusively by sending *messages* to the object, which causes it to invoke a corresponding method.

(4) Objects sharing the same structure and behavior are grouped into *classes*, where a class represents a 'template' for a set of similar objects. Each object is an instance of some class.

(5) A class can be defined as a specialization of one or more other classes. A class defined as a specialization forms a *subclass* and *inherits* both structure and behavior (i.e., attributes and methods) from its *superclasses*.

In the area of programming languages and also of software engineering, the introduction of these principles marked a radical departure from the conventional view (found in languages like Fortran and Algol) that *active functions operate on passive (data) objects*. Instead, the goal now is to have *active objects react to messages from other objects*. It was recognized that they are crucial for achieving *data abstraction* and *information hiding*, and for supporting *modularity*, *reusability* and *extensibility* in program designs.

Considering the success of the object-oriented paradigm in these areas, it is not surprising that a merger of object-orientation and database technology seems promising, basically for similar reasons that were mentioned in Section 2.6 as motivations for a merger of logic orientation and databases. While initially there has been a lot of confusion about what an *object-oriented database system* (OODBS) actually is, a working definition was established by Atkinson, Bancilhon, DeWitt, Dittrich, Maier & Zdonik [1989]: an OODBS is characterized by *modeling*, *language* and *system* properties, which capture the following features. First, the modeling capabilities of an OODBS must support complex objects, each of which has a unique identity [Khoshafian & Copeland, 1986], a (data) type and belongs to a class that is positioned in an inheritance hierarchy. Second, the language features support encapsulation of object behavior (into the corresponding class) and reusability in the form that message names may be *overloaded* or can be *overridden* in specializations (implying that *late binding* of methods to message names, i.e., at runtime, is necessary). New types can be defined from existing ones by using given constructors, and the language of the system combines ad-hoc query capabilities with the expressive power of a programming language. Finally, an OODBS should be a database system, meaning that it supports persistence, secondary storage management, concurrency control and recovery.

It is clear that these characteristics create many new challenges in terms of research and development, including data models for objects, operations on objects ('object algebras'), database design, evolution of database schemata, query languages, query processing and optimization, transaction processing, versioning, storage organization and performance evaluation. Some of these are discussed by Bancilhon [1989], Beeri [1990], Cattell [1991] and Kim [1990] as well as in the papers collected by Cardenas & McLeod [1990], Kim & Lochovsky [1989], and Zdonik & Maier [1990].

The current situation in the field is remarkably different from that of relational systems some 20 years ago, since the latter started from a strong theoretical foundation, but no consensus is yet in sight regarding a formal theory of OODBS (Agrawal [1991] is a survey of notable approaches in this direction). In spite of this, several OODBS are already commercially available, and many others close to being marketed (see Vossen [1991b] for details). Nevertheless, the general agreement seems to be that OODBS will constitute the next generation of database management systems, and that future releases of current systems will increasingly support features attributed to object-orientation. Indeed, the object-oriented paradigm has already been fruitfully applied to solving the data management problems in various new application domains [Gupta & Horowitz, 1991].

Acknowledgements

Most of this chapter was written while I was still affiliated with the Technical University of Aachen, where I have spent the last 10 years of my professional life (except for several visiting appointments). So it reflects what I have learned about databases and database management during my Aachen years, and I want to thank my former advisor, Prof. Walter Oberschelp, for all the ideas and support I received from him during this time. I am grateful to Kurt-Ulrich Witt, the editors of this volume and to an anonymous referee for constructive remarks on an earlier version of this chapter.

References

Abiteboul, S. (1988). Updates, a new frontier, *Proc. 2nd International Conference on Database Theory (ICDT)*, LNCS 326, Springer, Berlin, pp. 1–18.

Abiteboul, S., P.C. Fischer, H.J. Schek (eds.) (1989). *Nested Relations and Complex Objects in Database*, LNCS 361, Springer, Berlin.

Abiteboul, S., S. Grumbach (1991). A rule-based language with functions and sets. *ACM Trans. Database Systems* 16, 1–30.

Abiteboul, S., V. Vianu (1988). Equivalence and optimization of relational transactions. *J. ACM* 35, 70–120.

Abiteboul, S., V. Vianu (1990). Procedural languages for database queries and updates. *J. Comput. System Sci.* 41, 181–229.

Abiteboul, S., V. Vianu (1991). Datalog extensions for database queries and updates. *J. Comput. System Sci.* 43, 62–124.

Abiteboul, S., V. Vianu (1992). Expressive power of query languages, in: J.D. Ullman (ed.), *Theoretical Studies in Computer Science*, Academic Press, Boston, MA, pp. 207–251.

Agrawal, R. (ed.) (1991). Special issue on theoretical foundations of object-oriented database systems. *IEEE Computer Society Bulletin on Data Engineering* 14(2).

Aho, A.V., C. Beeri, J.D. Ullman (1979). The theory of joins in relational databases. *ACM Trans. Database Systems* 4, 297–314.

Aho, A.V., J.D. Ullman (1979). Universality of data retrieval languages, *Proc. 6th ACM Symposium on Principles of Programming Languages*, ACM, New York, pp. 110–120.

Apt, K.R., M.H. van Emden (1982). Contributions to the theory of logic programming. *J. ACM.* 29, 841–862.

Armstrong, W.W. (1974). Dependency structures of data base relationships, in: *Proc. IFIP Congress*, pp. 580–583.

Astrahan, M.M., M.W. Blasgen, D.D. Chamberlin, K.P. Eswaran, J.N. Gray, P.P. Griffiths, W.F. King, R.A. Lorie, P.R. McJones, J.W. Mehl, G.R. Putzolu, I.L. Traiger, B.W. Wade, V. Watson (1976). System/R: A relational approach to data base management. *ACM Trans. Database Systems* 1, 97–137.

Atkinson, M. (1990). Questioning persistent types, *Proc. 2nd International Workshop on Database Programming Languages*, Morgan Kaufmann, San Mateo, CA, pp. 2–24.

Atkinson, M., F. Bancilhon, D. DeWitt, K. Dittrich, D. Maier, S. Zdonik (1989). The object-oriented database system manifesto, *Proc. 1st International Conference on Deductive and Object-Oriented Databases*, pp. 40–57.

Atkinson, M., P. Buneman (1987). Types and persistence in database programming languages. *ACM Comput. Surveys* 19, 106–190.

Bachman, C.W. (1973). The programmer as navigator. *Commun. ACM* 16, 653–658.

Bancilhon, F. (1989). Query languages for object-oriented database systems: Analysis and a proposal, *Proc. 3rd GI/SI Conference on "Datenbank-Systeme für Büro, Technik und Wissenschaft"*, Informatik-Fachbericht No. 204, Springer, Berlin, pp. 1–18.

Bancilhon, F., P. Buneman (eds.) (1990). *Advances in Database Programming Languages*, Addison-Wesley, Reading, MA (ACM Press Frontier Series).

Bancilhon, F., S. Khoshafian (1989). A calculus for complex objects. *J. Comput. System Sci.* 38, 326–340.

Bancilhon, F., R. Ramakrishnan (1986). An amateur's introduction to recursive query processing strategies, *Proc. ACM SIGMOD International Conference on Management of Data*, ACM, New York, pp. 16–52.

Batini, C., S. Ceri, S.B. Navathe (1992). *Conceptual Database Design – An Entity-Relationship Approach*, Benjamin/Cummings, Redwood City, CA.

Batory, D.S., J.R. Barnett, J.F. Garza, K.P. Smith, K. Tsukuda, B.C. Twichell, T.E. Wise (1988). GENESIS: An extensible database management system. *IEEE Trans. Software Engrg.* SE-14, 1711–1729.

Batory, D.S., W. Kim (1985). Modeling concepts for VLSI CAD objects. *ACM Trans. Database Systems* 10, 322–346.

Batory, D.S., T.Y. Leung, T.E. Wise (1988). Implementation concepts for an extensible data model and data language. *ACM Trans. Database Systems* 13, 231–262.

Beeri, C. (1990). A formal approach to object oriented databases. *Data & Knowledge Engineering* 5, 353–382.

Beeri, C., P.A. Bernstein (1979). Computational problems related to the design of normal form relational schemas. *ACM Trans. Database Systems* 4, 30–59.

Beeri, C., P.A. Bernstein, N. Goodman (1978). A sophisticate's introduction to database normalization theory, *Proc. 4th International Conference on Very Large Data Bases*, Morgan Kaufmann, San Mateo, CA, pp. 113–124.

Beeri, C., P.A. Bernstein, N. Goodman (1989). A model for concurrency in nested transaction systems. *J. ACM* 36, 230–269.

Beeri, C., R. Fagin, J.H. Howard (1977). A complete axiomatization for functional and multi-valued dependencies, *Proc. ACM SIGMOD International Conference on Management of Data*, ACM, New York, pp. 47–61.

Beeri, C., H.J. Schek, G. Weikum (1988). Multi-level transaction management, theoretical art of practical need?, *Proc. 1st International Conference on Extending Database Technology (EDBT)*, LNCS 303, Springer, New York, pp. 134–154.

Bernstein, P.A. (1976). Synthesizing third normal form relations from functional dependencies. *ACM Trans. Database Systems* 1, 272–298.

Bernstein, P.A., N. Goodman (1983). Multiversion concurrency control – Theory and algorithms. *ACM Trans. Database Systems* 8, 465–483.

Bernstein, P.A., N. Goodman, V. Hadzilacos (1983). Recovery algorithms for database systems, in: R.E.A. Mason (ed.), *Information Processing 83*, Proc. IFIP Congress, North-Holland, Amsterdam, pp. 799–807.

Bernstein, P.A., N. Goodman, M.Y. Lai (1983). Analyzing concurrency control algorithms when user and system operations differ. *IEEE Trans. Software Engrg.* SE-9, 233–239.

Bernstein, P.A., V. Hadzilacos, N. Goodman (1987). *Concurrency Control and Recovery in Database Systems*, Addison-Wesley, Reading, MA.

Bertino, E., L. Martino (1991). Object-oriented database management systems: Concepts and issues. *IEEE Computer* 24(4), 33–47.

Bidoit, N. Negation in rule-based database languages: A survey. *Theoret. Comput. Sci.* 78, 3–83.

Biskup, J., U. Dayal, P.A. Bernstein (1979). Synthesizing independent database schemas, *Proc. ACM SIGMOD International Conference on Management of Data*, ACM, New York, pp. 143–151.

Bitton, D., D.J. DeWitt, C. Turbyfill (1983). Benchmarking database systems – A systematic approach, *Proc. 9th International Conference on Very Large Data Bases*, Morgan Kaufmann, San Mateo, CA, pp. 8–19.

Blasgen, M.W., M.M., Astrahan, D.D. Chamberlin, J.N. Gray, W.F. King, B.G. Lindsay, R.A. Lorie, J.W. Mehl, T.G. Price, G.R. Putzolu, M. Schkolnick, P.G. Selinger, D.R. Slutz, H.R. Strong, I.L. Traiger, B.W. Wade, R.A. Yost (1981). System/R: An architectural overview. *IBM Syst. J.* 20, 41–61.

Bry, F. (1990). Query evaluation in recursive databases: Bottom-up and top-down reconciled. *Data & Knowledge Engineering* 5, 289–312.

Cardenas, A.F., D. McLeod (eds.) (1990). *Research Foundations in Object-Oriented and Semantic Database Systems*, Prentice-Hall, Englewood Cliffs, NJ.

Carey, M.J., D.J. DeWitt (1987). An overview of the EXODUS project. *IEEE Computer Society Bulletin on Database Engineering* 10(2), 47–54.

Carey, M.J., M.R. Stonebraker (1984). The performance of concurrency control algorithms for database management systems, *Proc. 10th International Conference on Very Large Data Bases*, Morgan Kaufmann, San Mateo, CA, pp. 107–118.

Casanova, M.A., R. Fagin, C.H. Papadimitriou (1984). Inclusion dependencies and their interaction with functional dependencies. *J. Comput. System Sci.* 28, 29–59.

Casanova, M.A., L. Tucherman, A.L. Furtado, A.P. Braga (1989). Optimization of relational schemas containing inclusion dependencies, *Proc. 15th International Conference on Very Large Data Bases*, Morgan Kaufmann, San Mateo, CA, pp. 317–325.

Cattell, R.G.G. (1991). *Object Data Management – Object-Oriented and Extended Relational Database Systems*, Addison-Wesley, Reading, MA.

Ceri, S., G. Gottlob (1985). Translating SQL into relational algebra: Optimization, semantics, and equivalence of SQL queries. *IEEE Trans. Software Engrg.* SE-11, 324–345.

Ceri, S., G. Gottlob, L. Tanca (1989). What you always wanted to know about Datalog (and never dared to ask). *IEEE Transactions on Knowledge and Data Engineering* 1, 146–166.

Ceri, S., G. Gottlob, L. Tanca (1990). *Logic Programming and Databases*, Springer, Berlin.

Chandra, A.K. (1988). Theory of database queries, *Proc. 7th ACM SIGACT-SIGMOD-SIGART Symposium on Principles of Database Systems*, ACM, New York, pp. 1–9.

Chandra, A.K., D. Harel (1980). Computable queries for relational data bases. *J. Comput. System Sci.* 21, 156–178.

Chandra, A.K., D. Harel (1982). Structure and complexity of relational queries. *J. Comput. System Sci.* 25, 99–128.

Chen, P.P.-S. (1976). The entity-relationship model – Toward a unified view of data. *ACM Trans. Database Systems* 1, 9–36.

Chen, P.P.-S. (1985). Database design based on entity and relationship, in: Yao [1985], pp. 174–210.

Chimenti, D., R. Gamboa, R. Krishnamurthy, S. Naqvi, S. Tsur, C. Zaniolo (1990). The LDL System Prototype. *IEEE Trans. Knowledge and Data Engineering* 2, 76–90.

Clemons, E. (1985). Data models and the ANSI/SPARC architecture, in: Yao [1985], pp. 66–114.

CODASYL (1971). *Data Base Task Group April 71 Report*, ACM, New York.

CODASYL (1978). Report of the Data Description Language Committee. *Inf. Systems* 3, 247–320.

Codd, E.F. (1970). A relational model of data for large shared data banks. *Commun. ACM* 13, 377–387.

Codd, E.F. (1979). Extending the database relational model to capture more meaning. *ACM Trans. Database Systems* 4, 397–434.

Codd, E.F. (1982). Relational databases: A practical foundation for productivity. *Commun. ACM* 25, 109–117.

Codd, E.F. (1986). An evaluation scheme for database management systems that are claimed to be relational, *Proc. 2nd IEEE International Conference on Data Engineering*, IEEE Computer Society Press, Los Alamitos, CA, pp. 720–729.

Codd, E.F. (1990). *The Relational Model for Database Management Version 2*, Addison-Wesley, Reading, MA.

Database Architecture Framework Task Group. (1986). Reference model for DBMS standardization. *ACM SIGMOD Record* 15(1), 19–58.

Date, C.J. (1989). *A Guide to the SQL Standard, 2nd edition*, Addison-Wesley, Reading, MA.

Date, C.J. (1990). *An Introduction to Database Systems, Vol. 1, 4th edition*, Addison-Wesley, Reading, MA.

Dayal, U. (1988). Active database management systems, *Proc. 3rd International Conference on*

Data and Knowledge Bases: Improving Usability and Responsiveness, Jerusalem, Israel, Morgan Kaufmann, San Mateo, CA, pp. 150–169.

Du, W., A.K. Elmagarmid (1989). Quasi serializability: A correctness criterion for global concurrency in InterBase, *Proc. 15th International Conference on Very Large Data Bases*, Morgan Kaufmann, San Mateo, CA, pp. 347–355.

Elmagarmid, A. (ed.) (1991). Special issue on unconventional transaction management. *IEEE Computer Society Bulletin on Data Engineering* 14(1).

Elmagarmid, A., C. Pu (eds.) (1990). Special issue on heterogeneous databases. *ACM Comput. Surveys* 22(3).

Elmasri, R.A., S.B. Navathe (1989). *Fundamentals of Database Systems*, Benjamin/Cummings, Redwood, CA.

Eswaran, K.P., J.N. Gray, R.A. Lorie, I.L. Traiger (1976). The notions of consistency and predicate locks in a database system. *Commun. ACM* 19, 624–633.

Fagin, R. (1977). The decomposition versus the synthetic approach to relational database design, *Proc. 3rd International Conference on Very Large Data Bases*, Morgan Kaufmann, San Mateo, CA, pp. 441–446.

Fagin, R. (1983). Degrees of acyclicity for hypergraphs and relational database schemes. *J. ACM* 30, 514–550.

Fagin, R., M.Y. Vardi (1984). The theory of data dependencies – An overview, *Proc. 11th International Colloquium on Automata, Languages, and Programming (ICALP)*, LNCS 172, Springer, Berlin, pp. 1–22.

Fekete, A., N. Lynch, M. Merritt, W. Weihl (1990). Commutativity-based locking for nested transactions. *J. Comput. System Sci.* 41, 65–156.

Garcia-Molina, H. (1983). Using semantic knowledge for transaction processing in a distributed database. *ACM Trans. Database Systems* 8, 186–213.

Garcia-Molina, H., K. Salem (1987). Sagas, *Proc. ACM SIGMOD International Conference on Management of Data*, ACM, New York, pp. 249–259.

Gardarin, G., P. Valduriez (1989). *Relational Databases and Knowledge Bases*, Addison-Wesley, Reading, MA.

Gawlick, D. (1985). Processing 'hot spots' in high performance systems, *Proc. 13th IEEE COMPCON Spring Conference*, IEEE Computer Society Press, Los Alamitos, CA, pp. 249–251.

Goodman, N., O. Shmueli, Y.C. Tay (1984). GYO reductions, canonical connections, tree and cyclic schemas, and tree projections. *J. Comput. System Sci.* 29, 338–358.

Gray, J. (1978). Notes on data base operating systems, in: R. Bayer, M.R. Graham, G. Seegmüller (eds.), *Operating Systems – An Advanced Course*, LNCS 60, Springer, Berlin, pp. 393–481.

Gray, J. (1981). The transaction concept: Virtues and limitations, *Proc. 7th International Conference on Very Large Data Bases*, Morgan Kaufmann, San Mateo, CA, pp. 144–154.

Gray, J. (ed.) (1991). *The Benchmark Handbook for Database and Transaction Processing Systems*, Morgan Kaufmann, San Mateo, CA.

Günther, O., A. Buchmann (1990). Research issues in spatial databases. *ACM SIGMOD Record* 19(4), 61–68.

Gupta, R., E. Horowitz (eds.) (1991). *Object-Oriented Databases With Applications to CASE, Networks, and VLSI CAD*, Prentice-Hall, Englewood Cliffs, NJ.

Gyssens, M., D. van Gucht (1988). The powerset algebra as a result of adding programming constructs to the nested relational algebra, *Proc. ACM SIGMOD International Conference on Management of Data*, ACM, New York, pp. 225–232.

Gyssens, M., D. van Gucht (1991). A comparison between algebraic query languages for flat and nested databases. *Theoret. Comput. Sci.* 87, 263–286.

Hadzilacos, V. (1988). A theory of reliability in database systems. *J. ACM* 35, 121–145.

Hadzilacos, T., C.H. Papadimitriou (1986). Algorithmic aspects of multiversion concurrency control. *J. Comput. System Sci.* 33, 297–310.

Härder, T. (1988). Handling hot spot data in DB-sharing systems. *Inf. Systems* 13, 155–166.

Härder, T., A. Reuter (1983). Principles of transaction-oriented database recovery. *ACM Comput. Surveys* 15, 287–317.

Hull, R. (1987). A survey of theoretical research on typed complex database objects, in: J. Paredaens (ed.), *Databases*. Academic Press, London, pp. 193–256.

Hull, R., R. King (1987). Semantic database modeling: Survey, applications, and research issues. *ACM Comput. Surveys* 19, 201–260.

Immermann, N. (1986). Relational queries computable in polynomial time. *Inform. and Control* 68, 86–104.

Jäschke, G., H.J. Schek (1982). Remarks on the algebra of non first normal form relations, *Proc. 1st ACM SIGACT-SIGMOD Symposium on Principles of Database Systems*, ACM, New York, pp. 124–138.

Kanellakis, P.C. (1990). Elements of relational database theory, in: J. van Leeuwen (ed.), *Handbook of Theoretical Computer Science, Vol. B: Formal Models and Semantics*, North-Holland, Amsterdam, pp. 1073–1156.

Katz, R.H. (1985). *Information Management for Engineering Design*, Springer Berlin.

Katz, R.H. (1990). Toward a unified framework for version modeling in engineering databases. *ACM Comput. Surveys* 22, 375–408.

Kent, W. (1979). Limitations of record-based information models. *ACM Trans. Database Systems* 4, 107–131.

Kent, W. (1983). A simple guide to five normal forms in relational database theory. *Commun. ACM* 26, 120–125.

Khoshafian, S.N., R. Abnous (1990). *Object-Orientation – Concepts, Languages, Databases, User Interfaces*, Wiley, New York.

Khoshafian, S.N., G.P. Copeland (1986). Object identity, *OOPSLA '86 Proceedings*, pp. 406–416.

Kim, W. (1990). *Introduction to Object-Oriented Databases*, The MIT Press, Cambridge, MA.

Kim, W., F.H. Lochovsky (eds.) (1989). *Object-Oriented Concepts, Databases, and Applications*, Addison-Wesley, Reading, MA.

Kim, W., D.S. Reiner, D.S. Batory (eds.) (1985). *Query Processing in Database Systems*, Springer, Berlin.

King, R., D. McLeod (1985). Semantic data models, in: Yao [1985], pp. 115–150.

Korth, H.F., A. Silberschatz (1991). *Database System Concepts, 2nd ed.*, McGraw-Hill, New York.

Korth, H.F., G. Speegle (1988). Formal model of correctness without serializability, *Proc. ACM SIGMOD International Conference on Management of Data*, ACM, New York, pp. 379–386.

Laguna Beach Participants (1989). Future directions in DBMS research. *ACM SIGMOD Record* 18(1), 17–26.

Langerak, R. (1990). View updates in relational databases with an independent scheme. *ACM Trans. Database Systems* 15, 40–66.

Lien, Y.E. (1985). Relational database design, in: Yao [1985], pp. 211–254.

Lipski, W. (1977). Two NP-complete problems related to information retrieval, in: M. Karpinski (ed.), *Fundamentals of Computation Theory (Proc. of the FCT-Conference)*, LNCS 56, Springer, Berlin, pp. 452–458.

Lloyd, J.W. (1987). *Foundations of Logic Programming, 3rd edition*, Springer, Berlin.

Lockemann, P.C., A. Kemper, G. Moerkotte (1990). Future database technology: Driving forces and directions, *Proc. Database Systems of the 90s*, LNCS 466, Springer, Berlin, pp. 15–33.

Lynch, N. (1983). Multilevel atomicity – A new correctness criterion for database concurrency control. *ACM Trans. Database Systems* 8, 484–502.

Lynch, N., M. Merritt (1988). Introduction to the theory of nested transactions. *Theoret. Comput. Sci.* 62, 123–185.

Maier, D. (1983). *The Theory of Relational Databases*, Computer Science Press, Rockville, MD.

Maier, D., J.D. Ullman, M.Y. Vardi (1984). On the foundations of the universal relation model. *ACM Trans. Database Systems* 9, 283–308.

Maier, D., D.S. Warren (1988). *Computing with Logic – Logic Programming with Prolog*, Benjamin/Cummings, Menlo Park, CA.

Makinouchi, A. (1977). A consideration on normal form of not-necessarily-normalized relation in the relational data model, *Proc. 3rd International Conference on Very Large Data Bases*, Morgan Kaufmann, San Mateo, CA, pp. 447–453.

Minker, J. (ed.) (1988). *Foundations of Deductive Databases and Logic Programming*, Morgan Kaufmann, Los Altos, CA.

Mitchell, J.C. (1983). Inference rules for functional and inclusion dependencies, *Proc. 2nd ACM SIGACT-SIGMOD Symposium on Principles of Database Systems*, ACM, New York, pp. 58–69.

Moss, J.E.B. (1985). *Nested Transactions: An Approach to Reliable Distributed Computing*, MIT Press, Cambridge, MA.

Naqvi, S., S. Tsur (1989). *A Logical Language for Data and Knowledge Bases*, Computer Science Press, New York.

Özsoyoglu, Z.M., L.Y. Yuan (1987). A new normal form for nested relations. *ACM Trans. Database Systems* 12, 111–136.

Özsu, M.T., P. Valduriez (1991a). *Principles of Distributed Database Systems*, Prentice-Hall, Englewood Cliffs, NJ.

Özsu, M.T., P. Valduriez (1991b). Distributed database systems: Where are we now? *IEEE Computer* 24(8), 68–78.

Papadimitriou, C.H. (1979). The serializability of concurrent database updates. *J. ACM* 26, 631–653.

Papadimitriou, C.H. (1982). A theorem in database concurrency control. *J. ACM* 29, 998–1006.

Papadimitriou, C.H. (1983). Concurrency control by locking. *SIAM J. Comput.* 12, 215–226.

Papadimitriou, C.H. (1986). *The Theory of Database Concurrency Control*, Computer Science Press, Rockville, MD.

Papadimitriou, C.H., P.C. Kanellakis (1984). On concurrency control by multiple versions. *ACM Trans. Database Systems* 9, 89–99.

Papazoglou, M., W. Valder (1989). *Relational Database Management – A Systems Programming Approach*, Prentice-Hall, New York.

Paredaens, J., P. De Bra, M. Gyssens, D. van Gucht (1989). *The Structure of the Relational Database Model*, EATCS Monographs on Theoretical Computer Science No. 17, Springer, Berlin.

Peckham, J., F. Maryanski (1988). Semantic data models. *ACM Comput. Surveys* 20, 153–189.

Reiner, D. (ed.) (1990). Special issue on database connectivity. *IEEE Computer Society Bulletin on Data Engineering* 13(2).

Reiner, D. (1992). Database design tools, in: Batini, Ceri and Navathe [1992], pp. 411–454.

Reuter, A., H. Wächter (1991). The ConTract model, in: Elmagarmid [1991], pp. 39–43.

Richardson, J.E., M.J. Carey (1987). Programming constructs for database system implementation in EXODUS, *Proc. ACM SIGMOD International Conference on Management of Data*, ACM, New York, pp. 208–219.

Rissanen, J. (1977). Independent components of relations. *ACM Trans. Database Systems* 2, 317–325.

Rissanen, J. (1978). Theory of relations for databases – A tutorial survey, *Proc. 7th Symposium on Mathematical Foundations of Computer Science*, LNCS 64, Springer, Berlin, pp. 537–551.

Roth, M.A., H.F. Korth, D.S. Batory (1987). SQL/NF: A query language for ¬1NF relational databases. *Inf. Systems* 12, 99–114.

Roth, M.A., H.F. Korth, A. Silberschatz (1988). Extended algebra and calculus for nested relational databases. *ACM Trans. Database Systems* 13, 389–417.

Sagiv, Y. (1983). A characterization of globally consistent databases and their correct access paths. *ACM Trans. Database Systems* 8, 266–286.

Sagiv, Y., C. Delobel, D.S. Parker, R. Fagin (1981). An equivalence between relational database dependencies and a fragment of propositional logic. *J. ACM* 28, 435–453.

Schek, H.J., M.H. Scholl (1986). The relational model with relation-valued attributes. *Inf. Systems* 11, 137–147.

Schek, H.J., M.H. Scholl (1990). Evolution of data models, *Proc. Database Systems of the 90s*, LNCS 466, Springer, Berlin, pp. 135–153.

Schmidt, J.W., M.L. Brodie (1983). *Relational Database Systems – Analysis and Comparison*, Springer-Verlag, Berlin.

Schmidt, J.W., F. Matthes (1990). Language technology for post-relational data systems, *Proc. Database Systems of the 90s*, LNCS 466, Springer, Berlin, pp. 81–114.

Schwarz, P.M., A.Z. Spector (1984). Synchronizing shared abstract types. *ACM Trans. Computer Systems* 2, 223–250.

Shasha, D., N. Goodman (1988). Concurrent search structure algorithms. *ACM Trans. Database Systems* 13, 53–90.

Shaw, P. (1990). Database language standards: Past, present, and future, *Proc. Database Systems of the 90s*, LNCS 466, Springer, Berlin, pp. 55–80.

Shoshani, A., F. Olken, H.K.T. Wong (1984). Characteristics of scientific databases, *Proc. 10th International Conference on Very Large Data Bases*, Morgan Kaufmann, San Mateo, CA, pp. 147–160.

Silberschatz, A., M. Stonebraker, J.D. Ullman (eds.) (1990). Database systems: Achievements and opportunities. *ACM SIGMOD Record* 19(4), 6–22; see also *Commun. ACM* 34(10) (1991) 110–120.

Smith, J.M., D.C.P. Smith (1977a). Database abstractions: Aggregation. *Commun. ACM* 20, 405–413.

Smith, J.M., D.C.P. Smith (1977b). Database abstractions: Aggregation and generalization. *ACM Trans. Database Systems* 2, 105–133.

Snodgrass, R. (1990). Temporal databases: Status and research directions. *ACM SIGMOD Record* 19(4), 83–89.

Son, S.H. (ed.) (1988). Special issue on real-time database systems. *ACM SIGMOD Record* 17(1).

Stein, J., D. Maier (1988). Concepts in object-oriented data management. *Database Programming and Design* 1(4), 58–67.

Stonebraker, M. (ed.) (1986). *The INGRES Papers: Anatomy of a Relational Database System*, Addison-Wesley, Reading, MA.

Taylor, R.W., R.L. Frank (1976). CODASYL data-base management systems. *ACM Comput. Surveys* 8, 67–103.

Teorey, T.J. (1990). *Database Modeling and Design – The Entity-Relationship Approach*, Morgan Kaufmann, San Mateo, CA.

Teorey, T.J., D. Yang, J.P. Fry (1986). A logical design methodology for relational databases using the extended entity-relationship model. *ACM Computing Surveys* 18, 197–222.

The Committee for Advanced DBMS Function (1990). Third-generation database system manifesto. *ACM SIGMOD Record* 19(3), 31–44.

Thomas, S.J., P.C. Fischer (1986). Nested relational structures, in: P.C. Kanellakis, F.P. Preparata (eds.), *Advances in Computing Research, Vol. 3: The Theory of Databases*, JAI Press, Greenwich, CT, pp. 269–307.

Tsichritzis, D., A. Klug (1978). The ANSI/X3/SPARC DBMS framework report of the Study Group on Database Management Systems. *Inf. Systems* 3, 173–191.

Tsichritzis, D.C., F.H. Lochovsky (1976). Hierarchical database management: A survey. *ACM Comput. Surveys* 8, 67–103.

Tsur, S. (1991). Deductive databases in action, in: *Proc. 10th ACM SIGACT-SIGMOD-SIGART Symposium on Principles of Database Systems*, ACM, New York. pp. 142–153.

Ullman, J.D. (1983). Universal relation interfaces for database systems, in: R.E.A. Mason (ed.), ·*Information Processing 83* (*Proc. IFIP Congress*), North-Holland, Amsterdam, pp. 243–252.

Ullman, J.D. (1988). *Principles of Database and Knowledge-Base Systems, Vol. I*, Computer Science Press, Rockville, MD.

Ullman, J.D. (1989). *Principles of Database and Knowledge-Base Systems, Vol. II*, Computer Science Press, Rockville, MD.

User Facility Task Group of the ASC X3/SPARC Database System Study Group (1988). Reference model for DBMS user facility. *ACM SIGMOD Record* 17(2), 23–52.

Valduriez, P., G. Gardarin (1989). *Analysis and Comparison of Relational Database Systems*, Addison-Wesley, Reading, MA.

Van Emden, M.H., R.A. Kowalski (1976). The semantics of predicate logic as a programming language. *J. ACM* 23, 733–742.

Vardi, M.Y. (1982). The complexity of relational query languages, *Proc. 14th ACM Symposium on Theory of Computing*, ACM, New York, pp. 137–146.

Vardi, M.Y. (1988). Fundamentals of dependency theory, in: E. Börger (ed.), *Trends in Theoretical Computer Science*, Computer Science Press, Rockville, MD, pp. 171–224.

Vianu, V., G. Vossen (1988). Conceptual level concurrency control for relational update transactions (extended abstract), *Proc. 2nd International Conference on Database Theory (ICDT)*, LNCS 326, Springer, Berlin; pp. 353–367; *Theoret. Comput. Sci.* 95 (1992) 1–42.

Vianu, V., G. Vossen (1989). Goal-oriented concurrency control (extended abstract), *Proc. 2nd Symposium on Mathematical Fundamentals of Database Systems (MFDBS)*, LNCS 364, Springer, Berlin, pp. 398–414.

Vidyasankar, K. (1987). Generalized theory of serializability. *Acta Inform.* 24, 105–119.

Vidyasankar, K. (1991). Unified theory of database serializability. *Fund. Inform.* XIV, 147–183.

Vossen, G. (1991a). *Data Models, Database Languages and Database Management Systems*, Addison-Wesley, Workingham, England.

Vossen, G. (1991b). Bibliography on object-oriented database management. *ACM SIGMOD Record* 20(1), 24–46.

Vossen, G., K.U. Witt (1991). SUXESS: Towards a sound unification of extensions of the relational data model. *Data & Knowledge Engineering* 6, 75–92.

Weikum, G. (1991). Principles and realization strategies of multilevel transaction management. *ACM Trans. Database Systems* 16, 132–180.

Yang, C.C. (1986). *Relational Databases*, Prentice-Hall, Englewood Cliffs, NJ.

Yannakakis, M. (1984). Serializability by locking. *J. ACM* 31, 227–244.

Yannakoudakis, E.J., C.P. Cheng (1988). *Standard Relational and Network Database Languages*, Springer, Berlin.

Yao, S.B. (1979). Optimization of query evaluation algorithms. *ACM Trans. Database Systems* 4, 133–155.

Yao, S.B. (ed.) (1985). *Principles of Database Design, Vol. 1: Logical Organizations*, Prentice-Hall, Englewood Cliffs, NJ.

Zaniolo, C. (1990). Deductive databases – theory meets practice, *Proc. 2nd International Conference on Extending Database Technology (EDBT)*, LNCS 416, Springer, New York, pp. 1–15.

Zdonik, S.B., D. Maier (eds.) (1990). *Readings in Object-Oriented Database Systems*, Morgan Kaufmann, San Mateo, CA.

E.G. Coffman et al., Eds., *Handbooks in OR & MS, Vol. 3*

Chapter 5

Software Engineering

Raymond T. Yeh

International Software Systems, Inc., 9430 Research Boulevard, Bldg. 4, Suite 250, Austin, TX 78759, U.S.A.

Murat M. Tanik

Department of Computer Science and Engineering, Southern Methodist University, Dallas, TX 75275, U.S.A.

Wilhelm Rossak, Felicia Cheng, and Peter A. Ng

Institute for Integrated Systems Research, Department of Computer and Information Science, New Jersey Institute of Technology, Newark, NJ 07102, U.S.A.

1. Introduction and historical background

The last four decades have witnessed a tremendous growth in the computer production industry and in the diversity of computer applications throughout industry and everyday life. In the late 1940s it would have been difficult to imagine a software-controlled microprocessor placed inside an automobile or other consumer appliances. The cost of developing hardware has declined to the point that computers have become affordable for most households. Moreover, personalized computer network systems are now standard in industrial and academic institutions. However, the crucial factor in applications has proved to be the mapping of the customers needs to fully functional, stable and easy to use software. Indeed, the cost of a computer system is no longer determined so much by customized hardware as it is by the expense of developing the application software.

The explanation is twofold: the development of software is still a labor-intensive process with high personnel costs, and the software has to fit individual needs, whereas hardware tends to be standardized and prefabricated.

However, current research aims to make software an industrial product rather than a handcrafted piece of 'artwork', a goal that may be linked to an industrial revolution in the software development process. This chapter describes the present state of the art, including the underlying ideas and the methods for bringing software development to the level of engineered industrial production.

195

Before discussing the current issues in software development, let us first look at its history and background, so that its objectives may be more easily understood. The 1950s and 1960s were an era of hardware development. Hardware technology evolved from vacuum tube technology in the early 1950s, to transistor and integrated-circuit technology in the mid 1960s. Computer systems were viewed as general-purpose data processors and hardware was considered an expensive commodity. Software was usually designed for individual customers and had limited distribution. Thus, programs were usually 'homegrown' products; the same person designed, wrote, ran and debugged a software system. The design and the requirements the system had to fulfill were in the programmers head. Documentation rarely existed.

The 1970s marked a period of transition and a recognition of the importance of software development. The advanced hardware technology of the 1960s not only drove the hardware cost down, but also opened up a new level of software sophistication that increased demand in the 1970s. In particular, software packages were introduced and distributed to thousands of users. Suddenly, programmers found themselves in the role of service technicians, modifying existing software to suit a company's requirements and adapting software to a frequently changing hardware environment. Program maintenance absorbed (and absorbs today) a significant portion of the operating costs, severely limiting the funds available for new development. Furthermore, software in the 1970s was characterized as complex, error prone, extremely labor intensive, and expensive. Collectively, this phenomenon became known as the 'software crisis'.

Software was complex because there was no systematic procedure for handling the rapid growth in the size of applications. Increases in size rendered problems unmanageable by a single person.

Inadequate development and testing methods and incomplete documentation led to error-prone software. After a period of time, software was often not even comprehensible to its creator; modifications by others usually resulted in unexpected performance of sections of the software supposedly unaffected by the changes.

Software was highly labor intensive because software development was largely a manual process, requiring people to rework most of a program even when only minor changes occurred. Therefore, software became expensive and tended to be delivered too late. Furthermore, insufficient methods of formulating user requirements led to situations where products were outdated or inappropriate by the time they were finished. As a result, cost overrun was the norm rather than the exception.

In this situation, the term *software engineering* was coined at the 1968 NATO Conference. Software engineering was described as a set of techniques, tools, documents, and practices that were introduced to combat the software crisis. For the first time, software was considered an engineering product that required a phased approach consisting of planning, analysis, design, implementation, testing and maintenance. The major components of software engineering were identified as process models, methods, languages, and tools.

Methods define the procedures for handling software in the different phases of development. They support project planning and estimation, system and software requirements elicitation, systems analysis, design of functions and data structures, algorithm development, structured coding, testing and organized maintenance. Languages allow one to apply abstract methods and are of special importance as a means of communication among different groups of people in the usually team-oriented development process. They serve as a medium of communication between developer and customer and between programmer and machine. The language structures an analyst's thinking and shapes some features of the design. Tools expedite the development process and automate parts of the developer's work. Furthermore, in large systems tools are essential to the application of methods and languages in a structured and efficient way. They promote the necessary immediate feedback to manage the project properly. A process model is the glue that holds methods, languages and tools together. It defines both the sequence in which the methods are applied and the software products required. Together, the process models, methods, languages, and tools enable the developer to control the process of software development and they provide the developer with a guideline for producing high-quality software.

In the 1980s the main focus was on the integration of these different aspects of software technology and on the development of suitable tools. This period also marked a period of transition from a still manual approach to software development to an industrialized approach. Industry supported many of the labor-intensive development activities with software development tools, and used these tools to increase the quality of the software, reduce the development cost, and increase the productivity.

The 1980s and 1990s have seen the first results of the software industry's attempt to combine process models, methods, languages and tools into a 'software factory'. New and adapted paradigms like software reuse, prototyping, fourth-generation programming languages, end-user development and evolutionary development have been brought forward, evaluated and integrated into the software process, a process that has become more flexible and adaptable to the needs of varying types of software development units.

To give a step by step introduction and to provide an overview of the more prominent ideas, we have structured this chapter as follows. In Section 2, we shall discuss the waterfall model, which was the first process model to provide a systematic approach to software development. In Section 3, we shall look in more detail at some of the methodologies that lead to less effort being required for software development, to higher reliability, and to ease of modification. In particular we shall discuss the concept of structured programming introduced in the 1970s with the aim of reducing the complexity of the software at the programming level. In Section 4, we shall discuss the issues involved in the languages used in software engineering. Section 5 will elaborate on the industrial use of software tools to improve the productivity of software development; this section will also feature a small example. In Section 6, we shall examine a few of the ideas that introduce new paradigms into software development.

Space limitations will make it impossible for us to discuss every topic and detail of software engineering methodology. Therefore, our aim is to provide a sound framework of recognized ideas and concepts which will give the interested reader an improved understanding of what software engineering is or could be. As a source of more detailed information, we have attached an additional reading list at the end of the chapter.

2. The software life cycle

One of the basic concepts of software engineering is the so-called 'software life cycle'. This notion refers to the various phases through which software passes from the time it is conceived to the time it is discarded [ANSI, 1983]. Development, operation and maintenance are the major phases in the life cycle (Figure 1). Once the software has been developed, operation and maintenance form a cyclic pattern of use and modification throughout the service life of the system.

In most cases a definition phase precedes all the other phases that have been identified so far. It includes activities ranging from feasibility studies to the generation of the final software plane (Figure 2); that is the management structure of the project.

Development and maintenance are also split into more detailed activities or subphases. The development phase includes the architecture design, detailed design, coding and testing (Figure 3). The maintenance phase includes error correction and product improvement (Figure 4). These (sub)phases are not simple sequential structures but include feedback loops such as those in Figures

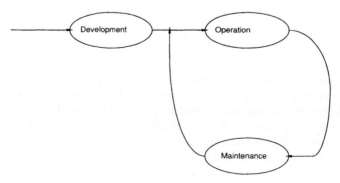

Fig. 1. A simplified software life cycle.

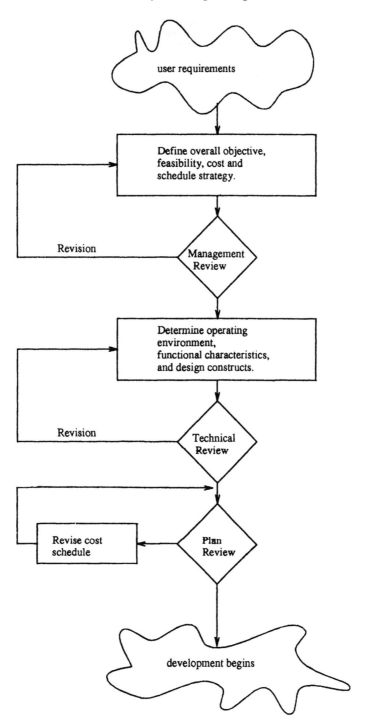

Fig. 2. The definition phase.

R.T. Yeh et al.

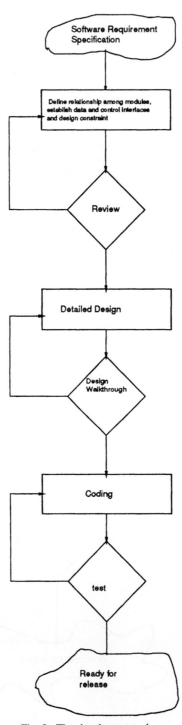

Fig. 3. The development phase.

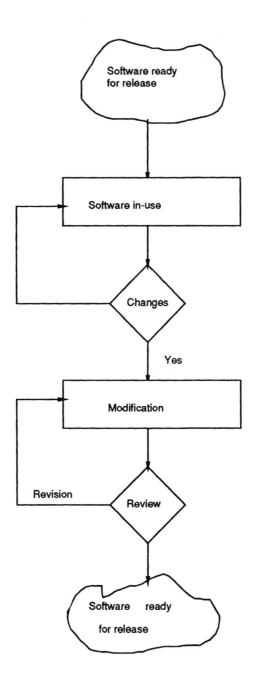

Fig. 4. The maintenance phase.

2 to 4. The operation phase can also be split into activities, but from our simplified point of view this is not necessary for the moment.

The basic concept of 'life cycle' makes it easier for researchers to invent frameworks (process models) for the control and review of the development project, to define the deliverables at each stage, to structure the documentation of the system and to discuss the applications of different methods and tools to support all the activities and phases in the development process. The waterfall model, which will be presented in the next section, was the first model to describe life cycles. Even though it is an oversimplification of the development and maintenance process, it still specifies the framework and basic components used in most of the later variations.

2.1. *The waterfall model*

The waterfall model was first introduced by Royce [1970] and later popularized and augmented by Boehm (see Boehm [1976, 1984]). The waterfall model accounts for all of the major transitions a piece of software might experience during its life cycle. It takes a stepwise approach to software development, following the concepts presented above, by breaking the development process into a sequence of units (Figure 5), called phases or stages.

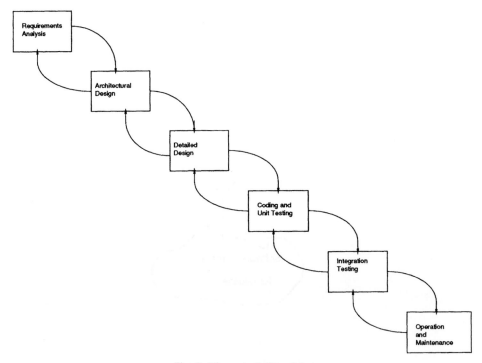

Fig. 5. The waterfall model.

The user requirements are elicited and specified during the first phase of the project. These stated requirements may not be changed later on and are used as a document that freezes the agreement between end user and developer. The job of the developer is to transform these requirements into a software system that reflects exactly the stated needs. As it is impossible to bridge the gap between requirements and computer in one step, a phased approach is used.

Each phase is related to a set of activities that take defined inputs and transform them into output items. Inputs and outputs are usually documents. The result of each stage is an intermediate form of the software system on its way from user requirements to a computer program and this serves either as the input to the next phase or as an error report requiring reconsideration of an earlier phase. This means that each output document is checked if it is – after all transformations and activities – still a valid representation of the input to the phase. Even though this implies a strict sequence of phases, improved water-fall-like models recognize that phases might have overlapping activities.

The sequence of tasks, as given in Figure 5, form a waterfall of evolving documents and phases. We discuss each phase in more detail by describing the basic activities and listing the input and output documents.

• *Requirements analysis* – the analysis of requirements focuses on studying the needs and expectations of end users, investigates the interfaces between hardware, software, and the given organizational and physical environment, and specifies the interconnection between user and system. It is used to understand the tradeoffs between conflicting constraints, to determine the available resources, and to specify the goals of the system.

Input – user requirements; project constraints.
Output – software plan; software requirements specification.

• *Architectural design* – the architectural design focuses on the overall structure of the system. The functional structure of the software and a conceptual data model are derived. The software structure should be modular. This is achieved by breaking the system up into smaller, self-contained parts and by describing the relationships and interfaces of these modules.

Input – system requirements specification.
Output – definition of modules and data; interfaces; test plans.

• *Detailed design* – detailed design refines the internal design of each module of the architectural design. This refinement is detailed enough to be matched later on to the programming language used during the coding phase.

Input – architectural design document.
Output – detailed design documents; detailed test plans.

• *Coding and unit testing* – coding translates the design representation to a program expressed in an appropriate language. Unit testing follows a basic test plan and focusses on the logic of the software, making sure that the input defined will produce the required output. The test plane should be already determined during the design phase. The units coded and tested during this phase are the modules of the architectural and detailed design. As there are modules at two different levels, we have two basic kinds of testing procedures: Testing low-level modules requires test drivers to simulate the environment. Testing higher-level modules eventually requires stubs to take the place of the missing low-level modules. Stubs are modules that offer only a reduced degree of functionality, but that provide the same interface as the fully functional units they replace.

Input – detailed design specification and module test procedures.
Output – tested modules.

• *Integration testing* – integration testing groups unit-tested modules according to the architectural design and then tests the entire system in a systematic manner. Integration testing reveals structural system errors missed in unit testing. This means not only that during this phase the implemented internal logic of the system is tested (white box test), but that the functionality of the system is checked, according to the given specification and without knowledge of the internal realization (black box test). There are two kinds of integration test strategies: top-down and bottom-up. Top-down integration testing begins with the higher-level modules. Then modules called by the higher-level modules are integrated into the system, forming packages of subsystems. Bottom-up integration reverses this process.

Input – unit-tested modules, test results.
Output – tested packages.

• *Operation and maintenance* – changes to software are the rule and not the exception. Changes may be due to errors uncovered while the software is in operation or due to changes in the external environment (e.g., changes in tax laws will require modifications to a payroll program that calculates the amount of tax to be deducted). There are three types of maintenance: (i) corrective maintenance corrects errors left undiscovered during testing; (ii) adaptive maintenance modifies the software to run in an altered environment; (iii) perfective maintenance enhances the existing functions to better fit user requirements.

The pie chart in Figure 6 shows the usual distribution of effort by activities over the life of software, derived from publications like [Boehm, 1984]. It is noteworthy that cumulative system costs are dominated by maintenance, and that coding is only a small portion of these costs.

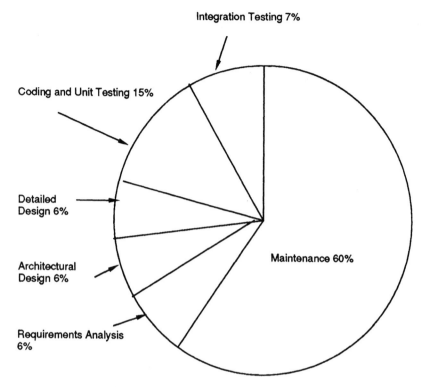

Fig. 6. Effort required by the various phases.

2.2. Alternatives and enhancements of the waterfall model

The waterfall model has undergone a set of changes and enhancements [e.g., Tonies, 1979], and has been successfully backed up with tool support [e.g., Denert & Hesse, 1980]. Furthermore, a wide variety of variations exists [Boehm, 1984]. However, the model has been a target of criticism in recent years (e.g., Agresti [1986], Gladden [1982], Hall [1982], Gidding [1984], McCracken & Jackson [1982], Martin [1984] and Swartout & Balzer [1982]). This is in most cases due to the fact that the model consists mainly of sequential phases; it assumes that all the functions of the system can be specified in the first step of the development phase and that subsequent phases can add the missing design details.

A basic assumption of the waterfall model is that users have the ability to specify their requirements adequately early in the development phase. This has proved to be rather unrealistic. Specification and implementation interact, so a partition of the model into two disjoint phases makes it difficult to capture the changes in specification and to reflect the changes in the implementation.

Incremental development is one possible way to improve this situation without losing the benefits of the waterfall model [Boehm, 1984]. Here, the basic idea is to break a large project into smaller subprojects as soon as a specification is written. These smaller projects are finished earlier, allow faster feedback to the end-user and provide opportunities for adjusting the specification to changing requirements before a new subproject is started.

Prototyping methodologies (see the discussion in Section 6.1.1) addresses a weakness of the waterfall model [Floyd, 1984] regarding the elicitation of requirements. However, the integration of pure prototyping methodologies seems to be adequate only for smaller and medium sized projects. With the rigid structure of a waterfall model, they need special attention and lead to a new version of a phased prototyping process, called the spiral model [Boehm, 1988].

Integration of techniques targeting reuse of existing software (see Section 6.1.2) in a waterfall model or in one of its variants seems to be easier to accomplish [Rossak, 1989a]. However, today the necessary commercially available tools supporting this development philosophy are lacking. Furthermore, organizational and psychological hurdles seem to prevent an easy introduction of already elaborated 'development with reuse' process models.

3. Elements of software development methodology

The software crisis has been characterized by increasing costs in software production and the relatively poor quality of the completed systems. In addition, it is evident within the software development community that a principle reason why maintenance takes up the majority of the development cost is that programmers spend a significant portion of their time reworking the code because of faulty logic and poor communication [Boehm, 1984].

Largely wasted efforts result from poor logical construction in the original design and from the difficulty of isolating software faults. This has led directly to a search for new methodologies that improve the programming and design stages in a software development cycle, and to the identification of a basic roster of software quality metrics that can be used to guide the development process and to evaluate the results.

3.1. Structured programming

Structured programming represents a major step towards easing and standardizing programming tasks [Dijkstra, 1972]. The term was coined in the early 1970s, when many publications were devoted to the idea of a structured and standardized way of designing and writing programs that eliminated the earlier rather chaotic handling of the implementation task.

The two basic concepts of structured programming are top-down program design and 'GOTO-less' programming. These are complemented by the idea of provably correct software.

Two propositions summarize the concepts of structured programming very accurately:

> Wirth [1974] stated that 'Structured Programming is the formulation of programs as hierarchical, nested structures of statements and objects of computations'.

> Dijkstra [1972] pointed out that the correctness of a program should and can be proved.

Thus, we can consider structured programming as the application of systematic decomposition methods for establishing a manageable hierarchical problem structure that can be implemented as a provably correct program. To reach this goal, the program is built exclusively from a small set of simple control and data structures the proof of the correctness of which is well understood. This set of programming primitives restricts the use of GOTO statements without restricting the class of implementable algorithms (each program with GOTO statements has an equivalent one without GOTO statements that uses only the basic primitives defined). This discipline of programming reduces the number of connections between different parts of a program and hence improves the comprehensibility and reliability of the program.

3.1.1. Basic control structures

An important issue related to structured programming is the concept of *proper programs*. A *proper program* is a program represented by a flowchart, such that
(1) there is exactly one input arc and exactly one output arc, and
(2) every node in the flowchart can be reached by the input and output arcs.
Mills and Linger [Linger, Mills & Witt, 1979] constructed an algorithm that converts every possible *nonstructured* program to a *structured* program that uses only the three basic control structures: sequence, selection, and iteration. A pictorial representation of the three constructs is shown in Figure 7.

Dijkstra pointed out that by using the above three control constructs, a programmer can construct any possible program without using GOTOs. Furthermore, the underlying structure of the program makes it readily comprehensible to other programmers. This ease of understanding is a critical attribute in software maintenance.

3.1.2. The information hiding principle

Information hiding [Parnas, 1972a,b] refers to the suppression of those design decisions within a module that have no effect on the interface between the module and its environment. When the concept of information hiding is applied to data, it refers to the encapsulation of the implementation details of a data item within a module; access to the data is restricted to predefined 'public' functions.

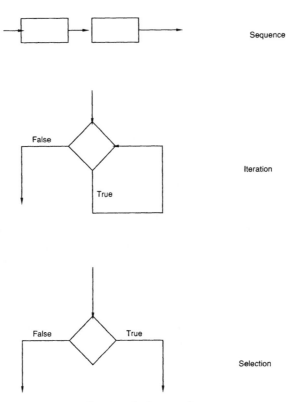

Sequence

Iteration

Selection

Fig. 7. The three basic control structures.

The actual application of information hiding in software development has proven to be important. Since the internal details of the procedure and data items are hidden from other parts of the system, modules are unable to circumvent the defined interface and to use the internal structures directly. The main effect is that errors introduced into one module of the system are less likely to affect other modules within the system. This effect is enhanced when modules are programmed to check the data provided by the interface thoroughly.

As an example, let us take a data object 'stack' together with two externally available functions PUSH and POP, which operate on the stack. A stack is usually implemented as a single module, so that the details of the internal structure of the stack can be encapsulated according to the ideas of information hiding, while the PUSH and POP operations allow a user to manipulate the stack without any knowledge of the implementation details. Hence, the implementation of the stack can be changed, if necessary, without affecting the calling module. This concept guarantees that the stack module can be independently coded, tested, verified, and enhanced.

3.1.3. Stepwise refinement

Stepwise refinement [Wirth, 1971] is the heart of structured programming. It is a procedure that decomposes a module into a set of submodules which, in the aggregate, perform the function of the original module. Each of these submodules is then independently decomposed into further submodules. The process continues until each submodule is at a level that can be expressed in a programming language.

Figure 8 shows the first two levels of a stepwise refinement intended to solve a small problem, that of printing those words of a text that being with 'c'.

Stepwise refinement is an attractive method for solving problems by a functional decomposition followed by a reintegration. It is widely used during the detailed design and implementation stage of software development. It allows a designer to concentrate on a set of progressively smaller and usually simpler problems, thereby reducing complexity and preparing for the integration of standard solutions.

3.1.4. Program verification

The major issue of program verification is to prove, at least in part, that a program functions according to its specification. There are basically two approaches to proofs of program correctness: the static approach and the constructive approach.

In the static approach, given a program and its specifications, mathematical proofs are developed to demonstrate that the logical behavior of a program is as specified, assuming that this logical behavior is completely characterized by a set of formal assertions. Formal techniques using assertions for the proof of the correctness of the program are (1) the verification methods in Floyd [1967], Hoare [1969], and Naur [1966], which are also known as inductive assertion methods, (2) the fixed-point method [Manna & Vuillemin, 1972; Manna, Ness & Vuillemin, 1972, 1973], which is known as computational induction, (3) recursion induction [McCarthy, 1963], (4) structural induction [Burstall, 1969], and (5) subgoal induction [Morris & Wegbrett, 1977].

For the inductive assertion methods, a programmer needs to capture the

```
level 1
    while not eof do
    print words that begin with a 'c'

level 2
    while not eof do
    for each line
        for each word
            if word begin with a 'c'
            then print word
            else skip word
```

Fig. 8. First step of refinement of a program that prints only words that begin with a 'c'.

'invariant' properties of a program at each node of a flowchart by means of a formal assertion, which is in principle a term in formal logic over the variables of the program. To prove that the program is consistent with its specification it is necessary to show that the input assertion at the start node implies the output assertion at the halt node, over all possible paths between the start and halt nodes.

Proof by recursion induction applies to recursive programs. The proof is carried out by mathematical induction, where the induction is on the recursion level. The induction method is related to recursion induction, but it depends on the inductive definition of the data structures manipulated by the program. Computational induction methods are those in which the induction is based on the computational steps of the recursive programs.

As an alternative or supplement to the commonly used inductive assertion method, the subgoal induction method decomposes the verification tasks into subtasks and tries to establish the validity of these subgoals. The proofs of subgoals can be pieced together to imply the validity of the original specification. The major virtue of the method is that it can be used to prove the correctness of a program loop directly from its input–output specification, without the use of an invariant.

Formal equivalences among the various proofs techniques have been established. Morris & Wegbrett [1977] showed the formal equivalence of computational induction and subgoal induction, and of inductive assertions and subgoal induction restricted to flowchart programs. Manna, Ness & Vuillemin [1973] showed the equivalence of structural and computational induction.

In addition to the methods mentioned so far there are a number of other approaches to proving the correctness of programs, such as the algebraic method of correctness proofs [Burstall & Landin, 1969] and the predicate transformation approach [Yeh, 1977; Basu & Yeh, 1975]. Verification of programs by predicate transformation is based on the concept of predicate transformation, as introduced by Dijkstra [1975]. A predicate transformer is used to define the formal semantics of programs by a mapping that transforms a set of states after the execution of a program to the set of all possible states before the execution of the same program. This technique of this proof differs from the other methods such as inductive assertions and subgoal induction. Both the inductive assertions and subgoal induction methods demonstrate program consistency (partial correctness) but require a separate proof of termination. Such proofs of termination of iterative programs can be found in Floyd [1967], Manna & McCarthy [1970], and Manna [1974]. In contrast, by the very nature of semantic definitions using predicate transformers, the predicate transformation method implicitly assumes that program termination is an inherent property of the algorithm that realizes the given program; termination and consistency can be handled by the same approach. An example of using the predicate transformation method for proving the correctness of programs is given by Basu & Yeh [1975].

The constructive approach lays stress on the correct development of the program [Dijkstra, 1976; Yeh, 1977]. Programming is seen as a problem-solving activity, filling the gaps between preconditions and postconditions (input and output assertions) with a program text that realizes the desired transformation. As such, it must deal with a spectrum of activities concerned with specifications, design, validation, modeling, and the structuring of programs and data. In the constructive approach testing is used to verify the correctness of the program constructed.

Under these circumstances the notions of reliability and validity are important in proving the correctness programs. A test criterion is reliable if any incorrectness of the program is revealed by testing all the requirements of the test criterion on any set of data. By choosing a test criterion that is both valid with regard to the program structure and reliable, it is guaranteed that any incorrectness of the program can be found.

Finally, formal specification techniques, such as those for describing data structures, can play a major role in the program construction process as well as in establishing the correctness of programs. A precise specification of what a program is intended to do should be given before the program is actually coded. When this is done, the correctness of the program can be established by proving that it is equivalent to the specification [Liskov & Zilles, 1974]. An example of the use of a formal specification technique to specify the stack data type can be found in Section 4.

3.2. Design principles and techniques

Much effort has been devoted to the development of programming and design techniques for the systematic construction of well-structured and reliable software architectures. All of these techniques seem to point to the concept of modularity. Several principles such as abstraction, information hiding and localization [Constantine & Yourdon, 1979; Ross & Goodenough, 1975; Liskov & Zilles, 1974; Parnas, 1972a,b] have emerged for the construction of modules with high quality standards.

However, modules must be integrated and organized to form a system. One of the major goals of module organization is to reduce dependencies between modules. By isolating the effects of each different decision made to achieve module organization, the modification of a system can be made relatively easily [Gilbert, 1983]. From this point of view the principles of abstraction, information hiding, and localization are principles of design aimed at ease of program modification. The design principles and related techniques will be briefly discussed in the following sections.

3.2.1. Structured design/analysis techniques

Structured analysis is a generic term for methodologies that approach system definition in a structured manner, based on the idea of leveled decomposition. Many papers, e.g., Stevens, Myers & Constantine [1974], De Marco [1978],

Constantine & Yourdon [1979] and Gane & Sarson [1979], have been written
in this area.

During the requirements phase the major task of the analyst is to identify
how a proposed system should operate in order to fulfill the customer's
requirements. Ideally, the customer can provide a detailed specification of the
system. However, in reality an analyst must very often use scenario techniques.
Scenario techniques use an interactive communication and prototyping process
to help the customer to describe his/her needs unambiguously. Structured
analysis supports this communication process by providing a means of writing
down and analyzing requirements.

In understanding the domain of the problem, an analyst, in consultation with
the customer, will model the existing system through a data flow diagram. Such
diagrams show the real-world data items used in the system and the processes
that act on them. The analyst then transforms this physical data flow diagram
into a logical diagram of the proposed system.

The tools used in structured analysis are the following.

• *Data flow diagram* – this diagram shows the changes that occur to the
system input data in order to achieve the desired output. The basic data flow
symbols consist of arrows indicating the flow of data, bubbles representing
processes that transform data from one form to another, straight lines representing files, and boxes indicating the sources or sinks of data. In order to
construct a data flow diagram, an analyst will first list all the system inputs and
outputs, and then identify a sequence of processes that define the transformation from input to output. Since it is rarely possible to represent all the details
of a large system in a single diagram, the overall system is usually represented
by a hierarchy of data flow diagrams. Level i subprocesses, which are formed
by decomposing processes at level $i - 1$, further refine the transformation of
inputs to outputs defined at level $i - 1$. The input/output interface of processes
at level i must preserve the interfaces at level $i - 1$. Figure 9 shows the first two
levels of a data flow diagram for an information retrieval/update system that
allows a credit department to check and update the credit of a customer. A
user has to provide a password in order to gain access to a database.
Depending on his privileges, a user may either display and/or update a
customer's credit.

• *Data dictionary* – the data dictionary defines the type and structure of the
data flowing through the system. In the process of developing a data flow
diagram, it is necessary to introduce names of each data flow, process and data
store. The data dictionary contains all these names along with the definitions
for structures and types. For example, consider the dictionary entry for
requests. As a minimum, such an entry should contain the type of operations
that are required and the name of the customer making the request. The only
two possible types of operation in our example are a retrieval or a combination
of retrieval and update. An example of a partial listing of a data dictionary is
shown in Figure 10.

• *Structured English* – a language is needed to describe the processes acting

LEVEL 1

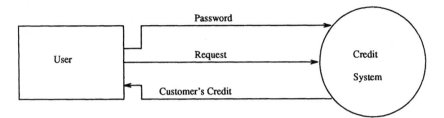

LEVEL 2   Request = (Update & Retrieval) OR (Retrieval)

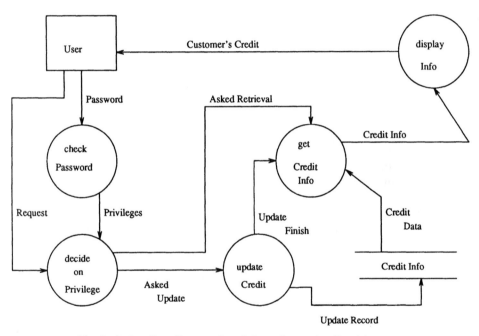

Fig. 9. A data flow diagram of an information retrieval/update system.

PASSWORD
  USER_ID
  PASSWORD_NUM
REQUEST
  OPERATION_TYPE
  CUSTOMER_NAME
  CUSTOMER_ID
  CREDIT
OPERATION_TYPE
  RETRIEVAL or (RETRIEVAL & UPDATE)

Fig. 10. Sample component of a data dictionary.

on data flows, for a data flow diagram shows only the flow of data not the sequence of events. In order to avoid the ambiguity inherent in natural language, the analyst relies on a restricted set of constructs to specify the function of a process. These constructs are again sequence, selection, and iteration. Figure 11 shows an example.

Structured design defines the structural relationships and interfaces between modules, data items and data stores that make up a system. The goal of structured analysis is a 'structure chart'.

A structure chart usually has a tree-like shape. It consists of labeled boxes (modules) that are joined by directed lines representing a reference or invocation of a subordinate module. The interface between modules is shown by labeled arrows indicating the flow of data or control information along module references. Each module is described separately in more detail, e.g., using structured English.

Figure 12 is the first top-level structure chart of the information retrieval/ update system. A predefined algorithm assists the engineer by transforming data flow diagrams into structure charts.

3.2.1.1. Creating a structured chart from a data flow diagram. Using 'transform analysis' [Pages-Jones, 1988] as one possible alternative, there is a natural progression from a data flow diagram to a structure chart. The top level of a data flow diagram is divided into three regions: (1) the efferent (input) region, (2) the transform region, and (3) the efferent (output) region. The input region is identified by tracing from the raw-source input to the point where the input data is in its most abstract form, but can still be considered as input. The output region is identified by tracing back from the final output to the point where the derived data is in an abstract, least-processed form, but is already considered as output. The transform region is the region between the input and the output region where the actual computation is done. This 'central transform' assumes that the data has been checked for correctness and consistency and has a format suitable for processing. All the checks and reformating activities belong to the afferent region; all the formating and layout activities belong to the efferent region.

Having been divided into these three regions, the data flow diagram is mapped onto a structure chart. This is done by selecting a process in the central transform as the top-level module and by extending the input and output branches of the data flow diagram downwards as subordinate modules.

> **If** password is valid
>   **then** check privilege
>   **If** privilege equals display-request
>   **then** display-request
>   **Else If** privilege equals update
>   **then** update

Fig. 11. Structured English.

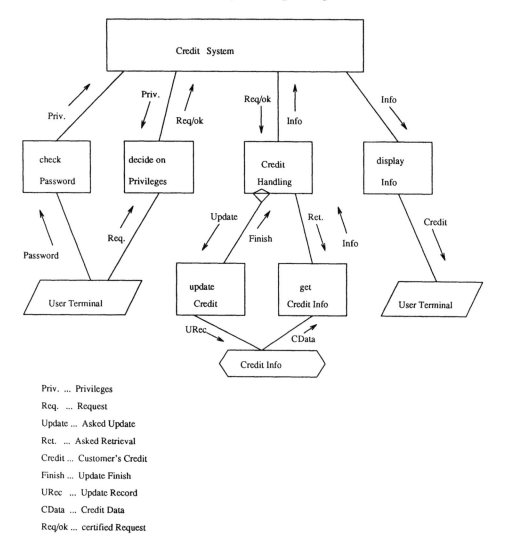

Priv. ... Privileges
Req. ... Request
Update ... Asked Update
Ret. ... Asked Retrieval
Credit ... Customer's Credit
Finish ... Update Finish
URec ... Update Record
CData ... Credit Data
Req/ok ... certified Request

Fig. 12. A structure chart of an information retrieval/update system.

These modules can then be decomposed according to the processes in the data flow diagram that define the single functions (transformations) in the input or output branches of the system and in the central transform. If none of the processes in the central transforms is a natural top-level module, an 'artificial' module of this type is introduced. The central transform, input and output branches are controlled by the new top-level module and decomposed in the next step.

During the 'factoring' stage, decomposition, and if necessary reintegration, continues as long as 'good' modules can be singled out. Details like reading and writing procedures, error handling, initialization, and terminations are

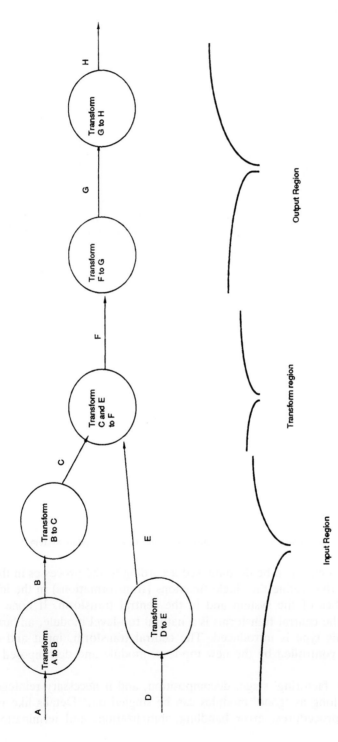

Fig. 13. A partitioned data flow diagram.

added. During 'packaging' the modules of the structure chart are grouped into programs, jobs and load units.

The process of mapping a data flow diagram to a top-level structure chart is shown schematically in Figures 13 and 14. We show only the flow of data and omit details like reading and error handling. Figures 9 and 12, describing the notational primitives of the data flow diagrams and the structure charts, give one more example of the top-level transformation process.

3.2.1.2. Criteria for structuring. During transform analysis, decomposition continued as long as 'good' modules could be defined. This means that we need criteria for measuring the quality of the design.

The two criteria by which a structured design is judged are: *modular strength* and *modular coupling*. Modular strength is a measure of how strongly related the elements are within a given module. Modular coupling is a measure of the strength of the relationship between different modules. A structured design that maximizes the modular strength and minimizes coupling is likely to be less prone to error and more easily incorporated into other systems [Page-Jones, 1988].

Modular strength. The stronger the relationship between elements of the same module, the more likely the module can be seen as a single unit. Myers [1978] has identified seven levels of modular strength. These levels are the following, in order of decreasing strength.

- *Functional strength* – all operations contribute to carrying out a single function.
- *Informational strength* – a module containing more than one functional-strength module acting on a common database (e.g., a data capsule).
- *Communicational strength* – all elements in a module are related to the same problem procedure and are coupled by the flow of data.
- *Procedural strength* – as in communicational strength, but coupling is by the flow of control.
- *Classical strength* – all operations in the module are logically similar and related in time (e.g., an initialization or termination module).
- *Logical strength* – instructions in a module are logically similar (e.g., all input instructions), but they need not be related in time.

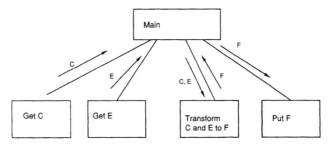

Fig. 14. Resulting structure chart.

• *Coincidental strength* – instructions are together in a module, but they are unrelated.

Modular coupling. This coupling measures the relationships that exist between system modules. Coupling is measured by the number of connections and the type of information communicated in the connections. The simpler and the fewer the interrelationships between modules, the more likely it is that the system will be robust, flexible and maintainable. Therefore, a low measure of coupling is desirable. The degrees of coupling are as follows.

• *Content coupling* – one module makes direct reference to the internal elements of another module.

• *Common coupling* – modules share a common unstructured database.

• *External coupling* – modules reference the same external and structured data items.

• *Control coupling* – one module controls the execution of another module.

• *Stamp coupling* – one module passes a full data structure to another as an argument, even though only parts of the structure are needed.

• *Data coupling* – one module calls another, none of the above coupling apply, and all arguments are data elements required by the function of the module.

3.2.2. *Other techniques*

As mentioned in the previous section, the term 'structured analysis and structured design' refers to a whole spectrum of very similar design techniques. In this section we shall briefly describe some of these related methodologies; each uses a diagram of one kind or another to enable the user to visualize a usually decomposed design. Martin & McClure [1985] contains a comprehensive discussion of these and other related methodologies. Readers are encouraged to consult the references for details.

Structure analysis and design techniques (SADT). SADT [Ross, 1987] is a methodology that provides a disciplined approach for examining the problem, defining system requirements and providing a rough design solution. The basic idea is to derive a blueprint-like picture of the system under development. SADT diagrams are organized into hierarchies of boxes, usually interpreted as activities, that decompose a given problem into its components or subactivities. An activity has input and output data, control information and a dedicated processor. SADT covers approximately the same phases as data flow diagrams, but there is no level of detail comparable to a structure chart.

Jackson diagrams – JSD and JSP. Jackson system development (JSD) [Jackson, 1983] identifies objects and actions on objects in the domain of the problem. It uses tree-shaped diagrams to show the relation between objects and actions in the object life cycle, and it includes the time dimension in its diagrams. These first diagrams are constructed of four basic components: sequence, selection, iteration, and elementary action boxes. Objects of the real world are then matched to objects (processes) of the data processing system. The procedure is completed by assigning input and output handling processes, and processes for internal organization. Processes communicate by two different data flows. Using object life cycles, data flows, and the description of the completed system, the detailed structure of the processes is derived. One way to accomplish this task is to use the Jackson structured programming (JSP) methodology [Jackson, 1975]. JSP first examines the input and output structures, and then designs a program to map the data structures at the input to those at the output.

Hierarchical input–process–output (HIPO). HIPO [IBM, 1974] is a very simple method for describing systems by input–output relations. HIPO diagrams are used mainly for the design and documentation of systems, even though the aim of a HIPO diagram is to describe what the system does rather than how its function is performed. HIPO diagrams use a set of simple techniques to show hierarchically the input, processing and output functions of a system or program, without placing emphasis on the integration of the parts into a system. HIPO diagrams have successfully described the top-down programming process, starting from a general system and then proceeding to program design. However, HIPO has been criticized for not having the same level of flexibility and comprehensiveness as other methodologies.

Warnier–Orr diagrams. Like structure charts a Warnier–Orr diagram [Warnier, 1981] provides a graphical representation of the hierarchical structure of a system or program design. It is mainly targeted at the design stage, in that it defines diagrams and data structures from which programs can be derived later on. This method is not so graphically oriented as SADT or JSP. It relies more on a notation that mixes structured English and graphical primitives.

3.3. Software metrics

Quantitative measures of software are needed during all phases of development. In the earlier phases, these measures only provide estimates, but in the later phases they give more precise measures of progress. Among the different measures, some are relatively easy to collect, once they are known. Such measures include the cost, lines of code, errors, effort, speed and size of memory. Others, such as quality, reliability, complexity, efficiency, and maintainability are more difficult to assess and can be measured only indirectly [Pressman, 1992].

Some metrics are based on the source code, whereas others may be applied in the design phase of the software development and maintenance. The following is an example using lines of code to determine the other metrics. However, it should be mentioned that this approach oversimplifies the issue. Measures, depending only on lines of code do not take into account many other cost factors; see Boehm [1975, 1984] for an evaluation of these factors. We restrict ourselves here to a basic introduction; a broader coverage can be found in the references.

The line-of-code (LOC) technique is based on the number of source lines

LOC projected for a system. From estimates of LOC, other software metrics can be computed.

For example, the cost of developing software can be estimated by the products of LOC and the average cost per line if we assume that the average cost per source line is independent of the size of the system. This metric further assumes that an average cost per line is known as the result of an evaluation of other, already completed projects in the company. LOC can also be determined by comparison with historical data collected from a similar project, or it can be estimated by techniques based on system design evaluations. Productivity can be determined by the LOC per person month. One aspect of the software quality is measured by the number of errors per line of code.

In general, software metrics can be divided into at least three categories: design metrics, code metrics and software quality metrics [GEC, 1986]. Design metrics focus on attributes associated with the structured software design. Code metrics are defined by the measurable attributes of program source code. Software quality metrics evaluate a system with respect to given non-functional requirements of the specification.

To evaluate development performance, one can use design metrics like the *function point* method supported with statistical data [Drummond, 1985]. The basic idea is to find the system parameters (function points) that are involved in the system development, e.g., the number and types of files. On the basis of these parameters an estimate is obtained, supported by data from existing systems with similar attributes.

Two prominent metrics measuring the system complexity have been proposed by Chapin [1979] and McCabe [1976]. Chapin's complexity measure uses a pattern of input to output data correspondences and is a function-based metric that determines the software productivity, quality and cost. McCabe develops the cyclomatic numbers, a measure for program complexity based on the pattern of control flow in the software.

The complexity measures of Halstead [1977] and Berlinger [1980] are examples of code metrics. By using counts of symbols found in the source code, Halstead formulated a theory of software science to compare different programming languages, to estimate the time and effort required to develop the computer programs, and to make predictions about the number of errors in a program.

Software quality measurement is important in software development as it enables a designer to predict the behavior of a product and to decide if non-functional system requirements are likely to be fulfilled at a given stage of development. There is a wide spectrum of software quality criteria; the quality goals adopted and the means by which they are measured and quantified depend very much on the project. Moreover, quality goals are very often contradictory rather than cooperative, such as performance and portability. Boehm, Brown & Lipow [1976] provides an in-depth discussion of issues related to software quality.

The following provides a partial listing of frequently used quality criteria.

• *Maintainability.* A measure of the effects of errors and of the time required to correct errors after the system has been accepted.

• *Reliability.* A measure of the number of errors designed or coded into the system.

• *Adaptability.* A measure of how difficult and costly it is to introduce new features into the software after release.

• *Security.* A measure of how difficult it is for unauthorized persons to gain access to the information in the computer system.

• *Installability.* A measure of how much time is spent in installing the system and restarting it after system failure.

• *Modifiability.* A measure of the cost of changing or extending the software after the development stage.

• *Simplicity.* A measure of the straightforwardness and directness of the design.

• *Portability.* A measure of how easy it is to transfer software to a different machine and/or a different system.

• *Usability.* A measure of how well the program satisfies its intended functions.

• *Understandability.* A measure of how easy it is for the users to use and understand the software.

• *Performance.* A measure of the efficiency of the software, in terms of storage requirement and execution speed.

These quality factors can be grouped according to three product activities: product operation, product revision and product transition [GEC, 1986]. Product operation includes factors like reliability, performance, security, understandability and usability. Maintainability, modifiability and installability are the factors influencing product revision. Adaptability, simplicity and portability apply to the transition activities in a software life cycle.

4. Language issues

In the 1960s the concept of higher level, more programmer-oriented languages was widely accepted as a means of easing the burden of writing source-code programs. In the late 1970s the shift was towards using higher level languages to document software and to improve the programming process itself through structured programming. Today, the objective is to generate software systems automatically from very high level languages that are especially designed to fit the needs of a particular problem domain. Typical systems in use or under development are directly interpretable specification, graphics, and pattern-based languages.

Languages have always played an important role as a medium of communication and as a basis of realizing the concepts and methodologies discussed in Section 3. In current software development, four types of languages exist: programming, specification, design, and prototyping languages.

The purpose of programming languages is to express the detailed design in a form that can be compiled and executed by a computer. Specification languages describe the desired properties of the system under development. In most cases this is done by defining the functions, the user interface, and the quality criteria of a software system. Design languages describe how the system is to achieve the goals set by the specification. They describe the architecture of a software system and its embedding in the given hardware and organizational environment. The 'structured methods' described in Section 3 are a typical example for the application of a wide variety of language concepts on the design level. Prototyping languages gain more and more importance as a means of supporting an alternative approach to specification and design.

During the last three decades, hundreds of programming languages have been developed to support the implementation of software systems; the designing of programming languages has emerged as a research domain in its own right. Thus, a detailed discussion of programming languages is far beyond the scope of this chapter. We limit ourselves here to the general characteristics of specification and design languages. Prototyping [Floyd, 1984] and the related language issues will be discussed in Section 6. The reader interested in programming languages is referred to Tucker [1986] and Pratt [1984].

4.1. Characteristics of specification languages

The purpose of a specification language is to document a conceptual model of the desired system and to provide a medium of communication between an analyst and the customer. Features of the language should make it easy to establish and maintain the model's conceptual integrity, e.g., correctness and consistency. There is much controversy [Gehani, 1982] regarding the tradeoffs between informal and formal notations in specification languages supporting both the rather informal communication requirements and the inherently more formal analysis and verification. In the light of the recent trends in software development, specification languages that provide a basic formal background have been widely accepted.

In Berzins & Luqi [1990] the following basic properties for a specification language are identified. In addition to precision, expressiveness, and simplicity, the following properties are emphasized.

Abstractness. It should be possible to define interface behaviors completely without considering the mechanisms that operate at lower levels.

Locality. The language should support description units with limited interaction with other units. Dependences between the units should be mechanically detectable.

Tractability. It should be possible to implement a wide variety of automated aids for analyzing, transforming, and implementing subsets of the specification language.

Adaptability. There should be provision for the description of general-purpose components and the adaptation of these components to particular situations.

There is a wide variety of different approaches for realizing specification languages. Some are based on algebras and some are based on logic or graphical notation. Detailed work on specification languages can be found in Burstall & Goguen [1981], Berzins & Gray [1985], and Guttag & Horning [1986]. We refer the interested reader to Luqi, Berzins & Yeh [1988] for a detailed discussion of the advantages and disadvantages of the various solutions.

However, to give an idea of what a non-graphic specification language might look like, Figure 15 shows an example using the algebraic specification of a stack. Algebraic specifications define a system by providing a set of interface procedures that define the functions of the system and the handling of internal data structures and abstract types. Mathematical equations describe the types of data items used and delivered by the procedures (the operational interface of the procedures). A second set of equations (the axioms) defines the behavior of the system when the interface procedures are applied. Each interface procedure is a function in the mathematical sense and can have no side effects on the system. The internal realization of the system is not discussed here; it remains hidden behind the system interface defined (see Section 3.1.2 on information hiding).

The algebraic specification in the example of Figure 15 has four sections. The *type* section specifies that the abstract data type is a stack. The *exception* section gives names to exceptional conditions that might occur during operation, like stack overflow caused by storage limitations. The *operation* section defines the argument types and the results, i.e., the interface, of available procedures necessary to assure normal operation. The procedure *push*, e.g., needs a stack and a stack element as input to produce a new stack. The *axioms* section defines the applications of interface procedures. The semantics of these definitions can be specified by interpreting them as a set of rewrite rules. By applying this concept, combined applications of interface procedures can be

```
type    stack[t]
exception    underflow, novalue
operations
     push(stack[t],e) : stack[t]
     pop(stack[t]) : stack[t]
     top(stack[t]) : e
     empty(stack[t]) : boolean
axioms
     pop(newstack) = underflow
     pop(push(s,e)) = s
     top(newstack) = novalue
     top(push(s,e)) = e
     empty(newstack) = true
     empty(push(s,e)) = false
end
```

Fig. 15. Algebraic specification of a stack.

described by deriving the mathematical expression equivalent to the sequence of procedure applications. This nested expression can then be reduced step by step by means of new rules.

The rewrite rules are an important aspect of abstract algebras. They reduce expressions systematically in the given algebra. The rules are of the form

'left-side expression' → 'right-side expression'

which defines a transformation or 'rewrite' of any expression containing 'left-side expression' by substitution of 'right-side expression'.

The *finite termination* property holds if the reduction process does not loop and comes to an end. The set of rewrite rules exhibits the *unique termination* property if the result of the reduction process is independent of the order in which the rules are applied. The reduction process is *convergent* if the termination is finite and unique.

An example for the application of a rewrite rule is given in Figure 16. The rule used for the rewrite step describes the fact that a 'pop' neutralizes the last 'push' on the stack. Using in the original expression 'push(newstack,e1)' as stack while applying the rule leads to the reduced expression shown.

4.2. Characteristics of design languages

A design is a concise and complete document of the concepts and relationships that embody a solution to some problem stated in a specification. This document is used for formulation, communication, analysis and planning. It bridges between the designers, the managers of the project and the programming group. Usually, the architecture or internal structure of a software system is described. This description enables the personnel involved to analyze many different design properties, such as correctness, performance and development cost. Ideally a design language should support the following activities with suitable notation and checks (see Section 3.2.1 for applications and examples).

Decomposition and aggregation. As we have noted, the development and design of a system is best approached by decomposing it into smaller units (modules). This process of decomposition should be guided by well-defined quality criteria and by methodological support. The design language must provide adequate means of describing the derived decomposition/aggregation

Original Expression:
push(pop(push(push(newstack,e1),e2)),e3)

Rule:
pop(push(s,e)) -> s

Reduced expression:
push(push(newstack,e1),e3)

Fig. 16. Application of a rewrite rule to reduce an expression.

relations between modules. Moreover, the background of the decision process that led to the given kind of structure, i.e., quality concerns and methodology-dependent design decisions, must be documented. It should be easy to see and to change the decomposition/aggregation structure of the design.

Specification of module interfaces. In a system aggregated of smaller units it is crucial to establish the relationships between modules that form the system as a whole. In traditional methods this results in an invocation structure, defining for each module which modules it controls and by which module it is controlled itself. The relationship also determines the streams of data and control between superordinate and subordinate modules. Structured design is a classical example of this approach [Constantine & Yourdon, 1979]. New design paradigms yield different approaches. Object-oriented methods, e.g., reduce interfaces between modules (programmed objects) basically to data items (messages) and related service functions [Kim & Lochovsky, 1989].

Abstraction. Functional abstraction and/or abstraction of data and control allow one to postpone the system design details. In traditional systems [Ross, 1987] the idea is very similar to decomposition. Different abstraction techniques, e.g., IS-A relations [Brachman, 1983], have become important elements in new approaches. In object-oriented design they are usually combined with inheritance algorithms [Kim & Lochovsky, 1989]. See Section 6.1.4 for a brief discussion.

Specification of alternative designs. Consider the implementation of level i in a hierarchical design process. There may exist a large number of modules that may be combined in various ways to produce alternative designs for level $i - 1$. The design language should enable the designer to document modules that (a) must appear together in designs, (b) represent alternatives to other modules, or (c) are optional in the design.

Historically, both high-level and detailed designs have been expressed in structured English. However, today one of the graphical notations associated with structured design methodologies is standard (see Section 3.2.1; Jackson [1975], Ross [1987], Constantine & Yourdon, [1979], Warnier [1981]).

For detailed design, i.e., the implementation of a single module, we have different prerequisites for a language. Flowcharts [Nassi & Schneiderman, 1973] and similar techniques are popular. In addition, a design language is often based on a high-level programming language, or on data declaration capabilities that correspond directly to programming constructs. An example is found in Radice [1975].

5. CASE

A decade after the introduction of an engineering discipline for software development, the members of the software development community still found themselves saddled with the so-called software backlog [Yeh, 1983]. A study of Musa [1985] indicated that from 1965 to 1985 the demand for software increased one hundredfold while software development productivity was increased only twofold. As productivity was obviously a bottleneck, one possible solution of the software crisis was to introduce a higher level of automation to support methodologies and languages, as had been done in other industries. The term describing these efforts is computer-aided software engineering (CASE).

The usual term for components of a CASE environment is 'tools'. Tools support the system developer by providing specialized functionality to handle programs, documents, communication, etc. A simple example for a tool is a compiler, automating the translation of high-level programming languages into a machine-dependent assembler.

5.1. Basic elements of CASE

The easiest way to introduce automation is to improve on already existing solutions in the programming phase. The concept of automatic programming dates back to the 1950s, when assemblers and compilers were introduced to support automation. They allowed one to write programs on a level abstracted from the actual machine architecture and to transform (compile) these programs automatically into machine language. The meaning of the term 'automatic programming' has evolved over time. Today, automatic programming refers more generally to the compiling process that takes a user's specification as input and automatically generates a program that satisfies this specification. However, even though very high level program generators for some narrow problem domains have been successfully produced, the development of an automatic programming system covering a wide range of applications appears to remain a long-term goal.

While academic research concentrated on general-purpose automatic programming systems, substantial progress was made in the commercial arena, with the introduction of so-called computer-aided software engineering environments [Rich & Waters, 1988a]. This less monolithic approach strives to improve productivity by usually focusing on only one phase of the development process; the tools developed in this approach are integrated into an environment that supports the full life cycle.

Today, software engineers have successfully developed tools that range from report generators to database management systems. However, studies done in the early 1980s indicate that there is either lack of awareness of the availability of software tools [Houghton, 1983] or the software tools are seldom used in industry [Yeh 1983, Zelkowitz, Yeh, Hamlet, Gannon & Basili, 1984]. The three broad categories of widely used software tools are as follows.

Design tools. These are graphics tools that help a user draw a 'blueprint' of a design based on a preselected methodology. They are generally user friendly and provide icons, menus, and fill-in-the-blank forms to help the user create the diagrams. They lack the capabilities of generating executable code. Earlier products were mostly mere drawing tools, but products in recent years have tended to cover more capabilities, such as consistency checking, and to allow one type of diagram to be integrated into another.

'Fourth-generation' tools. These tools are more than mere language processors; they are sets of integrated functions that enable the software developers to specify problems using alternative methods like nonprocedural languages. Typical tools of this type include database interfaces with different nonprocedural query capabilities and, for small systems, spreadsheet type application generators. Among the often used systems are the two products NOMAD and FOCUS.

COBOL code generators. A COBOL code generator draws upon a set of precoded COBOL shells. COBOL code is thus generated automatically from user-supplied specifications. Code generated in this way has been claimed to be reliable, but by their nature, COBOL code generators can only cover a narrow domain of application. Examples are APS, GAMMA and PACBASE.

With the advances of technology the challenge in CASE is not so much in developing individual tools as in integrating existing tools. An integrated CASE environment is shown in Figure 17. The innermost layer of the CASE environment is a database that contains all the information associated with the various projects. It contains managerial as well as technical data such as budget, personnel, schedules, specifications, designs and program code. This data is accessible by elements in the middle layer. Examples are tools such as compilers, debuggers, pretty printers, operating system utilities, consistency checkers and automatic-code generators. The outer layer consists of the interface components that directly interact with the end users. Examples of such components are graphics editors and diagrammers. Ideally, a user interacts with the environment only via the outer layer. The system should at least be able to generate a skeleton of the solution after a specification of the problem has been given.

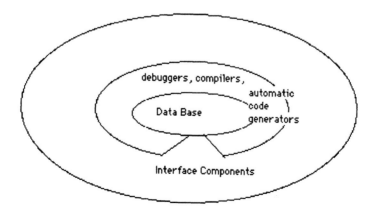

Fig. 17. A CASE environment.

5.2. An example

To increase individual productivity during a computerized process, software development should be treated as a problem definition process rather than a detailed coding process. That is, the development process should include design as in traditional software development but spare the user the coding and testing activities.

Within this class of software systems, MicroSTEP [Yeh, 1990] is an example that helps the user develop business applications directly from the specifications. There is no need to complete all of the steps in the specification process before building a working application that allows one to observe the behavior of the system. At a later stage, the specification can be modified to meet user-specific application requirements. In this way, MicroSTEP can be used effectively to produce prototype applications.

Basically, MicroSTEP consists of three major components: a graphics-based specification system, an application generation system, and an application runtime environment. A user works primarily with the specification system, choosing a few commands from a menu to generate and install the application, while programming and execution activities are handled by the application generation and runtime components.

5.3. Elements of next generation CASE

The concept of a computer-aided software engineering environment has made a radical change to the way software is developed. The trend towards greater automation is expected to continue in the next decade. There are at least two key components that will play a major role in the next generation of CASE: a user interface manager (UIM) and a design database.

The UIM consists of a number of subsystems that manage the different objects a user might need. Since users of future CASE systems might not be professional programmers, a UIM should provide capabilities that allow the user to customize the user interface. Remaining at the heart of any CASE environment, the design database will contain reusable components and domain-specific knowledge. The reusable components may be code, specifications, designs, or process guidelines and frameworks. The domain specific knowledge assists the user to apply reusable high-level application concepts when developing a specification. Domain knowledge and design rules can then be used for advanced checking of semantics and quality, validating the resulting specification in the context of a specific domain. Process frameworks strive for standardization and completeness.

The user of a good CASE environment can usually analyze, transform, and even synthesize several kinds of specifications. To provide such services a CASE environment must have the storage capacity necessary to maintain a large, growing set of interrelated specifications and applications. It should also have the following domain-independent functionalities.

(1) *User interface support.* The system must allow a user (analyst, designer,

specifier) to work with iconographic notations, similar to those used often in multiwindow systems. Apart from other such ease of use and learning attributes, the support subsystem should have the following characteristics.

(a) One should be able to develop applications incrementally, i.e., one can begin with a framework or skeleton and add the details when and where appropriate.

(b) Browsing or hierarchical navigation in a system of specifications whenever appropriate, should be possible.

(c) Design documentation, based on given specifications, should be generated automatically.

(d) It should be able to display specifications simultaneously in different formats and on different media (via a data/concept dictionary).

(e) It should be possible to selectively output skeletons of specifications.

(2) *Design support.* The primary functionality here is a semantics-preserving transformation of specifications, such as those derived from the methodologies discussed in Section 3.2. Examples include the mapping of one specification into an executable specification for prototyping purposes and the restructuring of a specification in order to improve its performance.

(3) *Verification and validation support.* The goal of verification is to ensure that a specification is complete and correct. The functionality of a support system should include checks to make use that no syntax error is contained in a specification and all interfaces are syntactically sound. Validation, on the other hand, is concerned with the consistency of one level of specification with respect to the next higher level of specification. Its ultimate goal is to assure that the specified application meets its intended purpose as stated in its requirements document, i.e., it should show in a formal way that the given specification is a properly transformed instantiation of the requirements document.

(4) *Project management support.* In this category there is a variety of functionalities that deal with technical and managerial concepts. Technical aspects include version and configuration control, maintenance of design decisions and design histories, and tracking of changes and support for quality assurance. Managerial aspects include measurement of progress, budget and staffing adjustment, workload planning and time scheduling. These features are crucial for any CASE environment to be effective in large projects.

The eventual future of CASE is more speculative than that for the other concepts we have discussed. However, it is important to recognize that the challenge of the future CASE environment is not only to provide the above-described functionalities, but to integrate existing tools so as to provide a migration path from the current system to the new system.

6. Alternative paradigms for software evolution

The traditional waterfall model is that of a phased refinement approach. In this approach, all system functionality is specified in the first step of development; subsequent implementation phases add prescribed design details. For many reasons, this approach is impractical for large projects. It is criticized for its high cost of maintenance, for poor motivation of system developers doing abstract tasks in early phases of development, and for complication of systems integration. With the complexity of the problem domains of today's software, there are increasingly many user requirements that do not admit a 'quick' solution. Even worse, the nature of the problem cannot be stated clearly by the user and thus cannot be recorded in a traditional requirements document. In these cases, a pilot version of the project or a different form of system modeling may provide the necessary assistance for a solution.

In this section we shall look at some of these new concepts and introduce an abstraction-based life cycle.

6.1. Emerging ideas

6.1.1. Rapid prototyping

A rapid prototype is an executable model (or pilot version) of the intended system. Prototyping is a process that enables the software developer to create in a short time a model of the software to be built, in order to gain insights into what the requirements and the design of the system should be, before the major development process starts. A prototype in software development is usually reduced in functionality and/or interface handling [Floyd, 1984], but it allows one to investigate specific parts of a system.

The purpose of rapid prototyping has been identified by Hekmatpour [1987] as

- a way to formulate the user requirements,
- a tool for experimenting with new design ideas,
- a safety factor in high-risk development (e.g., in hard real-time applications),
- a means of reacting to organizational changes,
- a means of encouraging user involvement in the development process, and
- a technique for easing the introduction of a system into an organization.

Three basic approaches to prototyping address different needs and functions [Hekmatpour, 1987; Floyd, 1984]; these are called throwaway prototyping, evolutionary prototyping, and incremental prototyping.

Throwaway prototyping addresses the fundamental issue of making sure that the product meets the user's requirements. First, the developer constructs a 'quick and dirty' partial implementation of the system. The potential users then evaluate the system by experimenting with it for a restricted period of time. They provide feedback to the developer on the potential of the system to meet their needs. Once the product has served its purpose of requirements elicitation, it is thrown away.

Evolutionary prototyping is an iterative process of constructing a fully operational system. It starts with a rough and simple implementation of the system that allows its potential users to use the system and provide feedback.

This first implementation is not thrown away, but is enhanced step by step, according to engineering design decisions and user feedback. This process continues until a fully operational system has been constructed and is ready for use.

Incremental prototyping is the process of constructing a system by dividing it, starting from a general first system specification, into self-contained parts. The full system is not implemented, but only one part at a time. After each implementation, the corresponding part of the system is delivered to the user. Feedback from the user on already installed and used system parts and on eventually changing requirements is integrated into the general specification of the system before the next part is implemented according to this changed specification in an adapted version.

In addition to these possible basic approaches prototypes can be classified according to which aspect of the system under development they are intended to model. We obtain three basic classes of prototypes, namely functional prototypes, behavioral or human interface prototypes, and performance-evaluating prototypes.

Functional prototyping addresses the logical capabilities of a proposed system. This permits debugging of the requirements and design. User-oriented functional prototyping may illustrate how the system would process user input information, how it would deal with erroneous cases, etc., without providing more than a model for these functions ('horizontal prototyping'). During a more system-architecture-oriented validation, implementation of selected system parts can demonstrate that the required functionality of certain components is feasible or that the interface mechanism between components is correct ('vertical prototyping'). See Floyd [1984] for a basic discussion.

Behavioral or human prototyping is a prototyping activity where the human interface factors of the system are studied in terms of screen layouts, the icons used, pop-up menus, etc. The main aim is to study the adequacy of the interface in the given user environment.

Performance prototyping can be viewed as a special class of vertical functional prototyping; in addition to functionality, the overall performance characteristics of the software are studied. Typical characteristics include the response time, execution time, interfacing subsystem timing rates, interfacing equipment capacities and the data environment (i.e., the frequency and pattern of changes of individual data items) that invariably affect the performance of the system.

In the past there have been disputes over the potential use of prototyping techniques. However, prototyping has gained a high level of acceptance in recent years for small- and medium-sized projects. It has been incorporated into the framework of existing, sometimes adapted, life cycle models [Boehm, 1988].

Specialized prototyping languages are necessary to support the process of rapid prototyping and its integration into different life cycles. Such a prototyping language is neither a specification, nor a design or programming language in the classical sense (see Section 4).

Berzins & Luqi [1990] have identified the most important attributes of a prototyping language. A prototyping language should have the following characteristics.

(1) It should be executable (at least machine interpretable), so that the customer can observe the operation of the prototype.

(2) It should support hierarchically structured prototypes, to simplify prototyping of a large and complex system (However, the descriptions used should be uniform at all levels of a prototype. The language should harmoniously support data abstraction, functional abstraction, and control abstraction).

(3) It should apply at both the specification and design levels to allow the designer to concentrate on designing the prototype without the distraction of translating one notation into another.

(4) It should be suitable for specifying the retrieval of reusable modules from a software base, to avoid creating multiple descriptions of each module.

(5) It should support both formal and informal module specification methods to allow the designer to work in the style most appropriate to the problem.

(6) It should contain a set of abstractions suitable for the problem area for which the prototyping language is designed, e.g., timing for real-time and embedded systems.

An example for such a prototyping language is PSDL, the prototyping systems definition language [Luqi, Berzins & Yeh, 1988]. PSDL is similar to algebraic design languages and modern programming languages. However, it supports design capabilities and executability at the same time. PSDL is part of an integrated prototyping environment that supports the prototyping process with additional features like a retrieval system for reusable modules, handling of timing constraints for real-time applications, etc.

6.1.2. Reuse

The concept of reuse plays a key role in several issues like productivity, maintainability, portability, quality, and standardization. Biggerstaff & Perlis [1989] provides an in-depth discussion of various approaches and practical examples.

Even though reuse can already be found in various forms in different development environments, e.g., in prototyping, a standardized model for the integration of reuse in structured development techniques that are life cycle oriented is still missing [Mittermeir & Rossak, 1990]. There are two basic concepts for software reuse that have to be applied simultaneously to reach optimal results [Mariani, Sommerville & Haddley, 1989]: development *with* Reuse and development *for* Reuse.

Development with reuse integrates reuse techniques with the development of a software system and focuses on the problem of specifying, locating, and adapting reusable components. Even though there are no standardized models software reuse can be applied to every phase of a traditional phase-oriented software development cycle; see, e.g., Rossak [1989], Rossak & Mittermeir [1989]. However, reuse during the upstream phases of development, such as requirements and design, pays off more than reuse, which is confined to the coding and testing phase.

Development for reuse and/or re-engineering of existing components concentrates on the development of software having a high likelihood of reuse and evaluates the necessary characteristics of such components. In order for a piece of software to be reusable, it should be interpretable, incorporable, or portable. Interpretable means that the potential users can obtain the information they need to understand the software's functionality, operational environment, and any other required attribute. Incorporable means that software is usable in building larger software systems. Portable means that the software can be adapted to different environments with different machines. Furthermore, specification and design of components have to meet strict quality criteria and should be evaluated by metrics. A further discussion of development for reuse is found in Caldiera & Basili [1990], Mittermeir & Rossak [1990], and Mittermeir & Oppitz [1987].

One can identify the current state of software reuse at three levels: the source code level, the level of systems and system parts, and higher levels.

Reuse of modules at the source code level refers to the incorporation of software modules into many different application programs. Typical examples at this level are the modules available in subroutine libraries. Advanced programming concepts like data abstractions, strict modularity and object orientedness support this kind of reuse.

Subroutine libraries are usually domain specific and confine their applicability to a single user or to a single project. Good examples are statistical packages such as SPSS. Data abstraction and modularity are supported by some modern programming languages such as Modula 2 [Wirth, 1985] and Ada [ADA, 1983]. Smalltalk [Goldberg & Robson, 1983] is an example of a language relying on the object-oriented paradigm (see Section 6.1.4). These languages allow a programmer to define data and procedural abstractions and to reuse them in different applications.

Generic program units are the most flexible reuse of program parts at the source code level. They introduce a new level of abstraction above the source code level, thus allowing for a more flexible handling of components. They lead directly to reuse of complete systems and system parts, instead of merely single modules.

A generic unit is a template of a program unit described at an abstract level that can be refined according to given needs. Therefore, it can be instantiated in a family of similar program units by defining the proper specializations. For example, one can write a generic sorting function for a list. The type of the elements and the precedence rule used in sorting can be generic. This generic function can then be instantiated (specialized) to sort a list of integers in ascending order, or to sort a list of strings in lexical order. Thus, generic units increase the modifiability of a program unit and allow a program part to adapt to many different but similar applications.

At the next level one defines not only single units but also a full system. This is done by providing a specification that represents the system structure and has 'open places' that can be filled with generic units, if these units fulfill the specification. This kind of system not only allows one to take advantage of generic units, but it adds the possibility to reason on the level of generic systems and subsystems as components of reuse. An example for a prototype of a system handling generic applications is the Software-Base [Mittermeir & Oppitz, 1987; Mittermeir & Rossak, 1987].

To be able to reuse components in other than the coding and testing phases it is necessary not only to handle source code and generics but to allow more generalized system descriptions like design and even requirements documents. Furthermore, a proper record of system aggregation/decomposition in subsystems, components and modules must be provided. Systems supporting this activity use generalization and aggregation taxonomies. These two basic classifications are enhanced by other notions, such as similarity or 'uses'-relations, and form a central knowledge base for classifying and describing reusable components. An engineer may browse, with or without automatic query support, through such a structure and retrieve components that fit his needs in a given phase of system development. Prototypes of reuse systems of this type are illustrated by the Software-Archive [Rossak & Mittermeir, 1989] and the LaSSIE system [Devanbu, Brachman, Selfridge & Ballard, 1990].

It is evident that a proper form of classification is a basic issue in all these systems. This classification scheme should allow software components to be retrieved and integrated into a complex system with ease. Many classification schemata have been discussed in the literature. In the simplest schema software components are classified by application and function. More sophisticated schemata are based on the idea of faceted classification [Prieto-Diaz & Freeman, 1987].

In addition to classifying and organizing components one must consider the requirements of the given problem domain. Today it is accepted as a standard that an analysis of the application domain for the derivation of a basic domain structure must be made before any components are defined or classified [Neighbours, 1984]. On the basis of this analysis and realizing that different projects in the same domain might use different classifications and forms of organization, flexible mechanisms have to be defined to provide interfaces between projects, see, e.g., Rossak & Mittermeir [1990].

However, methods, tools, languages, and standardized guidelines for software reuse deal only with the technical aspects of software reuse. It can be argued that organizational, financial, and psychological aspects have to be given as much weight as the more engineering-oriented aspects. See Tracz [1987, 1988] and Barnes, Durek, Gaffney & Pyster [1987] for a short introduction to these meta-issues of reuse.

6.1.3. Program transformation

Currently the most active area in automatic programming research is the use of a transformational approach to programming for supporting the program development process. Program development is an iterative process of successive transformation/refinement whereby the formal program specifications are gradually transformed into an efficient implementation [Balzer, 1981]. Transformations may involve generalizing a representation, selecting a data structure, or changing a control structure to improve program efficiency. A program transformation usually has three parts [Rich & Waters, 1988a,b]. An input pattern determines where to apply the transformation. A set of applicability conditions restricts the places where the transformation can be applied. A set of corresponding actions creates a new program to replace the text matched by the pattern.

There are many benefits of transformational programming [Agresti, 1986; Partsch & Steinbrugger, 1983]. The transformation can be automated and thus reduce the labor intensity of the software development, or by being coupled with flexible interactive programming, aid the selection of transformations at each iteration. To apply transformations is safe in that they can be expressed formally to preserve the correctness and freedom from side effects. Transformation also effectively eliminates final product testing, which is replaced by verification of the program specification.

However, the transformational approach is more than an alternative programming facility. It derives concrete programs from abstract ones. There are two principal interpretations of transformations [Jahinchen, 1986; Rich & Waters 1988]:

Lateral (*transformational*) transformations are regarded as a sequence of transitions that transforms a program (or specification) into a better one;

Vertical (*refinement*) transformations are regarded as a sequence of transitions replacing abstract parts of a program (or specification) by more detailed ones.

Both interpretations are often based on a language being rich enough to express both specifications and programs. They have to be supported by a development paradigm that includes the strategies and heuristics used by software experts to help transform a specification into a more efficient version, or automatically generate a more detailed program from abstract specifications. Unfortunately, users are unable to foresee all of the implications and interactions. As a result, transformation systems often create undesirable effects. In addition, dealing with incomplete specifications becomes a problem.

6.1.4. Object-oriented systems

Object orientedness, like prototyping, is an emerging alternative to classical development paradigms. However, while prototyping still results in systems that usually reflect the well known tree-like control structure, object-oriented methodologies are based on a different understanding of what a software system is. The essential idea is to build independent entities that communicate only by sending and accepting messages.

Beyond this general notion, there is no commonly accepted definition of the attributes that describe an object-oriented system. A good discussion of the various issues relating to object-oriented systems can be found in Kim & Lochovsky [1989]. This section briefly describes a kernel of basic concepts usually associated with object orientedness. Comments are also given on the state of the art of object-oriented design and languages. Because of space limitations, other aspects, such as object-oriented databases, are not covered.

Object-oriented systems create representations of entities in the problem domain of the real world and implement them as objects in the solution domain, i.e. the software system. An object consists of a set of structured data items and the operations (functions) on this internal data structure. An object can send or receive messages via its attached functions. On receiving a message, an object's data items are manipulated by the function addressed by the incoming message; the message is used as a set of parameters for that function. By sending a message, a function in one or more different objects of the system environment can be triggered.

As an example, consider a simple checking account as an object. The object is composed of data indicating the current balance, a list of authorized persons, and three functions, withdrawal and deposit of money, and authorization of use. An initial message authorizes a given person to use the account, by supplying a name to be included in the list of authorized persons. From this moment on, withdrawals and deposits, if signed with the proper name, can be sent to the account. If a withdrawal cannot be made because of an internal credit limit, a message indicating that fact is sent to a 'clerk' object for processing.

Object-oriented systems deal simultaneously with the modularization of functionality and data, rather than individually as classical systems. This means that object-oriented methods rely heavily on the standard principles of abstraction, information hiding, and modularity used in abstract datatypes, data capsules and traditional design languages (see Section 4). However, object-oriented systems do not define a strict hierarchical system structure based on component 'calls', as is done in most software engineering approaches. There is no general system structure with a static quality of its own; there is only a set of known objects and a dynamical flow of messages between them.

Apart from these concepts, most object-oriented systems rely on generalization and inheritance. Through generalization one constructs class hierarchies and differentiates between classes and instantiated objects.

In the above example, the 'checking account' is a class, describing in general what a checking account provides for a customer within the scope of the given problem domain. The checking account for Mr Smith is an instantiation of this class and it inherits all the structural and functional attributes of its superordinate class. To be exact, one must speak about a class instantiation in this example, for only instantiations normally send and receive messages.

Classes themselves are integrated into class hierarchies in which superordinate classes define common structural or functional properties of subordinate classes. In our example, the class 'checking account' and a class 'savings account' could have a common ancestor in the class hierarchy named 'account'.

'Account' specifies properties common to all accounts revealing differences between using checking and saving. This common description is inherited by 'checking account' and by 'savings account' and is automatically part of their definition. Special attributes for checking and saving can be added, and inherited attributes can be changed (specialized, eliminated). As an example, if 'account' specifies a general withdrawal procedure, 'checking account' could specialize this procedure to check withdrawals.

Class hierarchies and inheritance of attributes and functionality allow one to reuse objects already specified and to adapt them to given needs. Furthermore, it is easy to introduce a new class, when an already existing one can serve as an ancestor, e.g., 'checking account' could be an ancestor for a new class 'company account'. Prototyping and incremental development are natural to such environments.

However, from the point of view of software engineering other questions play a more important role. The proper objects in the application domain have to be identified, as to be transformed to procedures, message flows, and the class hierarchy. The dynamic relationship between different objects, based on the passing of messages during runtime, must be specified and implemented. There are several proposals how to handle object-oriented design, e.g., as described by Kim & Lochovsky [1989], Coad & Yourdon [1991], and Booch, [1991]. Traditional data-oriented methodologies like Jackson structured design [Jackson, 1983] identify objects and so-called activities, but they are not fully object oriented, as they lead ultimately to a traditional hierarchical system structure. Design languages like CML [Mittermeir, 1982] can be applied to object-oriented design, since they support the basic concept of a system of objects and messages.

Designers of programming languages have long recognized the importance of data abstraction, information hiding and modularity. Accordingly, there are several languages that provide features supporting some of these concepts. Examples are Ada [ADA, 1983] and Modula 2 [Wirth, 1985]. However, both of these languages are based on the concept of a predefined and mainly static hierarchical system structure comprised of modules related by invocation procedures (calls), import/export relations and synchronization mechanisms. The missing element is the 'distributed' aspect of object-oriented systems, where objects are related only by messages. C++ [Stroustrup, 1986] enriches the C programming language with object-oriented constructs and accommodates the concepts of both the traditional and the object-oriented world. The best known programming environment that is rigidly object oriented is Smalltalk [Goldberg & Robson, 1983].

To explore the flexibility of inheritance some object-oriented programming languages implement features like dynamic binding. Dynamic binding links an operation, e.g., withdrawal, to its implementation in a dynamic process during the runtime instead of in a more static way during compile time (as for traditional subroutines).

Ada, developed by the US Department of Defense, supports a rich set of language features that can be used to implement an object-oriented type of system with relatively conservative constructs. Programming units of Ada, such as subprograms, tasks and packages, consist of two parts: the specification and the body. The specification provides the information necessary for the correct use of the programming unit; the body provides the encapsulation of local variables and subprogram definitions. This concept permits access to modules through externally defined interfaces separated from the implementation. The interface is an external specification of data structures and related functions. The most valuable construct for object-oriented work in Ada seems to be the generic package, which is a variation of the generic components discussed in the section on software reuse (Section 6.1.2).

In Smalltalk a programmer can define object instantiations and classes of objects. Classes are organized in a generalization hierarchy with inheritance. Objects communicate only via messages; there is no static program structure other than a set of objects ready to communicate. The generalization hierarchy provides, like a well organized and structured library of components, a large number of reusable objects. Here, programming means to derive new objects from known classes rather than to build a tree-shaped structure of function-oriented modules.

6.2. An abstraction-based software life model

The shortcomings of the waterfall model (see Zvegintzov [1982] and Section 2.2) has encouraged researchers to seek new paradigms for software development [Yeh, 1983]. One such paradigm is the abstraction-based life model discussed in this section.

The process model of this paradigm is depicted in Figure 18. It differs from the traditional phase approach in that it concentrates on difficult problems in software, such as requirements, specification, and design, rather than coding. Of equal importance is the property that validation and evaluation are introduced as elements of the development process itself rather than at the completion of the development in each phase.

Central to this approach is the specification of software system functionality in a form that is precisely interpretable and yet does not oversimplify the implementation of the system design. This can be achieved by abstraction, whereby the functionality specification expresses constraints on the possible realizations that achieve different objectives in cost, performance, error tolerance, etc.

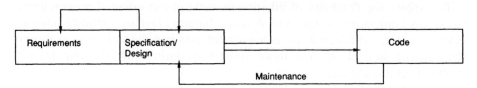

Fig. 18. A new paradigm for software evolution.

Function, data, and control are three types of abstractions that are essential in characterizing the functional attributes of any software system. Function abstractions hide certain properties of algorithms that perform transformations, hence allowing a function to be modified without affecting other functions. Data abstractions hide certain properties of the organization of a set of data structures; this allows the interface to be specified independently of its internal representation. Control abstractions hide certain properties of the order of execution of a set of operations and, thus, reduce the complexity of a system.

Given a precise statement of functionality, a set of evaluation and validation processes can be coupled closely with the design/development process. As shown in Figure 19, rapid functional prototyping, performance modeling and design testing are all part of this evaluation process. This permits the user an early review of the proposed capabilities of the system. It also helps users to better understand and express their needs. This early evaluation of the development serves to eliminate many of the causes for later system maintenance. With performance modeling at different stages of the design, performance issues can be identified before the system is completed. It also helps one trade off different design approaches. By checking interfaces and the degree of coupling between modules, design testing facilitates the early elimination of poor designs.

The code synthesis arrow in Figure 19 also implies that, in this evolution paradigm, code is synthesized at the highest level of specifications, by direct transformation or by utilizing previously developed component and subsystem designs. It avoids a common barrier to code reuse, namely that even if the functionality is correct, the implementation details might not apply in a new setting. The reusable component is described in terms of its functional abstraction. By this strategy, extensive reuse becomes the rule.

This paradigm incorporates two kinds of evolution: incremental delivery and maintenance. With the functionality structure directly determining the system implementation structure, it is convenient to add functional capability in-

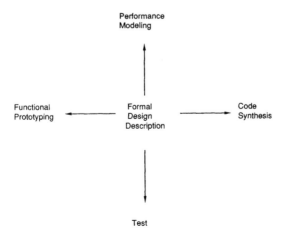

Fig. 19. Interactive design steps in the new paradigm.

crementally. It is often useful to realize an early implementation with limited capabilities. This achieves early usage of the system as an alternative to checking on specification errors. It also yields an early pass at system integration and the location of design defects and interface errors (see Section 6.1.1).

In summary, this abstraction-based model facilities the design of an executable specification by means of a design language based on abstraction. This allows one to integrate prototyping, transformation, and reuse techniques in a natural and easy manner.

References

Ada (1983). *Ada Programming Language*, U.S. Department of Defense, ANSI/MIL-STD-1815A.
Agresti, W.W. (1986). *New Paradigms for Software Development*, IEEE Tutorial.
ANSI (1983). *ANSI/IEEE Std 729-1983*, IEEE, New York.
Balzer, R. (1981). Transformation implementation: An example. *IEEE Trans. Software Engrg.* 7(1), 3–14.
Barnes, B., T. Durek, J. Gaffney, A. Pyster (1987). A framework and economic foundation for software reuse, *Proc. Workshop on Software Reusability and Maintainability*, Nat. Institute of Software Quality and Productivity, October 1987.
Basu, S.K., R.T. Yeh (1975). Strong verification of progrms. *IEEE Trans. Software Engrg.* 1(3), 339–345.
Berlinger, E. (1980). An information theory based complexity measure, *Proc. of the 1980 NCC*, AFIP Press, Arlington, VA, pp. 773–779.
Berzins, V., M. Gray (1985). Analysis and design in MSG.84: Formalizing functional specifications, *IEEE Trans. Software Engrg.* 11(8), 657–670.
Berzins, V., Luqi (1990). Languages for specification, design and prototyping, in: P. Ng., R.T. Yeh (eds.), *Modern Software Engineering*, Van Nostrand Reinhold, New York, pp. 83–118.
Biggerstaff, T.J., A.J. Perlis (1989). *Software Reusability, Vol. I and Vol. II*, ACM Press, New York, ACM 704894.
Boehm, B.W. (1975). Software and its impact: A quantitative assessment. *Datamation* 19(5), 48–59.
Boehm, B.W. (1976). Software engineering. *IEEE Trans. Comput.* 25(12), 1226–1241.
Boehm, B.W. (1984). Software life-cycle factors, in: C.R. Vick, C.V. Ramamoorthy (eds.), *Handbook of Software Engineering*, Van Nostrand Reinhold, New York.
Boehm, B.W. (1988). A spiral model of software development and enhancement. *IEEE Computer* 21(5), 61–72.
Booch, G. (1991). *Object Oriented Design with Applications*, Benjamin Cummings, Redwood City, CA.
Brachman, R.J. (1983). What IS-A is and isn't: An analysis of taxonomic links is semantic networks. *IEEE Computer* 16(10), 30–36.
Burstall, R.M. (1969). Proving properties of programs by structural induction. *Comput. J.* 12(1), 41–48.
Burstall, R.M., J.A. Goguen (1981). An informal introduction to specifications using clear, in: R.S. Boyer, J.S. Moore (eds.), *The Correctness Problem in Computer Science*, Springer, Berlin, pp. 185–213.
Burstall, R.M., P.J. Landin (1969). Programs and their proofs: An algebraic approach, in: B. Meltzer, D. Michie (eds.), *Machine Intelligence, Vol. 4*, Edinburgh University Press, pp. 17–43.
Caldiera, G., V.R. Basili (1990). Reengineering existing software for reusability, Institute for Advanced Computer Studies and Dept. of Computer Science, UMIACS-TR-90-3, CS-TR-2419, Univ. of Maryland, College Park, MD.
Chapin, N. (1979). A measure of softwrae complexity, *Proc. of the 1979 NCC*, AFIPS, Press, Arlington, VA, pp. 992–1002.

Coad, P., E. Yourdon (1991). *Object-oriented Design*, Yourdon Press Computing Series, Prentice-Hall, Englewood Cliffs, NJ.

Constantine, L.L., E. Yourdon (1979). *Structured Design: Fundamentals of a Discipline of Computer Program and Systems Design*, Prentice-Hall, Englewood Cliffs, NJ.

De Marco, T. (1978). *Structured Analysis and System Specification*, Yourdon Press, New York.

Denert E., W. Hesse (1980). Projektmodell und Projektbibliothek: Grundlagen zuverlaessiger Software-Entwicklung und Dokumentation. *Informatik Spektrum* 3, 215–228.

Devanbu, P.T., R.J. Brachman, P.J. Selfridge, B.W. Ballard (1990). LaSSIE – A knowledge-based software information system, *Proc. 12th ICSE*, Nice, France, IEEE Computer Soc. Press, Silver Spring, MD, pp. 249–261.

Dijkstra, E.W. (1972). Notes on structured programming, in: O.J. Dahl, E.W. Dijkstra, C.A.R. Hoare (eds.), *Structured Programming*, Academic Press, London.

Dijkstra, E.W. (1975). Guarded commands, non-determinancy and a calculus for the deviation of programs, *Commun. ACM* 18(8), 453–457.

Dijkstra, E.W. (1976). *A Discipline Programming*, Prentice-Hall, Englewood Cliffs, NJ.

Drummond, S. (1985). Measuring application development performance. *Datamation* 31(4), 102–108.

Floyd, R.W. (1967). Assigning meaning for programs, *Proc. of the American Mathematical Society Symposia in Applied Mathematics* 19 American Mathematical Society, Providence, RI, pp. 19–32.

Floyd, Ch. (1984). A systematic look at prototyping, in: R. Budde et al. (eds.), *Approaches to Prototyping*, Springer, Berlin, pp. 1–18.

Gane, C., T. Sarson (1979). *Structured Systems Analysis: Tools and Techniques*. Prentice-Hall, Englewood Cliffs, NJ.

GEC (1986). *Software Engineering Handbook*, Prepared by General Electric Company, Corporate Information Systems, Bridgeport, Connecticut, McGraw-Hill, New York.

Gehani, N.H. (1982). Specification: Formal and informal – A case study. *Software – Pract. Exper.* 12, 433–444.

Gidding, R.V. (1984). Accommodating uncertainty in software design, *Commun. ACM* 27(5), 428–434.

Gilbert, P. (1983). *Software Design and Development*, SRA, Chicago.

Gladden, G.R. (1982). Stop the life-cycle, I want to get off, *ACM SIGSOFT Software Engineering Notes* 7(2), 35–39.

Goldberg, A., D. Robson (1983). *Smalltalk-80: The Language and Its Implementation*, Addison-Wesley, Reading, MA.

Guttag, J.V., J.J. Horning (1986). Report on the Larch shared language. *Sci. Comput. Programming* 6, 103–134.

Hall, P.A.V. (1982). In defense of life cycles, *ACM SIGSOFT Software Engineering Notes* 7(3), p. 23.

Halstead, M.H. (1977). *Elements of Software Science*, North-Holland, New York.

Hekmatpour, S. (1987). Experience with evolutionary prototyping in a large software project, *ACM SIGSoft Software Engineering Notes* 12(1), 38–41.

Hoare, C.A.R. (1969). An axiomatic basis of computer programming, *Commun. ACM* 12(10), 576–583.

Houghton Jr., R.C. (1983). Software development tools; A profile. *IEEE Computer* 16(5), 63–70.

IBM (1974). *IBM HIPO*, A Design Aid and Documentation Technique, GC 20-185D, IBM Corp., White Plains, NY.

Jackson, M.A. (1975). *Principles of Program Design*, Academic Press, New York.

Jackson, M.A. (1983). *System Development*, Prentice-Hall, Englewood Cliffs, NJ.

Jahinchen, S. et al. (1986). Program development by transformation and refinement, in: G. Goos, J. Hartmanis (eds.), *Lecture Notes in Computer Science 244, Advanced Programming Environments*, Springer, Berlin.

Kim, W., F.H. Lochovsky (eds.) (1989). *Object-Oriented Concepts, Databases and Applications*, ACM Press, Frontier Series.

Linger, R.C., H.D. Mills, B.I. Witt (1979). *Structured Programming*, Addison-Wesley, Reading, MA.

Liskov, B.H., S.N. Zilles (1974). Programming with abstract data types, *Current Trends in Programming Methodology, Vol. 1*, Prentice-Hall, Englewood Cliffs, NJ, pp. 1–32.

Luqi, V. Berzins, R.T. Yeh (1988). A prototyping language for real-time software. *IEEE Trans. Software Engrg.* 14(10), 1409–1423.

Manna, Z. (1974). *Mathematical Theory of Computation*, McGraw-Hill, New York.

Manna, Z., J. McCarthy (1970). Properties of programs and partial function logic. *Mach. Intell.* 5, American Elsevier, New York, 27–37.

Manna, Z., S. Ness, J. Vuillemin (1972). Inductive methods for proving properties of programs, Proc. ACM Conference on Proving Assertions about Programs. *SIGPLAN Notices* 7(1), 27–50.

Manna, Z., S. Ness, J. Vuillemin (1973). Inductive methods for proving properties of programs. *Commun. ACM* 16(8), 491–502.

Manna, Z., J. Vuillemin (1972). Fixpoint approach to the theory of computation. *Commun. ACM* 15(7), 528–536.

Mariani, J.A., I. Sommerville, N. Haddley (1989). The dragon reuse toolset, Position Paper for Workshop on Software Reuse – Reports on Research in Progress, Utrecht, The Netherlands, November 1989.

Martin, J. (1984). *An Information Systems Manifesto*, Prentice-Hall, Englewood Cliff, NJ.

Martin, J., C. McClure (1985). *Diagramming Techniques for Analysts and Programmers*, Prentice-Hall, Englewood Cliffs, NJ.

McCabe, T.J. (1976). A complexity measure. *IEEE Trans. Software Engrg.* 2(4), 308–320.

McCarthy, J. (1963). A basis for a mathematical theory of computation, in: P. Baafort, D. Hirschberg (eds.), *Computer Programming and Formal Systems*, North-Holland, Amsterdam, pp. 33–70.

McCracken, D.D., M.A. Jackson (1982). Life cycle concept considered harmful. *ACM SIGSOFT Software Engineering Notes* 7(2), 29–32.

Mittermeir, R.T. (1982). CML-graphs – A notation for system development, *Proc. 6th European Meeting on Cybernetics and Systems Research*, North-Holland, Amsterdam, pp. 803–809.

Mittermeir, R.T., M. Oppitz, (1987). Software bases for the flexible composition of application systems. *IEEE Trans. Software Engrg.* 13(4), 440–460.

Mittermeir, R.T., W. Rossak (1987). Software-bases and software-archives – Alternatives to support software reuse, *Proceedings FJCC '87*, Dallas, TX, October 1987, IEEE Computer Soc. Press, Silver Spring, MD, pp. 21–28.

Mittermeir, R.T., W. Rossak (1990). Reusability, in: P. Ng, R.T. Yeh (eds.), *Modern Software Engineering*, Van Nostrand Reinhold, New York.

Morris, J.H. Jr., B. Wegbrett (1977). Subgoal induction. *Commun. ACM* 20(4) 209–222.

Musa, J.D. (1985). Software engineering; The future of a profession. *IEEE Software* 2(1), 55–62.

Nassi, I., B. Schneiderman (1973). Flowchart techniques for structured programming. *ACM SIGPLAN Notices* 8(8), 12–26.

Naur, P. (1966). Proof of algorithms by general snapshots. *BIT* 6(4), 310–316.

Neighbours, J.M. (1984). The DRACO approach to constructing software from reusable components, *IEEE Trans. Software Engrg.* 10(5), 564–574.

Page-Jones, M. (1988). *The Practical Guide to Structured Systems Design, 2nd edition*, Prentice-Hall, Englewood Cliffs, NJ.

Parnas, D.L. (1972a). A technique for the specification of software modules with examples. *Commun. ACM* 15(5), 330–336.

Parnas, D.L. (1972b). On the criteria to be used in decomposing systems into modules. *Commun. ACM* 15(12), 1053–1058.

Partsch, H., R. Steinbrugger (1983). Program transformation systems. *Comput. Surveys* 15(3), 199–236.

Pratt, T. (1984). *Programming Languages, 2nd edition*, Prentice-Hall, Englewood Cliffs, NJ.

Pressman, R.S. (1992). *Software Engineering: A Practitioner's Approach, 3rd edition*, McGraw-Hill Series in Software Engineering and Technology.

Prieto-Diaz, R., P. Freeman (1987). Classifying software for reusability. *IEEE Software* 4(1), 6–16.

Radice, R.A. (1975). Design programming language, IBM Tech. Rep. 21.604.

Rich, C., R.C. Waters, (1988a). Automatic programming: Myths and prospects. *IEEE Computer* 21(8), 40–51.

Rich, C., R.C. Waters (1988b). The programmer's apprentice: A research overview. *IEEE Computer* 21(11), 11–25.

Ross, D.T. (1987). Applications and extensions of SADT. *IEEE Computer* 18(4) 25–34.

Ross, D.A. J.B. Goodenough, C.A. Irvine (1975). Software engineering; Process, principles and goals. *IEEE Computer* 8(5), 17–27.

Rossak, W. (1989). Software development reusing existing components – The software archive, Proc. of the IEEE Phoenix Conference on Computers and Communications 89, Scottsdale AZ, March 1989, IEEE Computer Soc. Press. Silver Spring, MD, pp. 327–331.

Rossak, W., R.T. Mittermeir (1989). A DBMS based archive for reusable software components, *Proc. of the 2nd Internat. Workshop on Software Engineering and Its Applications*, Toulouse, France, December 1989, pp. 501–516.

Rossak, W., R.T. Mittermeir (1990). The user-view as basic concept for software reuse, *Proceedings of the Eighth International IASTED Symposium on Applied Informatics*, Innsbruck, Austria, February 1990, pp. 288–291.

Royce, W.W. (1970). Managing the development of large software systems: Concept and techniques, *Proc. WESCON*, AIEE, Aug. 1970.

Stevens, W.P., G.J. Myers, L.L. Constantine (1974). Structured design. *IBM Syst. J.* 13(2), 115–139.

Stroustrup, B (1986). *The C++ Programming Language*, Addison-Wesley, Reading, MA.

Swartout, W., R. Balzer (1982). On the inevitable intertwining of specification and implementation. *Commun. ACM* 25(7), 438–440.

Tonies, C.S. (1979). Project management fundamentals, in: R.W. Jensen, C.S. Tonies (eds.), *Software Engineering*, Prentice-Hall, Englewood Cliffs, NJ.

Tracz W. (1987). Software reuse: Motivators and inhibitors, *Proc. COMPCON S'87*, IEEE, Computer Soc. Press, Silver Spring, MD, pp. 358–363.

Tracz, W. (1988). Software reuse maxims. *Software Engineering Notes* 13(4), 28–31.

Tucker, A.B. (1986). *Programming Languages, 2nd edition*, McGraw-Hill, New York.

Warnier, J. (1981). *Logical Construction of Systems*, Van Nostrand Reinhold, New York.

Wirth, N. (1971). Program development by stepwise refinement. *Commun. ACM* 14(4), 221–227.

Wirth, N. (1974). On the composition of well-structured programs. *Comput. Surveys* 6(4), 247–259.

Wirth, N. (1985). *Programming in Modula 2, 3rd edition*, Springer, Berlin.

Yeh, R.T. (1977). Verification of programs by predicate transformation, in: R.T. Yeh (ed.), *Current Trends in Programming Methodology*, Prentice-Hall, Englewood Cliffs, NJ, pp. 228–247.

Yeh, R.T. (1983). Software engineering. *IEEE Spectrum*, November, 91–94.

Yeh, R.T. (1990). MicroSTEP: Your automated programmer for business application, in: P. Ng. R.T. Yeh (eds.), *Modern Software Engineering*, Van Nostrand Reinhold, New York.

Zelkowitz, M., R.T. Yeh, R.G. Hamlet, J.D. Gannon, V.R. Basili (1984). Software engineering practices in the US and Japan. *IEEE Computer* 17(6), 57–66.

Zvegintzov, N. (1982). What life? What cycle?, Proc. of the National Computer Conference, AFIPS Press, Reston, VA, pp. 563–568.

Additional reading

Software engineering

Pressman, R.S. (1992). *Software Engineering: A Practitioner's Approach, 3rd edition*, McGraw-Hill Series in Software Engineering and Technology.

Vick, C.R., C.V. Ramamoorthy (1984). *Handbook of Software Engineering*, Van Nostrand Reinhold Company, New York.

Ng, P.A., R.T. Yeh (1990). *Modern Software Engineering*, Van Nostrand Reinhold, New York.

CASE

Berzins, V., Luqi (1990). *Software Engineering with Abstractions*, Addison-Wesley, Reading, MA.

IEEE Software, (special issue on CASE) 5(2), 1988.

McClure, C. (1988). *CASE is Software Automation*, Prentice-Hall, Englewood Cliffs, NJ.

Bergland, G.D., R.D. Gordon (1981). *Software Design Strategies*, IEEE Tutorial, IEEE Computer Soc. Press, Silver Spring, MD, IEEE EH0184-2.

Tanik, M.M., E.S. Chan (1992). *Fundamentals of Computing for Software Engineers*, Van Nostrand Reinhold, New York.

Software reuse

Biggerstaff, T.J., A.J. Perlis (1989). *Software Reusability, Vol. I and Vol. II*, ACM Press, New York, ACM 704894.

Tracz, W. (1988). *Software Reuse: Emerging Technology*, IEEE Tutorial, IEEE Computer Soc. Press, Silver Spring, MD, IEEE EH0278-2.

Freeman, P. (1988). *Software Reusability*, IEEE Tutorial, IEEE Computer Soc. Press, Silver Spring, MD, IEEE EH0256-8.

Prototyping and integrated approaches

Budde, R. et al. (1984). *Approaches to Prototyping*, Springer, Berlin.

Boehm, B.W. (1988). A spiral model of software development and enhancements. *IEEE Computer* 21(5), 61–72.

IEEE Computer, (special issue on Prototyping) 22(5), 1989.

Object orientedness

Booch, G. (1991). *Object Oriented Design with Applications*, Benjamin Cummings, Redwood City, CA.

Coad, P., E. Yourdon (1991). *Object-Oriented Design*, Yourdon Press Computing Series, Prentice-Hall, Englewood Cliffs, NJ.

Kim, W., F.H. Lochovsky (1989). *Object-Oriented Concepts, Databases, and Applications*, ACM Press, New York, Frontier Series.

Programming environments

IEEE Software, (special issue on Seamless Systems) 22(11), 1989.

Proc. ACM SIGSOFT TAV3 '89, Symposium on Practical Software Development Environments, *Software Engineering Notes* 14(8), 1989.

Structured programming

Jensen, R.W. (1981). Tutorial series – 6: Structured programming. *IEEE Computer* 14(3), 31–48.

Linger, R.C., H.D. Mills, B.I. Witt (1979). *Structured Programming*, Addison-Wesley, Reading, MA.

Structured analysis and structured design

Yourdon, E., L.L. Constantine (1979). *Structured Design*, Prentice-Hall, Englewood Cliffs, NJ.
Ross, D.T. (1977). Structured analysis (SA): A language for communicating ideas. *IEEE Trans. Software Engrg.* 3(1), 16–33.
Jackson, M.A. (1975). *Principles of Program Design*, Academic Press, New York.
Warnier, J.D. (1974). *Logical Construction of Programs*, Van Nostrand Reinhold, New York.

Testing

Myers, G. (1979). *The Art of Software Testing*, Wiley, New York.
Miller, E., W.E. Howden, (1981). *Software Testing and Validation Techniques, 2nd edition*, IEEE Computer Soc. Press, Silver Spring, MD.

Software costing

Boehm, B.W. (1981). *Software Economics*, Prentice-Hall, Englewood Cliffs, NJ.
Boehm, B.W. (1975). The high cost of software, in: E. Horowitz (ed.), *Practical Strategies for Developing Large Software Systems*, Addison-Wesley, Reading, MA, pp. 4–14.

Software metrics

Albrecht, A.J., J.E. Gaffney (1983). Software function, source lines of code and development effort prediction: A software science validation. *IEEE Trans. Software Engrg.* 9(6), 639–648.
McCabe, T. (1976). A complexity measure. *IEEE Trans. Software Engrg.* 2(4), 308–320.

Fourth-generation languages

Martin, J. (1985, 1986). *Fourth Generation Languages, Vol. 1 to Vol. 3*, Prentice-Hall, Englewood Cliffs, NJ.

E.G. Coffman et al., Eds., *Handbooks in OR & MS, Vol. 3*

Chapter 6

A Survey of Matrix Computations

Charles Van Loan

Department of Computer Science, Cornell University, Ithaca, NY 14853-7501, U.S.A.

Preface

This chapter is a three-level introduction to the field of matrix computations. The first section is very informal and is designed to acquaint the reader with the basic tools of the trade. The tools range from the algorithmic (What is a Householder matrix and how can it be used to solve the least square problem?) to the analytic (What happens to the solution of a least square problem if we perturb the data?).

In the second section we discuss the matrix factorizations that figure heavily in numerical linear algebra. For each factorization we survey algorithms, associated mathematical properties, and applications. Sprinkled throughout this section are special topics that illustrate the power of the factorization paradigm.

In the final section we use one factorization (Cholesky) to illustrate various aspects of high performance matrix computations. Successful computing nowadays requires the design of codes that pay careful attention to the flow of data during execution. Our goal is to make the reader more aware of these data movement concerns.

Of course, it is impossible to do justice to the matrix computation field in just a few pages and so we have been careful to include ample pointers to the literature. But before delving into the research papers it is useful to be aware of some of the standard references. Books that attempt to cover the area include Hager [1988], Stewart [1973], Watkins [1991], and Golub & Van Loan [1989]. The last reference is particularly comprehensive – virtually everything we discuss may be found in that volume.

There are several good books that focus on some of the major problem areas such as linear systems, least squares fitting, and the eigenvalue problem. These include Forsythe & Moler [1967], Lawson & Hanson [1974], Parlett [1980], Varga [1962], and Wilkinson [1965].

Sparse matrix problems are increasingly important and so we mention the texts by Björck, Plemmons & Schneider [1981], Duff, Erisman & Reid [1986], and George & Liu [1981].

For those interested in the development or use of matrix computation software we recommend Coleman & Van Loan [1988], Smith, Boyle, Ikebe, Klema & Moler [1970], Garbow, Boyle, Dongarra & Moler [1972], Dongarra, Bunch, Moler & Stewart [1978], and Wilkinson & Reinsch [1971]. A new package called 'LAPACK' is due to be released soon and will be a milestone in practical scientific computing. The project is funded by the National Science Foundation and so all the codes will be in the public domain. LAPACK has all the functionality of the LINPACK and EISPACK packages plus many additional capabilities. LINPACK covers linear equations and least squares while EISPACK handles the eigenproblem. All of the dense matrix computations mentioned in this chapter can be handled by codes from these two packages.

Another software tool that is both widespread and indispensible is MATLAB. MATLAB is an interactive system that facilitates the design and testing of matrix algorithms. The MATLAB language is rapidly becoming the model for exposition in the field as it permits a very high level of specification.

At the time of writing (1992), it is possible to obtain software for many of the algorithms in the book by sending electronic mail to any of the following three addresses:

> netlib@ornl.gov
>
> netlib@research.att.com
>
> research!netlib

Typical messages include

> send index   {For a list of available libraries.}
>
> send index for linpack   {For a list of LINPACK codes.}
>
> send svd from eispack   {For the EISPACK svd code.}

The matrix computation literature is widely scattered, however, some of the more important journals include *SIAM J. Scientific and Statistical Computing*, *SIAM J. Matrix Analysis*, *SIAM J. Numerical Analysis*, *SIAM Review*, *Numerische Mathematik*, *J. Linear Algebra and its Applications*, *Mathematics of Computation*, *ACM Transactions on Mathematical Software*, and *IMA J. on Numerical Analysis*. We also mention that many interesting matrix methods surface in the engineering literature, particularly the IEEE journals.

Finally, a word about the level of linear algebra expertise that is required to understand this chapter. The reader should certainly be familiar with the concepts of basis, independence, transpose, inner product, span, null space, range, and inverse. No less important are the notions of norm, orthogonality, and eigenvalue although with these topics we start with definitions. Readers who wish to upholster their linear algebra background should consult Halmos [1958], Leon [1980], or Strang [1988].

1. Some tools of the trade

This section is an informal introduction to the analytic and computational tools that underpin numerical linear algebra. Low dimension examples are the rule with appropriate generalizations to follow. The central themes include (a) the language of matrix factorizations, (b) the art of introducing zeros into a matrix, (c) the exploitation of structure, and (d) the distinction between problem sensitivity and algorithmic stability.

1.1. Gaussian elimination

Perhaps the most important problem in scientific computing is the problem of solving a system of linear equations. The method of *Gaussian elimination* proceeds by systematically removing unknowns from equations. The core calculation is the multiplication of an equation by a constant and its addition to another equation. For example, if we are given the system

$$2x_1 - x_2 + 3x_3 = 13,$$
$$-4x_1 + 6x_2 - 5x_3 = -28,$$
$$6x_1 + 13x_2 + 16x_3 = 37,$$

then we start by multiplying the first equation by 2 and adding it to the second equation. This removes x_1 from the second equation. Likewise we can remove x_1 from the third equation by adding to it, -3 times the first equation. With these two reductions we obtain

$$2x_1 - x_2 + 3x_3 = 13,$$
$$4x_2 + x_3 = -2,$$
$$16x_2 + 7x_3 = -2.$$

We then multiply the (new) second equation by 4 and add it to the (new) third equation, obtaining

$$2x_1 - x_2 + 3x_3 = 13,$$
$$4x_2 + x_3 = -2, \tag{1}$$
$$3x_3 = 6.$$

In reverse order these three equations imply

$$x_3 = 6/3 = 2,$$
$$x_2 = (-2 - x_3)/4 = -1,$$
$$x_1 = (3 - 3x_3 + x_2)/2 = 3.$$

1.2. *LU factorization*

This description of Gaussian elimination can be succinctly described in matrix terms. In particular, the process finds a lower triangular matrix L and an upper triangular matrix U so that $A = LU$. In the preceding example, we have

$$A = \begin{bmatrix} 2 & -1 & 3 \\ -4 & 6 & -5 \\ 6 & 13 & 16 \end{bmatrix} = \begin{bmatrix} 1 & 0 & 0 \\ -2 & 1 & 0 \\ 3 & 4 & 1 \end{bmatrix} \begin{bmatrix} 2 & -1 & 3 \\ 0 & 4 & 1 \\ 0 & 0 & 3 \end{bmatrix} \equiv LU .$$

We call this the *LU factorization*. Notice that the subdiagonal entries in L are made up of the multipliers that arise during the elimination process. The diagonal elements of L are all equal to one and so we refer to L as a *unit lower triangular* matrix.

How does b fit into this matrix description of Gaussian elimination? Note that the transformed right-hand side in (1) is the solution to the lower triangular system

$$\begin{bmatrix} 1 & 0 & 0 \\ -2 & 1 & -0 \\ 3 & 4 & 1 \end{bmatrix} \begin{bmatrix} y_1 \\ y_2 \\ y_3 \end{bmatrix} = \begin{bmatrix} 13 \\ -28 \\ 37 \end{bmatrix} .$$

Thus, the overall technique has three stages:
- Apply the elimination process to A obtaining the factorization $A = LU$.
- Solve the lower triangular system $Ly = b$.
- Solve the upper triangular system $Ux = y$.

It all fits together nicely since $Ax = (LU)x = L(Ux) = Ly = b$.

In matrix computations, this language of 'matrix factorizations' has assumed a role of great importance. It enables one to reason about algorithms at a high level which in turn facilitates generalization and implementation on advanced machines. Thus, it is more appropriate to regard Gaussian elimination as a procedure for computing the LU factorization than as an $Ax = b$ solver.

1.3. *Solving triangular systems*

As evidenced by the above, the need to solve a triangular linear system of equations is an important problem. For upper triangular systems, the un- knowns are resolved in reverse order by a process known as *back substitution*. Lower triangular systems are solved via an analogous process called *forward substitution*. In this case the unknowns are resolved in forward order.

1.4. *Work and notation of a 'flop'*

Triangular system solving is a good setting for introducing *flop counting* as a method for anticipating performance. In an *n*-by-*n* unit lower triangular system

$Ly = b$, the kth unknown is prescribed by

$$y_k = b_k - \sum_{j=1}^{k-1} l_{kj} y_j .$$

This requires $k - 1$ multiplies and $k - 1$ adds for a total of $2(k - 1)$ *flops*. A flop is a floating point arithmetic operation (as opposed to an integer or logical operation). It follows that y requires $n^2 - n$ flops to compute. Now typically n is sufficiently large to ignore low order terms and so it is perfectly reasonable to say that n-by-n forward substitution costs n^2 flops.

A more complicated flop count reveals that Gaussian elimination requires $\frac{2}{3} n^3$ flops to produce the L and U factors. Thus, when a linear system is solved via this algorithm, the arithmetic associated with the triangular system solves is dominated by the arithmetic required for the factorization

Flop counting is a useful way to anticipate the performance of a matrix calculation but it has two shortcomings. First, on a modern computer the efficiency of a matrix code is more often determined by the nature of memory traffic than by flops. See Section 3 for further details. Second, matrix computations usually involve a large amount of integer arithmetic subscripting and this can dominate the actual cost of the floating point arithmetic. Nevertheless, the counting of flops is useful so long as one remembers that the volume of floating point arithmetic is but one of several factors that determine program efficiency.

1.5. Residual versus error

Consider the following innocuous linear system first point out to me by C. Moler:

$$\begin{bmatrix} 0.780 & 0.563 \\ 0.913 & 0.659 \end{bmatrix} \begin{bmatrix} x_1 \\ x_2 \end{bmatrix} = \begin{bmatrix} 0.217 \\ 0.254 \end{bmatrix}. \tag{2}$$

Without going into algorithmic details, suppose we apply two different methods and get two different solutions:

$$x^{(1)} = \begin{bmatrix} 0.341 \\ -0.087 \end{bmatrix}, \qquad x^{(2)} = \begin{bmatrix} 0.999 \\ -1.00 \end{bmatrix}.$$

Which one is preferred? An obvious way to compare the two solutions is to compute the associated *residuals*:

$$b - Ax^{(1)} = \begin{bmatrix} 0.0000001 \\ 0 \end{bmatrix}, \qquad b - Ax^{(2)} = \begin{bmatrix} 0.001343 \\ 0.001572 \end{bmatrix}.$$

On the basis of residuals, it is clear that $x^{(1)}$ is preferred. However, we are confronted with a dilemma when we learn that the exact solution is given by

$$x^{(\text{exact})} = \begin{bmatrix} 1 \\ -1 \end{bmatrix}.$$

Thus, $x^{(1)}$ renders a small residual while $x^{(2)}$ is much more accurate. Reasoning in the face of such a dichotomy requires care. We may be in a situation where how well Ax predicts b is paramount. In that case, we are after a small residual solution. In other settings, accuracy is critical in which case the focus is on nearness to the true solution. The point here is twofold: (a) the notion of a 'good' solution can be ambiguous, and (b) the intelligent appraisal of algorithms requires sharper tools.

1.6. Problem sensitivity and nearness

In our 2-by-2 problem above, the matrix A is very close to singular. Indeed,

$$\tilde{A} = \begin{bmatrix} 0.780 & 0.563001095\ldots \\ 0.913 & 0.659 \end{bmatrix}$$

is exactly singular. Thus, an $O(10^{-6})$ perturbation of the data renders our problem insoluble. Our intuition tells us that difficulties should arise if our given $Ax = b$ problem is 'near' to a singular $Ax = b$ problem. In that case we suspect that small changes in the problem data, i.e., A and b, will induce relatively large changes in the solution. It is clear that we need to be able to quantify notions such as 'nearness to singularity' and 'problem sensitivity.'

Notice that these concerns have *nothing* to do with underlying algorithms. They are mathematical issues associated with the $Ax = b$ problem. However, as we now show, they do clarify what we can expect from an algorithm in light of *rounding errors*.

A finite amount of hardware is devoted to the storage of each *floating point number*. A floating point number has a mantissa and an exponent. We focus on the former and for clarity assume that we are working on a base-10 machine with d-digit mantissas. We define the *unit roundoff* to be the largest floating point number such that the floating point addition of 1 and $\mathbf{u}$ equals 1. For d-digit arithmetic, $\mathbf{u} \approx 10^{-d}$. In general, a relative error of order $O(\mathbf{u})$ attends each floating point operation. However, errors arise even before we commence computation for data must be stored. For example, if $d = 4$ then π would have the representation 0.3142×10^1. In general, if $fl(x)$ denotes the stored version of a real number x, then

$$fl(x) = x + \varepsilon , |\varepsilon| \leq \mathbf{u} .$$

Let us return to the $Ax = b$ problem. Any algorithm that requires the storage of A (e.g., Gaussian elimination) 'sees' only the perturbed problem

$$(A + E)\hat{x} = b + f , \tag{3}$$

where $|e_{ij}| \leq \mathbf{u}|a_{ij}|$ and $|f_i| \leq \mathbf{u}|b_i|$. Since $\hat{x}$ is the 'best we can do', we ask two fundamental questions: (a) how can we guarantee that $A + E$ is nonsingular, and (b) how close is $\hat{x}$ to the true solution x?

1.7. Norms: Quantifying error and distance

To answer these questions we need the concept of a *norm*. Norms are one vehicle for measuring distance in a vector space. For vectors $x \in \mathbb{R}^n$ the 1, 2, and infinity norms are of particular importance:

$$\|x\|_1 = |x_1| + \cdots + |x_n| \, ,$$

$$\|x\|_2 = \sqrt{x_1^2 + \cdots + x_n^2} \, ,$$

$$\|x\|_\infty = \max\{|x_1|, \ldots, |x_n|\} \, .$$

For matrices $A \in \mathbb{R}^{m \times n}$ we have

$$\|A\|_1 = \max_{1 \leq j \leq n} \sum_{i=1}^m |a_{ij}| \, , \qquad \|A\|_2 = \max_{\|x\|_2 = 1} \|Ax\|_2 \, ,$$

$$\|A\|_\infty = \max_{1 \leq i \leq m} \sum_{j=1}^n |a_{ij}| \, , \qquad \|A\|_F = \sqrt{\sum_{i=1}^m \sum_{j=1}^n |a_{ij}|^2} \, .$$

It follows that the matrix of rounding errors E in (2) satisfies $\|E\|_1 \leq \mathbf{u}\|A\|_1$.

In the discussions that follow, whenever the choice of norm is a side issue, we drop subscripts. In examples with an order-of-magnitude theme, we choose whichever of the above norms is most convenient bearing in mind that for small problems, they do not differ by much. However, in serious applications the choice of a norm can be critical. This is especially true with weighted norms, e.g., $\|x\|_D = \|Dx\|_2$. Here, D is a nonsingular diagonal weighting matrix that may reflect our knowledge of underlying measurements.

1.8. Condition of linear systems

The $Ax = b$ sensitivity issues posed turn out to involve the *condition number*. In particular, if $A \in \mathbb{R}^{n \times m}$ then we say that

$$\kappa(A) = \|A\| \, \|A^{-1}\|$$

is the condition number of A *with respect to inversion*. If A is singular, then we assume $\kappa(A) = \infty$. Note that the condition number involves a choice of norm which we can stress through subscripting: $\kappa_1(A) = \|A\|_1 \|A^{-1}\|_1$. For $p = 1, 2, \infty$ we have $\kappa_p(A) \geq 1$.

It turns out that the perturbed system (3) is nonsingular if

$\mathbf{u}\kappa(A) < 1$,

meaning that A is not too badly conditioned with respect to the unit roundoff.

The condition number also figures in the bounding of the relative error in the stored system solution $\hat{x}$. In particular, if A and $A + E$ are nonsingular, then

$$\frac{\|\hat{x} - x\|}{\|x\|} \leq \mathbf{u}\kappa(A).$$

From this we reason that in the absence of additional information we have no right to expect an $Ax = b$ solver to obtain an accurate solution to an ill-conditioned linear system.

1.9. LU with pivoting

We return to Gaussian elimination. It can be shown that the computed solution $\tilde{x}$ satisfies a perturbed system $(A + \Delta A)\tilde{x} = b$, where $\|\Delta A\| \approx \mathbf{u}\| |\tilde{L}| |\tilde{U}| \|$. Here, $\tilde{L}$ and $\tilde{U}$ are the computed L and U. These quantities can be arbitrarily large as suggested by the 2-by-2 factorization

$$\begin{bmatrix} \varepsilon & 1 \\ 1 & 1 \end{bmatrix} = \begin{bmatrix} 1 & 0 \\ 1/\varepsilon & 1 \end{bmatrix} \begin{bmatrix} \varepsilon & 1 \\ 0 & 1 - \dfrac{1}{\varepsilon} \end{bmatrix}.$$

If we use 16-digit floating point arithmetic to solve

$$\begin{bmatrix} \varepsilon & 1 \\ 1 & 1 \end{bmatrix} \begin{bmatrix} x_1 \\ x_2 \end{bmatrix} = \begin{bmatrix} 1 + \varepsilon \\ 2 \end{bmatrix},$$

which has exact solution $x = \begin{bmatrix} 1 & 1 \end{bmatrix}^{\mathrm{T}}$, then in Table 1 is what we find for various ε. The troubling thing with this example is that the matrix A is well conditioned, e.g., $\kappa_2(A) = 1 + \mathrm{O}(\varepsilon)$. This means that Gaussian elimination introduces errors way above the level predicted by the mathematical sensitivity of the problem. This is because of the very small, $\mathrm{O}(\varepsilon)$, pivot that arises in the first step.

A simple way around this difficulty is to introduce *row interchanges*. For our example above, this means we apply Gaussian elimination to compute the LU

Table 1

ε	$\|x - \tilde{x}\| / \|x\|$
10^{-3}	$6 \cdot 10^{-16}$
10^{-6}	$2 \cdot 10^{-11}$
10^{-9}	$9 \cdot 10^{-8}$
10^{-12}	$9 \cdot 10^{-5}$
10^{-15}	$7 \cdot 10^{-2}$

factorization of A with its rows reversed

$$\begin{bmatrix} \varepsilon & 1 \\ 1 & 1 \end{bmatrix} \begin{bmatrix} x_1 \\ x_2 \end{bmatrix} = \begin{bmatrix} 2 \\ 1 + \varepsilon \end{bmatrix}.$$

The resulting algorithm is an example of Gaussian elimination with *partial pivoting*. A full precision answer is obtained. (Note that A is well conditioned.)

In general, partial pivoting involves a linear search at each elimination step. When x_k is being removed we search for the biggest coefficient for x_k in the remaining equations. That equation is then interchanged with the current kth equation. The resulting factorization has the form $PA = LU$, where P is a permutation matrix. A *permutation matrix* is the identity with its rows permuted. To solve $Ax = b$ we solve $Ly = Pb$ and then $Ux = y$. The application of P to b is an $O(n)$ operation.

1.10. Backwards stability

We say that a linear equation solver is *backwards stable* if it produces an $\hat{x}$ that solves a nearby problem exactly, i.e., $(A + E)\hat{x} = b + f$ with $\|E\| \approx \mathbf{u}\|A\|$ and $\|f\| \approx \mathbf{u}\|b\|$. This turns out to be the case for Gaussian elimination with pivoting. Two important heuristics follow from this:

$$\|A\tilde{x} - b\| \approx \mathbf{u}\|A\| \|\tilde{x}\| , \qquad \frac{\|\tilde{x} - x\|}{\|x\|} \approx \mathbf{u}\kappa(A) .$$

The first result essentially says the algorithm produces small relative residuals *regardless* of problem condition. The second heuristic shows the accuracy *does* depend upon problem condition. If a standard norm (such as $\|\cdot\|_\infty$) is involved and the unit roundoff and condition satisfy $\mathbf{u} \approx 10^{-q}$, and $\kappa_\infty(A) \approx 10^p$, then $\tilde{x}$ has approximately $q - p$ correct digits.

For the relative error bound to be of practical interest, we need an estimate of the condition. The central problem of *condition estimation* is to obtain a good estimate in $O(n^2)$ flops assuming the availability of a factorization such as $A = LU$ or $PA = LU$. This turns out to be possible, see Cline, Molder, Stewart & Wilkinson [1979], Cline, Conn & Van Loan [1982], Grimes & Lewis [1981], Hager [1984], Higham [1987], and Van Loan [1987].

1.11. Banded systems

We now turn our attention to the exploitation of structure, a very important theme in matrix computations. A matrix $A \in \mathbb{R}^{n \times n}$ has *upper bandwidth* q and *lower bandwidth* r if a_{ij} is zero whenever $j > i + q$ or $i > j + r$. Thus,

$$A = \begin{bmatrix} \times & \times & 0 & 0 & 0 \\ \times & \times & \times & 0 & 0 \\ 0 & \times & \times & \times & 0 \\ 0 & 0 & \times & \times & \times \\ 0 & 0 & 0 & \times & \times \end{bmatrix}$$

has upper and lower bandwidth equal to 1. In this case we also say that A is *tridiagonal*. It is often possible to exploit band structure during a factorization. For example, the L and U factors of a tridiagonal are bidiagonal:

$$L = \begin{bmatrix} \times & 0 & 0 & 0 & 0 \\ \times & \times & 0 & 0 & 0 \\ 0 & \times & \times & 0 & 0 \\ 0 & 0 & \times & \times & 0 \\ 0 & 0 & 0 & \times & \times \end{bmatrix}, \qquad U = \begin{bmatrix} \times & \times & 0 & 0 & 0 \\ 0 & \times & \times & 0 & 0 \\ 0 & 0 & \times & \times & 0 \\ 0 & 0 & 0 & \times & \times \\ 0 & 0 & 0 & 0 & \times \end{bmatrix}.$$

If pivoting is performed, then L is not lower bidiagonal but it does have the property that there is at most one nonzero below the diagonal in each column. The number of flops required to factor a matrix with upper and lower bandwidth equal to p is $O(np^2)$.

Further details concerning the manipulation of band matrices may be found in Golub & Van Loan [1989].

1.12. Symmetric systems

Symmetry is another important property that can be exploited in matrix computations. For example, if A is symmetric ($A = A^T$), then the amount of data that defines $x = A^{-1}b$ is halved. Let us see how this reduction is reflected in the LU factorization. If $A = LU$ is a nonsingular symmetric matrix with an LU factorization, then $LU = U^T L^T$ implies that $U^{-T}L = L^{-T}U \equiv D$ is diagonal. Thus, we can rewrite the LU factorization as $A = L(DL^T)$:

$$\begin{bmatrix} 4 & -8 & -4 \\ -8 & 18 & 14 \\ -4 & 14 & 25 \end{bmatrix} = \begin{bmatrix} 1 & 0 & 0 \\ -2 & 1 & 0 \\ -1 & 3 & 1 \end{bmatrix} \begin{bmatrix} 1 & 0 & 0 \\ 0 & 2 & 0 \\ 0 & 0 & 3 \end{bmatrix} \begin{bmatrix} 1 & -2 & -1 \\ 0 & 1 & 3 \\ 0 & 0 & 1 \end{bmatrix}.$$

Once obtained, the LDL^T factorization can be used to solve $Ax = b$ by solving $Ly = b$, $Dz = y$, and $Ux = z$.

This factorization need not be stable for the same reasons that the LU without pivoting may be unstable. Pivoting can rectify this but if we compute $PA = LU$ we can no longer expect U to be a diagonal scaling of L^T since PA is no longer symmetric. A possible way around this is to perform *symmetric pivoting*. In particular, we seek a permutation P so that the LDL^T factorization of PAP^T is stable. But notice that the diagonal of this matrix is a permutation of A's diagonal. It follows that if all of A's diagonal entries are small, then huge pivots can arise regardless of the choice of P.

There are two ways around this problem. In the approach of Bunch & Kaufman [1977] a permutation is found so that $PAP^T = LDL^T$, where L is unit lower triangular and D is a direct sum of 1-by-1 and 2-by-2 matrices, e.g.,

$$
PAP^T = \begin{bmatrix} 1 & 0 & 0 & 0 \\ \times & 1 & 0 & 0 \\ \times & 0 & 1 & 0 \\ \times & \times & \times & 1 \end{bmatrix} \begin{bmatrix} \times & 0 & 0 & 0 \\ 0 & \times & \times & 0 \\ 0 & \times & \times & 0 \\ 0 & 0 & 0 & \times \end{bmatrix} \begin{bmatrix} 1 & 0 & 0 & 0 \\ \times & 1 & 0 & 0 \\ \times & \times & 1 & 0 \\ \times & \times & \times & 1 \end{bmatrix}^T .
$$

The pivot strategy which determines P is rather complicated and involves a 2-column search at each step. The overall process is as stable as Gaussian elimination with pivoting and involves half the flops. Once obtained, the Bunch–Kaufman factorization can be used to solve a linear system in $O(n^2)$ flops as follows: $Lw = Pb$, $Dz = w$, $L^T v = z$, $x = P^T v$.

An alternative method for the stable factorization of an indefinite symmetric matrix is due to Aasen [1971] who developed an $\frac{1}{3}n^3$ algorithm for the factorization $PAP^T = LTL^T$, where T is tridiagonal and L is unit lower tridiagonal:

$$
PAP^T = \begin{bmatrix} 1 & 0 & 0 & 0 \\ \times & 1 & 0 & 0 \\ \times & \times & 1 & 0 \\ \times & \times & \times & 1 \end{bmatrix} \begin{bmatrix} \times & \times & 0 & 0 \\ \times & \times & \times & 0 \\ 0 & \times & \times & \times \\ 0 & 0 & \times & \times \end{bmatrix} \begin{bmatrix} 1 & 0 & 0 & 0 \\ \times & 1 & 0 & 0 \\ \times & \times & 1 & 0 \\ \times & \times & \times & 1 \end{bmatrix}^T .
$$

Once obtained, the Aasen factorization can be used to solve a linear system as follows: $Lw = Pb$, $Tz = w$, $L^T v = z$, $x = P^T v$. $O(n^2)$ flops are required.

1.13. Positive definiteness

A matrix $A \in \mathbb{R}^{n \times n}$ is *positive definite* if $x^T Ax > 0$ for all nonzero $x \in \mathbb{R}^n$. Symmetric positive definite matrices constitute a particularly important class and fortunately they submit to a particularly elegant factorization called the *Cholesky factorization*. In particular, if A is symmetric positive definite, then we can find a lower triangular G such that $A = GG^T$. In the 2-by-2 case if we equate entries in the equation

$$
\begin{bmatrix} a_{11} & a_{12} \\ a_{21} & a_{22} \end{bmatrix} = \begin{bmatrix} g_{11} & 0 \\ g_{21} & g_{22} \end{bmatrix} \begin{bmatrix} g_{11} & 0 \\ g_{21} & g_{22} \end{bmatrix}^T ,
$$

we obtain the equations

$$
a_{11} = g_{11}^2 \quad \Rightarrow \quad g_{11} = \sqrt{a_{11}} ,
$$
$$
a_{21} = g_{21} g_{11} \quad \Rightarrow \quad g_{21} = a_{21}/g_{11} ,
$$
$$
a_{22} = g_{21}^2 + g_{22}^2 \quad \Rightarrow \quad g_{22} = \sqrt{a_{22} - g_{21}^2} .
$$

Using the definition of positive definite it is not hard to show that the two square roots are square roots of positive numbers, thereby ensuring the production of a real G. Furthermore, $|g_{ij}| \leq \sqrt{a_{ii}}$ for all i and j, ensuring that no large numbers surface during the Cholesky reduction. Thus, pivoting is not necessary and Cholesky is backwards stable.

1.14. Orthogonality and the QR factorization

Orthogonality is a central concept in matrix computations. A set of vectors $\{x_1, \ldots, x_k\}$ is *orthogonal* if $x_i^T x_j = 0$ whenever $i \neq j$. Thus,

$$\left\{ \begin{bmatrix} 1 \\ -2 \\ 3 \end{bmatrix}, \begin{bmatrix} 4 \\ 5 \\ 2 \end{bmatrix} \right\}$$

is an orthogonal set. If in addition $x_i^T x_i = 1$, then they are referred to as *orthonormal*.

The computation of orthogonal bases via the *Gram–Schmidt* process is well known. If a_1 and a_2 are given vectors and we set

$$x_1 = a_1, \qquad\qquad q_1 = x_1 / \|x_1\|_2,$$
$$x_2 = a_2 - (q_1^T a_2) q_1, \qquad q_2 = x_2 / \|x_2\|_2,$$

then q_1 is orthogonal to q_2 and $\mathrm{span}\{a_1, a_2\} = \mathrm{span}\{q_1, q_2\}$.

For the data

$$a_1 = \begin{bmatrix} 1 \\ 2 \\ 2 \end{bmatrix}, \qquad a_2 = \begin{bmatrix} 8 \\ -1 \\ 14 \end{bmatrix},$$

we obtain

$$x_1 = \begin{bmatrix} 1 \\ 2 \\ 2 \end{bmatrix}, \qquad\qquad q_1 = \tfrac{1}{3} \begin{bmatrix} 1 \\ 2 \\ 2 \end{bmatrix},$$

$$x_2 = \begin{bmatrix} 8 \\ -1 \\ 14 \end{bmatrix} - \tfrac{34}{9} \begin{bmatrix} 1 \\ 2 \\ 2 \end{bmatrix}, \qquad q_2 = \tfrac{1}{3} \begin{bmatrix} -2 \\ -1 \\ 2 \end{bmatrix}.$$

This reduction can be expressed as a factorization:

$$\begin{bmatrix} 1 & -8 \\ 2 & -1 \\ 2 & 14 \end{bmatrix} = \begin{bmatrix} \tfrac{1}{3} & -\tfrac{2}{3} \\ \tfrac{2}{3} & -\tfrac{1}{3} \\ \tfrac{2}{3} & \tfrac{2}{3} \end{bmatrix} \begin{bmatrix} 3 & 6 \\ 0 & 15 \end{bmatrix} = \begin{bmatrix} \tfrac{1}{3} & -\tfrac{2}{3} & -\tfrac{2}{3} \\ \tfrac{2}{3} & -\tfrac{1}{3} & \tfrac{2}{3} \\ \tfrac{2}{3} & \tfrac{2}{3} & -\tfrac{1}{3} \end{bmatrix} \begin{bmatrix} 3 & 6 \\ 0 & 15 \\ 0 & 0 \end{bmatrix}.$$

We call this the *QR factorization* and it has an important role to play in least squares and eigenvalue computations.

The computations of the QR factorization is usually obtained through successive orthogonal transformations of the data. In particular, a product of 'simple' orthogonal matrices $Q = Q_1 \cdots Q_N$ is found so that $Q^T A = R$ is upper triangular. Two classes of such simple transformations are available to use: Householder reflections and Givens rotations.

1.15. Householder reflections

A *Householder reflection* has the form

$$H = I - 2vv^T, \quad v \in \mathbb{R}^n, \|v\|_2 = 1.$$

It is easy to confirm that H is orthogonal.
Suppose $x^T = [2 \quad -1 \quad 2]$ and we set $v = u/\|u\|_2$ where

$$u = \begin{bmatrix} 5 \\ -1 \\ 2 \end{bmatrix} = x + \begin{bmatrix} \|x\|_2 \\ 0 \\ 0 \end{bmatrix}.$$

It is easy to verify that if

$$H = I - 2vv^T = \tfrac{1}{15} \begin{bmatrix} -10 & 5 & -10 \\ 5 & 14 & 2 \\ -10 & 2 & 11 \end{bmatrix},$$

then

$$Hx = \begin{bmatrix} -3 \\ 0 \\ 0 \end{bmatrix}.$$

This illustrates how a Householder matrix can be called upon to zero all but the top component of a vector x. The *Householder vector* v has the form $x \pm \|x\|_2 e_1$, where e_1 is the first column of I_n. (The sign is chosen so that no cancellation ensues when forming the first component of v.)

Householder vectors are used to zero designated sub-columns and sub-rows in a matrix. For example, if

$$A = \begin{bmatrix} a_{11} & a_{12} & a_{13} \\ 0 & a_{22} & a_{23} \\ 0 & a_{32} & a_{33} \\ 0 & a_{42} & a_{43} \\ 0 & a_{52} & a_{53} \end{bmatrix},$$

and we wish to zero the subdiagonal portion of the second column, then we determine a Householder vector $v \in \mathbb{R}^4$ so that the corresponding Householder matrix $H \in \mathbb{R}^{4 \times 4}$ does the following:

$$
H \begin{bmatrix} a_{22} \\ a_{32} \\ a_{42} \\ a_{52} \end{bmatrix} = \begin{bmatrix} \tilde{a}_{22} \\ 0 \\ 0 \\ 0 \end{bmatrix}.
$$

If we define the 5-by-5 orthogonal matrix:

$$
\tilde{H} = \begin{bmatrix} 1 & 0 \\ 0 & H \end{bmatrix},
$$

then

$$
HA = \begin{bmatrix} a_{11} & a_{12} & a_{13} \\ 0 & \tilde{a}_{22} & \tilde{a}_{23} \\ 0 & 0 & \tilde{a}_{33} \\ 0 & 0 & \tilde{a}_{43} \\ 0 & 0 & \tilde{a}_{53} \end{bmatrix}.
$$

Here, the tildes denote updated entries. Note that $\tilde{H}$ is a Householder matrix itself associated with the vector $\tilde{v} = [0 \quad v]^{\mathrm{T}}$.

The product HA of an m-by-m Householder matrix and an n-by-k matrix involves $O(mk)$ flops if we invoke the formula

$$
HA = (I - 2vv^{\mathrm{T}})A = A - vw^{\mathrm{T}}, \quad w^{\mathrm{T}} = 2v^{\mathrm{T}}A .
$$

We see that the new A is a rank-one update of the old A.

Householder updates are backwards stable. This means that if we compute an update of the form $A \leftarrow HA$, then the result is an exact Householder update of a matrix near to the original A.

A 4-by-3 matrix can be upper triangularized by a product $Q = H_1 H_2 H_3$ of Householder matrices as follows:

$$
\begin{bmatrix} \times & \times & \times \\ \times & \times & \times \\ \times & \times & \times \\ \times & \times & \times \end{bmatrix} \xrightarrow{H_1} \begin{bmatrix} \times & \times & \times \\ 0 & \times & \times \\ 0 & \times & \times \\ 0 & \times & \times \end{bmatrix} \xrightarrow{H_2} \begin{bmatrix} \times & \times & \times \\ 0 & \times & \times \\ 0 & 0 & \times \\ 0 & 0 & \times \end{bmatrix} \xrightarrow{H_3} \begin{bmatrix} \times & \times & \times \\ 0 & \times & \times \\ 0 & 0 & \times \\ 0 & 0 & 0 \end{bmatrix} .
$$

This progressive introduction of zeros via Householder reflections is typical of several important factorization algorithms. These computations are backwards stable, e.g., the computed $\hat{R}$ satisfies $Q^{\mathrm{T}}(A + E)$ where Q is exactly orthogonal and $\|E\| \approx \mathbf{u}\|A\|$.

Various aspects of Householder manipulation are included in Golub & Van Loan [1989], Parlett [1971], and Tsao [1975].

1.16. Givens rotations

A 2-by-2 *Givens rotations* is an orthogonal matrix of the form

$$G(\theta) = \begin{bmatrix} c & s \\ -s & c \end{bmatrix}, \quad c = \cos(\theta), s = \sin(\theta).$$

If $x = [x_1 \ x_2]^T$, then it is possible to choose (c, s) such that if $y = G^T x$, then $y_2 = 0$. Indeed, all we have to do is set

$$c = x_1 / \sqrt{x_1^2 + x_2^2}, \quad s = -x_2 / \sqrt{x_1^2 + x_2^2}.$$

However, a preferred algorithm for computing the (c, s) pair would more likely resemble the following in which we assume that $x \neq 0$:

if $|x_1| > |x_2|$
  $\tau = x_2 / x_1; \ c = 1 / \sqrt{1 + \tau^2}; \ s = c \cdot \tau$
else
  $\tau = x_1 / x_2; \ s = 1 / \sqrt{1 + \tau^2}; \ c = s \cdot \tau$
end

In this alternative, we guard against the squaring of arbitrarily large numbers and thereby circumvent the problem of *overflow*. Overflow occurs when a floating operation leads to a result with an oversized exponent. Another benefit of this (c, s) determination is that square roots are always taken of numbers in this range $[1, 2]$. This restriction is sometimes helpful in the design of VLSI squareroot circuitry.

Givens rotations can be used to introduce zeros in a very selective fashion. Suppose that we want to compute the QR factorization of the structured matrix

$$A = \begin{bmatrix} r_{11} & r_{12} & r_{13} \\ 0 & r_{22} & r_{23} \\ 0 & 0 & r_{33} \\ v_1 & v_2 & v_3 \end{bmatrix}.$$

We first determine (c, s) so

$$\begin{bmatrix} c & s \\ -s & c \end{bmatrix}^T \begin{bmatrix} r_{11} \\ v_1 \end{bmatrix} = \begin{bmatrix} \tilde{r}_{11} \\ 0 \end{bmatrix}.$$

We say that

$$G(1, 4) = \begin{bmatrix} c & 0 & 0 & s \\ 0 & 1 & 0 & 0 \\ 0 & 0 & 1 & 0 \\ -s & 0 & 0 & c \end{bmatrix}$$

is a Givens rotation in the $(1, 4)$ plane. Note that

$$
G(1, 4)^\mathrm{T} A = \begin{bmatrix} \tilde{r}_{11} & \tilde{r}_{12} & \tilde{r}_{13} \\ 0 & r_{22} & r_{23} \\ 0 & 0 & r_{33} \\ 0 & \tilde{v}_2 & \tilde{v}_3 \end{bmatrix}.
$$

Here, the tildes denote updated matrix elements and the computation would continue with rotations in the $(2, 4)$ and $(3, 4)$ planes designed to remove $\tilde{v}_2$ and $\tilde{v}_3$. Note that 3 flops are associated with each updated element and so when a Givens update of the form $A \leftarrow G^\mathrm{T} A$ is performed, $O(n)$ work is involved where n is the number of columns. Similar comments apply to postmultiply updates of the form $A \leftarrow AG$.

Givens updates are backwards stable and various aspects of their implementation are discussed by Steward [1976a], Gentleman [1973], and Hammarling [1974]. See also Golub & Van Loan [1989].

1.17. The least squares problem

Given $A \in \mathbb{R}^{m \times n}$ and $b \in \mathbb{R}^m$ with $m \geq n$, consider the problem of finding $x \in \mathbb{R}^n$ so that $Ax = b$. This is an *overdetermined* system of equations and one must prepare for the fact that there may be no solution. However, if we seek an x so that $Ax \approx b$, then a number of possibilities arise. The *least squares* approach involves the minimization of $\| Ax - b \|_2$. Because the 2-norm is preserved under orthogonal transformations, we see that if Q is orthogonal, then

$$
\| Ax - b \|_2 = \| Q^\mathrm{T}(Ax - b) \|_2 = \| (Q^\mathrm{T}A)x - (Q^\mathrm{T}b) \|_2.
$$

Thus, the given least squares (LS) problem based upon (A, b) transforms to an equivalent LS problem based upon $(Q^\mathrm{T}A, Q^\mathrm{T}b)$. The transformed problem takes on a special form if $A = QR$ is the QR factorization. For example, in the $(m, n) = (4, 2)$ case that means

$$
\| A_x - b \|_2 = \left\| \begin{bmatrix} r_{11}x_1 + r_{12}x_2 - c_1 \\ r_{22}x_2 - c_2 \\ -c_3 \\ -c_4 \end{bmatrix} \right\|_2,
$$

where $Q^\mathrm{T}b = c$ is the transformed right-hand side. It follows that the optimum choice for x is that which solves the 2-by-2 upper triangular system

$$
\begin{bmatrix} r_{11} & r_{12} \\ 0 & r_{22} \end{bmatrix} \begin{bmatrix} x_1 \\ x_2 \end{bmatrix} = \begin{bmatrix} c_1 \\ c_2 \end{bmatrix}.
$$

Trouble arises in the QR solution of the LS problem if the columns of A are dependent. If this is the case, then one of the r_{ii} is zero and the back substitution process breaks down. However, it is possible to incorporate *column interchanges* during the Householder reduction with an eye towards maximizing $|r_{kk}|$ during the kth step. As a result of this, a set of independent columns is 'pushed up front'. For example, in a 4-by-3, rank 2 problem a factorization of the form

$$Q^T A \Pi = \begin{bmatrix} \times & \times & \times \\ 0 & \times & \times \\ 0 & 0 & 0 \\ 0 & 0 & 0 \end{bmatrix}$$

would be obtained. In this situation, the LS problem has an infinite number of solutions but one would be selected that attempts to predict b from the first two columns of $A\Pi$.

Of course, it is not likely that exact zeros would surface during the computation. This leads to the difficult problem of *numerical rank determination*. For example, suppose in the 4-by-3 problem above we emerge with

$$Q^T A \Pi = \begin{bmatrix} 1 & 2 & 3 \\ 0 & 10^{-6} & 10^{-7} \\ 0 & 0 & 10^{-9} \\ 0 & 0 & 0 \end{bmatrix}.$$

Whether or not we regard this as a matrix of rank 1, 2, or 3 depends upon (a) the precision of the underlying floating point arithmetic, and (b) the accuracy of the original a_{ij}. For example, if A is exact and $\mathbf{u} = 10^{-18}$, then we are on fairly firm ground to believe that $\text{rank}(A) = 3$. On the other and, if $\mathbf{u} = 10^{-8}$ then a case can be made for $\text{rank}(A) = 2$. If the a_{ij} are just correct to 3 digits, then it might be best to regard A as having rank 1. This spectrum of possibilities reveals that the intelligent handling of rank determination is tricky and not without a subjective component. The stakes are high too because radically different LS solutions result for different choice of numerical rank.

1.18. Eigenvalue problems

Orthogonal transformations are also useful in eigenvalue problems. In the simplest setting we have $A \in \mathbb{R}^{n \times n}$ and seek scalars λ so that $A - \lambda I$ is singular. These scalars are called *eigenvalues* and they are the roots of the *characteristic polynomial* $p(\lambda) = \det(A - \lambda I)$. It follows that an n-by-n real matrix has n (possibly complex) eigenvalues. We denote the set of eigenvalues by $\lambda(A)$. If $\lambda \in \lambda(A)$, then there exists a nontrivial vector called an *eigenvector* so that $Ax = \lambda x$. There is also a *left eigenvector* y so that $y^T A = \lambda y^T$.

Note that if T is nonsingular and $Ax = \lambda x$, then $(T^{-1} A T)(T^{-1} x) = \lambda(T^{-1} x)$. This shows that the *similar* matrices A and $T^{-1} A T$ have the same eigenvalues. The matrix T is called a *similarity transformation*.

From several points of view, orthogonal similarity transformations $A \leftarrow Q^T A Q$ are extremely attractive. They are backwards stable when based upon Householder and Givens transformations, i.e., the computed $Q^T A Q$ is orthogonally similar to $A + E$, where $\|E\| \approx \mathbf{u}\|A\|$. The inverse is easily obtained and well-conditioned: $Q^{-1} = Q^T$, $\kappa_2(A) = 1$.

An important family of eigenvalue methods involve computing an orthogonal Q such that the eigenvalues of $Q^T A Q$ are 'displayed'. For example, if $A \in \mathbb{R}^{2 \times 2}$ has real eigenvalues, then it is possible to find a cosine–sine pair (c, s) such that

$$\begin{bmatrix} c & s \\ -s & c \end{bmatrix}^T \begin{bmatrix} a_{11} & a_{12} \\ a_{21} & a_{22} \end{bmatrix} \begin{bmatrix} c & s \\ -s & c \end{bmatrix} = \begin{bmatrix} \lambda_1 & t \\ 0 & \lambda_2 \end{bmatrix}.$$

This is the $n = 2$ version of the *Schur decomposition*. Note that λ_1 and λ_2 are the eigenvalues of A. If y is an eigenvector of T, then $x = Qy$ is an eigenvector of A. It is easy to verify that

$$y_1 = \begin{bmatrix} 1 \\ 0 \end{bmatrix}$$

and

$$y_2 = \frac{1}{\sqrt{1 + \mu^2}} \begin{bmatrix} \mu \\ -1 \end{bmatrix}, \quad \mu = \frac{t}{\lambda_2 - \lambda_1},$$

are a pair unit 2-norm eigenvectors of T associated with λ_1 and λ_2, respectively. Note that if $t \neq 0$ and $\lambda_1 = \lambda_2$, then y_2 is not defined. In this case we see that T (and hence A) does not have a full set of n independent eigenvectors. Numerically, the independence of the eigenvector basis deteriorates as $\mu \to \infty$. Just observe that $y_2 \to y_1$ as $\mu \to \infty$.

The sensitivity of an eigenvalue to perturbation depends on 'how independent' its eigenvector is from the eigenvectors associated with other eigenvalues. For example, suppose $\lambda_1(\varepsilon)$ and $\lambda_2(\varepsilon)$ are the eigenvalues of the following perturbation of the T matrix above:

$$\tilde{T} = \begin{bmatrix} \lambda_1 & t \\ \varepsilon & \lambda_2 \end{bmatrix}.$$

It is not hard to show that for $i = 1, 2$, $\lambda_i'(0) \approx \mu$. Thus, for small ε, the eigenvalues are perturbed by $O(\mu \varepsilon)$.

If A is symmetric then this sensitivity cannot occur. This is because $T = Q^T A Q$ is symmetric and so t is zero. Indeed, a symmetric matrix always has a full set of orthonormal eigenvectors and it can be shown that symmetric $O(\varepsilon)$ perturbations induce just $O(\varepsilon)$ perturbations of the eigenvalues.

1.19. The singular value decomposition

We close with a few remarks about another very important factorization. If $A \in \mathbb{R}^{2 \times 2}$, then it is possible to find 2-by-2 orthogonal matrices U and V such that

$$U^T A V = \begin{bmatrix} \sigma_1 & 0 \\ 0 & \sigma_2 \end{bmatrix}.$$

This is called the *singular value decomposition* and in the $n = 2$ case it has a simple geometric description. In particular, the set

$$\{ y: y = Ax, \|x\|_2 = 1 \}$$

is an ellipse having semi-axes of length σ_1 and σ_2. Moreover, A maps the first and second columns of V onto $\sigma_1 u_1$ and $\sigma_2 u_2$, where u_1 and u_2 are the first and second columns of U. It can be shown that $\kappa^2(A) = \sigma_1/\sigma_2$ and so the more elongated the ellipse, the bigger the condition.

The singular value decomposition reveals a great deal of A's structure and turns out to be useful in a host of applications.

2. A catalog of matrix factorizations

Matrix factorizations that play a central role in numerical linear algebra are now presented. The discussion for each factorization is generally structured as follows. First, we state the factorization without proof and specify some of its more important related mathematical properties. Then we sketch associated algorithms and their numerical attributes. Finally, we describe a few important applications upon which the factorization has a bearing.

The classification of the matrix computation field by factorization is not too handy if you just want to see how a particular problem might be solved. So for those readers that are 'application driven', here is a more convenient classification in which we mention the relevant factorizations for each given problem:

• *General Linear Systems.* The LU factorization with pivoting and without. See Sections 2.2 and 2.3.

• *Positive Definite Systems.* The Cholesky and LDL^T factorizations. See Section 2.4 and 2.6.

• *Symmetric Indefinite Systems.* The Bunch–Kaufman and Aasen factorizations. See Sections 2.7 and 2.8.

• *Full Rank Least Squares Problems.* The Cholesky and QR factorizations. See Sections 2.4 and 2.9.

• *Rank Deficient Least Squares Problems.* The QR factorization with column pivoting and the singular value decomposition. See Sections 2.11 and 2.20.

- *The Unsymmetric Eigenvalue Problem.* The Schur, Partial Schur, Jordan, and Hessenberg decompositions. See Sections 2.12–2.15.
- *Symmetric Eigenvalue Problem.* The symmetric Schur and tridiagonal decompositions. See Sections 2.17 and 2.18.
- *The Eigenproblems* $Ax = \lambda Bx$ *and* $A^{\mathrm{T}}Ax = \mu^2 B^{\mathrm{T}}Bx$. The generalized Schur and the generalized singular value decompositions. See Sections 2.16, 2.22, and 2.23.

2.1. A word about notation

In the discussion that follows it is frequently necessary to be able to specify portions of a matrix column or row. A good notation for this is the *colon notation*. If $A \in \mathbb{R}^{m \times n}$, then $A(i, :)$ designates the ith row of A and $A(:, j)$ the jth column. This assumes that $1 \le i \le m$ and $1 \le j \le n$. We can specify parts of a row or column as well:

$$A(p{:}q, j) = [a_{pj} \cdots a_{qj}]^{\mathrm{T}},$$
$$A(i, p{:}q) = [a_{ip} \cdots a_{iq}].$$

If $A \in \mathbb{R}^{m \times n}$, then $[a_1 \cdots a_n]$ is a *column partitioning* if $a_k \in \mathbb{R}^m$ is the kth column of A.

We also need a notation for specifying submatrices. Suppose $A \in \mathbb{R}^{m \times n}$ and $u \in \mathbb{R}^M$ and $v \in \mathbb{R}^N$ are integer vectors whose components satisfy $1 \le \mu_i \le m$ and $1 \le v_i \le n$. By $A(u, v)$ we mean the M-by-N matrix whose (i, j)th entry is $A(u_i, v_j)$. Typically u and v are specified by the colon notation. For example, if $u = 2{:}4$ and $v = 7{:}8$, then

$$A(u, v) = A(2{:}4, 7{:}8) = \begin{bmatrix} a_{27} & a_{28} \\ a_{37} & a_{38} \\ a_{47} & a_{48} \end{bmatrix}.$$

A colon designation of the form $i{:}p{:}j$ means count from i to j with increment p. Thus, if $i = 4$, $p = 3$, and $j = 17$, then $u = i{:}p{:}j = (4, 7, 10, 13, 16)$. If a_j designates the jth column of $A \in \mathbb{R}^{m \times n}$, then

$$A(:, i{:}p{:}n) = [a_i, a_{i+p}, \ldots, a_r], \quad r = i + kp, k = \mathrm{floor}((n-1)/p).$$

Likewise, $A(1{:}2{:}m, 2{:}2{:}n)$ is the submatrix of A defined by its odd rows and even columns.

2.2. The LU factorization with pivoting

Theorem. *If* $A \in \mathbb{R}^{n \times n}$, *then there exists a permutation* $P \in \mathbb{R}^{n \times n}$ *such that* $PA = LU$, *where* L *is unit lower triangular with* $|l_{ij}| \le 1$ *and* U *is upper triangular.*

Mathematical notes

The determinant of A is given by $\pm u_{11} \cdots u_{nn}$. [The sign depends on $\det(P)$.] If A is singular, then the factorization still exists but some diagonal entry of U will be zero, say u_{kk}. This implies a dependence among the first k columns of A.

If A is banded, then U has the same upper bandwidth as A and $L(k + 1{:}n, k)$ has the same number of nonzeros as $A(k + 1{:}n, k)$.

Algorithmic and numerical notes

Gaussian elimination with row pivoting is the standard means for computing this factorization and it requires $\frac{2}{3}n^3$ flops. The classical way of determining P is via *partial pivoting*. Other pivot strategies are used in the sparse matrix setting where one typically relaxes the criteria for pivoting in order to control the *fill-in* of nonzero entries during the elimination process. In this context, factorizations of the form $PAQ = LU$ are often obtained because both columns and rows are permuted.

Sometimes it is possible to improve the quality of $\hat{x}$ through a process known as *iterative improvement*. Here, one computes the residual $r = b - A\hat{x}$ and then uses the factorization to solve $Az = r$. Under certain conditions the refined solution $\bar{x} = \hat{x} + z$ satisfies a perturbed system $(A + F)\bar{x} = b$, where $|f_{ij}| \approx \mathbf{u}|a_{ij}|$. The overall solution procedure is then said to be backwards stable in the componentwise sense.

Applications

• The most common use of the $PA = LU$ factorization is the solution of general linear systems $Ax = b$. Indeed if we solve the triangular systems $Ly = Pb$ and $Ux = y$, then $Ax = b$.

• The factorization can also be used to solve the *multiple right-hand side problem* $AX = B \in \mathbb{R}^{n \times p}$ column-by-column. Setting $B = I$ specifies the inverse, but this is rarely needed explicitly. For example, to compute something like $\alpha = c^T A^{-1} d$, compute $PA = LU$, solve $Az = d$ for z, and set $\alpha = c^T d$.

Further reading

Iterative refinement is a way of improving a computed solution to a linear system assuming that some factorization such as $PA = LU$ is available. See Arioli, Demmel & Duff [1989], Golub & Van Loan [1989], and Skeel [1980]. Various stability issues are covered by Higham & Higham [1988], and Trefethen & Schreiber [1987].

2.3. The LU factorization

Theorem. *If $A \in \mathbb{R}^{n \times n}$ has the property that $\det(A(1{:}k, 1{:}k)) \neq 0$ for $k = 1{:}n - 1$, then there exists a unit lower triangular L and upper triangular U such that $A = LU$.*

Mathematical notes

If A is banded, then L and U inherit the lower and upper bandwidth of A.

Algorithmic and numerical notes

Gaussian elimination *without* pivoting is the standard algorithm for computing this factorization. It requires the same amount of floating point work ($\frac{2}{3}n^3$ flops) but can often execute faster because pivoting can be disruptive in advanced computer systems. Moreover, it can sometimes destroy sparsity.

In the linear equation setting it is advisable to use this factorization only if it is known in advance that no small pivots arise. In particular, if Gaussian elimination without pivoting is used to solve a linear system, then it is essential that the resulting L and U factors be sufficiently bounded. Ideally, a rigorous proof covering the problem at hand would do this. Otherwise, one might be forced to rely on massive computational experience or some kind of dynamic monitoring of element growth. The crucial factor is $|\hat{L}||\hat{U}|$, the product of the absolute values of the computed triangular factors. If this matrix has entries significantly larger than $O(n)$, then you probably want to invoke some form of pivoting. Currently, researchers are investigating the possibility of using iterative improvement in conjunction with 'wreckless' LU computation.

Applications

● Diagonally dominant linear systems are an important class of problems for which pivoting is not necessary. Roughly speaking, $A \in \mathbb{R}^{n \times n}$ is *diagonally dominant* if $|a_{ii}| \geqslant \Sigma_{j \neq i} |a_{ij}|$ for $i = 1{:}n$ with at least one strict inequality. It can be shown that if A^T is diagonally dominant, then the LU factorization exists and the l_{ij} are bounded by 1.

● If

$$A = \begin{bmatrix} A_{11} & A_{12} \\ A_{21} & A_{22} \end{bmatrix}$$

and A_{11} is k-by-k and nonsingular, then the *Schur complement* of A_{11} in A is prescribed by $C = A_{22} - A_{21}A_{11}^{-1}A_{12}$. This matrix can be obtained as follows:

Compute the LU factorization $A_{11} = L_1 U_1$.
Solve $A_{21} = XU_1$ for $X \in \mathbb{R}^{(n-k) \times k}$.
Solve $A_{12} = L_1 Y$ for $Y \in \mathbb{R}^{k \times (n-k)}$.
Form $C = A_{22} - XY$.

Further reading

A sampling of papers that deal with LU factorizations of special matrices include Buckley [1974, 1977], de Boor & Pinkus [1977], Erisman & Reid [1974], Golub & Van Loan [1979], and Serbin [1980].

2.4. The Cholesky factorization

Theorem. *If $A \in \mathbb{R}^{n \times n}$ is symmetric and positive definite, then there exists a lower triangular $G \in \mathbb{R}^{n \times n}$ such that $A = GG^T$.*

Mathematical notes

The eigenvalues of A are the squares of the singular values of G. The largest entry in G is less than the square root of the largest entry of A (which must occur on the diagonal). The factorization also exists if A is just nonnegative definite, for if $a_{kk} = 0$, then it is easy to show that $A(k:n, k) = G(k:n, k) = 0$.

Algorithmic and numerical notes

An algorithm for computing the Cholesky factorization involves $\frac{1}{3}n^3$ flops and n square roots, about half the arithmetic associated with Gaussian elimination. If A has bandwidth p, then $O(np^2)$ flops are required and G has lower bandwidth p.

Solving symmetric positive definite systems via Cholesky is backwards stable. However, the process may breakdown if the condition of A has order $1/\mathbf{u}$. Here, 'breakdown' means that a square root of a negative number arises.

For (nearly) semidefinite problems it is sometimes helpful to introduce *symmetric pivoting*. Here, we compute the Cholesky factorization of a permuted version of A: $PAP^T = GG^T$. P is designed so that the last $n - r$ rows of G are zero, where r is the rank of A.

Applications

• Cholesky is useful for solving positive definite systems: $Gy = b$; $G^Tx = y \Rightarrow Ax = b$.

• In exact arithmetic, the Cholesky process breaks down if and only if A has a negative eigenvalue. Thus, the Cholesky procedure can be used to detect whether or not a symmetric matrix has a negative eigenvalue.

• If $A \in \mathbb{R}^{m \times n}$ has full column rank, then the solution x_{LS} to the least squares problem min $\| Ax - b \|_2$ is the solution of the *normal equations $A^TAx = A^Tb$*. If A is poorly conditioned or if $\| Ax_{LS} - b \|_2$ is fairly small, then one should solve the LS problem via the QR factorization or the SVD, see Sections 2.9, 2.11, and 2.20.

Further reading

Analyses of the Cholesky process appear in Higham [1989], Kielbasinski [1987], and Meinguet [1983].

2.5. Special topic: Updating Cholesky

Quasi-Newton methods for nonlinear optimization frequently require the updating of a Cholesky factorization. For example, at the current step we may have the Cholesky factorization of an n-by-n approximate Hessian:

$$H_c = L_c L_c^T .$$

At the next step a new approximate Hessian H_+ is obtained via a rank-2 update of H_c:

$$H_+ = H_c + U_c B_c U_c^T , \quad U_c \in \mathbb{R}^{n \times 2}, \ B_c = B_c^T \in \mathbb{R}^{2 \times 2} .$$

In this setting, the central problem is this: *can we find a lower triangular matrix* $L_+ \in \mathbb{R}^{n \times n}$ *in* $O(n^2)$ *flops so that* $H_+ = L_+ L_+^T$? Notice that H_+ need not be positive definite and so the sought after Cholesky factorization may fail to exist.

We outline a procedure which computes L_+ if it exists. More efficient methods exist but our approach has a simplicity which makes it easy to convey the central ideas behind updating.

We begin by solving the multiple right-hand side problem $L_c W = U_c$ for W. This involves $O(n^2)$ flops and it follows that

$$H^+ = L_c (I + W B_c W^T) L_c^T .$$

Next, we find Givens rotations $G_n, \ldots, G_2, J_n, \ldots, J_3$ so that if

$$V = (G_n \cdots G_2)(J_n \cdots J_3) ,$$

then

$$V^T W = \begin{bmatrix} R \\ 0 \end{bmatrix}, \quad R \in \mathbb{R}^{2 \times 2} .$$

Moreover, $G_k = G(k-1, k)$ and $J_k = J(k-1, k)$ are rotations in planes $k-1$ and k. An $n = 4$ schematic should illustrate the idea behind the reduction:

$$\begin{bmatrix} \times & \times \\ \times & \times \\ \times & \times \\ \times & \times \end{bmatrix} \xrightarrow{G(3,4)} \begin{bmatrix} \times & \times \\ \times & \times \\ \times & \times \\ 0 & \times \end{bmatrix} \xrightarrow{G(2,3)} \begin{bmatrix} \times & \times \\ \times & \times \\ 0 & \times \\ 0 & \times \end{bmatrix} \xrightarrow{G(1,2)} \begin{bmatrix} \times & \times \\ 0 & \times \\ 0 & \times \\ 0 & \times \end{bmatrix}$$

$$\xrightarrow{J(3,4)} \begin{bmatrix} \times & \times \\ 0 & \times \\ 0 & \times \\ 0 & 0 \end{bmatrix} \xrightarrow{J(2,3)} \begin{bmatrix} \times & \times \\ 0 & \times \\ 0 & 0 \\ 0 & 0 \end{bmatrix} = \begin{bmatrix} R \\ 0 \end{bmatrix} .$$

This requires $O(n^2)$ flops. It can be shown that V has upper bandwidth 2 and that if

$$\tilde{B} = I + V^T W B W^T V = \begin{bmatrix} R B R^T & 0 \\ 0 & I_{n-2} \end{bmatrix} ,$$

then

$$H_+ = (L_c V)\tilde{B}(L_c V)^{\mathrm{T}}.$$

Let U be a rotation in the (1,2) plane so

$$U^{\mathrm{T}}\tilde{B}U = \mathrm{diag}(d_1, d_2, 1, \ldots, 1) \equiv D.$$

The orthogonal matrix $Q = VU$ has upper bandwidth 2 and we have

$$H_+ = (L_c Q)D(L_c Q)^{\mathrm{T}}.$$

H_+ is positive definite if and only if d_1 and d_2 are positive. Assuming this to be the case, we then form $C = L_c Q D^{1/2}$. This can be done in $O(n^2)$ flops because Q is a product of Givens rotations. Note that C has upper bandwidth 2 and that $H_+ = CC^{\mathrm{T}}$.

The final step is to compute an orthogonal matrix Z (product of Givens rotations) such that $Z^{\mathrm{T}}C^{\mathrm{T}} = T$ is upper triangular. This proceeds as follows:

$$
\begin{bmatrix}
\times & \times & \times & \times \\
\times & \times & \times & \times \\
\times & \times & \times & \times \\
0 & \times & \times & \times
\end{bmatrix}
\xrightarrow{(2,3)}
\begin{bmatrix}
\times & \times & \times & \times \\
\times & \times & \times & \times \\
0 & \times & \times & \times \\
0 & \times & \times & \times
\end{bmatrix}
\xrightarrow{(3,4)}
\begin{bmatrix}
\times & \times & \times & \times \\
\times & \times & \times & \times \\
0 & \times & \times & \times \\
0 & 0 & \times & \times
\end{bmatrix}
$$

$$
\xrightarrow{(1,2)}
\begin{bmatrix}
\times & \times & \times & \times \\
0 & \times & \times & \times \\
0 & \times & \times & \times \\
0 & 0 & \times & \times
\end{bmatrix}
\xrightarrow{(2,3)}
\begin{bmatrix}
\times & \times & \times & \times \\
0 & \times & \times & \times \\
0 & 0 & \times & \times \\
0 & 0 & \times & \times
\end{bmatrix}
\xrightarrow{(3,4)}
\begin{bmatrix}
\times & \times & \times & \times \\
0 & \times & \times & \times \\
0 & 0 & \times & \times \\
0 & 0 & 0 & \times
\end{bmatrix}.
$$

This is a Givens QR factorization process, see Section 2.10. It involves $O(n^2)$ flops and it follows that

$$H_+ = (CZ)(CZ)^{\mathrm{T}} = T^{\mathrm{T}}T \equiv L_+ L_+^{\mathrm{T}}$$

is the required Cholesky factorization.

Further reading

We mention that there are also techniques for updating the factorizations $PA = LU$, $A = GG^{\mathrm{T}}$, and $A = LDL^{\mathrm{T}}$. Updating these factorizations, however, can be quite delicate because of pivoting requirements and because when we tamper with a positive definite matrix the result may not be positive definite. See Björck [1984], Bojanczyk, Brent, Van Dooren & de Hoog [1987], Bunch, Nielsen & Sorensen [1978], Gill, Golub, Murray & Saunders [1974], Stewart [1979], Bartels [1971], Daniel, Gragg, Kaufman & Stewart [1976], Gill, Murray & Saunders [1975], and Goldfarb [1976].

2.6. The LDL^T factorization

Theorem. If $A \in \mathbb{R}^{n \times n}$ is symmetric and has the property that $\det(A(1:k, 1:k)) \neq 0$ for $k = 1:n - 1$, then there exists a unit lower triangular L and a diagonal D such that $A = LDL^T$.

Algorithmic and numerical notes

If A is positive definite, then $LD^{1/2}$ is the Cholesky factor. If $U = DL^T$, then $A = LU$. Thus, we can think of LDL^T as a 'square root free' Cholesky or as natural symmetrization of the LU factorization.

It is generally not advisable to use this factorization unless A is positive definite. Otherwise, the same guidance applies that we offered in connection with LU without pivoting. Namely, the method is not backwards stable unless L and D are suitably bounded. This is assured, for example, if A is diagonally dominant.

Applications

• The main application of this factorization is in the solution of symmetric positive definite systems. Indeed, if $Ly = b$, $Dz = y$, and $L^Tx = z$, then $Ax = b$.

• In some nonlinear optimization problems, symmetric linear systems $As = -g$ arise which 'should be' positive definite A. (Here, s is a step direction, A is an approximate Hessian, and g is a gradient.) If LDL^T is used, then it is possible to dynamically determine a nonnegative diagonal matrix Δ so that no negative D_{kk} arise. The result is a factorization of the form $(A + \Delta) = LDL^T$. One then solves $(A + \Delta)s = -g$ instead of $As = -g$ and obtains a preferred s.

• In general, any application that calls for Cholesky can be solved via LDL^T. However, when solving a band positive definite systems it is better to rely on the latter factorization. The n square roots that surface in Cholesky can represent a significant portion of the arithmetic when A is banded. This is especially true if A is tridiagonal.

2.7. The Bunch–Kaufman factorization

Theorem. If $A \in \mathbb{R}^{n \times n}$ is symmetric, then there exists a permutation P such that $PAP^T = LDL^T$ where $L \in \mathbb{R}^{n \times n}$ is unit lower triangular with $|l_{ij}| \leq 1$ and D is a direct sum of 1-by-1 and 2-by-2 submatrices.

Algorithmic and numerical notes

The factorization is discussed by Bunch & Parlett [1971], but Bunch & Kaufman [1977] discovered a clever pivot strategy that results in a 'Cholesky speed' procedure, i.e., $\frac{1}{3}n^3$ flops and $O(n^2)$ compares. It is as stable as Gaussian elimination with partial pivoting. Because of the pivot strategy, it is not possible to exploit band structure if it is present.

Applications
• The leading application of this factorization is the solution of symmetric indefinite systems: $Lw = Pb$, $Dz = w$, $L^T y = z$, $x = Py \Rightarrow Ax = b$. Note that the $Dz = w$ system involves solving 1-by-1 and 2-by-2 indefinite symmetric systems.

• The *inertia* of a symmetric matrix is a triplet of nonnegative integers (P, Z, N) which are the number of positive, zero, and negative eigenvalues, respectively. A famous theorem due to Sylvester states that the inertia of A, and $X^T A X$ are the same if X is nonsingular. Thus, A and D have the same inertia and the inertia of the latter is easily computed. (Just examine the eigenvalues of the 1-by-1 and 2-by-2 blocks in D.)

Further reading
The main papers associated with the computation of this factorization include Bunch [1971], Bunch & Kaufman [1977], Bunch, Kaufman & Parlett [1976], and Bunch & Parlett [1971].

2.8. The Aasen factorization

Theorem. *If $A \in \mathbb{R}^{n \times n}$ is symmetric, then there exists a permutation P such that $PAP^T = LTL^T$ where $L \in \mathbb{R}^{n \times n}$ is unit lower triangular with $|l_{ij}| \leq 1$ and T is tridiagonal.*

Algorithmic and numerical notes
Early papers gave an algorithm requiring about $\frac{2}{3}n^3$ flops. Aasen [1971] showed how to halve the work. No efficient version for band problems currently exists. The procedure is backwards stable.

Applications
• Any problem that can be solved by the Bunch–Kaufman factorization can also be solved via the Aasen approach.

Further reading
The original reference for the Aasen algorithm is Aasen [1971]. Comparisons with the diagonal pivoting approach are offered by Barwell & George [1976].

2.9. The QR factorization

Theorem. *If $A \in \mathbb{R}^{m \times n}$ then there exists an orthogonal $Q \in \mathbb{R}^{m \times n}$ and an upper triangular $R \in \mathbb{R}^{m \times n}$ such that $A = QR$.*

Mathematical notes
If $\text{span}\{a_1, \ldots, a_n\}$ defines an n-dimensional subspace of $\mathbb{R}^m$ and $QR = [a_1, \ldots, a_n]$ is the QR factorization, then the columns of $Q(:, 1:k)$ form an

orthonormal basis for span$\{a_1, \ldots, a_k\}$ for $k = 1:n$. The columns of the matrix $Q(:, n + 1:m)$ are an orthonormal basis for span$\{a_1, \ldots, a_n\}^\perp$. If A is rank deficient, then the QR factorization still exists but then R has one or more zero diagonal entries.

Algorithmic notes

The factorization can be computed using Householder transformations. Here, $Q = H_1 \cdots H_n$ and the 'mission' of H_k is to zero the subdiagonal portion of the kth column of A. Givens rotations can also be used but this is advisable only if A is sparse or in certain parallel computation settings.

A careful implementation of the Gram–Schmidt process (known as *modified Gram–Schmidt*) can also be used to compute the QR factorization. If Householder or Givens transformations are used, then the computed Q is orthogonal to working precision. In modified Gram–Schmidt, the quality of Q's orthogonality depends upon the condition of A.

Applications

- The QR factorization is frequently used to compute an orthonormal basis for a subspace and/or its orthogonal complement. However, if the dimension is 'fuzzy', then the SVD (see Section 2.20) might be more appropriate.
- The least square solution of full rank overdetermined system of equations is a lead application for the QR factorization. Suppose $A \in \mathbb{R}^{m \times n}$ with $m \geq n$ and $b \in \mathbb{R}^m$ are given. It follows that if

$$Q^\mathrm{T} A = \begin{bmatrix} R_1 \\ 0 \end{bmatrix}, \qquad Q^\mathrm{T} b = \begin{bmatrix} c \\ d \end{bmatrix},$$

where $R_1 \in \mathbb{R}^{n \times n}$, $c \in \mathbb{R}^n$, and $d \in \mathbb{R}^{m-n}$, then

$$\| Ax - b \|^2 = \| Q^\mathrm{T}(Ax - b) \|^2 = \| R_1 x - c \|^2 + \| d \|^2 ,$$

and so the minimizing x_LS is prescribed by the upper triangular system $R_1 x_\mathrm{LS} = c$.

If $\hat{x}_\mathrm{LS}$ is the computed solution obtained in this fashion, then $\hat{x}_\mathrm{LS}$ solves a nearby LS problem and its relative error has the form

$$\frac{\| \hat{x}_\mathrm{LS} - x_\mathrm{LS} \|_2}{\| x_\mathrm{LS} \|_2} \approx \alpha \kappa_2(A) + \beta \| Ax_\mathrm{LS} - b \|_2 \kappa_2(A)^2 ,$$

where α and β are small constants. Note the $\kappa(A)^2$ term.

Further reading

An excellent overall reference for all aspects of the least squares problem is Björck [1988]. The intelligent implementation of the QR process via orthogonal transformations is discussed by Businger & Golub [1965] and Golub [1965].

Perturbation theory and associated error analyses for QR solution of the least squares problem is covered by Björck [1987], Gentleman [1973], and Stewart [1977]. Sparse/banded LS solution techniques are detailed by Cox [1981], Duff & Reid [1976], and Gill & Murray [1976].

2.10. Special topic: Equality constrained least squares

Consider the least squares problem with linear equality constraints:

$$\min_{Bx=d} \| Ax - b \|_2 .$$

Here $A \in \mathbb{R}^{m \times n}$, $B \in \mathbb{R}^{p \times n}$, $b \in \mathbb{R}^m$, $d \in \mathbb{R}^p$, and $\operatorname{rank}(B) = p$. We refer to this as the *LSE problem*. Assume for clarity that both A and B have full rank. Let

$$Q^{\mathrm{T}} B^{\mathrm{T}} = \begin{bmatrix} R \\ 0 \end{bmatrix} \quad \begin{matrix} p \\ n-p \end{matrix}$$

be the QR factorization of B^{T} and set

$$AQ = [A_1 \quad A_2], \qquad Q^{\mathrm{T}}x = \begin{bmatrix} y \\ z \end{bmatrix} \quad \begin{matrix} p \\ n-p \end{matrix} .$$

It is clear that with these transformations the LSE problem becomes

$$\min_{R^{\mathrm{T}}y=d} \| A_1 y + A_2 z - b \|_2 .$$

Thus, y is determined from the lower triangular constraint equation $R^{\mathrm{T}}y = d$ and the vector z is obtained by solving the *unconstrained* LS problem

$$\min_z \| A_2 z - (b - A_1 y) \|_2 .$$

Combining the above, we see that $x = Q\begin{bmatrix} y \\ z \end{bmatrix}$ is the required solution. See Golub & Van Loan [1989] for more details.

An alternative approach for solving the LSE problem, called the *method of weighting*, is attractive for its simplicity. In this method the unconstrained LS problem

$$\min_z \left\| \begin{bmatrix} A \\ \lambda B \end{bmatrix} x - \begin{bmatrix} b \\ \lambda d \end{bmatrix} \right\|_2$$

is solved. Intuitively, if λ is large, then the constraint equation $Bx = d$ will tend to be satisfied. A tricky feature associated with this method is the handling of large λ. See Barlow, Nichols & Plemmons [1988], Eldèn [1980], Lawson & Hanson [1974], and Van Loan [1985b] for further discussion.

2.11. The QR factorization with column pivoting

Theorem. If $A \in \mathbb{R}^{m \times n}$ then there exists an orthogonal $Q \in \mathbb{R}^{m \times m}$ and a permutation matrix $P \in \mathbb{R}^{n \times n}$, such that

$$Q^T A \Pi = R = \begin{bmatrix} R_{11} & R_{12} \\ 0 & 0 \end{bmatrix} \begin{array}{c} r \\ m - r \end{array} ,$$
$$\quad\quad\quad r \quad n-r$$

where $r = \mathrm{rank}(A)$ and R_{11} is upper triangular and nonsingular.

Mathematical notes
Any vector of the form

$$x = \Pi^T \begin{bmatrix} -R_{11}^{-1} R_{12} z \\ z \end{bmatrix} ,$$

where $z \in \mathbb{R}^{n-r}$, is in the null space of A.

Algorithmic and numerical notes
The factorization amounts to a QR factorization of a column-permuted version of A. There are several ways to determine Π. The usual procedure is to determine $\Pi = \Pi_1 \cdots \Pi_n$ as a product of exchange permutations. Π_j is computed at step j so that the 2-norm of the current $A(j{:}m, j)$ is maximized. As a result of this pivot strategy we have

$$r_{jj}^2 \geq \sum_{i=j}^{k} r_{ik}^2$$

for $k = j + 1{:}n$. Thus, the numbers in R diminish in size towards the bottom right-hand corner. This property is attractive with many triangular matrix condition number estimators.

Applications
- If $r = m < n$, then any vector of the form

$$x = \Pi \begin{bmatrix} K_{11}^{-1} Q^T b \\ 0 \end{bmatrix}$$

solves the *underdetermined* system $Ax = b$.
- The factorization can be used to solve rank-deficient least squares problems $\min \| Ax - b \|_2$. Suppose $A \in \mathbb{R}^{m \times n}$ has rank r. QR with column pivoting produces the factorization $A\Pi = QR$, where

$$R = \begin{bmatrix} R_{11} & R_{12} \\ 0 & 0 \end{bmatrix} \begin{array}{c} r \\ m - r \end{array} .$$
$$\quad\quad\quad r \quad n-r$$

Given this reduction, the LS problem can be readily solved. Indeed, for any

$x \in \mathbb{R}^n$ we have

$$
\begin{aligned}
\| Ax - b \|_2^2 &= \| (Q^T A \Pi)(\Pi^T x) - (Q^T b) \|_2^2 \\
&= \| R_{11} y - (c - R_{12} z) \|_2^2 + \| d \|_2^2 ,
\end{aligned}
$$

where

$$
\Pi^T x = \begin{bmatrix} y \\ z \end{bmatrix} \begin{array}{c} r \\ n - r \end{array} \quad \text{and} \quad Q^T b = \begin{bmatrix} c \\ d \end{bmatrix} \begin{array}{c} r \\ m - r \end{array} .
$$

Thus, if x is an LS minimizer, then we must have

$$
x = \Pi \begin{bmatrix} R_{11}^{-1}(c - R_{12} z) \\ z \end{bmatrix} .
$$

If z is set to zero in this expression, then we obtain the *basic solution*

$$
x_B = \Pi \begin{bmatrix} R_{11}^{-1} c \\ 0 \end{bmatrix} .
$$

Notice that x_B has at most r nonzero components and so the predictor Ax_B involves a subset of A's columns. Indeed, QR with column pivoting can be thought of as a heuristic method for selecting a 'strongly' independent subset of A's columns.

Further reading

Using QR with column pivoting in the rank-deficient LS setting is discussed by Chan [1987], and Businger & Golub [1965]. Deducing the condition of A from the condition of R is detailed by Anderson & Karasalo [1975]. Perturbation aspects of the rank deficient LS problem are covered by Stewart [1984, 1987], and Wedin [1973].

2.12. The partial Schur decomposition

Theorem. *Suppose $A \in \mathbb{R}^{n \times n}$ and that $Q \in \mathbb{R}^{n \times n}$ is orthogonal. If the columns of $Q_1 = Q(:, 1:p)$ define an invariant subspace, then*

$$
A^T A Q = \begin{bmatrix} T_{11} & T_{12} \\ 0 & T_{22} \end{bmatrix}
$$

and the eigenvalues of $T_{11} = Q_1^T A Q_1$ are also eigenvalues of A.

Mathematical notes

This decomposition splits the spectrum in that $\lambda(A) = \lambda(T_{11}) \cup \lambda(T_{22})$. The columns of $Q_2 = Q(:, p+1:n)$ do *not* define an invariant subspace unless T_{12} is zero.

If T_{11} and T_{22} have no eigenvalues in common, then the *Sylvester equation*

$$T_{11}Y - YT_{22} = -T_{12}, \quad Y \in \mathbb{R}^{n \times p}$$

has a solution. This permits block diagonalization for if we set

$$Z = \begin{bmatrix} I_p & Y \\ 0 & I_{n-p} \end{bmatrix},$$

then

$$Z^{-1}TZ = \begin{bmatrix} T_{11} & T_{11}Y - YT_{22} + T_{12} \\ 0 & T_{22} \end{bmatrix} = \begin{bmatrix} T_{11} & 0 \\ 0 & T_{22} \end{bmatrix}.$$

Complex versions of the above reductions are possible. The matrix Q is then complex and unitary. Note that complex quantities can arise in a real matrix eigenreduction because of possible complex conjugate eigenvalues.

Algorithmic notes

Suppose $|\lambda_1| \geqslant \cdots \geqslant |\lambda_n|$ is an ordering of $\lambda(A)$. If $|\lambda_p| > |\lambda_{p+1}|$, then a method known as *orthogonal iteration* can be used to compute a p-dimensional invariant subspace associated with the p largest eigenvalues. If $Q^{(0)} \in \mathbb{R}^{n \times p}$ is an initial guess, then the kth step in this iteration has the following form:

$$Z = AQ_1^{(k-1)}, \quad \text{matrix-matrix multiply},$$

$$Q_1^{(k)}R^{(k)} = Z, \quad \text{QR factorization}.$$

If $Q_1^{(0)}$ is not 'deficient', then the distance between $\text{ran}(Q_1^{(k)})$ and $\text{ran}(Q_1^{(0)})$ is bounded by a constant times $|\lambda_{p+1}/\lambda_p|^k$.

If $p = 1$, then the technique is known as the *power method*. If we replace A by A^{-1}, then the resulting iteration is called *inverse orthogonal iteration*. It can be used to find the small eigenvalues of A but it requires the solution of a linear system at each step.

Further reading

The connections among the various power iterations are discussed by Parlett & Poole [1973], Stewart [1975, 1976b], and Golub & Van Loan [1989].

2.13. The Schur decomposition

Theorem. *If $A \in \mathbb{R}^{n \times n}$ has no complex eigenvalues, then there exists an orthogonal $Q \in \mathbb{R}^{n \times n}$ such that $Q^{\mathrm{T}}AQ = T$ is upper triangular.*

Mathematical notes

The diagonal elements of T are the eigenvalues of A. The columns of Q are called *Schur vectors*. For $j = 1:n$, $\text{ran}(Q(:, 1:j))$ is an invariant subspace. The column $Q(:, j)$ is an eigenvector if and only if $T(1:j - 1, j) = 0$. T is diagonal if and only if A is *normal*, i.e., $A^H A = AA^H$.

If $A \in \mathbb{R}^{n \times n}$ has complex eigenvalues, then they occur in conjugate pairs and it is possible to determine an orthogonal $Q \in \mathbb{R}^{n \times n}$ so that T is *quasi-triangular*. This means that T is upper triangular with 2-by-2 'bumps' along the diagonal corresponding to the complex conjugate eigenpairs. In particular, if $t_{k,k-1} \neq 0$, then the eigenvalues of

$$T(k - 1:k, k - 1:k) = \begin{bmatrix} t_{k-1,k-1} & t_{k-1,k} \\ t_{k,k-1} & t_{kk} \end{bmatrix}$$

are complex conjugate eigenvalues of A. The real orthogonal reduction to quasi-triangular form is referred to as the *real Schur decomposition*.

If complex transformations are 'admissable', then we can find a unitary $Q \in \mathbb{C}^{n \times n}$ such that $Q^H A Q = T$ is upper triangular (and complex).

Algorithmic and numerical notes

The standard method for computing this decomposition is the QR iteration with shifts. A step in this procedure has the following form:

Determine approximate eigenvalues μ_1 and μ_2.
Compute the QR factorization $QR = (A - \mu_1 I)(A - \mu_2 I)$.
$A_{new} = Q^T A Q$.

The key to a successful implementation of this iteration involves (a) the preliminary reduction of A to upper Hessenberg form (see Section 2.14), (b) the intelligent selection of the *shifts* μ_1 and μ_2, and (c) a clever $O(n^2)$ method for computing A_{new} from Q to A. The overall reduction involves about $30n^3$ flops if Q is required, $15n^3$ if not.

Once a real Schur decomposition is obtained, the columns of Q and the diagonal entries of T can be cheaply re-ordered so that the eigenvalues appear in any prescribed order. This is important because we can then acquire an orthonormal basis for an invariant subspace associated with any subset of eigenvalues.

The QR iteration is backwards stable meaning that the computed $\hat{T}$ is exactly similar to a matrix near to A in norm. This does *not* mean that the computed eigenvalues are accurate. Indeed, if λ is a distinct eigenvalue of A, then its computed analog $\hat{\lambda}$ satisfies

$$|\lambda - \hat{\lambda}| \approx \frac{\mathbf{u}}{s(\lambda)} ,$$

where $s(\lambda) = |x^T y|$. Here, x and y are unit 2-norm right and left eigenvectors: $Ax = \lambda x$, $y^T A = \lambda y^T$. The reciprocal of $s(\lambda)$ can be thought of as a condition for λ. If λ is not distinct, then matters get complicated, see Golub & Van Loan [1989, Section 7.2].

Applications
  • Once the Schur decomposition is acquired, the eigenvectors of A can be found through a back substitution process. In particular, if t_{kk} is a distinct eigenvalue and we solve $(T(1{:}k-1, 1{:}k-1) - t_{kk}I)z = -T(1{:}k-1, k)$ for z, then

$$x = Q \begin{bmatrix} z \\ -1 \\ 0 \end{bmatrix}$$

satisfies $Ax = \lambda x$.
  • The Lyapunov equation $FX + XF^T = C$, where $F \in \mathbb{R}^{m \times m}$, and $C \in \mathbb{R}^{n \times n}$, can be solved by computing the Schur decomposition $U^T F U = T$. (For clarity we assume that F has real eigenvalues.) Note that with the Schur decomposition the original Lyapunov equation transforms to $TY + YT^T = \tilde{C}$ where $X = UYU^T$ and $\tilde{C} = U^T C U$. If $Y = [y_1, \ldots, y_n]$ and $\tilde{C} = [\tilde{c}_1, \ldots, \tilde{c}_n]$ are column partitioning, then for $k = 1{:}n$ we have

$$(T + t_{kk}I)y_k = \tilde{c}_k - \sum_{j=k+1}^{n} t_{kj}y_j .$$

Y can be resolved by invoking this formula for $k = n, n-1, \ldots, 1$.

Further reading
  The mathematical properties of the algebraic eigenvalue problem and related perturbation theory are covered by Golub & Van Loan [1989].
  Practical invariant subspace computation is detailed by Golub & Wilkinson [1976], Stewart [1976a], and Bavely & Stewart (1979). Various aspects of eigenvector computation are treated by Chan & Parlett [1977], Symm & Wilkinson [1980], and Van Loan [1987].

2.14. The Hessenberg decomposition

Theorem. *If $A \in \mathbb{R}^{n \times n}$ then there exists an orthogonal $Q \in \mathbb{R}^{n \times n}$ such that $Q^T A Q = H$ is upper Hessenberg. In other words, $h_{ij} = 0$ whenever $i > j + 1$.*

Mathematical notes
  If no subdiagonal entry of H is zero, then H is *unreduced*. If H is unreduced and $\lambda \in \lambda(A)$, then $\text{rank}(A - \lambda I) = n - 1$. This implies that if H is unreduced, then there is at most one independent eigenvector per eigenvalue.
  If q_i is the ith column of Q, then $\{q_1, \ldots, q_j\}$ is an orthonormal basis for the *Krylov subspace* $\text{span}\{q_1, Aq_1, \ldots, A^{j-1}q_1\}$ assuming the latter subspace has dimension j.

Algorithmic and numerical notes
  The standard method for computing the factorization is via Householder matrices. In particular, $Q = Q_1 \cdots Q_{n-2}$ where Q_j is a Householder matrix

whose mission is to zero $A(j + 2{:}n, j)$. This procedure requires $\frac{10}{3}n^3$ flops and is backwards stable.

If A is large and sparse the method of Arnoldi is of interest. After k steps of the Arnoldi process the leading k-by-k portion of H is available and its eigenvalues can be regarded as approximate eigenvalues of A. The Arnoldi algorithm requires only matrix–vector products involving A and thus has potential for large sparse problems.

Applications

• The Hessenberg reduction is usually applied to A before computing the real Schur form. The QR iteration preserves Hessenberg form, a property that reduces work per iteration by an order of magnitude.

• If one has to solve $(A - \mu I)x = b$ for many different $\mu \in \mathbb{R}$ and $b \in \mathbb{R}^n$, then the volume of computation can be greatly reduced if A is first reduced to Hessenberg form. Note that if we solve $(H - \mu I)y = Q^T b$ and set $x = Qy$, then $(A - \mu I)x = b$. This involves a pair of matrix–vector products and a Hessenberg system solve implying $O(n^2)$ flops.

• The *Sylvester equation* $FX + XG = C$, where $F \in \mathbb{R}^{m \times m}$, $G \in \mathbb{R}^{n \times n}$, and $C \in \mathbb{R}^{m \times n}$, can be solved by computing the Hessenberg decomposition $U^T F U = H$ and the Schur decomposition $V^T G V = S$. (For clarity we assume that G has real eigenvalues.) The original Sylvester equation now transforms to $HY + YS = \tilde{C}$, where $X = UYV^T$ and $\tilde{C} = U^T C V$. If $Y = [y_1, \ldots, y_m]$ and $\tilde{C} = [\tilde{c}_1, \ldots, \tilde{c}_m]$ are column partitionings, then for $k = 1{:}n$ we have

$$(H + s_{kk}I)y_k = \tilde{c}_k - \sum_{j=1}^{k-1} s_{jk}y_j \,.$$

Thus, if $y_1, \ldots, y_n$ are computed in turn, then we obtain Y.

• If $\hat{\lambda}$ is a computed eigenvalue of H, then a corresponding eigenvector can be found via *inverse iteration*. In this procedure, the nearly singular Hessenberg system $(H - \hat{\lambda})x = c$ is solved for a random c. The solution x is very often rich in the desired eigendirection.

Further reading

The Householder reduction to Hessenberg form is discussed by Dongarra, Kaufman & Hammarling [1986], and Businger [1969, 1971].

For a survey of applications where the decomposition has proven to be very useful, see Golub, Nash & Van Loan [1979], Laub [1981], and Van Loan [1982b].

2.15. Jordan canonical form

Theorem. *If $A \in \mathbb{C}^{n \times n}$ then there exists a nonsingular $X \in \mathbb{C}^{n \times n}$ such that $X^{-1}AX = \mathrm{diag}(J_1, \ldots, J_t)$ where*

$$J_i = \begin{bmatrix} \lambda_i & 1 & \cdots & 0 \\ 0 & \lambda_i & \ddots & \vdots \\ \vdots & & \ddots & 1 \\ 0 & \cdots & 0 & \lambda_i \end{bmatrix}$$

is n_i-by-n_i and $n_1 + \cdots + n_t = n$.

Mathematical notes

The J_i are referred to as *Jordan blocks*. The number and dimensions of the Jordan blocks associated with each distinct eigenvalue is unique, although their ordering along the diagonal is not. If a Jordan block is bigger than 1-by-1, then the associated eigenvalue is said to be *defective*. This means that A has fewer than n independent eigenvectors. If this is not the case, then A is said to be *diagonalizable*.

Algorithmic and numerical notes

Because it involves a set of numerical rank decisions, computation of the JCF is tricky and involves use of the singular value decomposition (see Section 2.20) to resolve difficult questions that concern eigenvalue multiplicity.

Further reading

Some intelligent algorithms that address the difficulties associated with JCF computation include Ruhe [1969], Kagstrom & Ruhe [1980a,b], and Demmel [1983].

2.16. The generalized Schur decomposition

Theorem. *If $A \in \mathbb{C}^{n \times n}$ and $B \in \mathbb{C}^{n \times n}$, then there exist unitary $Q, Z \in \mathbb{C}^{n \times n}$ such that $Q^H A Z = T$ and $Q^H B Z = S$ are upper triangular.*

Mathematical notes

The λ which make $A - \lambda B$ singular are called the *generalized eigenvalues* of the *pencil* $A - \lambda B$. Since

$$\det(A - \lambda B) = \det(Q^H Z)\det(T - \lambda S) = \det(Q^H Z) \prod_{k=1}^{n} (t_{kk} - \lambda s_{kk}) \,,$$

it follows that the quotients t_{kk}/s_{kk} are generalized eigenvalues. If $s_{kk} = 0$ then $A - \lambda B$ has an infinite eigenvalue. If for some k, $t_{kk} = s_{kk} = 0$, then $\lambda(A, B) = \mathbb{C}$.

If B is nonsingular then $Q^H A B^{-1} Q = T S^{-1}$ is the Schur decomposition of $C = A B^{-1}$.

The columns of $Z_1 = Z(:, 1:p)$ define what is called a *deflating subspace* for the matrix pencil $A - \lambda B$. In particular, $\text{ran}(AZ_1) = \text{ran}(BZ_1)$.

Algorithmic and numerical notes

A generalization of the QR algorithm called the QZ algorithm is the standard approach to this problem. The algorithm is backwards stable and is *not* effected by singularity in A or B.

Applications

• The main application of the QZ algorithm is the computation to generalized eigenvalues and their associated eigenvectors. Indeed, the eigenvectors of the triangular pencil $T - \lambda S$ can be found via back substitution analogous to how one proceeds with the standard Schur decomposition.

Further reading

Many theoretical and practical aspects of the $A - \lambda B$ problem are covered by Kågström & Ruhe [1983], and Stewart [1972]. Various aspects of the QZ algorithm are detailed by Moler & Stewart [1973], Ward [1975], and Golub & Van Loan [1989].

2.17. The symmetric Schur decomposition

Theorem. *If $A \in \mathbb{R}^{n \times n}$ is symmetric, then there exists an orthogonal $Q \in \mathbb{R}^{n \times n}$ such that $Q^T A Q = D = \mathrm{diag}(\lambda_i)$.*

Mathematical notes

Because symmetric matrices have a diagonal Schur form, the columns of Q are eigenvectors: $AQ(:, j) = Q(:, j)\lambda_j$.

The stationary values of the *Rayleigh quotient*

$$r(x) = \frac{x^T A x}{x^T x}$$

are the eigenvalues of A. Moreover, if $\lambda_1 \geq \lambda_2 \geq \cdots \geq \lambda_n$, then

$$\lambda_k(A) = \max_{\dim(S)=k} \min_{0 \neq y \in S} r(y).$$

This result can be used to show that if $\lambda \in \lambda(A)$, then there exists an eigenvalue $\tilde{\lambda} \in \lambda(A + E)$ such that $|\lambda - \tilde{\lambda}| \leq \|E\|_2$. Unlike the unsymmetric eigenvalue problem, $O(\varepsilon)$ perturbations of A induce $O(\varepsilon)$ perturbations of the eigenvalues.

Algorithmic and numerical notes

If A is tridiagonal (see Section 2.18), then a symmetrized version of the QR iteration described in Section 2.13 is an effective method for computing the decomposition. A divide-and-conquer technique based on tearing is an alternative method of interest.

If A is full, then the Jacobi iteration can be used. Jacobi's idea is to compute the real Schur decomposition via a sequence of 2-by-2 problems. In particular, updates of the form

$$A \leftarrow J_{pq}^{\mathrm{T}} A J_{pq}$$

are repeatedly performed, where J_{pq} is a Givens rotation in the (p, q) plane. With each update the Frobenius norm of the off-diagonal portion of A is strictly reduced. By choosing the rotation indices (p, q) carefully it is possible to introduce significant amounts of parallelism.

Applications
  ● In certain optimization algorithms one would like to translate the system $Ax = b$ so that the solution is suitably bounded. In particular, we are given $A = A^{\mathrm{T}} \in \mathbb{R}^{n \times n}$, $b \in \mathbb{R}^n$, and $\delta > 0$ and we seek $\sigma \geq 0$ such that the solution $x(\sigma)$ to $(A + \sigma I)x = b$ satisfies $\|x(\sigma)\|_2 \leq \delta$. This problem transforms to an equivalent diagonal problem via the symmetric Schur decomposition: $(D + \sigma I)y(\sigma) = \tilde{b}$ subject to $\|y(\sigma)\|_2 \leq \delta$. Since $y_i(\sigma) = \tilde{b}_i/(\lambda_i + \sigma)$ the optimum y is readily found.
  ● The maximization of $r(x)$ over a subspace is the largest eigenvalue of $U^{\mathrm{T}} A U$ where the columns of U are an orthonormal basis for the subspace.

Further reading
  The book by Parlett [1980] covers many aspects of the symmetric eigenvalue problem. See also Golub & Van Loan [1989] for algorithmic details.

2.18. Orthogonal tridiagonalization

Theorem. *If $A \in \mathbb{R}^{n \times n}$ is symmetric, then there exists an orthogonal $Q \in \mathbb{R}^{n \times n}$ such that $Q^{\mathrm{T}} A Q = T$ is tridiagonal, i.e., $t_{ij} = 0$ if $|i - j| > 1$.*

Mathematical notes

  If T has no zero subdiagonal elements, then A has no repeated eigenvalues. Let $T_r = T(1:r, 1:r)$ denote the leading r-by-r principal submatrix of

$$T = \begin{bmatrix} \alpha_1 & \beta_1 & \cdots & & 0 \\ \beta_1 & \alpha_2 & & \ddots & \vdots \\ \vdots & & \ddots & \ddots & \\ & & \ddots & \ddots & \beta_{n-1} \\ 0 & \cdots & & \beta_{n-1} & \alpha_n \end{bmatrix},$$

and define the polynomials $p_r(x) = \det(T_r - xI)$, $r = 1:n$. A simple determinantal expansion can be used to show that

$$p_r(x) = (\alpha_r - x)p_{r-1}(x) - \beta_{r-1}^2 p_{r-2}(x)$$

for $r = 2{:}n$ if we define $p_0(x) = 1$.

Algorithmic and numerical notes

For dense problems, Q is usually computed as a product of Householder transformations: $Q = Q_1 \cdots Q_{n-2}$. The resulting algorithm is backwards stable.

The *method of Lanczos* is a technique for computing T without resorting to updates of A, see Section 2.19.

Because the polynomial $p_n(x)$ can be evaluated in $O(n)$ flops, it is feasible to find its roots by using the method of bisection.

Applications

● Given a general symmetric matrix A, it is customary to tridiagonalize it first before applying the QR iteration for eigenvalues.

● Some of the applications of the Hessenberg decomposition (Section 2.14) can be solved via tridiagonalization if A is symmetric. For example, if we must solve symmetric systems of the form $(A - \sigma I)x = b$ for many different σ and b.

Further reading

The tridiagonalization of a symmetric matrix is detailed by Golub & Van Loan [1989].

2.19. Special topic: The Lanczos and conjugate gradient algorithms

A different method for computing the tridiagonalization can be derived by comparing columns in the equation $AQ = QT$. With the notation of the previous section and the column partitioning $Q = [q_1, \dots, q_n]$ we obtain

$$Aq_j = \beta_{j-1}q_{j-1} + \alpha_j q_j + \beta_j q_{j+1} \quad (\beta_0 q_0 \equiv 0)$$

for $j = 1{:}n - 1$. The orthonormality of the q_i implies $\alpha_j = q_j^T A q_j$. Moreover, if $r_j = (A - \alpha_j I)q_j - \beta_{j-1}q_{j-1}$ is nonzero, then $q_{j+1} = r_j/\beta_j$, where $\beta_j = \pm \|r_j\|_2$. Collecting these observations we obtain the *Lanczos iteration*:

$r_0 = q_1; \ \beta_0 = 1; \ q_0 = 0; \ j = 0$
while $\beta_j \neq 0$
$\quad q_{j+1} = r_j/\beta_j; \ j = j + 1; \ \alpha_j = q_j^T A q_j$
$\quad r_j = (A - \alpha_j I)q_j - \beta_{j-1}q_{j-1}; \ \beta_j = \|r_j\|_2$
end

See Golub & Van Loan [1989, p. 478]. The q_j are called *Lanczos vectors*.

Notice that the matrix A is involved only through matrix–vector multiplication. This is important in large sparse problems because the Householder approach can lead to an unacceptable level of fill-in. If $\beta_j = 0$ then $q_1, \ldots, q_j$ define an invariant subspace for A associated with the eigenvalues of $T(1:j, 1:j)$.

Unfortunately, the computed Lanczos vectors are usually far from orthogonal and a great deal of research has been devoted to handle this problem. On the positive side, the extreme eigenvalues of $T(1:j, 1:j)$ tend to be very good approximations of A's extreme eigenvalues even for relatively small j making the Lanczos procedure very attractive in certain settings.

The Lanczos procedure can also be used to solve sparse symmetric positive definite systems $Ax = b$. Indeed the sequence of vectors x_j produced by the iteration

$$r_0 = b; \ \beta_0 = \|b\|_2; \ q_0 = 0; \ j = 0; \ x_0 = 0$$
while $\beta_j \neq 0$
$\quad q_{j+1} = r_j/\beta_j; \ j = j+1; \ \alpha_j = q_j^T A q_j$
$\quad r_j = (A - \alpha_j I)q_j - \beta_{j-1}q_{j-1}; \ \beta_j = \|r_j\|_2$
$\quad$ **if** $j = 1$
$\quad\quad d_1 = \alpha_1; \ c_1 = q_1; \ \rho_1 = \beta_0/\alpha_1; \ x_1 = \rho_1 q_1$
$\quad$ **else**
$\quad\quad \mu_{j-1} = \beta_{j-1}/d_{j-1}; \ d_j = \alpha_j - \beta_{j-1}u_{j-1}$
$\quad\quad c_j = q_j - \mu_{j-1}c_{j-1}; \ \rho_j = -\mu_{j-1}d_j - {}_1\rho_{j-1}/d_j$
$\quad\quad x_j = x_{j-1} + \rho_j c_j$
$\quad$ **end**
end
$x = x_j$

have the property that they minimize $\phi(x) = \frac{1}{2}x^T Ax - x^T b$ over span$\{q_1, \ldots, q_j\}$. It follows that $Ax_n = b$ since $x = A^{-1}b$ is the global minimizer of ϕ. However, it turns out that x_j tends to be a very good approximate solution for relatively small j. This method, known as the *method of conjugate gradients* has found wide applicability. (The above specification is taken from Golub & Van Loan [1989, p. 497]).

A technique known as *preconditioning* is often crucial to the process. The preconditioned conjugate gradient algorithm is very similar to the above iteration only during each step, a vector z_j defined by $Mz_j = r_j$ must be computed. M is the preconditioner and it must satisfy two constraints:

- Linear systems involving M must be easily solved.
- M must approximate A either in the norm sense or in the sense that $M - A$ has low rank.

Further reading

Good 'global' references for the Lanczos algorithm include Parlett [1980], Cullum & Willoughby [1985a,b], and Golub & Van Loan [1989]. The rapid convergence of the Lanczos process is discussed by Kaniel [1966], Paige [1971, 1980], and Saad [1980]. Practical details associated with the implementation of the Lanczos procedure are discussed by Parlett & Nour-Omid [1985]; Parlett, Simon & Stringer [1982], and Scott [1979].

Interesting papers that pertain to the method of conjugate gradients include Axelsson [1985], Concus, Golub & Meurant [1985], Concus, Golub & O'Leary [1976], and Golub & Meurant [1983]. Representative papers that are concerned with preconditioning include Elman [1986], Manteuffel [1979], Meijerink & Van der Vorst [1977], and Rodrigue & Wolitzer [1984]. The idea of adapting the method to unsymmetric problems is explored by Saad [1981], and Faber & Manteuffel [1984]. Implementation strategies for high performance computers are set forth in Meurant [1984], Poole & Ortega [1987], Seager [1986], and Van der Vorst [1982a,b]. The GMRES scheme due to Saad & Schultz [1986] is one of the most widely used sparse unsymmetric system solvers. The survey by Saad [1989] is recommended for further insight into GMRES and related Ktylov subspace methods.

2.20. The singular value decomposition

Theorem. *If $A \in \mathbb{R}^{m \times n}$ then there exists an orthogonal $U \in \mathbb{R}^{m \times m}$ and $V \in \mathbb{R}^{n \times n}$ such that $U^T A V = \Sigma$ is diagonal. The diagonal elements of Σ are the singular values and the columns of U and V are left and right singular vectors.*

Mathematical notes

If $\sigma_r > \sigma_{r+1} = 0$, then $r = \text{rank}(A)$. If $U = [u_1, \ldots, u_m]$ and $V = [v_1, \ldots, v_n]$ are column partitionings, then $\{v_{r+1}, \ldots, v_n\}$ is an orthonormal basis for null(A) and $\{u_1, \ldots, u_r\}$ is an orthonormal basis for ran(A). Moreover, if

$$A_{\tilde{r}} = \sum_{j=1}^{\tilde{r}} \frac{u_j v_j^t}{\sigma_j} \, ,$$

then $A = A_r$ and $B_{\text{opt}} = A_{\tilde{r}}$ minimizes $\| A - B \|_2$ subject to rank(B) = $\tilde{r} \leqslant r$.

Algorithmic and numerical notes

A variant of the symmetric QR algorithm is the standard means for computing the SVD of a dense matrix. A is first reduced to bidiagonal form (see Section 2.21) and then the symmetric QR iteration is *implicitly* applied to the tridiagonal matrix $A^T A$.

Jacobi procedures also exist. These involve solving a sequence of 2-by-2 SVD problems which make A progressively more diagonal.

Applications

● The rank deficient least squares problem is handled nicely through the SVD. If $u_i = U(:, i)$ and $v_i = V(:, i)$, then

$$x_{LS} = \sum_{i=1}^{r} \frac{u_i^T b}{\alpha_i} \, v_i \,, \quad r = \text{rank}(A) \,.$$

• In exact arithmetic, if $r = \text{rank}(A)$, then $\sigma_r > \sigma_{r+1} = \cdots = \sigma_n = 0$. However, this is an unworkable criterion in the face of fuzzy data and inexact arithmetic. So a more realistic approach to numerical rank determination is to choose a parameter ε and then say A has ε-rank $\hat{r}$ if

$$\hat{\sigma}_{\hat{r}} > \hat{\sigma}_1 \varepsilon \geq \hat{\sigma}_{\hat{r}+1} \,,$$

where the 'hats' designate computed quantities.
• Given $A, B \in \mathbb{R}^{m \times p}$ the problem

$$\text{minimize} \quad \|A - BQ\|_F$$

$$\text{subject to} \quad Q^T Q = I_p$$

is solved by $Q = UV^T$ where $U^T CV$ is the SVD of $C = B^T A$.
• Suppose $A \in \mathbb{R}^{m \times n}$ and $B \in \mathbb{R}^{p \times n}$ are given and that we want to compute an orthonormal basis for $\text{null}(A) \cap \text{null}(B)$. Using the SVD, first compute a matrix V_A whose columns are an orthonormal basis for $\text{null}(A)$. Then use the SVD again to compute a matrix V_C whose orthonormal columns span the null space of $C = BV_A$. The columns of V_C can be shown to span the required null space.
• Suppose the columns of $Q_S \in \mathbb{R}^{n \times p}$ and $Q_T \in \mathbb{R}^{n \times p}$ are orthonormal and define a pair of subspaces S and T. The singular values of $C = Q_S^T Q_T$ are situated in $[0, 1]$ and so we may write $\sigma_i = \cos(\theta_i)$ for $i = 1{:}p$ with $0 \leq \theta_1 \leq \cdots \leq \theta_p \leq \frac{1}{2}\pi$. The θ_i are called the *principal angles* between the subspaces S and T. If $0 = \theta_1 = \cdots = \theta_p < \theta_{p+1}$ and $U^T CV = \Sigma$ is the SVD, then $\text{ran}(V(:, 1{:}p)) = \text{ran}(U(:, 1{:}P)) = S \cap T$.
• If error is also present in the 'data matrix' A, then instead of solving the ordinary least squares problem it may be more natural to consider the problem

$$\min_{b + r \in \text{range}(A + E)} \|D[E \quad r]T\|_F, \quad E \in \mathbb{R}^{m \times n}, r \in \mathbb{R}^m, \tag{5}$$

where $D = \text{diag}(d_1, \ldots, d_m)$ and $T = \text{diag}(t_1, \ldots, t_{n+1})$ are nonsingular. This problem is referred to as the *total least squares* (TLS) problem. If $U^T CV = \Sigma$ is the SVD of $C = D[A \quad b]T$, then $[E_{\text{opt}} \quad r_{\text{opt}}] = -\sigma_{n+1} u_{n+1} v_{n+1}^T$ and $(A + E_{\text{opt}}) x_{\text{TLS}} = b + r_{\text{opt}}$, where

$$x_{\text{TLS}} = -V(1{:}n, n+1)/V(n+1, n+1)$$

is the total least squares fit.

Further reading

All aspects of the SVD are discussed by Golub & Van Loan [1989]. The standard means for computing the SVD is a modification of the symmetric QR algorithm for eigenvalues. Appropriate references include Chan [1982], Golub & Kahan [1965], and Golub & Reinsch [1970].

A modification of the symmetric Jacobi algorithm can also be used. See Brent, Luk & Van Loan [1985], Forsythe & Henrici [1960], Kogbetliantz [1955], and Van Dooren & Paige [1986].

Using the SVD to solve the canonical correlation problem was originally proposed by Björck & Golub [1973].

The TLS problem is discussed by Golub & Van Loan [1980], and Van Huffel [1987, 1988]. If some of the columns of A are known exactly, then it is sensible to force the TLS perturbation matrix E to be zero in the same columns. Aspects of this constrained TLS problem are discussed by Van Huffel & Vandewalle [1988].

2.21. Orthogonal bidiagonalization

Theorem. *If $A \in \mathbb{R}^{m \times n}$ then there exist orthogonal $U \in \mathbb{R}^{m \times m}$ and orthogonal $V \in \mathbb{R}^{n \times n}$ such that $U^T A V = B$ is upper bidiagonal.*

Mathematical notes

A and B have the same singular values. If A is rank deficient, then B has at least one zero on its diagonal. Note that V tridiagonalizes $A^T A$ and U tridiagonalizes $A A^T$.

Algorithmic and numerical notes

The standard method for bidiagonalization uses Householder transformations. The reduction is backwards stable and requires $2mm^2 + n^3$ flops.

2.22. The CS decomposition

Theorem. *If*

$$Q = \begin{bmatrix} Q_{11} & Q_{12} \\ Q_{21} & Q_{22} \end{bmatrix} \begin{matrix} k \\ j \end{matrix}$$
$$\quad\;\, k \quad\; j$$

is orthogonal with $k \geq j$, then there exist orthogonal matrices $U_1, V_1 \in \mathbb{R}^{k \times k}$ and orthogonal matrices $U_2, V_2 \in \mathbb{R}^{j \times j}$ such that

$$\begin{bmatrix} U_1 & 0 \\ 0 & U_2 \end{bmatrix}^T \begin{bmatrix} Q_{11} & Q_{12} \\ Q_{21} & Q_{22} \end{bmatrix} \begin{bmatrix} V_1 & 0 \\ 0 & V_2 \end{bmatrix} = \begin{bmatrix} I_{k-j} & 0 & 0 \\ 0 & C & S \\ 0 & -S & C \end{bmatrix},$$

where

$$C = \text{diag}(c_1, \ldots, c_j) \in \mathbb{R}^{j \times j}, \quad c_i = \cos(\theta_i),$$

$$S = \text{diag}(s_1, \ldots, s_j) \in \mathbb{R}^{j \times j}, \quad s_i = \sin(\theta_i),$$

and $0 \leq \theta_1 \leq \theta_2 \leq \cdots \leq \theta_j \leq \frac{1}{2}\pi$.

Mathematical notes

Paige & Saunders [1981] have explored a variation of the above concerned with the SVDs of the blocks of

$$Q = \begin{bmatrix} Q_1 \\ Q_2 \end{bmatrix},$$

where Q has orthonormal columns. No assumption that Q_1 be square is required.

Algorithmic and numerical notes

Algorithms for the CS decomposition algorithm may be found in Stewart [1983], and Van Loan [1985a]. SVDs and QR factorizations are involved. They are all backwards stable.

Applications

• The CS decomposition is useful in the analysis of many problems that involve distances between subspaces.

• Some generalized SVD problems can be solved using the Paige–Saunders variant, see Section 2.24.

Further reading

The CS decomposition has many applications associated with subspace nearness. See Davis & Kahan [1970].

2.23. *Generalized SVD*

Theorem. *If we have* $A \in \mathbb{R}^{m \times n}$ *with* $m \geq n$ *and* $B \in \mathbb{R}^{p \times n}$, *then there exist orthogonal* $U \in \mathbb{R}^{m \times m}$ *and* $V \in \mathbb{R}^{p \times p}$ *and an invertible* $X \in \mathbb{R}^{n \times n}$ *such that*

$$U^\mathsf{T} A X = C = \text{diag}(c_1, \ldots, c_n), \quad 1 \geq c_1 \geq \cdots \geq c_n \geq 0$$

and

$$V^\mathsf{T} B X = S = \text{diag}(s_1, \ldots, s_q), \quad s_i \geq 0, s_i^2 + c_i^2 = 1,$$

where $q = \min(p, n)$.

Algorithmic and numerical notes

A sequence of carefully chosen QR factorizations and SVDs can be used to compute the generalized SVD. For stability it is sometimes better to compute X^{-1} rather than X, see Section 2.24.

Applications

• Consider the least squares problem with quadratic inequality constraint (LSQI):

$$\text{minimize} \quad \|Ax - b\|_2$$
$$\text{subject to} \quad \|Bx - d\|_2 \leq \alpha ,$$

where $A \in \mathbb{R}^{m \times n}$ $(m \geq n)$, $b \in \mathbb{R}^m$, $B \in \mathbb{R}^{p \times n}$, $d \in \mathbb{R}^p$, and $\alpha \geq 0$. The generalized singular value decomposition sheds light on the solvability of the LSQI problem. Indeed, if

$$U^T A X = \text{diag}(\alpha_1, \dots, \alpha_n) , \quad U^T U = I_m ,$$
$$V^T B X = \text{diag}(\beta_1, \dots, \beta_q) , \quad V^T V = I_p, \ q = \min\{p, n\}$$

is the generalized singular value decomposition of A and B, then the original LSQI problem transforms to

$$\text{minimize} \quad \|D_A y - \tilde{b}\|_2$$
$$\text{subject to} \quad \|D_B y - \tilde{d}\|_2 \leq \alpha ,$$

where $\tilde{b} = U^T b$, $\tilde{d} = V^T d$, and $y = X^{-1} x$. The simple diagonal form of the objective function and the constraint equation facilitate the analysis of the LSQI problem. Here, $r = \text{rank}(B)$.

• The problem of finding nontrivial solutions to the generalized eigenvalue problem $A^T A - \lambda B^T B$ is called the *generalized singular value problem*. It is easy to show that if we have the above generalized SVD, then the λ we seek are the zeros of $\det(C^T C - \lambda S^T S) = \Pi_{k=0}^n (c_k^2 - \lambda s_k^2)$.

Further reading

Various aspects of the generalized singular value decomposition are discussed by Golub & Van Loan [1989], Kågström [1985], Paige [1986], Stewart [1983], Paige & Saunders [1981], and Van Loan [1976].

2.24. Special topic: Avoiding inverses and cross-products

We have seen several instances where the avoidance of explicit inverse computation results in methods with superior numerical properties. We would like to expand upon this critical point as it is a symbol of intelligent matrix computations. We consider a problem that arises in signal processing, see Speiser & Van Loan [1984].

Suppose $A \in \mathbb{R}^{m \times n}$ and $B \in \mathbb{R}^{p \times n}$ with $m, n \geqslant p$ and that

$$\text{null}(A) \cap \text{null}(B) = \{0\} \ .$$

This condition can be relaxed but with a loss of clarity. Suppose

$$\lambda_1 \geqslant \lambda_2 \geqslant \cdots \geqslant \lambda_n \geqslant 0$$

are the generalized eigenvalues of $A^T A - \lambda B^T B$. We wish to find an orthonormal basis for the subspace

$$S_{\min} = \{x \colon A^T A x = \lambda_n B^T B x\} \ .$$

This is the subspace associated with smallest generalized singular value of the pair (A, B). If

$$U^T A X = C = \text{diag}(c_1, \ldots, c_n), \quad 0 \leqslant c_1 \leqslant \cdots \leqslant c_n \ ,$$

$$V^T B X = S = \text{diag}(s_1, \ldots, s_n), \quad s_1 \geqslant \cdots \geqslant s_n \geqslant 0$$

is the generalized SVD with $c_i^2 + s_i^2 = 1$ and

$$c_1 = \cdots = c_q < c_{q+1} \ ,$$

then

$$S_{\min} = \text{span}\{x_1, \ldots, x_q\} \ ,$$

where $X = [x_1, \ldots, x_n]$ is a column partitioning of X. Thus, our problem is solved once we obtain the QR factorization of $X(:, 1:q)$.

We proceed as follows. First we compute the QR factorization

$$\begin{bmatrix} A \\ B \end{bmatrix} = \begin{bmatrix} Q_1 \\ Q_2 \end{bmatrix} R \ ,$$

where Q_1 and Q_2 have the same size as A and B, respectively. Because A and B have trivially intersecting nullspaces, we know that R is nonsingular.

We then compute the Paige–Saunders CS decomposition

$$\begin{bmatrix} U & 0 \\ 0 & V \end{bmatrix}^T \begin{bmatrix} Q_1 \\ Q_2 \end{bmatrix} Z = \begin{bmatrix} C \\ S \end{bmatrix} \ ,$$

where $C = \text{diag}(c_i)$ and $S = \text{diag}(s_i)$. Assume that the c_i and s_i are ordered as above. It follows that

$$\begin{bmatrix} U & 0 \\ 0 & V \end{bmatrix}^{\mathrm{T}} \begin{bmatrix} A \\ B \end{bmatrix} = \begin{bmatrix} C \\ S \end{bmatrix} Z^{\mathrm{T}} R,$$

and so $X = R^{-1}Z$.

Now one approach is to compute the QR factorization of an explicitly formed $X(:, 1:q)$. This involves solving $RX(:, 1:q) = Z(:, 1:q)$ and is thus subject to great error if R is ill-conditioned, i.e., if the nullspaces of A and B nearly intersect. However, we can avoid the inversion of R as follows:

Form $W = Z^{\mathrm{T}}R$. Note that $W = X^{-1}$ and that all we have here is a stable orthogonal matrix times matrix multiplication.

Compute an orthogonal Y such that $WY = T$ is upper triangular. This can be accomplished by a minor modification of the Householder QR process in which the rows of W are zeroed bottom-up via Householder matrices.

Since $X = W^{-1} = (TY^{\mathrm{T}})^{-1} = YT^{-1}$ we see that the first q columns of Y define the required orthonormal basis.

This example is typical of many applications in control theory and signal processing where calculations are put on a much sounder footing through the use of stable matrix factorizations.

3. High performance matrix computations

New computer architectures have brought about a change in how efficient matrix algorithms are designed. *We are now compelled to pay as much attention to the flow of data as to the amount of arithmetic.* A ramification of this is that flop counting is no longer adequate as a mechanism for anticipating performance. A careless implementation of Gaussian elimination (for example) can be ten times slower than one is organized around the careful control of memory traffic.

Our goal is to delineate the scope of the memory management problem in high performance matrix computations. By 'high performance' we mean any computer whose speed when performing an operation is a strong function of data locality. This applies to a multiprocessor where one processor may be forced into idleness as it waits for data that happens to reside somewhere else in the network. But it is also an issue in a uniprocessor with hierarchical memory. The schematic in Figure 1 depicts such a memory system. Movement of data between two levels in the hierarchy represents a communication overhead. A submatrix that climbs its way to the top of the hierarchy should be involved in as much constructive computation as possible before it returns to its niche further down in the memory system.

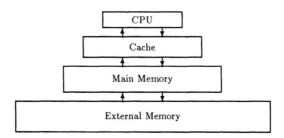

Fig. 1. A hierarchical memory system.

From the standpoint of clarifying these issues, matrix–matrix multiplication and the fast Fourier transform are great teaching algorithms. Both procedures can be arranged in numerous ways and this enables one to resolve many of the computational dilemmas that typify high performance matrix manipulation. However, in this section we have chosen to frame the discussion in terms of the Cholesky factorization, which is simple mathematically and can be organized in several ways like matrix multiplication and the FFT.

Much of what we say carries over to other matrix factorizations and to general scientific computing as well. By the end of the discussion the reader should acquire a practical intuition about high performance computing. We start by deriving several versions of the Cholesky procedure. These highlight the issues of stride and data re-use and motivate four different parallel implementations. The parallel versions of Cholesky that we discuss are chosen for what they reveal about algorithmic thinking in multiprocessor environments.

Before we begin it should be stressed that memory traffic has been a central concern in matrix computations for many years. For example, one can find papers written in the early 1950s that are concerned with the 'out of core' solution of linear systems. However, a hallmark of the current situation is that we must pay attention to memory traffic even for relatively small, dense problems.

3.1. A 'point' derivation of Cholesky

One way to derive the Cholesky algorithm is to compare entries in the equation $A = GG^{\mathrm{T}}$. If $i \geqslant j$, then

$$a_{ij} = \sum_{k=1}^{j} g_{ik} g_{jk} \, ,$$

and so

$$g_{ij} g_{jj} = a_{ij} - \sum_{k=1}^{j-1} g_{ik} g_{jk} \equiv s_{ij} \, .$$

Thus, $g_{ij} = s_{ij}/g_{jj}$ if $i > j$ and $g_{jj} = \sqrt{s_{jj}}$ if $i = j$. By computing the lower triangular matrix G row-by-row we have:

Algorithm 1.
```
for i = 1:n
  for j = 1:i
    s ← A(i, j)
    for k = 1:j − 1
      s ← s − G(i, k)G(j, k)
    end
    if j < i
      G(i, j) ← s/A(j, j)
    else
      G(j, j) ← √s
    end
  end
end
```

A flop count reveals that this implementation of Cholesky involves $\frac{1}{3}n^3 + O(n^2)$ flops.

3.2. Level-1 operations

Notice that the k-loop in Algorithm 1 oversees an inner product between subrows of G. To highlight this and the fact that the lower triangular portion of A can be overwritten with the lower triangular portion of G, we rewrite the algorithm as follows.

Algorithm 1'.
```
for i = 1:n
  for j = 1:i
    s ← A(i, j) − A(i, 1:j − 1)A(j, 1:j − 1)ᵀ
    if j < i
      A(i, j) ← s/A(j, j)
    else
      A(j, j) ← √s
    end
  end
end
```

An inner product is an example of a *level-1* linear algebra operation. Level-1 operations involve $O(n)$ work and $O(n)$ data. Inner products, vector scaling, vector addition, and saxpy's are level-1 operations. (A *saxpy* is a vector operation of the form $y \leftarrow ax + y$ where x and y are vectors and α is a scalar.)

It is important to be able to identify level-1 operations. A class of processors known as *vector processors* are often able to execute level-1 operations faster than what would be expected from consideration of individual, 'free-standing' scalar operations. For example, the successful vectorization of a length n vector addition $z \leftarrow x + y$ would require much less time than an n-fold increase in the time for a single $z_i \leftarrow x_i + y_i$ operation.

The philosophy of vector processing is identical with the philosophy of an automobile assembly line whose mission is the production of $car(1), \ldots, car(n)$. It is much more efficient to pipeline the assembly than to assign *all* the workers (functional units) to $car(1)$, then to $car(2)$, etc.

3.3. Stride

Arrays are stored in column major order in Fortran. This means that the entries that define an array column are contiguous in memory while those within a row are not. For example, if A is a matrix stored in a 100-by-50 array, then $A(4, 2)$ is 100 memory units 'beyond' $A(4, 1)$.

Now observe that the vectors which define the inner product in Algorithm 1' are not contiguous in memory because both of the vectors involved in the operation, i.e., $A(i, 1:j-1)$ and $A(j, 1:j-1)$, are matrix subrows. If A is stored in an array with row dimension *lda*, then we say that *lda* is the *stride* of these vectors. Unit stride code organization can enhance performance because the cost of accessing n contiguous memory locations that house a vector may be much less than the cost of accessing n individual scalars. To make an analogy, suppose a file cabinet contains a thousand folders. It is easy for a human being to extract adjacent folders 101 through 200 than non-adjacent folders 2, 12, 22, $\ldots$, 982, 992.

3.4. A vector derivation

Notice that the nonunit stride problem in Algorithm 1' would be solved if either i or j was the inner loop variable. To derive such a procedure we compare jth columns in the equation $A = GG^\mathrm{T}$ and get

$$A(:, j) = \sum_{k=1}^{j} G(:, k)G(j, k).$$

Focussing on components j through n in this vector equation we obtain

$$G(j{:}n, j)G(j, j) = A(j{:}n, j) - \sum_{k=1}^{j-1} G(j{:}n, k)G(j, k) \equiv v(j{:}n).$$

Since $G(j, j) = \sqrt{v(j)}$ it follows that $G(j{:}n, j) = v(j{:}n)/\sqrt{v(j)}$ and so with overwriting we have the following specification of the Cholesky process.

Algorithm 2.
 for $j = 1:n$
  $v(j:n) \leftarrow A(j:n, j)$
  for $k = 1:j - 1$
   for $i = j:n$
    $v(i) \leftarrow v(i) - G(i, k)G(j, k)$
   end
  end
  $G(j:n, j) \leftarrow v(j:n)/\sqrt{v(j)}$
 end

Notice that as i ranges from j to n, the kth column of A is accessed in the inner loop. Thus, Algorithm 2 is a unit stride Cholesky procedure. From the flop point of view, it is identical to Algorithm 1.

3.5. Level-2 operations

Recognize that the inner two loops in Algorithm 2 oversee a matrix–vector product. Indeed, from the derivation of the algorithm we see that

$$v(j:n) = A(j:n, j) - \begin{bmatrix} G(j, 1) \cdots G(j, j-1) \\ \vdots \qquad \vdots \\ G(n, 1) \cdots G(n, j-1) \end{bmatrix} \begin{bmatrix} G(j, 1) \\ \vdots \\ G(j, j-1) \end{bmatrix}$$

$$= A(j;n, j) - G(j:n, 1:j - 1)G(j, 1:j - 1)^{\mathrm{T}} .$$

Substituting this observation into Algorithm 2 gives:

Algorithm 2'.
 for $j = 1:n$
  $v(j:n) \leftarrow A(j:n, j) - A(j:n, 1:j - 1)A(j, 1:j - 1)^{\mathrm{T}}$
  $A(j:n, j) \leftarrow v(j:n)/\sqrt{v(j)}$
 end

Matrix–vector multiplication is a *level-2* operation. Such operations are characterized by quadratic work and quadratic data, e.g., for m-by-n matrix–vector multiplication, $O(mn)$ data and $O(mn)$ flops are involved.

From a certain standpoint, a matrix–vector product is 'just a bunch' of level-1 saxpy operations. Indeed, the computation of

$$u \leftarrow u + Av = u + \sum_{j=1}^{n} v(j)A(:, j)$$

has the form:

for $j = 1{:}n$
   $u \leftarrow u + v(j)A(:, j)$
end

However, one should think of u as a *vector accumulator*. It is a running vector sum which can be built up in a vector register without any writing to lower level memory until the summation is complete. Thus, there are $n + 1$ vector reads and only one vector write. In contrast, if each saxpy is executed without an awareness of the overall mission of the loop, then $2n$ vector reads and $2n$ vector writes are involved.

A matrix–vector product is referred to as a *gaxpy* operation. Use of the term tacitly implies vector accumulation as discussed above.

3.6. An inductive derivation

Consider the following blocking of the matrix equation $A = GG^{\mathrm{T}}$:

$$\begin{bmatrix} \alpha & w^{\mathrm{T}} \\ w & B \end{bmatrix} = \begin{bmatrix} \beta & 0 \\ v & G_1 \end{bmatrix} \begin{bmatrix} \beta & 0 \\ v & G_1 \end{bmatrix}^{\mathrm{T}}.$$

Here $\alpha, \beta \in \mathbb{R}$, $w, v \in \mathbb{R}^{n-1}$, and $B, G_1 \in \mathbb{R}^{(n-1)\times(n-1)}$. We illustrate a third 'methodology' for developing a matrix factorization algorithm by equating entries in the above:

$$\alpha = \beta^2 \qquad\qquad \Rightarrow \beta = \sqrt{\alpha}\ ,$$
$$w = \beta v \qquad\qquad \Rightarrow v = w/\beta\ ,$$
$$B = vv^{\mathrm{T}} + G_1 G_1^{\mathrm{T}} \Rightarrow G_1 G_1^{\mathrm{T}} = B - vv^{\mathrm{T}}\ .$$

It can be shown that the symmetric matrix $B - vv^{\mathrm{T}}$ is positive definite and so by induction on n we can find its Cholesky factor G_1 as required above.

Note that $G(2{:}n, 2) = G_1(1{:}n - 1, 1)$. Thus, repitition of the square root, the scaling, and the update of B leads to yet another formulation of Cholesky:

Algorithm 3.
  for $k = 1{:}n$
    $G(k{:}n, k) \leftarrow A(k{:}n, k)/\sqrt{A(k, k)}$
    for $j = k + 1{:}n$
      for $i = j{:}n$
        $A(i, j) \leftarrow A(i, j) - G(i, k)G(j, k)$
      end
    end
  end

The inner loop oversees a unit stride saxpy. The overall procedure involves exactly the same amount of floating point arithmetic as Algorithms 1 and 2.

3.7. Outer product

The inner two loops of Algorithm 3 feature a level-2 operation referred to as an *outer product*. If $A \in \mathbb{R}^{m \times n}$, $u \in \mathbb{R}^m$, and $v \in \mathbb{R}^n$, then an update of the form $A \leftarrow A \pm uv^T$ is an outer product update. Notice that this involves $2n$ vector reads and $2n$ writes. Each column is an outer product update is a saxpy $[A(:, j) \leftarrow A(:, j) \pm v(j)u]$ and there is *no* opportunity for vector accumulation in contrast to the gaxpy operation.

Algorithm 3 features a *symmetric outer product update*, i.e., an update of the form $B \leftarrow B \pm uu^T$ where $B = B^T$. To emphasize this we rewrite Algorithm 3 and incorporate overwriting:

Algorithm 3'.
  for $k = 1:n$
    $u(k:n) \leftarrow A(k:n, k)/\sqrt{A(k, k)}$
    $A(k:n, k) \leftarrow u(k:n)$
    $A(k + 1:n, k + 1:n) \leftarrow A(k + 1:n, k + 1:n) - u(k + 1:n)u(k + 1:n)^T$
  end

We assume that symmetry is exploited during the symmetric outer product update of the submatrix $A(k + 1:n, k + 1:n)$.

3.8. Loop reorderings

Algorithms 1, 2, and 3 are identical with respect to arithmetic but different with respect to the ordering of the three loops. For example, Algorithm 1 can be through of as *ijk* Cholesky and Algorithms 2 and 3 are the *jki* and *kji* variants, respectively. There are actually three other versions: *jik* (via permutation of the first two loops in Algorithm 1), *ijk* (the row-by-row analog of Algorithm 2), and *kij* (which computes the outer product updates by row in Algorithm 3). Each loop ordering features certain linear algebraic operations and has distinct memory reference patterns. In general, the *jki* version (Algorithm 2) has the best attributes in terms of stride and the potential for vector accumulation.

3.9. Recursion

The notion of a *recursive procedure* is increasingly important in matrix computations. Roughly speaking, a recursive procedure is able to call itself.

Recursion makes the specification of some matrix algorithms particularly concise. Here is a recursive version of Algorithm 3 stated in quasi-Matlab style:

```
function  G = chol(A, n)
   G(1, 1) ← √(A(1, 1))
   if n > 1
      G(2:n, 1) ← A(2:n, 1)/G(1, 1)
      G(2:n, 2:n) ← chol(A(2:n, 2:n) − G(2:n, 1)G(2:n, 1)ᵀ, n − 1)
   end
end chol
```

Leading examples of recursion in matrix computations include Strassen matrix multiply, cyclic reduction, and the Cuppen–Dongarra–Sorensen divide and conquer algorithm for the symmetric tridiagonal eigenproblem. These procedures are all discussed by Golub & Van Loan [1989].

3.10. Level-3 operations

For many architectures, matrix–matrix multiplication is the operation of choice. There are two reasons for this: it is a highly parallelizable computation and it has a favorable 'computation-to-communication' ratio. The latter aspect needs additional comment. Consider the n-by-n matrix multiplication $C = AB$. This computation involves the reading and writing of $O(n^2)$ data. However, $2n^3$ flops are expended. Thus, in a loose manner of speaking, the ratio of arithmetic to data movement is $O(n)$. As n grows the overhead associated with the accessing of data diminishes. This explains the current interest in *block matrix algorithms* by which we mean algorithms that are rich in matrix multiplication. Matrix operations that involve $O(n^2)$ data and $O(n^3)$ work are referred to as *level-3* operations. Matrix multiplication updates of the form $C \leftarrow \alpha AB + \beta C$ and the multiple triangular system solve $C \leftarrow \alpha T^{-1}C$ are examples of frequently occurring level-3 operations. (Here, α and β are scalars and T is triangular.) See Golub & Van Loan [1989] for a discussion of the latter problem and why it is rich in matrix multiplication.

In many computing environments, level-3 operations can be executed at near peak speed in contrast to matrix/vector computations at the first and second level. Thus, the goal of designing good block algorithms is the extraction of *level-3 performance* from the underlying architecture.

3.11. Block Cholesky

We show how to organize the Cholesky computation so that all but a small fraction of the arithmetic occurs in the context of matrix multiplication. This rather surprising result can be accomplished in several ways. For simplicity, we have chosen to develop a block version of Algorithm 1. Assume for clarity that

$n = Nr$ and partition A and G into r-by-r blocks as follows:

$$A = \begin{bmatrix} A_{11} & \cdots & A_{1N} \\ \vdots & & \vdots \\ A_{N1} & \cdots & A_{NN} \end{bmatrix}, \qquad G = \begin{bmatrix} G_{11} & \cdots & 0 \\ \vdots & \ddots & \vdots \\ G_{N1} & \cdots & G_{NN} \end{bmatrix}.$$

Comparing (i, j) blocks in the equation $A = GG^{\mathrm{T}}$ with $i \geqslant j$ gives

$$A_{ij} = \sum_{k=1}^{j} G_{ik} G_{jk}^{\mathrm{T}},$$

and so

$$G_{ij} G_{jj}^{\mathrm{T}} = A_{ij} - \sum_{k=1}^{j-1} G_{ik} G_{jk}^{\mathrm{T}} \equiv S_{ij}.$$

Corresponding to the derivation of Algorithm 1 we see that G_{ij} is the solution of $XG_{jj}^{\mathrm{T}} = S_{ij}$ if $i > j$ and G_{jj} is the Cholesky factor of S_{jj}. We therefore obtain:

Algorithm 4.
  for $i = 1:N$
    for $j = 1:i$
      $S \leftarrow A_{ij}$
      for $k = 1:j - 1$
        $S \leftarrow S - G_{ik} G_{jk}^{\mathrm{T}}$
      end
      if $j < i$
        Solve $G_{ij} G_{jj}^{\mathrm{T}} = S$ for G_{ij}
      else
        Compute the Cholesky factorization $S = G_{jj} G_{jj}^{\mathrm{T}}$
      end
    end
  end

Notice again that each subdiagonal block is the solution of a multiple right-hand side triangular system while the diagonal blocks are obtained as r-by-r Cholesky factorizations. Most importantly, the matrix S is the consequence of a matrix–matrix product

$$S_{ij} = A_{ij} - [G_{i1}, \ldots, G_{i,j-1}][G_{j1}, \ldots, G_{j,j-1}]^{\mathrm{T}}.$$

Algorithm 4 involves the same number of flops as Algorithms 1, 2, and 3. The only flops that are *not* level-3 flops are those associated with the computation of the r-by-r Cholesky factors $G_{11}, \ldots, G_{NN}$. This accounts for approximately $Nr^3/3$ flops. Thus, the fraction of flops that are associated with level-3 computation is given by:

$$L_3 \approx 1 - \frac{Nr^3/3}{n^3/3} = 1 - \frac{1}{N^2} .$$

We say that L_3 is the *level-3 fraction* associated with Algorithm 4.

A tacit assumption in all this is that the block size r is large enough so that true level-3 performance is extracted during the computation of S. Intelligent block size determination is a function of algorithm and architecture and typically involves careful experimentation.

3.12. Block algorithm development: The LAPACK Project

The search for good block algorithms is an active area of current research. Block algorithms that are rich in matrix multiplication like the above Cholesky procedure have been found for

● The LU factorization with or without partial pivoting.
● The Bunch–Kaufman and Aasen factorizations.
● The QR factorization with and without pivoting. [Bischof & Van Loan, 1987; Bischof, 1988.]

The best block algorithm for the Hessenberg reduction has a level-3 fraction equal to one-half. However, with some regrouping of the Householder transformations significant improvements to the standard level-2 procedure can be realized. To date, no effective block algorithms (in the level-3 sense) have been found for the QR family of iterations (QR, SVD, QZ, etc.) although again, it is possible to improve upon level-2 performance via some clustering of the matrix–vector operations.

The mission of the LAPACK Project is to develop a library of level-3 algorithms for the LINPACK and EISPACK codes. These packages handle linear systems and the eigenproblem, respectively. The efficient implementation of this block library on a particular machine requires an optimized *level-3 BLAS library*. 'BLAS' stands for Basic Linear Algebra Subprograms. Level-1 and 2 BLAS libraries exist as well. Details may be found in Dongarra, du Croz, Hammarling & Hanson [1988a,b], Dongarra, du Croz, Duff & Hammarling [1988], Lawson, Hanson, Kincaid & Krogh [1979a,b], and Kågström, Ling & Van Loan [1991].

Further elaboration of the notion of 'level' and what it means for the design of efficient matrix code is discussed by Dongarra, Gustavson & Karp [1984], Gallivan, Jalby & Meier [1987], Gallivan, Jalby, Meier & Sameh [1988], and Kågström & Ling [1988].

The high-level LAPACK codes for things like Cholesky are written in terms of these BLAS and 'automatically' perform well if the underlying level-3 fraction is close to 1 *and* the level-3 BLA routines are fine-tuned to the underlying architecture.

3.13. Parallel computation

We next discuss the parallel computation of the Cholesky factorization. Two types of multiprocessors are considered: those with *shared memory* and those with *distributed memory*. In either case, an individual processor (sometimes called a *node*) comes complete with processing units and its own *local memory*. In a shared memory machine each individual processor is able to read and write to a typically large *global memory*. This enables one processor to communicate with another. A distributed memory machine has no global memory. Instead, each node is connected to some subset of the remaining nodes. The overall *distributed network* supports communication via the routing of messages between nodes.

Throughout the remainder of this section, p will stand for the number of processors in the system. For us, the act of designing a parallel algorithm is the act of designing a *node algorithm* for each of the participating processors. We suppress very important details such as (a) the downloading of data and programs into the nodes, (b) the subscript computations associated with local array access, and (c) the formatting of messages. We designate the μth processor by $\text{Proc}(\mu)$. The μth node program is usually a function of μ. For example, in the n-by-n matrix–vector product problem $y = Ax$, $\text{Proc}(\mu)$ might be assigned the computation of $y(\mu:p:n) = A(\mu:p:n, :)x$.

To illustrate the differences and similarities between shared and distributed memory computing and the crucial role of block matrix notation, we consider the two-processor calculation of the n-by-n matrix multiply update $C \leftarrow C + AB$. Assume $n = 2m$ and consider the block matrix equation

$$[C_1 \quad C_2] \leftarrow [C_1 \quad C_2] + [A_1 \quad A_2] \begin{bmatrix} B_{11} & B_{12} \\ B_{21} & B_{22} \end{bmatrix},$$

where we assume $A_1, A_2, C_1, C_2 \in \mathbb{R}^{n \times m}$ and $B_{11}, B_{12}, B_{21}, B_{22} \in \mathbb{R}^{m \times m}$ are situated in global memory. A shared memory implementation can be organized as follows:

Proc(1):

$C_{\text{loc}} \leftarrow C_1$
$A_{\text{loc}} \leftarrow A_1$
$B_{\text{loc}} \leftarrow B_{11}$
$C_{\text{loc}} \leftarrow C_{\text{loc}} + A_{\text{loc}} B_{\text{loc}}$
$A_{\text{loc}} \leftarrow A_2$
$B_{\text{loc}} \leftarrow B_{12}$
$C_{\text{loc}} \leftarrow C_{\text{loc}} + A_{\text{loc}} B_{\text{loc}}$
$C_1 \leftarrow C_{\text{loc}}$

Proc(2):

$C_{\text{loc}} \leftarrow C_2$
$A_{\text{loc}} \leftarrow A_2$
$B_{\text{loc}} \leftarrow B_{22}$
$C_{\text{loc}} \leftarrow C_{\text{loc}} + A_{\text{loc}} B_{\text{loc}}$
$A_{\text{loc}} \leftarrow A_1$
$B_{\text{loc}} \leftarrow B_{21}$
$C_{\text{loc}} \leftarrow C_{\text{loc}} + A_{\text{loc}} B_{\text{loc}}$
$C_2 \leftarrow C_{\text{loc}}$

The 'loc' subscript is used to indicate local arrays. Notice that each processor has 5 global-to-local matrix reads, two matrix multiplies, and a single local-to-global matrix write.

A distributed memory procedure is similar. However, instead of data flowing back and forth between the local memories and the global memory, it moves along the channels that connect the processors themselves. The primitives **send** and **recv** are used for this purpose and they have the following syntax:

$$\textbf{send}(\{matrix\}, \{destination\ node\}) \qquad \textbf{recv}(\{matrix\}, \{source\ node\})$$

If a processor invokes a **send**, then we assume that execution resumes immediately after the message is sent. If a **recv** is encountered, then we assume that execution of the node program is suspended until the requested messages arrives. We also assume that messages arrive in the same order that they are sent.

Now in our $p = 2$ problem let us assume that for $j = 1{:}2$, Proc(j) houses C_j, A_j, and

$$\begin{bmatrix} B_{1j} \\ B_{2j} \end{bmatrix}$$

in the local arrays C_{loc}, A_{loc}, and B_{loc}. We then have:

Proc(1):

$$C_{\text{loc}} \leftarrow C_{\text{loc}} + A_{\text{loc}}B_{\text{loc}}(1{:}m, :)$$
$$\textbf{send}(A_{\text{loc}}, 2)$$
$$\textbf{recv}(A_{\text{loc}}, 2)$$
$$C_{\text{loc}} \leftarrow C_{\text{loc}} + A_{\text{loc}}B_{\text{loc}}(m + 1{:}n, :)$$
$$\textbf{send}(A_{\text{loc}}, 2)$$
$$\textbf{recv}(A_{\text{loc}}, 2)$$

Proc(2):

$$C_{\text{loc}} \leftarrow C_{\text{loc}} + A_{\text{loc}}B_{\text{loc}}(m + 1{:}n, :)$$
$$\textbf{send}(A_{\text{loc}}, 1)$$
$$\textbf{recv}(A_{\text{loc}}, 1)$$
$$C_{\text{loc}} \leftarrow C_{\text{loc}} + A_{\text{loc}}B_{\text{loc}}(1{:}m, :)$$
$$\textbf{send}(A_{\text{loc}}, 1)$$
$$\textbf{recv}(A_{\text{loc}}, 1)$$

The last **send**/**recv** is executed so that upon completion, A is distributed in its original manner. This could be avoided with the introduction of additional local workspaces. However, one tends to be stingy with work spaces in distributed environments because local memory is often limited.

Notice that in the distributed memory case, each processor has two **send**s, two **recv**s, and two matrix multiplies.

We now make a few comments about parallel computations in general using the above parallel algorithms for illustration. We say that a parallel procedure is *load balanced* if each processor has roughly the same amount of arithmetic and communication. The above procedures have this property. However, this would not be the case if $B_{12} = 0$ for although both processors would be equally loaded, the B_{12} computations are superfluous. Hence, a revision of the node programs would be required so that each node had equal amounts of *meaningful* work and communication.

The *speed-up* associated with a parallel program is a quotient:

$$\text{speed-up} = \frac{\text{time required by the best single-processor program}}{\text{time required for the } p\text{-processor implementation}}.$$

In this definition we do not just set the numerator to be the $p = 1$ version of the parallel code because the best uniprocessor algorithm may not parallelize. Ideally, one would like the speed-up for an algorithm to equal p. In the above 2-processor example, speed-up will approach 2 as the communication overhead is reduced compared to the time required for the actual matrix multiplication. In particular, if the time for communication is proportional to $O(n^2)$, then speed-up approaches 2 as n gets large.

At times it is sufficient to quantify communication overheads in an order of magnitude sense. On other occasions we need a little more precision. To that end we assume that the communication of a length r floating point vector requires $\alpha + \beta r$ seconds. Here, α represents a start-up overhead and β reflects the rate of transmission. The communication may be between local and global memory, between main memory and a disk, or between two neighbor processors in a distributed network. The values of α and β relative to computation speed have a great effect on the design of a parallel matrix code.

Before we go on to illustrate Cholesky in shared and distributed memory environments, we mention that in practice one often has to work with a system that embodies a mixture of these multiprocessor designs. However, our goal is to paint the parallel matrix computation picture with broad strokes capturing just the central ideas. Nothing much is lost by considering the purely shared and purely distributed systems.

For additional overviews of the parallel matrix computation area, see Dongarra & Sorensen [1986], Gallivan, Plemmons & Sameh [1990], Heller [1978], Hockney & Jesshope [1988], and Ortega & Voigt [1985]. See also Golub & Van Loan [1989, Chapter 6].

3.14. *Shared memory computation*

A schematic of a shared memory multiprocessor is given in Figure 2. During execution, data flows back and forth between the nodes and the global memory. All computation takes place on data situated in the node.

Two shared memory implementations of the Cholesky factorization are

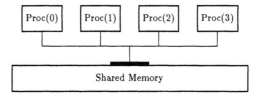

Fig. 2. A 4-processor shared memory system.

given. In the first each processor's portion of the overall computation is determined in advance. This is an example of *static scheduling*. The strategy in the second implementation is different in that the overall computation is broken down into a sequence of tasks with *no* a priori assignment of tasks to processors. A queue of remaining tasks is then maintained during the computation. When a processor finishes a task it goes to the queue and obtains (if possible) the next available task. This is an example of the *pool-of-tasks* approach to *dynamic scheduling*.

3.15. Shared memory Cholesky with static scheduling

Suppose $B = B^T \in \mathbb{R}^{m \times m}$ and $v \in \mathbb{R}^m$ reside in a global memory that is accessible to p processors and that we wish to overwrite B with $B - vv^T$. One way to approach the parallel computation of this symmetric outer product update is to have $\text{Proc}(\mu)$ update the columns designated by the integer vector $\mu:p:m$:

$v_{\text{loc}} \leftarrow v$
for $j = \mu:p:m$
   $b_{\text{loc}}(j:m) \leftarrow B(j:m, j)$
   $b_{\text{loc}}(j:m) \leftarrow b_{\text{loc}}(j:m) - v_{\text{loc}}(j:m)v_{\text{loc}}(j)$
   $B(j:m, j) \leftarrow b_{\text{loc}}(j:m)$
end

A few comments are in order. Each processor needs a copy of v and this is accomplished outside the loop with the global to local assignment $v_{\text{loc}} \leftarrow v$. Within the j-loop we see repetition of the following activity:
- The *global to local reading* of the original $B(j:m, j)$ into $b_{\text{loc}}(j:m)$.
- The *local computation* of the saxpy $b_{\text{loc}}(j:m) \leftarrow b_{\text{loc}}(j:m) - v_{\text{loc}}(j:m)v_{\text{loc}}(j)$.
- The *local to global writing* of $b_{\text{loc}}(j:m)$ into $B(j:m, j)$.

This 3-step pattern of reading from global memory, local computation, and writing to global memory is typical. The reading and the writing represent communication overheads and hence, one tries to design shared memory procedures so that the amount of local computation is significant compared to the amount of data that goes back and forth between the local memories and shared memory.

Our parallel outer product update is load balanced. To see this, assume $m = pM$ for clarity and note that jth saxpy involves $2(m - j + 1)$ flops. Thus, $\text{Proc}(\mu)$ must perform

$$\sum_{j+\mu:p:m} 2(m - j + 1) = \frac{m^2}{p} + m\left(3 + \frac{2(1 - \mu)}{p}\right) \approx \frac{m^2}{p}$$

flops, i.e., one pth of the arithmetic.

$\text{Proc}(\mu)$'s communication overhead is proportional to

$$\alpha \frac{2m}{p} + \beta \left(\frac{m^2}{p} + m \left(\frac{2(1-\mu)}{p} + 1 \right) \right) \approx \alpha \frac{2m}{p} + \beta \left(\frac{m^2}{p} \right),$$

where α and β capture the nature of communication between local and global memory. Because this is independent of μ we see that the overall procedure is load balanced from the communication point of view.

Note that we could not make these loading balancing claims if Proc(μ) is assigned the update of contiguous columns, i.e., $B(j:m, j)$ for $j = (\mu - 1)M + 1:\mu M$. This is because the work and communication associated with the jth saxpy is a decreasing function of j.

We now apply these ideas to the design of a shared memory version of outer product Cholesky (Algorithm 3). Recall that this algorithm is structured as follows:

for $k = 1:n$
    Perform a square root and a vector scale
    Perform a symmetric outer product update of $A(k + 1:n, k + 1:n)$
end

Our strategy is to let a single designated processor handle the square root and the scaling and to let all the processors participate in the outer product updates as discussed above. However, some synchronization is necessary so that the correct Cholesky factor emerges:

• A processor cannot begin its share of the kth outer product update until the kth column of G is available.

• The computation of $G(k + 1:n, k + 1)$ should not begin until the kth outer product update is completed.

To ensure that these 'rules' are enforced we use the **barrier** construct in the following algorithm.

Algorithm 5.
    for $k = 1:n$
        if $\mu = 1$
            $g_{\text{loc}}(k:n) \leftarrow A(k:n, k)$
            $g_{\text{loc}}(k:n) \leftarrow g_{\text{loc}}(k:n)/\sqrt{g_{\text{loc}}(k)}$
            $A(k:n, k) \leftarrow g_{\text{loc}}(k:n)$
        end
        barrier
        $v_{\text{loc}}(k + \mu:n) \leftarrow A(k + \mu:n, k)$
        for $j = (k + \mu):p:n$
            $a_{\text{loc}}(j:n) \leftarrow A(j:n, j)$
            $a_{\text{loc}}(j:n) \leftarrow a_{\text{loc}}(j:n) - v_{\text{loc}}(j:n)v_{\text{loc}}(j)$
            $A(j:n, j) \leftarrow a_{\text{loc}}(j:n)$
        end
        barrier
    end

This procedure overwrites the lower triangular portion of A (in global memory) with the lower triangular portion of G.

Here is how the **barrier** construct works. When a processor encounters a **barrier** during the execution of its node program, computation is suspended. It resumes as soon as *every* other processor reaches its **barrier**. In that sense the **barrier** is like a stream to be traversed by p hikers. For safety, no one proceeds across the stream until *all* p hikers arrive at its edge. In Algorithm 5, the first **barrier** ensures that the kth outer product update does not begin until $G(k + 1:n, k)$ is ready. The second **barrier** forces all the processors to wait until the kth update is completely finished before work commences with the next update.

Algorithm 5 is load balanced for the same reasons that the above outer product update algorithm is load balanced. (The square root and scaling assigned to Proc(1) do not appreciably overload this processor so long as $n \gg p$, a reasonable assumption.)

3.16. Shared memory Cholesky with dynamic scheduling

For some simple computations static scheduling is adequate. However, it is important to recognize that a **barrier** forces global idleness and therefore fosters a certain inefficiency. For this reason, dynamic scheduling using the pool-of-task paradigm is often attractive. This style of shared memory programming begins with an identification of computational tasks. The tasks are then executed in a prescribed order by the individual processors. Various synchronization problems must typically be solved along the way.

We illustrate this by implementing Algorithm 4, block Cholesky. We refer to the computation of the Cholesky block G_{ij} as task(i, j). Following the order of G_{ij} resolution in Algorithm 4, we perform the tasks in the following order:

$$(1, 1), (2, 1), (2, 2), (3, 1), (3, 2), (3, 3), \dots , (N, 1),$$
$$\dots , (N, N - 1), (N, N) .$$

We assume the existence of a function **next.task** that is invoked by a processor whenever it wants to acquire a new task. A pair of special pointers **row** and **col** is updated with each call, i.e.,

```
function (i, j) = next.task(·)
    col ← col + 1
    if col = N + 1
        row ← row + 1; col ← 1
    end
    i ← row; j ← col
end next.task
```

If we assume that **row** = 1 and **col** = 0 at the start and that at any instant only one processor can be executing **next.task**, then we can structure each node program as follows:

$(i, j) \leftarrow$ **next.task**$(\cdot)$
while $i \leq N$
   Perform task(i, j)
   $(i, j) \leftarrow$ **next.task**$(\cdot)$
end

The assumption that only one processor at a time can be executing **next.task** ensures that each task is assigned to exactly one processor. A node program terminates as soon as **row** has value $N + 1$. This happens when a task is requested after task(N, N) is assigned. Thus, all node programs eventually terminate.

Now returning to the development of a parallel version of Algorithm 4, recall that task(i, j) requires the computation of

$$ S_{ij} = A_{ij} - \sum_{k=1}^{j-1} G_{ik} G_{jk}^{\mathrm{T}} . $$

Note that a simple summation of the form

$S_{\mathrm{loc}} \leftarrow A_{ij}$
for $k = 1 : j - 1$
   $B_{\mathrm{loc}} \leftarrow A_{ik}$
   $C_{\mathrm{loc}} \leftarrow A_{jk}$
   $S_{\mathrm{loc}} \leftarrow S_{\mathrm{loc}} - B_{\mathrm{loc}} C_{\mathrm{loc}}^{\mathrm{T}}$
end

is not guaranteed to work since we have no way of knowing that A_{ik} and A_{jk} actually house G_{ik} and G_{jk} at the time they are requested from global memory. For this reason we assume the existence of a function **get.block**(q, r) which returns the contents of A_{qr} *only* if it houses G_{qr}. If G_{qr} is not available, then the invoking processor is placed in a state of idle waiting to be broken only when the requested block is available. When this happens the requested G-block is read into local memory and execution resumes with the next statement in the node program.

One way to implement this scheme is for **get.block** to maintain a binary scoreboard $done(1:N, 1:N)$ with the convention that $done(q, r)$ is zero or one depending upon the availability of G_{qr}.

We are not quite ready to specify the overall procedure in that we have yet to indicate how the scoreboard is updated. Once a processor has computed the matrix sum S_{ij} it proceeds with the computation of G_{ij}. If $i = j$ then G_{jj} is the Cholesky factor of S_{ij} and a local computation ensues. If $j < i$ then G_{jj} is required for the resolution of $G_{ij}G_{jj}^{\mathrm{T}} = S_{ij}$ and **get.block** must be invoked. In either case once G_{ij} is computed it can be written to global memory. For this process we need another function **put.block**$(i, j, \{local\ matrix\})$ which writes the specified local matrix to a shared memory block A_{ij}. In addition, **put.block** updates the scoreboard by changing the value of $done(i, j)$ from a zero to one. Combining all these ideas and assuming that A is to be overwritten by G in global memory, we obtain the following node program:

Algorithm 6.

```
(i, j) ← next.task(·)
while i ≤ N
    S_loc ← A_ij
    for k = 1:j − 1
        B_loc ← get.block(i, k)
        C_loc ← get.block(j, k)
        S_loc ← S_loc − B_loc C_loc^T
    end
    if j < i
        B_loc ← get.block(j, j)
        Solve XB_loc = S_loc for X; B_loc ← X
    else
        Compute the Cholesky factorization XX^T = S_loc; B_loc ← X
    end
    A_ij ← put.block(i, j, B_loc)
    (i, j) ← next.task(·)
end
```

As with the updating of the task indices **row** and **col** in shared memory, the updating of the scoreboard must be carefully controlled. In particular, we must never allow the scoreboard to be manipulated by more than one processor at a time. These restrictions coupled with the ability of **get.block** and **put.block** to purposely delay an invoking processor imply that these functions are more than just functions in the sense of $\sin(\theta)$. The 'computer science' aspects associated with the design of these synchronization tools (and the **barrier** as well) are discussed by Andrews & Schneider [1983], and Boyle, Butler, Disz, Glickfield, Lusk, Overbeek, Patterson & Stevens [1987].

3.17. Comments

We have stepped through the design of two shared memory Cholesky procedures. While we have depicted the kind of logic associated with shared memory computing, we are a long way from being able to predict performance. Although we can model the rate of floating point arithmetic and the time required for local–global communication, we suppressed a number of important hardware factors such as the bandwidth between local and global memory. Without knowledge of the local/global memory interface we cannot anticipate what happens when two nodes wish to access global memory at the same time.

We also have made no attempt to quantify the synchronization overheads, i.e., the cost of invoking the **barrier**'s in Algorithm 5 and the 'synchronization functions' **next.task**, **get.block**, and **put.block** in Algorithm 6. An understanding of these factors would most likely be acquired through intelligent experimentation.

Further references for the shared memory computation of matrix factorizations include Chen, Dongarra & Hsuing [1984], Dongarra & Hewitt [1986], Dongarra & Hiromoto [1984], Dongarra, Kaufman & Hammarling [1986], Dongarra, Sameh & Sorensen [1986], and George, Heath & Liu [1986]. See also Golub & Van Loan [1989].

3.18. Distributed memory computing

We now turn out attention to the design of matrix algorithms in a distributed memory environment. Of central importance is the *topology* of the underlying processor network, i.e., how the processors are interconnected. Popular schemes include the ring, the mesh, the tree, the torus, and the hypercube. In this section we consider the implementation of Cholesky on a ring. In this situation, each processor has a left and a right neighbor (see Figure 3). For

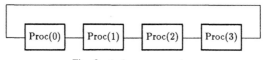

Fig. 3. A 4-processor ring.

notational convenience we assume the existence of local integer variables *left* and *right* so that commands of the form

$$\textbf{send}(\{\text{local matrix}\}, \textit{left})$$

$$\textbf{send}(\{\text{local matrix}\}, \textit{right})$$

instruct the executing node to send the named local matrix to the left and right neighbors, respectively. (Similarly for **recv**.) Thus, if $p = 4$ and Proc(2) executes **send**(A_{loc}, *left*), then a copy of A_{loc} is send to Proc(1). (Proc(2) retains a copy of A_{loc}.)

The distributed Cholesky procedures that we are about to develop involve only nearest-neighbor communication meaning that whenever a message is sent, it is always to a neighbor in the network. This minimizes reliance on the *routing algorithms* that oversee the message passing and generally helps to control communication overheads.

For any network topology there are usually several natural *distributed data structures* for matrices and vectors. Consider the storage of

$$A = [A_1 \quad \cdots \quad A_N], \quad A_i \in \mathbb{R}^{n \times n_i}, n_i + \cdots + n_N = n,$$

on a p-processor ring. With a *wrap block column* data structure Proc(μ) houses block columns A_i, where $i = \mu{:}p{:}N$. Note that if $N = p$, then each processor houses a contiguous set of columns, namely, the columns of A_μ. If $N = n$, then A has a *wrap column* distribution.

3.19. Distributed memory Cholesky on ring

We now develop a ring implementation of Algorithm 2. Recall that in that version of Cholesky, the generation of $G(j{:}n, j)$ requires the computation of

$$s_j = A(j{:}n, j) - \sum_{k=1}^{j-1} G(j{:}n, k)G(j, k),$$

followed by the scaling $G(j{:}n, j) \leftarrow s_j / \sqrt{s_j(1)}$.

Assume for clarity that $n = pN$ and that Proc(μ) initially houses $A(i{:}n, i)$ for $i = \mu{:}p{:}n$ in a local array A_{loc}. The mission of Proc(μ) in our ring Cholesky procedure is to overwrite this array with the nonzero portion of $G(:, \mu{:}p{:}n)$. This involves using the columns of A_{loc} as running vector sums for building up the s_j that are to be used locally.

Notice that a G-column generated by one processor is generally needed by all the other processors. So suppose Proc(μ) generates $G(j{:}n, j)$. This vector is then circulated around the ring in merry-go-round fashion 'stopping' at Proc($\mu + 1$), ..., Proc(p), Proc(1), ..., Proc($\mu - 1$) in turn. At each stop the visiting G-column is incorporated into all the local s_k for which $k \geq j$.

By counting the number of received G-columns a processor can determine whether or not it is ready to take its turn in G-column generation. For example, if Proc(μ) has received $k - 1$ G-columns and $k \in \{\mu, \mu + p, \ldots, \mu + (N-1)p\}$, then it 'knows' that it is time to generate $G(k{:}n, k)$.

Here is the program to be executed by Proc(μ). It assumes that the local variables *left* and *right* contain the indices of the left and right neighbor and that $n = pN$.

Algorithm
```
    k ← 0; j ← 0
    last ← μ + (N − 1)p
    j̃ ← 1
    while j ≠ last
        if k + 1 ∈ {μ, μ + p, ..., last}
            j ← k + 1
            Generate G(j:n, j) and copy into g_loc(j:n) and A_loc(j:n, j̃)
```

```
    if j < n
        send( g_loc( j:n), right)
        Update A_loc(:, j̃ + 1:N)
        k ← k + 1
    end
    j̃ ← j̃ + 1
else
    recv( g_loc(k:n), left)
    if k ∉ {right, right + p, . . . , right + (N − 1)p}
        send( g_loc(k:n), right)
    end
    k ← k + 1
    Update A_loc(:, j̃:N)
end
end
```

We make a few observations about this node program:

• The number of received G-column updates is maintained in the variable k. Note that k is incremented when a G-column is received and when a G-column is locally generated.

• The index of the last locally generated G-column is maintained in j. If $j = last$, then there is nothing let for $\text{Proc}(\mu)$ to do.

• $j̃$ points to the next column of A_{loc} that will produce a G-column.

• A circulating G-column is not sent to $\text{Proc}(right)$ if $\text{Proc}(right)$ is the generator of the G-column.

Notice that when early g-columns circulate, the local computation associated with each message is of order $O(n^2/p)$. However, as the algorithm proceeds the circulating g-columns get shorter and there are fewer local columns to update. Thus, towards the end of the algorithm, $O(k)$ flops are performed per received g-column of length $O(k)$. The unfavorable computation/communication balance can be improved by implementing a *block column* version of the above. The messages are now block columns of G and local computation is more nearly level-3.

Additional details on ring factorization procedures may be found in Geist & M.T. Heath [1986], Ipsen, Saad & Schultz [1986], Bischof [1988], Golub & Van Loan [1989, Chapter 6], and Geist & Heath [1985]. An important related topic is the parallel solution of triangular systems. See Romine & Ortega [1988], Heath & Romine [1988], Li & Coleman [1988], and Eisenstat, Heath, Henkel & Romine [1988].

Acknowledgement

This research was partially supported by the U.S. Army Research Office through the Mathematical Sciences Institute, Cornell University.

References

Aasen, J.O. (1971). On the reduction of a symmetric matrix to tridiagonal form. *BIT* 11, 233–242.
Anderson, N., I. Karasalo (1975). On computing bounds for the least singular value of a triangular matrix. *BIT* 15, 1–4.
Andrews, G., F.B. Schneider (1983). Concepts and notations for concurrent programming. *Comput. Surv.* 15, 1–43.
Arioli, M., J.W. Demmel, I.S. Duff (1989). Solving sparse linear systems with sparse backward error, Report CSS 214, Computer Science and Systems Division, AERE Harwell, Didcot, England.
Ashby, S., T.A. Manteuffel, P.E. Saylor (1988). A taxonomy for conjugate gradient methods, Report UCRL-98508, Lawrence Livermore National Laboratory, Livermore, CA.
Axelsson, O. (1985). A survey of preconditioned iterative methods for linear systems of equations. *BIT* 25, 166–187.
Barlow, J.L., N.K. Nichols, R.J. Plemmons (1988). Iterative methods for equality constrained least squares problems. *SIAM J. Sci. Statist. Comput.* 9, 892–906.
Bartels, R.H. (1971). A stabilization of the simplex method. *Numer. Math.* 16, 414–434.
Barwell, V., J.A. George (1976). A comparison of algorithms for solving symmetric indefinite systems of linear equations. *ACM Trans. Math. Software* 2, 242–251.
Bavely, C., G.W. Stewart (1979). An algorithm for computing reducing subspaces by block diagonalization. *SIAM J. Numer. Anal.* 16, 359–367.
Bischof, C.H. (1988). A parallel QR factorization algorithm with local pivoting, Report ANL/MCS-P21-1088, Argonne National Laboratory, Argonne, IL.
Bischof, C.H., C. Van Loan (1986). Computing the SVD on a ring of array processors, in: J. Cullum, R. Willoughby (eds.), *Large Scale Eigenvalue Problems*, North-Holland, Amsterdam, pp. 51–66.
Bischof, C.H., C. Van Loan (1987). The WY representation for products of householder matrices. *SIAM J. Sci. Statist. Comput,* 8, s2–s13.
Björck, Å. (1984). A general updating algorithm for constrained linear least squares problems. *SIAM J. Sci. and Statist. Comput.* 5, 394–402.
Björck, Å. (1987). Stability analysis of the method of seminormal equations. *Linear Algebra Appl.* 88/89, 31–48.
Björck, Å. (1988). *Least Squares Methods: Handbook of Numerical Analysis, Vol. 1: Solution of Equations in R^N*, North-Holland, Amsterdam.
Björck, Å., G.H. Golub (1973). Numerical methods for computing angles between linear subspaces. *Math. Comp.* 27, 579–594.
Björck, Å., R.J. Plemmons, H. Schneider (1981). *Large-Scale Matrix Problems*, North-Holland, New York.
Bojanczyk, A.W., R.P. Brent, P. Van Dooren, F.R. de Hoog (1987). A note on downdating the Cholesky factorization. *SIAM J. Sci. Statist. Comput.* 8, 210–221.
Boyle, J., R. Butler, T. Disz, B. Glickfield, E. Lusk, R. Overbeek, J. Patterson, R. Stevens (1987). *Portable Programs for Parallel Processors*, Holt, Rinehart & Winston, New York.
Brent, R.P., F.T. Luk, C. Van Loan (1985). Computation of the singular value decomposition using mesh connected processors. *J. VLSI Computer Systems* 1, 242–270.
Buckley, A. (1974). A note on matrices $A = 1 + H$, H skew-symmetric. *Z. Angew. Math. Mech.* 54, 125–126.
Buckley, A. (1977). On the solution of certain skew-symmetric linear systems. *SIAM J. Numer. Anal.* 14, 566–570.
Bunch, J.R. (1971). Analysis of the diagonal pivoting method. *SIAM J. Numer. Anal.* 8, 656–680.
Bunch, J.R., L. Kaufman (1977). Some stable methods for calculating inertia and solving symmetric linear systems. *Math. Comp.* 31, 162–179.
Bunch, J.R., L. Kaufman, B.N. Parlett (1976). Decomposition of a symmetric matrix. *Numer. Math.* 27, 95–109.

Bunch, J.R., C.P. Nielsen, D.C. Sorensen (1978). Rank-one modification of the symmetric eigenproblem. *Numer. Math.* 31, 31–48.

Bunch, J.R., B.N. Parlett (971). Direct methods for solving symmetric indefinite systems of linear equations. *SIAM J. Numer. Anal.* 8, 639–655.

Businger, P.A. (1969). Reducing a matrix to Hessenberg form. *Math. Comp.* 23, 819–821.

Businger, P.A. (1971). Numerically stable deflation of Hessenberg and symmetric tridiagonal matrices, *BIT* 11, 262–270.

Businger, P.A., G.H. Golub (1965). Linear least squares solutions by Householder transformations. *Numer. Math.* 7, 269–276.

Chan, S.P., B.N. Parlett (1977). Algorithm 517: A program for computing the condition numbers of matrix eigenvalues without computing eigenvectors. *ACM Trans. Math. Software* 3, 186–203.

Chan, T.F. (1982). An improved algorithm for computing the singular value decomposition. *ACM Trans. Math. Software* 8, 72–83.

Chan, T.F. (1987). Rank-revealing QR factorizations. *Linear Algebra Appl.* 88/89, 67–82.

Chen, S., J. Dongarra, C. Hsuing (1984). Multiprocessing linear algebra algorithms on the Cray X-MP-2; Experiences with small granularity. *J. Parallel and Distributed Computing* 1, 22–31.

Cline, A.K., A.R. Conn, C. Van Loan (1982). Generalizing the LINPACK condition estimator, in: J.P. Hennart (ed.), *Numerical Analysis*, Lecture Notes in Mathematics, no. 909, Springer–Verlag, New York.

Cline, A.K., C.B. Moler, G.W. Stewart, J.H. Wilkinson (1979). An estimate for the condition number of a matrix. *SIAM J. Numer. Anal.* 16, 368–375.

Coleman, T., C. Van Loan (1988). *Handbook for Matrix Computations*, SIAM Philadelphia, PA.

Concus, P., G.H. Golub, G. Meurant (1985). Block preconditioning for the conjugate gradient method. *SIAM J. Sci. Statist. Comput.* 6, 220–252.

Concus, P., G.H. Golub, D.P. O'Leary (1976). A generalized conjugate gradient method for the numerical solution of elliptic partial differential equations, in: J.R. Bunch, D.J. Rose (eds.), *Sparse Matrix Computations*, Academic Press, New York.

Cox, M.G. (1981). The least squares solution of overdetermined linear equations having band or augmented band structure. *IMA J. Numer. Anal.* 1, 3–22.

Cullum, J., R.A. Willoughby (1985a). *Lanczos Algorithms for Large Symmetric Eigenvalue Computations. Vol. I: Theory*, Birkhauser, Boston.

Cullum, J., R.A. Willoughby (1985b). *Lanczos Algorithms for Large Symmetric Eigenvalue Computations, Vol. II: Programs*, Birkhauser, Boston.

Daniel, J., W.B. Gragg, L. Kaufman, G.W. Stewart (1976). Reorthogonalization and stable algorithms for updating the Gram–Schmidt QR factorization. *Math. Comp.* 30, 772–795.

Davis, C., W.M. Kahan (1970). The rotation of eigenvectors by a perturbation III. *SIAM J. Numer. Anal.* 7, 1–46.

De Boor, C., A. Pinkus (1977). A backward error analysis for totally positive linear systems. *Numer. Math.* 27, 485–490.

Demmel, J.W. (1983). A numerical analyst's Jordan canonical form, Ph.D. Thesis, Univ. of California, Berkeley.

Dongarra, J.J., J.R. Bunch, C.B. Moler, G.W. Stewart (1978). *LINPACK Users Guide*, SIAM, Philadelphia, PA.

Dongarra, J.J., J. Du Croz, I.S. Duff, S. Hammarling (1988). A set of level 3 basic linear algebra subprograms, Report ANL-MCS-TM-88, Argonne National Laboratory, Argonne, IL.

Dongarra, J.J., J. Du Croz, S. Hammarling, R.J. Hanson (1988a). An extended set of Fortran basic linear algebra subprograms. *ACM Trans. Math. Software* 14, 1–17.

Dongarra, J.J., J. Du Croz, S. Hammarling, R.J. Hanson (1988b). Algorithm 656: An extended set of Fortran basic linear algebra subprograms: Model implementation and test programs. *ACM Trans. Math. Software* 14, 18–32.

Dongarra, J.J., F.G. Gustavson, A. Karp (1984). Implementation linear algebra algorithms for dense matrices on a vector pipeline machine. *SIAM Rev.* 26, 91–112.

Dongarra, J., T. Hewitt (1986). Implementing dense linear algebra algorithms using multi-tasking on the Cray X-MP-4 (or approaching the gigaflop). *SIAM J. Sci. Statist. Comput.* 7, 347–350.

Dongarra, J.J., R.E. Hiromoto (1984). A collection of parallel linear equation routines for the Denelcor HEP. *Parallel Comput.* 1, 133–142.

Dongarra, J.J., L. Kaufman, S. Hammarling (1986). Squeezing the most our of eigenvalue solvers on high performance computers. *Linear Algebra Appl.* 77, 113–136.

Dongarra, J.J., A. Sameh, D. Sorensen (1986). Implementation of some concurrent algorithms for matrix factorization. *Parallel Comput.* 3, 25–34.

Dongarra, J.J., D.C. Sorensen (1986). Linear algebra on high performance computers. *Appl. Math. and Comput.* 20, 57–88.

Duff, I.S., A.M. Erisman, J.K. Reid (1986). *Direct Methods for Sparse Matrices*, Oxford University Press, Oxford.

Duff, I.S., J.K. Reid (1976). A comparison of some methods for the solution of sparse over-determined systems of lienar equations. *J. Inst. Math. Its Appl.* 17, 267–280.

Eisenstat, S.C., M.T. Heath, C.S. Henkel, C.H. Romine (1988). Modified cyclic algorithms for solving triangular systems on distributed memory multiprocessors. *SIAM J. Sci. Statist. Comput.* 9, 589–600.

Eldèn, L. (1980). Perturbation theory for the least squares problem with linear equality constraints. *SIAM J. Numer. Anal.* 17, 338–350.

Elman, H. (1986). A stability analysis of incomplete LU factorization. *Math. Comp.* 47, 191–218.

Erisman, A.M., J.K. Reid (1974). Monitoring the stability of the triangular factorization of a sparse matrix. *Numer. Math.* 22, 183–186.

Faber, V., T. Manteuffel (1984). Necessary and sufficient conditions for the existence of a conjugate gradient method. *SIAM J. Numer. Anal.* 21, 352–362.

Forsythe, G.E., P. Henrici (1960). The cyclic Jacobi method for computing the principal values of a complex matrix. *Trans. Amer. Math. Soc.* 94, 1–23.

Forsythe, G.E., C.B. Moler (1967). *Computer Solution of Linear Algebraic Systems*. Prentice-Hall, Englewood Cliffs, NJ.

Funderlic, R.E., A. Geist (1986). Torus data flow for parallel computation of missized matrix problems. *Linear Algebra Appl.* 7, 149–164.

Gallivan, K., W. Jalby, U. Meier (1987). The use of BLAS3 in linar algebra on a parallel processor with a hierarchical memory. *SIAM J. Sci. Statist. Comput.* 8, 1079–1084.

Gallivan, K., W. Jalby, U. Meier, A.H. Sameh (1988). Impact of hierarchical memory systems on linear algebra algorithm design. *Int. J. Supercomputer Appl.* 2, 12–48.

Gallivan, K., R.J. Plemmons, A.H. Sameh (1990). Parallel algorithms for dense linear algebra computations. *SIAM Rev.* 32, 54–135.

Garbow, B.S., J.M. Boyle, J.J. Dongarra, C.B. Moler (1972). *Matrix Eigensystem Routines: EISPACK Guide Extension*, Springer, New York.

Geist, G.A., M.T. Heath (1985). Parallel Cholesky factorization on a hypercube multiprocessor, Report ORNL 6190, Oak Ridge Laboratory, Oak Ridge, TN.

Geist, G.A., M.T. Heath (1986). Matrix factorization on a hypercube, in: M.T. Heath (ed.), *Hypercube Multiprocessor*, SIAM, Philadelphia, PA, 161–180.

Gentleman, W.M. (1973). Least squares computations by Givens transformations without square roots. *J. Inst. Math. Appl.* 12, 329–336.

Gentleman, W. M., H.T. Kung (1981). Matrix triangularization by systolic arrays. *SPIE Proceedings* 298, 19–26.

George, J.A., M.T. Heath, J. Liu (1986). Parallel Cholesky factorization on a shared memory multiprocessor. *Linear Algebra Appl.* 77, 165–187.

George, J.A., J.W. Liu (1981). *Computer Solution of Large Sparse Positive Definite Systems*, Prentice-Hall, Englewood Cliffs, NJ.

Gill, P.E., G.H. Golub, W. Murray, M.A. Saunders (1974). Methods for modifying matrix factorizations. *Math. Comp.* 28, 505–535.

Gill, P.E., W. Murray (1976). The orthogonal factorization of a large sparse matrix, in: J.R. Bunch, D.J. Rose (eds.), *Sparse Matrix Computations*, Academic Press, New York, pp. 177–200.

Gill, P.E., W. Murray, M.A. Saunders (1975). Methods for computing and modifying the LDV factors of a matrix. *Math. Comp.* 29, 1051–1077.

Goldfarb, D. (1976). Factorized variable metric methods for unconstrained optimization. *Math. Comp.* 30, 796–811.

Golub, G.H. (1965). Numerical methods for solving linear least squares problems. *Numer. Math.* 7, 206–216.

Golub, G.H. (1969). Matrix decompositions and statistical computation, in: R.C. Milton, J.A. Nelder (eds.), *Statistical Computation*, Academic Press, New York, pp. 365–397.

Golub, G.H. (1973). Some modified matrix eigenvalue problems. *SIAM Rev.* 15, 318–344.

Golub, G.H., W. Kahan (1965). Calculating the singular values and pseudo-inverse of a matrix. *SIAM J. Num. Anal. Ser. B* 2, 205–224.

Golub, G.H., G. Meurant (1983). *Résolution Numérique des Grandes Systèmes Linéaires*, Collection de la Direction des Etudes et Recherches de l'Electricité de France, Vol. 49, Eyolles, Paris.

Golub, G.H., S. Nash, C. Van Loan (1979). A Hessenberg–Schur method for the matrix problem $AX + XB = C$. *IEEE Trans. Auto. Cont.* AC-24, 909–913.

Golub, G.H., C. Reinsch (1970). Singular value decomposition and least squares solutions. *Numer. Math.* 14, 403–420. See also Wilkinson & Reinsch [1971, pp. 134–151].

Golub, G.H., C.F. Van Loan (1979). Unsymmetric positive definite linear systems. *Linear Algebra Appl.* 28, 85–98.

Golub, G.H., C.F. Van Loan (1980). An analysis of the total least squares problem. *SIAM J. Number. Anal.* 17, 883–893.

Golub, G.H., C.F. Van Loan (1989). *Matrix Computations, 2nd edition*, Johns Hopkins Uinversity Press, Baltimore, MD.

Golub, G.H., J.H. Wilkinson (1976). Ill-conditioned eigensystems and the computation of the Jordan canonical form. *SIAM Rev.* 18, 578–619.

Grimes, R.G., J.G. Lewis (1981). Condition number estimation for sparse matrices. *SIAM J. Sci. Statist. Comput.* 2, 384–388.

Hager, W. (1984). Condition Estimates. *SIAM J. Sci. Statist. Comput.* 5, 311–316.

Hager, W. (1988). *Applied Numerical Linear Algebra*, Prentice-Hall, Englewood Cliffs, NJ.

Halmos, P. (1958). *Finite Dimensional Vector Spaces*, Van Nostrant Reinhold, New York.

Hammarling, S. (1974). A note on modifications to the Givens plane roation. *J. Inst. Math. Appl.* 13, 215–218.

Heath, M.T. (ed.) (1986). *Proceedings of First SIAM Conference on Hypercube Multiprocessors*, SIAM, Philadelphia, PA.

Heath, M.T. (ed.) (1987). *Hypercube Multiprocessors*, SIAM, Philadelphia, PA.

Heath, M.T., C.H. Romine (1988). Parallel solution of triangular systems on distributed memory multiprocessors. *SIAM J. Sci. Statist. Comput.* 9, 558–588.

Heath, M.T., D.C. Sorensen (1986). A pipelined method for computing the QR factorization of a sparse matrix. *Linear Algebra Appl.* 77, 189–203.

Heller, D. (1978). A survey of parallel algorithms in numerical linear algebra. SIAM Rev. 20, 740–777.

Heller, D.E., I.C.F. Ipsen (1983). Systolic networks for orthogonal decompositions, *SIAM J. Sci. Statist. Comput.* 4, 261–269.

Higham, N.J. (1987). A survey of condition number estimation for triangular matrices. *SIAM Rev.* 29, 575–596.

Higham, N.J. (1988). Computing a nearest symmetric positive semidefinite matrix. *Linear Algebra .Appl.* 103, 103–118.

Higham, N.J. (1989). Analysis of the Cholesky decomposition of a semi-definite matrix, in: M.G. Cox, S.J. Hammarling (eds.), *Reliable Numerical Computation*, Oxford University Press, Oxford.

Higham, N.J., D.J. Higham (1989). Large growth factors in Gaussian elimination with pivoting. *SIAM J. Matrix Anal. Appl.* 10, 155–164.

Hockney, R.W., C.R. Jesshope (1989). *Parallel Computers 2*, Adam Hilger, Bristol and Philadelphia.

Ipsen, I.C.F., Y. Saad, M. Schultz (1986). Dense linear systems on a ring of processors. *Linear Algebra Appl.* 77, 205–239.

Kågström, B. (1985). The generalized singular value decomposition and the general $A - \lambda B$ problem. *BIT* 24, 568–583.

Kågström, B., P. Ling (1988). Level 2 and 3 BLAS routines for the IBM 3090 VF/400: Implementation and experiences, Report UMINF-154.88, Univesity of Umeå, Inst. of Inf. Proc., S-901 87 Umeå, Sweden.

Kågström, B., P. Ling, C. Van Loan (1991). High performance GEMM-based level-3 BLAS: Sample routines for double precision real data, Report UMINF-91.09, University of Umeå, Inst. of Inf. Proc., S-901 87 Umeå, Sweden.

Kågström, B., A. Ruhe (1980a). An algorithm for numerical computation of the Jordan normal form of a complex matrix. *ACM Trans. Math. Software* 6, 398–419.

Kågström, B., A. Ruhe (1980b). Algorithm 560 JNF: An algorithm for numerical computation of the Jordan normal form of a complex matrix. *ACM Trans. Math. Software* 6, 437–443.

Kågström, B., A. Ruhe (1983). *Matrix Pencils*, Proc. Pite Havsbad, 1982, Lecture Notes in Mathematics 973, Springer, New York and Berlin.

Kaniel, S. (1966). Estimates for some computational techniques in linear algebra. *Math. Comp.* 20, 369–378.

Kielbasinski, A. (1987). A note on rounding error analysis of Cholesky factorization. *Linear Algebra Appl.* 88/89, 487–494.

Kogbetlianztz, E.G. (1955). Solution of linear equations by diagonalization of coefficient matrix. *Quart. Appl. Math.* 13, 123–132.

Laub, A.J. (1981). Efficient multivariable frequency response computations. *IEEE Trans. Auto. Contr.* AC-26, 407–408.

Lawson, C.L., R.J. Hanson (1974). *Solving Least Squares Problems*, Prentice-Hall, Englewood Cliffs, NJ.

Lawson, C.L., R.J. Hanson, D.R. Kincaid, F.T. Krogh (1979a). Basic linear algebra subprograms for FORTRAN usage. *ACM Trans. Math. Software* 5, 308–323.

Lawson, C.L., R.J. Hanson, D.R. Kincaid, F.T. Krogh (1979b). Algorithm 539: Basic linear algebra subprograms for FORTRAN usage. *ACM Trans. Math. Software* 5, 324–325.

Leon, S. (1980). *Linear Algebra with Applications*, MacMillan, New York.

Li, G., T. Coleman (1988). A parallel triangular solver for a distributed-memory multiprocessor. *SIAM J. Sci. Statist. Comput.* 9, 485–502.

Lusk, E., R. Overbeek (1983). Implementation of monitors with macros: A programming aid for the HEP and other parallel processors, Argonne Report 83–97.

Manteuffel, T.A. (1977). The Tchebychev iteration for nonsymmetric linear systems. *Numer. Math.* 28, 307–327.

Manteuffel, T.A. (1979). Shifted incomplete Cholesky factorization, in: I.S. Duff, G.W. Stewart (eds.), *Sparse Matrix Proceedings, 1978*, SIAM, Philadelphia, PA.

Meijerink, J.A., H.A. Van der Vorst (1977). An iterative solution method for linear equations systems of which the coeffceint matrix is a symmetric M-matrix. *Math. Comp.* 31, 148–462.

Meinguet, J. (1983). Refined error analyses of Cholesky factorization. *SIAM J. Numer. Anal.* 20, 1243–1250.

Meurant, G. (1984). The block preconditioned conjugate gradient method on vector computers. *BIT*, 24, 623–633.

Moler, C.B., G.W. Stewart (1973). An algorithm for generalized matrix eigenvalue problems. *SIAM J. Numer. Anal.* 10, 241–256.

O'Leary, D.P., G.W. Stewart (1985). Data flow algorithms for parallel matrix computations. *Comm. ACM* 28, 841–853.

Ortega, J.M., R.G. Voigt (1985). Solution of partial differential equations on vector and parallel computers. *SIAM Rev.* 27, 149–240.

Paige, C.C. (1971). The computation of eigenvalues and eigenvectors of very large sparse matrices, Ph.D. thesis, London University, London, England.

Paige, C.C. (1980). Accuracy and effectiveness of the Lanczos algorithm for the symmetric eigenproblem. *Linear Algebra Appl.* 34, 235–258.

Paige, C.C. (1986). Computing the generalized singular value decomposition. *SIAM J. Sci. Statist. Comput.* 7, 1126–1146.

Paige, C.C., M. Saunders (1981). Towards a generalized singular value decomposition. *SIAM J. Numer. Anal.* 18, 398–405.

Parlett, B.N. (1971). Analysis of algorithms for reflections in bisectors. *SIAM Rev.* 13, 197–208.

Parlett, B.N. (1980). *The Symmetric Eigenvalue Problem*, Prentice-Hall, Englewood Cliffs, NJ.

Parlett, B.N., B. Nour-Omid (1985). The use of a refined error bound when updating eigenvalues of tridiagonals. *Linear Algebra Appl.* 68, 179–220.

Parlett, B.N., W.G. Poole (1973). A geometric theory for the QR, LU, and power iterations. *SIAM J. Numer. Anal.* 10, 389–412.

Parlett, B.N., H. Simon, L.M. Stringer (1982). On estimating the largest eigenvalue with the Lanczos algorithm. *Math. Comp.* 38, 153–166.

Poole, E.L., J.M. Ortega (1987). Multicolor ICCG methods for vector computers. *SIAM J. Number. Anal.* 24, 1394–1418.

Rodrigue, G. (ed.) (1982). *Parallel Computations*, Academic Press, New York.

Rodrigue, G., D. Wolitzer (1984). Preconditions by incomplete block cyclic reduction. *Math. Comp.* 42, 549–566.

Romine, C.H., J.M. Ortega (1988). Parallel solution of triangular systems of equations. *Parallel Comput* 6, 109–114.

Ruhe, A. (1969). An algorithm for numerical determination of the structure of a general matrix. *BIT* 10, 196–216.

Saad, Y. (1980). On the rates of convergence of the Lanczos and the block Lanczos methods. *SIAM J. Numer. Anal.* 17, 687–706.

Saad, Y. (1981). Krylov subspace methods for solving large unsymmetric linear systems. *Math. Comp.* 37, 105–126.

Saad, Y. (1982). The Lanczos biorthogonalization algorithm and other oblique projection methods for solving large unsymmetric systems. *SIAM J. Numer. Anal.* 19, 485–506.

Saad, Y. (1984). Practical use of some Krylov subspace methods for solving indefinite and nonsymmetric linear systems. *SIAM J. Sci. Statist. Comput.* 5, 203–228.

Saad, Y. (1989). Krylov subspace methods on supercomputers. *SIAM J. Sci. Statist. Comput.* 10, 1200–1232.

Saad, Y., M. Schultz (1986). GMRES: A generalized minimal residual algorithm for solving nonsymmetric linear systems. *SIAM J. Sci. Statist. Comput.* 7, 856–869.

Schreiber, R., B.N. Parlett (1987). Block reflectors: Theory and computation. *SIAM J. Numer. Anal.* 25, 189–205.

Schreiber, R., C. Van Loan (1989). A storage efficient WY representation for products of Householder transformations. *SIAM J. Sci. Statist. Comput.* 10, 53–57.

Scott, D.S. (1979). Block Lanczos software for symmetric eigenvalue problems, Report ORNL/CSD-48, Oak Ridge National Laboratory, Union Carbide Corporation, Oak Ridge, TN.

Seager, M.K. (1986). Parallelizing conjugate gradient for the Cray X-MP. *Parallel Comput.* 3, 35–47.

Serbin, S. (1980). On factoring a class of complex symmetric matrices without pivoting. *Math. Comp.* 35, 1231–1234.

Skeel, R.D. (1979). Scaling for numerical stability in Gaussian elimination. *J. ACM* 26, 494–526.

Skeel, R.D. (1980). Iterative refinement implies numerical stability for Gaussian elimination. *Math. Comp.* 35, 817–832.

Skeel, R.D. (1981). Effect of equilibration on residual size for partial pivoting. *SIAM J. Numer. Anal.* 18, 449–455.

Smith, B.T., J.M. Boyle, Y. Ikebe, V.C. Klema, C.B. Moler (1970). *Matrix Eigensystem Routines: EISPACK Guide, 2nd edition*, Springer, New York.

Speiser, J., C. Van Loan (1984). Signal processing computations using the generalized singular value decomposition, *Proc. SPIE Vol. 495*, SPIE Int'l Conf., San Diego, CA, 1984.

Stewart, G.W. (1971). Error bounds for approximate invariant subspaces of closed linear operators. *SIAM J. Numer. Anal.* 8, 796–808.

Stewart, G.W. (1972). On the sensitivity of the eigenvalue problem $Ax = \lambda Bx$. *SIAM J. Numer. Anal.* 9, 669–686.

Stewart, G.W. (1973). *Introduction to Matrix Computations*, Academic Press, New York.

Stewart, G.W. (1975). Methods of simultaneous iteration for calculating eigenvectors of matrices, in: J.H. Miller (ed.), *Topics in Numerical Analysis II*, Academic Press, New York, pp. 185–196.

Stewart, G.W. (1976a). The economical storage of plane rotations. *Numer. Math.* 25, 137–138.

Stewart, G.W. (1976b). Simultaneous iteration for computing invariant subspaces of non-Hermitian matrices. *Numer. Math.* 25, 12–36.

Stewart, G.W. (1977). On the perturbation of pseudo-inverses, projections, and linear least squares problems. *SIAM Rev.* 19, 634–662.

Stewart, G.W. (1979). The effects of rounding error on an algorithm for downdating a Cholesky factorization. *J. Inst. Math. Its Appl.* 23, 203–213.

Stewart, G.W. (1983). A method for computing the generalized singular value decomposition, in: B. Kågström, A. Ruhe (eds.), *Matrix Pencils*, Springer, New York, pp. 207–220.

Stewart, G.W. (1984). Rank degeneracy. *SIAM J. Sci. Statist. Comput.* 5, 403–413.

Stewart, G.W. (1987). Collinearity and least squares regression. *Statist. Sci.* 2, 68–100.

Strang, G. (1988). *Linear Algebra and Its Applications, 3rd edition*, Harcourt, Brace and Jovanovich, San Diego.

Symm, H.J., J.H. Wilkinson (1980). Realistic error bounds for a simple eigenvalue and its associated eigenvector. *Numer. Math.* 35, 113–126.

Trefethen, L.N., R.S. Schrieber (1987). Average case stability of Gaussian elimination, Numer. Anal. Report 88-3, Department of Mathematics, MIT.

Tsao, N.K. (1975). A note on implementating the Householder transformation. *SIAM J. Numer. Anal.* 12, 53–58.

Van der Sluis, A. (1969). Condition numbers and equilibration matrices. *Number. Math.* 14, 14–23.

Van der Sluis, A. (1970). Condition, equilibration, and pivoting in linear algebraic systems. *Numer. Math.* 15, 74–86.

Van der Vorst, H.A. (1982a). A vectorizable variant of some ICCG methods. *SIAM J. Sci. Statist. Comput.* 3, 350–356.

Van der Vorst, H.A. (1982b). A generalized Lanczos scheme. *Math. Comp.* 39, 559–562.

Van Dooren, P., C.C. Paige (1986). On the quadratic convergence of Kogbetliantz's algorithm for computing the singular value decomposition. *Linear Algebra Appl.* 77, 301–313.

Van Huffel, S. (1987). Analysis of the total least squares problem and its use in parameter estimation, Doctoral Thesis, Department of Electrical Engineering, K.U. Leuven.

Van Huffel, S., J. Vandewalle (1988). The partial total least squares algorithm. *J. Comp. and App. Math.* 21, 333–342.

Van Loan, C.F. (1976). Generalizing the singular value decomposition. *SIAM J. Numer. Anal.* 13, 76–83.

Van Loan, C.F. (1982a). A generalized SVD analysis of some weighting methods for equality-constrained least squares, in: B. Kagstrom, A. Ruhe (eds.), *Proceedings of the Conference on Matrix Pencils*, Springer, New York.

Van Loan, C.F. (1982b). Using the Hessenberg decomposition in control theory, in: D.C. Sorensen, R.J. Wets (eds.), *Algorithms and Theory in Filtering and Control*, Mathematical Programming Study no. 18, North-Holland, Amsterdam, pp. 102–111.

Van Loan, C.F. (1985a). Computing the CS and generalized singular value decomposition. *Numer. Math.* 46, 479–492.

Van Loan, C.F. (1985b). On the method of weighting for equality constrained least squares problems. *SIAM J. Numer. Anal.* 22, 851–864.

Van Loan, C.F. (1987). On estimating the condition of eigenvalues and eigenvectors. *Linear Algebra Appl.* 88/89, 715–732.

Varga, R.S. (1962). *Matrix Iterative Analysis*, Prentice-Hall, Englewood Cliffs, NJ.

Walker, H.F. (1988). Implementation of the GMRES method using Householder transformations. *SIAM J. Sci. Statist. Comput.* 9, 152–163.

Ward, R.C. (1975). The combination shift QZ algorithm. *SIAM J. Numer. Anal.* 12, 835–853.

Watkins, D.S. (1991). *Fundamentals of Matrix Computations*, Wiley, New York.

Wedin, P.Å. (1972). Perturbation bounds in connection with the singular value decomposition. *BIT* 12, 99–111.

Wedin, P.Å. (1973). On the almost rank-deficient case of the least squares problem. *BIT* 13, 344–354.

Wilkinson, J.H. (1961). Error analysis of direct methods of matrix inversion. *J. ACM.* 10, 281–330.

Wilkinson, J.H. (1965). *The Algebraic Eigenvalue Problem*, Clarendon Press, Oxford.

Wilkinson, J.H. (1971). Modern error analysis. *SIAM Rev.* 14, 548–568.

Wilkinson, J.H. (1972). Note on matrices with a very ill-conditioned eigenproblem. *Numer. Math.* 19, 176–178.

Wilkinson, J.H., C. Reinsch (eds.) (1971). *Handbook for Automatic Computation, Vol. 2: Linear Algebra*, Springer, New York. (Here abbrevated as *HACLA*.)

E.G. Coffman et al., Eds., *Handbooks in OR & MS, Vol. 3*

Chapter 7

Fundamental Algorithms and Data Structures

Jan van Leeuwen

Department of Computer Science, University of Utrecht, P.O. Box 80.089, 3508 TB Utrecht, The Netherlands

Peter Widmayer

Institut für Theoretische Informatik, ETH Zentrum, CH-8092 Zürich, Switzerland

In this tutorial, we describe in detail some fundamental data structures and operations, and we discuss the techniques and arguments involved. Our intention is to provide the reader both with a toolbox of data structures, serving as building blocks for algorithms, and some knowledge to build his own problem-specific data structures and algorithms. We present data structures and operations for the dictionary problem with and without access probabilities, for priority queues, and for the set union problem. The topics we discuss include linear lists, skip lists, red–black trees, finger search trees, the move-to-front heuristic for linear lists, the move-to-root heuristic for binary trees, splay trees, elementary hashing, pairing heaps, binomial queues, relaxed heaps, path-length reduction techniques for set union structures, amortization, and persistence. Since we emphasize detailed explanations of concepts, we necessarily do not cover many of the basic issues found in almost any textbook on algorithms and data structures. We do not discuss sorting, multidimensional keys, keys in a bounded universe, implicit data structures, external storage structures, dynamization techniques for static structures, and the design and analysis of algorithms in general; the latter is treated in a different chapter of this volume.

1. Introduction

This chapter deals with algorithms and data structures that are fundamental in solving algorithmic problems efficiently. Algorithmic problems abound in many different fields of study and application. More and more efficient and sophisticated solutions to the ever growing body of problems keep the field of *algorithms and data structures* under constant change. To some extent, this development is documented in textbooks [Aho, Hopcroft & Ullman, 1974, 1983; Baase, 1988; Brassard & Bratley 1988; Cormen, Leiserson & Rivest,

1990; Gonnet & Baeza-Yates, 1991; Harel, 1987; Horowitz & Sahni 1983, 1984; Kingston, 1990; Knuth, 1973a,b, 1981; Lewis & Denenberg, 1991; Manber, 1989; Mehlhorn, 1984a,b,c; Sedgewick, 1988; Standish, 1980; Wirth, 1976] on algorithms and data structures in general, as well as in more specific textbooks on combinatorial algorithms, graph algorithms, computational geometry, and mathematical algorithms, to name but a few. Volume A of the Handbook of Theoretical Computer Science [van Leeuwen, 1990] with close to one thousand pages is entirely devoted to algorithms and complexity; it offers an up-to-date in depth view of the recognized core areas of the field.

An algorithm describes a sequence of operations to be performed on the given data; hence, the efficiency of an algorithm depends on the efficiency of these operations. For sets of data elements, the efficiency of operations in turn depends on the data structure. An operation with the data in a data structure is again described by an algorithm – of a more basic type, so to speak. In this chapter, we focus on operations and data structures that are basic for a large number of algorithms – we consider these as fundamental algorithms and data structures. Among the large variety of fundamental algorithms and data structures we present some of those where the data structuring method is of interest, since the data structure may serve as a building block in an algorithm designed by the reader. For all interesting algorithms excluded from consideration, like sorting algorithms, several mathematical and combinatorial algorithms, and many more, we refer the reader to the textbooks mentioned above and to the open literature.

1.1. A not so fundamental algorithm

As an example, let us look at Dijkstra's well-known algorithm for single-source shortest paths [Dijkstra, 1959]; we base our presentation loosely on Fredman & Tarjan [1987], and Tarjan [1983a]. Let $G = (V, E)$ be an undirected, connected *graph*, where V is the set of *vertices*, $E \subseteq V \times V$ is the set of *edges*, and each edge $(v, w) \in E$ has a nonnegative *length* $l(v, w)$. The *length of a path* in G is the sum of the lengths of its edges. A *shortest path* between two vertices v and w is a path of minimum length among all paths in G between v and w; this length is the *distance* between v and w in G. For a distinguished vertex $s \in V$, the *source*, the *single-source shortest paths* problem is the problem of finding a shortest path from s to each other vertex in V.

Dijkstra's algorithm finds shortest paths of increasing length by adding single edges to shortest paths that have already been found. At each stage of the computation, each vertex is either *seen* or *unseen*; initially, only s is seen, all other vertices are unseen. A vertex v changes its state from unseen to seen when a path from s to v is first detected. For any seen vertex v, $v.dist$ is the length of a path between v and s; $v.seen$ is a label of v, telling whether or not v is seen. Whenever $v.dist$ is minimum among all seen vertices, $v.dist$ is the distance between v and s, i.e., a shortest path between v and s has been found. Then v is removed from the set of vertices under consideration. More precisely, Dijkstra's algorithm can be formulated as follows in Pascal-like notation (indentation denotes *begin–end* blocks):

{Dijkstra's algorithm for single-source shortest paths}
$s.dist := 0;$
$s.seen := true;$
for all $v \in V \setminus \{s\}$ **do**
   $v.dist := \infty;$
   $v.seen := false;$
initialize VC;
   {VC is the set of vertices under consideration, initially empty}
insert s into VC according to $s.dist$;
while VC is not empty **do**
   return a vertex v with minimum $v.dist$ in VC,
     and then delete it from VC;
   for each edge $(v, w) \in E$ **do**
    if $v.dist + l(v, w) < w.dist$ **then**
      if $w.seen$ **then**
        decrease $w.dist$ in VC to the new value $v.dist + l(v, w)$
      else
        $w.seen := true;$
        $w.dist := v.dist + l(v, w);$
        insert w into VC according to $w.dist$;
{for each $v \in V$, $v.dist$ is the distance between s and v}

1.2. Fundamental operations

The efficiency of Dijkstra's algorithm depends, among other things, on the efficiency of the operations on VC. As an *abstract data type*, we can describe what is needed for VC as follows. The *data* is a set of items, each with a *key* from some ordered universe, say the real numbers with the $<$-ordering. The *operations* are the following, where s denotes a set, i denotes an item with key component $i.key$, and k denotes a key:

initialize (s)	: create empty set s;
insert (i, s)	: insert item i according to $i.key$ into set s;
isempty (s)	: return true, if s is empty, and false otherwise;
deletemin (s)	: return an item i with minimum $i.key$ among the items in s, and delete it from s;
decreasekey (i, k, s)	: decrease the key of item i to the new value $k < i.key$ in s.

This abstract data type is known as *priority queue*; we will present efficient implementations for it – that is, data structures and algorithms – in Section 3. To avoid permanent explicit consideration of error conditions, we assume that whenever a requested item does not exist, a special null item will be returned, and whenever a requested modification of set s cannot be carried out, s will be left unchanged. For instance, a deletemin operation on an empty priority queue will return the null item and leave the priority queue empty.

Other operations that are of very general interest for single sets include the following:

search (k, s) : return item i in s with $i.key = k$;
predecessor (k, s) : return item i in s with largest $i.key < k$;
successor (k, s) : return item i in s with smallest $i.key > k$;
min (s) : return item i in s with smallest $i.key$;
max (s) : return item i in s with largest $i.key$;
deletemax (s) : return an item i with maximum $i.key$ among the items in s, and delete it from s;
delete (k, s) : delete item i with $i.key = k$ from s.

Not many algorithms will need all of these operations on a set simultaneously. As a consequence, efficient implementations for important subsets of these operations have been proposed. We will describe some of them in the next sections. On the other hand, there are algorithms for which the described operations are not sufficient. In particular, an algorithm may perform operations that involve more than one set simultaneously. Here, a set is identified by a label, and the following operations are carried out on labelled sets:

makeset (i, l) : create a set with label l, containing item i as its single element; here, i must not be in a set initially;
findlabel (i) : return the label of the set containing item i;
unite (i, j) : combine the set containing item i with the set containing item j, and give it the label of the old set containing i; here, i and j have to be in different sets initially.

For sorted sets of elements, we additionally define operations that join two sets into one and that split one set into two:

join (l, l') : combine the sets labelled l and l' into a new set labelled l; here, all keys of items in set l have to be smaller than all keys of items in set l';
split (l, k, l') : partition the set labelled l into two new sets labelled l and l', with set l containing all items with key at most k, and set l' containing all items with key greater than k.

To illustrate the use of these operations, let us briefly look at Kruskal's algorithm for computing a minimum spanning tree of a connected, undirected graph with nonnegative edge lengths [Kruskal, 1956]. A minimum spanning tree is a connected subgraph of minimum total length, containing all vertices of the given graph. Kruskal's algorithm constructs a minimum spanning tree by considering all edges in order of increasing length and selecting those that do not form a cycle with already selected edges. More precisely, it can be described as follows, where $V = \{v_1, \ldots, v_n\}$:

{Kruskal's algorithm for minimum spanning trees}
for $i := 1$ **to** n **do**
  makeset(v_i, i);
$T := \emptyset$;
  {T contains the edges of the part of the minimum spanning tree constructed
  thus far}
for each edge $(v, w) \in E$ in order of increasing length **do**
  if *findlabel*$(v) \neq$ *findlabel*(w) **then**
    $T := T \cup \{(v, w)\}$;
    unite(v, w);
{the edges in T form a minimum spanning tree}

Again, it is clear that the efficiency of the operations *makeset, findlabel*, and *unite* is crucial for the efficiency of the described algorithm. The problem of supporting these operations efficiently is known as the *set union* problem or the *disjoint set union* problem, since the constraint on operation *makeset* implies that all sets are disjoint. We will describe efficient implementations for it in Section 4.

1.3. Costs of computations

Before we can claim that an algorithm solves a problem efficiently or even optimally, we need a clear concept of efficiency. We restrict ourselves in this chapter to deterministic algorithms, designed for a computer with a single processor. The resources of interest are the *runtime* and the *storage space* requirements of an algorithm, depending on the problem input. The computer model we use is the *random access machine* [Cook & Reckhow, 1973] for real numbers, *realRAM* for short. The memory of a realRAM is an array of storage cells, each of them able to store an arbitrary real number. In a single computation step, a realRAM can perform an elementary arithmetic or boolean operation on the contents of two storage cells, given by their respective array indices, and store the result in another cell. Elementary arithmetic operations are addition, subtraction, multiplication and division (for integer operands, we may opt for integer division); elementary boolean operations are all kinds of comparisons ($<, \leq, =, \geq, >, \neq$). Charging only unit computation time to any of these operations is called the *uniform cost assumption*; it is an abstraction from existing computers that is justified only if we do not exploit it to the limit, e.g., by encoding many small numbers into a large one.

The realRAM is quite a powerful machine, since it can perform address arithmetic, i.e., a storage cell index can be the result of an arithmetic operation. In contrast, *pointer machines* allow memory access only through explicit reference [Kolmogorov, 1953; Kolmogorov & Uspenskii, 1958; Knuth, 1973a; Schönhage, 1980; Tarjan, 1979], similar to pure pointer mechanisms in programming languages. A review of early issues and concepts in defining what is a step in a computation and what is a reasonable machine model can be found in Cook [1982].

The number of elementary operations, *computation steps* or *runtime* for short, and the storage space needed are measured relative to the length of the input and the output for a given problem instance, where the length is the number of storage cells needed to store the data. That is, we view a sequence of n real numbers as having length n. Instead of directly measuring elementary steps of an algorithm, we might as well measure specific operations. For instance, if Kruskal's algorithm as described above is run on a graph with n vertices and m edges, $2m$ *findlabel* operations and $n - 1$ *unite* operations will be carried out. Most often, we will only be interested in the order of growth of the runtime as a function of the input and output length, the *asymptotic efficiency*. Instead of identifying a single function, we therefore content our-selves with identifying a class of functions that bound the growth from above. For two nonnegative, real-valued functions g and f on nonnegative integers, let $O(g) = \{f \mid \exists c > 0,\ c \in \mathbb{R}^+,\ n_0 > 0,\ n_0 \in \mathbb{N} \text{ s.t. } 0 \le f(n) \le c \cdot g(n) \text{ for all } n \ge n_0,$ $n \in \mathbb{N}\}$. In our example, the number of *unite*-operations in Kruskal's algorithm is in $O(n)$ or, a weaker statement, in $O(n^2)$. Instead of $f \in O(g)$ we usually write $f = O(g)$, an established convention in the analysis of algorithms. To bound the growth of a function from below, we define $\Omega(g) = \{f \mid \exists c > 0,$ $n_0 > 0, \text{ s.t. } 0 \le c \cdot g(n) \le f(n) \text{ for all } n \ge n_0\}$. That is, $f = O(g)$ if and only if $g = \Omega(f)$. For any two functions f and g, we define $f = \Theta(g)$ if and only if $f = O(g)$ and $f = \Omega(g)$. In our example, Kruskal's algorithm performs $\Theta(n)$ *unite* and $\Theta(m)$ *findlabel* operations.

In general, the runtime of an algorithm need not be asymptotically the same for all inputs of a certain length. A typical example is sorting: if the sequence of n numbers presented to a sorting algorithm is already sorted, the algorithm should take only $O(n)$ steps to complete its job, whereas for an unsorted sequence it may take up to $O(n \log n)$ steps. In this chapter, log denotes the base 2 logarithm.

We are interested in the runtime and storage space requirements of al-gorithms in the *worst case*, i.e., for the input that makes the algorithm as inefficient as possible, because this gives us a guarantee for the behavior of the algorithm. Certainly, a worst-case bound should be as tight as possible to be meaningful. This entails a problem when we use fundamental algorithms and data structures as building blocks for more complex algorithms: just adding up worst-case costs for single operations, like *findlabel* or *unite* in our example of Kruskal's algorithm, may lead to overly pessimistic worst-case cost estimates for the overall algorithm. Here, *amortization* of costs, i.e., averaging the costs of operations over a worst-case sequence of operations, may help. The *amortized cost* of an operation is defined in such a way that for any sequence of operations on an initially empty data structure, the total of the amortized costs is an upper bound on the total of the actual costs of the operations. For a single operation in the sequence, however, the actual cost may well be higher than the amortized cost. Amortization is useful whenever the worst-case cost of an operation can vary considerably, such that the amortized cost is of a lower order of growth than the worst-case cost of an operation. In Tarjan [1985a], amortization is treated in detail; we will use the technique in Section 2. In a different type of complexity analysis, the *average case* analysis, the average is taken over all problem instances, on the basis of an underlying probability distribution of problem instances [see van Leeuwen, 1990, Chapter 9]; we will not analyze average case costs of algorithms in this chapter.

In the next section, we will describe data structures for the most prominent abstract data type, the *dictionary*. We will also discuss the situation that search frequencies vary widely for different items. For concreteness, in the remainder of this chapter we assume that an item consists of an integer key only, since any other information associated with an item (like a vertex identification in our example) is irrelevant for our purposes.

2. Dictionaries

A *dictionary* is an abstract data type that supports the operations *search*, *insert*, and *delete* on a set of items with unique key values, in addition to the operation *initialize* needed for any abstract data type. Data structures for dictionaries support searching either by ordering items according to their key value and comparing keys, or by performing arithmetic on the key value to directly calculate a storage cell address for an item. The latter methods are called *key transformation methods* or *hashing techniques*; they form an interesting type of dictionary implementations with often good average-case performance, but bad worst-case efficiency. In this chapter, we will emphasize comparison-based methods and discuss elementary hashing techniques only briefly.

2.1. Linear lists and skip lists

Perhaps the simplest implementation of dictionaries is to chain all items into a single list, where each list element – a *node* in the list – references the next node in the list by a pointer (see Figure 1).

In Pascal, a list may be defined as follows:

```
type listptr = ↑listnode;
     listnode = record
                     key: integer; {represents an item}
                     next: listptr
                end
```

Fig. 1. A linear list.

If items are kept in the list in sorted order, and the pointer of the last node is
nil, the search for a key k in a list with head pointer *head* can be described as
follows:

$p := head$;
while ($p \neq$ **nil**) **and** ($p\uparrow.key < k$) **do**
  $p := p\uparrow.next$;
if $p \neq$ **nil then**
  successful search: k is in $p\uparrow$
else unsuccessful search: k is not in the list

Here, we assume that expressions are evaluated from left to right only as far as
necessary; in the above program fragment, the boolean expression ($p\uparrow.key <$
k) is not evaluated if ($p =$ **nil**), and hence illegal dereferencing of pointers is
avoided.

Even though a linear list is asymptotically storage space efficient – it uses
$\Theta(n)$ space for n keys – a search operation is not very fast in the worst case.
For n keys, a search may take up to $O(n)$ steps, among them $O(n)$ key
comparisons. The same bound holds for insert and delete, since the position in
the list of the key to be inserted or deleted has to be determined.

A faster way of getting to the desired position in a list is to skip some of the
list elements; this is possible only if the list contains extra pointers. In Pugh
[1990], *skip lists* are proposed as a way of organizing extra pointers. Let a
perfect skip list be a sorted, linked list, where each 2^i'th node has a pointer to
the node 2^i positions ahead of it in the list, for $i = 0, \ldots, \lfloor \log n \rfloor$, where n is
the number of nodes in the list (see Figure 2). That is, each node has a pointer

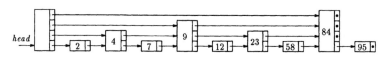

Fig. 2. A perfect skip list.

to the next node in the list; every other node has a pointer to the node two
positions ahead in the list, and so on. Call a node with $k + 1$ pointers a *level-k
node*, and call the pointer in a level-k node pointing 2^j positions ahead a *level-j
pointer*, $0 \leq j \leq k$. The maximum level of any node is then $\lfloor \log n \rfloor$, and the list
has $\lfloor \log n \rfloor + 1$ head pointers, one to the first node of each level. To simplify
the description of operations, let *head* be a pointer to a dummy level $\lfloor \log n \rfloor$
node containing the head pointers. As compared with a simple linear list, the
number of pointers in a perfect skip list only doubles, but the worst-case cost
for a search goes down to $O(\log n)$, if we follow pointers of decreasing levels,
starting at level $\lfloor \log n \rfloor$. More precisely, if component *next*[j] denotes the
level-j pointer of a node, a search for key k in the list can be described as

follows:

$p := head;$
for $j := \lfloor \log n \rfloor$ **downto** 0 **do**
  {examine level j pointer}
  if $(p\uparrow.next[j] \neq \textbf{nil})$ **and** $(k \geq p\uparrow.next[j]\uparrow.key)$ **then**
    $p := p\uparrow.next[j];$
if $(p \neq head)$ **and** $(p \neq \textbf{nil})$ **and** $(p\uparrow.key = k)$ **then**
  successful search: k is in $p\uparrow$
else unsuccessful search: k is not in the list

In contrast to searching, insertion and deletion is inefficient in a perfect skip list, since it requires the whole list to be reorganized in the worst case. On the average, if the probability of an element being inserted in some list position is the same for all positions and all elements, roughly half the list needs to be reorganized; the same holds for deletion.

To lower the average case runtime of $O(n)$ for insertions and deletions, a *randomized* version of perfect skip lists, the *skip lists*, have been proposed [Pugh, 1990]. When a node is inserted into a skip list, its level is chosen randomly, in the same proportions as for perfect skip lists. That is, roughly half the nodes are level 0, roughly one fourth are level 1, and so on. The level-j pointer of a node, instead of pointing 2^j nodes ahead, points to the next node in the list of level j or higher. The level of a node is never changed. Now, insertions and deletions only affect the pointers local to the respective position in the list (see Figure 3).

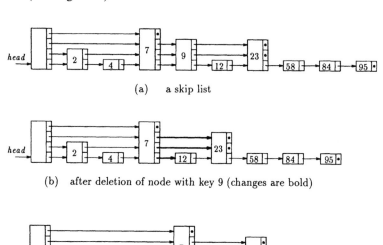

(a)   a skip list

(b)   after deletion of node with key 9 (changes are bold)

(c)   after insertion of node with key 5 and randomly chosen level 2

Fig. 3.

Detailed algorithms for insertion and deletion, additional considerations and implementation details as well as an average-case analysis can be found in Pugh [1990]. Of course, unfortunate choices of levels can result in poor performance, but, due to the randomization, no sequence of operations consistently leads to bad behavior of skip lists. The expected cost of any of the operations search, insert and delete in skip lists is $O(\log n)$, and it is very unlikely that any operation takes substantially longer than expected [Papadakis, Munro & Poblete, 1990; Pugh, 1990].

2.2. Balanced binary search trees

Like skip lists, binary search trees are a generalization of linear lists, where each node may have more than one pointer to other nodes. Unlike skip lists, the number of pointers of a node to other nodes is at most two, and the directed graph structure of the nodes and pointers is a tree. In a binary tree there is one node, the *root*, from which each node can be reached through a directed path. The root serves as an entry point for operations on trees, similar to the head pointer of a linear list. If there is an arc in the tree (a pointer in the data structure) from a node v to a node w, w is called a *child* of v, and v is the *parent* of w. We distinguish between the at most two children of a node in a binary tree: one is the *left* child, the other is the *right* child. A node with no children is a *leaf*; a node with at least one child is an *interior node*. A *full binary tree* is a binary tree in which every node has two children or none. Binary trees can be used as data structures, if we store a key (or, more generally, an item having a key component) in a node. In Pascal, a binary tree may be defined as follows:

```
type treeptr = ↑treenode;
     treenode = record
                    key: integer; {represents an item}
                    left, right: treeptr
                end
```

Figure 4 shows an example binary tree.

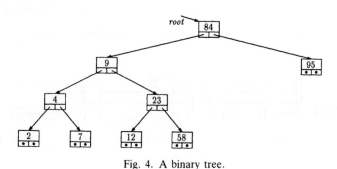

Fig. 4. A binary tree.

For a node v in a binary tree, the *left* (*right*) *subtree of* v is the tree rooted at the left (right) child of v. In a *binary search tree*, for each node v, all keys in the left subtree are smaller than the key stored at v, which in turn is smaller than all keys in the right subtree of v. Figure 4 actually shows a binary search tree; note the striking similarity of the perfect skip list in Figure 2 and the binary search tree in Figure 4. The *inorder* (or *symmetric*) *traversal* of the tree corresponds to the sorted order of keys:

```
procedure inorder( p: treeptr);
begin {initially, let p be the root pointer}
   if p ≠ nil then
      inorder( p↑.left);
      deliver p↑.key;
      inorder( p↑.right)
end {inorder}
```

Searching for key k in a binary search tree with root pointer r is simple: exclude one of the two subtrees of the node from further consideration and search recursively in the other, unless the current node already contains k:

```
procedure search(k: integer {key}; p: treeptr);
begin {initially, let p be the root pointer}
   if p = nil then
      unsuccessful search: k is not in the tree
   elsif k < p↑.key then
      search(k, p↑.left)
   elsif p↑.key < k then
      search(k, p↑.right)
   else successful search: k is in p↑
end {search}
```

In the worst case, the runtime of this procedure is proportional to the maximum number of arcs on any path from the root to a leaf – the *height* of the tree. The *depth* of a node is the number of arcs on the (unique) path from the root to that node. All nodes of depth i together form level i of the tree (note that this definition counts levels just the other way round, when compared with skip lists). As an example, the height of the tree in Figure 4 is 3; two nodes are on level 1, two are on level 2, and four are on level 3 – as always, the only vertex on level 0 is the root. In order to get an efficient search procedure, we aim at keeping the height of binary search trees reasonably small. Since a binary tree of height h has at most $2^{h+1} - 1$ vertices, any binary search tree for n keys needs to have height at least $\lfloor \log n \rfloor$. Hence, a search time of $O(\log n)$ is asymptotically optimal.

Over the years, a considerable number of classes of search trees that guarantee a logarithmic upper bound on the tree height have been developed;

they are known as *balanced search trees*, since they somehow balance the right versus the left subtree of any node. Balancing criteria are the relative weights of subtrees [Nievergelt & Reingold, 1973; Nievergelt & Wong, 1972, 1973] or the relative heights of subtrees [Adel'son-Vel'skii & Landis, 1962; Bayer, 1972; Bayer & McCreight, 1972; Guibas, McCreight, Plass & Roberts, 1978; Huddleston & Mehlhorn, 1982; Icking, Klein & Ottmann, 1987; Olivié, 1982; Ottmann & Six, 1976; Ottmann & Wood, 1989; Tarjan, 1983b; van Leeuwen & Overmars, 1983]. Let us look at an interesting class more closely, the *red–black trees* [Guibas & Sedgewick, 1978], with a modified deletion algorithm [Tarjan, 1983b], as presented, e.g., by Sarnak & Tarjan [1986].

2.2.1. Red–black trees

A *red–black tree* is a binary search tree where each node is either *red* or *black*, such that the following conditions are satisfied:

(1) *black height condition*: the number of black nodes is the same on any path from the root to a leaf;

(2) *red condition*: no red node has a red parent;

(3) *leaf condition*: each leaf is black.

By induction on the height of a red–black tree, it can be shown easily that $O(\log n)$ is an upper bound on the height of a red–black tree with n nodes. Hence, if the red–black tree conditions can be maintained dynamically, i.e., under insertions and deletions of nodes, red–black trees are an efficient search structure. To simplify the description of insertion and deletion, we only use interior nodes to store keys; each leaf represents an interval between two stored keys. Hence, a leaf is not stored explicity. For balancing purposes, we can therefore conceptually strip the red–black tree of the leaf level and disregard the leaf condition. Nevertheless, we will use the existence of leaves in the description of insertion and deletion. With this convention, Figure 4 does not show the leaves of the tree; they are represented by **nil**-pointers and correspond to intervals $(-\infty, 2)$, $(2, 4)$, $(4, 7)$, $(7, 9)$, $(9, 12)$, $(12, 23)$, $(23, 58)$, $(58, 84)$, $(84, 95)$ and $(95, +\infty)$.

To insert a node with key k into a red–black tree, we first search for k in the tree. Searching in a red–black tree is the same as searching in an unbalanced binary search tree, i.e., node color information is disregarded. Since we assume that k is not present in the tree, the search ends at the leaf whose interval contains k. Now we replace the leaf by a new interior red node storing k; the two children of the new node are leaves. Figure 5 shows the tree of Figure 4, colored to fulfill the red–black tree conditions, and the insertion of key 30; red nodes are shown as boxes, black nodes as circles, and leaves are not shown.

This preserves the black height condition, but may violate the red condition. In the latter case, the parent of the inserted node is red (see Figure 5). If the parent has a red sibling (a *sibling* is the other child of the same parent), we color both black, and color the parent of both, which must have been black, red (see Figure 6, where the trees shown may be parts of a larger tree, and the

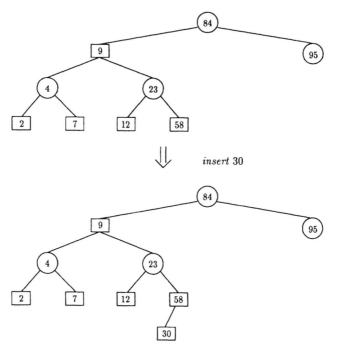

insert 30

Fig. 5. A red–black tree insertion starting.

Fig. 6. Shifting up a red violation.

two symmetric cases are not shown). This preserves the black height condition, but potentially shifts the red violation two levels up the tree (see, e.g., Figure 5, where this happens). We repeatedly shift up the red violation in this way, until this is no longer possible.

If there is still a red violation, and the red parent is the root, we color the root black; this restores the red–black tree conditions. Otherwise, the red parent has a black brother or no brother, and a restructuring operation (pointer change) plus some color changes restore the red–black tree conditions, as shown in Figure 7 ($\triangle$ denotes a subtree; node d may be missing). That is, after a constant number of structural changes and a logarithmic number of color flips, the red–black tree conditions are restored after an insertion.

The structural changes illustrated in Figure 7 can be expressed in elementary structural changes that have been used in numerous classes of balanced trees – the rotations. A *rotation* of a tree edge between a child v and its parent w makes v the new parent and w the new child. To retain the symmetric order

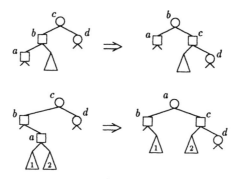

Fig. 7. Restructuring after insertion.

(inorder), *w* becomes *v*'s right child if *v* was *w*'s left child (a *right rotation*), and similarly, *w* becomes *v*'s left child if *v* was *w*'s right child (a *left rotation*). Pictorially, in a right rotation, the tree edge rotates clockwise, in a left rotation it rotates counter-clockwise. In Figure 7, the first restructuring is a right rotation of the tree edge between nodes *b* and *c* – we call this a right rotation at *c*; the second restructuring is a left rotation at *b*, followed by a right rotation at *c*. Hence, an insertion into a red–black tree causes at most two rotations.

In the example of Figure 5, shifting the red violation two levels up the tree, and then applying a left rotation to the node with key 9 (node 9, for short), followed by a right rotation at node 84, restores the red–black tree conditions and yields the tree shown in Figure 8.

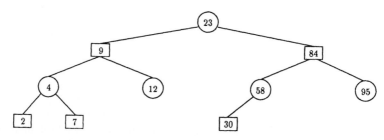

Fig. 8. The red–black tree of Figure 5 after insertion.

Deletion is similar, but slightly more complicated. Essentially, if the node *v* with key *k* to be deleted has two children, we copy the key *k'* of the successor of *k* in symmetric order from its node *v'* into *v*, and then we delete node *v'*. Node *v'* can be reached from *v* by following once the right child pointer and then successively left child pointers, until a node with no left child is found. In Figure 8, deleting node 23 hence amounts to copying value 30 to the root and then deleting the red node 30. The deletion of a node that has at most one child is carried out by deleting this node and replacing it in the tree with its child (if any). If the deleted node was red, the resulting tree is a red–black tree. Otherwise, the black height condition will be violated. With color changes along the path to the root and at most three rotations, the red–black tree conditions can be restored [Sarnak & Tarjan, 1986].

Altogether, red–black trees are a data structure for implementing dictionaries, with the following efficiency for a dictionary containing *n* keys:
– storage space requirements are $\Theta(n)$; for any key, two pointers plus one bit of color information are needed (contrary to other balanced search tree structures, no balance information is stored explicitly);
– *search, insert, delete, min, max, deletemin, deletemax, predecessor, successor* operations all take time $O(\log n)$ in the worst case;
– *insert* and *delete* take $O(1)$ rotations in the worst case, plus $O(\log n)$ color flips; *amortized* over a sequence of operations, each insert or delete takes only $O(1)$ color flips [see Huddleston & Mehlhorn, 1982; Maier & Salveter, 1981; and Tarjan, 1985a, where a nice amortization argument is presented].

Logarithmic worst-case search, insertion and deletion cost are achieved by many balanced search tree structures. Constant worst-case restructuring cost (pointer changes) for insertion and deletion is a more distinguished feature; it makes red–black trees especially suitable as building blocks in other dynamical data structures, such as persistent search trees [Sarnak & Tarjan, 1986] or priority search trees [McCreight, 1985]. In terms of worst-case time for insert or delete, red–black trees are outperformed by a balanced search tree with $O(1)$ update cost, once the position of the inserted or deleted node is known [Levcopoulos & Overmars, 1988]; however, it is not known whether this structure is well suited as a building block for other types of search trees. For instance, search trees may be used in situations where the keys of any two consecutive operations tend to be fairly close (in the symmetric order), i.e., operations exhibit some locality pattern [Tarjan & van Wyk, 1988]. To exploit such a pattern, it is natural to keep one or more pointers to nodes of interest – the *fingers*.

2.2.2. Finger search trees

A *finger search tree* is a binary search tree with extra level links [Brown & Tarjan, 1980; Hoffmann, Mehlhorn, Rosenstiehl & Tarjan, 1986; Huddleston & Mehlhorn, 1982]; other finger search tree suggestions can be found in Guibas, McCreight, Plass & Roberts [1977], and Tsakalidis [1985]. Red–black trees are a good basis for level-linked trees; for the purpose of linking levels, let us define the level concept for black nodes. The *black height* of a node is the number of black nodes on the path to the root, including the node itself and the root. The black nodes of the same black height form a *black level* (in these terms, the black height condition requests that all leaves of a red–black tree are on the same black level). A *left* (*right*) *black neighbor* of a black node v is a black node immediately preceding (following) v in the symmetric order of the black nodes on the same black level. In a level-linked red–black tree, each node points to its children and its parent; in addition, each black node points to its left and right black neighbor. Figure 9 shows the level-linked version of the red–black tree of Figure 5, where leaves are shown explicitly.

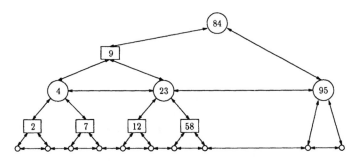

Fig. 9. A level-linked red–black tree; leaves are denoted as ○.

Starting from an arbitrary node in the tree, identified by a finger, a search for a node with given key follows parent and neighbor pointers in the appropriate direction, until a subtree is found that must contain the given key; then the search follows child pointers, as usual. Let d be the number of keys between the key of the starting node and the search key in symmetric order. Then a search takes $O(\log d)$ steps in the worst case.

In an update, the extra time needed to adjust level links is only $O(1)$ for each local transformation, i.e., for each color flip or rotation. Hence, the worst-case time bound for insertions and deletions is $O(\log n)$, since, e.g., color flips may bubble up an entire path to the root. The amortized cost of an insertion or deletion, however, is bounded by $O(\log d)$, since the amortized cost for color flips and link changes is $O(1)$, and searching costs $O(\log d)$.

Finger search trees can be used, for instance, if the relative access frequency of keys varies over time, by keeping one or more fingers to the most recently accessed nodes. This makes repeated, consecutive access to the same node cheap. However, for different access frequencies of keys, there exist search structures that dynamically adjust themselves to the data.

2.3. Self-adjusting search structures

Self-adjusting search structures try to efficiently solve the dictionary problem for keys with different *access frequencies* that vary over a sequence of operations, without maintaining explicit frequency information. Varying access frequencies are quite common; consider, for instance, the names of variables in a program to be the keys, and consider each occurrence of a name in the program to be an access, as in a compilation. A self-adjusting structure adjusts itself to the access frequencies of the elements; that is, access frequencies need not be known in advance. These structures are efficient only in an amortized sense, i.e., a single access may be very inefficient but, averaged over a sequence of accesses, performance is good. The best self-adjusting structures are asymptotically as good as *optimum binary search trees*: these are binary search trees built for a static set of keys whose access frequencies are fixed and known in advance. In an optimum binary search tree, the average length of search paths, weighted with the access frequencies of keys, is minimum among all possible binary search trees [Hu & Tucker, 1971; Knuth, 1971]. If keys are stored in leaves only, and interior nodes merely guide the search to the appropriate leaf (these trees are called *leaf search trees*), optimum trees [Garsia & Wachs, 1977; Kingston, 1988] can be used, e.g., to assign variable-length codes to letters of an alphabet so as to minimize the expected length of a coded message, for given, fixed relative frequencies of letters [Huffmann, 1952].

2.3.1. Move-to-front in linear lists

If keys are organized in a linear list, a simple heuristic that makes the list adjust itself to access frequencies is asymptotically as good as the optimal static strategy [Bentley & McGeoch, 1985] and even as good as any arbitrary dynamic strategy [Sleator & Tarjan, 1985b]. The heuristic is the *move-to-front rule* [McCabe, 1965]: after an access, move the accessed node to the front of the list, without changing the relative positions of the other nodes. In the list shown in Figure 1, a search for node 58 results in the list shown in Figure 10. Note that keys are not sorted, and in fact, a total order on the keys need not even exist.

Fig. 10. A self-adjusting linear list with move-to-front heuristic.

The move-to-front rule and other heuristics have been studied in detail [Bitner, 1979; Chung, Hajela & Seymour, 1988; Gonnet, Munro & Suwanda, 1981; Hester & Hirschberg, 1985, 1987; McCabe, 1965; Rivest, 1976; Oommen, Hansen & Munro, 1990; Oommen & Hansen, 1987] and used, e.g., in data compression methods [Bentley, Sleator, Tarjan & Wei, 1986; Lelewer & Hirschberg, 1987].

2.3.2. Move-to-root in binary search trees

If keys are ordered and stored in a binary search tree, the idea of moving an accessed node to the head pointer naturally leads to a *move-to-root* heuristic [Allen & Munro, 1978; Bitner, 1979]: after an access, move the accessed node to the root, by repeatedly rotating the edge to its current parent. For the binary search tree of Figure 4, the effect of accessing node 58 is shown in Figure 11.

With the move-to-root heuristic, frequently accessed nodes will often be close to the root; if the access frequencies are fixed and accesses are independent, the asymptotic expected access time is within a constant factor of that of an optimum static binary search tree [Allen & Munro, 1978]. In the worst case, however, move-to-root is not that efficient: there exist arbitrarily long access sequences for which the time for each access is $\Theta(n)$; recall that n is the number of nodes of the tree.

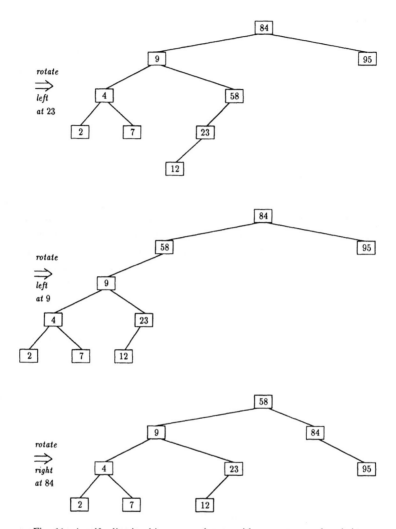

Fig. 11. A self-adjusting binary search tree with move-to-root heuristic.

2.3.3. Splay trees

Splay trees [Sleator & Tarjan, 1985a; Tarjan, 1983a] use a different heuristic, called *splaying*, to achieve good amortized efficiency. They are asymptotically as good as optimum binary search trees in the static case and adapt extremely well to varying access frequencies. *Splaying* is similar to move-to-root in that it also rotates an accessed element up to the root. It is different, however, in that it performs rotations in pairs. After an access to a node v we *splay at v* by repeating the following *splaying step at v* until v is the root:

(zig) If the parent w of v is the root, we rotate the edge between v and w. This terminates the splay at v (see Figure 12a).

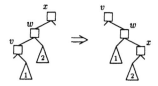

(a) zig: rotate at w

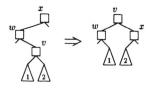

(b) zig-zig: rotate at x; rotate at w

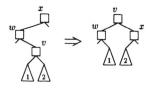

(c) zig-zag: rotate at w; rotate at x

Fig. 12. Three possible cases in a splaying step.

(zig–zig) If the parent w of v is not the root, and v and w are either both left or both right children, first rotate the edge between w and its parent, and then rotate the edge between v and w (see Figure 12b).

(zig–zag) If the parent w of v is not the root, and v is a left and w is a right child, or v is a right and w is a left child, first rotate the edge between v and w, and then rotate the edge between v and its new parent (see Figure 12c).

For the binary search tree of Figure 4, the effect of splaying at node 58 is shown in Figure 13. Splaying at a node of depth d clearly takes time $\Theta(d)$. The difference between splaying and move-to-root is in the zig–zig case, and in the pairing of rotations. In addition to moving the accessed vertex v to the root, splaying roughly halves the depth of every node on the access path; this is not the case with move-to-root.

2.3.3.1. Amortized efficiency analysis. To prove the *amortized efficiency* of splay tree accesses, we present the arguments of Sleator & Tarjan [1985a], in the *banker's view* [Huddleston & Mehlhorn, 1982; Tarjan, 1985a] of amortization, used implicitly by Brown & Tarjan [1980]. We define a bank account for a data structure, and we associate operations on the data structure with deposits into and withdrawals from the bank account. A bound on the total cost of a sequence of operations follows by relating the deposits and withdrawals with the initial and final balances of the account. In this setting, the computer can

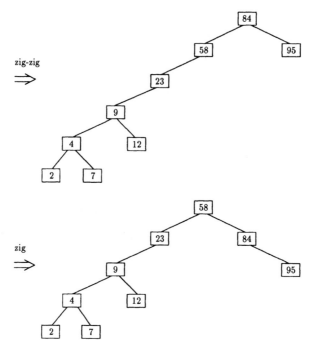

Fig. 13. Self-adjustment by splaying.

be viewed as a coin-operated machine, where each coin pays for a fixed, constant amount of runtime. We assign a certain number of coins to each operation – its *amortized cost* – , and we pay for the *actual cost* of the operation by giving away the money for the amortized cost; if the actual cost is higher than the amortized cost, we withdraw the necessary extra money from the bank account, if it is lower, we deposit the spare money into the account.

More precisely, assign to each possible configuration of the data structure a real value b called bank account *balance*. The *amortized cost* am of an operation is am $=$ act $+ b' - b$, where act is the *actual cost* of the operation, b is the balance before the operation, and b' is the balance after the operation. For a sequence of m operations, let am_i and act_i be the amortized and actual cost of operation $i, 1 \leq i \leq m$, let b_0 be the initial balance, and let b_i be the balance after the execution of operation i. Then the total actual cost of the sequence is

$$\sum_{i=1}^{m} act_i = \sum_{i=1}^{m} (am_i - b_i + b_{i-1}) = \sum_{i=1}^{m} am_i + b_0 - b_m \, .$$

Hence, if the final balance is no less than the initial balance, the amortized cost is an upper bound on the actual cost of the sequence.

In the amortized analysis of splay trees [Sleator & Tarjan, 1985a], let each item i have an arbitrary, but fixed positive weight $w(i)$, and let the *size* $s(v)$ of a node v be the sum of the weights of all items in nodes in the subtree rooted at v. Let the *rank* $r(v)$ of node v be defined as $\log s(v)$. The *balance* b of a tree is the sum of the ranks of all its nodes. The *actual cost* of a splaying operation is measured in the number of performed rotations, i.e., we charge unit cost per rotation; if no rotation is performed, we charge unit cost. The following lemma [Sleator & Tarjan, 1985a] serves as a basis for several results on splay tree behavior.

Access Lemma. *The amortized cost to splay a tree with root t at a node v is at most* $3(r(t) - r(v)) + 1 = O(\log(s(t)/s(v)))$.

Proof. If no rotation is performed, the bound follows directly. Consider any single splaying step, and let s and s', r and r' denote the size and rank functions just before and just after the splaying step, respectively. Let w be the parent of v and x the parent of w, if it exists, before the splaying step. Now consider the three cases:

(zig) The actual cost is 1, since one rotation is performed. Only v and w can change rank; therefore, the balance will change by $r'(v) - r(v) + r'(w) - r(w)$. Hence, the amortized time is

$$\text{am} = 1 + r'(v) - r(v) + r'(w) - r(w) \,.$$

Since w loses some of the nodes in its subtree in the rotation, $r(w) \geq r'(w)$, and hence am $\leq 1 + r'(v) - r(v)$, where $r'(v) - r(v) \geq 0$.

(zig–zig) Two rotations, plus rank changes at v, w, and x result in

$$\text{am} = 2 + r'(v) - r(v) + r'(w) - r(w) + r'(x) - r(x) \,.$$

Since $r'(v) = r(x)$,

$$\text{am} = 2 - r(v) + r'(w) - r(w) + r'(x) \,.$$

With $r'(v) \geq r'(w)$ and $r(w) \geq r(v)$ we get

$$\text{am} \leq 2 - 2r(v) + r'(v) + r'(x) \,.$$

To see that this is at most $3(r'(v) - r(v))$, i.e., that $-2r'(v) + r(v) + r'(x) \leq -2$, we argue as follows. By definition,

$$r(v) - r'(v) + r'(x) - r'(v) = \log(s(v)/s'(v)) + \log(s'(x)/s'(v)) \,.$$

From $s(v) + s'(x) \leq s'(v)$ we get $s(v)/s'(v) + s'(x)/s'(v) \leq 1$, $0 \leq s(v)/s'(v) \leq 1$, and $0 \leq s'(x)/s'(v) \leq 1$. Since $\log(s(v)/s'(v)) + \log(s'(x)/s'(v))$ is maximized at value -2 for arguments $s(v)/s'(v) = \frac{1}{2} = s'(x)/s'(v)$, we get am $\leqslant 3(r'(v) - r(v))$.

(zig–zag) Two rotations, plus rank changes at v, w, and x, together with the facts that $r'(v) = r(x)$ and $r(v) \leqslant r(w)$ yield am $\leqslant 2 + r'(w) + r'(x) - 2r(v)$. To see that this is at most $2(r'(v) - r(v))$, i.e., that $-2r'(v) + r'(w) + r'(x) \leqslant -2$, our arguments are similar to the zig–zig case. By definition,

$$r'(w) - r'(v) + r'(x) - r'(v) = \log(s'(w)/s'(v)) + \log(s'(x)/s'(v)) \; ;$$

with $s'(w) + s'(x) \leqslant s'(v)$, this is maximized at value -2, and hence am $\leqslant 2(r'(v) - r(v))$.

Hence, in each of the nonterminating cases (zig–zig, zig–zag), am $\leqslant 3(r'(v) - r(v))$, and in the terminating case (zig), am $\leqslant 3(r'(v) - r(v)) + 1$. The sum of these amortized cost estimates over the entire splaying operation yields the claimed value. $\square$

A number of results follow from the Access Lemma for sequences of operations by arguing on various choices of the item weights $w(i)$. Consider a sequence of m accesses to a splay tree with n nodes. The size of the node containing item i is at least $w(i)$ and at most $W = \Sigma_{i=1}^{n} w(i)$. If item weights remain fixed throughout the sequence of operations, the net balance decrease over the sequence is at most $\Sigma_{i=1}^{n} \log(W/w(i))$.

To see that splay trees are asymptotically as good as optimum binary search trees, consider a sequence of operations within which each item is accessed at least once. Let the absolute access frequency of item i be $f(i)$, i.e., item i is accessed $f(i)$ times in the sequence. Then we have [Sleator & Tarjan, 1985a]:

Static Optimality Theorem. *Total access cost for the described sequence of operations is* $O(m + \Sigma_{i=1}^{n} f(i) \log(m/f(i)))$.

Proof. Choose $w(i) = f(i)/m$. Then $W = 1$, and the Access Lemma implies an amortized access cost for accessing item i of $O(\log(m/f(i)))$. The balance decrease over the sequence is at most $\Sigma_{i=1}^{n} \log(m/f(i))$, and the upper bound is proved. Optimality follows from the noiseless coding theorem of information theory. $\square$

But even if access frequencies are not important, splay trees can be used for solving the dictionary problem. In the amortized sense, they are asymptotically as good as any form of uniformly balanced binary search tree, and they avoid the overhead of maintaining balance information [Sleator & Tarjan, 1985a]:

Balance Theorem. *Total access cost for a sequence of m operations on a splay tree of n items is* $O(m + (m + n) \log n)$.

Proof. Choose $w(i) = 1/n$. Then $W = 1$, the amortized access cost per item is $3 \log n + 1$, and the net balance decrease is $n \log n$. $\square$

Similarly, one can show that splay trees support accesses in the vicinity of a fixed finger with the same amortized efficiency as finger search trees; additional interesting properties of splay trees are described by Cole [1990], Sleator & Tarjan [1985a], and Tarjan [1985b].

2.3.3.2. Operations. The attentive reader may have noticed that we did not define rigorously which nodes are *accessed* in an operation; so far, we only dealt with successful search operations, implying that the node storing the search key is accessed. Let us now define how to implement operations on splay trees.

A *search* for an item with key k starts at the root of the splay tree and proceeds towards a leaf, as described earlier. If the search reaches a node storing the desired item, we splay at that node. As a result, *search* returns a pointer to the root of the splay tree. If the search reaches a leaf, no item with key k is in the tree. In that case, we splay at the last interior node on the search path and return a **nil**-pointer.

Insert and *delete* are based on *join* and *split*. For labelled sets of items, each set forms its own splay tree; the label of the set is the pointer to the root.

We *join* two splay trees with root pointers p and q, where all keys in tree p are smaller than all keys in tree q, by searching for the item with maximum key in p. After the search, the maximum is in the root, and hence the root has no right child. We complete the join operation by making q the right child of the new root of tree p (see Figure 14a).

Split at key k is performed by searching for k. Then either k or its predecessor or its successor in sorted order is in the root. We break the right or the left link of the root and return the two trees (see Figure 14b).

For *insert* with key k, we *split* at key k, and then we place k in a new root, making the two trees created by *split* the children of the new root (see Figure 14c).

To *delete* an item with key k from a splay tree, we *search* for k, moving it to the root. We remove the root node and *join* its two children (see Figure 14d).

An amortized analysis of these operations reveals that the cost of an *insertion* or *deletion* is $O(\log n)$ in an n-node splay tree, for equal access frequencies of keys; *split* and *join* asymptotically cost the same as *search* [Sleator & Tarjan, 1985a]. Even if access frequencies are different, amortized costs are good for all operations.

Variations of the splaying technique and applications of splaying to *lexicographic trees* and so-called *link-/cut-trees*, used in maximum network flow and minimum cost network flow algorithms, are presented by Sleator & Tarjan [1985a]. Due to their conceptual elegance, splay trees are of interest for other operations than the ones described [see, e.g., Port & Moffat, 1989] and other types of trees [see, e.g., Sherk, 1989]. Lexicographic splay trees have been used, e.g., in the implementation of approximation algorithms for finding shortest common superstrings [Turner, 1989]. Splay trees can also be used in data compression, yielding fast, locally adaptive algorithms [Jones, 1988].

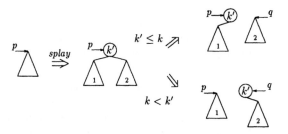

(a) A splay tree *join* operation

(b) A splay tree *split* operation

(c) A splay tree *insert* operation with key k

(d) A splay tree *delete* operation with key k

Fig. 14. Splay tree operations.

2.4. Hashing

In a technique that is fundamentally different from the previous ones, we make use of the power of the realRAM by computing an array index directly from a given key, instead of tracing pointers, depending on key comparisons. The *hash function* takes the key as its argument and computes an index in the *hash table* as its result. Let the hash table t be an array of m elements, indexed from 0 to $m - 1$, and let the hash function h map each key k in the universe K of keys to an index $h(k)$ with $0 \leq h(k) \leq m - 1$. Then, it is natural to store a data item with key k at $t[h(k)]$. Since usually $|K| \gg m$, there is always the possibility that $h(k) = h(k')$ for two different keys k and k' to be stored in the hash table; this event is called a *collision*, and k and k' are called *synonyms*. Therefore, storing k at $t[h(k)]$ is generally possible only if a hash table element can hold more than one item; hashing with *chaining* does so by using a linear list for each table element. Many other *collision resolution techniques* have been proposed for hash tables where each element holds just one item. In *open addressing*, the insertion of a key k whose home location $t[h(k)]$ is already occupied leads to a sequence of probes of other locations, of which the first empty one is taken to store k. A simple and practical strategy, *double hashing*, is close to best possible: in case of a collision, use a second hash function h' to determine the distance to the next location to be probed. That is, in the ith probe, see whether $t[(h(k) + i \cdot h'(k)) \bmod m]$ is occupied. Clearly, the choices of h and h' are critical: h should return all possible locations $0, \ldots, m - 1$ with equal probability, even if the distribution of keys taken from K is skewed, and h' should be such that all locations of t will eventually be probed. The latter can be achieved by choosing h' such that $h'(k)$ is relatively prime to m, which in turn is achieved by choosing m to be prime. The former condition cannot be guaranteed in general: for any given hash function h, there is always a set of keys in which any two keys map to the same location. This fact leads to a bad worst case guarantee of $O(n)$ for search, insert and delete operations on a set of n keys.

With a good choice of h, however, hashing is excellent on the average: the number of probes in hashing with chaining is roughly $1 + \frac{1}{2}\alpha$ for a successful search (and hence a deletion), where $\alpha = n/m$ is the *load factor* of the hash table, and is roughly α for an unsuccessful search (and hence an insertion). Furthermore, a good hash function can be chosen in a way that makes it very unlikely for a sequence of keys to lead to worst case behavior. This is achieved by picking a hash function at random from a suitable class of hash functions: a class of hash functions is *universal*, if any two different keys are synonyms under at most the mth fraction of the functions in the class [Carter & Wegman, 1979]. Hence, for any function picked from the universal class, the probability that any two given keys are synonyms is at most $1/m$; that is, no bad pairs of keys exist. This is the best that can be achieved by any hashing method in general; i.e., universal hash functions are expected to avoid collisions of keys in the best possible way, even if the key distribution is skewed.

In a simple example of a universal class of hash functions, let K be the set of integers from 0 up to some maximum $N - 1$, where N is prime. Then for any $a \in \{1, \ldots, N - 1\}$ and $b \in \{0, \ldots, N - 1\}$, $h_{a,b}(k) = ((a \cdot k + b) \bmod N) \bmod m$ is a hash function, and $H = \{h_{a,b} \mid a \in \{1, \ldots, N - 1\}, b \in \{0, \ldots, N - 1\}\}$ is a universal class of hash functions. Then, a function in the class can be chosen at random by choosing a and b at random.

Numerous other types of hash functions and methods of resolving collisions have been studied, including combinations of chaining and open addressing or dynamic hashing for external storage blocks [Enbody & Du, 1988]; we refer the interested reader to the textbooks mentioned in the introduction.

3. Priority queues

Apart from hashing, the data structures for the dictionary problem presented in Section 2 not only support the operations *search*, *insert*, and *delete*. For instance, red–black trees also support *min, max, deletemin, deletemax, succes-sor, predecessor*, and even *decreasekey* in O(log n) time, for a tree of n nodes; finger search trees with a finger to the maximum and a finger to the minimum key are even faster. Hence, red–black trees can be used to implement *priority queues* with a worst-case cost of O(log n) for each operation. In addition to the simple priority queue operations *insert, deletemin*, and *decreasekey*, such an implementation also supports *search* operations; we therefore call it a *search-able priority queue*. Some simple priority queue structures can be modified to support searches for and deletions of both the minimum and the maximum key [Atkinson, Sack, Santoro & Strothotte, 1986]; in this chapter, we will restrict ourselves to priority queues for the *minimum* key. Sometimes we request that two priority queues be united into one (similar to *unite* for labelled sets); the corresponding operation is

meld(p, q): combine priority queues *p* and *q* into one priority queue named *p*,

sometimes called *concatenate*, and the data type is called *concatenable queue*.

Priority queues can be used in a number of combinatorial optimization algorithms, like, e.g., Dijkstra's algorithm, as presented in Section 1. Here it is crucial that the execution time of a decreasekey operation is low, since many of these operations may be requested (one for each edge of the graph). Searching and melding are not needed in our example, if we use the knowledge of the position of an item in the data structure as input to the decreasekey operation. *Deletion* of keys is also supported by some data structures for priority queues, again with the position of the item given as an input parameter of the operation. If searching is not required, more relaxed structures can be used instead of search trees to implement priority queues. We will have a closer look at some data structures, maintaining families of heap-ordered trees. A *heap-ordered tree* is a tree of nodes containing keys such that for any two nodes w and v, where w is the parent of v, the *heap condition* $w.key \leq v.key$ is satisfied.

3.1. Implicit heaps

In the classical *heapsort* algorithm, a heap-ordered tree is maintained *implicitly*, i.e., without storing pointers, in an array [Floyd, 1964; Williams, 1964]. The array is indexed from 1 to n, for an n-item *implicit heap*. The root of the tree, containing the minimum key, is at index 1. The children of a node at index i are at index $2i$ and $2i + 1$; if $2i > n$ or $2i + 1 > n$, the corresponding child does not exist (see Figure 15).

In Gonnet & Munro [1986] it is shown that in an n-item implicit heap, an item can be inserted surprisingly fast, namely with O(log log n) comparisons; *deletemin* takes O(log n) steps. Due to their fixed structure, however, implicit heaps do not support all concatenable queue operations very efficiently. Let us therefore look at more relaxed explicit collections of heaps.

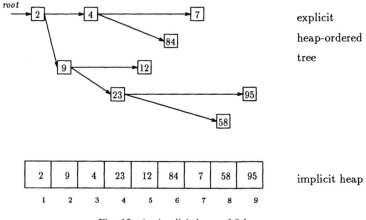

explicit

heap-ordered

tree

implicit heap

Fig. 15. An implicit heap of 9 keys.

3.2. Pairing heaps

The *pairing heap* [Fredman, Sedgewick, Sleator & Tarjan, 1986] realizes a concatenable queue by a collection of heap-ordered trees, in general not binary trees. A primitive for combining two heap-ordered trees is *linking*: the root of larger key is made a child of the root of smaller key (see Figure 16); the result is one heap-ordered tree.

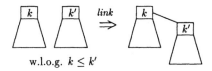

w.l.o.g. $k \leq k'$

Fig. 16. Linking two heap-ordered trees.

To implement pairing heaps efficiently, let us maintain such a heap-ordered tree in the *binary tree representation* [Knuth, 1973a], also called the *child–sibling representation* [Fredman, Sedgewick, Sleator & Tarjan, 1986]. In the heap-ordered tree, consider the children of each node to be ordered, and let us refer to the order as *age*. In the binary tree representation, each node has a left and a right pointer; the left pointer points to the node's first child, and the right pointer points to the node's next older sibling. For a heap-ordered tree, this representation leads to a binary tree where the key in each node is no greater than any key in its left subtree (see Figure 17) – we call the binary tree *half-ordered*. The root of the binary tree has an empty right subtree. In addition, each node has a parent pointer to make *decreasekey* and *delete* operations efficient.

The concatenable queue operations can then be carried out as follows,

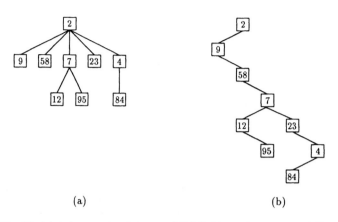

Fig. 17. (a) A heap-ordered tree, and (b) its binary tree representation.

expressed in terms of heap-ordered trees:

initialize(p)   : make *p* the empty tree;
insert(i, p)   : make a tree of one node for item *i*, and link it with tree
                        p;
isempty(p)   : return true, if *p* is the empty tree, and false otherwise;
min(p)   : return the root of tree *p*;
meld(p, q)   : link *p* and *q*, and let *p* be the resulting tree;
decreasekey(i, k, p) : set the key of item *i* to value *k*; if *i* is not the root, *cut*
                        the edge joining *i* to its parent, and *link* the two trees
                        formed by the cut;
delete(k, p)   : the node *i* with key *k* must be given; if node *i* is the root
                        of tree *p*, perform *deletemin(p)*; otherwise, *cut* the edge
                        joining *i* to its parent, perform a *deletemin* on the tree
                        rooted at *i*, and *link* the resulting tree with the other
                        tree formed by the cut;
deletemin(p)   : remove the root of the tree; this produces a collection of
                        heap-ordered trees, one for each child of the former
                        root; combine these trees with the *pairing method* de-
                        scribed below.

   The *pairing method* for combining heap-ordered trees, rooted at the children
of a (former) common parent (the deleted root in a *deletemin operation*),
considers the trees in the order in which they have been linked to their parent.
This information is maintained in each heap-ordered tree by always making a
newly linked node the new first child of its parent; i.e., for each node, the first
child is the most recently linked one, and all children are ordered according to
their linking date. The pairing method links the first and second child, the third
and fourth child, and so on, of the deleted root; starting from *j* trees (the
deleted node had *j* children), this leaves us with $\lceil j/2 \rceil$ trees $t_1, \ldots, t_{\lceil j/2 \rceil}$. Now

link each remaining tree to the last one, in reverse order of the first linking pass; i.e., link to $t_{\lceil j/2 \rceil}$ first $t_{\lceil j/2 \rceil - 1}$, then $t_{\lceil j/2 \rceil - 2}$, and so on, until t_1 is linked and all trees have thus been combined into one (see Figure 18).

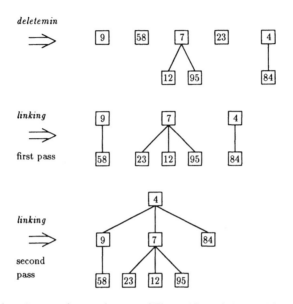

Fig. 18. A *deletemin* operation on the tree of Figure 17a and the resulting linking passes.

The linking passes in the combination of subtrees of a deleted root have been chosen carefully with the aim of achieving an amortized runtime of $O(\log n)$ for a *delete* or a *deletemin* operation in a pairing heap of n items, and $O(1)$ for all other operations. These amortized bounds, however, have only been conjectured, but not proved [Fredman, Sedgewick, Sleator & Tarjan, 1986]; they have been proved to hold in case no *decreasekey* operations are performed [Stasko & Vitter, 1987]. With *decreasekey*, pairing heaps are known to support *initialize*, *isempty*, and *min* in $O(1)$ and all other operations in $O(\log n)$ amortized runtime [Fredman, Sedgewick, Sleator & Tarjan, 1986]. This can be seen by observing that in the half-ordered binary tree representation, the linking after a *deletemin* has essentially the effect of a splay, and by using the same bank account balance function as for splay trees (see Section 2.3.3.1) in a similar amortized analysis [Fredman, Sedgewick, Sleator & Tarjan, 1986].

Since *decreasekey* is a frequent operation in algorithms of interest, we do not content ourselves with these amortized bounds. Even though pairing heaps seem to be a good practical concatenable queue, other data structures with better, known amortized costs (Fibonacci-heaps [Fredman & Tarjan, 1987]) or even worst-case costs (relaxed heaps [Driscoll, Sarnak, Sleator & Tarjan, 1988]) exist. Relaxed heaps achieve the bounds conjectured for pairing heaps, even in the worst case per operation.

3.3. Relaxed heaps

Relaxed heaps are based on *binomial trees* and *binomial queues* [Vuillemin, 1978].

3.3.1. Binomial queues and relaxed heap structure

A *binomial tree* of type B_r, $r \geq 1$, is a tree consisting of two trees of type B_{r-1}, where the root of one is the last child of the other; B_0 is a single node (see Figure 19).

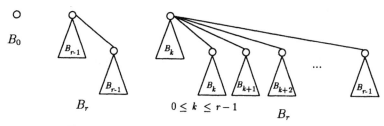

Fig. 19. Binomial trees: two equivalent illustrations.

The *rank* of a node v in a binomial tree is the index r of the (maximal) subtree of type B_r rooted at v, or, equivalently, the number of children of v. Children in a binomial tree are *ordered* by increasing rank; the *first child* is depicted left-most, the *last child* (the child of highest rank) rightmost. A *binomial queue* of n nodes is a collection of binomial trees B_i, one for each position i in the binary representation of n in which the bit value is 1; since a tree B_i has 2^i nodes, the number of nodes adds up to n. To make *decreasekey* operations as efficient as possible, relaxed heaps do not insist on the heap condition for all keys in binomial trees. A node v that violates the heap condition with its parent w, i.e., for which $v.key < w.key$, is called *bad*, all other nodes are called *good*. In our subsequent arguments, we use a superset of all bad nodes, the set of *active* nodes, since a bad node may happen to become good as a side-effect of an operation. A *relaxed binomial tree* is a binomial tree in which some nodes are *active*, and any bad node is active. A *relaxed heap* (*run relaxed heap* in Driscoll, Sarnak, Sleator & Tarjan [1988]) is a collection of τ relaxed binomial trees with a total of n nodes, where $\tau \leq \lfloor \log n \rfloor + 1$ and the total number α of active nodes is at most $\lfloor \log n \rfloor$.

Technically, each node of a relaxed heap has a *rank* field and pointers to its last child, its two neighboring siblings, and its parent, in addition to the stored item with its key. A dummy node ρ is the root of the entire collection of binomial trees; the root of each binomial tree is a child of ρ. Figure 20 shows a relaxed heap of 25 items. It consists of $\tau = 4 \leq \lfloor \log n \rfloor + 1 = 5$ trees and has $\alpha = 4 \leq \lfloor \log n \rfloor = 4$ active nodes, depicted as boxes in Figure 20. Undirected edges are pointers in both directions; directed edges point in only one direction. *Sibling* pointers go horizontally, *parent* pointers go up, and *last child* pointers go down. *Rank* fields are not shown.

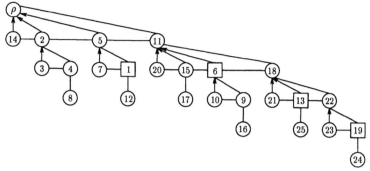

Fig. 20. A relaxed heap of 25 items.

For the purpose of guaranteeing $\tau \leqslant \lfloor \log n \rfloor + 1$, we keep a *tree pointer* T_r for each rank $r, 0 \leqslant r \leqslant \lfloor \log n \rfloor$, to a binomial tree with a rank r root. Pairs of trees with the same rank are not referenced by T_r, but instead kept in a doubly linked *tree pair list*. In the example of Figure 20, T_4 points to node 11, the only rank 4 root; T_0 points to node 14, while nodes 5 and 2 are the only pair entry in the pair list (T_1, T_2, and T_3 are **nil**-pointers).

3.3.2. Relaxed heap operations

We will treat in detail only *insert*, *deletemin*, *delete*, *min*, and *decreasekey*; the other operations are similar. We will use the relaxed heap in Figure 20 as our running example.

3.3.2.1. Insert.

To insert an item with key k, we make a B_0-tree for this item, and then *add* the B_0-tree to the relaxed heap.

To *add* a B_r-tree to a relaxed heap, we check the T_r pointer: if it is **nil**, we let it point to B_r. Otherwise, we have a pair of trees of equal rank, namely B_r and the tree referenced by T_r, that we add to the tree pair list; then, T_r is set to **nil**. After adding the new B_0-tree to the relaxed heap, we try to decrease the number of trees by *pairing* two trees into one.

We *pair* two relaxed binomial trees of equal rank by removing a pair from the tree pair list, *linking* the corresponding trees to a new tree, and *adding* the new tree to the relaxed heap.

We *link* two binomial trees of equal rank by making the tree whose root has the larger key the last child of the root with the smaller key.

In the example of Figure 20, adding an item with key 26 first creates a new B_0-tree with key 26 in its single node. Since there is already a B_0-tree ($T_0 \neq$ **nil**), the two trees are added to the pair list, and T_0 is set to **nil**. We then remove a pair from the pair list, say the rank 2 pair with roots 5 and 2, and link the two trees, giving a rank 3 tree with root 2. Since there is no single rank 3 tree yet ($T_3 =$ **nil**) we add the rank 3 tree by letting T_3 point to it. As a result, we get the relaxed heap of Figure 21.

Hence, by performing only one linking operation per insertion, we arrive at

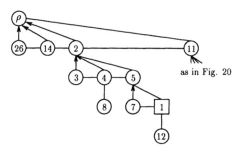

Fig. 21. Insertion into a relaxed heap.

a worst-case cost of $O(1)$ for inserting an item into a relaxed heap. An insertion does not change the number of bad nodes, i.e., $\alpha \leqslant \lfloor \log n \rfloor$ is preserved. An insertion may increase the number τ of trees by one. However, τ cannot grow beyond $\lfloor \log n \rfloor + 1$ since $\tau > \lfloor \log n \rfloor + 1$ implies that the pair list contains an entry, and linking a pair of trees decreases τ by one, making it equal to the value of τ before insertion.

3.3.2.2. Deletemin, delete, and min. Before deleting the minimum, we first find it by scanning through all roots of binomial trees and through all active nodes. Let v be the node storing the minimum key.

To *delete* a node v from a relaxed heap, we proceed as follows. If v is the root of a binomial tree, for each child v' of v, we *add* the subtree rooted at v' to the collection of trees and *pair* two trees in the tree pair list, if possible; then, the tree rooted at v is *removed* from the collection. *Removing* a tree with root v of rank r from the collection implies adjusting T_r and the tree pair list, if necessary: if the tree is in the tree pair list, let w be the root of its partner in the pair. Delete the pair from the list, and let T_r point to w. Otherwise, i.e., for v not in the tree pair list, T_r points to v; in this case, set T_r to **nil**. Since the maximum rank of any node in a relaxed heap of n nodes is $\lfloor \log n \rfloor$, the runtime for deleting a root node is $O(\log n)$. By the same arguments as for insert, τ cannot grow beyond $\lfloor \log n \rfloor + 1$, and the number of active nodes cannot increase (it can decrease however).

If the node v storing the item with minimum key is not the root of a binomial tree, it must be an active node. We take a root x of least rank and *delete* it. Then we replace v by x in the following way. We successively *link* the single node x and all children of v in the order of increasing rank, i.e., we repeatedly *link* the two trees of smallest rank. The two trees of smallest rank have the same rank, since the children of v have ranks $0, 1, \ldots$ up to the rank of v. This linking procedure ends with a tree that replaces the subtree rooted at v. By the same arguments as above, the resulting relaxed heap is found in $O(\log n)$ steps in the worst case.

Note that the *delete* procedure in a *deletemin* operation can be used to *delete* any given node in a tree. For instance, in the example of Figure 20, deletion of node 18 is carried out by linking the trees rooted at nodes 21 and 14, 14 and 13,

13 and 22, and then replacing the subtree with root 18 by the subtree with root 13 (this changes node 13 from bad to good).

We still need to show how active nodes can be scanned efficiently. To keep track of active nodes for *deletemin* and also for *decreasekey*, we distinguish two situations for active nodes. A consecutive sequence of at least two active siblings is called a *run*; an active node that is not in a run is called a *singleton*. Each active node is *marked* by an *active bit*. For each rank *r*, we maintain a *singleton list* S_r of rank *r* singletons. With an intention similar to pairing trees, we store in a *node pair list* all ranks with at least two singletons. Each run is represented by its node of largest rank in the run; these nodes are stored in a *run list*. All lists are doubly linked, and there is a two-way link between each node and its occurrence in a list (if any). The lists together are called the *run-singleton structure*. It is straightforward, but lengthy, to describe how the run-singleton structure can be updated when nodes are rearranged or bad nodes become good or good nodes become bad. We will leave the details to the reader and assume that all necessary run-singleton structure updates are performed in all operations. In a *deletemin* operation, active nodes can be found by scanning the singleton lists of all ranks and the run list. For each node in the run list, the other nodes of the run can be found by following sibling pointers in the respective binomial tree. Since there are·at most $\lfloor \log n \rfloor$ active nodes, a node of minimum key can be found (operation *min*) in $O(\log n)$ steps in the worst case. Hence, the total worst-case runtime for a *deletemin* operation is $O(\log n)$.

3.3.2.3. Decreasekey. The *decreasekey* operation is of special importance, since its worst-case time bound of $O(1)$ that we will show to hold is instrumental for the efficiency of many network algorithms. For instance, in the version of Dijkstra's algorithm presented in Section 1, $O(|E|)$ *decreasekey* operations may be performed, but only $O(|V|)$ *deletemin* and *insert* operations. Relaxed heaps are therefore suitable for implementing Dijkstra's algorithm in worst-case time $O(|E| + |V| \log |V|)$, since at most $|V|$ items are ever in the relaxed heap.

In a *decreasekey* operation, the node *v* of the item whose key must be decreased to its new value *k* is given. *Decreasekey* first sets the key in *v* to *k*. Then it checks whether by this change *v* has become bad and, at the same time, if the number α of active nodes has increased above $\lfloor \log n \rfloor$. If so, a *transform* is carried out; otherwise, the decreasekey operation terminates with a correct relaxed heap.

The *transform* operation serves to restore the condition that $\alpha \leq \lfloor \log n \rfloor$ in a situation where $\alpha = \lfloor \log n \rfloor + 1$. It does so by fixed restructuring operations in the relaxed heap that decrease the number of active nodes by one. If the node pair list is not empty, a rank *r* is removed from it, and a *singleton transformation* as described below is performed for the first two nodes *v* and v' in the singleton list S_r. This reduces α by at least one. If S_r still contains two nodes or more after the singleton transformation, *r* is added to the node pair list. If the run list is not empty, a node v is removed from the run list, and a *run transformation* as described below is performed for the run ending at v. If this leaves one or more nodes of the previous run, the appropriate update to the singleton list or the run list is made. Since $\alpha = \lfloor \log n \rfloor + 1$, either a singleton transformation or a run transformation can be performed. We will show that each transformation carries out $O(1)$ steps in the worst case and reduces α by at least one; this will complete the description of the *decreasekey* operation. As in the other operations, updates of the run-singleton structure are not described explicitly. Both transformations do not change the collection of binomial trees in the relaxed heap, hence we do not incur costs for updating tree pair lists and tree pointers.

In any transformation, we may assume w.l.o.g. that all considered active nodes are actually bad. Otherwise, we would simply change the state of an active good node to *not active*, thereby decreasing α, and terminate the transformation.

For two active singleton nodes v and v' of equal rank r, let p and p' (g and g') be the parent (grandparent) of v and v', respectively. A *singleton transformation* distinguishes three cases, depending on whether *both* v and v', *one* of v and v', or *none* are last children:

(both) Both v and v' are last children (Figure 22); in the example of Figure 20, choose nodes 1 and 19 for v and v'. Apply a *pair transformation* to v and v'. A *pair transformation* removes v and v' from their parents, so p and p' both have rank r. W.l.o.g. assume $p.key \leqslant p'.key$. Make p' the rank-r child of p; this makes p a rank-$(r+1)$ node. Link v and v' to form a B_{r+1}-tree with root $min(v, v')$ and rank-r son $max(v, v')$, where $min(v, v')$ is a node of smallest key among v and v', and $max(v, v')$ is the other. Make $min(v, v')$ the rank-$(r+1)$ son of g'. This makes $max(v, v')$ good, and it possibly makes $min(v, v')$ good as well, but not necessarily. Also, p' is good, no matter whether it was bad before the transformation. All other nodes' states are unchanged (see Figure 22, where $\square$ denotes a bad node, $\bigcirc$ denotes a good node, and $\boxdot$ denotes a node that may be good or bad). Altogether, the number of active nodes decreases by at least one.

(one) Exactly one of v and v' is not a last child. W.l.o.g. assume v is not a last child and v' is. Then v has a rank-$(r+1)$ sibling s. Since v is a singleton, s is good. Let c be the last child of s. We distinguish whether c is bad (see Figure 23) or good (see Figure 24).

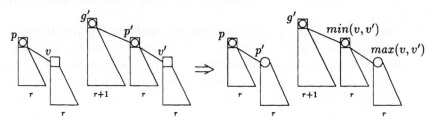

Fig. 22. A pair transformation for v, v', with $p.key \leqslant p'.key$.

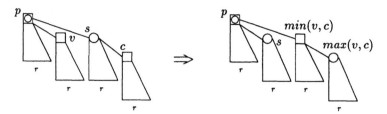

Fig. 23. A pair transformation for v, c.

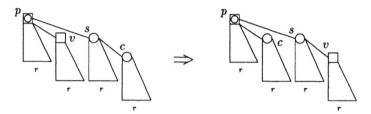

Fig. 24. Exchanging trees to make v last child.

(c bad) In the example of Figure 20, choose nodes 13, 22, 19, and 1 for $v, s, c,$ *and* v', respectively. Apply a *pair transformation* to v and c. The effect is illustrated in Figure 23. The number of active nodes decreases by one.

(c good) In the example of Figure 20, choose nodes 6, 18, 22, and 1 for $v, s, c,$ and v', respectively. Exchange the B_r-trees rooted at v and at c (see Figure 24). The number of active nodes is unchanged but v is now last child of its parent. Hence, v and v' are both last children, and a *pair transformation* for v and v' [see Case (both)] decreases α by one.

(none) None of v and v' is a last child; in the example of Figure 20, choose nodes 13 and 6 for v and v', respectively. Process v as in Case (one). If the pair transformation [Case (c bad)] applied, it decreased α by one, and the singleton transformation terminates. Otherwise, process v' as in Case (one). Again, if the pair transformation applied, it decreased α by one, and the singleton transformation terminates. Otherwise, the pair transformation applies to v and v', since they are both last children, and decreases α by one, terminating the singleton transformation.

Hence, singleton transformation is guaranteed to decrease α by at least one. Note that a pair transformation is applicable even if v or v' are in a run, and that Cases (one) and (none) may actually use this property when resorting to the pair transformation after a rearrangement of nodes. In all cases, the run-singleton structure can be updated without difficulty.

A *run transformation* is applied if no singleton transformation is applicable. Let v be the largest rank child of a run, having rank r, parent p, and grandparent g. Let t be the rank-$(r-1)$ sibling of v; since v is last in a run, t is active. As in the sibling transformation, an active node that is not bad decreases α by one, with changes only to the run-singleton structure. That is, w.l.o.g. t and v are bad. Distinguish whether v is a last child or not:

(last) is the last child of p (see Figure 25). Cut t and v from p; p and t are now the roots of B_{r-1}-trees. Link p and t; t is the root of the created B_r-tree. Link t and v; this makes $min(t, v)$ the root of the B_{r+1}-tree. Replace p as the rank-$(r+1)$ son of g by $min(t, v)$. This transformation changes the number of bad nodes among p, t, and v from at least two to at most one; hence, α decreases by at least one.

(not last) v is not the last child of p (see Figure 26). Then v has a rank-$(r+1)$ sibling s. Since v is last in its run, s is good. Let a be the rank-$(r-1)$ child and b the rank-r child of s, respectively. Cut a and b from s, and cut t, v, and s from p. Make a and b the rank-$(r-1)$ and rank-r children of p, respectively. Now link the B_{r-1}-trees rooted at t and s, and link the resulting

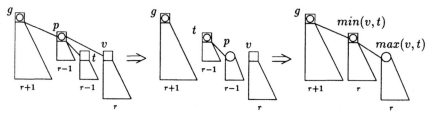

Fig. 25. Run transformation for active last child.

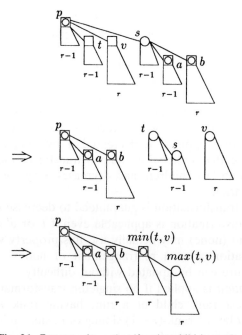

Fig. 26. Run transformation if active child is not last.

B_r-tree rooted at t with the tree rooted at v. The number of bad nodes among t and v decreases from two to at most one, since $min(t, v)$ may remain bad; s remains good. Because s was good, a and b do not change their states (active or not), and therefore α decreases by at least one.

This completes our description of transformations applied to maintain a relaxed heap under *decreasekey* operations.

To summarize, relaxed heaps support the operations *insert* and *decreasekey* in time $O(1)$ and the operations *min*, *delete*, and *deletemin* in time $O(\log n)$ for an n-item relaxed heap in the worst case.

In Driscoll, Gabow, Shrairman & Tarjan [1988] it is demonstrated how relaxed heaps can be used to implement various network algorithms on parallel computers. Fibonacci heaps [Fredman & Tarjan, 1987] are an alternative to relaxed heaps in many network optimization algorithms (single-source shortest paths, all-pairs shortest paths, weighted bipartite matching, minimum spanning trees), because worst-case time bounds are no better than amortized time bounds for sequences of operations performed in algorithms. If the keys to be stored in the priority queue are known to be of moderate size, better solutions for single operations and for sequences of operations are possible. An interesting structure, the *radix heap* [Ahuja, Mehlhorn, Orlin & Tarjan, 1990], supports Dijkstra's algorithm for single-source shortest paths in time $O(m + n\sqrt{\log C})$, where C is maximum of the nonnegative integer edge costs of the given graph.

4. Set union algorithms

In the previous sections, we have seen how one set of elements can be maintained so as to support various operations. The need for maintaining a collection of sets has been illustrated in Section 1 at the example of Kruskal's algorithm. Certainly, a collection of data structures for sets can be used for this purpose, depending on the operations that need to be performed on single sets. For instance, *join* and *split* for splay trees have already been described in Section 2.3.3.2. In Port & Moffat [1989], an algorithm for *melding* splay trees is presented that works in time $O(n \log n)$ for any sequence of $n - 1$ meld operations, performed on a collection of n single node splay trees initially; a *meld* operation creates a splay tree containing the union of two sets of elements stored in two given splay trees. While this performance is optimal for creating a splay tree of n elements – they can be sorted by reading them off the splay tree in inorder in linear additional time – it need not be optimal if searching for keys is not required. Other structures, like level-linked finger search trees in the red–black variety [Tarjan & van Wyk, 1988] or in a multiway variety [Huddleston & Mehlhorn, 1982], as well as concatenable queue structures [e.g., Fredman & Tarjan, 1987], support split, join, and meld operations efficiently.

If *makeset*, *findlabel*, and *unite* are the only operations, like in Kruskal's algorithm, fairly straightforward techniques may sometimes be good enough, and algorithmically simple methods are best possible [Tarjan & van Leeuwen, 1984]. In an algorithm for the set union problem, we represent each set with an arbitrary, but fixed element, called the *canonical element* of the set. The label of a set is associated with the canonical element. Operations *findlabel* and *unite* can be carried out by using two operations on sets with canonical elements:

find(*i*)   : return the canonical element of the set containing *i*;
link(*i*, *j*) : combine the two sets whose canonical elements are *i* and *j* into one
                set whose canonical element is either *i* or *j*; the label of the new set
                is the label of the former set containing *i*.

The restriction on *makeset*, requiring that a new element must not already be in a set, ensures that sets are disjoint, and hence canonical elements of different sets are different. The operations *findlabel* and *unite* can immediately be expressed through *find* and *link*:

findlabel(*i*) : return the label of *find*(*i*);
unite(*i*, *j*)   : *link*(*find*(*i*), *find*(*j*)).

Find operations are supported by implementing each set as a rooted tree, where each node is a set element and the root is the canonical element; each node *i* has a pointer *i.parent* to its parent, and the root points to itself. Figure 27 depicts two trees for two sets of 13 and 14 elements. In the example of Figure 27, *find*(*x*) = *find*(*w*) = *find*(*u*) = *u* ≠ *v* = *find*(*v*) = *find*(*y*).

The operations on this *compressed tree* representation [Galler & Fisher, 1964] can be implemented as follows:

makeset(*i*, *l*) : {naive}
                i.parent := *i*;
                i.label := *l*;

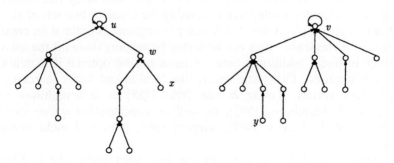

Fig. 27. Two compressed trees.

find(*i*)   : {naive}
            if *i.parent* = *i* **then**
                find := *i*
            else *find* := *find*(*i.parent*);
link(*i*, *j*)   : {naive}
            j.parent := *i*.

Let n denote the number of *makeset*, m the number of *find* and k the number of *link* operations. To analyze the worst-case behavior of a sequence of operations, note that each *makeset* and *link* costs $O(1)$ time. A *find* in general costs time proportional to the number of nodes on a find path, i.e., $O(n)$. Now consider a sequence of *makeset*, *find*, and *link* operations; clearly, $k \leq n - 1$. After k *link* operations, at most $2k$ elements are not in singleton sets; since a *find* in a singleton set costs $O(1)$ time, assume w.l.o.g. that $2k \geq n$ – intuitively speaking, elements that remain in singleton sets do not contribute to the worst case. If the sequence of operations results from a sequence of *makeset*, *findlabel*, and *unite* operations, as in Kruskal's algorithm, each *link* needs two *finds*, i.e., $m \geq 2k$; since $2k \geq n$, we get $m \geq n$. In total, n *makeset*, m *find*, and k *link* operations can be carried out in time $O(n + mn + k) = O(n + mn)$; we do not assume $m \geq n$ here. By building a tree that is a path of n nodes and then performing m find operations on it, we can see that this bound is tight [Fisher, 1972] for the described algorithm.

A lower bound for the set union problem in the pointer machine model has been based on the *separation assumption*: loosely speaking, there are pointers between elements of the same set, but no pointer leads from one set to the other [Banachowski, 1980; Tarjan, 1979; Tarjan & van Leeuwen, 1984]. It has been shown that any set union algorithm obeying the separation assumption must require $\Omega(n + m\alpha(m + n, n))$ time in the worst case, where α is the functional inverse of Ackermann's function [Ackermann, 1929]. Ackermann's function $A(i, j)$ for $i, j \geq 1$ is defined as:

$$A(i, j) = \begin{cases} 2^j & \text{if } i = 1, \ j \geq 1, \\ A(i - 1, 2) & \text{if } i \geq 2, \ j = 1, \\ A(i - 1, A(i, j - 1)) & \text{if } i, j \geq 2. \end{cases}$$

Its functional inverse α is $\alpha(m, n) = \min\{i \geq 1 \mid A(i, \lfloor m/n \rfloor) > \log n\}$; for all practical purposes, α is a constant no larger than four. The separation assumption can imply a loss of efficiency, as compared with a general pointer machine algorithm [Mehlhorn, Näher & Alt, 1988]. In La Poutré [1990], the lower bound has been generalized to arbitrary pointer machine algorithms, without the separation assumption.

Note that the gap between the upper bound for set union derived from the proposed naive algorithm and the lower bound is considerable. Various techniques have been suggested to speed up the naive algorithm by making find paths shorter; we will have a closer look at methods that reduce path lengths in connection with *link* and in connection with *find* operations.

4.1. Path length reduction during link

4.1.1. Link by size

We use the freedom in the operation $link(i, j)$ to let either i point to j or else j point to i as follows: let the root of the smaller tree point to the root of the larger tree. In the example of Figure 27, make v the new parent of u. This is called *linking by size* or *weighted union* [Galler & Fisher, 1964]. If a field *size* of a root node stores the tree size, *makeset* and *link* can be described as follows (*find* is not affected):

$makeset(i, l)$: {link by size}
           $i.parent := i$;
           $i.label := l$;
           $i.size := 1$;
$link(i, j)$: {link by size}
           if $i.size \geq j.size$ **then**
               $j.parent := i$;
               $i.size := i.size + j.size$
           else
               $i.parent := j$;
               $j.size := i.size + j.size$;
               $j.label := i.label$.

After a sequence of *link by size* operations, starting with singleton sets, for each node i, $i.size \geq 2^{i.rank}$, where $i.rank$ is the maximum number of nodes on any path from a leaf to i (i.e., the height of the subtree rooted at i). This can be seen easily by induction on the number of *link* operations: it is true before the first *link*, and each *link* that increases the rank of i by letting j point to i also increases the size of i, to at least twice the size of j. As a consequence, no find path has length exceeding $\log n$. Hence, linking by size guarantees an upper bound of $O(\log n)$ for each *find*. Then, a sequence of n makeset, m find and k link operations can be performed in $O(n + m \log n + k) = O(n + m \log n)$ time. This bound can be seen to be tight by observing that a binomial tree (cf. Figure 19) B_i of size 2^i and height i can be constructed with any linking rule from two isomorphic trees B_{i-1}. Performing m find operations on the path of length $i = \lfloor \log n \rfloor - 1$ yields a bound of $\Theta(n + m \log n)$. This bound, although not optimal, is asymptotically satisfactory for Kruskal's algorithm, if a preparatory sorting step on the edge lengths is performed. Note, however, that the proposed implementation of Kruskal's algorithm is not the best one can do to compute minimum spanning trees; an algorithm similar to Dijkstra's shortest path algorithm can be made to run in time $O(m + n \log n)$, and even faster solutions exist [Fredman & Tarjan, 1987].

4.1.2. Link by rank

Linking by rank achieves the same effect as linking by size, but uses less storage space: instead of storing its size with each node, we store its rank. This brings the extra number of bits per node from log n (for storing numbers up to n) down to log log n (for storing numbers up to log n). In a *link* operation, we let the node of smaller rank point to the node of larger rank [Galler & Fisher, 1964]:

makeset(i, l) : {link by rank}
                 $i.parent := i$;
                 $i.label := l$;
                 $i.rank := 0$;
link(i, j) : {link by rank}
                 if $i.rank > j.rank$ **then**
                     $j.parent := i$;
                 elsif $i.rank = j.rank$ **then**
                     $j.parent := i$;
                     $i.rank := i.rank + 1$
                 else {$i.rank < j.rank$}
                     $i.parent := j$;
                     $j.label := i.label$.

In the example of Figure 27, make u the new parent of v. The runtime bounds derived for linking by size also hold for linking by rank, as can be seen with similar arguments [Galler & Fisher, 1964; Tarjan & van Leeuwen, 1984].

4.1.3. Collapsing during linking

Yet another way of making find paths shorter is *collapsing* during linking [Aho, Hopcroft & Ullman, 1974], perhaps the most straightforward technique. Here, two trees are linked by making every node in one tree point to the root of the other (see Figure 28). Each *find* takes $O(1)$ time, but each link takes time proportional to the number of elements in one of the two sets. It should be clear that collapsing with linking by size or by rank takes time $O(n \log n + m)$ for the set union problem, with arbitrary m and n.

4.2. Path length reduction during find

In addition to keeping paths short by linking by size or rank, we may rearrange a tree during a *find* operation.

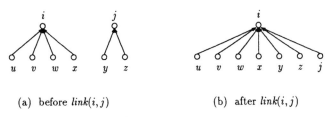

    (a) before *link*(i, j) (b) after *link*(i, j)

Fig. 28. Collapsing during linking.

4.2.1. Path compression

The *path compression* method due to McIlroy and Morris [Hopcroft & Ullman, 1973] changes all parent pointers on the find path to point to the root (see Figure 29):

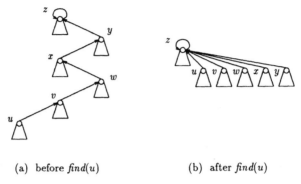

(a) before *find(u)*   (b) after *find(u)*

Fig. 29. Path compression.

find(i) : {compression}
    if *i.parent* = *i* **then**
        find := *i*
    else
        i.parent := *find(i.parent)*;
        find := *i.parent*.

The recursion corresponds to two scans along the find path in an iterative version of *find*. If path compression is used together with linking by rank, the rank value of a node gives only an upper bound on its height, namely the height the node would have without path compression.

Naive linking and path compression with $m = O(n)$ takes time $\Theta(n \log n)$ in the worst case; the lower bound is due to Fisher [1972], the upper bound to Paterson [Meyer & Fisher, 1973]. If each sequence of $n - 1$ link operations that unites n singleton sets into one set is equally likely, the expected performance is $O(n)$ [Yao, 1985]. In the worst case, for linking by size and path compression, a sequence of operations with $m \geqslant n$ has been shown to run in time $O(m\alpha(m, n))$ [Tarjan, 1975]; this is asymptotically optimal for pointer machines [LaPoutré, 1990].

To avoid the need for two passes over a find path, *path splitting* and *path halving* [van der Weide, 1980; van Leeuwen & van der Weide, 1977] have been proposed.

4.2.2. Path splitting

In *path splitting*, we let each node (except the two last ones on the path) point two nodes past itself (see Figure 30):

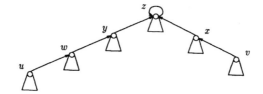

Fig. 30. Path splitting when *find(u)* is applied to Figure 29a.

find(i) : {path splitting}
  { *j* is a local variable}
  while *i.parent.parent* ≠ *i.parent* **do**
    j := *i.parent*;
    i.parent := *i.parent.parent*;
    i := *j*.

Splitting breaks a find path into two of roughly equal length.

4.2.3. Path halving

In *path halving*, we let every other node (except the two last ones on the path) point two nodes past itself (see Figure 31):

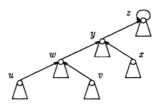

Fig. 31. Path halving when *find(u)* is applied to Figure 29a.

find(i) : {path halving}
    while *i.parent.parent* ≠ *i.parent* **do**
      i.parent := *i.parent.parent*;
      i := *i.parent*.

Halving needs only half as many pointer changes as splitting and keeps the nodes on the find path together; subsequent *find* operations may lead to shorter paths. Linking by rank or by size, combined with path compression, splitting or halving runs in time $O(n + m\alpha(m + n, n))$ for arbitrary m and n, and is therefore asymptotically optimal for pointer machines [La Poutré, 1990].

4.2.4. Reversals

Another method, *reversal* [van Leeuwen & van der Weide, 1977], turns out to be not as efficient, contrary to the first impression one might have. A *reversal of type 1* lets each node on the find path except the first and the last (the root) point to the first node, and lets the first node point to the root (see Figure 32):

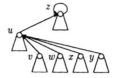

Fig. 32. Type-1 reversal when *find(u)* is applied to Figure 29a.

find(i) : {type-1 reversal}
        { *j, first* are local variables}
        first := *i*;
        while *i* ≠ *i.parent* **do**
            j := *i*;
            i := *i.parent*;
            j.parent := *first*;
        first.parent := *i*.

Combined with linking by rank or by size, type-1 reversal solves the set union problem for arbitrary *m* and *n* in time $O(n + m \log n)$, i.e., no better than linking alone [Tarjan & van Leeuwen, 1984]. Other types of reversals are discussed by Tarjan & van Leeuwen [1984]; although some are more interesting than type-1 reversal, none is asymptotically optimal.

In Tarjan & van Leeuwen [1984], additional set union algorithms obeying the separation assumption have been investigated; for practical applications, either halving or compression with linking by rank seems the method of choice. These methods achieve almost linear performance; it remains open, however, whether the general set union problem can be solved in linear time.

In the special case where the structure of the unions is known in advance, linear time for the disjoint set union problem can be achieved [Gabow & Tarjan, 1985]. The precondition here is that a *union tree* be given of which every node is in a singleton set initially; each *link* operation is restricted to link a node to its parent. Hence, sets and subtrees correspond; the root of a subtree is the canonical element of the set. A sequence of intermixed find and link operations can be carried out in linear time by taking advantage of the power of a random access machine. The applications of this special case of the set union problem – the *static tree set union* – are numerous: they cover scheduling and matching problems, and many more [Gabow & Tarjan, 1985].

The performance of general set union algorithms has been stated for sequences of operations rather than single operations. Until recently, in spite of the almost linear time complexity of a sequence of *findlabel* and *unite* operations, only algorithms with $\Omega(\log n)$ single operation complexity have been known. In Blum [1986], a data structure, the *union-find tree*, of size $O(n)$ has been proposed that supports each *unite* in time $O(f + \log_f n)$ and each *findlabel* in time $O(\log_f n)$; here, f is a parameter that may depend on n. The *improved union-find-tree* proposed by Smid [1990] achieves $O(f)$ time for *unite*, without changing the $O(\log_f n)$ time for findlabel and the size $O(n)$ of the data structure. For a very general class of data structures containing all pointer machine implementations, a single operation worst-case time bound of $O(g)$ for *unite* implies that there is a *findlabel* operation that needs time $\Omega(\log n/ (\log g + \log \log n))$ [Blum, 1986]. As a consequence, for each data structure in this class there is either a *findlabel* or a *unite* that takes $\Omega(\log n/\log \log n)$ time.

5. Concluding remarks

In this chapter, we have presented several fundamental data structures and operations. Instead of sketching a large number of results rather briefly, we have tried to describe a small number of techniques in detail so as to lay a foundation for the reader to invent his own problem-specific data structures and operations, and to study on his own more advanced methods found in the literature. As an example for the latter, we pick one of the settings that generalize the operations we have discussed so far.

The data structures presented in the preceding sections are *ephemeral* in the sense that a change to the data structure destroys the old version of the data structure. Even though parts of the old version of the structure may be unchanged, e.g., some subtree in a red–black tree after an insertion may be the same as before, operations referring to older versions cannot be handled. However, a number of algorithms, especially in computational geometry [Preparata & Shamos, 1985; Sarnak & Tarjan, 1986], operate on the versions that a data structure takes over a sequence of *insert* and *delete* operations, induced, e.g., by a sweeping line that cuts the plane into slices. We call a data structure *partially persistent* if it supports insertions and deletions in the present and search operations in the present and the past; it is *fully persistent* if it also supports insertions and deletions in the past. An introduction to the problem, with references to specific persistent data structures, can be found in Driscoll, Sarnak, Sleator & Tarjan [1989]. The fully general approaches described in Overmars [1981] either copy the entire data structure for each version, i.e., after each update operation, or store the entire sequence of update operations – they are assumed to be applied to the initially empty structure. In the former case, each update costs $\Omega(n)$ time and space in the worst case, where n is the total number of updates. In the latter case, for each operation the full sequence of updates is reconsidered to construct the appropriate version of the data structure, taking $\Omega(n)$ time in the worst case, even for search operations. Between these extremes, it is possible to store every kth version of the data structure, in addition to storing the full sequence of updates.

In Driscoll, Sarnak, Sleator & Tarjan [1989], a general technique is proposed for making ephemeral linked data structures persistent. All versions of the ephemeral structure are embedded in some way into one linked persistent structure. Instead of copying all nodes of the ephemeral linked structure, it is here sufficient to copy nodes that change; of course, all nodes that point to a copied node must also be copied. For instance, in a binary search tree, after each insertion a path from the root to the new leaf is copied; access to the appropriate root may be provided through an array of access pointers (see Figure 33).

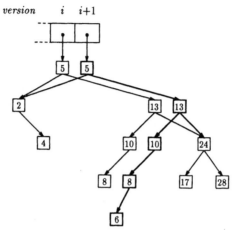

Fig. 33. Path copying: into version *i*, node 6 is inserted.

By growing nodes arbitrarily fat, a change to a node can be stored in the node itself; hence, pointers to changed nodes are not affected by the change. In arbitrarily fat nodes, searching for the pointer to follow is not a constant time operation; furthermore, an arbitrarily fat node must itself be implemented as a linked data structure. This overhead can be avoided by letting each node grow only by a constant amount of extra storage space, and by copying a node if it becomes too big. For instance, each node in a binary search tree may store its version number (time), a fixed number of *extra entries*, and a *copy pointer* linking the node to its copy, if any. An *extra entry* consists of a version number, a field name, and a value. Figure 34a shows the effect of an insertion of key 6 into the version-*i* tree, creating the version-$(i + 1)$ tree with node copying, and Figure 34b details node 8 with one extra entry.

The amortized cost for partial persistence obtained by node-copying for an arbitrary linked data structure is $O(1)$ additional space per update operation and a constant factor in access time per operation, provided that the number of pointers to any node is bounded by a constant [Driscoll, Sarnak, Sleator & Tarjan, 1989]. A variant of node copying achieves full persistence at the same extra cost [Driscoll, Sarnak, Sleator & Tarjan, 1989]. Node copying can be used to make red–black trees and finger search trees partially persistent [Driscoll, Sarnak, Sleator & Tarjan, 1989; Sarnak & Tarjan, 1986] with linear space (amortized constant space per operation) and logarithmic time per

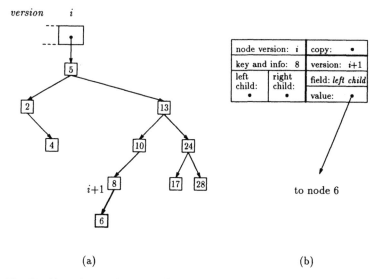

Fig. 34. (a) Node copying, and (b) a suitable node structure, detailing node 8.

operation in the worst case. Full persistence is achieved at a cost of linear space, logarithmic worst-case access time, and logarithmic amortized update time.

Acknowledgements

Thanks are due to Trudi Halboth for typesetting this chapter, and to Gabriele Reich for helpful discussions and for producing the figures.

References

Ackermann, W. (1929). Zum Hilbert'schen Aufbau der reellen Zahlen. *Math. Ann.* 99, 118–133.

Adel'son-Vel'skii, G.M., Y.M. Landis (1962). An algorithm for the organization of information. *Dokl. Akad. Nauk* 146, 263–266.

Aho, A.V., J.E. Hopcroft, J.D. Ullman (1974). *The Design and Analysis of Computer Algorithms*, Addison-Wesley, Reading, MA.

Aho, A.V., J.E. Hopcroft, J.D. Ullman (1983). *Data Structures and Algorithms*, Addison-Wesley, Reading, MA.

Ahuja, R.K., K. Mehlhorn, J.B. Orlin, R.E. Tarjan (1990). Faster algorithms for the shortest path problem. *J. Assoc. Comput. Mach.* 37, 213–223.

Allen, B., J.I. Munro (1978). Self-organizing binary search trees. *J. Assoc. Comput. Mach.* 25, 526–535.

Atkinson, M.D., J.-R. Sack, N. Santoro, T. Strothotte (1986). Min–max heaps and generalized priority queues. *Comm. Assoc. Comput. Mach.* 29, 996–1000.

Baase, S. (1988). *Computer Algorithms: Introduction to Design and Analysis, 2nd edition*, Addison-Wesley, Reading, MA.

Banachowski, L. (1980). A complement to Tarjan's result about the lower bound on the complexity of the set union problem. *Inform. Process. Let.* 11, 59–65.

Bayer, R. (1972). Symmetric binary B-trees: Data structure and maintenance algorithms. *Acta Inform.* 1, 290–306.

Bayer, R., E.M. McCreight (1972). Organization and maintenance of large ordered indexes. *Acta Inform.* 1, 173–189.

Bentley, J.L., C.C. McGeoch (1985). Amortized analysis of self-organizing sequential search heuristics. *Comm. Assoc. Comput. Mach.* 28, 405–411.

Bentley, J.L., D.D. Sleator, R.E. Tarjan, V.K. Wei (1986). A locally adaptive data compression scheme. *Comm. Assoc. Comput. Mach.* 29, 320–330.

Bitner, J.R. (1979). Heuristics that dynamically organize data structures. *SIAM J. Comput.* 8, 82–110.

Blum, N. (1986). On the single-operation worst-case time complexity of the disjoint set union problem. *SIAM J. Comput.* 15, 1021–1024.

Brassard, G., P. Bratley (1988). *Algorithmics: Theory and Practice*, Prentice-Hall, Englewood Cliffs, NJ.

Brown, M.R., R.E. Tarjan (1980). Design and analysis of a data structure for representing sorted lists. *SIAM J. Comput.* 9, 594–614.

Carter, J.L., M.N. Wegman (1979). Universal classes of hash functions. *J. Comput. System Sci.* 18, 143–154.

Chung, F.R., D.J. Hajela, P.D. Seymour (1988). Self-organizing sequential search and Hilbert's inequalities. *J. Comput. System Sci.* 36, 148–157.

Cole, R. (1990). On the dynamic finger conjecture for splay trees, *Proc. 27th Annual Symposium on Theory of Computing*, pp. 8–17.

Cook, S.A. (1982). An overview of computational complexity, Turing Award Lecture 1982, in: *ACM Turing Award Lectures: The First Twenty Years*, ACM, New York and Addison-Wesley, Reading, MA, 1987.

Cook, S.A., R.A. Reckhow (1973). Time-bounded random access machines. *J. Comput. System Sci.* 7, 354–375.

Cormen, T.H., C.E. Leiserson, R.L. Rivest (1990). *Introduction to Algorithms*, MIT Press, Cambridge, MA.

Dijkstra, E.W. (1959). A note on two problems in connexion with graphs, *Numer. Math.* 1 269–271.

Driscoll, J.R., H.N. Gabow, R. Shrairman, R.E. Tarjan (1988). Relaxed heaps: An alternative to Fibonacci heaps with applications to parallel computation. *Comm. Assoc. Comput. Mach.* 31, 1343–1354.

Driscoll, J.R., N. Sarnak, D.D. Sleator, R.E. Tarjan (1989). Making data structures persistent. *J. Comput. System. Sci.* 38, 86–124.

Enbody, R.J., H.C. Du (1988). Dynamic hashing schemes. *ACM Comput. Surveys* 20, 85–113.

Fisher, M.J. (1972). Efficiency of equivalence algorithms, in: R.E. Miller, J.W. Thatcher (eds.), *Complexity of Computer Computations*, Plenum Press, New York, pp. 153–168.

Floyd, R.W. (1964). Algorithm 245 (treesort). *Comm. Assoc. Comput. Mach.* 7, 701.

Fredman, M.L., R. Sedgewick, D.D. Sleator, R.E. Tarjan (1986). The pairing heap: A new form of self-adjusting heap. *Algorithmica* 1, 111–129.

Fredman, M.L., R.E. Tarjan (1987). Fibonacci heaps and their uses in improved network optimization algorithms. *J. Assoc. Comput. Mach.* 34, 596–615.

Gabow, H.N., R.E. Tarjan (1985). A linear-time algorithm for a special case of disjoint set union. *J. Comput. System Sci.* 30, 209–221.

Galler, B.A., M.J. Fisher (1964). An improved equivalence algorithm. *Comm. Assoc. Comput. Mach.* 7, 301–303.

Garsia, A.M., M.L. Wachs (1977). A new algorithm for minimum cost binary trees. *SIAM J. Comput.* 6, 622–642.

Gonnet, G.H., R. Baeza-Yates (1991). *Handbook of Algorithms and Data Structures, 2nd edition*, Addison-Wesley, Reading, MA.

Gonnet, G.H., J.I. Munro (1986). Heaps on heaps. *SIAM J. Comput.* 15, 964–971.

Gonnet, G.H., I. Munro, H. Suwanda (1981). Exegesis of self-organizing linear search. *SIAM J. Comput.* 10, 613–637.

Guibas, L.J., E.M. McCreight, M.F. Plass, J.R. Roberts (1977). A new representation for linear lists, *Proc. 9th Annual ACM Symp. on Theory of Comput.*, pp. 49–60.

Guibas, L.J., R. Sedgewick (1978). A dichromatic framework for balanced trees, *Proc. of the 19th Annual Symposium on Foundations of Computer Science*, pp. 8–21.

Harel, D. (1987). *Algorithmics: The Spirit of Computing*, Addison-Wesley, Reading, MA.

Hester, J.H., D.S. Hirschberg (1985). Self-organizing linear search. *ACM Comput. Surveys* 17, 295–311.

Hester, J.H., D.S. Hirschberg (1987). Self-organizing search using probabilistic back-pointers. *Comm. Assoc. Comput. Mach.* 30, 1074–1079.

Hoffmann, K., K. Mehlhorn, P. Rosenstiehl, R.E. Tarjan (1986). Sorting Jordan sequences in linear time using level-linked search trees. *Inf. Control* 68, 170–184.

Hopcroft, J.E., J.D. Ullman (1973). Set-merging algorithms. *SIAM J. Comput.* 2, 294–303.

Horowitz, E., S. Sahni (1983). *Fundamentals of Data Structures*, Computer Science Press, Rockville, MD.

Horowitz, E., S. Sahni (1984). *Fundamentals of Computer Algorithms*, Computer Science Press, Rockville, MD.

Hu, T.C., A.C. Tucker (1971). Optimal computer search trees and variable-length alphabetical codes. *SIAM J. Appl. Math.* 21, 514–532.

Huddleston, S., K. Mehlhorn (1982). A new data structure for representing sorted lists. *Acta Inform.* 17, 157–184.

Huffmann, D.A. (1952). A method for the construction of minimum redundancy codes. *Proc. IRE* 40, 1098–1101.

Icking, C., R. Klein, T. Ottmann (1987). Priority search trees in secondary memory, in: *Graphtheoretic Concepts in Computer Science, Staffelstein*, Lecture Notes in Computer Science 314, Springer, Berlin, 84–93.

Jones, D.W. (1988). Application of splay trees to data compression. *Comm. Assoc. Comput. Mach.* 31, 996–1007.

Kingston, J.H. (1988). A new proof of the Garsia–Wachs algorithm. *J. Algorithms* 9, 129–136.

Kingston, J.H. (1990). *Algorithms and Data Structures: Design, Correctness, Analysis*, Addison-Wesley, Reading, MA.

Knuth, D.E. (1971). Optimum binary search trees. *Acta Inform.* 1, 14–25.

Knuth, D.E. (1973a). *The Art of Computer Programming, Vol. I: Fundamental Algorithms*, 2nd edition, Addison-Wesley, Reading, MA.

Knuth, D.E. (1973b). *The Art of Computer Programming, Vol. III: Sorting and Searching*, Addison-Wesley, Reading, MA.

Knuth, D.E. (1981). *The Art of Computer Programming, Vol. II: Seminumerical Algorithms*, 2nd edition, Addison-Wesley, Reading, MA.

Kolmogorov, A.N. (1953). On the notion of algorithm. *Uspekhi Mat. Nauk* 8, 175–176.

Kolmogorov, A.N., V.A. Uspenskii (1958). On the definition of an algorithm. *Uspekhi Mat. Nauk* 13, 3–28; English translation in *Amer. Math. Soc. Transl. Ser. 2* 29, 1963, 217–245.

Kruskal, J.B. (1956). On the shortest spanning subtree of a graph and the traveling salesman problem. *Proc. Amer. Math. Soc.* 7, 48–50.

LaPoutré, J.A. (1990). Lower bounds for the union-find and the split-find problem on pointer machines, *Proc. 27th Annual Symposium on Theory of Computing*, pp. 34–44.

Lelewer, D.A., D.S. Hirschberg (1987). Data compression. *ACM Comput. Surveys* 19, 261–296.

Levcopoulos, C., M.H. Overmars (1988). A balanced search tree with O(1) worst-case update time. *Acta Inform.* 26, 269–277.

Lewis, H.R., L. Denenberg (1991). *Data Structures and their Algorithms*, Harper Collins Publishers, New York.

Maier, D., C. Salveter (1981). Hysterical B-trees. *Inform. Process. Lett.* 12, 199–202.

Manber, U. (1989). *Introduction to Algorithms: A Creative Approach*, Addison-Wesley, Reading, MA.

McCabe, J. (1965). On serial files with relocatable records. *Oper. Res.* 12, 609–618.

McCreight, E.M. (1985). Priority search trees. *SIAM J. Comput.* 14, 257–276.

Mehlhorn, K. (1984a). *Data Structures and Algorithms 1: Sorting and Searching*, Springer, Berlin.

Mehlhorn, K. (1984b). *Data Structures and Algorithms 2: Graph Algorithms and NP-Completeness*, Springer, Berlin.

Mehlhorn, K. (1984c). *Data Structures and Algorithms 3: Multidimensional Searching and Computational Geometry*, Springer, Berlin.

Mehlhorn, K., S. Näher, H. Alt (1988). A lower bound for the complexity of the union-find-split problem. *SIAM J. Comput.* 17, 1093–1102.

Meyer, A.R., M.J. Fisher (1973). MIT class notes, Course 6.851J, MIT Cambridge, MA.

Nievergelt, J., E.M. Reingold (1973). Binary search trees of bounded balance. *SIAM J. Comput.* 2, 33–43.

Nievergelt, J., C.K. Wong (1972). On binary search trees, *Proc. IFIP Congress 71*, North-Holland, Amsterdam, pp. 91–98.

Nievergelt, J., C.K. Wong (1973). Upper bounds for the total path length of binary trees. *J. Assoc. Comput. Mach.* 20, 1–6.

Olivié, H.J. (1982). A new class of balanced search trees: Halfbalanced search trees, *RAIRO Inform. Théor. Appl.* 16, 51–71.

Oommen, B.J., E.R. Hansen (1987). List organizing strategies using stochastic move-to-front and stochastic move-to-rear operations. *SIAM J. Comput.* 16, 705–716.

Oommen, B.J., E.R. Hansen, J.I. Munro (1990). Deterministic optimal and expedient move-to-rear list organizing strategies. *Theoret. Comput. Sci.* 74, 183–197.

Ottmann, T., H.-W. Six (1976). Eine neue Klasse von ausgeglichenen Bäumen. *Angew. Inf.* 18, 395–400.

Ottmann, T., D. Wood (1989). How to update a balanced binary tree with a constant number of rotations, *2nd Scandinavian Workshop on Algorithm Theory, Bergen, Norway*, Lecture Notes in Computer Science 447, Springer, Berlin, 1990, pp. 122–131.

Overmars, M.H. (1981). Searching in the past II: General transforms, Tech. Report RUU-CS-81-9, Department of Computer Science, Rijksuniversiteit Utrecht, Utrecht.

Papadakis, T., J.I. Munro, P.V. Poblete (1990). Analysis of the expected search cost in skip lists, *2nd Scandinavian Workshop on Algorithm Theory, Bergen, Norway*, Lecture Notes in Computer Science 447, Springer, Berlin, 1990, pp. 160–172.

Port, G., A. Moffat (1989). A fast algorithm for melding splay trees, *Workshop Algorithms and Data Structures, Ottawa, Canada*, Lecture Notes in Computer Science 382, Springer, Berlin, 1989, 450–459.

Preparata, F.P., M.I. Shamos (1985). *Computational Geometry: An Introduction*, Springer, Berlin.

Pugh, W. (1990). Skip lists: A probabilistic alternative to balanced trees. *Comm. Assoc. Comput. Mach.* 33, 668–676.

Rivest, R. (1976). On self-organizing sequential search heuristics. *Comm. Assoc. Comput. Mach.* 2, 63–67.

Sarnak, N., R.E. Tarjan (1986). Planar point location using persistent search trees. *Comm. Assoc. Comput. Mach.* 29, 669–679.

Schönhage, A. (1980). Storage modification machines. *SIAM J. Comput.* 9, 490–508.

Sedgewick, R. (1988). *Algorithms, 2nd edition*, Addison-Wesley, Reading, MA.

Sherk, M. (1989). Self-adjusting *k*-ary search trees, *Workshop Algorithms and Data Structures, Ottawa, Canada*, Lecture Notes in Computer Science 382, Springer, Berlin, pp. 381–392.

Sleator, D.D., R.E. Tarjan (1985a). Self-adjusting binary search trees. *J. Assoc. Comput. Mach.* 32, 652–686.

Sleator, D.D., R.E. Tarjan (1985b). Amortized efficiency of list update and paging rules. *Comm. Assoc. Comput. Mach.* 28, 202–208.

Smid, M.H.M. (1990). A data structure for the union-find problem having good single-operation complexity. *Algorithms Rev.* 1, 1–11.

Standish, T.A. (1980). *Data Structure Techniques*, Addison-Wesley, Reading, MA.

Stasko, J.T., J.S. Vitter (1987). Pairing heaps: Experiments and analysis. *Comm. Assoc. Comput. Mach.* 30, 234–249.

Tarjan, R.E. (1975). Efficiency of a good but not linear set union algorithm. *J. Assoc. Comput. Mach.* 22, 215–225.

Tarjan, R.E. (1979). A class of algorithms which require nonlinear time to maintain disjoint sets. *J. Comput. System Sci.* 18, 110–127.

Tarjan, R.E. (1983a). *Data Structures and Network Algorithms*, Society for Industrial and Applied Mathematics, Philadelphia, Pennsylvania.

Tarjan, R.E. (1983b). Updating a balanced search tree in O(1) rotations. *Inform. Process. Lett.* 16, 253–257.

Tarjan, R.E. (1985a). Amortized computational complexity. *SIAM J. Alg. Disc. Meth.* 6, 306–318.

Tarjan, R.E. (1985b). Sequential access in splay trees takes linear time. *Combinatorica 5*, 367–378.

Tarjan, R.E., J. Van Leeuwen (1984). Worst-case analysis of set union algorithms. *J. Assoc. Comput. Mach.* 31, 245–281.

Tarjan, R.E., C.J. Van Wyk (1988). An O(n log log n)-time algorithm for triangulating a simple polygon. *SIAM J. Comput.* 17, 143–178 and 1061.

Tsakalidis, A.K. (1985). AVL-trees for localized search. *Inform. and Control* 67, 173–194.

Turner, J.S. (1989). Approximation algorithms for the shortest common superstring problem. *Inform. and Comput.* 83, 1–20.

Van der Weide, T. (1980). *Datastructures: An Axiomatic Approach and the Use of Binomial Trees in Developing and Analyzing Algorithms*, Mathematisch Centrum, Amsterdam.

Van Leeuwen, J. (ed.) (1990). *Handbook of Theoretical Computer Science, Vol. A: Algorithms and Complexity*, North-Holland, Amsterdam and MIT Press, Cambridge, MA.

Van Leeuwen, J., M. Overmars (1983). Stratified balanced search trees. *Acta Inform.* 18, 345–359.

Van Leeuwen, J., T. Van der Weide (1977). Alternative path compression techniques, Tech. Report RUU-CS-77-3, Rijksuniversiteit Utrecht, Utrecht.

Vuillemin, J. (1978). A data structure for manipulating priority queues. *Comm. Assoc. Comput. Mach.* 21, 309–314.

Wirth, N. (1976). *Algorithms + Data Structures = Programs*, Prentice-Hall, Englewood Cliffs, NJ.

Williams, J.W.J. (1964). Algorithm 232 (heapsort). *Comm. Assoc. Comput. Mach.* 7, 347–348.

Yao, A.C. (1985). On the expected performance of path compression algorithms. *SIAM J. Comput.* 14, 129–133.

E.G. Coffman et al., Eds., *Handbooks in OR & MS, Vol. 3*

Chapter 8

Design (with Analysis) of Efficient Algorithms

Dan Gusfield

Department of Computer Science, University of California, Davis,
CA 95616, U.S.A.

1. Introduction

This chapter is an introduction to the design (with analysis) of efficient computer algorithms. The main theme of this chapter will be to illustrate the interelationship between mathematical insight, data structures, and the design (with analysis) of 'provably' efficient algorithms. The process of designing an efficient algorithm is interwoven with its analysis, the analysis of the data structures to be used, and often with the discovery of mathematical structure underlying the problem that the algorithm is to solve.

The approach taken in this chapter is an experiment. We have chosen not to survey the entire (huge) field of algorithmic design, for to do so would not permit rigorous treatment of any topic. We have chosen instead to discuss a large range of current and historical issues by focusing on a single set of related problems. We will look in detail at the task of calculating a *maximum flow* and a *minimum cut* in a network, along with several associated problems. The intention is not to provide a comprehensive or completely up-to-date discussion of network flow algorithms, but rather to use this focus as a means to discuss in some detail many major ideas in the design or analysis of efficient algorithms, and the computational models that these algorithms are designed for.

We will start with the most basic network flow algorithm for a sequential machine and show how it has been successively improved and changed by additional insights into the network flow problem itself, by new algorithmic ideas, by new data structures, by new methods of analysis, by changes in the accepted notion of 'efficiency', and by changes in the assumed computational model. In this way we will see how related questions are answered under most of the computational settings of current interest. We will discuss sequential algorithms, parallel algorithms, randomized algorithms, parametric algorithms, distributed algorithms, amortized time analysis, approximation algorithms, all-for-one results, results based on preprocessing, and strong versus weak polynomial time algorithms.

2. Maximum network flow on a sequential machine

In this first section we examine the problem of efficiently computing a maximum network flow and minimum-cut, where the computation is to be done on a sequential machine (RAM model) and the measure of goodness of an algorithm is its worst-case running time. We will follow in spirit an abridged history of the improvements, allowing us to illustrate the interplay between the unfolding mathematics of the flow problem, the data-structures proposed, and the resulting algorithmic ideas. However, the history will be apocryphal in places, and it will not detail sparse versions of the results, nor the most recent advances in this field. For a comprehensive discussion of these more recent improvements, see Goldberg, Tardos & Tarjan [1990] and Ahuja, Magnanti & Orlin [1989].

Definitions. Let $G = (N, E)$ be a *directed* graph on the set of nodes N and set of edges E, and let $c(i, j)$ be a positive real number on directed edge (i, j), called the *capacity* of (i, j). In our notation, the edge is directed from the first node in the pair to the second node. We designate two particular nodes s and t as the *source* and the *sink*, respectively. A *flow* f is an assignment of real numbers to edges such that the following conditions are satisfied:

(1) For every edge (i, j), $0 \leq f(i, j) \leq c(i, j)$. This is called the *capacity constraint*.

(2) For every node i other than s or t,

$$\sum_{j:\,(j,i)\in E} f(j, i) = \sum_{j:\,(i,j)\in E} f(i, j) .$$

In other words, the flow into i equals the flow out of i. This constraint is called the *conservation constraint*.

It is easy to prove that in any flow f, $\Sigma_i f(s, i) - \Sigma_i f(i, s) = \Sigma_i f(i, t) - \Sigma_i f(t, i)$, and we call this the *value* of flow f, and denote it by $f_{s,t}$, or by f when the source and sink are clear by context. Intuitively, the flow value is the net amount of flow that is sent out of s and also the net amount of flow that is received at t. We will henceforth assume that there are no edges directed into s or out of t, since such edges are useless in computing a maximum s, t flow. Consequently the flow value $f_{s,t} = \Sigma_i f(s, i) = \Sigma_i f(i, t)$.

An s, t *cut* of G is a partition (X, Y) of the nodes of G where $s \in X$ and $t \in Y$. The *capacity* of the cut (X, Y), denoted $C(X, Y)$, is the sum of the capacities of the edges directed from X to Y, i.e., $C(X, Y) = \Sigma_{i\in X, j\in Y} c(i, j)$. Given a flow f, and an s, t cut (X, Y), the net flow across the cut, denoted $f_{(X.Y)}$, is

$$\sum_{i\in X, j\in Y} f(i, j) - \sum_{i\in Y, j\in X} f(i, j) .$$

The connection between s, t flows and s, t cuts is very fundamental. The first fact, which follows immediately from the definitions, is that for any s, t cut (X, Y) and any s, t flow f, $f_{(X,Y)} \leq C(X, Y)$. That is, the net flow across any cut cannot exceed the capacity of the cut. The next fact, which is intuitive, is that for any s, t flow f and any s, t cut (X, Y), $f_{s,t} \leq f_{(X,Y)}$. That is, the flow from s to t cannot exceed the net flow across any s, t cut. This fact is physically intuitive, and we omit a formal proof of it, although in general in this field it is not a good idea to rely exclusively on physical intuition.

Combining the above two facts we have the following lemma and the theorem that follows immediately from it.

Lemma 2.1. *For any flow f and any s, t cut (X, Y), $f_{s,t} \leq C(X, Y)$.*

Theorem 2.1. *If there is an s, t cut (X, Y) and an s, t flow f such that $f_{(X,Y)} = C(X, Y)$, then f is a maximum s, t flow and (X, Y) is a minimum capacity s, t cut.*

In the next section we will show that the converse of this theorem also must hold.

2.1. First methods

A history of maximum flow algorithms will normally begin with the Ford–Fulkerson algorithm, although there were related mathematical theorems and even algorithmic methods that precede that method.

The Ford–Fulkerson method starts with an assignment of zero flow f to each edge, i.e., $f(i, j) = 0$ for each edge (i, j). At a general iteration of the algorithm there is a flow f which is not necessarily maximum. From that flow f, the algorithm constructs a graph G^f, called the *residual* graph of f, according to the following rules:

(1) If $f(i, j) > 0$, then create the edge (j, i) in G^f and assign it a capacity of $f(i, j)$. Edges of this type are called *backward* edges.

(2) If $f(i, j) < c(i, j)$, then create the edge (i, j) in G^f and assign it a capacity of $c(i, j) - f(i, j)$. Edges of this type are called *forward* edges.

Note that every edge in the residual graph has a strictly positive capacity. The residual graph is used to determine whether f is a maximum flow, and if not, to indicate how to augment the flow. These two tasks are accomplished in the Ford–Fulkerson algorithm by details suggested in the following theorem.

Theorem 2.2. *The flow f is a maximum s, t flow if and only if there is no directed path from s to t in G^f.*

Proof. Let S be the set of nodes which are reachable from s via some directed path in G^f, and let $T = V - S$.

Suppose first that $t \notin S$, so that (S, T) is an s, t cut. Consider the capacity of the cut. For every edge (i, j) in G where $i \in S$ and $j \in T$, it must be that

$f(i, j) = c(i, j)$, for otherwise edge (i, j) would be a forward edge in G^f and so j would be reachable from s and hence j would be in S. Similarly, for every edge (i, j) where $i \in T$ and $j \in S$, it must be that $f(i, j) = 0$, for otherwise edge (j, i) would be a backward edge in G^f and i would be in S. Hence

$$f_{(S,T)} = \sum_{i \in S, j \in T} f(i, j) - \sum_{i \in T, j \in S} f(i, j) = \sum_{i \in S, j \in T} c(i, j) = c(S, T).$$

Then, by Lemma 2.1, f is a maximum s, t flow and (S, T) is a minimum s, t cut.

For the converse, suppose that $t \in S$ and consider a directed simple path (one with no cycles) P in G^f from s to t that starts at s and ends at t. Let δ be the minimum capacity in G^f of the edges on P. We will show that the total flow from s to t can be increased to $f'_{s,t} = f_{s,t} + \delta$. To accomplish this, for every edge (i, j) on P which is a forward edge in G^f, set $f'(i, j)$ to $f(i, j) + \delta$; for every edge (i, j) on P which is backward edge in G^f, set $f'(j, i)$ to $f(j, i) - \delta$; for every other edge on G, set $f'(i, j)$ to $f(i, j)$.

We will show that f' is an $s - t$ flow of value $f_{s,t} + \delta$. First, note that s is incident with exactly one edge (directed out of s) on P, t is incident with exactly one edge (directed into t) on P (and both must be forward edges), hence $\sum_i f'(s, i) = \delta + \sum_i f(s, i)$ and $\sum_i f'(i, t) = \delta + \sum_i f(i, t)$.

Next, note that for every other node i on P is incident with exactly one edge on P directed in, and exactly one of P directed out of i. We will show that f' satisfies the conservation constraint at each such node i. If both the edges of P incident with i are forward edges, exactly one is into i and one is out of i, so

$$\sum_{j: (j,i) \in E} f'(j, i) = \delta + \sum_{j: (j,i) \in E} f(j, i)$$

and

$$\sum_{j: (i,j) \in E} f'(i, j) = \delta + \sum_{j: (i,j) \in E} f(i, j).$$

Since f is a flow, it follows that

$$\sum_{j: (j,i) \in E} f'(j, i) = \sum_{j: (i,j) \in E} f'(i, j).$$

A similar argument holds if both are backward edges. Now if the edge of P into i is a forward edge, and the edge of P put of i a backward edge, then

$$\sum_{j: (j,i) \in E} f'(j, i) = \delta - \delta + \sum_{j: (j,i) \in E} f(j, i)$$

and

$$\sum_{j: (i,j) \in E} f'(i, j) = \sum_{j: (i,j) \in E} f(i, j)$$

hence

$$\sum_{j:\,(j,i)\in E} f'(j,i) = \sum_{j:\,(i,j)\in E} f'(i,j) .$$

A similar argument holds if the in-edge of P at i is a backward edge and the out-edge of P at i is a forward edge. So the assignment f' satisfies the conservation requirement.

The only thing left to check is that $0 \le f'(i,j) \le c(i,j)$ for each edge (i,j). Recall that δ is the minimum of capacities in G^f of the edges on P. So, if (i,j) is a forward edge, then

$$0 \le f(i,j) + \delta = f'(i,j) \le f(i,j) + c(i,j) - f(i,j) \le c(i,j) .$$

If (i,j) is a backward edge, then

$$c(j,i) \ge f(j,i) \ge f'(j,i) = f(j,i) - \delta \ge f(j,i) - f(j,i) = 0 .$$

Hence we have shown that f' is an s,t flow, and since $\Sigma_i f'(i,t) = \delta + \Sigma_i f(i,t)$, and $\delta > 0$, it follows that $f'_{s,t} > f_{s,t}$, and f is not a maximum flow. □

The Ford–Fulkerson method

All the essential elements of the Ford–Fulkerson method, and most of the proof of correctness, have been outlined in the proof of Theorem 2.2. In detail, the algorithm is the following:

(1) Set $f(i,j) = 0$ for every edge (i,j).
(2) Construct the residual graph G^f from f.
(3) Search for a directed path P from s to t in G^f. If there is none, then stop, f is a maximum flow.
Else, find the minimum capacity δ in G^f of any of the edges on P.
(4) If (i,j) is a forward edge on P, then set $f(i,j)$ to $f(i,j) + \delta$. If (i,j) is a backward edge on P, then set $f(j,i)$ to $f(j,i) - \delta$.
(5) Return to Step 2.

2.2. Termination

Since $\delta > 0$, every iteration of the Ford–Fulkerson algorithm increases the amount of flow $f_{s,t}$ sent from s to t. Further, since edge capacities are only changed by addition and subtraction operations, if all the edge capacities in G are integral, then δ is always integral and hence at least one. Since the maximum flow is bounded by the capacity of any s,t cut (Lemma 2.1), we have the following theorem.

Theorem 2.3. *If all the edge capacities are finite integers, then the Ford–Fulkerson algorithm terminates in a finite number of steps.*

By the same reasoning, it is also easy to see that the theorem holds when all the capacities are rational. However, the theorem does not hold for irrational capacities. We will see later how to fix this.

Now, in the proof of Theorem 2.2, *if* the algorithm terminates, the final flow f saturates the s, t cut S (defined in the proof of Theorem 2.2), so that f is a maximum flow of value $f_{s,t}$ and $(S, V - S)$ is a minimum s, t cut of capacity $f_{s,t}$. So for the case when the capacities of G are rational, we have proved the converse to Theorem 2.1, the famous *max-flow min-cut theorem*:

Theorem 2.4. *The maximum s, t flow value is equal to the minimum capacity of any s, t cut.*

Theorem 2.4 is an example of a *duality theorem* or *min = max* theorem. Such duality theorems appear extensively in combinatorial optimization, and often are the key to finding efficient methods, and to their correctness proofs.

There is a problem in extending the theorem to the case of irrational capacities: we do not yet have a proof that the Ford–Fulkerson algorithm terminates when capacities are irrational. In fact, it is known that the algorithm, as given, might not terminate in this case. This issue will be resolved in Section 3.3 and then the max-flow min-cut theorem for any capacities will have been proven.

Efficiency

Eventual termination is not the only issue. We want the algorithm to terminate as quickly as possible. Unfortunately, even in the case that all the capacities are integral, and hence the algorithm terminates, the Ford–Fulkerson algorithm can require as many as $f_{s,t}$ iterations of Step 3 [Ford & Fulkerson, 1962]. Hence the only provable time bound for the algorithm (with integer capacities) is $O(ef_{s,t})$, where e is the number of edges. Each residual graph and augmenting path can certainly be found in $O(e)$ time.

The time bound of $O(ef_{s,t})$ is not considered a polynomial time bound in either a strong or a weak sense. To be a (weakly) polynomial time bound, it must grow no faster than some polynomial function of the total number of bits used to represent the input. But a family of examples can be constructed where the capacities of the edges can be represented in $O(\log f_{s,t})$ bits, and where the algorithm uses $\Omega(f_{s,t})$ iterations. Hence, the number of iterations is exponentially larger than the number of bits used in the input.

A stronger notion of a polynomial bound would require that the bound grow no faster than some polynomial function of the number of items in the input, i.e., $e + n$. The bound $O(ef_{s,t})$ certainly does not fit that criterion since $f_{s,t}$ is not even a function (let alone a polynomial) of n and e. We will discuss the distinction between strong and weak polynomial bounds more deeply in Section 14.

The first strongly polynomial bound for network flow was shown by Dinits [1970] and independently by Edmonds & Karp [1972], who both proposed a modification of the Ford–Fulkerson algorithm to be discussed below. They proved that the modified algorithm terminates correctly within $O(n^5)$ time, where $n = |N|$. This time bound is correct even if the edge capacities are irrational. We will examine the Edmonds–Karp method as we derive the even faster Dinits method.

3. Ford–Fulkerson leads 'naturally' to Dinits

In this section we develop the Dinits algorithms for network flow. We also show a continuity of ideas that leads 'naturally' from the Ford-Fulkerson and Edmonds–Karp methods to the Dinits method. The word 'naturally' is in quotes because the continuity was seen only in retrospect, and because the Dinits algorithm actually predates that of Edmonds–Karp. The Dinits method was developed in the Soviet Union in 1970, but became known in the West only in the later part of that decade. During that time a different algorithm containing some of the ideas of the Dinits method was independently developed in the West by Jack Edmonds and Richard Karp, but the ideas were not as fully developed as in the Dinits method. In fact, it was not even recognized, when the Dinits method first became known in the West, that the Dinits methods could be viewed as a natural refinement of the Ford–Fulkerson method – it looked very different at first. We now see it as essentially a more efficient implementation of the Ford–Fulkerson method.

The Ford–Fulkerson (FF) method is a fairly natural algorithm not far removed from the definitions of flow. The Edmonds–Karp (EK) and Dinits algorithms to be discussed can be derived from the FF algorithm by exploiting deeper observations about the behavior of the FF algorithm. As a result, these algorithms are less natural and farther removed from the basic definitions of flow.

3.1. Path choice for the Ford–Fulkerson method

The Ford-Fulkerson algorithm builds a succession of residual graphs, finds an augmentation path in each, and uses the path to augment the flow. However, there can be more than one s, t path in a residual graph, and the method does not specify which path to use. It is easy to construct networks [Ford & Fulkerson, 1962] where the Ford–Fulkerson method could use just a few augmenting paths, but if it chose paths unwisely, it would use a huge number of paths. Hence the question of which paths to select is important. One reasonable suggestion is to pick the path that increases the flow by the largest amount. This idea was explored in the early 1970s [Edmonds & Karp,

1972], but a different idea was found to be better. The idea is to choose the augmentation path with the *fewest* edges. This is the first idea of the Dinits method, and is also the key idea in the Edmonds–Karp method [Edmonds & Karp, 1972]. Later, this same idea was applied to the bipartite matching problem, yielding the fastest known method for that problem [Hopcroft & Karp, 1973].

We hereafter refer to the Ford–Fulkerson algorithm where each augmentation path is the shortest s, t path in the residual graph, as the EK algorithm.

We now explore the idea of choosing the augmentation path with fewest edges (the EK algorithm), and show how the Dinits algorithm evolves naturally from it, although we note again that this exposition is a corruption of the true history of network flow algorithms.

Definition. For i from 1 to r, let G^i be the ith residual graph constructed by the EK algorithm, and let P_i be the s, t path found by the algorithm in G^i. Then for node v, let $D^i(v)$ be the smallest number of edges of any v, t path in G^i, and let $d_i = D^i(t)$. Any v, t path with $D^i(v)$ edges will be called a *shortest* v, t path.

The following two facts are easy to verify, and are left to the reader (these facts are true for the Ford–Fulkerson algorithm as well as for the EK algorithm).

Fact 1. *The capacity in G^{i+1} of an edge (x, y) is less than its capacity in G^i if and only if edge (x, y) is on P_i.*

Fact 2. *The capacity in G^{i+1} of an edge (x, y) is greater than its capacity in G^i if and only if the edge (y, x) is in G^i and is on P_i. As a special case of this, any edge (x, y) is in $G^{i+1} - G^i$ only if the edge (y, x) is in G^i and is on P_i.*

As a consequence of these facts, the capacities of all edges not in P_i are the same in G^i and G^{i+1}.

Lemma 3.1. *For i from 1 to r, and for any node v, $D^i(v) \leq D^{i+1}(v)$, and so $1 \leq d_1 \leq d_2 \leq \cdots \leq d_r \leq n$.*

Proof. Let P_i be a shortest s, t path in G^i. The EK algorithm augments flow on P_i, and then creates G^{i+1} from G^i by changing some edge capacities, by deleting any edges whose capacities fall to zero, and by possibly adding some new edges not in G^i.

To see how $D^{i+1}(v)$ compares to $D^i(v)$, we create G^{i+1} from G^i in two steps: first, delete all the edges in $G^i - G^{i+1}$; second, add in all the edges in $G^{i+1} - G^i$. After the first step, $D^{i+1}(v) \geq D^i(v)$, since deletion of edges from G^i certainly does not decrease any D value. We will add the new edges in one at a time and see that after each addition the D values remain the same or increase, but never decrease.

Let (x, y) be a new edge added. By Fact 2, edge (x, y) in G^{i+1} is the reversal of an edge (y, x) on P_i in G^i. But, P_i is a shortest s, t path in G^i, and so $D^i(y) = D^i(x) + 1$. (If $D^i(y) \leq D^i(x)$, there is an s, t path of fewer edges than P_i, by following P_i to y and then going from y to t with $D^i(y)$ edges.) Clearly, the addition of (x, y) does not decrease the distance from y. Further, since $D^i(y) > D^i(x)$, any path from any node z to t using edge (x, y) will have distance greater than $(D^i(z, x) + D^i(x)) \geq D^i(z)$, where $D^i(z, x)$ is the shortest distance from z to x in the ith augmentation graph. Therefore, the addition of (x, y) cannot decrease the distance to t from any node, and so $D^i(v) \leq D^{i+1}(v)$, for all nodes v, and in particular $d_i \leq d_{i+1}$. Further, $d_r \leq n$, since no simple path can be longer than n, the number of nodes in the graph. $\square$

Given Lemma 3.1, we can partition the execution of the EK algorithm into *phases*, where in each phase, all the augmentation paths used by the algorithm have the same number of edges, and all the augmentations of that length are in that single phase. More formally:

Definition. A *phase* of the EK algorithm is a maximal portion of the execution of the algorithm where all the augmentation paths have equal length. If G^i is the first residual graph and G^k is the last residual graph in a phase, then $d_{i-1} < d_i = d_k < d_{k+1}$.

It follows immediately from Lemma 3.1 that in the EK algorithm there are at most n phases.

The idea of the Dinits algorithm is to efficiently find the augmentation paths inside a single phase. We will argue that inside a phase we can streamline the way each successive augmentation graph is constructed from its predecessor. In particular, we will see that inside a phase we can completely ignore any edges whose residual capacities are increased by the EK algorithm, including all the new residual edges that the EK algorithm adds. This streamlining may at first seem only a cosmetic improvement, but, in fact, it holds the key to a significant speed up.

Lemma 3.2. *For any node v, let $P(v)$ be any shortest v, t path in G^{i+1}. If $P(v)$ contains at least one edge of $G^{i+1} - G^i$, then $P(v)$ has at least $D^i(v) + 1$ edges.*

Proof. Let (x, y) be the closest edge to t on $P(v)$ such that $(x, y) \in G^{i+1} - G^i$. By Fact 2, (y, x) must have been on P_i. P_i is a shortest s, t path in G^i, so $D^i(y) = D^i(x) + 1$, and it follows that $D^{i+1}(x) = 1 + D^{i+1}(y) \geq 1 + D^i(y)$ since all the edges from y to t on $P(v)$ are in G^i. But $1 + D^i(y) = D^i(x) + 2$, so $D^{i+1}(x) > D^i(x)$. Now let (x', y') be the next closest edge to t on $P(v)$ such that (x', y') is in $G^{i+1} - G^i$. Again (y', x') must have been on P_i, and $D^{i+1}(x') = 1 + D^{i+1}(y') > 1 + D^i(y')$. The inequality follows from the fact that all the edges on $P(v)$ from y' to x are also in G^i, and that $D^{i+1}(x) > D^i(x)$. Iterating this argument along edges on P_i that are in $G^{i+1} - G^i$, we obtain the lemma. $\square$

The following corollary is immediate.

Corollary 3.1. *If for some $i < j$, $P(v)$ contains at least one edge of $G^j - G^i$, then $P(v)$ has at least $D^i(v) + 1$ edges.*

A short digression

Digressing briefly from the exposition of the Dinits algorithm, we can now bound the running time for the EK algorithm.

Corollary 3.2. *The Edmonds–Karp algorithm runs in $O(n^5)$ time.*

Proof. In any augmentation path P_i, at least one edge (x, y) becomes saturated and hence does not appear in any successive residual graphs until (y, x) is used on an augmentation path P_j for some $j > i$. But, by Corollary 3.1, $D^j(y) < D^i(y)$. Hence the reappearance of edge (x, y) in G^{j+1} is associated with an increase in $D(y)$. As $D(y)$ is bounded by n, edge (x, y) can be saturated at most $n + 1$ times, and this holds for each edge into y. Further, there are at most n edges into y, so the total number of times that the edges into y can be saturated by an augmentation in algorithm EK is $O(n^2)$. Therefore, the total number of augmentations of the EK algorithm is $O(n^3)$, and since each augmentation takes $O(e)$ time, the total time for the algorithm is $O(n^3 e) = O(n^5)$. Note that this bound can also be shown to be $O(ne^2)$. $\square$

Back to the Dinits method

Dinits improved upon the EK algorithm, obtaining a running time of $O(n^4)$, by more fully exploiting Lemma 3.2. In particular, by setting v to s in Lemma 3.2 we get:

Corollary 3.3. *Any s, t augmentation path in G^{i+1} which contains an edge in $G^{i+1} - G^i$ has at least $d_i + 1$ edges.*

The importance of this corollary is that if a directed edge (x, y) in G^i is not on any shortest s, t path at the start of a particular phase in the EK algorithm, it will not be on any shortest s, t path during *any* part of the phase. So suppose that a new phase of the EK algorithm has just begun, i.e., the previous augmentation path had been some length d, but there are no length-d augmentation paths in the current residual graph. Let G^i be the residual graph at the start of the phase. Then Corollary 3.3 says that we can execute the entire phase using residual graph G^i, without ever adding new edges to G^i. In fact, Corollary 3.3 says that we might as well remove from G^i any edge that is not on some shortest s, t path in G^i – we can execute the entire phase on this reduced graph without affecting the correctness of the EK algorithm! We now make this idea precise.

Definition. The *layered* graph LG^i for G^i is the graph obtained from G^i by removing all edges which are not on some shortest s, t path in G^i.

Note that in a layered graph, all s, t paths have the same length, so every s, t path is a shortest s, t path. It is easy to find the layered graph LG^i for G^i in $O(e)$ time by *breadth-first search* (BFS). Breadth-first search will give each node v a number $l(v)$ which is the minimum number of edges from s to v along any s, v path in G^i. Then LG^i consists of all edges (u, v) in G^i such that $l(u) = l(v) - 1$, and $l(v) < l(t)$. Once the node labels have been assigned, the proper edges can be selected by scanning through them in $O(e)$ time. Below we give the BFS algorithm for assigning node labels.

Breadth-first search

Let Q be a *queue*, i.e., a list in which new elements are added at the end, and elements are removed from the top. A queue is also known as a *first-in first-out* list.

(1) Set $l(s) = 0$; mark s and add it to Q.

(2) While Q is not empty, execute Steps 3 and 4.

(3) Remove the top node w from Q.

(4) For each unmarked node u connected from w by a directed edge in G^i, mark u, add it to Q, and set $l(u) = l(w) + 1$.

It is easy to prove by induction, that the assigned node labels are correct.

Using the definition of a layered graph, we can summarize the observations so far: if G^i is the augmentation graph at the start of a phase, then the entire phase of the EK algorithm can be executed on the layered graph LG^i in place of G^i. LG^i can be found by breadth-first search in $O(e)$ time.

The algorithmic importance of this may not be at first apparent. The EK algorithm spends $O(e)$ time to build each augmentation graph, and $O(e)$ time to find a shortest s, t path in it. The above observations show that we only need to build a new (layered) augmentation graph at the start of each phase, and this reduces the time involved in building augmentation graphs. But does it lead to an overall speedup in the EK algorithm? If the costs of finding augmentation paths are not reduced, then the answer is 'no' since each path continues to cost $O(e)$. The importance of layered graphs is that they do in fact allow augmentation paths to be found faster, as follows.

Since any s, t path in LG^i is a shortest s, t path, and it can have at most $n - 1$ edges, a shortest s, t augmentation path in LG^i can be found myopically in $O(n)$ time: just follow any sequence of edges from s to t in LG^i. So to implement a phase we do the following:

The Dinits algorithm for a single phase
Repeat
  Myopically follow any path P from s, keeping track of the minimum residual edge capacity δ along that path. If the path reaches t, then execute Step A. Else execute Step B.
Until all edges have been removed from LG^i.

Step A (when t is reached): augment the flow f in G along the edges of P by

δ units, and reduce the capacity of these edges in LG^i by δ units. The capacity of at least one edge in LG^i on P will become zero. Remove any such edges from LG^i.

Step B (when the path in LG^i from s reaches a node v which has no edges out of it): remove all edges into v from LG^i.

Lemma 3.3. *The Dinits algorithm for a single phase correctly implements a phase of the EK algorithm, and it runs in time* $O(ne)$.

Proof. First note that if edge (x, y) is in LG^i, then edge (y, x) cannot be in LG^i. This means that during a phase of the EK algorithm executed on LG^i, the capacities of the edges of LG^i never increase. Therefore, once the capacity of an edge becomes zero, the edge can be removed. The correctness of the algorithm then follows from Lemma 3.3.

For the time bound, note that each myopic search for a path takes $O(n)$ time, since the length of any path is at most n. Each such myopic search ends with the removal of at least one edge of LG^i, and hence there are at most e such searches. □

The Dinits *network* flow algorithm is the EK algorithm where each phase is implemented as above. Since in each phase the length of the s, t path increases, there can be at most n phases. Hence, we have:

Theorem 3.1. *The Dinits network flow algorithm runs in time* $O(n^2 e) = O(n^4)$.

To review, the speed-up of the Dinits algorithm over the EK algorithm comes first from understanding how successive augmentation paths are related, leading to the notion of a phase, and second from the ability to implement an entire phase on a single layered graph, leading to an $O(n)$ method to find each augmenting path. The EK algorithm needs $\Theta(e)$ time to find each augmentation path because it searches in an arbitrary residual graph, while the Dinits algorithm restricts its search to a layered graph. This illustrates the main theme of this chapter, how mathematical insight and algorithm analysis (in this case of an existing algorithm) leads to the design of a more efficient algorithm.

3.2. An $O(n^3)$ network flow algorithm

We now show how to reduce the time for computing a maximum flow from $O(n^2 e)$ to $O(n^3)$ by reducing the time for a single phase computation from $O(ne)$ to $O(n^2)$. The idea will be to look further at the set of augmentation paths that *could have* been found in a phase of the EK or the Dinits algorithm. That is, instead of trying to find the paths one at a time during a phase, as the EK and Dinits methods both do, we try to find a subset of edges, and flows on those edges, which could have been obtained from the superposition of augmentation paths found in a phase. It turns out that we can find such a set faster than by actually finding individual augmentation paths, and since this set of edges could have come from the Dinits or EK algorithm, we can correctly use them in the network flow algorithm.

Before we delve into the details, we have to slightly switch our view of what is being computed on a residual graph.

Definition. For a layered graph LG^i used during phase i of the EK or Dinits algorithms, define $g(u, v)$ to be $c(u, v) - \bar{c}(u, v)$, where $c(u, v)$ is the capacity in LG^i of edge (u, v) at the start of phase i, and $\bar{c}(u, v)$ is its capacity at the end of the phase.

In the Dinits method the flow f is modified in Step A immediately after each augmentation path is found. These modifications are related to, but distinct from, the ongoing modifications of LG^i. Suppose we only make the modifications on LG^i, and delay changing the flow f until the end of the phase. What we would know at the end of the phase is the flow f which is correct for the start of the phase, and the function g. From that we could easily obtain the flow f', the correct flow for the end of the phase, by *superimposing* f and g:

If (u, v) is a forward edge in LG^i, then set $f'(u, v)$ to

$$f(u, v) + g(u, v) \,.$$

If (u, v) is a backward edge in LG^i, then set $f'(u, v)$ to

$$f(u, v) - g(u, v) \,.$$

So instead of finding augmenting paths one at a time, if we had some other method for determining the function g we could simulate a phase of the Dinits algorithm (which itself simulates a phase of the EK algorithm). So is there any easy way to find the function g? To answer that, we look a little more closely at what g is.

It is easy to verify that the function g is an s, t *flow* in LG^i. However, it is not necessarily a maximum flow, since for any edge (u, v) in LG^i, $g(u, v)$ starts at zero and only increase during a phase. That is, if we consider a phase of the Dinits or EK method to be computing an s, t flow g in LG^i, then that computation never decreases the flow in any edge of LG^i, and by simple example, such an algorithm cannot be guaranteed to find a maximum flow. Instead, g is something called a *blocking flow*.

Definition. A blocking flow in a graph is a flow in which at least one edge on every s, t path is saturated. It is easy to construct examples illustrating that a blocking flow is not necessarily a maximum flow.

Clearly, g is a blocking flow in LG^i, for if it was not blocking, then additional s, t paths in LG^i could be found, and the phase would not be complete. We would like to say that conversely any blocking flow in LG^i can be used to simulate a phase of the Dinits method. Unfortunately this is not quite correct unless we modify Step A of the Dinits method as follows: after finding a path P with minimum capacity δ', set δ to be any positive value less or equal to δ', and use δ as before. It is easy to see that even with this change the maximum flow is still correctly computed, although one might suspect that if we were to modify the Dinits method in this way, the algorithm would become very inefficient. We will see that this need not be the case.

Lemma 3.4. *Let f and LG^i be as above. If g is any blocking flow in LG^i, then the superimposition of f and g gives a flow f' which could have been obtained by the execution of a phase of the (modified) Dinits algorithm on LG^i.*

Proof. Given g we will find s, t paths which could have been found by the modified Dinits method. First remove any edge (u, v) where $g(u, v) = 0$. There are s, t paths in LG^i, and g is a blocking flow, so there must be at least one edge (s, u) such that $g(s, u) > 0$. Then, since g is a flow, there must be an edge (u, v) where $g(u, v) > 0$. LG^i is acyclic and all paths end at t, so repeating this reasoning, we find an s, t path P in LG^i among edges with positive flow g. Let ε be the smallest g value among the edges on P. Now decrease $g(u, v)$ by ε for every edge on P. What remains is again an s, t flow, so we can again find an s, t path. Repeating this operation, we can decompose g into a set of s, t paths, and for each such path $\varepsilon > 0$. Clearly, these paths could have been found (in any order) by an execution of the modified Dinits method, provided that it chose δ to be ε. Finally, since g is a blocking flow, such an execution of the Dinits algorithm would terminate after finding these flows. $\square$

Hence any phase of the Dinits algorithm can be simulated if we have a blocking flow for the layered graph of that phase. Then, one way to speed up the Dinits algorithm is to find a blocking flow in a layered graph in time faster than $O(ne)$. The first solution [in time $O(n^2 + e)$] to this was proposed by Karzanoff [1974]. A simpler method was later discussed by Malhotra, Kumar & Maheshwari [1978], and many additional methods have since been found. In this section, we follow the method called the *wave* method due to Tarjan [1983], which is itself a simplification of the Karzanoff method.

3.3. The wave algorithm

All of the above methods for finding a blocking flow in a layered graph are *preflow* methods. A preflow is a relaxation of a flow; it is an assignment of non-negative real numbers to edges of the graph satisfying the capacity constraints, but the original conservation constraint is replaced by the following relaxed constraint:

For every node i other than s or t,

$$\sum_{j:\,(j,i)\in E} f(j, i) \geq \sum_{j:\,(i,j)\in E} f(i, j).$$

In other words, the flow into i is greater or equal to the flow out of i.

We define $e(v)$ (*excess* at v) to be the total flow into v minus the total flow out of v. In a preflow f, node v ($v \neq s, t$) is called *unbalanced* if the excess is positive, and is called *balanced* if the excess is zero. The residual graph G^f for a preflow f is defined exactly as a flow f. That is, if $f(u, v) > 0$, the directed edge (v, u) is in the residual graph with capacity $f(u, v)$; if $f(u, v) < c(u, v)$, the directed edge (u, v) is in the residual graph with capacity $c(u, v) - f(u, v)$.

The wave method uses preflows until it ends, at which time each node is balanced, and hence the ending preflow is a flow; we will see that it is in fact a blocking flow. During the algorithm, each node will be called either *blocked* or *unblocked*. Initially s is blocked, but all other nodes are unblocked; when a node becomes blocked, it never again becomes unblocked.

The algorithm tries to balance an unbalanced *unblocked* node v by *increasing* the flow out of v, and to balance an unbalanced *blocked* node v by *decreasing* the flow into v. The algorithm operates by repeatedly alternating a wave of increase steps (where flow is pushed towards t) and a wave of decrease steps (where flow is pushed back towards s). We will describe the increase and decrease steps in detail below, but before we do, we give the high-level description of the algorithm.

The wave algorithm for a blocking flow g in a layered graph

(0) Set $g(u, v) = 0$ for every edge (u, v) in the layered graph LG^i.

(1) Saturate all edges out of s.

(2) Find a topological ordering of the nodes of the layered graph. That is, find an ordering of the nodes such that for any directed edge (u, v), u appears before v in the ordering.

(3) Repeat Steps 4 through 7 until stopped.

(4) Examine each node v in the established topological order, and execute Step 4a.

    (4a) If v is unblocked and unbalanced, then attempt to balance it by executing the *Increase Step* for v. If v cannot be so balanced, then declare it *blocked*.

(5) If there is any unbalanced blocked node, then go to Step 6. If there is not such a node, then stop the algorithm.

(6) Examine each node v in reverse topological order and execute Step 6a.

    (6a) If v is blocked and unbalanced, then balance it by executing the *Decrease Step* for v. Note that v will always become balanced in this step.

(7) If there is an unblocked, unbalanced node, then go to Step 4, else stop the algorithm.

We can now describe in detail the increase and decrease steps executed while examining a node v.

Increase Step. Repeat the following operation for each neighboring node w of v until either v is balanced, or no further neighboring nodes of v exist.

If w is an unblocked node, and $g(v, w) < c(v, w)$, then increment $g(v, w)$ by $\min[e(v), c(v, w) - g(v, w)]$.

Decrease Step. Repeat the following operation for each neighboring node u until v is balanced:

If (u, v) is an edge with flow $g(u, v) > 0$, then decrease $g(u, v)$ by $\min[g(u, v), e(v)]$.

We prove the correctness and the time bound for the wave method with the following lemmas. Note first that once a node becomes blocked in the algorithm, it never becomes unblocked.

Lemma 3.5. *If node v is blocked, then there is a saturated edge on every path from v to t.*

Proof. The proof is by induction on the order that the nodes become blocked. Node s is initially blocked, and all edges out of s are saturated. So the lemma holds at this point. Suppose it holds after the kth node becomes blocked. Now before the $k + 1$ node becomes blocked some flow could be decreased from a node v to a blocked node w, but this happens only in Step 6a, and only if v is blocked. Hence by the induction assumption, all paths from w contain a saturated edge. The $k + 1$ node v becomes blocked only in Step 4a, and only after all the edges out of v are saturated, hence the inductive step holds. □

Lemma 3.6. *If the method halts, all nodes are balanced and the preflow is a blocking flow.*

Proof. Note that after Step 4, there are no unbalanced unblocked nodes, so if the algorithm terminates in Step 5, then all nodes are balanced. Similarly, after Step 6 there are no unbalanced blocked nodes, so if the algorithm halts in Step 7, all nodes are balanced. Hence if the algorithm terminates, then the preflow is a flow. To see that the flow is blocking, note that for every edge (s, v) out of s, either (s, v) is saturated or v is blocked, since v had to be blocked before flow on (s, v) could be decreased. But if v is blocked, then by Lemma 3.5 all v to t paths are blocked. □

Theorem 3.2. *The wave algorithm computes a blocking flow in a layered graph in $O(n^2)$ time.*

Proof. Nodes only become blocked in Step 4a, and once blocked remain blocked forever. Further, when a blocked node becomes unbalanced in Step 4a, it is immediately balanced in the next execution of Step 6a, and no new unbalanced nodes are created in Step 6. So the algorithm terminates unless at least one new node becomes blocked in each execution of Step 4; hence, there are at most $n - 1$ executions of Step 4 and at most $n - 2$ of Step 6. In each such step, we attempt to balance $n - 2$ nodes, so there are $O(n^2)$ times when the algorithm attempts to balance nodes. Each such attempt (at a node v, say) either succeeds or results in saturating all edges out of v.

To bound the running time of the algorithm it is not enough to bound [by $O(n^2)$] the number of attempts to balance the nodes, since in each attempt to balance a node v, several edges out of v are examined. We now examine how many edges are examined by the algorithm. The flow on an edge (v, w) is increased only if w is unblocked, and is decreased only if w is blocked, hence the flow on (v, w) increases for some time, then decreases, but never again increases. During the increase part, each flow increase either balances v or saturates (v, w). Any edge can be saturated only once, so over the entire algorithm there can be at most $O(n^2 + e)$ edges examined during the Increase Step. Similarly, during the decrease part, each flow decrease on (v, w) either reduces its flow to zero (which can happen only once) or ends an attempt to balance w. Hence there can be at most $O(n^2 + e) = O(n^2)$ edges examined during the Decrease Step. The number of edges examined dominates the running time of the method, so the theorem follows. □

3.4. Section summary

To summarize this section, the maximum s, t flow and minimum cut can be found in $O(n^3)$ time by the Dinits network flow method if the wave algorithm is used to execute each phase. The Dinits method executes at most n phases, where in a phase a blocking flow in a layered graph must be found. The wave algorithm finds a blocking flow in a layered graph in $O(n^2)$ time, so a total time bound of $O(n^3)$ is achieved.

4. The breakdown of phases: Goldberg's preflow-push algorithm

The idea of a *phase* was central to the speedup of the Dinits and wave methods over the Ford–Fulkerson and EK methods. The basic observation was that when shortest augmenting paths are used, the computation naturally partitions into at most n phases, and in each phase a blocking flow in a layered graph is computed; the speedups then resulted from implementing a phase more efficiently. The overall time bound was just the *product* of the bound on the number of phases and an *independent* upper bound on the worst-case running time of phase. But maybe there is some important *interaction* between phases. Perhaps the number of phases affects the total time taken by the phases, or perhaps when one phase takes a long time, the next phases take less than the worst-case upper bound on an arbitrary phase. As long as the worst-case time bounds are obtained by multiplying a bound on the number of phases by an independent bound on the worst-case running time of a phase, no analysis of such interaction is possible.

Goldberg [1987] introduced a network flow algorithm that had the same dense worst-case running time, $O(n^3)$, as the best previous algorithms, but whose analysis did not divide the algorithm into phases. Hence the time bound for the algorithm is not just a bound on the number of phases times a bound on the time per phase. This sort of analysis, where the bound comes from analyzing an *entire* sequence of operations is often called an *amortized* analysis. Hence the analysis of the Goldberg algorithm differs from that of the Dinits algorithm in that the former analysis is more amortized than the latter. We will see other amortized analyses below when we consider parametric flow, and in a later section when we discuss the problem of computing the connectivity of a graph.

Goldberg's method was modified by Goldberg & Tarjan [1988] and is now generally referred to as the Goldberg–Tarjan (GT) method. The amortized analysis of the GT method allows additional advances, one of which, parametric flow, will be discussed in detail in the next section. Another advance, by Goldberg & Tarjan [1988], was the improvement of the running time to $O(ne \log(n^2)/e)$, which is $O(n^3)$ for dense graphs, and $O(ne \log n)$ for sparse graphs. This second advance relies heavily on the use of a data structure called a *dynamic tree* and will not be discussed in this article.

4.1. The generic algorithm

The Goldberg method is a preflow method, maintaining a preflow until the end of the algorithm when it becomes a (maximum) flow. During the algorithm each vertex v has an associated label $d(v)$ which is always between 0 and $2n - 1$. These d labels are called *valid* for the current preflow f if $d(s) = n$, $d(t) = 0$, and $d(u) \leq d(v) + 1$ for any edge (u, v) in the current residual graph for f. Throughout the algorithm the d labels never decrease and are always kept valid (a fact that we will prove later). A directed edge (u, v) is called *admissible* if and only if it is in the current residual graph and $d(u) = d(v) + 1$.

The basic step of the Goldberg algorithm is called a *node examination* of an active node. In a node examination of active node u, all the excess at u is pushed along *admissible* edges out of u to neighbors of u in the current residual graph. If at any point in the examination, the active node u has no more admissible edges out of it, then $d(u)$ is changed to $\min[d(v) + 1: (u, v)$ is an edge in the current residual graph]. It is easy to prove, by induction on the number of pushes say, that any active node has a residual edge out of it. So the relabeling is always possible and creates an admissible edge from u to v allowing additional flow from u to be pushed to v. Hence, the node examination of u ends only when all excess at u has been pushed out of u, at which point u is no longer active. After a push, of amount δ say, has been made along edge (u, v), we change the preflow f along the edge as follows: if (u, v) is a forward edge (i.e., an original edge in G), then $f(u, v)$ gets increased by δ. If (u, v) is a backward edge, then $f(v, u)$ gets decreased by δ. These changes of f are considered part of the node examination of u.

As an implementation detail, any push along an edge is required to push as much as possible, i.e., an amount equal to the minimum of the node's excess and the capacity of the edge. A push is called *saturating* if the push fills the residual edge (either forward or backward) to capacity, and *non-saturating* otherwise.

We can now describe the generic Goldberg algorithm.

The generic Goldberg algorithm

Push flow out of s to neighbors of s so that all edges out of s are saturated. {This makes all neighbors of s active.}

Set $d(s) = n$, $d(t) = 0$, and $d(u)$ equal to the number of edges on the shortest path from u to t in the graph.

While there are any active nodes other than s or t

begin

    Pick an active node u other than s or t and perform a node examination of u.

end.

Note that the notion of the residual graph is important in the algorithm even though it is not explicitly in the algorithm description. It is important because the definition of an admissible edge ultimately depends on the current residual graph. Hence the residual graph must be (explicitly or implicitly) updated as the computation proceeds (after each node examination).

It is easy to see that the algorithm always maintains a preflow. Clearly then, if the algorithm terminates, the preflow is a flow, because when a node has no excess the flow into it equals the flow out of it. We will show that the algorithm does terminate after some additional implementation detail is presented. But with the help of the following lemma, we can already prove that at termination the flow is a maximum flow.

Lemma 4.1. *Throughout the algorithm, the d node labels are valid.*

Proof. It is immediate that the initial d values are valid. Now consider the first point in time where an invalid labeling occurs, and suppose it is $d(u) > d(v) + 1$ for a residual edge (u, v). What could have happened between the time all labels were valid, and the point of first invalidity? There are three things that could have happened: either (u, v) was already a residual edge and $d(u)$ changed or $d(v)$ changed, or (u, v) was not a residual edge but residual edge (u, v) got created the point of invalidity. Whenever the value $d(u)$ is changed it is set to $\min[d(v) + 1: (u, v)$ is an edge in the current residual graph], hence this does not create an invalid node label. If $d(v)$ is changed it must increase (since node labels never decrease); but just before that point $d(v) \leq d(v) + 1$, since (u, v) was a residual edge and the node labels are valid. When a new edge (u, v) is added to the residual graph it is because of a push from v to u in the residual graph. But this means that the edge (v, u) was admissible, so $d(v) = d(u) + 1$. Certainly then $d(u) \leq d(v) + 1$, the requirement for validity on the new edge (u, v) entering the residual graph. Edges leaving the residual graph have no affect on validity.   □

Theorem 4.1. *Assuming the algorithm terminates, the preflow at termination is a maximum flow.*

Proof. We have already noted that at termination the preflow is a flow, hence the residual graph is then a residual graph for an s, t flow. The flow will be maximal if and only if there is no s to t path in that residual graph. Since the node labels are always valid and $d(s) = n$ and $d(t) = 0$ throughout the algorithm, any path from s to t in the residual graph would have to have n edges, hence $n + 1$ nodes, which is not possible. Hence there is no s to t path in the residual graph at termination (or ever), and so the preflow is a maximum flow.   □

4.2. Additional implementation details

Before we can completely prove termination and worst-case time bounds, there are two important implementation details to discuss: how admissible edges are searched for during a node examination, and which active node to examine if there are choices. We first address the admissible edge question.

How to search for an admissible edge
For each node v, the algorithm keeps a list $I(v)$ in arbitrary but fixed order, containing every node w such that either edge (v, w) or (w, v) is in G. Hence $I(v)$ represents all the edges (v, w) which could possibly be admissible. At any point during the algorithm there is a pointer $p(v)$ into $I(v)$. At the start of the algorithm each $p(v)$ points to the top of $I(v)$. When node v is examined the algorithm finds admissible edges out of v by searching through $I(v)$ in order, starting at $p(v)$, advancing $p(v)$ each time a new node of $I(v)$ is considered. Further, the algorithm will only consider updating $d(v)$ when it has passed the bottom of $I(v)$. The algorithm remains correct, because in the generic algorithm $d(v)$ is changed when there are no admissible edges out of v, and although that might happen before $p(v)$ is at the bottom of $I(v)$, it certainly cannot hurt to explicitly check all the remaining potential residual edges. So the algorithm will only consider changing $d(v)$ when $p(v)$ passes the bottom of $I(v)$. This detail by itself does not imply that $d(v)$ will definitely change at that point, however, we will prove that implication. That is, we will show that if the bottom node of $I(v)$ is passed, then there are no admissible edges out of v. At that point then, $d(v)$ is changed to $\min[d(w) + 1: (v, w)$ is an edge in the current residual graph], $p(v)$ is set to the top of $I(v)$, and the examination of v continues.

Since the change of $d(v)$ creates a new admissible edge out of v, this cycling scan through $I(v)$ always results in all excess being pushed out of v during an examination of v. Note that at most one non-saturating push (the last one, if any) from v occurs during a single examination of v.

Lemma 4.2. *When the bottom of $I(v)$ is passed (but before $d(v)$ is changed), there are no admissible edges out of node v in the current residual graph.*

Proof. For any node w on $I(v)$, $p(v)$ passes w during a node examination of v only when edge (v, w) is not admissible. Since that time, the algorithm might have examined nodes other than v, and so we have to see what effect this might have on the admissibility of (v, w).

At the moment that $p(v)$ passes w edge (v, w) is not admissible, so either edge (v, w) was not in the residual graph, or $d(v)$ was strictly less than $d(w) + 1$. In the latter case $d(v)$ is still strictly less than $d(w) + 1$ when $p(v)$ passes the bottom of $I(v)$, because $d(v)$ has not changed and $d(w)$, if changed, has only increased. In the former case, it may be that edge (v, w) is in the current residual graph, although it was not in the residual graph when $p(v)$ passed w. This can only happen if there was a push from w to v in the meantime; at that time $d(w)$ equaled $d(v) + 1$. But this again implies that $d(v) < d(w) + 1$ when $p(v)$ passes the bottom, so (v, w) is still inadmissible. Since w was arbitrary, we have proved that there are no admissible edges out of v when $p(v)$ passes the bottom of $I(v)$. $\square$

Note we have actually shown something a little stronger which will be needed later. We have shown that if w is above $p(v)$ in $I(v)$, then edge (v, w) is inadmissible.

We can now complete a little of the timing analysis, and hence also a little of the termination argument.

Lemma 4.3. *For any node v, $d(v)$ is always less than $2n$.*

Proof. First, only node labels of active nodes are changed, so once a node becomes permanently inactive its node label is fixed. So we only need to show what happens to active nodes.

Next, we claim that for any active node v there is a directed path in the current residual graph from v to s. For suppose not, and let W be the set of nodes which are reachable from v along any directed path from v in the current residual graph. Let $\bar{W} = V - W$. By assumption $s \in \bar{W}$. By the maximality of W, all $f(x, y) = 0$ for all $x \in W$, $y \in \bar{W}$, otherwise there would be a residual edge from $\bar{W}$ to W. But if there is no flow (or preflow) into W from $\bar{W}$, there certainly cannot be any excess at any node in W. So there is a directed path from v to s in the current residual graph. Let w be the node adjacent to s on this path. Because $d(s) = n$, and node labels are always valid, it follows that $d(w) \leq n + 1$. Repeating this argument along the path to v, and using the fact that there are only n nodes, we see that $d(v) < 2n$. $\square$

Lemma 4.4. *The generic algorithm does at most $O(n^2)$ node relabel operations, and at most $O(ne)$ saturating pushes.*

Proof. Since $d(v) < 2n$ for each node v, and each relabel of v increases $d(v)$, the total number of relabels is bounded by $2n^2$. Now $d(v)$ increases each time the bottom of $I(v)$ is passed, since there are no admissible edges out of v at that point, so the bottom of v can be passed at most $2n$ times. Each saturating push along an edge out of v advances $p(v)$ by one position, so the total number of saturating pushes out of v is $2n$ times $|I(v)|$ (which is the number of neighbors of v in G). Summing this over all nodes bounds the total number of saturating pushes by $2ne$. $\square$

To complete the time analysis of the algorithm we essentially need only consider the number of non-saturating edge pushes. This is most easily done by adding computational implementation detail given below.

4.3. How to chose among active nodes

There are two well-studied specialized versions of the generic algorithm. In the FIFO version, nodes are placed on the end of a queue as they become active, and are picked for examination off the top of the queue. In the max-d version, the active node picked for examination is always the one with the largest d label. Both methods lead to an $O(n^3)$ time algorithm, but the max-d method is easier to analyze (following an argument given by Cheriyan & Maheshwari [1989]), and has additional applications we will discuss later.

Note that Lemmas 4.3 and 4.4 remain valid for the max-d version of the algorithm since they did not rely in any way on how active nodes were chosen. The next lemma does rely on the max-d version of the algorithm, and nearly completes the remaining time analysis.

Lemma 4.5. *The* max-d *algorithm performs only* $O(n^3)$ *non-saturating pushes.*

Proof. In the max-d algorithm, at most n consecutive node examinations can occur without at least one node label increasing. To see this, note that excess is always pushed from the highest labeled active node to a lower labeled node (since it is pushed along admissible edges). So, since each node pushes out all its excess when examined, if no node labels change during n node examinations, then all excess in the network will either be pushed forward to t or backward to s. At that point the algorithm terminates with a maximum flow, since there will be no active nodes. Each node examination can do at most one non-saturating push, so there can be at most n non-saturating pushes between node label increases. Each node label is bounded by $2n$, and node labels never decrease, so there can be at most $O(n^3)$ non-saturating pushes. $\square$

Theorem 4.2. *The* max-d *version of the Goldberg algorithm finds a maximum flow in* $O(n^3)$ *worst case time.*

Proof. The time analysis is divided between the time for all the non-saturating pushes, and the time for all-other-work. Lemma 4.5 showed that the total number of non-saturating pushes is bounded by $O(n^3)$, and each can clearly be done in $O(1)$ time.

Ignoring for now the time to find the max-d active node, the time for 'all-other-work' is just $O(ne)$ as follows. Each operation other than a non-saturating push or a relabeling causes $p(v)$ to advance for some v, and $d(v)$ advances every time $p(v)$ passes the bottom of $I(v)$. Since $d(v) < 2n$, and $|I(v)|$ is the sum of the in and out degrees of v in G, the total advancement of all n p-pointers is bounded by $2n \sum_v |I(v)| = O(ne)$. Relabeling also only costs $O(ne)$ since a node gets relabeled at most $2n$ times, and the time for each relabel is bounded by the sum of its in and out degrees. So the time for all-other-work is $O(ne)$.

Now we discuss how to find an active node of maximum d label. To do this efficiently, the algorithm keeps a set A of $2n - 1$ linked lists of active nodes, each indexed by a number from 1 to $2n - 1$. List j keeps all the active nodes whose d label is j. A is used to locate an active node of maximum d label. If there is more than one, then the node picked for examination is the first one on the list. Each push from a node v must be to a node with d label equal to $d(v) - 1$, so finding the next active node of maximum d value takes constant time. Further, updating A after a node relabeling involves only constant work, so A can be maintained and used in $O(n^2)$ time plus $O(1)$ time per push. □

5. Parametric flow: The value of amortizing across phases

The worst-case (dense) running time of the Goldberg algorithm presented above is no better than that of earlier algorithms. However, the analysis of the Goldberg algorithm is not divided into phases and this amortization across phases can be very useful in analyzing more complex applications of network flow algorithms. In this section we give one example in detail.

5.1. The problem

One of the most useful applications of network flow is in the solution of combinatorial problems by a *sequence* of maximum flow or minimum cut calculations. For examples of such problems, see Picard & Queyranne [1982], Gusfield & Martel [1989], Gusfield & Tardos [1991], Gusfield [1991], Cunningham [1985], and Gallo, Grigoriadis & Tarjan [1989]. In many problems the networks in the sequence are similar and differ only by a systematic change in some of the edge capacities. In particular, the edge capacities are often functions of a single parameter λ, and the particular combinatorial problem is solved by finding the value of λ whose corresponding maximum flow or minimum cut meets some side constraint(s). Hence problems of this type are solved by searching over the possible values of λ (in some efficient manner), solving a maximum flow problem for each fixed value of λ generated.

Of course, for each fixed value of λ in the generated sequence we could solve the corresponding maximum flow problem from scratch, but the similarity of the problems can often be exploited to solve the entire sequence faster. For a large and important class of such problems, we will see that a sequence of $O(n^2)$ maximum flow problems can be solved with the same worst case time bound as just a single maximum flow problem. The use of the Goldberg (and Goldberg–Tarjan) algorithms in parametric analysis was initiated by Gallo, Grigoriadis & Tarjan [1989] who showed that a sequence of $O(n)$ maximum flow problems can be solved in the worst-case time bound for only a single flow. The result given here is an improvement on that result and is taken from Gusfield [1990b], and Gusfield & Tardos [1991].

Definition. In a *monotone parametric flow network* G, the capacities of the edges out of s are *non-decreasing* functions of the real parameter λ, and the capacities of the edges into t are *non-increasing* functions of λ. All other edge capacities are fixed, as in a normal flow network. For a given value λ^*, we define $G(\lambda^*)$ as the ordinary flow network that results from plugging in λ^* into the capacity functions of the edges out of s and into t. Given a sequence of values $\lambda_1 < \lambda_2 < \cdots < \lambda_k$ (in sorted order), the *parametric flow problem* is to compute the maximum flow and minimum cut in $G(\lambda_1), \ldots, G(\lambda_k)$. We will let f_j denote a maximum flow in $G(\lambda_j)$.

5.2. The central idea

In $G(\lambda_{j+1})$ the edge capacities out of s increase and those into t decrease compared to $G(\lambda_j)$, so f_j is a legal preflow in $G(\lambda_{j+1})$, and we can start the computation of f_{j+1} with the initial preflow f_j rather than starting from the zero flow. This 'common-sense' idea has been around (in use with other flow algorithms) for a long time. What is new is that by using this idea together with the max-d version of the Goldberg algorithm, it can be proved that the total work involved in the k network flow computations is at most $O(n^3 + kn)$.

The fundamental result of Gallo, Grigoriadis & Tarjan [1989] is the following:

Theorem 5.1. *In a monotone parametric flow network G, if the values $\lambda_1 < \lambda_2 < \cdots < \lambda_k$ (or $\lambda_1 > \lambda_2 > \cdots > \lambda_k$) are specified in this order, then a maximum flow and a minimum cut in each of the networks $G(\lambda_1), \ldots, G(\lambda_k)$ can be computed on line in $O(n^3 + kn^2)$ total time.*

Thus for $k = O(n)$, all the flows can be done in the same worst-case time as the fastest known algorithm for a single flow. This result has many applications and leads to the fastest solutions of many combinatorial problems. It is important to note that in all of these applications it is the minimum cut that is needed; the maximum flow is computed in order to find the minimum cut. Martel [1989] showed that the $O(n^3 + kn^2)$ bound can also be obtained by using either the Karzanoff or the wave versions of the Dinits maximum flow algorithm in place of the GT algorithm.

The GGT algorithm [Gallo, Grigoriadis & Tarjan, 1989] (establishing Theorem 5.1) is based on the idea that the maximum flow in $G(\lambda_i)$ can be used to obtain a good initial preflow in $G(\lambda_{i+1})$ and that, if care is taken, the last d labels in $G(\lambda_i)$ remain valid for this initial preflow. In detail, for each i, the initial preflow in $G(\lambda_{i+1})$ is obtained from the maximum flow in $G(\lambda_i)$ by increasing the flow in every edge (s, v) to $c_v(\lambda_{i+1})$ if $d(v) < n - 1$, by reducing the flow in every edge (v, t) to $c_v(\lambda_{i+1})$, and by leaving all other edge flows as they are in the maximum flow in $G(\lambda_i)$. Each $d(v)$ is unchanged from its last value in $G(\lambda_i)$.

It is easy to verify, by the fact that $\lambda_i < \lambda_{i+1}$ and the monotonicity of the capacity functions, that this initial flow assignment is a preflow in $G(\lambda_{i+1})$; it is also easy to verify that the d labels are valid for this preflow. After the initial preflow is set, the maximum flow in $G(\lambda_{i+1})$ is found by resuming the GT flow algorithm and running it to completion.

5.3. Parametric flow with the max-d *version*

Theorem 5.2. *In a monotone parametric flow network G, if the values $\lambda_1 < \lambda_2 < \cdots < \lambda_k$ (or $\lambda_1 > \lambda_2 > \cdots > \lambda_k$) are specified in this order, then a maximum flow and a minimum cut in each of the networks $G(\lambda_1), \ldots, G(\lambda_k)$ can be computed on line in $O(n^3 + kn)$ total time.*

Proof. As mentioned above, we use the max-d version of the Goldberg algorithm. However, we note two additional implementation details that are needed for this result. First, when beginning the flow computation in $G(\lambda_{i+1})$, the initial position of each $p(v)$ is its ending position in the flow computation in $G(\lambda_i)$. Second, s must be at the bottom of any $I(v)$ list that it is in, and similarly for t. The first modification is needed for the time analysis below, and the second modification is needed for the correctness of the method. The reason is the following. For the correctness of the Goldberg algorithm, whenever $d(v)$ changes there must be no admissible edges out of v. From the comment after Lemma 4.2 we know that for a single flow computation if w is a node above $p(v)$ in $I(v)$, then (v, w) is not admissible; so when $p(v)$ passes the bottom of $I(v)$ there are no admissible edges out of v. To ensure that after a capacity change, edge (v, w) is still inadmissible if w is above $p(v)$, we always put s and t at the bottom of any list they are in, since an inadmissible edge not incident with s or t is clearly still inadmissible after a capacity change.

For the time analysis, we note how the $O(n^3)$ bound for a single flow computation is affected when k flows are computed by the method described above. Again, the analysis is divided into time for non-saturating pushes, and all-other-work. In the above parametric method, the d labels never decrease, and each is bounded by $2n$ no matter how large k is. Further, $p(v)$ is not moved when the edge capacities change. So the analysis for all-other-work *inside* the k flow computations is unchanged, and the time is again O(ne). The time for making the capacity changes is certainly bounded by O(kn) as is the time to set up A after each capacity change. Note that A is empty at the end of each flow computation. So all-other-work inside and between flow computations is bounded by O($ne + kn$). Note that we have amortized over the entire sequence of k flows. Had we just taken the O(n^3) bound on the time for any single flow and multiplied by k, our desired bound would be impossible.

To analyze the number of non-saturating pushes, note that *inside* any of the k flows there cannot be more than n non-saturating pushes before a d label increases, for precisely the same reason as in a single flow. However, there may be $n - 1$ non-saturating pushes, then a capacity change, and then another $n - 1$ non-saturating pushes, all without a label change. So each time the capacities change the bound on the total number of allowed non-saturating pushes increases by n. Hence the total number of non-saturating pushes over k flows is bounded by O($n^3 + kn$). Therefore, the time to compute the k flows is O($n^3 + kn$). The analysis here is again amortized over all the k flows.

We now discuss how to find the k minimum cuts. Define S_i to be the set of nodes reachable from s in the residual graph obtained from the maximum flow in $G(\lambda_i)$; let $T_i = N\backslash S_i$. It is known [Ford & Fulkerson, 1962] that S_i, T_i is the unique 'leftmost' minimum s, t cut. That is, if S', T' is another minimum s, t cut in $G(\lambda_i)$, then $S_i \subseteq S'$. We will find S_i, T_i in each $G(\lambda_i)$, but we cannot search naively from s since that would take $\Omega(km)$ total time. We note the following two facts. First, $S_i \subseteq S_{i+1}$ for every i [Stone, 1978; Gallo, Grigoriadis & Tarjan, 1989]; second, if w is in $S_{i+1}\backslash S_i$, then w must be reachable in the $G(\lambda_{i+1})$ residual graph from a node $v \in S_{i+1}\backslash S_i$ such that (s, v) is an edge in G and $c_v(\lambda_{i+1}) > c_v(\lambda_i)$ [Gallo, Grigoriadis & Tarjan, 1989]. To search for S_{i+1} we start at from such nodes v, and we delete any edge encountered that is into S_i. Hence the search for S_{i+1} examines some edges not previously examined in any search for $S_j, j < i$, plus at most n edges previously examined. So, the time to find all the k cuts is O($m + kn$). □

5.4. Parametric flow for parameters given out of order

In Theorem 5.2 the values of λ changed monotonically and there are many applications where this is the case. However, it is even more useful to be able to handle the case when the λ values change in no ordered manner. It was shown by Gusfield & Martel [1989] that a sequence of flows determined by k values of λ given in any order can be computed in O($n^3 + kn^2$) time; later this was improved to O($n^3 + kn$) by Gusfield [1990b] and Gusfield & Tardos [1991]. We will not give either result here, but examine an important special case where the values of λ are given out of order.

The special case of binary search

We consider the special case where the λ values are generated by some binary search over the space of possible λ values (this is the case in several of the applications). What is special about such a sequence of λ values is that at any instant there is an interval $[\lambda_l, \lambda_r]$ such that the next λ value is guaranteed to fall into this interval, and such that either λ_l or λ_r will next be set to λ. Hence λ_l monotonically increases, λ_r monotonically decreases, and the intervals are nested over time. The nested interval property will make the algorithm and the analysis particularly simple: we will be able to charge all the flow computations to exactly two monotone sequences of continued flows.

The binary search process iterates the following until the desired value of λ is found or $\lambda_l = \lambda_r$. Assume initially that λ_l and λ_r are known, that the maximum flows $f(\lambda_l)$ and $f(\lambda_r)$ in $G(\lambda_l)$ and $G^R(\lambda_r)$, respectively, are also known.

(1) Given a new value λ^* between λ_l and λ_r, dovetail the following two computations: compute the maximum flow in $G(\lambda^*)$ by continuing the flow computation from $f(\lambda_l)$ (this corresponds to increasing λ to λ^*); compute the maximum flow in $G^R(\lambda^*)$ by continuing the computation from $f(\lambda_r)$ (i.e., decreasing λ to λ^*). Stop as soon as either of these flow computations finishes, and call the resulting flow $f(\lambda^*)$.

(2) Use $f(\lambda^*)$ to determine (in the binary search process) which of λ_l or λ_r should be changed to λ^*, and make the change.

If it is λ_l that changed to λ^*, and the dovetailed flow computation from $f(\lambda_l)$ finished, then set $f(\lambda_l)$ to $f(\lambda^*)$; if it is λ_l that changed but the dovetailed computation from $f(\lambda_l)$ did not finish, then finish it, and set $f(\lambda_l)$ to the resulting flow.

If it is λ_r that changed and the dovetailed flow computation from $f(\lambda_r)$ finished, then set $f(\lambda_r)$ to $f(\lambda^*)$; if it is λ_r that changed but the dovetailed computation from $f(\lambda_r)$ did not finish, then finish it and set $f(\lambda_r)$ to the resulting flow.

Time analysis

Consider an iteration when λ_l is changed to λ^* (in Step 2). The work in that iteration is either involved in finding $f(\lambda^*)$ by continuing the flow from $f(\lambda_l)$ (the value of λ_l is before Step 2), or in finding (or attempting to find) $f(\lambda^*)$ by continuing the flow from $f(\lambda_r)$ (λ_r before Step 2). Because of the dovetailing, the amount of the latter work is dominated by the amount of the former work and so the total work in the iteration is at most twice the amount used to continue the flow from $f(\lambda_l)$. By symmetry, the same conclusion holds when λ_r changes to λ^*.

We will identify two sequences of λ values, one increasing and one decreasing, such that the associated flows for each sequence can be charged as in Theorem 5.2, and such that all other work is dominated by the work done in these two sequences. The first sequence (of increasing λ values) will be called S_l, and the other sequence (of decreasing λ values) will be called S_r. The first values of S_l and S_r are the first λ_l and λ_r values used in the binary search.

In general, whenever λ_l is changed to λ^* (in Step 2), add λ^* to the end of S_l, and whenever λ_r is changed to λ^*, add λ^* to the end of S_r. By construction, if λ_i and λ_j are two consecutive values in S_l, then $f(\lambda_j)$ is computed in the algorithm by continuing the flow from $f(\lambda_i)$. Hence all of the flows associated with S_l form one (increasing) sequence, and Theorem 5.2 applies. Similarly, all the flows associated with S_r form one (decreasing) sequence and Theorem 5.2 again applies. By the comment in the first paragraph, all other work is dominated by the work involved in computing the flows in these two sequences. Hence we have the following.

Theorem 5.3. *In a binary search that probes k values of* λ, *the total time for all the flows is* $O(n^3 + kn)$. *So if the binary search is over D possible values for* λ, *then the time for the binary search is* $O(n^3 + n \log D)$.

5.5. An application: Network reliability testing

In a communication network $G = (V, E)$, each node v can test $k(v)$ incident lines per day, and each line e must be tested $t(e)$ times. The problem is to find a schedule to minimize the number of days to finish the tests. This problem can be solved as a parametric network flow problem in the following bipartite network GB: there are n nodes (one for each node of V) on one side and m nodes (one for each edge of E) on the other side; there is an edge (v, e) from node v to node e in GB if and only if node $v \in V$ is an endpoint of edge $e \in E$ of graph G. Each edge (e, t) in GB has capacity $t(e)$, and each edge (s, v) capacity $k(v)$. If we multiply the capacity of each (s, v) edge by a parameter λ, then the problem is to find the minimum integer value of λ such that there is a flow saturating the edges into t.

A direct method to solve this problem is to search for the proper λ by binary search. Let $T = \Sigma_e \, t(e)$; then the binary search would solve $O(\log T)$ network flow problems. These flows are in the form assumed for Theorem 5.3, hence the optimal schedule can be found in $O(n^3)$ time for $T = O(2^{n^2})$.

6. Computing edge connectivity: The amortization theme writ small

The edge connectivity of a connected undirected graph is the minimum number of edges needed to be removed in order to disconnect the graph, i.e., after the edges are removed, at least two nodes of the graph have no path between them. The set of disconnecting edges of minimum size is called a *connectivity cut*. The computation to find edge connectivity, and a connectivity cut, is based on network flow but we will see that by exploiting properties of the problem, and by *amortizing* the analysis, we can obtain a much faster algorithm than at first may be suspected.

The most direct way to compute edge connectivity is to put a unit capacity on each edge, and then consider the $\binom{n}{2}$ minimum cut problems obtained by varying the choice of source and sink pair over all possibilities. The smallest of these pairwise cuts is clearly a connectivity cut. With this approach, the edge connectivity can be computed in $O(n^2 F(n))$ time, where $F(n)$ is the time to find a minimum cut between a specified source–sink pair in a graph with n nodes. In a graph where all the edges have capacity of one, it is known [Even & Tarjan, 1975] that the Dinits algorithm will have at most $O(n^{2/3})$ phases, rather than the general bound of n phases. So, for the connectivity problem $F(n) = O(n^{2/3}e)$, and the edge connectivity and a connectivity cut can be found in $O(n^{2+2/3}e)$ time.

The first improvement over this direct method is to note that only $n - 1$ flows need to be computed. To achieve the bound of only $n - 1$ flows, simply pick a node v arbitrarily and compute a minimum cut between v and each of the other $n - 1$ nodes. The minimum cut over these $n - 1$ cuts will be a connectivity cut because a connectivity cut must separate at least one node w from v, and clearly no v, w cut can be smaller than the connectivity cut. Hence the minimum cut separating v from w is also a connectivity cut. So a time bound of $O(n^{1+2/3}e)$ is achieved.

6.1. An $n - 1$ flow method allowing amortization

There are actually several ways, different than the approach above, to organize the flow computations so that only $n - 1$ total flows are necessary. We will follow one such method that will allow us to amortize the time for these $n - 1$ flows, achieving a total running time bounded by $O(ne)$. Not only is this a speed up over the above approach based on the Dinits method, but the algorithm will be considerably simpler than the Dinits method.

Let us assume an arbitrary ordering of the nodes $v_1, v_2, \ldots, v_n$, and define V_i to be the set $\{v_1, v_2, \ldots, v_i\}$. The graph G_i is the graph obtained from the original graph G by contracting the set V_i into a single node called v_0. That is, the nodes V_i are removed and a node v_0 is added, and any edge (v_j, v_k) from a node $v_j \notin V_i$ to a node in $v_k \in V_i$ is replaced by an edge from v_j to v_0. Note that G_i could also be defined as the graph obtained from G_{i-1} by contracting v_i into v_0. Let C_i denote a minimum cut between v_{i+1} and v_0 in G_i.

Lemma 6.1. *The smallest of the cuts C_i $(i = 1, \ldots, n - 1)$ is a connectivity cut of G.*

Proof. Let C be a connectivity cut in G, and let $k + 1$ be the smallest integer such that v_1 and v_{k+1} are on opposite sides of C. Hence all the nodes of V_k are on one side of C and v_{k+1} is on the other side. Note that for any i, any cut in G separating V_i from v_{i+1} is a v_0, v_{i+1} cut in G_i and conversely. So C and C_k must have the same number of edges, and C_k must be a connectivity cut in G. $\square$

Now we consider the total time to compute the $n - 1$ C_i cuts. As should be expected, each C_i will be obtained from a maximum v_{i+1}, v_0 flow in G_i. To compute these flows efficiently, we will use a slight variation of the Ford–

Fulkerson algorithm, differing from the original Ford–Fulkerson algorithm in two implementation details.

First, for every iteration $i = 1, \ldots, n - 1$, after the maximum v_{i+1}, v_0 flow and minimum cut C_i are found in G_i, we scan the current adjacency list of v_{i+1}, and for any node $v_j \neq v_0$ adjacent to v_{i+1} we mark v_j and the edge v_j, v_{i+1}. Then we contract v_{i+1} into v_0, updating the appropriate adjacency lists, thus creating graph G_{i+1}. Note that at this point the set of nodes which are adjacent to v_0 in G_{i+1} and the edges incident with v_0 are all marked.

Second, when computing a maximum v_{i+1}, v_0 flow in G_i we start by searching for paths of length one or length two in G_i and flow one unit on each such path found. These paths will be called *short* paths. Note that these paths are in G_i and not in a residual graph. The node and edge markings discussed above make this search particularly easy: simply scan the current adjacency list of v_{i+1} for either v_0 or a marked node (note that v_0 can appear more than once because of previous node contractions). Every occurrence of v_0 indicates an edge between v_{i+1} and v_0, and every marked node $w \neq v_0$ indicates a path of length two from v_{i+1} to v_0. In particular, this path consists of the unique edge (v_{i+1}, w) followed by one of the possibly many (due to previous contractions) edges (w, v_0). Note that the node and edge markings allow each node w to be processed in constant time.

The search for short paths ends when all paths of length one or two are blocked. Because each edge saturated at this point is either connected to v_0 or v_{i+1}, there is no need to ever undo flow on these edges, so we can remove from further consideration any edges that are saturated at this point. This will be important for the time analysis below.

To complete the v_{i+1}, v_0 maximum flow in G_i we follow the original Ford–Fulkerson algorithm, i.e., successively building residual graphs (ignoring the saturated edges on short paths found above), finding augmentation paths, and augmenting the flow by one unit for each such path. All paths found during this part of the algorithm will have length three or more, and are called *long* paths.

6.2. Analysis

The modified Ford–Fulkerson method clearly finds a maximum v_{i+1}, v_0 flow, and C_i is easily obtained from it, as shown in Theorem 2.2. Then by Lemma 6.1, the connectivity and connectivity cut are correctly obtained from the smallest of these $n - 1$ cuts.

Theorem 6.1. *The total time for computing the $n - 1$ C_i cuts is $O(ne)$.*

Proof. Note first that the time for computing any particular cut C_i cannot be bounded by $O(e)$, but rather the $O(ne)$ bound will be obtained by amortizing over all the flows. The time needed to find a minimum cut given a maximum flow is clearly just $O(e)$ per flow, as is the time to mark nodes and edges and do the updates to create the next G_i. Hence the total time for these tasks is $O(ne)$.

Now in any iteration i, the short paths in G_i are found in time $O(n)$, since the size of v_{i+1}'s adjacency list is at most size $n-1$, and, by use of the markings, processing of any node on the list takes constant time. Hence over the entire algorithm the time for these tasks is $O(ne)$, although a closer analysis gives an $O(e)$ time bound.

So the key to the time analysis is to show that the searches for long paths (done by using the original Ford–Fulkerson method) take only $O(ne)$ total time over the $n-1$ flows. Each search for a long augmentation path takes $O(e)$ time, and we will show that at most $n-1$ such long searches are done over the entire algorithm.

In iteration i, suppose a long augmentation path begins with the edge (v_{i+1}, w). At the end of iteration i node v_{i+1} is contracted into v_0, so node w will be adjacent to v_0 thereafter. Hence in any iteration $j > i$, if v_{j+1} is adjacent to w in G_j, then there is a path of length two from v_{j+1} to v_0 through w. The edge (v_{j+1}, w) is unique and so will become saturated during the search for paths of lengths one or two. The flow in that edge will not be decreased, so in iteration j, w cannot be the second node on a long augmentation path. It follows that over the entire algorithm a node can be the second node on a long augmentation path at most once. Hence the number of long augmentation paths is at most $n-1$, and the theorem is proved. □

The amortization in the above analysis is on the number of long augmentation paths. In any of the n iterations the number of long augmentations might approach $n-1$, but over the entire algorithm the total number of long augmentations is never more than that number.

6.3. Historical note

The history of the above $O(ne)$ connectivity algorithm is similar to the history of the first $O(n^4)$ and $O(n^3)$ network flow algorithms, which were discovered in the Soviet Union in the early 1970s, but were unknown to the western researchers for some time after that. The $O(ne)$ connectivity algorithm discussed in this section is due to Podderyugin [1973] [see Adelson-Velski, Dinits & Karzanov, 1975] who developed it in 1971. However, it was only published in Russian, and, as far as we know, the method was never discussed in the western literature until now (this article). In the meantime, Matula [1987] independently developed an $O(ne)$ connectivity algorithm in 1986 which incorporates many of the same ideas as the above method, but which will in general do fewer than $n-1$ flows. Matula further showed that connectivity can be found in $O(\lambda n^2)$ time, where λ is the connectivity of the graph. Note that since $\lambda \leqslant e/n$, $\lambda n^2 \leqslant ne$.

7. Matching: Optimal, greedy and optimal-greedy approaches

A *matching* in a graph is a set of edges such that no two edges have a node in common. A *maximum cardinality matching*, or maximum matching for short, in a matching with the largest number of edges over all matchings. A *perfect* matching is one where every node is incident with an edge in the matching. In many problems solved by matching, each edge of the graph has a *weight*, and the problem is to find a matching maximizing the sum of the edges in the matching. We call this the *weighted matching problem*.

7.1. Cardinality matching

The cardinality matching problem in a bipartite graph $G = (N_1, N_2, E)$ can be solved by general network flow algorithms as follows. Let N_1 and N_2 denote the nodes in the two sides of bipartite graph G. We introduce two new nodes, s and t, connecting every node in N_1 to s and every node in N_2 to t. The resulting graph consists of all the original edges of G plus these new edges. Let H denote the new graph, and give every edge a capacity of one.

Theorem 7.1. *An integral maximum s, t flow in H defines a maximum matching.*

Proof. Note that because all edge capacities are one, and the maximum flow is integral, the flow can be decomposed into node-disjoint s, t paths consisting of three edges. The set of middle edges on these paths clearly defines a matching. Conversely if the matching is not maximum, then there is some edge (v, w) with $v \in N_1$ and $w \in N_2$ which can be added to the matching. But, since all edge capacities are one and the flow is integral, the path s, v, w, t with flow one could then also be added to the flow, contradicting the assumption that it is a maximum flow. Hence the matching defined by the flow is maximum. □

Since network flow on n nodes runs in $O(n^3)$ time, maximum cardinality bipartite matching can be computed in $O(n^3)$ time. However, we will show that the Dinits algorithm only uses $O(\sqrt{n})$ phases in H, rather than the general bound of n phases. Each phase can still be implemented in $O(n^2)$ time, hence bipartite matching runs in $O(n^{2.5})$ worst-case time using Dinits algorithm. We begin with the following lemma.

Lemma 7.1. *Let H be as above, and let F be the maximum flow value in H, and let F' be the maximum flow value after phase $i - 1$ of Dinits algorithm. Then $i \leqslant n/(F - F')$.*

Proof. The total flow F in H can be obtained by superimposing the flow of value F' in H obtained at the end of phase $i - 1$ with the maximum s, t flow obtained in the residual graph G^i defined from F'. Further, we can think of the maximum flow problem in G^i as a new flow problem on a graph with zero flow, and we know that it will have a maximum flow of value $F - F'$. In H every node either has one edge into it from s or one edge out of it to t, and all edges in G have capacity one. Further, the Dinits algorithm always maintains an integral flow, so every edge either has flow one or zero. Now consider a node $v \in N_1$. If there is any flow from s to v at this point, then in G^i there will be no (s, v) edge (since it is saturated) but there will be exactly one edge into v from a node $w \in V_2$ (w is the node that v sent its unit flow to). If there is no flow into v at this point, then there is exactly one edge, namely (s, v) into v. Similarly, for any node w on the t side of H there is exactly one edge out of w. It follows that the maximum integral s, t flow in G^i is partitioned into s, t paths that share no nodes except for s and t. Since there are only n nodes in G^i, the shortest of these paths must be less than or equal to $n/(F - F')$. Hence the length of the layered graph LG^i obtained from G^i is at most $n/(F - F')$. Since the length of the layered graphs grow by at least one in each phase, $i \leq n/(F - F')$. $\square$

Theorem 7.2. *In graph H defined above the Dinits algorithm can only use $2\sqrt{n}$ phases.*

Proof. Assume the total flow value F is greater than $\sqrt{n}$, since otherwise the theorem is immediate. Now consider the phase i in which the flow reaches or exceeds $F - \sqrt{n}$. At the start of phase i the flow F' is less than $F - \sqrt{n}$, so $F - F' > \sqrt{n}$. By Lemma 7.1, $i \leq n/(F - F') < \sqrt{n}$. Further, at the end of phase i, the flow is at least $F - \sqrt{n}$ so there can be at most $\sqrt{n}$ additional phases, and the theorem follows. $\square$

This theorem is of importance in its own right, but it also illustrates a common theme in the design of efficient algorithms: seeking out and taking advantage of special structure. There is no fancy name or philosophy suggesting how to identify which structures will be the most useful, but digging for structure and exploiting what is found is certainly one of the most productive techniques in finding efficient algorithms. We will see another example of this later in this section.

We should also mention that a maximum cardinality matching in a general graph can be found in $O(n^{2.5})$ time by a much more complex algorithm.

7.2. Weighted matching and the greedy paradigm

We now look at a simple and very fast heuristic, *the greedy method*, for finding a maximum weight matching in any graph. The heuristic does not always produce an optimal matching, but it is guaranteed to find one with weight at least *one half* that of the optimal.

Greedy matching

Input: A weighted graph $G = (N, E)$; $w(e)$ represents the weight of edge e.

Output: A matching M, with total weight at least half that of the maximum weight matching.

(1) Set M to the empty set, and set A to E.

(2) While A is not empty do

　　Begin

　　　　(2.1) Pick the edge e in A with the largest weight $w(e)$ of all edges in A.

　　　　(2.2) Put edge e in set M; delete e and all edges incident with it from A.

　　End

(3) Output edge set M.

Theorem 7.3. *Let M' be the optimal matching in G, and let $c(M')$ and $c(M)$ denote the weights of the optimal and the greedy matchings, respectively. Then $c(M)/c(M') \geqslant \frac{1}{2}$.*

Proof. Initially, every edge of M' is in A. Each time an edge e is chosen for M, the only edges of M' that get deleted from A are those edges incident with an endpoint of e. M' is a matching, and so at most two edges, e_1 and e_2, of M' are deleted from A at each step. Since e is chosen over both e_1 and e_2, $w(e) \geqslant w(e_1)$ and $w(e) \geqslant w(e_2)$, so $w(e) \geqslant \frac{1}{2}(w(e_1) + w(e_2))$. Eventually, A is empty; at that point, every edge e' in M' is associated with an edge e in M, such that $w(e) \geqslant w(e')$, and at most two edges in M' are associated with the same edge in M. Hence $c(M) \geqslant \frac{1}{2}c(M')$. □

Corollary 7.1. *M' has cardinality at least one half that of the maximum cardinality matching in G.*

In fact, if edges are picked arbitrarily in Step 2.1, the resulting matching has cardinality at least one half the maximum. This is easy to prove, and is left as an exercise.

It should be clear why this approach to matching is called a 'greedy algorithm'. Another suggestive term for it is a 'myopic algorithm'. Greedy algorithms are generally fast, but in most cases give results that deviate from the optimal solutions by large or even unbounded amounts. A very elegant theory based on matroids has been developed which explains and predicts when a certain type of greedy approach will be guaranteed to yield an optimal solution [see Lawler, 1976]. However, not all greedy methods can be explained by matroid theory. The example below is such a case.

7.3. A problem where the greedy algorithm finds the optimal matching

Weighted matching is a very important problem because many, varied, combinatorial problems can be cast and solved in term of weighted matching.

Sometimes the problem being solved via matching can be shown to have special structure, and this structure can be exploited to speed up finding the optimal weighted matching. Below we can discuss a case where the edge weights have special structure allowing the optimal weighted matching to be found in O(e) time via a greedy approach.

The box inequality

Let u, u', v, v' be four nodes in a complete bipartite graph $G = (N_1, N_2, E)$ (a complete bipartite graph is one where there is an edge between every node in N_1 and every node in N_2) such that u and u' are in N_1 and v and v' are in N_2. Suppose w.l.o.g. that $w(u, v) \geq \max[w(u, v'), w(u', v), w(u', v')]$. If $w(u, v) + w(u', v') \geq w(u, v') + w(u', v)$, then these four nodes satisfy the *box inequality*. A complete bipartite graph is said to satisfy the box inequalities if the box inequality is satisfied for any two arbitrary nodes from N_1 together with any two arbitrary nodes from N_2.

Below we will discuss a problem solved by weighted bipartite matching, where the graph satisfies the box inequality. But for now we show the following theorem.

Theorem 7.4. *If the complete bipartite graph satisfies the box inequalities, and all weights are non-negative, then the greedy matching is a maximum weight matching.*

Proof. Let M be the matching found by the greedy algorithm. If there is more than one maximum weight matching, then let M' be a maximum weight matching which contains the largest number of edges also in M. Suppose M' has weight strictly greater than M. Since G is a complete bipartite graph and all weights are non-negative, both M and M' will be perfect matchings.

Let $M \oplus M'$ be the symmetric difference of the sets of edges in M and in M'. That is, $M \oplus M'$ is the set of edges which are in exactly one of the two matchings M or M'. $M \oplus M'$ must be non-empty for otherwise $M = M'$. Since both matchings are perfect, any edge in $M \oplus M'$ is part of an even length *alternating cycle* where every other edge is from M (M'). Let C be such an alternating cycle, and let $e = (u, v)$ be the first edge in C considered by the greedy algorithm. We claim edge e must be in M. If not, then at the time e was considered either edge (u, v') and (u', v) was in M, for some nodes u', v'. W.l.o.g. say that (u, v') was in M. Then v' is not in C, since e is the first edge on C considered by the algorithm. But this is not possible, because u is in C so the other endpoint (v') of the edge in M touching u must, by definition, also be in C. Hence $e = (u, v)$ is in M.

Let (u, v') and (u', v) be the edges of M' in C that touch u and v. We know these edges exist since C must have at least four edges. Since (u, v) is the first edge in C considered by the greedy algorithm, $w(u, v) \geq \max[w(u, v'), w(u', v)]$. We claim also that $w(u, v) \geq w(u', v')$. This is clearly true if $(u', v') \in M$, since it then would be in C. So suppose (u', v') is not in M. But both u' and v' are in C, so neither were matched at the time (u, v) was examined, so if $w(u, v) < w(u', v')$, then (u', v') would have been taken into M, a contradiction. Hence $w(u, v) \geq \max[w(u, v'), w(u', v), w(u', v')]$, and by the box inequality, $w(u, v) + w(u', v') \geq w(u, v') + w(u', v)$.

Now consider the matching formed from M' that omits edges (u', v) and (u, v') and includes edges (u, v) and (u', v'). It is immediate that this is still a perfect matching, that it contains one more edge of M than did M', and (by the box inequality) that it has weight greater or equal to that of M'. But that contradicts the choice of M', proving the theorem.   □

A matching problem in molecular biology where the box inequalities hold

A central task in molecular biology is determining the nucleotide sequence of strings of DNA. For our purposes, DNA is just a string composed from an alphabet of four symbols (nucleotides): A, T, C, or G. Efficient methods exist for determining the sequence of short strings of DNA, but in order to sequence long strings (which are of more interest) the long strings of DNA must first be cut into smaller strings. Known ways of cutting up longer strings of DNA result in the pieces becoming randomly permuted. Hence, after obtaining and sequencing each of the smaller strings one has the problem of determining the correct order of the small strings. The most common approach to solving this problem is to first make many copies of the DNA, and then cut up each copy with a different cutter so that the pieces obtained from one cutter overlap pieces obtained from another. Then, each piece is sequenced, and by studying how the sequences of the smaller pieces overlap, one tries to reassemble the original long sequence.

Given the entire set of strings, the problem of assembling the original DNA string has been *modeled* as the *shortest superstring problem*: find the shortest string which contains each of the smaller strings in the set as a contiguous substring. In the case when the original DNA string is linear, the problem of finding the shortest superstring is known to be NP-complete but there are approximation methods which are guaranteed to find a superstring at most three times the length of the shortest string [Blum, Jiang, Li, Tromp & Yannakakis, 1991].

The methods discussed by Blum, Jiang, Li, Tromp & Yannakakis [1991] are heavily based on weighted matching, where weight $w(u, v)$ is the length of the longest suffix of string u that is identical to a prefix of string v. In the initial part of the method, the weight $w(u, v)$ is computed for each ordered pair (this can be done in linear time [Gusfield, Landau & Schieber, 1992]), and a bipartite graph $G = (N_1, N_2, E)$ is created with one node on each side of the graph for each of the small DNA strings. The weight of edge (u, v), $u \in N_1$, $v \in N_2$ is set to $w(u, v)$, and a maximum weight matching is found. This matching is then used to construct a superstring which is at most four times the length of the optimal superstring. This error bound is then reduced to three, by another use of weighted matching using suffix–prefix lengths derived from strings obtained from the factor-four solution.

The point of interest here is that for weights equaling the maximum suffix–prefix overlap lengths, as above, the weights satisfy the box inequality, and hence the two matchings needed in the above approximation method can be found by the greedy algorithm.

Theorem 7.5. *Let graph G with weights w be obtained from a set of strings as defined above. Then G satisfies the box inequalities. That is, if $w(u, v) \geqslant \max[w(u, v'), \ w(u', v), \ w(u', v')]$, then $w(u, v) + w(u', v') \geqslant w(u, v') + w(u', v)$, for any nodes u, u' in N_1 and v, v' in N_2.*

Proof. Assume w.l.o.g. that $w(u', v) \geqslant w(u', v')$. We divide the proof into two cases. Either $w(u', v') = 0$ or $w(u', v') > 0$. The first case is shown in Figure 1. Since it is a suffix of u' that matches a prefix of v, the left end of u' cannot be to the right of the left end of v. Also, since $w(u, v) \geqslant w(u', v)$, the right end of u' can also not be to the right end of u. So, we define $x = w(u', v) \leqslant w(u, v)$. With the lengths x, y, z as shown in the figure,

$$w(u, v) + w(u', v') = x + y + z \geqslant z + x = w(u, v') + w(u', v).$$

The second case when $w(u', v') > 0$ is shown in Figure 2. With x, y, z as shown in the figure

$$w(u, v) + w(u', v')$$
$$= (x + y + z) + y \geqslant (y + z) + (x + y) = w(u, v') + w(u', v). \qquad \square$$

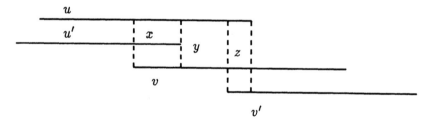

Fig. 1. First case.

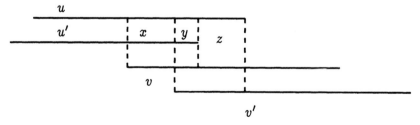

Fig. 2. Second case.

8. Parallel network flow in $O(n^2 \log n)$ time

In this section we discuss how to compute network flow on a parallel computer. But first, we have to define what we mean by a parallel computer. There are many ways that parallel computers have been defined and modeled, some more realistic than others. The most critical differences have to do with whether more than one processor can read or write the same memory cell concurrently, and how the processors communicate. One model that is generally agreed as meaningful is the concurrent read exclusive write parallel random access machine (CREW PRAM).

In the CREW PRAM model there are k processors that are identical except that they each have a unique identifying number. These processors can execute their programs in parallel, and each processor is a general purpose sequential computer, in particular a RAM (random access machine). The processors are assumed to work in lock-step synchrony following a central clock that divides the work of the processors into discrete time units. The processors may have separate memories, but they share a common memory that any of them can read from or write into. Each processor can read or write a single memory cell in a single time unit. We assume that the hardware allows any number of processors to read the same memory cell concurrently (concurrent read), but if more than one processor tries to write to the same cell in the same time step, then the result is unassured (exclusive write). Hence any program for this parallel system should avoid concurrent writes. The processors communicate with each other via the shared memory. The parallel time for a parallel algorithm refers to the number of primitive time units (each of which is enough for a single step of the algorithm on any processor) that have passed from the initiation of the algorithm to its termination, no matter how many processors are active at any moment.

Below we will describe an implementation of the max-d GT algorithm on a CREW PRAM using $k = O(e)$ processors, and a shared memory of size $O(e)$ cells. In particular, there will be a constant number of memory cells and a constant number of independent processors for each node and each edge of G. The algorithm will run in $O(n^2 \log n)$ parallel time. This speed up over $O(n^3)$ is not very dramatic, however, it is the best that is known (for dense graphs) and has been obtained by a variety of different methods, suggesting that improving the bound may be a difficult problem. This bound was first obtained by Shiloah and Vishkin [1982] using only $O(n)$ processors. We will follow ideas that are closer to those given by Goldberg & Tarjan [1988], but again using $O(e)$ processors rather than $O(n)$ processors.

The parallel GT algorithm will be broken up into stages, and each stage will be broken up into four substages. In the first substage of a stage, the label of any active node v is set to $\min[d(w) + 1: (v, w)$ is an edge in the current residual graph]. In the next substage, all the active nodes of max-d label are identified. In the third substage each such node v will, in parallel with the others, push excess out along admissible incident edges until either v has no more excess or until v's label must be incremented. In the final substage, each node 'receives' its new flow (if any) and recomputes its excess. After this, the stage ends. The algorithm ends in the stage when there are no active nodes. We will provide implementation details and justify the time bound below, but first we establish the following.

Theorem 8.1. *The parallel GT algorithm introduced above correctly computes a maximum flow.*

Proof. In the sequential algorithm, it was easy to establish that if the algorithm terminated, then it terminated with a maximum flow. The key to this was that the node labels were always valid. It is easy to verify that in the parallel GT algorithm, the node labels are valid after the first substage in each stage. Hence it is again easy to see that, if the algorithm terminates, it terminates with a maximum flow. We will establish termination below by bounding the number of stages. □

Lemma 8.1. *In the parallel max-d algorithm, there can be at most $O(n^2)$ stages.*

Proof. Between two consecutive stages either the max-d value will increase, remain constant, or decrease. In the first two cases the node label of at least one node will increase, and hence there can be at most $2n^2$ stages of this type (the second case is a little more subtle than the first, but is not hard). For the third case, note that since the max-d label of any active node is between $2n$ and 0 (this follows from validity), at any point in time the number of stages that end with max-d decreasing can be at most $2n$ larger than the number of stages that end with max-d increasing. Since there can be only $O(n^2)$ increasing cases, there can be at most $O(n^2)$ stages of the third type as well. □

Below we will show how to implement a stage in $O(\log n)$ parallel time using $O(e)$ processors, yielding an $O(n^2 \log n)$ parallel time algorithm.

8.1. Parallel implementation

We will discuss each substage and show how it can be implemented in $O(\log n)$ parallel time. The central idea in each substage is the same, the use of a binary tree with at most n leaves. The easiest conceptual way to think of the tree is that each vertex in the tree contains a dedicated processor. Since the tree is binary, the number of processors in any tree is $O(n)$, and the height of the tree is $O(\log n)$.

How to update node labels in parallel

A node v can compute its updated $d(v)$ label during the first substage as follows: it signals the processors associated with the possible residual edges out of v to determine (in parallel) which of them are residual edges. Each edge processor can do that because it knows the current flow on the edge. A processor representing residual edge (v, w) then reads $d(w)$ and inserts it into a leaf in a binary tree for v, in a predefined leaf specified for (v, w). A processor representing a possible residual edge out of v which is not in the current residual graph enters a value large than $2n$ in its predefined leaf. This tree has d_v leaves, where $d_v = |I(v)|$, the number of possible residual edges out of v. Then in $O(\log d_v)$ parallel time, the minimum of the values at the leaves is computed by the obvious tournament computation. That is, once the value is known for each of the two children of a vertex in the tree, the value at that vertex is set to the minimum of the value of its children. The value at the root of the tree is the overall minimum. If the root value is greater than $2n$, then there are no residual edges out of v, and $d(v)$ is unchanged. Otherwise, the processor at the root changes $d(v)$ to one plus the value at the root.

For any node v of G, the total number of processors needed to implement the tournament is $O(d_v)$ since the binary tree contains only that many vertices. So the number of processors involved in this substage is $\Sigma_v\, d_v = O(e)$.

How to find the active nodes of max-d label

The processor for any node v knows the current excess at v and the updated $d(v)$. Each processor associated with an active node inserts the current d value in a predefined leaf of a binary tree. Then by the tournament method again, and in $O(\log n)$ time using $O(n)$ processors, the maximum of these values is found and placed in a memory cell. All the active node processors then read this cell in unit time to determine if their node is of max-d.

How to push in parallel

For each node v in G, we will again use a binary tree with d_v leaves, where each leaf in the tree is associated with a possible residual edge out of v. Again, each vertex in the tree has an assigned dedicated processor. Hence over all the trees there are $O(e)$ processors assigned. Essentially, the leaves of the tree correspond to the list $I(v)$ described in Section 4.2.

We will determine in $O(\log d_v)$ parallel time which edges v should use to push out its excess, and how much to push on each edge. At the start of this substage, the processor for the leaf corresponding to edge (v, w) determines whether (v, w) is admissible (by reading $d(v), d(w)$ and knowing whether (v, w) is a residual edge), and what the capacity $c(v, w)$ in the current residual graph is. If the edge is admissible, then its current capacity is written at the leaf. If the edge (v, w) is not admissible, then a zero will be written instead of its capacity.

Processing the vertices of the tree bottom up from the leaves, we collect at each vertex the sum of the numbers written at the leaves in its subtree. This process is completed in $O(\log d_v)$ parallel time, since the entry at a vertex is the just the sum of the two entries of its two children, and the depth of the tree is $O(\log d_v)$. At this point, all the processors associated with leaves of v's tree can read, in unit time, the sum at the root, to determine if all their associated edges will become saturated or not.

If the number at the root is smaller or equal to $e(v)$, then every admissible edge out of v will get saturated. This message is sent back down the tree to the leaf processors which make the flow changes on their associated edges.

If the sum at the root of v's tree is greater than $e(v)$, then only some of the admissible edges out of v will be used. However, at most one edge will get new flow without getting saturated. The allocation to edges is done in $O(\log d(v))$ time by working down from the root. Essentially, we will write at each vertex x of the tree the amount of flow to be pushed from node v along edges associated with leaves in the subtree of x. Hence the number written at a leaf for edge (v, w) is the amount to be pushed along edge (v, w) in the residual graph. In detail, we do the following: let $n(x)$ denote the number presently written at tree vertex x. First change $n(r)$, the number written at the root, to $e(v)$. For any tree vertex x, let x' be the right child of r and x'' be its left child. Set $n(x')$ to the minimum of $n(x')$ and $n(r)$; then set $n(x'')$ to the maximum of $n(r) - n(x')$ and zero. Once the numbers at the leaves have been written, the processors associated with those edges can make the flow changes on these edges in parallel.

How to receive flow

In the previous substage flow was pushed along certain edges. The amount pushed out of a node v is known during the substage and so the excess at v is updated then. However, the total flow entering a node w must also be determined. This is again easily computed in $O(\log n)$ parallel time using a binary tree for each node, where each leaf is associated with a possible residual edge into w. We omit the details.

8.2. Final result

Since there are $O(n^2)$ stages in the parallel method and each can be implemented to run in $O(\log n)$ parallel time with $O(e)$ processors, we get the following theorem.

Theorem 8.2. *A maximum flow can be computed in* $O(n^2 \log n)$ *parallel time using* $O(e)$ *processors.*

8.3. Work versus time

In the above implementation we used $O(e)$ processors to compute maximum flow in $O(n^2 \log n)$ parallel time. If we were to convert this parallel algorithm to a sequential one we would immediately obtain a sequential time bound of $O(en^2 \log n)$, which is much larger than the known $O(n^3)$ bounds. This leaves the intuition that a 'better' parallel algorithm may be possible, one which either uses fewer processors or has a smaller worst-case bound.

To examine this issue we define the *work* of a parallel algorithm to be the product of the parallel time bound and the maximum number of processors needed by the algorithm. There are network flow algorithms which run in $O(n^2 \log n)$ time using only $O(n)$ processors, hence using only $O(n^3 \log n)$ work [Shiloah & Vishkin, 1982], and similar results have been obtained for sparse graphs [Goldberg & Tarjan, 1988]. The notion of work is important not only as a way of distinguishing between equally fast parallel algorithms, but because the number of assumed processors may not be available. In that case the degradation of the running time is related to the assumed number of processors; the smaller the number of assumed processors, the smaller the degradation.

In addition to reducing the work needed by the parallel algorithm, most parallel algorithms for network flow have been implemented on the EREW PRAM model. In that model only one processor can read (exclusive read) any memory cell in one unit. Since this is a more restrictive assumption than for a CREW PRAM, results on EREW PRAMs are considered more realistic, or at least more likely to be implementable on real parallel machines.

9. Distributed algorithms

In this section we briefly discuss another form of parallel computation, namely *distributed computation*. There are numerous particular models of distributed computation but they all try to capture the notion of several autonomous, often asynchronous, processors each with their own memory solving some problem by their joint actions and restricted or local communication. This is in contrast to the single processor model, and even in contrast to models of synchronous parallel computation, where there is an assumed common clock, shared memory, and possibly a very rich or highly structured communication network. In particular, in the distributed model, computation on any processor is considered to be much faster than interprocessor communication, and so it is the later time that is to be minimized.

The efficiency of a distributed algorithm is usually measured in terms of the number of messages needed, and the complexity of the computations that each processor does. Alternatively, one can measure the worst-case, or average-case, parallel time for the system to solve its problem. To make this measure meaningful, we usually assume some maximum fixed time that a processor will wait after it has all the needed inputs, before executing a single step of the algorithm. However, it is possible to sometimes relax even this assumption, and there also are general techniques for converting asynchronous distributed algorithms to synchronous ones with only a small increase in the number of messages used.

In this article we can only give some flavor of the nature of distributed computation, and will examine only a very simple problem, the *shortest path communication* problem. Although simple, this problem actually arises in some distributed versions of the Goldberg–Tarjan network flow algorithm.

9.1. *Shortest path communication*

Consider the situation where each node v on a directed graph must repeatedly send messages to a fixed node t, and so wants to send the message along a path with the fewest number of edges (a shortest path). The nodes are assumed only to know who their neighbors are in the graph. In order to know how to route a message on a shortest v to t path, v only needs to know the first node w after v on such a shortest path, since the edge (v, w) followed by a shortest w to t path is shortest v to t path. When the system first starts up, or after some edges have been removed, the distances to t increase, no node can be sure of the shortest path from it to t. The goal at that point is for the system to begin some asynchronous, distributed computation, so that at the end of the computation, every node v learns which one of its neighbors is the first node on the shortest path from v to t. We ignore for now the question of how the nodes know to start this process. In the KE, Dinits or GT network flow algorithms, the distance to t from a node v in the evolving residual graph does only increase as was shown earlier.

We first assume that a central clock is available, so that the actions of the processors can be divided into distinct iterations. Later we will remove this assumption. Let H be any directed graph with designated nodes s and t. For any node v, let $D(v)$ denote the number of edges on the shortest v to t path in H.

Lemma 9.1. *For each node v, let $\hat{D}(v)$ be a number assigned to node v, such that $\hat{D}(t) = 0$. If for every node v, $\hat{D}(v) = 1 + \min[\hat{D}(w): (v, w)$ is a directed edge in $H]$, then $\hat{D}(v)$ is the distance of the shortest (directed) path from v to t in H.*

Proof. Suppose not, and let v be the closest node to t such that $\hat{D}(v) \neq D(v)$, the true distance from v to t. Let P_v be the shortest path from v to t and let w be the node after v on P_v. By assumption $\hat{D}(w) = D(w)$. But then $\hat{D}(v) \leq \hat{D}(w) + 1 = D(w) + 1 = D(v)$. So, suppose that $\hat{D}(v) < D(v)$; then there is an edge (v, u) to a node u such that $\hat{D}(u) < \hat{D}(w)$ and, by assumption, $\hat{D}(u) = D(u)$. But that would contradict the assumption that P_v is the shortest v to t path. Hence $\hat{D}(v) = D(v)$ for every node v. □

We will use the above lemma to compute the shortest distances from each node to t. Suppose we start off with numbers $\hat{D}(v)$, where for all v $\hat{D}(v) \leq D(v)$, and $\hat{D}(v) \leq 1 + \min[\hat{D}(w): (v, w)$ is a directed edge in $H]$. We call a node v *deficient* if the second inequality above is strict. We can think of $\hat{D}(v)$ as an underestimate of $D(v)$. We will modify the $\hat{D}(v)$ values in the following algorithm, then show that the algorithm terminates, and that at termination, $\hat{D}(v) = D(v)$ for each v.

Distance estimate algorithm
Repeat
   Step A. For at least one node v such that the current $\hat{D}(v)$ is less than $1 + \min[\hat{D}(w): (v, w)$ is an edge in $H]$, i.e., v is deficient, set $\hat{D}(v) = 1 + \min[\hat{D}(w): (v, w)$ is an edge in $H]$.
Until $\hat{D}(v) = 1 + \min[\hat{D}(w): (v, w)$ is an edge in $H]$ for every node v.

Note that if more than one deficient node is selected in Step A (any number are possible), then the updates to the $\hat{D}$ values are made in parallel.

Theorem 9.1. *The distance estimate algorithm terminates, and upon termination* $\hat{D}(v) = D(v)$ *for all* v.

Proof. First we show that $\hat{D}(v) \leq D(v)$ throughout the algorithm. Suppose not, and let v be the first node set to a value above $D(v)$. As before, let w be the first node after v on P_v. Then at the point that $\hat{D}(v)$ is set above $D(v)$, $\hat{D}(w) \leq D(w)$, so $\hat{D}(v) \leq 1 + D(w) = D(v)$, which is a contradiction. Now the algorithm must terminate since each time a $\hat{D}(v)$ value is changed it is increased by a least one, and $\hat{D}(v)$ is bounded by $D(v)$. At termination, the conditions of Lemma 9.1 are satisfied, hence the theorem is proved. $\square$

We now add implementation detail to the distance update algorithm so that it runs efficiently. We will assume that at the beginning of the algorithm the minimum of $\{\hat{D}(w): (v, w)$ is a directed edge in $H\}$ is known for each v, and hence that all the initially deficient nodes are known. Note that a deficient node remains deficient until its $\hat{D}$ value is increased.

Although we assume that initially deficient nodes are known, we will need an efficient way to identify nodes which become, or become again, deficient during the algorithm. It is not efficient to have each node scan the $\hat{D}$ values of its neighbors at each iteration of Step A. That would take $O(e)$ messages per iteration. Instead, whenever a $\hat{D}(v)$ is changed, the updated $\hat{D}(v)$ is sent to each node u such that (u, v) is a directed edge in H. If a node u receives such a message in one iteration, in the next iteration it compares its current $\hat{D}(u)$ against one plus the values it received in the previous iteration. The smaller of these candidate values is then taken as the current $\hat{D}(u)$. We associate the work to send these messages and then to do the comparisons, to the nodes of the previous iteration whose values have changed. In this way, the total amount of work involved in such checking is just $O(n)$ times the number of nodes whose $\hat{D}$ value changed in the previous iteration. Hence we have the following theorem.

Theorem 9.2. *Let* $\hat{D}(v)$ *be the initial values given to each node* v, *and let* $S = \Sigma_v[D(v) - \hat{D}(v)]$, *where* $D(v)$ *is the correct* v *to* t *distance. Ignoring the work to locate the initially deficient nodes, the distance estimate algorithm uses at most* $O(nS)$ *message passes.*

9.2. The asynchronous case

The distance estimate algorithm is more sequential than is permitted in the distributed model. The problem is that in the above discussion of the distance estimate algorithm there are definite iterations of Step A, and there is a centralized clock that establishes the starts and ends of each iteration. The implementation specified that every node receiving one or more messages from its neighbors in one iteration should use this information to update its $\hat{D}$ value in the next iteration. But in the distributed model, the processors run at differing speeds, and there is no central clock, so the notion of iterations is not applicable. This difficulty is easily handled.

We change the implementation of the algorithm so that whenever a node v decides to update its distance estimate, it simply uses its knowledge of who its neighbors are (this knowledge is assumed to be current), and the $\hat{D}$ values that it has received *since $\hat{D}(v)$ was last changed*. The algorithm with this modification is truly distributed, and the estimates will converge to the correct distances. The proof of this is almost identical to that of Theorem 9.1. Hence if $D(v)$ is the correct distance from v to t, and $\hat{D}(v)$ is the initial estimate, then the system will converge to the correct distance values using only $n \sum_v [D(v) - \hat{D}(v)] = nS$ messages.

Although the $\hat{D}$ values will converge to the correct distances, how will the nodes in the system know when this has happened? Whenever a node v adjacent to t sees that $\hat{D}(v) = 1$, it knows that $\hat{D}(v) = D(v)$. This will eventually happen for every node v whose shortest path to t is the single edge (v, t), and there certainly must be one such v. When a node realizes it has the correct D value, it sends an appropriate message to its neighbors. In general, any node v which learns that the true distance of all its neighbors have been established, and which sees that $\hat{D}(v) = 1 + \hat{D}(w)$ for its neighbor w with minimum $\hat{D}(v)$, knows that $\hat{D}(v) = D(v)$ and should send a message to its neighbors. In this way, all the nodes in the system eventually realize that the correct distances have been found, and only e additional messages have been passed. So the total number of messages used is $nS + e$.

We leave to the reader the problem of modifying the distance estimate algorithm so that it can work even when path distances decrease, and in the case that edge distances can take values other than one.

10. Many-for-one results

10.1. Introduction

It often happens that a sequence of related instances of a problem must be solved. In some cases, each instance must be solved from scratch, but in many notable cases it is possible to solve all the instances at a cost which is substantially less than the total cost of solving each instance from scratch.

Results of this type are called *many-for-one* results, or *quantity-discount* results. If one can solve all the problem instances for the price of one, then the result is called an *all-for-one* result. We have actually already seen such a result, namely the parametric flow problem. There we saw that $O(n)$ problem instances, in a highly structured sequence of problem instances, could be solved in $O(n^3)$ time, which is the best (dense) bound presently known for even one problem instance. Here we consider another important class of flow related problems for which there is an elegant many-for-one result.

To start, we consider the problem of computing the maximum flow value for each of the $\binom{n}{2}$ possible source–sink pairs in an undirected, capacitated graph G. If each pair were considered separately, then $\binom{n}{2}$ solutions of a network flow problem would be required. However, we will show that all $\binom{n}{2}$ flow values can be determined after computing the flow between only $n-1$ source–sink pairs. Hence the total computation is a factor of n faster than the straightforward approach.

This result was originally obtained by Gomory & Hu [1961]. Their method produces an edge weighted tree with n nodes, such that the value of the maximum flow in G for any pair of nodes, say s and t, is the minimum weight of the edges on the path between s and t in the tree. A tree which represents the flow values in this way is called an *equivalent-flow tree*. Gomory and Hu's method in fact constructs a special equivalent flow tree called a *cut-tree* with an additional desirable feature: for any pair of nodes (s, t) if you remove the minimum weight edge on the path from s to t, then the resulting partition of nodes defines a minimum (s, t) cut in G. Hence a cut-tree not only compactly represents flow *values*, but also compactly represents one easily extracted minimum cut for each pair of nodes. It is not true that every equivalent-flow tree for G is also a cut-tree for G.

The key algorithmic feature of the Gomory–Hu method is the maintenance of 'non-crossing' cuts. In the method, if a minimum cut $(X, \bar{X})$ has been found between a pair of nodes, then every successive cut $(Y, \bar{Y})$ computed by the method (for any other pairs of nodes) must have the property that either all of X, or all of $\bar{X}$ is on one side of the $(Y, \bar{Y})$ cut. That is, the $(Y, \bar{Y})$ cut splits only one side of the $(X, \bar{X})$ cut. The implementation detail to enforce this non-crossing property of the cuts makes the method complicated to program.

Simpler methods which avoid the need to find non-crossing cuts, and which also require only $n-1$ flow computations, were later obtained [Gusfield, 1990c] for finding equivalent-flow trees and cut-trees. These methods work with any minimum cuts, whether they cross or not. Although the algorithms do not need to maintain non-crossing cuts, their *existence* is central to the *proofs* of correctness used by Gusfield [1990c].

Recently, the role of non-crossing cuts has been further reduced with the development, by Cheng & Hu [1989], of a new, equally efficient algorithm, that produces a tree called an *ancestor cut-tree*. This tree has all the advantages of an equivalent-flow tree (and others as we will see), but lacks some of the advantages of a true cut-tree.

10.2. The Cheng–Hu method for ancestor cut-trees

We will represent the minimum cut values of a graph G, containing n nodes, with a binary tree T. Each internal vertex of T will be labeled with a source–sink pair (p, q), and will be associated with a minimum (p, q) cut in G; each leaf of T will be labeled by one node in G, and each node in G will label exactly one leaf of T. Further, for any two nodes i, j in G, if the least common ancestor of i and j in T is labeled by the pair (p, q), then the associated minimum (p, q) cut is a minimum (i, j) cut as well. Hence this tree represents the maximum flow values for every pair of nodes, and allows the retrieval of one minimum cut for any pair of nodes. However, it is not as compact as a cut-tree, for a cut-tree takes only $O(n)$ space, while the cuts associated with an ancestor cut-tree are stored explicitly and hence take $\Omega(n^2)$ space.

As an example, the graph shown in Figure 3a has an ancestor cut-tree shown in Figure 3e.

Note that for clarity, the word 'node' refers to a point in G, while 'vertex' refers to a point in an ancestor cut-tree.

The algorithm builds successive trees $T_0, T_1, \ldots, T_{n-1} = T$, each containing one more leaf than its predecessor. The following fact about any T_i will be proved in Lemma 10.1 later.

Fact. *If v is any internal vertex of T_i labeled with the pair (s, t), and its two children are labeled with the pairs (i, j) and (p, q), then i and j are together on one side of the (s, t) minimum cut associated with v, and p and q are together on the other side of the cut.*

In order to describe the algorithm, we first define T_i' to be the subgraph of T_i consisting of the internal vertices of tree T_i, and describe how to place the leaves of T_i, given tree T_i'. This process is called *sorting* the nodes of G into T_i'.

Starting at the root of T_i', we separate the nodes of G according to the cut specified at the root node. For example, if the cut at the root is an (s, t) cut, then we place on one branch out of the root all the nodes of G on the s side of the cut, and on the other branch out of the root we place all the nodes of G on the t side of the cut. There still is a question of which edge to use for which set. Suppose the two children of the root are labeled with the pairs (i, j) and (p, q). Given the fact stated above, we use the following rule to assign the two parts of the (s, t) cut to the two edges out of the root of T_i': the part of the (s, t) cut containing i and j is placed on the edge from the root to its child labeled with the (i, j) cut, and the part containing p and q is placed on the other edge out of the root.

In general, at any vertex x to T_i', we split the nodes of G that are on the edge leading to x into the two edges out of x, according to how the cut at x separates these nodes. To decide which set goes on which of the two edges out

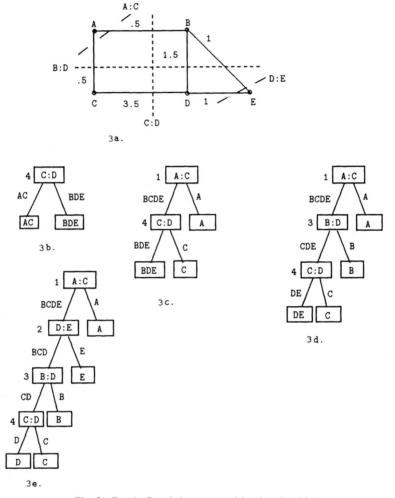

Fig. 3. Graph *G* and the cuts used by the algorithm.

of *x*, we follow the same rule stated for the root. If *x* is a leaf of T_i', then the nodes of *G* on the edge entering *x* are split into two children of *x* according to how the cut labeling *x* splits these nodes. The children of *x* are then leaves in T_i.

For example, in Figures 3b through 3e, the nodes written on the edges of the intermediate trees show the sorting process.

An added feature of any tree T_i, which will be maintained inductively, is that after each iteration of the algorithm, the set of nodes contained in any leaf will have exactly one designated node called the *representative* of that set.

The full algorithm is now the following.

The Cheng–Hu algorithm

Set k to 0.

The initial tree T_0 consists of a single leaf containing all the nodes of G. Arbitrarily set one of the nodes to be the representative of this leaf.

Repeat

Pick a leaf x of T_k which contains more than one node of G; suppose i is the representative of x, and let j be any other node of G in x. Declare j to be a representative.

Find a minimum cut $(X, \bar{X})$ between i and j; let its value be $f(i, j)$, and assume that $i \in X$.

Find the closest ancestor vertex y of x in T_k whose cut value is less than or equal to $f(i, j)$; let z be the vertex below y on the path from y to x in T. Create a vertex labeled with (i, j), and place it between y and z in T_k. Remove all the leaves of T_k, creating tree T'_{k+1}; then sort the nodes of G into T'_{k+1}, creating tree T_{k+1}. Set $k := k + 1$.

Until each leaf node of T contains only a single node of G.

Note that z may be a leaf of T_k. Note also that at least one of the children of vertex x is a leaf of T_{k+1}.

Correctness of the algorithm

The key to the correctness of the algorithm is that every intermediate tree T'_{k+1} is sortable. For a tree to be sortable, we need that the (s, t) cut (say) at any internal vertex x partitions the nodes on the edge coming into x such that all nodes in labels of the internal vertices in the left subtree of x are on one side of the (s, t) cut, and all nodes in labels in the right subtree of x are on the other side of the cut. If this condition is satisfied, then the tree is sortable. To prove that the tree is always sortable, we start with the following definition.

Definition. For a vertex x in T_k, let p and q be any two nodes of G which are each used in some label (not necessarily the same label) of a vertex in the subtree of T_k rooted at x. We say that p and q are *connected* in the subtree of x, if there exists a sequence $(p, v_1), (v_1, v_2), \dots, (v_j, q)$, where the second node in each pair is the first node in the succeeding pair, and each pair is a label of a vertex in the subtree of x.

For example, in Figure 3e let x be the root of the tree, and let p be A and q be B. Then p and q are connected in the subtree rooted at x through the path $(A, C), (C, D), (D, E)$.

Lemma 10.1. *Any intermediate tree T'_{k+1} produced by the algorithm is sortable. In addition, all of the nodes in pairs labeling the vertices in the subtree of x are connected.*

Proof. We prove the lemma inductively. T_0 is clearly sortable, and since it has no internal nodes, it has the claimed connectedness property. Suppose T'_k is sortable and has the connectedness property. Let (i, j) be the source–sink pair used by the algorithm to create T_{k+1}, where i is a representative of a leaf w in T_k. Let x denote the new vertex created, labeled with the pair (i, j).

Suppose first that in T'_{k+1}, x takes the place that w occupied in T_k, then T'_{k+1} is sortable since T'_k was, and the new (i, j) cut simply splits the nodes coming into x into two branches. Further, the label of the parent of x must contain either i or j (by the way that representatives of leaves are created, and the fact that T'_k was sortable). Suppose, w.l.o.g., its label is (i, s). Then, there is a sequence (s, i), (i, j) in T_{k+1}, so j is also connected to s in T_{k+1}. Since the connectedness property holds for T_k, s is connected to all nodes in labels of the subtree of x in T_{k+1}.

Now suppose that x is inserted between two internal vertices y and z, where y is the parent of z. We first show that T'_{k+1} is sortable. All nodes that were on the incoming edge into z in T_k are now on the incoming edge into x in T'_{k+1}. Hence, all vertex labels of the subtree rooted at x are contained on the set of nodes coming into x. In particular, i and j are on that edge.

For any internal vertex, labeled (s, t), in the subtree rooted at x, $f(s, t) > f(i, j)$, and therefore the (i, j) cut cannot separate s from t. Further, by induction, all nodes used in labels in this subtree are connected, so it follows that the (i, j) cut cannot separate any two nodes p and q which are used as labels in this subtree. For suppose that the (i, j) cut did separate p from q. Then the (i, j) cut must also separate two nodes in a label on the chain of labels connecting p and q, a contradiction. Thus, the cut at x partitions the incoming nodes into two sets, such that one set contains all labels in the subtree of x. The part of the cut containing these nodes is passed on to z, while the other part becomes a leaf of T_{k+1} below vertex x. From z downwards, the tree is certainly sortable as before.

To show that the connectedness property holds for T_{k+1}, consider an arbitrary subtree of T_{k+1}. If it does not contain the new vertex x, then the claim clearly holds for it. If it does contain x, then it must contain the immediate ancestor of leaf w in T_k. As before, assume that the label of that ancestor is (i, s). Now (i, s), (i, j) is a sequence in the subtree of T_{k+1} rooted at x. Further, by the induction hypothesis, in T_k, s and t are connected in the subtree of z if t is used in a vertex label in the subtree of z. It follows that i and t and j and t are connected in the subtree of x in T_{k+1}, and the connectedness property holds. □

Lemma 10.2. *If the least common ancestor of nodes i and j has label (p, q), then the associated minimum (p, q) cut separates i and j, and so $f(i, j) \leq f(p, q)$.*

Proof. Follows immediately from the sorting process. □

Lemma 10.3. *Let $S = (i, v_1), (v_1, v_2), \ldots, (v_k, j)$ be a sequence of node pairs, where the second node of each pair is the first node of the succeeding pair. Then $f(i, j) \geq \min[f(x, y): (x, y) \text{ is a pair in } S]$.*

Proof. Let $(X, \bar{X})$ be a minimum (i, j) cut. Since $i \in X$ and $j \in \bar{X}$, there must be a pair $(v_h, v_{h+1}) \in S$ such that $v_h \in X$ and $v_{h+1} \in \bar{X}$, and hence $f(v_h, v_{h+1}) \leq f(i, j)$, and the lemma follows. $\square$

Theorem 10.1 *For any nodes i and j in G, the cut (p, q) at the least common ancestor x of i and j in T is a minimum (i, j) cut in G.*

Proof. By Lemma 10.2, $f(i, j) \leq f(p, q)$. Now consider the set of vertex labels in the subtree of T rooted at x. By applying the connectedness property shown in Lemma 10.1, we can connect *all* the vertex labels in the subtree of x into a single sequence $(i, v_1), (v_1, v_2), \ldots, (v_k, j)$ (vertex labels may be repeated). Then by Lemma 10.3, $f(i, j) \geq \min[f(u, v): (u, v) \text{ is a vertex label in the subtree of } x]$. But by construction of T, x has a smaller associated cut than any vertices in its subtree, and so $f(p, q) \leq f(u, v)$ for any label (u, v) in the subtree of x. Therefore $f(i, j) \geq f(p, q)$, and the theorem follows. $\square$

So the ancestor cut-tree can be built with $n - 1$ flow computations, takes $O(n)$ space, and can be used to retrieve in $O(n)$ time the minimum cut value of any pair of nodes in G. In fact, any value could be retrieved in $O(1)$ time after an initial preprocessing phase taking $O(n)$ time. This is accomplished by using a fast *least common ancestors* algorithm [Harel & Tarjan, 1984, Schieber & Vishkin, 1988] that will be briefly discussed in the next section. If simpler methods are desired, it is not difficult to devise a method to collect all the $\binom{n}{2}$ values from the tree in $O(n^2)$ time. Hence the ancestor cut tree has all the advantages of an equivalent-flow tree. Further, by Lemma 10.2, for any pair of nodes (i, j), the tree can be used to retrieve an actual (i, j) minimum cut. However, $n - 1$ minimum cuts need to be explicitly stored, so it does not have all the advantages of a cut-tree.

We should note that the use of representatives in the algorithm makes the correctness proof easier, but their use is not essential. In fact, the algorithm would be correct if we arbitrarily select any pair of nodes in a leaf. Also, if the values for only a subset of the node pairs are needed, then the algorithm can be terminated early. We leave the details to the reader.

10.3. Additional uses of the ancestor cut-tree

Closer examination of the proof of Theorem 10.1 yields the following important observation made by Cheng & Hu [1989]. Suppose that instead of defining the value of a cut $(X, \bar{X})$ as the sum of the edge capacities crossing the cut, we give the cut an arbitrary value. Then for a pair of nodes (i, j) we define $f(i, j)$ as the minimum value of all the cuts separating i from j. Under this definition of $f(i, j)$, all of the lemmas and theorems in the preceding section remain valid, for all of them depend only on the fact that $f(i, j)$ is the minimum value of the cuts separating i from j. Hence there exists ancestor cut-trees for any such values applied to cuts in G. Further, if it is possible to efficiently find a cut of value $f(i, j)$ when a pair (i, j) is specified, then an ancestor cut-tree for these cut values can be found efficiently, with only $n - 1$ calls to the routine which gives the cut values and the cuts.

There are many applications of this more general cut framework. As one useful application, let G be a *directed* graph with edge capacities, let $C(X, \bar{X})$ be the sum of the capacities of the edges crossing from X to $\bar{X}$, and let $C(\bar{X}, X)$ be the sum of the capacities of edges from $\bar{X}$ to X. Then we define the *value* of the cut (partition) $X, \bar{X}$ to be the minimum of $C(X, \bar{X})$ and $C(\bar{X}, X)$, and we define $f(i, j)$ as before to be the minimum *value* of all the cuts which separate i from j. By the max-flow min-cut theorem $f(i, j) = \min[F(i, j), F(j, i)]$, where $F(i, j)$ is the maximum flow value from i to j, and $F(j, i)$ is the maximum flow value from j to i. Since G is directed, $F(i, j)$ need not be equal to $F(j, i)$. This particular function $f(i, j)$ was studied by Schnorr [1979] who called the function $\beta(i, j)$ and used it in computing the directed connectivity of a graph. He showed that all the $\beta(i, j)$ values could be computed with $O(n \log n)$ minimum cut calculations in a graph of n nodes, although these flows can be implemented to run in $O(n^4)$ amortized time. However, the ancestor cut-tree, when G has been given the above cut values, clearly also represent $\beta(i, j)$. Moreover, for any i and j, $\beta(i, j)$ and the associated cut can be found with only two network flow computations – the maximum flow from i to j, and the maximum flow from j to i. Hence, an ancestor cut-tree for the β function can be constructed in $2n - 2$ flow computations on G. This achieves the same overall time bound as the Schnorr method, $O(n^4)$, but it does not need any of the involved implementation details that the Schnorr method uses to achieve that amortized bound. Further, when the graph has special properties allowing a specialized faster than general network flow method to be used, the time to build the ancestor-tree is automatically improved, while the Schnorr method may not be able to exploit the faster flow.

One of the applications of the β function is in the area of data security [Gusfield, 1988], where it is shown how to compute the tightest upper bounds on a secure matrix entry (i, j) by computing $\beta(i, j)$ in a directed graph derived from the matrix. Hence the tightest upper bounds on all the cell values can be computed with only $O(n)$ flow computations, even though there may be $\Omega(n^2)$ upper bounds that need to be determined. The time to determine all these values is then the time for just $n - 1$ flow computations, plus a total of $O(n^2)$ time. Full details of this application are given by Gusfield [1990a].

11. The power of preprocessing: The least common ancestor problem

The previous section discussing the Cheng–Hu algorithm stated that the least common ancestor of any two leaves of a tree can be found in *constant* time, after a *linear* time amount of preprocessing. That is, the tree is first preprocessed in linear time, and thereafter each least common ancestor query takes only constant time, no matter how large the tree is. Without preprocessing, the best worst-case time bound for a single query is linear, so this is a most surprising and useful result. Since it has applications in network algorithms and it illustrates the tremendous speedup that can sometimes be achieved through preprocessing, we will briefly discuss some of the ideas used for this method.

The actual method we will present is not 'correct' because it needs a few (probably realistic) assumptions and needs to allocate (but not use) more than linear space. Still, it will capture the spirit of the correct method and will be practical for reasonable sized problems.

11.1. An 'incorrect' method

Suppose first that the tree T is a rooted binary tree, so that every internal node has exactly two children. Let d be the length of the longest path from the root to a leaf in T and let n be the number of nodes in T. We will first label each node v in T with a description of the unique path from the root to node v as follows. Counting from the leftmost bit of the desired node label, the ith bit corresponds to the ith edge on the path from the root to v; a zero in bit i indicates that the ith edge goes to a left child, and a one in bit i indicates a right child. So for example a path that goes left twice then right and then left again ends at a node which will be given the label 0010. We will now extend these node labels so that the root also has a label and so that all labels consist of $d + 1$ bits. To do this we add a 1-bit to the right end of every label, and then add 0-bits to the right of each label so that each resulting label has exactly $d + 1$ bits. We will use $L(v)$ to denote the resulting label of node v.

It is not difficult to see how to set these labels in $O(n)$ time during a depth first traversal of T, if we assume that multiplication by a number as big as 2^d can be done in constant time. During the depth first traversal, we construct the path label of v by shifting the path label of its parent v' one bit to the left (multiplying by two) and adding one if v is a right child of v'. To get the final label for v we multiply its label by two, add one, and then multiply by 2^{d-k} (shift left by $d - k$ bits).

We keep $L(v)$ at node v in T, so that when given v we can retrieve $L(v)$ in constant time. Conversely, we will also need to be able to find any node v from its label $L(v)$ in constant time. One simple, but very space inefficient way to do this is to reserve a space A of 2^{d+1} words addressed by all the possible binary numbers of length $d + 1$. Whenever a label $L(v)$ is computed, we write v in $A(L(v))$. So the total time we set up this space is only $O(n)$. A more practical approach would be to hash the L labels into a space much smaller than A.

Now suppose we want to find the least common ancestor of nodes x and y, and say that it is node z. We first take the *exclusive or* (XOR) of $L(x)$ and $L(y)$ and look for the leftmost 1-bit in the resulting number. The XOR of two bits is 1 if and only if the two bits are different. The XOR of two numbers, each of which consists of $d + 1$ bits, is just the XOR of the $d + 1$ pairs of bits taken independently. For example, XOR of 00101 and 10011 is 10110.

Suppose that the leftmost 1-bit in the XOR of $L(x)$ and $L(y)$ is in position k counting from the left. Then the leftmost $k - 1$ bits of $L(x)$ and $L(y)$ are the same, and hence the paths to x and y agree for the first $k - 1$ edges, and then diverge. It follows that $L(z)$ consists of the leftmost $k - 1$ bits of $L(x)$ [or $L(y)$] followed by a 1-bit followed by $d + 1 - k$ zeroes. We assume that our machine can find the leftmost 1-bit in a number in constant time. Again, this is not an unreasonable assumption on most machines, depending on how big n is. So $L(z)$ can be found in constant time. Given $L(z)$ we find z in entry $A(L(z))$ in constant time.

11.2. How to handle non-binary trees

If the original tree T is not binary we modify any node with more than two children as follows. Suppose node v has children $v_1, v_2, \ldots, v_k$. Then we replace the children of v with two children v_1 and v^* and make nodes $v_2, \ldots, v_k$ children of v^*. We repeat this until each original child v_i of v has only one sibling, and we place a pointer from v^* to v for every new node v^* created in this process. Later, whenever any such a new node v^* is returned by the least common ancestor algorithm, the pointer at v^* leads to the true least common ancestor v in T. Note that the transformed tree has at most $2n$ nodes.

So assuming a shift (multiply) by up to d bits can be done in constant time, that XOR on d bits can be done in constant time, that the leftmost 1-bit can be found in constant time, and that we have space of size 2^{d+1}, the above gives a linear time preprocessing method, and constant time look-up method for the least common ancestor problem. All these assumptions are reasonable for reasonable values of n, except for the space required. However, we can still obtain a practical method (but lacking the theoretical constant time guarantee) if we use hashing for A, since we only hash n numbers.

11.3. A peek at a correct method

The deficiencies of the above method are: we must allow word sizes to be $d + 1$ bits which in worst case is $n + 1$ bits (although in any actual case of $d = n$, the ancestor problem is trivial); we assume the ability to shift (by at most d bits), to do XOR and to find the leftmost 1-bit in constant time; and we need space 2^{d+1} or must use hashing.

The correct method avoids all of these deficiencies with the same idea. It efficiently maps the nodes of T into a *balanced* binary tree B with n nodes in such a way that if x maps to $B(x)$ and y maps to $B(y)$, then the least common ancestor of $B(x)$ and $B(y)$ in B can be used to quickly find the least common ancestor of x and y in T. Since B is balanced its maximum depth d is O($\log n$). That means that only O($\log n$) bits need to be used for L labels, and that the other assumptions needed in the first method need not be made. The way that the mapping is done is complex, and is a major achievement.

This peek at the correct method has not done justice to the real method, and the interested reader is referred to the paper by Schieber & Vishkin [1988]. The fact that the problem can be solved in constant time was first shown by Harel & Tarjan [1984].

12. Randomized algorithms for matching problems

We will now consider the use of randomization in algorithms. In particular we will discuss how randomization can be used in a fast parallel algorithm for *constructing* a maximum cardinality matching in a bipartite graph. The major focus is randomization, but the specific topic will also allow an additional look at parallel algorithms.

Recall from Section 7 that a maximum cardinality matching can be computed in $O(n^{2.5})$ time by maximum flow in a graph where all edges have capacity one. This is faster than the $O(n^3)$ bound for flow in general graphs. As another distinction between flow in this special bipartite graph and general maximum flow, we will discuss here very efficient (polylog time) parallel randomized algorithms for bipartite matching, while we saw earlier that the best available (deterministic) parallel algorithm for network flow runs in $O(n^2 \log n)$ time. Even when randomization is allowed, no one knows a fast parallel algorithm for the general network flow problem.

We will discuss in detail matching under the *Monte Carlo* model, but also introduce the other common model, the *Las Vegas model*. The matching result is due to Mulmuley, Vazirani & Vazirani [1987]. In our discussion we will first assume that a perfect matching exists in the bipartite graph, discuss how to find such a perfect matching, and then discuss how to reduce the problem of constructing a maximum cardinality matching to the perfect matching problem. Along the way we will also see how to test if a graph has a perfect matching.

12.1. The Monte Carlo model

By randomization we mean that the algorithm (not the input) has some random component. Typically there is some point where the algorithm randomly generates a number according to some distribution, and then uses that number to direct its computation in some way. It may seem strange at first that certain problems can be efficiently 'solved' by a randomized algorithm, but not efficiently by any known deterministic algorithm. Parallel matching is one such problem.

To define a *Monte Carlo* algorithm we restrict attention to decision problems, i.e., problems which have either a 'yes' answer or a 'no' answer. A $T(n)$ time Monte Carlo algorithm is a randomized algorithm which outputs either 'yes' or 'no' and has the following three properties.

(1) On any input of size n, the algorithm halts in $O(T(n))$ time.

(2) For any input, if the algorithm answers 'yes', then 'yes' is definitely the correct answer.

(3) For any input, if the algorithm answers 'no', then 'no' is the correct answer with probability at least one-half.

Notice that the probability in the last statement is taken over the randomized executions of the algorithm, and *not* over the distribution of the input – the probability of one-half holds for *any* input. This is the novel and surprising aspect of randomizing the algorithm. Notice also that each time the algorithm is run, the probability of an incorrect 'no' answer is independent of all other executions of the algorithm so if we run the algorithm 100 times, say, and get a 'no' answer each time, then the probability that 'no' is incorrect is less than $1/2^{100}$.

A parallel algorithm which always terminates in $O(\log^k n)$ time, for some fixed k, is said to run in *polylog* parallel time. A Monte Carlo algorithm which runs in polylog time on a parallel machine (PRAM model) with at most a polynomial number of processors (as a function of n), is said to be in the complexity class RNC. An algorithm in class RNC is referred to as an RNC algorithm.

The Monte Carlo model has been defined for 'yes/no' problems, but its definition can be easily extended to optimization problems or construction problems. In that case the algorithm produces a proposed solution which is correct with probability at least one-half.

12.2. Self-reduction in sequential and parallel environments

A natural approach to designing a parallel algorithm is to divide the problem into *independent* pieces so that the solution to the original problem can be constructed quickly from information obtained about each piece. Independence of the pieces means that work on the pieces can be done in parallel. Of course, the key problem is to find such a nice division.

One idea for dividing up the matching problem was suggested by the early result that the following *decision question* can be solved, as we will see below, by an RNC algorithm.

Decision problem. For any fixed edge e, is e in some perfect matching in G?

Now in the sequential environment, the ability to answer this decision question can easily be used to *construct* a perfect matching as follows. Order the edges arbitrarily as $e_1, e_2, \ldots, e_m$. Test if e_1 is in *some* perfect matching of G, and if so modify G by deleting the endpoints of e_1 and all incident edges from G. Next test whether e_2 (if it has not been removed) is in some perfect matching in the new G. In general, for every edge e_k there is a current G, and if e_k is in a perfect matching in the current G, then G gets modified as above. When all edges have been removed, the set of edges which were found to be in some perfect matching of their associated G, form a perfect matching in the original G. This process of constructing a solution by repeatedly solving a decision question is called *self-reduction*.

Difficulties in the parallel environment

Although we will see that the above *decision* question for matching can be solved fast in parallel, the self-reduction used seems to be a very sequential process, so it is not clear how to use it to *construct* a perfect matching fast in parallel. A natural response to this difficulty is to ask all the decision questions in parallel, i.e., for each edge *e* determine whether there is a perfect matching in the *original G* containing *e*. These questions are independent and so can be solved in parallel. But now the set of edges which are in some perfect matching may not themselves form a matching. The problem is that the perfect matching may not be unique, and two adjacent edges in *G* may be in separate perfect matchings. However, the above method would work *if* there were only one perfect matching in *G*.

Given the problem of non-unique matchings, the next immediate idea is to find a way to distinguish the perfect matchings so that one of them is unique. An easy way of doing this is to introduce edge weights that make the *minimum weight* perfect matching unique. In particular, give edge e_k weight 2^k. Then the sum of the weights in any edge set is different from the sum for any other edge set. Hence there can be no ties for the minimum weight perfect matching. With this idea the appropriate decision question is the following.

Weighted decision question. Given a fixed edge *e*, is *e* in some minimum weight perfect matching?

We can ask this decision question about each edge *e* in parallel, because the questions are independent of each other. Further, since the minimum weight perfect matching is unique, the set of edges which are in some minimum weight perfect matching form the unique perfect matching. So *if* we could solve the above weighted form of the decision question fast in parallel we would have a good parallel method to construct a perfect matching.

The problem with the above idea is that we do not know how to solve the stated decision question fast in parallel *when the weights are so large*. However, the decision question can be solved fast in parallel (as we will see) when the weights are 'small' (polynomial in *m*). But then the minimum weight perfect matching is not always unique, and when it is not unique the 'yes' answers to all the questions asked in parallel do not specify a matching. So we seem to have taken one step forward and one step back.

Here is where the power of randomization comes in. We will show that the minimum weight perfect matching is unique *with high probability* if the weights are chosen *uniformly* over the interval 1 through 2*m*. This is the basis for the following randomized matching method.

Randomized matching algorithm

(1) For each edge *e* choose a weight *w(e)* uniformly from the interval 1 through 2*m*.

(2) For each edge e test whether e is in some minimum weight perfect matching for the above weights. If yes, place e in set S.

We will see that S is a perfect matching (always assuming that one exists in G) with probability at least one-half. We will also see how to solve Step 2 fast in parallel.

If we want to exclude the possibility that S is not a perfect matching, then we should add an additional Step 3: check whether S is a perfect matching, and if not, return to Step 1. Since the weight assignments in each execution of Step 1 are independent and the probability that an execution gives a perfect matching is at least one-half, the *expected* number of iterations until S is a perfect matching is at most two. With Step 3, the algorithm becomes a very fast *expected* time parallel method.

We now begin the detailed investigation of these claims.

Lemma 12.1. *If each edge weight $w(e)$ is selected uniformly from the integers in the range 1 to $2m$, then the minimum weight perfect matching is unique with probability greater than one-half.*

Proof. There are $(2m)^m$ equally likely assignments of integers to the edges of G. We will estimate how many of them have more than one minimum weight perfect matching. Fix a particular edge e and then fix an assignment Q of weights for all edges *other than* e. Since there are $2m$ choices for $w(e)$, there are $2m$ assignments of weights to all the edges which agree with Q. Given Q, let $M(e)$ be the minimum weight of any perfect matching which excludes e, and let $M'(e)$ be the total weight of the edges other than e in any minimum weight perfect matching which contains e. $M(e)$ is defined to be some large finite number if there is no perfect matching excluding e, and similarly for $M'(e)$. If both perfect matchings exist, then the second one will have the same weight as the first only when $w(e)$ is exactly $M'(e) - M(e)$. This happens in at most one of the $2m$ assignments which agree with Q. So there is a minimum weight perfect matching containing e and a minimum weight perfect matching not containing e, in at most one of these $2m$ assignments. Letting Q vary over all possible assignments, we conclude there is both a minimum weight perfect matching containing e and one not containing e in at most $1/2m$ of the $(2m)^m$ weight assignments.

Now for any fixed assignment of edge weights, the minimum weight perfect matching is unique unless there is at least one 'witness' edge e where the minimum weight perfect matchings with and without e have equal weight. As shown above, any fixed edge e is the 'witness' of non-uniqueness in at most $1/2m$ of the weight assignments. Since there are only m edges, at most one-half of all the assignments have such a witness, and the lemma follows.   □

Corollary 12.1. *For any graph G containing a perfect matching, the random matching algorithm constructs a perfect matching with probability at least one-half.*

Proof. When the minimum weight perfect matching is unique, the 'yes' answers to the weighted decision questions, asked in parallel, specify a perfect matching. With the edge weights selected as above, the minimum weight perfect matching is unique with probability at least one-half. □

Note that the lemma and corollary hold for non-bipartite graphs as well as bipartite graphs. However, the details of how to solve the decision question are more involved for the non-bipartite case, and for convenience we will only discuss the bipartite case.

12.3. How to solve the decision problem

We now begin to show how to solve the weighted decision question. Given a set of edge weights in the range 1 to $2m$, and assuming that G has a unique minimum weight perfect matching M, is e in M?

For any edge $e = (i, j)$, let $G(e) = (X, Y, E)$ be the graph obtained from G by deleting i and j and all incident edges. We assume that the nodes of X are renumbered consecutively from 1 to $|X|$, and similarly for the nodes of Y. Hence the correspondence of numbers to nodes in each $G(e)$ may be different from each other and from G. We let M be the unique minimum weight perfect matching in G, and let w denote its weight. We also assume for now that we know w (but of course not M); we will see how to compute w below.

The solution to the decision problem is based on the relationship between matchings in a bipartite graph and the determinant of a certain matrix obtained from it. The method will be applied both to G and to $G(e)$ for each e, but we will focus on $G(e)$; the case of G is simpler. We start with an idea that does not quite work and then add in the needed modification.

The simple matrix A

Let the two sides of a bipartite graph $G(e)$ be denoted by X and Y, where $|X| = |Y|$. Let A be the adjacency matrix of $G(e)$, i.e., $a_{i,j} = 1$ if $i \in X, j \in Y$ and $(i, j) \in G(e)$; $a_{i,j} = 0$ otherwise. Now the determinant of A is defined as

$$\sum_\sigma s(\sigma) \prod a_{i,\sigma(i)} ,$$

where σ is a permutation of the integers from 1 to $|X|$, and $s(\sigma)$ is a function which evaluates to either $+1$ or -1. Details of this function are not needed in this discussion.

It is useful to consider a particular permutation σ as describing a 'potential' perfect matching containing the potential edges $(i, \sigma(i))$ for $i \in X, \sigma(i) \in Y$. Since σ is a permutation, each node $i \in X$ and $\sigma(i) \in Y$ is incident with exactly one of the 'potential' edges described by σ. If $(i, \sigma(i))$ is an edge in $G(e)$ for each $i \in X$, then the potential matching is a perfect matching in $G(e)$, and $\prod a_{i,\sigma(i)} = 1$. If $(i, \sigma(i))$ is not an edge in $G(e)$ for some i, then $\prod a_{i,\sigma(i)} = 0$ and σ does not describe a perfect matching in $G(e)$.

Hence if the det A is not zero, then $G(e)$ must contain a perfect matching, although the converse does not hold. Each perfect matching contributes either a $+1$ or -1 to the determinant, and by cancellation the determinant could be zero even when $G(e)$ has a perfect matching. So with the current A, we cannot determine from det A whether $G(e)$ has a perfect matching. We will modify A so that this, and more, will be possible.

A modified matrix A

Matrix A is now defined as follows: set $a_{i,j} = 2^{w(i,j)}$ if (i, j) is an edge in $G(e)$, and $a_{i,j} = 0$ otherwise. Then we have the following.

Theorem 12.1. *If* det $A = 0$, *then e is not in M. If* det $A \neq 0$, *then $e \in M$ if and only if $2^{w - w(e)}$ is the largest power of two which evenly divides* det A.

Proof. If $e \in M$ then let σ be the permutation of the integers in X which describes the perfect matching $M - e$ in $G(e)$. Then in A, $\Pi\, a_{i,\sigma(i)} = 2^{w - w(e)}$.

Since M is the unique minimum weight perfect matching in G, the minimum weight perfect matching in $G(e)$ (if one exists) has weight at least $w - w(e)$. Further, it has exactly that weight only if $e \in M$. Therefore, any permutation $\sigma' \neq \sigma$ contributes either a zero term to det A [when σ' does not describe a perfect matching in $G(e)$], or contributes a term of $\pm 2^k$ with $k > w - w(e)$. Hence no subset of these other terms can sum to $\pm 2^{w - w(e)}$. It follows that if $e \in M$, then det $A \neq 0$, and so det $A = 0$ implies that $e \notin M$. The first statement of the theorem is proved.

For the second part, recall that all terms in det A are powers of two with absolute value larger or equal to $2^{w - w(e)}$. So $2^{w - w(e)}$ divides det A when it is not zero. Now $2^{w - w(e) + 1}$ does not divid det A (assumed to be non-zero) if and only if $\pm 2^{w - w(e)}$ is a term in det A (this follows simply from the fact that det A is the sum of numbers which are powers of two). But the only permutation that can contribute $\pm 2^{w - w(e)}$ is σ, so $M - e$ must be a perfect matching in $G(e)$, so $w^{w - w(e) + 1}$ does not divide det A if and only if $e \in M$. $\square$

At this point we can also describe a randomized method for the decision question: is e in some perfect matching in G, assuming that G has a perfect matching? This is equivalent to asking if there is a perfect matching in $G(e)$, which is answered by the following immediate corollary of Theorem 12.1.

Corollary 12.2. *Assume that G has a perfect matching. If* det $A \neq 0$ *then there is a perfect matching in $G(e)$. If* det $A = 0$ *then the probability that [*det $A = 0$ *and $G(e)$ has a perfect matching] is at most one-half.*

How to compute w

Replace $G(e)$ with G in the above discussion and let A be defined for G. Since M is the unique minimum weight perfect matching in G, det A will not be zero, and $\pm 2^w$ will be the smallest term. Therefore, 2^w will be the largest power of two that divides det A. To obtain w, simply test in parallel powers of two to find the largest which divides det A. The number of such independent tests is bounded by log(det A), which is polynomial in m, so only a polynomial number of processors are needed.

Summary of the method

The one detail that we cannot explain here is that the determinant of a symmetric n by n matrix can be computed fast in parallel, in fact by an NC^2 algorithm. An NC^2 algorithm is a deterministic parallel algorithm which uses a polynomial number of processors and runs in $O(\log^2 n)$ parallel time. With that assumption, it should be clear that the following algorithm can be implemented to run in parallel in $O(\log^2 n)$ time with just a polynomial (in m) number of processors.

(1) Select edge weights uniformly from 1 to $2m$.
(2) Form A from G and compute w, the weight of the (assumed unique) minimum weight perfect matching in G.
(3) For each edge e in G form A [conceptually from $G(e)$] and compute det A. If det $A = 0$ then place e into set S. If det $A \neq 0$ then find the largest power of two, z, which divides det A. If $z = 2^{w - w(e)}$ then place e in S.

We have shown that S is the perfect matching M under the assumption that G has a unique minimum weight perfect matching, and that this happens with probability at least one-half for the edge weights chosen. So we have an NC^2 method which is guaranteed to find a perfect matching with probability at least one-half, assuming there is a perfect matching in G. Note that this gives an RNC method to determine if a graph has a perfect matching (when we cannot assume that it does): run the above algorithm and examine S; if S is a perfect matching, then 'yes' is definitely the correct answer; if S is not a perfect matching, then 'no' is the correct answer with probability at least one-half.

The reader should consider at this point why we cannot make the above method deterministic? We mentioned earlier that if we set $w(e_k) = 2^k$, then the minimum weight perfect matching is definitely unique, so the only source of randomness in the above method would be eliminated. So why did we not use these weights? The problem is that $a_{i,j}$ would then be 2^{2^k} for $(i, j) = e_k$. These numbers would then not be representable in polynomial space as a function of n, and operations on them would require more than polynomial time in n. So such large numbers simply violate the basic model of what kinds of numbers are permitted. Because of the requirement to use numbers in the correct range, we needed to introduce randomization into the method.

12.4. The cardinality matching problem

We started with the problem of constructing in parallel a maximum cardinality matching, but have focussed above on the perfect matching problem. How do we use the latter to solve the former?

Suppose that the maximum cardinality matching in G is $n - k$, where each side of G has n nodes. Let $G(k)$ be obtained from G by adding k nodes to each side of G and connecting each of them to all the n nodes on the other side. Then there is a perfect matching in $G(k)$. So the maximum cardinality matching in G can be obtained by finding the smallest k such that $G(k)$ has a perfect matching. We saw above how to test if $G(k)$ has a perfect matching so that the probability of an incorrect 'no' answer is at most one-half. Each iteration of this test is independent of the others, so if it gives a 'no' answer q times, the probability of error $[G(k)$ has a perfect matching but the algorithm did not find one] is less than $1/2^q$. So if we test each k in parallel say 100 times, and k' is the smallest value such that the test for $G(k')$ found a perfect matching, the probability that the maximum matching is greater than $n - k'$ is less than $1/2^{100}$. So we can use this method to quickly find a matching which, with very high probability, is a maximum cardinality matching.

If we run the Monte Carlo perfect matching algorithm just on a single $G(k)$, then we have a fast parallel Monte Carlo method for the decision question: is there a matching of size $n - k$ or more? When the method says 'yes' it is certainly correct, and when it says 'no' it is correct with probability at least one-half.

12.5. A Las Vegas extension

The method above has the property that when it says 'yes' there is a matching of size $n - k$ or more, it is certainly correct, but when it says 'no', it could be wrong with some small probability. If we could construct a symmetric algorithm that was surely right when it said 'no' and wrong with some small probability when it said 'yes', then we could dovetail the two computations to get a method that was already right. This approach leads to the idea of a Las Vegas algorithm.

A Las Vegas algorithm also has a random component, but compared to a Monte Carlo algorithm it is a more reliable algorithm, although not as certain to be fast. In particular, a randomized 'yes/no' algorithm is called a $T(n)$-time Las Vegas algorithm if it satisfies the following two properties:

(1) *If* the algorithm halts, then it definitely outputs the correct answer.

(2) For *any* input of size n, the *expected* running time of the algorithm is bounded by $O(T(n))$, where the expectation is taken over the random choices of the algorithm.

More generally, an optimization algorithm, such as one which finds a maximum cardinality matching, is called a $T(n)$-time Las Vegas algorithm if it is randomized and has the properties: (a) if it halts then it has the optimal solution; (b) the expected running time, averaged over the random choices of the algorithm, is bounded by $O(T(n))$.

In the case of bipartite graphs, we can very simply turn the Monte Carlo algorithm we have for finding the maximum cardinality matching into a Las Vegas algorithm for maximum matching.

Las Vegas bipartite matching

(0) Set $k' = 0$.

(1) Repeat the Monte Carlo decision algorithm once, in parallel, for each $G(k)$, $k \le n - k'$, in parallel.

(2) In parallel, examine each output set of edges S, checking for a matching. If no matching is found, repeat Step 1. Else let M be the largest matching found.

(3) If the size of M is less than n, then test whether a larger matching is possible as follows:

(3a) Considering the matching problem as a flow problem as detailed at the start of Section 7, build the residual graph for the flow corresponding to matching M.

(3b) Search for an s to t directed path in the residual graph. In other words, test whether t can be reached from s via a directed path.

(3c) If there is no path, then M must be the maximum cardinality, so report with certainty that M is optimal and stop.

(3d) If there is a path, then a larger matching is possible. Set $k' = |M| + 1$ and return to Step 1.

The expected number of iterations of Step 1 before the maximum cardinality matching is found is two. When M is the maximum cardinality matching, Step 2 will determine that for sure and stop the algorithm. So the method is Las Vegas. Steps 2 and 3 can be implemented to run in polylog time with a polynomial number of processors (we leave the details as an exercise). Hence the method is a polylog parallel Las Vegas algorithm using only a polynomial number of processors to find a maximum cardinality matching in a bipartite graph. Notice that in this Las Vegas algorithm the only randomness comes in the phase where matchings are constructed. The test of optimality is deterministic.

For non-bipartite graphs Karlof [1986] extended the Monte Carlo matching algorithm to a polylog parallel Las Vegas algorithm using only a polynomial number of processors. He first developed a complementary RNC Monte Carlo algorithm to solve the decision question: does G have a perfect matching. Karloff's algorithm is complementary to the one we discussed in that when it says 'no' it is certainly correct, and when it says 'yes' it is correct with probability at least one-half. So if you alternate running the two Monte Carlo algorithms until either the first one says 'yes' or the second one says 'no', the resulting answer will certainly be correct. If the correct answer is 'yes', then the expected time before the first algorithm halts is within two iterations; similarly if the correct answer is 'no', then the expected time for the second algorithm to halt is within two iterations. The dovetailed algorithm therefore has expected running time of no more than two iterations. Hence it runs in expected polylog time with a polynomial number of processors, and if it halts it always gives the correct answer. The dovetailed algorithm is therefore a Las Vegas algorithm for testing for a perfect matching. The extension to the maximum cardinality case is left for the reader.

13. A matching problem from biology illustrating dynamic programming

Having discussed several variants of the matching problem on different
machine models, we turn now to a very special variant that arises in biology.
This problem will allow us to introduce and discuss an important algorithmic
technique, namely *recursive programming* and a speedup of it known as
dynamic programming.

The following is a simple version of a problem that arises in predicting the
secondary folding structure of transfer RNA molecules. Let L be a string of n
binary characters, i.e., each character is either 0 or 1. We define a *matching* as
set of pairs of characters in L, each pair containing *exactly* one one and one
zero, such that no character appears in more than one pair. We say that
characters i and j of L are *matchable* if and only if exactly one of them is a one
and the other is a zero.

We consider the string L to be arrayed around a circle and define a *nested
matching* as a matching where each matched pair is connected by a line inside
the circle such that no two lines cross each other. That is, for any positions $i < j$
in L, if the character in position i is matched to the character in position j, then
no character below i or above j can be matched to a character between i and j.
The problem is to find a nested matching of largest cardinality. It is the nesting
property of the matching that makes this problem interesting; without that
constraint, the problem is easily cast and solved as a maximum flow problem.
We will solve the problem by *recursive programming* and show how that leads
to a *dynamic programming* solution.

13.1. A recursive solution

Define $C(i, j)$ as the value of the optimal nested matching on the substring
defined by characters in positions i through j of L. Clearly then, we seek the
value $C(1, n)$. For the base case, $C(i, i + 1) = 1$ if the two characters are
different and $C(i, i + 1) = 0$ if they are the same.

We approach the problem of computing $C(1, n)$ by thinking recursively,
starting with the question: what are the possible matches for character 1?
Either character 1 is not involved in a match, or it matches with some character
$k \leq n$, where characters 1 and k are matchable. In the first case $C(1, n) =
C(2, n)$. In the second case $C(1, n) = 1 + C(2, k - 1) + C(k + 1, n)$, where we
define $C(p, q) = 0$ if $p \geq q$.

So $C(1, n) = \max[C(2, n), \max_{k \leq n}[1 + C(2, k - 1) + C(k + 1, n)]$: i and k
are matchable].

Of course, this leaves the question of what $C(2, n)$ is and what $C(k + 1, n)$ is
for each $k \leq n$. Still, with only this small effort and little notation, we could
actually program a computer to compute $C(1, n)$, provided that we use a
programming language that allows recursion, i.e., that allows a function with
parameters to be defined in terms of itself. For example, we can write the
following recursive 'program' to compute $C(i, j)$ for $i < j$.

If $i = j$ Then $C(i, j):= 0$ Else
  Begin
  If $i = j - 1$ Then
    Begin
    If characters i and j are different
    Then $C(i, j):= 1$
    Else $C(i, j):= 0$
    End
  Else
    Begin
    $K:= C(i + 1, j)$
    For k between $i + 1$ and $j - 1$
      Begin
      If characters i and k are matchable
      Then $K:= \max[K, C(i + 1, k - 1) + C(k + 1, j) + 1]$
      End
    End
  $C(i, j) = K$
  End

13.2. Defects of the recursive solution

Then we can start the recursive program by calling $C(1, n)$, sit back and wait for the output. The computer will make all the subsequent required recursive calls, stacking all pending calls, until the base cases are reached. Then it climbs back up the tree of pending calls filling in the computed values, etc., until $C(1, n)$ is learned. This recursive program is easy to think up and program, and it leaves all the drudge work to the computer (a good use for a computer), but it is not satisfactory for large n because of the time it takes to execute. The call to $C(1, n)$ makes about $2n$ calls to compute other values of C, and in general $C(i, j)$ makes about $2(j - 1)$ calls to other C values. So the number of calls in total when computing $C(1, n)$ in this way is $\Omega(n!)$, a very unsatisfactory growth rate.

The reason for this large growth is that any particular $C(i, j)$ can be called a very large number of times in the above recursive program. And yet, there are only $O(n^2)$ distinct choices for the pair i and j. This suggests that if we can avoid duplicate calls to the function with the same choice of parameters, then we can speed up the solution. Indeed, it is possible to avoid all duplicate calls in a *top–down* manner, i.e., using the above top–down recursive method that starts by calling $C(1, n)$. This leads to a solution that runs in $O(n^3)$ time for the RNA folding problem. Further, it is possible to write a general recursion implementing system which will automatically avoid duplicate calls, and hence find by itself an efficient implementation of the otherwise inefficient recursive program. However, this approach is not usually taken. Instead, a different, slightly more efficient but less automatic method is often used to overcome the problem of duplicate calls. That method is called *dynamic programming*.

13.3. Dynamic programming

In the context of the RNA folding problem, dynamic programming is simply the above recursive solution to computing $C(1, n)$, but with the modification that the $C(i, j)$ values are computed *bottom–up* rather than *top–down*. That is, we start by computing $C(i, i + 1)$ for each i, and continue computing $C(i, j)$ in order of increasing difference $j - i$. In this way, once $C(i, j)$ has been computed and stored for each pair i, j where $j - i < t$, then we have all the needed values to compute $C(i, j)$ for $j - i = t$, using only $O(j - 1)$ table look-ups per pair. Hence $C(i, j)$ can be computed for all pairs i, j in $O(n^3)$ total time.

The approach to RNA folding is typical of problems solved by dynamic programming. The problems often have a fairly direct recursive solution, but direct recursive implementation of the solution solves the problem top–down and hence duplicates calls to subproblems. However, if the structure of the subproblems is regular enough so that the subproblems can be nicely ordered, then the subproblems can be solved and their values tabulated in a bottom–up manner. This bottom–up tabling of solutions to subproblems is called dynamic programming. In this view, dynamic programming is a way to efficiently *implement* recursive programming, and it works when the structure of the subproblems is sufficiently well behaved. The reader should be aware however that this view of dynamic programming as an implementation technique, reducing its importance as a conceptual technique, is somewhat non-standard.

14. Min-cost flow: Strong versus weak polynomial time

In this section we will briefly discuss a generalization of the network flow problem called the *min-cost flow* problem. As in the case of the original network flow problem, we will first develop a finite time algorithm which is not necessarily polynomially bounded. Then we will discuss some recent developments showing how this algorithm can be converted into a (strongly) polynomial time solution. That solution will be related to the first, merely finite, solution in a way that is very analogous to the relationship of the Edmonds–Karp network flow algorithm to the Ford–Fulkerson algorithm. Finally, we will discuss an earlier, yet still valuable, approach to the problem which first lead to a (weakly) polynomial time solution. This method, also developed by Edmonds & Karp [1972], is called *scaling*.

In an instance of the min-cost flow problem each directed edge (i, j) has an associated cost $w(i, j)$ as well as the normal capacity $c(i, j)$. The *cost* of a flow f from source s to sink t is

$$\sum_{(i,j)} f(i, j) \times w(i, j) .$$

The min-cost flow problem is to find an s, t flow of maximum value which has minimum cost among all maximum value s, t flows. The problem was shown in 1972 to be solvable in polynomial time using scaling by Edmonds & Karp [1972], but the result is not totally satisfying to some because it is not strongly polynomial.

An algorithm is considered *strongly polynomial* if the *number* of primitive operations of the algorithm is bounded by a polynomial function of the *number of input elements* alone, always with the implicit assumption that the time of each operation is bounded by a polynomial in the size of the input. That is, if some of the input elements consist of numbers, then the polynomial bound on the number of operations is independent of how large the numbers are. In the case of the maximum flow problem, the EK, Dinits, GT and wave algorithms are all strongly polynomial – in each case the worst-case number of primitive operations (additions, subtractions, comparisons, data movements) is a function of the number of nodes and edges of the graph, and not of the size of the edge capacities. Of course, the time to carry out a given operation will be affected by the size of the numbers, but not the number of such operations.

For contrast, recall that an algorithm is considered polynomial if the worst case number of operations is bounded by a polynomial in the *total size* of the input, i.e., the number of bits needed to represent the input. In this model, the number of arithmetic operations need not be related to the number of input elements, just to their total size.

In the first polynomial method for min-cost flow, the scaling method [Edmonds & Karp, 1972], the number of primitive operations is $O(n^4 \log U)$, where U is the largest edge capacity in the graph. This bound is a polynomial function of the size of the input, because the input takes at least $n + m + \log U$ bits.

Now there is a school of thinking which might be called the 'bit-is-a-bit-is-a-bit' school, which considers the polynomial bound of $O(n^4 \log U)$ to be every bit as good as a bound which does not contain U, but many people find themselves in the opposite camp. For them, a strongly polynomial time bound is superior, and so the question of whether the min-cost flow problem could be solved in strongly polynomial time was an attractive open problem for some time. Indeed, the same question is still open for linear programming – polynomial time algorithms are known, but not strongly polynomial ones. The min-cost flow question was solved by Tardos [1985]. We will not describe her solution, but will briefly describe a different strongly polynomial solution. But first we develop a finite method for the problem.

14.1. Finite time solution for min-cost circulation

In discussing min-cost flow algorithms it is convenient to first generalize the problem to the min-cost *circulation* problem. A *circulation* is a generalization of a flow where all the conditions for flow must apply, but additionally the inflow must equal the outflow at *all* nodes, i.e., including nodes s and t. The min-cost circulation problem is to find a circulation f of minimum total cost $\Sigma_{(i,j)} f(i, j) w(i, j)$.

Now the min-cost circulation problem is a true generalization of the min-cost flow problem since not all min-cost circulations will be maximum s, t flows, but a min-cost maximum s, t flow can be achieved as a min-cost circulation as follows: add an edge from t to s with infinite capacity and cost $M < 0$, where $|M|$ is larger than $\Sigma_{(i,j)\neq(t,s)}\, w(i, j)$. A min-cost circulation in this network will consist of a min-cost (maximum) s, t flow of some value, say v, and a flow along edge t, s of v units. So the min-cost circulation problem generalizes the min-cost flow problem.

An early finite method [Röck, 1980] for solving the min-cost circulation problem is the following.

Cycle augmentation algorithm

(1) Find a circulation f (possibly all zeros) in G. Let G^f be the residual graph.

(2) For every forward edge (i, j) in G^f associate the weight $w(i, j)$, and for every backward edge (i, j) in G^f associate the weight $-w(j, i)$.

(3) Search for a negative weight cycle C in G^f. If there are none, then stop; f is a min-cost circulation.

(4) If C exists, then let u be the minimum residual capacity of any edge in C. For every forward edge (i, j) in C set $f(i, j)$ to $f(i, j) + u$. For every backward edge (i, j) in C set $f(j, i)$ to $f(j, i) - u$. The new f is still a circulation, but it has less cost than the previous f.

(5) Go to Step 2.

It is not difficult to prove that this algorithm is correct, and assuming that all edge costs are rational, that it terminates in finite time. Searching for a negative weight cycle is also not a difficult task; it can be done by a modification of the dynamic programming based shortest path algorithms that allow negative as well as positive distances.

Analogies to Ford–Fulkerson

To see how the above algorithm is analogous to the Ford–Fulkerson maximum flow method, consider how to use it just to find a maximum flow. One simple way is to set the cost of edge (t, s) to -1 and the cost of all other edges to zero. Then if we start with the zero circulation, each negative weight cycle in the residual graph is actually an s, t path in the residual graph, followed by the t, s edge. The Ford–Fulkerson maximum flow algorithm allows *any* (s, t) residual path to be used, and the above algorithm allows *any* negative weight cycle to be used. Further, as in the Ford–Fulkerson method, the number of iterations of the algorithm, although finite, may be exponential in terms of n and m alone.

The final, but very recent, analogy is that the number of iterations in the above circulation method can be made polynomial (in fact strongly polynomial) by a rule for choosing negative weight cycles which generalizes the shortest augmenting path rule of the Edmonds–Karp method. The rule is to use the negative weight cycle of smallest *mean* weight. That is, if cycle C has total weight $w(C) < 0$ and has k edges, its mean weight is $w(C)/k$. There are strongly polynomial methods for finding the smallest mean weight cycle [Karp, 1978], so this gives a strongly polynomial method for min-cost flow. This approach was discovered by Goldberg & Tarjan [1989]. It is not the fastest presently known solution to min-cost flow, but it is perhaps the most satisfying in the way it ties together the history of the maximum flow and the minimum cost flow problems.

The minimum cycle-mean method is the proper generalization of the EK maximum flow method which augments along shortest s, t paths in the residual graph. Put a cost of zero on all original edges and a cost of -1 on the (t, s) edge; then the minimum cost circulation gives a maximum s, t flow, and the minimum cycle-mean rule specializes to the shortest s, t path rule of the EK algorithm.

14.2. An earlier polynomial method based on scaling

Despite the analogies developed above between the history of the maximum flow and the min-cost flow problems, there is one major difference between the two stories. The first polynomial time methods for maximum flow were also strongly polynomial, while the first polynomial time method for min-cost flow [Edmonds & Karp, 1972] was not strongly polynomial. A strongly polynomial time method did not appear for more than ten years after that [Tardos, 1985]. The first polynomial min-cost flow method introduced a technique called *scaling* which has continued to be an important technique in its own right. For that reason we will now examine a polynomial (but not strongly polynomial) time scaling method for the min-cost flow problem. In particular, we will discuss the capacity scaling method of Röck [1980] modified by Andrew Goldberg.

The idea of the method is to solve the min-cost flow problem on successively closer approximations of the original capacities. Let U be the largest edge capacity and let $J = \lfloor \log_2 U \rfloor + 1$. J is the number of bits used to represent U in binary. The method consists of J iterations. The purpose of iteration k is to compute the min-cost flow where the approximate edge capacity of any edge is the number created by the leftmost k bits of its original capacity. So for example, at the end of the first iteration any original edge capacity equal to or greater than 2^J will be approximated by 1, and all other approximate edge capacities will be zero.

At the end of iteration k, the circulation will be a min-cost circulation for capacities given by the leftmost k bits of the true capacities. At the start of iteration $k + 1$ the current flow assignment and edge capacity of every edge is doubled. Note that the circulation is still min-cost for these new capacities. At this point the edge capacity of any edge is at most one less than the number given by the leftmost $k + 1$ bits of its true capacity. An edge will be called *deficient* if its capacity is less than its $k + 1$ bit capacity. One by one we will increase the edge capacity of each deficient edge by one unit, and update the circulation to be a min-cost circulation. Iteration $k + 1$ ends when there are no remaining deficient edges.

What remains is to explain how to efficiently update the min-cost circulation. Suppose the capacity of edge $e = (i, j)$ is increased by one. If edge (i, j) is already in the residual graph or is new but no negative cycles get created, then the current circulation is optimal. If edge (i, j) is new and its addition to the residual graph creates a negative cycle, then we find the *most negative* cycle C and augment around it by exactly one unit, the residual capacity of edge (i, j). We will show that the resulting circulation is min-cost for the current capacities. Note first that C must contain (i, j) and therefore C is obtained from the shortest path from j to i [excluding edge (j, i)] in the current residual graph. To find that path we delete edges (i, j) and (j, i) from the residual graph; the resulting graph has no negative cycles (although it has negative edges), so dynamic programming methods such as Floyd's method can find the most negative path P from j to i in $O(n^3)$ time.

Lemma 14.1. *After augmenting around the most negative cycle C by one unit, the resulting residual graph contains no negative cycles.*

Proof. Before increasing the capacity of (i, j) the circulation is min-cost, so any negative cycle created (when the capacity of (i, j) is increased) must contain edge (i, j). Suppose that the augmentation around C creates another negative cycle C' in the resulting residual graph. C' must contain at least one edge which was not in the residual graph before C was augmented. Let X be the set of such new edges in C' and note that each of these must be in C but in the opposite direction then they are in C'.

Suppose edge (p, q) is the first edge on the j to i path P such that its reverse [edge (q, p)] is in X. Then consider the j to i path P' formed by taking P until p followed by path C' until q and then P until j. Now both C and C' have negative total weight, and edge (p, q) has a weight which is the negative of the weight of (q, p), so the cycle P' plus edge (i, j) is more negative than C. Note that the cycle P' plus edge (i, j) has fewer edges in X than does C'. Iterating this argument until there are no edges from X on the cycle, we obtain a cycle that only contains edges of the residual graph before C was augmented, and which is more negative than C – a contradiction. $\square$

There are m edges, so every iteration takes $O(mn^3)$ operations, and since there are only $\log U$ iterations, the method uses $O(mn^3 \log U)$ operations, and with a closer analysis the bound can be reduced to $O(n^4 \log U)$. A polynomial but not strongly polynomial time bound.

14.3. Edge cost scaling

The idea of the method is to solve the min-cost flow problem on successively closer approximations of the original costs. Let Cmax be the largest edge cost and let $J = \lfloor \log_2 \text{Cmax} \rfloor$. J is the number of bits used to represent Cmax in binary. The method consists of J iterations. The purpose of iteration k is to compute the min-cost flow where the approximate edge cost of any edge is the number formed from the leftmost k bits of its original cost. So for example, at the end of the first iteration any original edge equal to or greater than 2^J will be approximated by 1, and all other approximate edge costs will be zero. In iteration $k + 1$ the approximate edge costs are updated by doubling the approximate edge costs of iteration k and adding one to the cost of any edge whose original cost has a one in bit $k + 1$. Then the min-cost flow from iteration k is used as a starting point to efficiently find a min-cost flow for the $k + 1$ bit costs. It is not obvious and we will not go into details, but the $(k + 1)$st min-cost flow can be found from the previous one using at most n network flow calculations (these do not involve costs) each on a graph that is efficiently derived from the original graph and the most recent flow. So every iteration takes $O(n^4)$ operations, and since there are only $\log(\text{Cmax})$ iterations, the method uses $O(n^4 \log \text{Cmax})$ operations. Another polynomial but not strongly polynomial bound.

15. Weighted node cover: Approximation algorithms based on network flow

In this section we consider a common approach that is taken to problems which are known to be NP-hard. We will illustrate the approach with the node cover problem, and a polynomial-time approximation algorithm for it based on network flow.

15.1. The node cover problem

Let G be an undirected graph with each node i given weight $w(i) > 0$. A set of nodes S is a *node cover* of G if every edge of G is incident to at least one node of S. The *weight* of a node cover S is the summation of the weights, denoted $w(S)$, of the nodes in S; the weighted node cover problem is to select a node cover with minimum weight.

The node cover problem (even when all weights are one) is known to be NP-hard, and hence we do not expect to find a polynomial-time (in terms of worst-case) algorithm that is always correct. Therefore, we relax somewhat the insistence that the method be both correct and efficient for all problem instances. There are many types of relaxations that have been developed for NP-hard problems. The most common is the constant-factor, polynomial-time approximation algorithm.

For a graph G with node weights, let $S^*(G)$ denote the minimum weight node cover. Let A be a polynomial time algorithm that always finds a node cover, but one that is not necessarily minimum; let $S(G)$ denote the node cover of G that A finds. Then A is called a *constant-error polynomial-time approximation algorithm* (or approximation algorithm for short) if for any graph G, $S(G)/S^*(G) \leq c$ for some fixed constant c.

For the node cover problem we will give an approximation algorithm, based on network flow, with $c = 2$. First, we observe that the node cover problem has a nice solution when the graph G is bipartite.

For a bipartite graph $G = (N, N', E)$, connect all nodes in N to a new node s, and connect all nodes in N' to a new node t. For every node $i \in N$, set the capacity of edge (s, i) to $w(i)$, and for $i \in N'$, set the capacity of edge (i, t) to $w(i)$. Set the capacity of all original edges in E to be infinity. Call the new graph $\hat{G}$.

Theorem 15.1. *A minimum s, t cut in $\hat{G}$ defines a minimum node cover of G.*

Proof. Let C be a minimum s, t cut in $\hat{G}$. To get a node cover $S^*(G)$ of G we use the rule that if $i \in N$ and edge (s, i) is cut by C or if $i \in N'$ and edge (i, t) is cut by C, then i is in $S^*(G)$. Set $S^*(G)$ is clearly a node cover of G, for if there is an edge (u, v) with neither u or v in $S^*(G)$, then the path s, u, v, t is not cut by C in $\hat{G}$. To see that $S^*(G)$ is a minimum node cover, note that any node cover S' of G defines an s, t cut C' of $\hat{G}$ of equal cost: if $i \in N \cap S'$, then $(s, i) \in C'$, and if $i \in N' \cap S'$, then $(i, t) \in C'$. Since C is a minimum s, t cut, its cost is less than or equal to the cost of any minimum node cover of G, so the node cover $S^*(G)$ is a minimum node cover of $\hat{G}$. □

15.2. The approximation algorithm for general graphs

Given G, create bipartite graph $B = (N, N', E)$ as follows: for each node i in G, create two nodes i and i', placing i on the N side, and i' on the N' side of B; give both of these nodes the weight $w(i)$ of the original node i in G. If (i, j) is an edge in G, create an edge in B from i to j' and one from j to i'. Now find a minium cost node cover $S^*(B)$ of graph B. From $S^*(B)$, create a node cover $S(G)$ in G as follows: for any node i in G, if either i or i' is in $S^*(B)$, then put i in $S(G)$.

It is easy to find examples where $S(G)$ is not a minimum node cover of G, and where $S(G)/S^*(G) = 2$ for any G and any choice of node weights. However, no worse error ever happens.

Theorem 15.2. $S(G)/S^*(G) \leq 2$ *for any G and any choice of node weights for G.*

Proof. If node i is in $S^*(G)$, then put both nodes i and i' of B into a set Q. It is easy to see that Q is a node cover of B, and that its costs is twice that of $S^*(G)$. Hence the minimum node cover of B has cost at most twice that of $S^*(G)$. Now let $S^*(B)$ denote the minimum node cover of B, and for every node i in G, if i or i' of B is in $S^*(B)$, then put node i of G in a set S. It is easy to verify that S is a node cover of G, and its cost is at most the cost of $S^*(B)$. Hence S has cost at most $2S^*(G)$. □

Now the time for this approximation algorithm is $O(n^3)$, the time to find the minimum cut in B. In addition to the above method, there are approximation methods for the node cover problem which also achieve a factor-two approximation and which are not based on network flow. Some of these run in $O(n)$ time [Bar-Yehuda & Even, 1981; Gusfield & Pitt, 1986].

15.3. A small (worst-case) improvement in the approximation

We now examine a modification of the heuristic that improves slightly the worst-case approximation bound, but might be much more effective in practice. First observe that we do not need to double the occurrence of each edge of G. That is, for each edge (i, j) of G, put into B either the edge (i, j') or the edge (j, i'), but not both. It should be clear that with this sparser graph B, a node cover of B still defines a node cover $S(G)$ of G such that $S(G)/S^*(G) \leq 2$. This seems intuitively better than the original construction because the number of edges has been reduced by half, so intuitively the node cover of B should be smaller. However, every node of G still 'appears' twice in B. This doubling can be reduced with the following rule.

First, pick any edge (i, j) in G and place i (but not i') in B. Then for every neighbor k of i in G (including j), place k' (but not k) in B, and put the edge (i, k') into B. Similarly, for every neighbor k (including i) of j in G, put k (but not k') in B, and put the edge (k, j') into B. Then neither i' nor j appears in B, and each neighbor of i or j in G appears only once in B. After putting in these nodes and edges, add all nodes which are not neighbors of i or j, and for each edge (u, v) of G which does not yet appear in B, place either edge (u, v') or (u', v) into B.

Theorem 15.3. *Letting $S(G)$ be the node cover of G defined by the node cover $S^*(B)$, and assuming all nodes have positive weight, $S(G) < 2S^*(G)$.*

Proof. First, any node cover of B defines a node cover of G of no greater cost, since every edge in G is in B and its end points correspond to its correct endpoints in G. Hence the cost of $S(G)$ is no more than $S^*(B)$. Now suppose that edge (i, j) in G is the one picked by the modified method, so that neither i' nor j are in B. Consider any optimal node cover $S^*(G)$ of G. It certainly must include either i or j, since (i, j) is in G. Now create a node cover S' of B from $S^*(G)$ by taking into S' any node k if k is in B and $S^*(G)$, and any node k' if k' is in B and $S^*(G)$. Hence some nodes in $S^*(G)$ may be taken twice into S', but neither of i or j can be taken twice. Since one of i or j must be in $S^*(G)$, at least one of its nodes is taken only once into S', and hence S' cannot be as much as double the cost of $S^*(G)$. Therefore $S(G) \leq S^*(B) \leq S' < 2S^*(G)$. In fact, $S(G) \leq 2S^*(G) - \min[w(i), w(j)]$. $\square$

The best edge to pick (to get the best guaranteed approximation result) is the edge (i, j) in G where $\min[w(i), w(j)]$ is maximized. The heuristic can be improved by iterating, as long as every edge of G ends up in B at least once. It is an interesting open question how nodes and edges should be picked in order to optimize the effectiveness of this heuristic.

16. Summary and thesis

In this chapter we have discussed a large range of current and historical issues in algorithm design and analysis by focusing on network flow and related problems. In this way we have looked at many computational models, algorithm design and analysis techniques, and general design paradigms. Perhaps more important, we have seen many different types of questions that have been addressed by research in algorithm design and analysis. The field is not just concerned with worst- (or even average-) case running times on algorithms that are always correct, deterministic, run on sequential machines, and assume that all data appear at the start of the algorithm and disappear at its end. It is difficult to set out a taxonomy of all the types of questions, results, computational models and techniques that were discussed, but it is instructive to try, and also to try to set out some conclusions.

16.1. Models

We summarize the broad computational models that were discussed in this chapter. We first used the most familiar model, the random access machine (RAM) model, when we examined the Ford–Fulkerson algorithm, the Edmonds–Karp algorithm, the Dinits and wave algorithm and the Goldberg–Tarjan algorithm in Sections 2, 3, 3.3, 4. Parallel random access machines (PRAMs) were introduced when discussing parallel implementation of the Goldberg–Tarjan algorithm in Section 8 and again in Section 12 where we discussed randomized matching on a parallel machine. In Section 8 we distinguished between concurrent read concurrent write (CRCW) programs and exclusive read exclusive write (EREW) programs. We also introduced there the notion of parallel work. The notion of a distributed computation, in both the synchronous and asynchronous case, was introduced in Section 9 on shortest path communication problems. Randomized algorithms and the class RNC were introduced in Section 12, where randomized methods for finding maximum cardinality matchings were discussed. In that section we looked both at Monte Carlo and Las Vegas randomized models. In Section 14 on minimum cost flow, we introduced strong versus weak polynomial time, addressing the issue of how input should be represented. Since running times of algorithms are expressed as a function of the input size, the question of input size is central to what running times are established.

16.2. Questions

The standard question asked is about the worst-case running time of a sequential algorithm that must always be correct, and where no two instances of the problem can be assumed to be related. This was the assumption during most of the chapter, e.g., in the discussions on maximum flow algorithms on sequential machines. However, in Sections 5, 10 and 11 we discussed parameterized algorithms, many-for-one results, and a method based on preprocessing, where a sequence of problems must be solved, and where the times obtained were significantly better than by solving each instance from scratch. In Section 12 on randomized algorithms we dropped the insistence that the algorithm and its analysis be deterministic, and that it always be right. Further, we distinguished between Monte Carlo randomization where the algorithm must be fast but it can be wrong in certain ways with certain probabilities, and Las Vegas randomization where the algorithm must always be right, but it must only be fast in expectation. In Section 15 we considered approximation algorithms, where the method must be fast in worst-case, but can make errors as long as the maximum deviation from the optimal is bounded by a constant ratio. We distinguished between strong and weak polynomial time and algorithms, where the central issue is whether the algorithm runs in polynomial time as a function of the number of objects in the input, or just in the total size of the input.

16.3. Design and analysis paradigms and techniques

It is sometimes difficult to separate design techniques from analysis techniques since the analysis often guides the design, and the design often suggests the analysis. Still we can identify some broad paradigms and specific techniques.

The most classic design paradigm is to break a problem into smaller pieces or units that one can better understand and effectively solve than the whole original problem. These units must have the property that a solution to the original problem can be obtained either by iterating through a series of solutions to these small problems, or by taking the solutions to a set of smaller problems and using these solutions to construct a solution to the original problem. The former case is illustrated many times in this chapter. The latter case is usually called 'divide and conquer', and almost none of the algorithms in this chapter fall into that description. We will return to this point below.

The paradigm of solving a problem by solving a series of smaller more manageable units was first seen in the Ford–Fulkerson algorithm which iteratively solves the smaller problem: can a given flow be augmented, and if so, how? The problem of computing a flow was understood by Ford–Fulkerson in terms of the repetitive solving of that more limited augmentation problem. The Edmonds–Karp algorithm maintains that essential structure. Dinits expanded the basic unit to a phase, in which a maximal flow is computed on a layered graph, but still the algorithm and analysis is understood as the solving of a sequence of phases. Many other examples of this paradigm are contained in the chapter. Breaking down a problem and analysis into manageable pieces is clearly the most important paradigm in tackling a hard problem, but it might only be a starting point. More will be said on this later.

Another broad design paradigm illustrated in this chapter was that of exploiting special structure of properties of the problem to obtain faster algorithms. This was certainly important in the discussion on parametric flow, bipartite matching, computing sets of minimum cuts with ancestor trees, optimal greedy matching with box inequalities, and edge connectivity.

More technically and narrowly we saw many identifiable design and analysis techniques. We saw *breadth-first search* in the FF algorithm; the use of *max-min duality* to direct an algorithm and prove its correctness; algorithm termination proofs by appeal to *finite progress*; the idea of *amortized analysis* in many examples; *greedy algorithms* for matching; more general than greedy algorithms, we saw *hill climbing* or *local improvement* methods such as in the FF algorithm or *scaling* methods for minimum cost flow, where the methods move from one flow to the next in a greedy manner; algorithms that use *preprocessing*; *self-reduction* in the randomized matching method; and *recursive programming* which led to *dynamic programming*.

16.4. A thesis: Combine and prosper versus divide and conquer

In contrast to the idea of breaking problems and analyses down into small easily solved concatenable units, is the technique of grouping or combining units together and solving them more efficiently as a whole. This design technique is often accompanied and encouraged by the very important analysis technique of amortization.

Dinits saw that the work done during a series of certain augmentations in the FF method could be grouped together into a larger unit, a phase, and computed more efficiently as maximal flow in a layered graph. Hence the basic unit of the FF algorithm (a single augmentation) was expanded and optimized. By considering a larger unit, the time for a set of augmentation operations was amortized over all the operations, and hence improved. The wave algorithm then sped up the work per phase keeping the phase as the basic unit. The Goldberg–Tarjan algorithm took the next step, breaking down phases entirely and amortizing the work over the entire flow computation. This allowed further amortization over a sequence of flows in the parametric setting, with the resulting faster time bounds compared to solving each problem from scratch. There the basic unit of a single flow was broken down and all the flows analyzed together. Along similar lines, the efficiency of the connectivity algorithm presented in Section 6 was established by amortizing over all the $n - 1$ specific flow computations. Taking the worst-case of single flow, and then multiplying by the number of flows would have given much inferior time bounds for both the parametric and connectivity problems. Computation of the ancestor tree in Section 10 illustrates the same point. The output of that computation could be gotten by independent flow computations. But instead of breaking down the problem into its $\binom{n}{2}$ natural pieces, Cheng and Hu addressed how to compute the entire constellation of flows, with the resulting speed up.

We see this same moral in dynamic programming compared to recursive programming or divide and conquer. Recursive programming and divide and conquer are *top–down* techniques. In the divide and conquer paradigm one can design an algorithm by just describing how to efficiently divide the problem into smaller pieces and how to efficiently combine the solutions to these smaller pieces to obtain the solution to the original problem. Following this paradigm, the algorithm designer is allowed to assume that the solutions to the smaller pieces will be obtained 'by recursion'. Dynamic programming can be understood as recursive programming with an implementation trick that works in highly structured settings. The trick is that of tabulating and reusing subresults, or evaluating the recursion tree bottom up. The trick is needed, because the top–down dividing method is often not efficient. But in comparison to the divide and conquer paradigm, the dynamic programming trick requires analyzing, understanding and exploiting the interrelationships between the recursively called subproblems. It requires an examination of the entire sequence of computations and recursive calls that a top–down algorithm would invoke, and reorganizing those computations to avoid redundant work.

The idea of breaking down a problem and analysis into easily solved units is an important one, and it may be the most effective way to make early progress. But the examples in this chapter, and the history generally of flow and flow related algorithms suggest that as a problem is better understood, further improvements are made by fuzzing or enlarging the boundaries of the basic unit, or combining units into larger ones, or considering the computation over the whole set of units. In other words, combine and prosper.

Acknowledgement

I would like to thank Jan Karel Lenstra for his patience, and David Shmoys for reading an early draft and making many helpful suggestions.

References

Adelson-Velski, G.M., E.A. Dinits, A.V. Karzanov (1975). *Flow algorithms*, Science, Moscow.

Ahuja, R.K., T.L. Magnanti, J.B. Orlin (1989). Network flows, in: G.L. Nemhauser, A.H.G. Rinnooy Kan, M.J. Todd (eds.), *Handbooks in Operations Research and Management Science, Vol. 1: Optimization*, North-Holland, Amsterdam, pp. 211–369.

Bar-Yehuda, R., S. Even (1981). A linear time approximation algorithm for the weighted vertex cover problem. *J. Algorithms* 2, 198–203.

Blum, A., T. Jiang, M. Li, J. Tromp, M. Yannakakis (1991). Linear approximation of shortest superstrings, *Proceedings of the twenty-third annual ACM symposium on theory of computing*, pp. 328–336.

Cheng, C.K., T.C. Hu (1989). Ancestor tree for arbitrary multiterminal cut functions, Technical Report CS88-148, Department of Computer Science, University of California, San Diego, CA.

Cheriyan, J., S.N. Maheshwari (1989). Analysis of preflow push algorithms for maximum network flow. *SIAM J. Comput.* 18, 1057–1086.

Cunningham, W.H. (1985). Optimal attack and reinforcement of a network. *J. ACM* 32, 549–561.

Dinits, E.A. (1970). Algorithm for solution of a problem of maximum flow in networks with power estimations. *Soviet Math. Dokl.* 11, 1277–1280.

Edmonds, J., R.M. Karp (1972). Theoretical improvements in algorithmic efficiency for network flow problems. *J. ACM* 19, 242–264.

Even, S., R.E. Tarjan (1975). Network flow and testing graph connectivity. *SIAM J. Comput.* 4, 507–508.

Ford, L.R., D.R. Fulkerson (1962). *Flows in Networks*, Princeton University Press, Princeton, NJ.

Gallo, G., M. Grigoriadis, R.E. Tarjan (1989). A fast parametric network flow algorithm. *SIAM J. Comput.* 18, 30–55.

Goldberg, A. (1987). Efficient graph algorithms for sequential and parallel computers, Ph.D. thesis, M.I.T.

Goldberg, A.V., E. Tardos, R.E. Tarjan (1990). Network flow algorithms, in: B. Korte, L. Lovász, H.J. Prömel, A. Schrijver (eds.), *Paths, Flows and VLSI-Design*, Springer, Berlin, pp. 101–164.

Goldberg, A., R.E. Tarjan (1988). A new approach to the maximum flow problem. *J. ACM* 35, 136–146.

Goldberg, A., R.E. Tarjan (1989). Finding minimum cost circulations by cancelling negative cycles. *J. ACM* 36, 873–886.

Gomory, R.E., T.C. Hu (1961). Multi-terminal network flows. *SIAM J. Appl. Math.* 9, 551–570.

Gusfield, D. (1988). A graph theoretic approach to data security. *SIAM J. Comput.* 17, 552–571.

Gusfield, D. (1990a). Faster detection of compromised cells in a 2-d table, *Proceedings of the 1990 IEEE computer society symposium on security and privacy*, pp. 86–94.

Gusfield, D. (1990b). A faster parametric minimum cut algorithm, Technical Report CSE-90-11, Computer Science Division, University of California, Davis, CA.

Gusfield, D. (1990c). Very simple methods for all pairs network flow analysis. *SIAM J. Comput.* 19, 143–155.

Gusfield, D. (1991). Computing the strength of a graph. *SIAM J. Comput.* 20, 639–654.

Gusfield, D., G. Landau, B. Schieber (1992). An efficient algorithm for the all pairs suffix-prefix problem. *Inf. Process. Lett.* 41, 181–185.

Gusfield, D., C. Martel (1989). A fast algorithm for the generalized parametric minimum cut problem and applications, Technical Report CSE-89-21, University of California, Davis, CA.

Gusfield, D., L. Pitt (1986). Equivalent approximation algorithms for node cover. *Inf. Process. Lett.* 22, 291–294.

Gusfield, D., E. Tardos (1991). A faster parametric minimum cut algorithm. *Algorithmica*, to appear.

Harel, D., R.E. Tarjan (1984). Fast algorithms for finding nearest common ancestors. *SIAM J. Comput.* 13, 338–355.

Hopcroft, J.E., R.M. Karp (1973). An $n^{5/2}$ algorithm for maximum matching in bipartite graphs. *SIAM J. Comput.* 2, 225–231.

Karlof, H. (1986). Las Vegas RNC algorithm for maximum matching. *Combinatorica* 6(4), 387–391.

Karp, R.M. (1978). A characterization of minimum cycle mean in a digraph. *Discrete Math.* 23, 309–311.

Karzanov, A.V. (1974). Determining the maximal flow in a network by the method of preflows. *Soviet Math. Dokl.* 15, 434–437.

Lawler, E.L. (1976). *Combinatorial Optimization: Networks and Matroids*, Holt, Rinehart and Winston, New York.

Malhotra, V.M., M.P. Kumar, S.N. Maheshwari (1978). An $o(n^3)$ algorithm for finding maximum flows in networks. *Inf. Process. Lett.* 7, 277–278.

Martel, C. (1989). A comparison of phase and non-phase network algorithms. *Networks* 19, 691–705.

Matula, D. (1987). Determining edge connectivity in o(nm), *Proceedings of the 28th Annual IEEE Symposium on Foundations of Computer Science*, pp. 249–251.

Mulmuley, K., U.V. Vazirani, V.V. Vazirani (1987). Matching is as easy as matrix inversion. *Combinatorica* 7, 105–131.

Picard, J., M. Queyranne (1982). Selected applications of minimum cuts in networks. *INFOR J. (Can. J. Oper. Res. Inf. Process.)* 20, 394–422.

Podderyugin, B.D. (1973). An algorithm for determining edge connectivity of a graph. Soviet Radio.

Röck, H. (1980). Scaling techniques for minimal cost network flows, in: U. Pape (ed.), *Discrete Structures and Algorithms*, pp. 181–191.

Schieber, B., U. Vishkin (1988). On finding lowest common ancestors: Simplifications and parallelization. *SIAM J. Comput.* 17, 1253–1262.

Schnorr, C.P. (1979). Bottlenecks and edge connectivity in unsymmetrical networks. *SIAM J. Comput.* 8, 265–274.

Shiloah, Y., U. Vishkin (1982). An $o(n^2 \log n)$ parallel maximum flow algorithm. *J. Algorithms* 3, 128–146.

Stone, H.S. (1978). Critical load factors in two-processor distributed systems. *IEEE Trans. Software Engrg.* 3, 254–258.

Tardos, E. (1985). A strongly polynomial minimum cost circulations algorithm. *Combinatorica* 5, 247–255.

Tarjan, R.E. (1983). *Data Structures and Network Algorithms*, SIAM, Philadelphia, PA.

E.G. Coffman et al., Eds., *Handbooks in OR & MS, Vol. 3*

Chapter 9

Computational Complexity

Larry J. Stockmeyer

Department K53/802, IBM Almaden Research Center, 650 Harry Road, San Jose, CA 95120-6099, U.S.A.

1. Overview

The computational complexity of a problem is a measure of the computational resources, typically time, required to solve the problem. The computational complexity of a problem should not be confused with the time used by a particular algorithm for the problem. While the analysis of a particular algorithm can provide a useful upper bound on the problem's complexity, another important part of the picture is a lower bound which shows that a certain amount of time is used by *any* algorithm for the problem. The term 'inherent complexity' is sometimes used to emphasize that the complexity of a problem is a property of the problem itself, rather than a property of a particular algorithm.

The study of computational complexity began as a rigorous mathematical discipline in the early 1960s. Since then the foundations of the theory have been established, and important paradigms and questions have been identified. Many basic results about computational complexity have been proved; for example, it is known that there exist infinite hierarchies of problems of strictly increasing complexity. Regarding the complexity of specific problems, there has been some success in placing reasonably close upper and lower bounds on the computational complexity of certain problems in formal logic and other areas of mathematics. For a great many problems of interest in Operations Research, however, there are presently large gaps between known upper and lower bounds. Nevertheless, progress has been made in showing that many of these problems can be grouped into classes such that all of the problems in the same class are of similar complexity. The most important of these classes, the class of NP-complete problems, is one of the principal subjects of this chapter. Before proceeding with the details, it is useful to look at some examples.

We consider four problems. In each, a particular input includes a connected undirected graph G. Imagine that vertices correspond to cities and that edges represent roads connecting various pairs of cities.

(1) *Traveling Salesman Problem*. In addition to a graph G, we are given, for

each edge e, a positive integer $d(e)$ which represents the distance between the two cities connected by e. The objective is to find a path through the graph which visits every city at least once and returns to its starting point, and which minimizes the total distance traveled.

(2) *Chinese Postman Problem.* This problem is similar to the previous one, except that the path must traverse every road at least once; the objective, as before, is to minimize the total distance traveled.

(3) *Vertex Cover Problem.* A vertex cover of a graph G is a set U of vertices such that every edge has at least one of its endpoints in U. Given G, the objective is to find a vertex cover containing the smallest number of vertices. This is a type of facility location problem, where the objective is to place the smallest number of facilities in certain cities so that every road has a facility at one (or both) of its endpoints.

(4) *Edge Cover Problem.* This problem is similar to the previous one, except that the objective is to find a set of edges, containing as few edges as possible, so that every vertex is an endpoint of some edge in the cover set.

All of these problems have a similar form, which is shared by many problems in Operations Research: given an input I, optimize (i.e., minimize or maximize, depending on the particular problem) the 'value' $c(s)$ of a solution s over all solutions s belonging to some set $\mathcal{F}(I)$ of 'feasible solutions'. In the case of the vertex cover problem, e.g., $\mathcal{F}(G)$ is the set of vertex covers of G, and $c(s)$ is the number of vertices in the vertex cover s. For all four problems, as well as many others of this type, the number of solutions grows exponentially in the size of the input; for the present discussion we can take the 'size' n of an input to be the number of vertices of G. For this reason, solving these problems by exhaustive enumeration of all solutions is impractical for all but small values of n.

Despite the similarities of definition between problems 1 and 2 and between problems 3 and 4, our present knowledge of the complexities of these problems suggests that the actual similarities are between problems 1 and 3 and between problems 2 and 4. Deeper understanding of problems 2 and 4 has yielded algorithms, due to Edmonds, which operate quite differently than exhaustive enumeration and which run within time proportional to n^3 on inputs of size n [see, e.g., Lawler, 1976]. These are examples of *polynomial-time algorithms*, algorithms which run within time proportional to n^k for some fixed constant k. The class of problems having polynomial-time algorithms is viewed as a paradigm for the class of 'tractable' problems; the reasons behind this view, as well as some drawbacks, are discussed in Section 2.3.

Although much excellent work has been done to improve upon exhaustive enumeration for the traveling salesman problem, and particular instances with several thousand cities have been solved to optimality, no general polynomial-time algorithm for this problem is known. On the other hand, there is no proof that one does not exist. The situation for the vertex cover problem is similar: it is not known whether it can be solved in polynomial time. Problems 1 and 3 have much more in common, however, than our ignorance of their complexity.

It is known that if either one of these problems has a polynomial-time algorithm then the other does also. Even more can be said. If either of these problems has a polynomial-time algorithm, then so does *any* problem of the form

$$\text{optimize } c(s) \text{ over } s \text{ in } \mathcal{F}(I)\,, \tag{1.1}$$

provided that c and $\mathcal{F}(I)$ satisfy certain mild technical conditions which will be described later. (Informally, these conditions say that it should not be too difficult to compute $c(s)$ or to decide whether a given s is feasible.) This property of problems 1 and 3 can be viewed as an *implicit* lower bound on the inherent complexity of problems 1 and 3: they are at least as hard as any optimization problem of the general form (1.1). The problems of this form, after being redefined as problems with a yes/no answer, belong to an important class called NP, and problems 1 and 3 (after similar redefinition) are examples of NP-complete problems. Intuitively, the complete problems in a class are the hardest problems in that class. The theory of NP-complete problems is described in Sections 2 and 3. Besides the class NP, complexity theorists have identified other fundamental classes with corresponding complete problems. Some of this work is covered in Section 5.

By adopting polynomial time as our model of efficiency, we are taking a rather broad view of computational complexity in this chapter. Determining whether or not a certain problem has a polynomial-time algorithm provides a rough first cut at its complexity. If a problem has a polynomial-time algorithm, the next step is to seek more detailed information about its complexity, e.g., whether time proportional to n, or n^2, or n^3, etc. is sufficient. Techniques for designing efficient polynomial-time algorithms can be found in many texts such as Aho, Hopcroft & Ullman [1974] and Cormen, Leiserson & Rivest [1989], as well as in Chapters 7 and 8 of this volume. On the other hand, if the problem is NP-complete we have strong evidence that finding a polynomial-time algorithm will be difficult, or perhaps even impossible, since such an algorithm would immediately give polynomial-time algorithms for many other optimization problems, such as integer programming and the traveling salesman problem, which have resisted solution by polynomial-time algorithms despite much research. Nevertheless, there are many avenues for coping with such problems, e.g., by settling for slightly nonoptimal solutions. A few such avenues and some related theory are mentioned in Section 4, although the details of such methods fall within the scope of Chapter 8 of this volume and several chapters in the first volume of this series [Nemhauser, Rinnooy Kan & Todd, 1989].

In the final section of this chapter we give a brief introduction to an emerging theory of parallel computation. We address another fairly broad question: given that a problem can be solved in polynomial time using one processor, can it be solved in time proportional to $(\log n)^k$ using n^b parallel processors for some constants k and b? More information about parallel algorithms can be found in Chapter 8 of this volume.

The primary reference on the subject of NP-complete problems is the book by Garey & Johnson [1979]. Several topics in this chapter are covered there in more depth.

2. Basic definitions

The purpose of this section is to specify more precisely terms such as problem, algorithm, and running time, and to define other concepts used in the theory of NP-complete problems. We first define some basic notation. We let $\mathbb{N}$ denote the set of nonnegative integers, $\mathbb{N}^+$ the set of positive integers, $\mathbb{Z}$ the set of integers, and $\mathbb{Q}$ the set of rational numbers. If S is a finite set, $|S|$ denotes the cardinality of S. Unless noted otherwise, graphs are undirected and have no multiple edges or self loops. The notation $G = (V, E)$ means that V is the set of vertices of G and E is the set of edges. We let $[u, v]$ denote the edge connecting vertices u and v. The edge $[u, v]$ is *incident* on u and on v. The *degree* of a vertex v is the number of edges incident on v, and the *degree* of a graph is the maximum degree of its vertices. By a *polynomial* of one variable n we mean a function of the form an^k for some positive constants a and k. A polynomial of two variables, n and m, has the form $an^{k_1}m^{k_2}$ for some constants a, k_1, and k_2. Logarithms with no specified base are taken to the base 2.

2.1. Problems and encodings

From the informal discussion in the Overview, it should be clear that by a 'problem', e.g., the vertex cover problem, we do not mean the problem of finding a smallest vertex cover for a single particular graph G. We mean rather the *general* problem: given an arbitrary G find an optimum vertex cover for this G. A particular G is called an *instance* of the general problem.

For the purposes of the theory, it is often more convenient to deal with *decision problems*, i.e., problems with a yes/no answer, rather than optimization problems. Any optimization problem of the general form (1.1) can be turned into a decision problem by including a target value K with the instance I, and asking whether or not there is a feasible solution $s \in \mathcal{F}(I)$ with $c(s) \leq K$ in the case of a minimization problem, or $c(s) \geq K$ in the case of a maximization problem. Using the vertex cover problem as an example, we illustrate these types of problems and also describe an intermediate problem where the goal is to find the optimum value without necessarily finding an s which achieves it.

VERTEX COVER OPTIMIZATION
Instance: A graph G.
Answer: A vertex cover of smallest size.

VERTEX COVER EVALUATION
Instance: A graph G.
Answer: The number of vertices in a smallest vertex cover.

VERTEX COVER DECISION
Instance: A graph G and a positive integer K.
Answer: 'yes' if there is a vertex cover of size $\leq K$, 'no' otherwise.

Any set U of vertices given as an answer to VERTEX COVER OPTIMIZA-
TION on instance G supplies an answer to VERTEX COVER EVALUA-
TION on instance G, with a small amount of extra work: simply count the
number of vertices in U. Similarly, any answer l to VERTEX COVER
EVALUATION gives an answer to VERTEX COVER DECISION by com-
paring l with K. This is a simple example of a *reduction* from one problem,
VERTEX COVER DECISION, to another, VERTEX COVER OPTIMIZA-
TION. As a consequence of this reduction, VERTEX COVER OPTIMIZA-
TION is at least as difficult as VERTEX COVER DECISION, to within the
small extra work (counting and comparison) needed to perform the reduction.
Therefore, to give a lower bound, either explicit or implicit, on the complexity
of some optimization problem, it suffices to establish the lower bound for the
associated decision problem. The concept of reduction between problems is
one of the cornerstones of complexity theory, and we consider this idea in
more detail in Section 2.5.

Instances of problems typically involve a variety of mathematical objects
such as graphs, matrices, vectors, sets, numbers, etc. In order to solve a
problem by an algorithm, each instance must be *encoded*, i.e., put into a form
suitable as input to the algorithm. For our purposes, it is convenient to assume
that each instance is encoded as a string of symbols. The details of the
encoding are not important, provided that a few general rules are followed.
One rule is that the encoding of an instance should mimic the structure of the
instance. This is more a common sense rule than a precise definition; for
example, it would clearly be cheating to encode an instance of a problem by its
answer. Two more concrete rules are (i) the symbols should come from some
fixed finite set or *alphabet*, and (ii) for problems which involve numbers, the
numbers should be represented in binary notation.

To illustrate how an encoding could be done, consider the problem VER-
TEX COVER DECISION. Given an instance (G, K), number the vertices of
the graph $G = (V, E)$ from 1 to l in some order. For $1 \leq i < j \leq l$, let $b_{i,j} = 1$ if
there is an edge $[i, j]$ in E, or let $b_{i,j} = 0$ if there is no edge $[i, j]$. Let $b(K)$ be
the binary representation of K. Then the encoding of the instance (G, K) is

$$b_{1,2}\$b_{1,3}\$\cdots\$b_{1,l}\#b_{2,3}\$b_{2,4}\$\cdots\$b_{2,l}\#$$
$$\cdots\#b_{l-2,l-1}\$b_{l-2,l}\#b_{l-1,l}\#b(K) .$$

In this way, each instance is encoded as a string of symbols over the alphabet

{0, 1, \$, #}. Instances of the traveling salesman problem could be encoded in a similar way except that, for each edge $e = [i, j]$, $b_{i,j}$ would be the binary representation of the distance $d(e)$. (If distance can be zero, we could introduce another symbol, other than 0, to indicate there is no edge $[i, j]$.)

Having specified an encoding scheme for a decision problem, the problem is then formally defined as the set of encoding of instances having the answer 'yes'. A finite string of symbols from some alphabet Σ is called a *word*, and a set of words is called a *language*. The set of all words with symbols from Σ is denoted Σ^*. In this terminology, a decision problem is a language, a subset of Σ^* for some alphabet Σ. By further encoding symbols as binary words, we can assume without loss of generality that $\Sigma = \{0, 1\}$.

For optimization and evaluation problems, answers are also encoded. These types of problems belong to a general class of problems often referred to as 'search problems'. A *search problem* is a set S of pairs, $S \subseteq \Sigma^* \times \Sigma^*$, such that for each $x \in \Sigma^*$ there is at least one y such that $(x, y) \in S$. For each $x, (x, y) \in S$ iff y is a possible answer for instance x. For certain problems (such as optimization problems) there could be more than one answer (optimum solution) for a single instance. A decision problem can also be viewed as a search problem; in this case y takes only two values, and there is a unique y for each x.

The *length* of the word x, denoted $|x|$, is the number of occurrences of symbols in x. We view the 'size' of an instance as the length of its encoding. The *length* of an integer z is the length of its binary representation $(= \lceil \log_2(z + 1) \rceil$ if z is positive).

Finally, we should mention that, while the notion of encoding is useful for giving uniform formal definitions of many basic concepts such as 'decision problem', encodings rarely come up in dealing with particular problems. When working with a particular problem (e.g., VERTEX COVER DECISION) we speak in terms of the same objects (e.g., graphs and numbers) which were used to define the problem in the first place.

2.2. Models of computation and time complexity

In order to define the time complexity of an algorithm, we must first specify a computing device on which algorithms are executed. In general, the time taken by the algorithm will depend on the details of the device. But since we are concerned mainly with understanding whether problems are solvable in polynomial time, we have considerable freedom in choosing a model of computation. The definitions of two such models are outlined next.

The first model, the *random access machine* or RAM, is based on actual digital computers. The literature contains a variety of formal definitions of this model, differing in the machine instructions allowed and in the conventions for input and output. A key component common to all definitions is an addressable (or random access) memory. The following simple definition captures key features of the model. A particular RAM consists of a finite program and an infinite sequence of *registers*, $r_1, r_2, r_3, \ldots$, each of which holds an integer. A program is a finite sequence of labeled instructions of the following types:

$r_i \leftarrow r_j$, transfers the contents of register r_j to register r_i;

$r_i \leftarrow r_j @ r_k$, where @ is one of the four arithmetic operations $+, -, \times, \div$ (when $\div$ produces a nonintegral result, it is truncated to an integer);

go to LABEL if $r_i ? r_j$, where ? is $=, \neq, <, >$, etc., transfers execution to the instruction labeled LABEL if the test $r_i ? r_j$ holds;

Halt, causes the machine to halt.

In any of the above instructions, a register name can be replaced by some fixed integer or by an *indirect address* $*r_j$ meaning the register r_k where k is the contents of r_j.

Let $\Sigma = \{0, 1\}$. Let $x \in \Sigma^*$ and write $x = x_1 \cdots x_n$, where $x_i \in \Sigma$ for $1 \le i \le n$ and $n = |x|$. The word x is *written in* the registers if, for some constant b (depending on the particular machine), register r_{b+i} contains the integer $x_i + 1$ for $1 \le i \le n$, and the other registers contain 0. (This permits registers $r_1, \ldots, r_b$ to be used for other purposes.) The word x is given as input to the RAM by writing x in the registers. When the program halts, the answer should be written in the registers. We are concerned only with algorithms which halt on all inputs.

Defining the running time of a RAM requires a little care. Although it is natural to equate time with the number of instructions executed, a difficulty is that, by executing t multiplication instructions, a machine can generate numbers of length 2^t, and it would be unreasonable to charge one unit of time for operations on numbers this large. Some treatments of RAMs handle this by charging each instruction an amount of time proportional to the lengths of the numbers involved. The approach taken here, which is similar to one taken by Angluin & Valiant [1979], is to require that all RAMs M satisfy the following:

> There is a constant a such that, for any input x, the computation of M on x generates numbers of length at most $a \cdot \log t$, where t is the number of instructions executed in this computation.

The bound $a \cdot \log t$ avoids the build-up of excessively large numbers, while still permitting (indirect) access to a large space of registers (of size about t^a).

Let $\text{time}_M(x)$ be the number of instructions executed by the computation of M on input x. The *time complexity* of M is the function

$$t(n) = \max\{\text{time}_M(x) \mid |x| = n\}. \tag{2.1}$$

M runs within time $T(n)$ if $\text{time}_M(x) \le T(|x|)$ for all x.

The O-*notation* is often used when stating upper bounds on time complexity. If $f(n)$ and $g(n)$ are numerical valued functions, $f(n) = O(g(n))$ if there are constants $a, n_0 > 0$ such that $f(n) \le a \cdot g(n)$ for all $n \ge n_0$.

The second model we consider is the *Turing machine* or TM. A particular Turing machine consists of a fixed number of tapes which serve as the machine's memory and a finite state control which serves as the machine's program; see Figure 1. Each tape is divided into *cells*, and each cell can hold a single symbol from some *tape alphabet*. Each tape is scanned by a single head which can read and write symbols on the tape and move left and right one cell at a time. Initially, the input word x is written on the first tape, the other tapes are blank, and the control is in a special initial state. At each step, based on the current state and the symbols scanned by all the heads, the program instructs the machine to enter a new state, change some or all of the symbols under the heads, and move some or all of the heads. This continues until the machine halts, at which point the answer is written on the first tape. The *time complexity* of the TM M is defined as in (2.1), except that $time_M(x)$ is the number of steps in the computation of M on input x.

The Turing machine is actually the model of choice for much research in complexity theory. This is due in part to historical reasons. Complexity theory grew out of computability theory where the Turing machine was one standard model used to define the computable functions. A more important reason is that the TM is easier than the RAM to deal with mathematically since the effect of one step of a TM is localized around the heads and the finite control; the effect of one RAM instruction is relatively complicated.

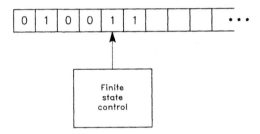

Fig. 1. A Turing machine with one tape.

Nevertheless, results about TMs can sometimes be translated to results about RAMs, and vice versa, by taking into account the time needed by one of these models to simulate the other. Let $\mathcal{M}_1$ and $\mathcal{M}_2$ be classes of computational models (e.g., TMs and RAMs) with associated notions of time complexity. The class $\mathcal{M}_2$ can *polynomially simulate* the class $\mathcal{M}_1$ if there is a constant b such that, for any machine $M_1 \in \mathcal{M}_1$ of time complexity $T_1(n) \geq n$, there is a machine $M_2 \in \mathcal{M}_2$ of time complexity $O((T_1(n))^b)$ such that M_2 has the same input–output behavior as M_1. The classes $\mathcal{M}_1$ and $\mathcal{M}_2$ are *polynomially related* if each can polynomially simulate the other. The following result is implicit in work of Cook & Reckhow [1973].

Theorem 2.1. *RAMs and TMs are polynomially related.*

Remark. $b = 3$ suffices for the simulation of RAMs by TMs, and $b = 1$ works for the simulation of TMs by RAMs.

Any reasonable computational model which comes to mind will likely be polynomially related to RAMs and TMs. For example, the RAM instruction set can be extended to include other instructions used in real computers, or models can be defined based on programming languages. More information about RAMs, TMs, and other models of computation can be found, e.g., in Aho, Hopcroft & Ullman [1974, Chapter 1] or in Van Emde Boas [1990].

To close the discussion of time complexity, we should point out that the definition of time complexity given above is a *worst-case* measure. Even though the running time of an algorithm could vary widely over the instances of length n, the time complexity $t(n)$ is defined to be the largest of these running times. This way of measuring the efficiency of algorithms has been developed as an alternative to empirical methods which evaluate the efficiency of algorithms by trying them on test cases. Discussion of the history of this development can be found in the Turing Award papers of Hopcroft [1987] and Tarjan [1987]. Yet another method is average-case analysis, where the instances are assumed to be produced according to some specific probability distribution. All three methods have their own advantages and drawbacks. While worst-case analysis might give an overly pessimistic bound on an algorithm's efficiency, the average case could be overly optimistic if the instances are not, in fact, being generated according to the assumed distribution. The results of empirical analysis can depend heavily on the particular choice of test cases. One advantage of worst-case analysis, over both average-case and empirical analysis, is that it provides an absolute guarantee of an algorithm's performance, and therefore provides a guaranteed upper bound on the time needed to solve a problem.

2.3. The class P

P is the class of decision problems solvable by polynomial-time algorithms. More precisely,

$$P = \{L \mid L \text{ is solvable by some RAM of time complexity } O(n^k) \text{ for some constant } k\} .$$

Papers of Cobham [1965] and Edmonds [1965] were the first to formally define this complexity class as a model of the tractable, or efficiently solvable, problems. There are good reasons to choose P for this role, although, like many mathematical idealizations of reality, the model breaks down if pushed too far. Some advantages and shortcomings of this model are discussed next, beginning with the advantages.

The first reason to view polynomial-time algorithms as efficient is that, as n increases, polynomial functions grow much more slowly than exponential functions. Algorithms which solve optimization problems by searching large parts of the solution space usually have exponential time complexities. For any polynomial function an^k and any exponential function c^n where $c > 1$, there is a cross-over point n_0 such that $an^k < c^n$ for all $n \geq n_0$. The distinction between polynomial and exponential algorithms becomes more apparent when we consider the ability of these algorithms to take advantage of increases in the speed of computers. Suppose that we have two algorithms, one of time complexity an^k and the other of complexity c^n. Suppose that we obtain a new computer which runs twice as fast as our old one. Comparing the size of instances which can be solved in the same amount of time on the two computers, the size of instances which can be solved by the polynomial-time algorithm increases by the multiplicative factor $\sqrt[k]{2}$, whereas the increase for the exponential-time algorithm is only by the additive amount $\log_c 2$.

Another advantage of P is its *robustness*, meaning that its definition is not very sensitive to changes in the model of computation or encoding scheme. For example, although we defined P in terms of RAMs, we could have defined it equivalently in terms of Turing machines or any other computational model polynomially related to RAMs. This robustness also permits us to be somewhat vague about encoding schemes for particular problems. For example, instead of the encoding scheme for VERTEX COVER DECISION described in Section 2.1, we could have encoded an instance (G, K) by giving, for each vertex i of G, a list of the edges incident on vertex i. If G has l vertices and m edges, and if B is the length of the encoding of the target K, then the length n of the original encoding is proportional to $l^2 + B$, whereas the length n' of the new encoding is proportional to $l + m \log m + B$. Since $m \leq l^2$ it follows that there are constants a and b such that

$$a\sqrt{n} \leq n' \leq bn \log n .$$

So VERTEX COVER DECISION belongs to P under one encoding iff it belongs to P under the other encoding.

Robustness suggests that polynomial time is a fundamental concept around which a general and unified theory can be built. (Of course, this generality is obtained at the cost of a loss of precision. In obtaining more detailed information about a problem's complexity, the model of computation and the encoding scheme must be specified in more detail.)

A final advantage is that obtaining a polynomial-time algorithm for a particular optimization problem usually signals that a deeper understanding of the problem has been reached. While study of a particular problem often leads to 'less exponential' algorithms, making the jump from exponential time to polynomial time typically requires a breakthrough in understanding.

The model which equates P with tractability breaks down when the crossover n_0 mentioned above is very large. It goes without saying that an exponential-time algorithm with running time 1.01^n would be preferable in practice to a polynomial-time algorithm with running time n^{100}. Such extreme situations rarely occur in reality, however. For many important problems which are known to have polynomial-time algorithms, such as the assignment problem and the max-flow problem, the degree of the polynomial is at most 3. Even so, equating P with tractability cannot be taken completely literally.

On the other hand, if a problem is not in P, its solution is not necessarily a hopeless task. The definition of P is based on a *worst-case* view of complexity, as discussed at the end of Section 2.2. Even though a problem cannot be solved efficiently in the worst case, it might still be solved efficiently on most of the 'typical' instances which arise in practice. In order to deal with this precisely, however, the 'typical' instances must be specified in some way. One way to do this is to say that a typical instance is a randomly chosen instance, and then consider the average-case complexity of an algorithm instead of its worst-case complexity. (This approach might not be realistic, since a random instance may be no more typical than a worst-case instance.) Another way would be to specify the typical instances in terms of some structural restrictions. For problems which involve graphs, e.g., the graphs which arise in practice might always be planar or have a small degree. Recognizing a suitable restriction can sometimes reduce the complexity of a problem. We return to the subjects of restricted problems and average-case analysis in Sections 3.3 and 4.3, respectively.

2.4. The class NP

Many decision problems which are based on optimization problems have the following property. For each 'yes' instance, there is a short witness which proves that the answer is indeed 'yes', and the proof can be verified in polynomial time. Consider, e.g., VERTEX COVER DECISION. If (G, K) is an instance such that G has a vertex cover of size at most K, then the witness can be any such vertex cover. The witness can be encoded by writing the names of vertices in the cover U, and the witness can be verified by checking that $|U| \leq K$ and that every edge of G is incident on some vertex in U. If, on the other hand, (G, K) is a 'no' instance of VERTEX COVER DECISION, then no such witness exists; that is, there is no vertex cover U with $|U| \leq K$. The class NP is defined to capture problems with this property.

A *P-relation* is a function $R : \Sigma^* \times \Sigma^* \to \{0, 1\}$ such that (i) R is computable in polynomial time, and (ii) there is a polynomial $p(n)$ such that, for all $x, w \in \Sigma^*$, if $|w| > p(|x|)$, then $R(x, w) = 0$.

Definition. Let L be a decision problem, $L \subseteq \Sigma^*$. Then L belongs to the class NP if there is a P-relation R such that

$$L = \{x \mid \text{there exists a } w \text{ such that } R(x, w) = 1\} . \tag{2.2}$$

$R(x, w)$ performs the polynomial-time verification that w is (the encoding of) a valid witness that $x \in L$. R is called a 'relation' because it expresses a relationship between instances x and witnesses w. The condition (ii) in the definition of a P-relation says that, for each x, there are no very long witnesses (longer than some polynomial in the length of x). Obviously, $P \subseteq NP$.

If $L \in NP$, then L can be solved by an algorithm of time complexity $O(c^{p(n)})$

for some polynomial p and constant c. Given an input x, this algorithm computes $R(x, w)$ for all $w \in \Sigma^*$ with $|w| \leq p(|x|)$ until a w with $R(x, w) = 1$ is found; if no such w is found then the algorithm answers 'no'. It would be very surprising if each L in NP could be solved in polynomial time, although there is presently no proof that this is impossible. The following question plays a central role in what follows.

Open Question. Does $P = NP$?

NP can be defined equivalently in terms of *nondeterministic* algorithms. The notation NP stands for 'nondeterministic polynomial time'. Nondeterminism means that there can be many ways for the computation to proceed. Formally, we can define a *nondeterministic RAM (NRAM)* by allowing another type of instruction:

Split(LABEL1, LABEL2) .

Whenever the machine executes such an instruction, we imagine that it splits into two machines, or offspring; one continues execution at the instruction labeled LABEL1 and the other continues at LABEL2. Each offspring can then split again, and so on. The answer of the original parent machine is 'yes' if at least one of the offspring answers 'yes'. It is not hard to see that NP is the class of decision problems solvable in polynomial time by NRAMs, where the *time* of a computation is defined as the maximum number of instructions executed along any *single path* of this branching computation. For example, suppose that $L \in NP$ as defined above, and let x be an input of length n. By splitting $O(p(n))$ times along each path, an NRAM can produce $c^{p(n)}$ offspring such that each one computes $R(x, w)$ for a different w and answers 'yes' if $R(x, w) = 1$.

The adjective *deterministic* is sometimes used with machines to emphasize that the computation of the machine can proceed in only one way. For example, RAMs as defined in Section 2.2 are deterministic RAMs.

2.5. *Reducibility and NP-completeness*

Let L_1 and L_2 be decision problems, $L_1, L_2 \subseteq \Sigma^*$. Then L_1 is *polynomial-time transformable* to L_2, written $L_1 \propto L_2$, if there is a function $f : \Sigma^* \to \Sigma^*$ such that:
(1) f is computable in polynomial time,
(2) $x \in L_1$ iff $f(x) \in L_2$ for all $x \in \Sigma^*$.
This concept is useful for the following reason.

Proposition 2.2. *If $L_1 \propto L_2$ and $L_2 \in P$, then $L_1 \in P$.*

Proof. Suppose that L_2 is solved by a RAM M within time $p(n)$ and that f is computed by a RAM M_f within time $q(n)$, where p and q are polynomials. The following RAM M' solves L_1. Let x be an input to M' and let $n = |x|$. The machine M' first runs M_f to compute $f(x)$. This takes time at most $q(n)$ and produces the word $f(x)$. Since M_f can change at most one register per step, $|f(x)| \leq q'(n)$, where $q'(n) = q(n) + n$. M' then runs M on input $f(x)$. This takes time at most $p(|f(x)|) \leq p(q'(n))$. Since $x \in L_1$ iff $f(x) \in L_2$, the machine M' gives the correct answer. The total time, $O(q(n) + p(q'(n)))$, is bounded above by some polynomial in n. $\square$

A very similar proof, which we do not give, establishes the following useful property of $\propto$.

Proposition 2.3. $\propto$ *is transitive; that is,*

$$\text{if } L_1 \propto L_2 \text{ and } L_2 \propto L_3 , \quad \text{then } L_1 \propto L_3 .$$

Definition. $\text{NP} \propto L$ if $L' \propto L$ for all $L' \in \text{NP}$. The decision problem L is *NP-complete* if both $L \in \text{NP}$ and $\text{NP} \propto L$.

The importance of this concept is captured in the following fact, which is the formal statement that the NP-complete problems are the hardest problems in NP.

Proposition 2.4. *Let L be NP-complete. Then $L \in \text{P}$ if and only if* $\text{P} = \text{NP}$.

Proof. (if) Assuming $\text{P} = \text{NP}$, we have $L \in \text{P}$ because $L \in \text{NP}$.

(only if) Assume that $L \in \text{P}$. Since $\text{P} \subseteq \text{NP}$, it suffices to show that $\text{NP} \subseteq \text{P}$. Let L' be an arbitrary problem in NP. Since $\text{NP} \propto L$, we have $L' \propto L$. So, by Proposition 2.2, $L' \in \text{P}$. $\square$

It follows from this fact that if L_1 and L_2 are any two NP-complete problems, then either both belong to P or both do not belong to P. To answer the general question of whether $\text{P} = \text{NP}$, we can focus on any NP-complete problem L.

In the everyday business of proving that problems are NP-complete, the definition is seldom applied directly. Instead of proving that $\text{NP} \propto L$, it is usually easier to start with a known NP-complete problem L' and show that $L' \propto L$. The justification for this alternative is given by the next fact. The proof follows immediately from the definitions and the transitivity of $\propto$.

Proposition 2.5. *Let L' be NP-complete. If $L \in \text{NP}$ and $L' \propto L$, then L is NP-complete.*

Although $\propto$ suffices for many applications, there is another, more general, type of reducibility which is based on the notion of subroutines. To show that a decision problem L' is polynomial-time reducible to a problem L, one designs an algorithm which solves L' and which, during the course of its computation, calls a subroutine for L; moreover, the algorithm should run within polynomial time assuming that each subroutine call is counted as just one instruction. Since each subroutine call takes only unit time, we imagine that the subroutine's answers are provided by an 'oracle'. More precisely, define an *oracle RAM* to be a RAM which has an additional set of *oracle registers* $o_1, o_2, \ldots$ and an additional instruction 'Call-Oracle'. The computation of an oracle RAM depends not only on the input x, but also on a particular *oracle problem* which could be a decision problem $L \subseteq \Sigma^*$, a function $f : \Sigma^* \to \Sigma^*$, or in general any search problem. Whenever the Call-Oracle instruction is executed, the word y written in the oracle registers is viewed as an instance of the oracle problem; in one step, y is replaced by the answer to the oracle problem on this instance. This answer can then be used by the RAM to generate a new instance of the oracle problem, and so on.

L_1 is *polynomial-time Turing reducible* to L_2, written $L_1 \propto_T L_2$, if L_1 is solvable by a polynomial-time oracle RAM using oracle problem L_2. The decision problem L is *NP-hard* if $L' \propto_T L$ for every $L' \in$ NP. L is *NP-easy* if there is some $L' \in$ NP such that $L \propto_T L'$. L is *NP-equivalent* if L is both NP-hard and NP-easy. The next proposition collects some easy facts about these new notions.

Proposition 2.6.
  (1) *If $L_1 \propto L_2$, then $L_1 \propto_T L_2$.*
  (2) *$\propto_T$ is transitive.*
  (3) *If $L_1 \propto_T L_2$ and $L_2 \in$ P, then $L_1 \in$ P.*
  (4) *If L is NP-hard and $L \in$ P, then P = NP.*
  (5) *If L is NP-easy and P = NP, then $L \in$ P.*
  (6) *If L is NP-equivalent, then $L \in$ P iff P = NP.*

The evaluation version of an optimization problem can usually be reduced to the decision version. Consider the vertex cover problem. Given an instance $G = (V, E)$ of VERTEX COVER EVALUATION, call an oracle for VERTEX COVER DECISION on (G, K) for $K = 1, 2, 3, \ldots, |V|$ until the oracle first answers 'yes'. By using binary search instead of linear search, the worst-case upper bound on the number of oracle calls can be reduced from $O(|V|)$ to $O(\log |V|)$. (In binary search, the range of possible values for the optimum K is halved with each oracle call. If the current range is $[a, b]$, then the oracle is called with $c = \lfloor \frac{1}{2}(a + b) \rfloor$, and the range is replaced by either $[a, c]$ or $[c + 1, b]$.) Although binary search is not needed to perform this reduction in polynomial time for the vertex cover problem, it is needed in cases where solution values are exponential in the size of the instance. This can occur, e.g., in the traveling salesman problem with distances encoded in binary.

Many optimization problems have a *self-reducibility* property which permits the optimization problem to be reduced to the evaluation version, and hence, by transitivity of $\propto_T$, to the decision version. Consider again the vertex cover problem as an example. Let $\tau(G)$ be the size of a smallest vertex cover of G. If v is a vertex of G, let G_v be the graph obtained from G by deleting the vertex v together with all edges incident on v. It is easy to see that (i) $\tau(G) - 1 \leq \tau(G_v) \leq \tau(G)$, and (ii) for every G having at least one edge there exists a v such that $\tau(G_v) = \tau(G) - 1$. To see (ii), let v be any vertex in a smallest vertex cover of G. The reduction from VERTEX COVER OPTIMIZATION to VERTEX COVER EVALUATION is as follows. Let G be an instance of the former problem. The reduction algorithm first calls an oracle for VERTEX COVER EVALUATION to find $\tau(G)$. The algorithm then calls the oracle on G_v for all v until it finds a v with $\tau(G_v) = \tau(G) - 1$. It then puts v into the optimum vertex cover being constructed, replaces G by G_v, and continues by finding an optimum vertex cover of G_v in the same way.

Historically, the concept of reducibility has deep roots in computer science, going back to the development of computability theory in the 1930s. For example, one can prove that a problem L is undecidable by showing that the halting problem is reducible to L. In this context, the time complexity of the reduction does not matter. In the 1960s, there appeared several isolated results giving *efficient* reductions between particular problems. For example, Danzig [1960] shows that certain problems can be expressed as integer programming problems. In a groundbreaking paper, Cook [1971] introduced the idea of showing that L is a 'hardest' problem in NP by showing that any problem in NP is polynomial-time reducible to L. Cook also showed two particular problems to be NP-complete. Similar ideas were introduced independently by Levin [1973] then in the Soviet Union. The importance of this idea was solidified in a paper of Karp [1972] who proved NP-completeness of (decision versions of) many classical optimization problems such as integer programming and the traveling salesman problem. The terminology NP-complete, NP-equivalent, etc. developed after the appearance of the papers of Cook and Karp, however. Since $\propto_T$ and $\propto$ were first defined in the papers of Cook and Karp, respectively, $\propto_T$ is sometimes called *Cook reducibility* and $\propto$ is sometimes called *Karp reducibility*. The notations $\propto$ and $\propto_T$ are taken from Garey & Johnson [1979]; other notations are often found in the literature.

2.6. Optimization problems

We can now give the formal statement and justification of the fact, mentioned in the Overview, that if any NP-complete problem belongs to P, then every optimization problem of the form (1.1) can be solved in polynomial time. We first define this class of optimization problems more precisely. The two parts of the definition are a relation $F(x, s)$, which specifies the (encoded) solutions s which are feasible for the instance x, and an objective function c. Say that a P-relation F is *total* if for every x there is at least one s such that $F(x, s) = 1$. The following defines a minimization problem; the definition of a maximization problem is similar.

Definition. A *P-optimization problem* is a pair (F, c) such that F is a total P-relation and c is a polynomial-time computable function, $c : \Sigma^* \to \mathbb{N}$. For $x \in \Sigma^*$, define:

$$\text{opt}(x) = \min\{c(s) \mid F(x, s) = 1\} .$$

An algorithm *solves* (F, c) if, when given x, it produces some s such that $F(x, s) = 1$ and $c(s) = \text{opt}(x)$. We require F to be total, i.e., we require each instance to have at least one feasible solution, to ensure that $\text{opt}(x)$ is always defined. This causes no loss of generality since we can always include a 'default' solution for every instance.

Proposition 2.7. *Let L be any* NP-*complete decision problem and let (F, c) be any* P-*optimization problem. If $L \in$ P, then (F, c) can be solved in polynomial time.*

Proof (*sketch*). The proof is a generalization of the reduction from VERTEX COVER OPTIMIZATION to VERTEX COVER DECISION described above. Assume that $\Sigma = \{0, 1\}$. Since $L \in$ P, we have P = NP.
   First consider the following decision problem D:

$$D = \{(x, K) \mid \text{opt}(x) \leq K\} .$$

It is easy to see that $D \in$ NP: if $(x, K) \in D$, a witness is any s such that $F(x, s) = 1$ and $c(s) \leq K$. Therefore, $D \in$ P. Since c is computable in polynomial time and F is a P-relation, the length of $c(s)$ is bounded above by some polynomial in $|x|$ for all s with $F(x, s) = 1$. Therefore, $\text{opt}(x) \leq 2^{q(|x|)}$ for some polynomial q.
   Let x be a given input for the problem (F, c) and let $n = |x|$. First, $\text{opt}(x)$ can be found by doing binary search on K while calling a polynomial-time algorithm for D at most $q(n) + 1$ times.
   Consider now the decision problem D' defined to be the set of all (x, r, K) (where $r \in \Sigma^*$) for which there exists an s such that $F(x, s) = 1$, $c(s) = K$, and r is a prefix of s. Since $D' \in$ NP, we have $D' \in$ P. Let $s_1, s_2, \ldots, s_m$ stand for the symbols of the optimum solution to be constructed; $m \leq p(n)$ for some polynomial p. By calling a polynomial-time algorithm for D', ask whether $(x, 0, \text{opt}(x)) \in D'$. If the answer is 'yes', then set $s_1 = 0$; otherwise, set $s_1 = 1$. Now ask whether $(x, s_1 0, \text{opt}(x)) \in D'$. Set the value of s_2 according to the same rule. In general, a satisfactory value for s_i is found by asking whether $(x, s_1 s_2 \cdots s_{i-1} 0, \text{opt}(x)) \in D'$. Continuing in this way, all the symbols of some optimum solution are found.   □

3. NP-complete problems

3.1. Cook's Theorem

The most common way to show a particular problem $L \in NP$ to be NP-complete is to show $L' \propto L$ where L' is already known to be NP-complete (Proposition 2.5). To get off the ground, however, the NP-completeness of at least one problem L must be established by showing $NP \propto L$. The first examples of NP-complete problems were provided by Cook [1971] and Levin [1973]. The problem considered by Cook was the satisfiability problem for propositional logic. Cook was interested in understanding the inherent complexity of theorem proving, and the satisfiability problem is a combinatorial problem which lies at the heart of automatic theorem proving. In retrospect, it makes sense that one of the first NP-complete problems would be a decision problem in logic; since computers are essentially logical devices, logic provides a convenient 'language' for describing computations.

A particular instance of the satisfiability problem consists of a finite set of *clauses*, where each clause is a subset of *literals* drawn from the set $\{X_1, \bar{X}_1, \ldots, X_l, \bar{X}_l\}$ for some l. Each literal X_i is a variable which can take the value either *true* or *false*. For each i, $\bar{X}_i$ is the negation of X_i, so $\bar{X}_i$ takes the value *false* if X_i takes the value *true*, and vice versa. Given a particular assignment of truth values to the literals, a particular clause C is *satisfied* by the assignment if some literal in C is assigned the value *true*. A set of clauses is *satisfiable* if there is an assignment which satisfies all clauses simultaneously. For example, the set containing the three clauses

$$\{X_1, X_2, X_3\}, \qquad \{\bar{X}_1, \bar{X}_2\}, \qquad \{X_2, \bar{X}_3\}$$

is satisfiable; one satisfying assignment is $X_1 = true$ and $X_2 = X_3 = false$. The satisfiability problem can be viewed as a type of hitting problem, as the following definition illustrates.

SATISFIABILITY (SAT)
Instance: A set of clauses $C_1, \ldots, C_m \subseteq \{X_1, \bar{X}_1, \ldots, X_l, \bar{X}_l\}$ for some l and m.
Question: Does there exist a set $T \subseteq \{X_1, \bar{X}_1, \ldots, X_l, \bar{X}_l\}$ (the true literals) such that $|T \cap \{X_i, \bar{X}_i\}| = 1$ for $1 \leq i \leq l$ and $T \cap C_j \neq \emptyset$ for $1 \leq j \leq m$?

Note that $SAT \in NP$, since a witness for a satisfiable instance can be any satisfying truth assignment.

Theorem 3.1 (Cook). *SAT is* NP-*complete.*

The proof that $NP \propto SAT$ is technical, although the basic idea can be explained simply. Let L be any decision problem in NP, and let R be a

P-relation which defines L, i.e., $x \in L$ if and only if there exists a witness w such that $R(x, w) = 1$. Let M be a Turing machine with one tape which computes R in polynomial time. (It is known that one-tape TMs are polynomially related to general TMs.) The goal is to construct, for each x, an instance I_x of SAT such that $x \in L$ iff I_x is satisfiable. Fix some x. For each time step t, a *configuration* of M consists of the state of the finite control, the symbols written on the tape, and the position of the head on the tape. A sequence S_t of literals is associated with each time step t. Each possible configuration of M at step t is encoded by some assignment of truth values to the literals in S_t. For the initial configuration, i.e., $t = 0$, the truth values of the literals which encode the portion of the tape containing x are fixed according to the symbols of x. The literals which encode the witness w are left 'free'. For each time step t, a set of clauses involving the literals in S_t and S_{t+1} is constructed so that these clauses are satisfied by an assignment of truth values iff one step of M takes it from the configuration encoded by S_t to the configuration encoded by S_{t+1}. (The locality feature of Turing machine computations is useful here.) Another set of clauses is constructed to be satisfied iff M produces the answer 1. It follows that the entire set I_x of clauses is satisfiable iff there exists a witness w such that M produces the answer 1 on input (x, w). The polynomial time complexity of M is used to show that the transformation from x to I_x can be computed in polynomial time. (A detailed proof can be found, e.g., in Garey & Johnson [1979].)

The following restricted version of the satisfiability problem is also NP-complete.

3SAT
Instance: An instance of SAT such that each clause C_j contains exactly 3 literals.
Question: Same as for SAT.

Part of the transformation SAT $\propto$ 3SAT is done as follows. For each clause C_j, if C_j contains more than 3 literals, then C_j is replaced by a set of clauses, each containing 3 literals, in such a way that C_j is satisfied iff the new set of clauses is satisfiable. For example, the clause $\{X_1, X_2, X_3, X_4, X_5\}$ is replaced by the three clauses

$$\{X_1, X_2, Y_1\}, \quad \{X_3, \bar{Y}_1, Y_2\}, \quad \{X_4, X_5, \bar{Y}_2\},$$

where the literals Y_1 and Y_2 and their negations appear nowhere else in the clauses. Other tricks can be used to increase the size of a clause to 3 if necessary [see, e.g., Garey & Johnson, 1979].

3.2. Examples of NP-complete problems

The purpose of this section is to give more examples of NP-complete decision problems and to illustrate a few polynomial-time transformations between problems. The list of known NP-complete problems extends well into the hundreds. Some of these problems have turned out to be more useful than others as starting points for transformations to other problems. The problems SAT and 3SAT are examples of such 'basic' NP-complete problems, and several others are included in the examples given next. Many of the problems described in this section will also serve as examples in later sections.

We begin with a simple type of covering problem, the vertex cover problem.

VERTEX COVER
Instance: A graph $G = (V, E)$ and a positive integer K.
Question: Does G have a vertex cover of size at most K, i.e., a set $U \subseteq V$ with $|U| \leq K$ such that every edge in E is incident on some vertex in U?

It is clear that VERTEX COVER belongs to NP. To prove NP-completeness, it suffices to show that 3SAT $\propto$ VERTEX COVER. A general strategy for finding a polynomial-time transformation f from L' to L, where L and L' are both in NP, is to set up a correspondence between witnesses that prove $x \in L'$ and witnesses that prove $f(x) \in L$. Returning to the specific example 3SAT $\propto$ VERTEX COVER, witnesses for the satisfiability problem are truth assignments which satisfy all the clauses, and witnesses for the vertex cover problem are vertex covers of a certain maximum size.

Let the clauses $C_1, \ldots, C_m$ be an instance of 3SAT where each clause contains exactly 3 literals from the set $\{X_1, \bar{X}_1, \ldots, X_l, \bar{X}_l\}$. This instance is transformed to an instance (G, K) of the vertex cover problem as follows. The construction is illustrated in Figure 2. Suppose that the graph G contains two vertices, labeled X_i and $\bar{X}_i$, which are connected by an edge. At least one of these two vertices must belong to any vertex cover of G. If the instance (G, K) is so constrained that any vertex cover of size K can contain at most one of

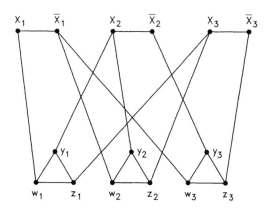

Fig. 2. The graph G which results from transforming the 3SAT instance consisting of clauses $\{X_1, X_2, X_3\}$, $\{\bar{X}_1, X_2, X_3\}$, and $\{\bar{X}_1, \bar{X}_2, \bar{X}_3\}$. Since there are $l = 3$ variables and $m = 3$ clauses, $K = 3 + 2 \cdot 3 = 9$. For example, the satisfying truth assignment $X_1 = true$, $X_2 = false$, $X_3 = true$ corresponds to the vertex cover $\{X_1, \bar{X}_2, X_3, y_1, z_1, w_2, y_2, w_3, z_3\}$ or $\{X_1, \bar{X}_2, X_3, w_1, y_1, w_2, z_2, w_3, z_3\}$.

these two vertices, then there is a natural correspondence between the vertex cover restricted to these two vertices and the truth assignment to the variable X_i: if the vertex labeled X_i is in the vertex cover, then X_i is *true* (and $\bar{X}_i$ is *false*); if the vertex $\bar{X}_i$ is in the vertex cover, then $\bar{X}_i$ is *true* (and X_i is *false*). To give a correspondence for the truth assignment to all the literals, the graph G should contain l pairs of vertices. For each i, the two vertices in the ith pair, labeled X_i and $\bar{X}_i$, are connected by an edge.

Another part of the graph G must be constructed to check that the vertex cover, restricted to these l pairs, corresponds to a satisfying truth assignment for the clauses. For each clause C_j, the graph contains a triangle of vertices, w_j, y_j, and z_j, and edges $[w_j, y_j]$, $[w_j, z_j]$, $[y_j, z_j]$. To cover the three edges interconnecting w_j, y_j, and z_j, at least two of these vertices must belong to any vertex cover. Choosing $K = l + 2m$ ensures that any vertex cover of size K contains exactly one vertex from each pair $\{X_i, \bar{X}_i\}$ and exactly two vertices from each triangle $\{w_j, y_j, z_j\}$. For each j, let W_j, Y_j, and Z_j denote the three literals in clause C_j. To complete the construction, for every j, the 'checking' edges $[w_j, W_j]$, $[y_j, Y_j]$, and $[z_j, Z_j]$ are added to G (see Figure 2).

It is not difficult to see that G has a vertex cover of size K if and only if the given clauses are satisfiable. For example, suppose that G has a vertex cover U of size K, and consider the corresponding truth assignment to the literals. If this assignment does not satisfy some clause C_j, then the three vertices labeled W_j, Y_j, and Z_j are not in U. Since at most two of the vertices w_j, y_j, and z_j can be in U, it follows that some checking edge has neither of its endpoints in U, contradicting the assumption that U is a vertex cover. The other direction, going from a satisfying truth assignment to a vertex cover, is similar. This completes the transformation.

The vertex cover problem can be easily transformed to two other closely related basic NP-complete problems, the maximum independent set problem and the maximum clique problem. Given a graph $G = (V, E)$, a subset U of the vertices is an *independent set* if no two vertices in U are connected by an edge in E, and U is a *clique* if every two distinct vertices in U are connected by an edge in E.

CLIQUE
Instance: A graph G and a positive integer K.
Question: Does G have a clique containing at least K vertices?

The definition of the INDEPENDENT SET problem is similar.

Note that U is an independent set in $G = (V, E)$ iff $V - U$ (the set of vertices in V that are not in U) is a vertex cover for G. Also, U is an independent set in G iff U is a clique in $\bar{G} = (V, \bar{E})$, the complement of G; for every pair of distinct vertices u and v, $[u, v] \in \bar{E}$ iff $[u, v] \notin E$. This shows that

VERTEX COVER $\propto$ INDEPENDENT SET $\propto$ CLIQUE

and establishes the NP-completeness of the latter two problems.

We next consider two versions of the integer programming problem.

INTEGER LINEAR PROGRAMMING (ILP)
Instance: An $m \times n$ integer matrix A, an integer m-vector b, an integer n-vector c, and an integer B.
Question: Is there an integer n-vector $x \geq 0$ such that $Ax \leq b$ and $c \cdot x \geq B$?

0–1 INTEGER LINEAR PROGRAMMING (01ILP)
Instance: Same as for ILP.
Question: Is there an n-vector x of 0's and 1's such that $Ax \leq b$ and $c \cdot x \geq B$?

In other words, c describes a linear objective function to be maximized subject to the system $Ax \leq b$ of m constraints.

ILP is the first problem we have encountered which is not obviously in NP. It is natural to use the vector x as a witness for each 'yes' instance. For this to fit the definition of NP, however, it must be that, whenever there is an x satisfying $Ax \leq b$ and $c \cdot x \geq B$, there is such an x of polynomial length; more precisely, the sum of the lengths of the integers appearing in x must be bounded above by some fixed polynomial in the sum of the lengths of the integers appearing in A, b, c, and B. As several people have observed, such a polynomial bound does exist; a simple proof is given by Papadimitriou [1981].

It is well known that many combinatorial optimization problems can be expressed as integer programming problems. It is easy to show, e.g., that CLIQUE $\propto$ 01ILP. Let (G, K) be an instance of the clique problem. Assume that the vertices of G are labeled $\{1, 2, \ldots, n\}$ for some n. The 01ILP instance will involve n 0–1 variables $x_1, \ldots, x_n$, where $x_i = 1$ means that vertex i is in the clique and $x_i = 0$ means that vertex i is not in the clique. If i and j are two distinct vertices which are not connected by an edge of G, then at most one of i and j can be in the same clique. Therefore, the system $Ax \leq b$ contains the constraint $x_i + x_j \leq 1$ for each such i and j. To complete the 01ILP instance, set $c = (1, 1, \ldots, 1)$ and $B = K$. The transformation 01ILP $\propto$ ILP is straight-forward.

Both ILP and 01ILP remain NP-complete when restricted to instances having one constraint $a \cdot x \leq b$ where a is an n-vector of positive integers and b is a positive integer, in addition to the inequality $c \cdot x \geq B$ where c is an n-vector of positive integers. These restricted versions are called *knapsack problems*. The problems can be further restricted by taking $a = c$ and $b = B$. The 0–1 knapsack problem, restricted in this way, amounts to asking whether some subset of the elements of a sums to B.

SUBSET SUM
Instance: A vector a of positive integers and a positive integer B.
Question: Is there a vector x of 0's and 1's such that $a \cdot x = B$?

We show that CLIQUE $\propto$ SUBSET SUM by continuing the transformation

CLIQUE $\propto$ 01ILP above. The transformation is illustrated in Figure 3. For a given instance of the clique problem, let $Ax \leqslant b$ and $c \cdot x = K$ be the instance of 01ILP constructed above. Recall that A has 0–1 entries and that b and c are vectors of all 1's. Say that A is $m \times n$. By introducing a new slack variable into each constraint and by viewing $c \cdot x = K$ as an $(m + 1)$st constraint, we obtain an $(m + 1) \times (n + m)$ 0–1 matrix A' and an $(m + 1)$-vector b' of positive integers such that the pair $Ax \leqslant b$ and $c \cdot x = K$ has a 0–1 solution x iff $A'y = b'$ has a 0–1 solution y. Letting v_i denote the ith column of A' for $1 \leqslant i \leqslant n + m$, this is equivalent to asking whether $\Sigma_{i=1}^{n+m} y_i v_i = b'$ has a solution in the 0–1 variables $y_1, \ldots, y_{n+m}$. Now each vector v_i is transformed to an integer a_i as follows. Writing $v_i = (v_{i,1}, \ldots, v_{i,m+1})$,

$$a_i = \sum_{j=1}^{m+1} v_{i,j} 4^{j-1}.$$

Another way of viewing this is that the binary representation of a_i is divided into $m + 1$ blocks, where the m low order blocks contain 2 bits each. For

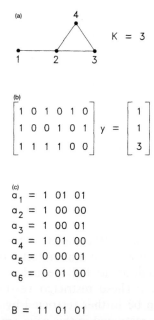

Fig. 3. An instance (a) of the maximum clique problem is transformed to a system (b) of linear equalities $A'y = b'$, and then to an instance (c) of the subset sum problem. The vertices of G correspond to the first four columns of A' which correspond in turn to a_1, a_2, a_3, a_4. The last two columns of A' correspond to slack variables. The binary representations of the a_i and B are broken into blocks of size 2 for illustration. The clique $\{2, 3, 4\}$ corresponds to the solution
$$a_2 + a_3 + a_4 = B.$$

$1 \le j \le m + 1$, $v_{i,j}$ is the rightmost (lower order) bit of the jth block, numbering the blocks from low order to high order; see Figure 3. Since the first m rows of A' have row-sum 3, it follows that, if we add any subset of the a_i's, carries from the addition in any block will not spill over into an adjoining block. Therefore, addition of any subset of the vectors v_i is mimicked by addition of the corresponding subset of the integers a_i. To finish the transformation, the integer B is constructed from the vector b' in the same way that a_i is constructed from v_i.

Note that $a_i \ge 4^m$. Therefore, it is crucial that integers can be encoded by their binary representations, so that the lengths of the encoding of the a_i and B are polynomial in m. The effect of restricting the sizes of the a_i is considered in Section 3.3.

The subset sum problem is useful in proving NP-completeness of certain problems which involve packing different sized objects into constrained spaces. An example is the following.

BIN PACKING
Instance: A number K of bins, a bin size S, a set $W = \{w_1, \ldots, w_n\}$ of objects, and the size $s_i \in \mathbb{N}^+$ of each object w_i.
Question: Is there a partition of W into K disjoint parts such that the sum of the sizes of the objects in each part does not exceed S?

This problem is the decision version of two related optimization problems. The optimization problem which holds S fixed and attempts to minimize K is a version of the classical stock cutting problem. The other problem, which holds K fixed and attempts to minimize S, is a type of *multiprocessor scheduling problem* where the bins correspond to the processors, each object w_i is a job which takes time s_i to be performed on any processor, and the goal is to assign the jobs to the processors while minimizing the time to perform all the jobs.

To show SUBSET SUM $\propto$ BIN PACKING, let $a = (a_1, \ldots, a_m)$ and B be an instance of the subset sum problem. Let $D = \sum_{i=1}^{m} a_i$. Let $s_i = a_i$ for $1 \le i \le m$, $s_{m+1} = 2D - B$, $s_{m+2} = D + B$, $S = 2D$, and $K = 2$. In any bin packing, the objects of size s_{m+1} and s_{m+2} must go into different bins, since $s_{m+1} + s_{m+2} = 3D$ exceeds the bin size $2D$. After this is done, we are left with two partial bins, of size B and $D - B$, into which the remaining objects must be (tightly) packed. This packing can be done iff there is a subset of the a_i's which sums to B.

The next group of NP-complete problems often arise in various types of routing or sequencing problems.

HAMILTONIAN CYCLE
Instance: A graph G.
Question: Is there a Hamiltonian cycle in G, i.e., a cycle which visits each vertex exactly once?

TRAVELING SALESMAN (TSP)

Instance: A set of 'cities' $\{1, 2, \ldots, n\}$, a distance $d_{i,j} \in \mathbb{N}^+$ for each pair i and j of cities such that $d_{i,j} = d_{j,i}$, and an integer D.

Question: Is there a *tour*, i.e., a permutation $\pi : \{1, \ldots, n\} \to \{1, \ldots, n\}$, such that

$$\sum_{i=1}^{n-1} d_{\pi(i),\pi(i+1)} + d_{\pi(n),\pi(1)} \le D?$$

△TSP

Instance: An instance of TSP where the distances satisfy the *triangle inequality*, i.e., for each triple (i, j, k) of distinct cities, $d_{i,k} \le d_{i,j} + d_{j,k}$.

Question: Same as for TSP.

The version of the traveling salesman problem mentioned in the Overview, where finite distances need not be given for every pair of cities but where the tour can visit cities more than once, is equivalent to (the optimization version of) △TSP.

The known transformations proving NP-completeness of the Hamiltonian cycle problem are more involved than the transformations presented above. A transformation from 3SAT to the Hamiltonian cycle problem can be found, e.g., in Papadimitriou & Steiglitz [1982].

The transformation HAMILTONIAN CYCLE $\propto$ △TSP is easy. Given an instance G of the Hamiltonian cycle problem having n vertices, set $d_{i,j} = 1$ (respectively $d_{i,j} = 2$) if there is (respectively is not) an edge between vertex i and vertex j in G, and take $D = n$.

The problems considered so far in Section 3.2 were first shown to be NP-complete by Karp [1972], with the exception of the maximum clique problem and the knapsack (one constraint) version of ILP which were shown NP-complete by Cook [1971] and Lueker [1975], respectively.

Although proofs of NP-completeness are usually done for problems one at a time, there are some results which prove NP-completeness for large classes of related problems. An example of this is a result of Lewis & Yannakakis [1980] on checking whether a graph has a large induced subgraph with a certain property. If $G = (V, E)$ and $H = (V', E')$, then H is an *induced subgraph* of G if $V' \subseteq V$ and, for every $u, v \in V'$, $[u, v] \in E'$ iff $[u, v] \in E$. Let Π be a property of graphs.

INDUCED SUBGRAPH WITH PROPERTY Π

Instance: A graph G and a positive integer K.

Question: Does G have an induced subgraph H such that H has property Π and H has at least K vertices?

For example, if Π is the property 'H is a clique', then this problem is exactly the problem CLIQUE defined above. Lewis & Yannakakis [1980] show that the induced subgraph problem is NP-hard for any property Π which satisfies the following two conditions:

(1) Π is nontrivial, i.e., there are infinitely many graphs for which Π holds and infinitely many graphs for which Π does not hold;

(2) Π is hereditary on induced subgraphs, i.e., if Π holds for G then Π holds for every induced subgraph of G.

Examples of properties meeting these two conditions are 'H is planar', 'H is bipartite', and, for any fixed positive integer d, 'H has degree at most d'. If, in addition, the property Π can be tested in polynomial time, then the resulting induced subgraph problem is NP-complete. These two conditions do not completely characterize the properties for which the induced subgraph problem is NP-hard: if Π is the property 'H is a simple path', then the induced subgraph problem for Π is NP-hard, but Π is not hereditary on induced subgraphs.

Other results do provide a dichotomy into the NP-complete cases and the cases solvable in polynomial time. Let H be any fixed connected graph. The H-factor problem is defined as follows: an instance is a graph G, and the question is whether there are vertex-disjoint subgraphs $H_1, H_2, \ldots, H_k$ of G such that the vertices of $H_1, \ldots, H_k$ partition the vertices of G and such that H_i is isomorphic to H for $1 \le i \le k$. If H has only one vertex, this problem is trivial. If H is the graph which has two vertices with an edge connecting them, then the H-factor problem is just the problem of deciding whether G has a perfect matching, and this can be solved in polynomial time [Edmonds, 1965]. Kirkpatrick & Hell [1983] show that if H is any connected graph having at least 3 vertices, then the H-factor problem is NP-complete.

3.3. Restricted problems

The consequences of NP-completeness toward the difficulty of solving a problem can be misinterpreted if the instances actually fall into some special case of the problem. If they do, it could happen that the special case can be solved in polynomial time, even though the general problem is NP-complete. As a simple example, suppose that one wants to find a clique of maximum size in a planar graph. Even though the maximum clique problem is NP-complete, this special case, restricting to planar graphs, can be solved in polynomial time. Since no planar graph can contain a clique on five vertices, the special case can be solved in time $O(|V|^4)$ by enumerating and checking all subsets of four vertices. Similarly, if the clique problem is restricted to graphs of degree three, then the maximum clique has at most four vertices and the same algorithm works.

In general, the decision problem L' is a *restriction* of the decision problem L if the instances of L' form a subset of the instances of L, and the question to be decided for L' is the same as that for L. For a given NP-complete problem and a given restriction, the goal is to either prove that the restricted problem remains NP-complete or find a polynomial-time algorithm for it. For restrictions which involve a numerical parameter, such as the restriction to graphs of degree d, it is sometimes possible to identify a sharp boundary, or threshold, which separates the NP-complete cases from the cases solvable in polynomial time. For example, the satisfiability problem remains NP-complete when restricted to instances having three literals per clause, but this problem can be solved in polynomial time if there are only two literals per clause.

3.3.1. Restricted graph problems

We have observed that the clique problem can be solved in polynomial time when restricted either to planar graphs or to graphs of degree three. On the other hand, it is not clear how the planarity or degree-three restrictions can be exploited to give polynomial-time algorithms for the vertex cover, independent set, or Hamiltonian cycle problems. In fact, these problems remain NP-complete when restricted to planar graphs of degree three. This was proved by Garey & Johnson [1977] for vertex cover and independent set, and by Garey, Johnson & Tarjan [1976] for Hamiltonian cycle. It is easy to see that these problems can be solved in polynomial time for graphs of degree two. There is a substantial body of research studying NP-complete graph problems on restricted families of graphs. Besides planar and degree-restricted graphs, other families which have been studied include trees, bipartite graphs, and chordal graphs. See Johnson [1985] for a survey.

3.3.2. Restricted number size and strong NP-completeness

An interesting type of restriction concerns problems that involve numbers in their instances. Examples of such problems considered so far are integer programming, subset sum, bin packing, and traveling salesman. Motivation for restricting the magnitudes of numbers is provided by the following algorithm for the subset sum problem. This algorithm uses dynamic programming, a technique which is covered further in Chapter 8 of this volume. Let $a = (a_1, a_2, \ldots, a_m)$ and B be an instance of the subset sum problem, where $a_i \leq B$ for all i. The algorithm computes sets $S_1, \ldots, S_m$ of numbers where S_i is the set of all numbers $z \leq B$ which can be generated as 0–1 linear combinations of $a_1, \ldots, a_i$. Starting with $S_1 = \{0, a_1\}$, the sets are computed in sequence by

$$S_i = S_{i-1} \cup \{z \mid z \leq B \text{ and } z = s + a_i \text{ for some } s \in S_{i-1}\} \, .$$

The algorithm stops if it discovers that $B \in S_i$. If $B \notin S_i$ for $1 \leq i \leq m$, then the algorithm answers 'no'. Since the numbers a_i are encoded by their binary representations, this is not a polynomial-time algorithm. For example, by taking $a_i = 2^i$ for $1 \leq i \leq m$ and $B = 2^{m+1} - 2$, the length of the encoding of the instance is roughly m^2, whereas the set S_m contains 2^m numbers and so requires time 2^m to compute. Although this algorithm does not run in time polynomial in the length of the encoding of the instance, the algorithm can be implemented on a RAM of time complexity $O(mB)$, since each set S_i can be computed in time $O(B)$. The algorithm could therefore be useful if B is not too large. This is an example of a *pseudo-polynomial-time* algorithm, an algorithm whose time complexity can depend polynomially on the *magnitude* of the numbers appearing in the instance as well as on the total *length* of the instance.

To define this type of algorithm more precisely, some notation will be useful. If I is an instance of some problem, let $\max(I)$ be the maximum absolute value of an integer appearing in the instance; if I does not involve numbers, then $\max(I) = 1$. Let $\text{length}(I)$ be the length of the encoding of I. An algorithm is a *pseudo-polynomial-time* algorithm if there is a polynomial $p(\cdot, \cdot)$ such that the algorithm uses time at most $p(\max(I), \text{length}(I))$ on input I.

Since the subset sum problem has a pseudo-polynomial-time algorithm, we would not expect this problem to remain NP-compete when restricted to instances with 'small' numbers. In particular, if it remained NP-complete on instances $(a_1, \ldots, a_m)$, B with $B \leq m^d$ for some constant d, then, since the pseudo-polynomial-time algorithm runs in time polynomial in m on such instances, we would have $P = NP$. We have seen other problems, such as ILP, 01ILP, TSP, and $\triangle$TSP, which remain NP-complete when restricted to instances containing only small numbers.

Formally, L is *NP-complete in the strong sense* if there is a polynomial p such that L is NP-complete when restricted to instances I satisfying

$$\max(I) \leq p(\text{length}(I)) \,. \tag{3.1}$$

We say that a problem uses *small numbers* if all instances satisfy (3.1) for some fixed polynomial p.

The transformations described in Section 3.2 for proving NP-completeness of ILP, 01ILP, TSP, and $\triangle$TSP actually show that these problems are NP-complete in the strong sense. We would not expect any of these problems to have even pseudo-polynomial-time algorithms, due to the following easy fact which is the analogue for pseudo-polynomial time of Proposition 2.4.

Proposition 3.2. *Let L be* NP-*complete in the strong sense. Then L can be solved by a pseudo-polynomial-time algorithm iff* $P = NP$.

The transformation from SUBSET SUM to BIN PACKING given in Section 3.2 does not prove that BIN PACKING is NP-complete in the strong sense. Garey & Johnson [1975] give a different transformation (starting from another NP-complete problem) which shows that the following restricted version of BIN PACKING is NP-complete in the strong sense.

3-PARTITION
Instance: A number K of bins, a bin size S, a set $W = \{w_1, \ldots, w_{3K}\}$ of objects, and the size $s_i \in \mathbb{N}^+$ of each object w_i, where $\frac{1}{4}S < S_i < \frac{1}{2}S$ for all i and $\sum_{i=1}^{3K} s_i = KS$.
Question: Is there a partition of W into K disjoint parts such that the sum of the sizes of the objects in each part equals S?

The framework and terminology described in Section 3.3.2 was introduced by Garey & Johnson [1978]; see also Garey & Johnson [1979, Section 4.2].

3.3.3. A case study – Integer programming

In this section, several restricted versions of the problem ILP are considered and classified as being either NP-complete or polynomial-time solvable. Identical results hold for 01ILP. Each restriction is obtained as some combination of the following four restrictions:

(1) The number of variables, n, is held fixed.
(2) The number of constraints, m, is held fixed.
(3) The number of variables per constraint is held fixed.
(4) The problem is restricted to small numbers.

First, Lenstra [1983] has shown that, for every fixed n, ILP can be solved in polynomial time. The running time does depend exponentially on n, but this should be expected since ILP is NP-complete for unrestricted n. This is a remarkable result since, even with a fixed number of variables, the number of feasible solutions can grow exponentially in the size of the instance. (The analogous result for 01ILP is trivial, since the number of feasible solutions is at most 2^n.) The theoretical running time of Lenstra's algorithm has been improved by Kannan [1987]. In the remaining cases, n is not restricted.

If m is unrestricted, then the transformation from CLIQUE to ILP described in Section 3.2 shows that ILP is NP-complete even with small numbers and with two variables per constraint. With only one variable per constraint, ILP becomes trivial.

If m is fixed, then the number of variables per constraint cannot be fixed, since if it were fixed then n would also be fixed. There are only two remaining cases, depending on whether or not numbers are small. If numbers are not restricted to be small, then NP-completeness of the knapsack problem shows that ILP is NP-complete even for $m = 1$. By generalizing the algorithm for SUBSET SUM described above, Papadimitriou [1981] gives a pseudo-polynomial-time algorithm for ILP for every fixed m. It follows that ILP can be solved in polynomial time if m is fixed and numbers are small.

3.3.4. Restricted witness size

The final type of restriction we consider concerns the sizes of witnesses for the 'yes' instances. An example of a problem where a restriction on witness size arises naturally is provided by work of Megiddo & Vishkin [1988] on finding a minimum dominating set in a tournament. Here we consider directed graphs. We say that the vertex u *dominates* the vertex w if there is an edge directed from u to w. A *tournament* is a directed graph $T = (V, E)$ such that, for every pair u and w of distinct vertices, either u dominates w or w dominates u, but not both. (Imagine that the edges represent the outcomes of the games in a round-robin tournament where each vertex represents a player.) A *dominating set* in T is a set $D \subseteq V$ such that for every $w \in V - D$ there is some $u \in D$ that dominates w.

DOMINATING SET IN A TOURNAMENT (DOMT)

Instance: A tournament T and a positive integer K.

Question: Does T have a dominating set containing at most K vertices?

It is not hard to show that any tournament on n vertices has a dominating set of size at most $\lceil \log n \rceil$. First, a simple counting argument shows that there must be some vertex u which dominates at least $\lceil \frac{1}{2}(n - 1) \rceil$ other vertices. By placing u in the dominating set and removing from T the vertex u and all vertices dominated by u, we increase the size of the dominating set by one, but we cut the number of vertices in half. Continuing in this way, the size of the dominating set will be at most $\lceil \log n \rceil$ when the size of the remaining tournament becomes zero.

This upper bound on the size of a dominating set effectively restricts the witnesses for the 'yes' instances of DOMT to sets D containing at most $\lceil \log n \rceil$ vertices. (In contrast, witnesses for CLIQUE could contain cn vertices for some positive constant c.) The bound implies that DOMT can be solved in time $n^{O(\log n)}$: if $K \geqslant \lceil \log n \rceil$, then answer 'yes'; if $K < \lceil \log n \rceil$, then check for the existence of a dominating set D of size K by enumerating and checking all sets of size K.

By modifying the proof of Proposition 2.2, it follows that if DOMT were NP-complete, then every problem in NP could be solved in time $n^{O(\log n)}$. As a function of n, this time bound grows much more slowly than the best known time bound $2^{p(n)}$, some polynomial p, for solving a general problem in NP. On the other hand, Megiddo & Vishkin [1988] show that if DOMT can be solved in polynomial time, then the satisfiability problem can be solved in time $2^{O(\sqrt{v})}m^d$ for some constant d, where m and v are the number of clauses and variables, respectively, in the instance being checked for satisfiability. No algorithm with this time bound is known for satisfiability; in particular, testing satisfiability by exhaustive enumeration takes time at least 2^v. If it is true that any algorithm for the satisfiability problem has time complexity at least 2^{cv} for some constant $c > 0$, then DOMT is neither NP-complete nor solvable in polynomial time.

3.4. Problems between P and NP-complete

The problem DOMT appears to be neither solvable in polynomial time nor NP-complete. Although there is no proof that this particular problem lies 'between' P and NP-complete, Ladner [1975a] has proved that such problems do exist, assuming that $P \neq NP$. If $P \neq NP$, he shows that there is a decision problem L such that $L \notin P$ and L is not NP-complete. This problem is constructed specifically to have the desired property. There are no known examples of natural problems with this property. Other than DOMT, a candidate for a natural problem between P and NP-complete is the problem of deciding whether two graphs are isomorphic. This problem is discussed further in Section 5.9.

4. Coping with NP-complete problems – Related theory

Suppose that a solution to some optimization problem is needed and the decision version of the problem is NP-complete. The message of NP-complete-ness is that one should not try to find an algorithm which uses polynomial time in the worst case and which always finds an optimum solution (unless one is actually trying to prove that $P = NP$). There are several ways of relaxing this goal while still obtaining a satisfactory solution. One possibility which should be explored is that the instances which arise in practice all belong to some restricted subproblem which can be solved efficiently. Another alternative is to use an enumerative algorithm. If the instances to be handled are sufficiently small, then enumerative algorithms can be useful, even though they might use exponential time. Techniques such as branch-and-bound and dynamic programming can often be used to perform the enumerative search in a more intelligent way, thereby increasing the size of instances which can be handled. We mention three other ways of coping with NP-complete problems: approximation algorithms, local search, and average-case analysis. Although the design of algorithms using these methods lies outside the scope of this chapter, we mention them here since they have led to some interesting theory, e.g., to new types of reducibility and complete problems.

4.1. Approximation algorithms

Recall that an optimization problem Φ consists of a set of instances and a set of solutions. With each instance I is associated a set $\mathcal{F}(I)$ of feasible solutions, and each solution s has a value $c(s)$. In this section we assume that solution values are always positive integers. For each I, $\text{opt}(I)$ is the optimum, i.e., minimum or maximum, value of s over all $s \in \mathcal{F}(I)$. An algorithm A is an *approximation algorithm* for Φ if, for any given I, A returns some feasible solution $s \in \mathcal{F}(I)$. Define $A(I) = c(s)$, where s is the solution returned by A on input I. One way to measure the goodness of a solution is by the ratio of its value to the optimum value. To this end, define $R_A(I) = A(I)/\text{opt}(I)$ for minimization problems and $R_A(I) = \text{opt}(I)/A(I)$ for maximization problems. The approximation algorithm A has *ratio bound* r if $R_A(I) \leq r$ for all instances I. So $r \geq 1$, and $r = 1$ iff A gives an optimum solution for every I.

Different optimization problems are susceptible to varying degrees of approximation, measured by how close r is to 1. Problems can be roughly grouped into four classes. In the following, we assume $P \neq NP$; otherwise, every P-optimization problem can be solved by a polynomial-time algorithm A with $A(I) = \text{opt}(I)$ for all I (Proposition 2.7).

(1) For no constant r does the problem have a polynomial-time approximation algorithm with ratio bound r.

(2) There are constants $1 < r_1 < r_2$ such that the problem has a polynomial-time approximation algorithm with ratio bound r_2 but no polynomial-time approximation algorithm with ratio bound r_1.

(3) There is an approximation algorithm A which takes a parameter $\varepsilon > 0$ together with an instance I. For each fixed value of ε, A is a polynomial-time approximation algorithm with ratio bound $1 + \varepsilon$. Such an A is called a *polynomial-time approximation scheme*.

(4) There is an A as in (3) whose running time on inputs ε and I is polynomial in length(I) and $1/\varepsilon$. Such an A is called a *fully polynomial-time approximation scheme*.

Note that if the running time of A is $(\text{length}(I))^{1/\varepsilon}$, then A would be a polynomial-time, but not fully polynomial-time, approximation scheme. For problems in the first category (no constant r exists), it is useful to let r be a function of the size of I, although we do not pursue this generalization here.

The theory of NP-completeness has been used to determine how well certain problems can be approximated. One general result, due to Garey & Johnson [1978], is the following.

Theorem 4.1. *Let Φ be an optimization problem where there is a polynomial q such that* $\text{opt}(I) \leqslant q(\text{length}(I), \max(I))$ *for all instances I. Assume that* $P \neq NP$. *If the decision version of Φ is NP-complete in the strong sense, then Φ has no fully polynomial-time approximation scheme.*

The assumption in the first sentence of this theorem is quite natural. The proof of this result goes along the following lines. Let L be the decision version of Φ restricted to small numbers, so L is NP-complete. Restricting the optimization problem to small numbers, we have $\text{opt}(I) \leqslant q'(\text{length}(I))$ for some polynomial q'. Suppose there is a fully polynomial-time approximation scheme A. When A is given inputs I and $\varepsilon = (q'(\text{length}(I)) + 1)^{-1}$, we have $\text{opt}(I) < 1/\varepsilon$. Since solution values are positive integers, the condition $A(I) \leqslant (1 + \varepsilon)\,\text{opt}(I)$ (for a minimization problem) or $\text{opt}(I) \leqslant (1 + \varepsilon)A(I)$ (for a maximization problem) implies that $A(I) = \text{opt}(I)$. On inputs of this form, A runs in time polynomial in length(I) and $1/\varepsilon$, so by choice of ε the time is polynomial in length(I). Therefore, A can be used to solve L in polynomial time, contradicting the assumption that $P \neq NP$.

For example, since BIN PACKING is NP-complete in the strong sense, it follows that the multiprocessor scheduling problem defined in Section 3.2 has no fully polynomial-time approximation scheme. Hochbaum & Shmoys [1987] show that this scheduling problem does have a polynomial-time approximation scheme. Ibarra & Kim [1975] give a fully polynomial-time approximation scheme for the knapsack problem. (This problem has a pseudo-polynomial-time algorithm, so it is not NP-complete in the strong sense, unless $P = NP$.)

Other results place lower bounds on the minimum r or show that no constant r can exist. An example is the following, due to Sahni & Gonzalez [1976].

Theorem 4.2. *If $P \neq NP$, then for no constant r is there a polynomial-time approximation algorithm with ratio bound r for TSP Optimization, i.e., the problem of minimizing the distance of a tour, given the intercity distances.*

Proof. Suppose there were an approximation algorithm A with ratio bound r. We can assume r is an integer. Given an instance $G = (V, E)$ of the Hamiltonian cycle problem, construct an instance I of TSP by setting $d_{i,j} = 1$ (respectively $d_{i,j} = r|V|$) if there is (respectively is not) an edge in E between vertex i and vertex j. If G has a Hamiltonian cycle, then there is a tour of total distance $|V|$, so $A(I) \leqslant r|V|$. If G does not have a Hamiltonian cycle, then since A must return some tour and since any tour must use at least one of the distances $d_{i,j} = r|V|$, we have

$$A(I) \geqslant (|V| - 1) + r|V| > r|V| .$$

Therefore, by comparing $A(I)$ with $r|V|$, A can be used to solve the NP-complete Hamiltonian cycle problem in polynomial time. $\square$

The instances of TSP constructed in this proof do not satisfy the triangle inequality. In the case that the triangle inequality must be observed, Christofides [1976] gives a polynomial-time approximation algorithm with ratio bound $\frac{3}{2}$ for the optimization version of $\triangle$TSP. It is not known whether the constant $\frac{3}{2}$ can be improved.

Arora & Safra [1992], building on work of Feige, Goldwasser, Lovász, Safra & Szegedy [1991], show that the maximum clique problem cannot be approximated with any constant ratio in polynomial time, assuming that $P \neq NP$. Building further on this work, Arora, Lund, Motwani, Sudan & Szegedy [1992] show that if an optimization problem is hard for MAX SNP, as defined by Papadimitriou and Yannakakis [1991], then the problem does not have a polynomial-time approximation scheme, assuming again that $P \neq NP$. Examples of such problems are minimum vertex cover and minimum $\triangle$TSP tour. Both of these problems have polynomial-time approximation algorithms with a constant ratio bound.

The reducibilities defined in Section 2 and used in Section 3 are not designed to preserve closeness of solution values to the optimum. It is possible to define stronger types of reducibility which do preserve closeness. There are a number of papers which define such reducibilities and use them to show how a good approximation algorithm for one problem can be used to give good approximation algorithms for other problems; two early examples are Ausiello, D'Atri & Protasi [1980] and Paz & Moran [1981], and a more recent paper is Papadimitriou & Yannakakis [1991]. This and related work on the structure of optimization problems is surveyed by Bruschi, Joseph & Young [1991].

4.2. Local search

Several optimization problems have been successfully attacked in practice by the technique of local search. The basic idea of local search is to associate with every solution s a neighborhood $N(s)$ of solutions such that optimizing the value of s' over all s' in $N(s)$ can be done in a reasonable amount of time.

Consider, e.g., TSP. A solution for a given instance is a tour which visits every city exactly once. One neighborhood structure which has been used is the k-change neighborhood: the neighborhood of a tour s is the set of all tours which can be obtained from s by changing at most k edges. For each fixed k, the neighborhood of any s can be searched in polynomial time. The standard local search procedure for a minimization problem begins with some solution s (which might be found by a greedy approach). It then searches $N(s)$ for some $s' \in N(s)$ with $c(s') < c(s)$. If such an s' is found, the procedure replaces s by s' and continues. If no such s' is found, then the procedure has found a *local optimum*, that is, an s such that $c(s') \geq c(s)$ for all $s' \in N(s)$.

There are two potential difficulties with this local search procedure. First, since $N(s)$ is typically much smaller than the entire space of feasible solutions, the procedure could find a local optimum which is not a global optimum. Second, if the solution values belong to an exponentially large range, as they do for example in TSP with distances encoded in binary, the procedure could take exponential time to find a local optimum. If so, it is then natural to ask whether there is some completely different procedure which finds a local optimum in polynomial time. For examining questions of the type, Johnson, Papadimitriou & Yannakakis [1988] have presented a framework which is analogous in many ways to the framework of NP-completeness.

In the framework of Johnson et al., the formal definition of a *polynomial-time local search problem* (*PLS-problem*) is obtained by adding two new ingredients to the definition of a P-optimization problem (Section 2.6). As before, there is a P-relation F such that $F(x, s) = 1$ iff the solution s is feasible for the instance x, and there is a function c giving the value $c(s)$ of solution s. The new ingredients are polynomial-time algorithms A and C. When given x, A produces some 'starting solution' s with $F(x, s) = 1$. When given x and s, either C produces an s' with $F(x, s') = 1$ and $c(s') < c(s)$, or C reports that s is locally optimal. (The definition for a maximization problem is similar.) An algorithm *solves* this local search problem if, when given an x, it produces some s which is locally optimal for x. The PLS-problem Φ_1 is *PLS-reducible* to the PLS-problem Φ_2 if there are two polynomial-time computable functions f and g such that (i) the function f maps each instance x of Φ_1 to an instance $f(x)$ of Φ_2, and (ii) the function g maps each pair (solution for $f(x)$, x) to a solution for x so that, if s is a local optimum for $f(x)$, then $g(s, x)$ is a local optimum for x. A PLS-problem Φ is *PLS-complete* if every PLS-problem PLS-reduces to Φ. Two basic facts are: PLS-reducibility is transitive; and if Φ is PLS-complete, then Φ can be solved in polynomial time iff every PLS-problem can be solved in polynomial time. Johnson, Papadimitriou & Yannakakis [1988] show PLS-completeness of a particular PLS-problem which is based on a famous local search method of Kernighan & Lin [1970] for solving a graph partitioning problem. More recently, Krentel [1989] has shown that, for a sufficiently large k, TSP optimization under the k-change neighborhood structure is PLS-complete. Additional examples of PLS-complete problems are given by Schäffer & Yannakakis [1991].

A variation of local search, which attempts to deal with the local optimum vs. global optimum difficulty, is *simulated annealing* [Kirkpatrick, Gelat & Vecchi, 1983]. In this approach, a solution s is sometimes replaced by a *worse* solution s' in the neighborhood of s, thereby permitting the procedure to break out of local optima. The probability of adopting a worse s' decreases exponentially in $|c(s') - c(s)|$ and also depends on a parameter which is varied as the search procedure progresses so that the probability of choosing a worse s' decreases with time.

4.3. Average-case analysis

Average-case analysis of algorithms copes with difficult problems essentially by adopting a less stringent criterion for 'efficiency'. In order to define the average running time of an algorithm for a particular problem, the definition of the problem must also specify the probability $\mu(x)$ of each instance x. The average, or expected, running time of machine M on instances of size n is then the sum of $\mu(x) \cdot \text{time}_M(x)$ over all x of size n, assuming that μ has been normalized so that the instances of size n have total probability 1. There is a large body of research giving algorithms which run in polynomial expected time for various problems, including some NP-complete problems, using natural uniform distributions on instances. For example, a popular distribution for problems on graphs is the *random graph* model: given the number n of vertices and an edge probability p (possibly depending on n), the random graph $G_{n,p}$ has n vertices and, for each pair of vertices u and v, the edge $[u, v]$ is present with probability p; the choices are done independently for each edge $[u, v]$. Some of this work is surveyed by Johnson [1984a]. (Such results do not prove that P = NP since an algorithm which runs in polynomial expected time can also use exponential time in the worst case.) This raises the question of whether there are hardest problems in NP for average-case complexity just as the NP-complete problems are hardest problems in NP for worst-case complexity.

Levin [1986] has introduced a theory of average-case complexity and has exhibited a hardest, or complete, problem. The new concepts of the theory are average polynomial time (Average-P), Random-NP, and an extension of polynomial-time transformability which takes into account the probability distributions associated with problems. We deal here with decision problems where instances are encoded as words in $\{0, 1\}^*$. A *problem* is, therefore, a pair (L, μ) where $L \subseteq \{0, 1\}^*$ and μ is a probability distribution on $\{0, 1\}^*$. Define (L, μ) to be in *Average-P* if there is a machine (either a RAM or a TM) M and a constant k such that M solves L and $\Sigma_x \mu(x) \cdot \text{time}_M(x)^{1/k}/|x|$ converges, where the sum is over all $x \in \{0, 1\}^*$. This definition was chosen because it is robust under changes in the model of computation and the encoding scheme (cf. Section 2.3). The problem (L, μ) is in *Random-NP* if $L \in \text{NP}$ and the cumulative distribution function $\mu^*(x) = \Sigma_{y \leq x} \mu(y)$ can be computed in polynomial time, where $<$ here denotes lexicographic order on binary words. Finally, the definition of polynomial-time transformation should be such that (i) it is transitive, and (ii) if (L_1, μ_1) is transformable to (L_2, μ_2) and if (L_2, μ_2) belongs to Average-P, then (L_1, μ_1) belongs to Average-P. Regarding condition (ii), we must be careful that x's with large $\mu_1(x)$ are not transformed to y's with tiny $\mu_2(y)$. Otherwise, if the running time of the algorithm M for (L_2, μ_2) were very large on input y, this would contribute only a small amount to the average time of M (since $\mu_2(y)$ is tiny), but it would contribute a large amount to the average time of the algorithm M' for (L_1, μ_1), where M' first transforms x to y and then runs M on y. Formally, (L_1, μ_1) is *polynomial-time transformable* to (L_2, μ_2) if there is a function f computable in polynomial time and a constant k such that,

(1) for all x, $x \in L_1$ iff $f(x) \in L_2$,
(2) for all y, $\mu_2(y) \geq \Sigma_{f(x)=y} \mu_1(x) / |x|^k$.

A problem (L, μ) is *Random-NP-complete* if (L, μ) belongs to Random-NP and every problem in Random-NP is polynomial-time transformable to (L, μ). A consequence of completeness should by now be familiar: (L, μ) is in Average-P iff every problem in Random-NP is also in Average-P. Levin [1986] shows that a certain 'tiling' problem is Random-NP-complete, Gurevich [1991] gives other examples of Random-NP-complete problems and also provides evidence that certain problems (L, μ) are *not* Random-NP-complete. Say that μ is *flat* if there is a constant $d > 0$ such that, for all x, $\log \mu(x) \leq -|x|^d$. Many of the natural 'uniform' distributions, under which average-case analyses have been done, are flat. For example, the random graph distribution is flat, provided that the edge probability p is not too close to either 0 or 1. Under a certain assumption, Gurevich shows that if μ is flat, then (L, μ) is not Random-NP-complete. The assumption is that some nondeterministic algorithm of time complexity 2^{n^d}, for some constant d, can solve a decision problem which cannot be solved by any deterministic algorithm of time complexity 2^{n^b} for any constant b. This assumption is regarded as likely; it is believed that nondeterministic algorithms are more powerful than deterministic ones at each level of time complexity, polynomial, exponential, etc. Venkatesan & Levin [1988] have countered this result by liberalizing the definition of transformation to include transformations computed by machines using random numbers. Using the more liberal definition, there is a Random-NP-complete (L, μ) (a type of graph coloring problem) with a flat μ. The consequence of completeness is somewhat weaker, however: if (L, μ) is in Average-P, then every problem in Random-NP can be solved in polynomial average time by an algorithm using random numbers.

Additional information on this theory of average-case complexity can be found in Gurevich [1991].

5. The world beyond NP

Although many problems have been classified as being NP-complete, other important problems are not known to be in NP. To classify such problems, complexity theorists have defined and studied other general classes of problems. In many cases, particular problems of interest have been shown to be complete in some general class.

Let $\mathscr{C}$ be a class of decision problems, and let L be a decision problem. Then $\mathscr{C} \propto L$ if $L' \propto L$ for every $L' \in \mathscr{C}$. The problem L is $\mathscr{C}$-complete (under $\propto$ reducibility) if $L \in \mathscr{C}$ and $\mathscr{C} \propto L$. The class $\mathscr{C}$ is closed under $\propto$ provided that, if $L \in \mathscr{C}$ and $L' \propto L$, then $L' \in \mathscr{C}$. For example, Proposition 2.2 is the statement that P is closed under $\propto$. It is also easy to see that NP is closed under $\propto$. The results of Section 2.5 have analogues in this more general setting. For example, the following are generalizations of Propositions 2.4 and 2.5, respectively.

Proposition 5.1. Let $\mathscr{C}$ and $\mathscr{D}$ be classes of problems such that $\mathscr{D}$ is closed under $\propto$, and let L be $\mathscr{C}$-complete. If $L \in \mathscr{D}$ then $\mathscr{C} \subseteq \mathscr{D}$. If in addition $\mathscr{D} \subseteq \mathscr{C}$, then $L \in \mathscr{D}$ iff $\mathscr{D} = \mathscr{C}$.

Proposition 5.2. Let L' be $\mathscr{C}$-complete. If $L \in \mathscr{C}$ and $L' \propto L$, then L is $\mathscr{C}$-complete.

Some classes $\mathscr{C}$ have the property that P = NP implies P = $\mathscr{C}$. In this article, we call such classes *collapsible*, since they collapse to P if P = NP. If follows that if L is $\mathscr{C}$-complete where $\mathscr{C}$ is collapsible and NP $\subseteq \mathscr{C}$, then $L \in$ P iff P = NP. We also mention one class which is known to be different from P; call such classes *noncollapsible*. (The terms 'collapsible' and 'noncollapsible' are being used here for expositional purposes to describe a current state of knowledge; they should not be viewed as technical definitions. For example. if P $\neq$ NP in reality, then the term 'collapsible' is meaningless.) Figure 4 illustrates known containment relations among the classes described below, and shows which classes are known to be collapsible or noncollapsible. Many of these containments are obvious from definitions and are not mentioned explicitly in the text. All of the classes shown in Figure 4 are closed under $\propto$. A more extensive survey of complexity classes is given by Johnson [1990].

Before proceeding, a note on terminology should be given. The definition of $\mathscr{C}$-complete given above in terms of $\propto$ is used for classes $\mathscr{C}$ where P $\subseteq \mathscr{C}$ and where it is possible that P $\neq \mathscr{C}$. For classes $\mathscr{C}$ with $\mathscr{C} \subseteq$ P, the definition must be given in terms of more stringent types of reducibility. For example, the concept of a 'P-complete' problem is covered in Section 7.

5.1. co-NP

If L is a decision problem, the complement of L, denoted $\bar{L}$, has the same instances as L, but 'yes' instances are interchanged with 'no' instances. If $\mathscr{C}$ is a class of problems, define

$$\text{co-}\mathscr{C} = \{\bar{L} \mid L \in \mathscr{C}\} .$$

For example, the complement of VERTEX COVER is the set of (G, K) such

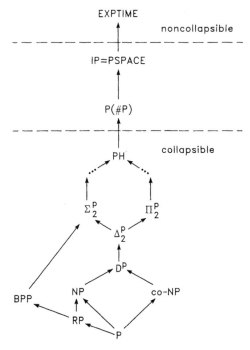

Fig. 4. Containments among complexity classes. Classes below the lower dashed line are collapsible, the class above the higher dashed line is noncollapsible, and the classes between the two dashed lines are not known to be either collapsible or noncollapsible.

that G does *not* have a vertex cover U with $|U| \leq K$. With regard to ordinary (deterministic) algorithms, a problem and its complement have very similar complexity: given any algorithm M for L, we can obtain an algorithm for $\bar{L}$ by first running M and then complementing its answer. In particular, P is closed under complementation. On the other hand, if $L \in$ NP it does not follow that $\bar{L} \in$ NP. Consider, for example, $\overline{\text{VERTEX COVER}}$. If (G, K) is an instance such that G does not have a vertex cover of size K, it is not at all obvious how to give a short (polynomial length) witness to this fact. It is an open question whether or not NP equals co-NP. It follows from Proposition 5.1 that if any NP-complete problem belongs to co-NP, then NP = co-NP. It is also easy to see that if L is NP-complete then $\bar{L}$ is co-NP-complete.

5.2. D^P

Some problems involve a combination of an NP question and a co-NP question. One type of problem asks, given an instance of some optimization problem and some K, whether the optimum solution value is *exactly* K. A particular example is EXACT CLIQUE: an instance is a pair (G, K), and the question is whether the largest clique in G has exactly K vertices. Note that the answer is 'yes' iff G has a clique of size K and G does not have a clique of size $K + 1$. Leggett & Moore [1981] observed that many such 'exact problems' have embedded in them both an NP-complete problem and a co-NP-complete problem. They used this fact to show, for many exact problems including EXACT CLIQUE, that the problem belongs to neither NP nor co-NP assuming that NP $\neq$ co-NP. Leggett and Moore did not, however, show these exact problems to be complete in a class.

Papadimitriou & Yannakakis [1984] later introduced the following class D^P which precisely captures the complexity of many exact problems:

$$D^P = \{ L \mid L = L_1 \cap L_2 \text{ for some } L_1 \in \text{NP and } L_2 \in \text{co-NP} \} .$$

Papadimitriou & Yannakakis [1984] show that EXACT CLIQUE is D^P-complete. They also give a basic D^P-complete problem, SAT–UNSAT, defined as the set of all pairs (S, S') where S and S' are sets of clauses such that S is satisfiable and S' is not satisfiable.

D^P has been useful in classifying two other types of problems, critical problems and facet problems. An example of a critical problem is MAXIMUM NON-HAMILTONIAN GRAPH, defined as the set of graphs G such that G does not have a Hamiltonian cycle but adding any new edge to G produces a graph with a Hamiltonian cycle. Facet problems arise in the field of polyhedral combinatorics, one of whose goals is to solve combinatorial optimization problems by better understanding the structure of their associated polytopes; see Pulleyblank [1989]. Consider, for example, TSP. The solutions, i.e., tours, for an n-city instance of TSP can be represented as points in m-dimensional space where $m = \frac{1}{2}n(n - 1)$; there is one coordinate for each pair $[i, j]$ of distinct cities. Each tour is represented by the 0–1 vector whose 1's correspond to the edges $[i, j]$ traversed by the tour. The convex hull of the points representing all tours is the TSP polytope (for n cities). A *facet* of this polytope is a face whose dimension is one lower than the dimension of the polytope itself. Each facet is defined by a unique (up to multiplication by a constant) linear equality which is satisfied by all points on the facet. Let TSP FACETS be the set of linear equalities which define the facets of some TSP polytope. A complete characterization of these linear equalities has been a long-standing open question in combinatorics. Papadimitriou & Wolfe [1988] show that MAXIMUM NON-HAMILTONIAN GRAPH and TSP FACETS are both D^P-complete.

5.3. Δ_2^P and the complexity of evaluation problems

Note that any problem in D^P can be solved in polynomial time by an oracle RAM which makes two calls to an oracle for some problem in NP. The class Δ_2^P generalizes this by allowing many oracle calls. This class lies at the second level of a 'hierarchy' of classes defined in Section 5.4.

If $\mathscr{C}$ is a class of problems, define $P(\mathscr{C})$ to be the class of all decision problems which can be solved by oracle RAMs in polynomial time using some problem in $\mathscr{C}$ as the oracle problem. Then $\Delta_2^P = P(NP)$. (So Δ_2^P is exactly the class of decision problems defined as NP-easy in Section 2.5.) The power of Δ_2^P is useful for certain decision problems whose solution can be based on the solution of some optimization problem. Consider, e.g., the problem UNIQUE-LY OPTIMAL TSP: an instance is an instance of TSP, and the question is whether there is a unique tour which achieves the optimum value, i.e., the minimum distance. It is easy to see that this problem belongs to Δ_2^P as follows. As in the proof of Proposition 2.7, an oracle RAM can find some optimum tour T using any NP-complete problem as the oracle. With one more oracle call, the RAM can determine if there exists another tour $T' \neq T$ with the same distance as T. Papadimitriou [1984] shows that UNIQUELY OPTIMAL TSP is Δ_2^P-complete.

The class of functions computable in polynomial time using NP oracles can be refined by placing upper bounds on the number of oracle calls. In this way, Krentel [1988] has refined the classification of several evaluation problems. Recall that in the evaluation version of an optimization problem, the goal is to compute the value of an optimum solution. For $z : \mathbb{N} \to \mathbb{N}$, let $FP^{NP}[z(n)]$ be the class of functions $f : \Sigma^* \to \mathbb{N}$ which can be computed in polynomial time by an oracle RAM using some NP oracle, where, for each input x, at most $z(|x|)$ oracle calls are made in the computation on input x. If (F, c) is a P-optimization problem and ν is a function such that $\mathrm{opt}(x) \leq \nu(|x|)$ for all x, then the function $\mathrm{opt}(x)$ belongs to $FP^{NP}[O(\log \nu(n))]$ (use binary search). For example, CLIQUE EVALUATION is in $FP^{NP}[O(\log n)]$ and TSP EVALUA-TION is in $FP^{NP}[n^{O(1)}]$. Krentel shows that these two evaluation problems are complete in these two classes, respectively, under a type of reduction, called metric reduction, which is an appropriate generalization of $\propto$ to transformations between functions. A *metric reduction* from g to h is a pair of polynomial-time computable functions, f_1 and f_2, such that $g(x) = f_2(x, h(f_1(x)))$ for all x. By using a sophisticated approximation algorithm for bin packing due to Karmarkar & Karp [1982], Krentel observes that BIN PACKING EVALUA-TION, i.e., the problem of finding the minimum number of fixed-size bins sufficient to pack the given objects, belongs to $FP^{NP}[O(\log \log n)]$. Krentel also shows that if $P \neq NP$, then

$$FP^{NP}[O(\log \log n)] \neq FP^{NP}[O(\log n)] \neq FP^{NP}[n^{O(1)}].$$

Therefore, in a technical sense, TSP EVALUATION is harder than CLIQUE EVALUATION which is in turn harder than BIN PACKING EVALUATION. In particular, there is no metric reduction from TSP EVALUATION to CLIQUE EVALUATION, or from CLIQUE EVALUATION to BIN PACK-ING EVALUATION, assuming $P \neq NP$.

Let OptP be the class of functions $\mathrm{opt}(x)$ defined by all P-optimization problems. Since $\mathrm{OptP} \subseteq FP^{NP}[n^{O(1)}]$, TSP EVALUATION is OptP-complete under metric reductions. The evaluation version of 0–1 integer programming is also OptP-complete.

5.4. The polynomial-time hierarchy

While NP is useful for classifying problems which involve an existential quantifier $\exists$ (e.g., there exists a clique of size K), and co-NP is useful for problems which involve a universal quantifier $\forall$ (e.g., every clique has size less than K), the polynomial-time hierarchy is useful for problems involving a fixed number of alternations of quantifiers, such as $\exists\forall$. Alternating quantifiers arise, e.g., in games. Consider the following game between two players. Player I (who moves first) controls 0–1 variables $x_1 = (x_{1,1}, \ldots, x_{1,n})$ and Player II controls 0–1 variables $x_2 = (x_{2,1}, \ldots, x_{2,n})$. The constraints of the game are given by $A_1 x_1 + A_2 x_2 \le b$ where A_1 and A_2 are $m \times n$ matrices and b is an m-vector. Assume that for every choice of x_1 there is at least one choice of x_2 satisfying the constraints. Player I is trying to maximize an objective function $c(x_1, x_2) = c_1 \cdot x_1 + c_2 \cdot x_2$ where c_1 and c_2 are n-vectors, while Player II is trying to minimize this function. The value of the game, from Player I's point of view, is therefore

$$\max_{x_1} \min_{x_2} c(x_1, x_2) \quad \text{over } \{(x_1, x_2) \mid A_1 x_1 + A_2 x_2 \le b\} \,.$$

An instance of the decision problem GAME consists of A_1, A_2, b, c_1, c_2 together with an integer K; the question is whether the value of the game is at least K. If we try to place GAME in NP, it is natural to use an optimal move x_1 of Player I as a witness. The difficulty is that checking a particular witness x_1 requires checking that there does not exist a 0–1 x_2 such that $A_2 x_2 \le b - A_1 x_1$ and $c_2 \cdot x_2 < K - c_1 \cdot x_1$. This is an instance of the *complement* of 01ILP, so the checking requires solving a co-NP-complete problem. This would pose no difficulty if the checking algorithm had an oracle for 01ILP.

If $\mathscr{C}$ is a class of problems, define NP($\mathscr{C}$) to be the class of decision problems solvable by nondeterministic oracle RAMs in polynomial time using some problem in $\mathscr{C}$ as the oracle problem. Equivalently, $L \in \text{NP}(\mathscr{C})$ if there is a relation R, a problem $Q \in \mathscr{C}$, and a polynomial p, such that R is computable in polynomial time by a (deterministic) oracle RAM with oracle Q, and $x \in L$ iff there exists a witness w with $|w| \le p(|x|)$ and $R(x, w) = 1$. Define $\Sigma_2^P = \text{NP}(\text{NP})$. It is easy to see that GAME is in Σ_2^P.

In fact, GAME is Σ_2^P-complete. This can be proved by a simple transformation from a basic Σ_2^P-complete problem B_2. An instance of B_2 is a set of clauses $C_1, \ldots, C_m$ involving the Boolean variables $\mathscr{X}_1 = \{X_{1,1}, \ldots, X_{1,l}\}$, $\mathscr{X}_2 = \{X_{2,1}, \ldots, X_{2,l}\}$, and their negations; the question is whether there exists an assignment of truth values to $\mathscr{X}_1$ such that, for all assignments of truth values to $\mathscr{X}_2$, the clauses are not satisfied by the combined assignment.

The definitions of Σ_2^P and Δ_2^P can be extended to give an entire 'hierarchy' of classes called the *polynomial-time hierarchy*. Starting with $\Sigma_0^P = \text{P}$, define for all $k \ge 1$,

$$\Sigma_k^P = \text{NP}(\Sigma_{k-1}^P)\,, \qquad \Delta_k^P = \text{P}(\Sigma_{k-1}^P)\,, \qquad \Pi_k^P = \text{co-}\Sigma_k^P \,.$$

Let PH $= \bigcup_k \Sigma_k^P$. In particular, $\Sigma_1^P = NP$ and $\Pi_1^P = co\text{-}NP$. The class Σ_k^P contains problems involving k alternating quantifiers starting with $\exists$. The problem B_2 can be generalized to a problem B_k which is Σ_k^P-complete. The problem B_k involves k different types of variables $\mathscr{X}_j = \{X_{j,1}, \ldots, X_{j,l}\}$ for $1 \le j \le k$ and k alternating quantifiers $\exists \mathscr{X}_1 \, \forall \mathscr{X}_2 \, \exists \mathscr{X}_3 \, \forall \mathscr{X}_4 \cdots$; it corresponds to a k-move game between two players, where I controls $\mathscr{X}_1, \mathscr{X}_3, \ldots$, II controls $\mathscr{X}_2, \mathscr{X}_4, \ldots$, and the objective of Player I is that the clauses should be satisfied (respectively not satisfied) if k is odd (respectively even). Jeroslow [1983] has considered multi-player games where each player is trying to maximize her own objective function. He classifies the complexity of such games in terms of the polynomial-time hierarchy, where the level in the hierarchy depends on the number of players.

Just as it is not known whether P equals NP, it is not known, for any k, whether Σ_k^P equals Σ_{k+1}^P. Stockmeyer [1977] has observed that if $\Sigma_k^P = \Pi_k^P$ for some $k \ge 1$, then $\Sigma_k^P = \Sigma_j^P$ for all $j > k$. In particular, if P = NP, then P = PH, so PH is collapsible. The converse is not known to be true: it is conceivable that $P \ne NP$ and yet the hierarchy extends only to a finite number of distinct levels. To the extent that people believe that $P \ne NP$, it is also believed that the classes Σ_k^P do form a proper hierarchy. There are several results which provide evidence for some conjecture C by proving that the negation of C implies that the hierarchy collapses to the kth level for some particular k, i.e., that $PH \subseteq \Sigma_k^P$. The polynomial-time hierarchy was first defined by Meyer & Stockmeyer [1972]; the concept was also known to Karp [1972]. More information about the hierarchy and basic complete problems can be found in Stockmeyer [1977] and Wrathall [1977].

5.5. Counting problems

Some problems require counting the number of objects having a certain property. Valiant [1979] has defined the class #P to capture such problems. #P is a class of functions. For a P-relation R, let

$$C_R(x) = |\{w \mid R(x, w) = 1\}| .$$

Then #P is the class of all functions C_R for all P-relations R. Every decision problem in NP of the form 'Does there exist a w such that $R(x, w)$?' has a corresponding counting problem in #P of the form 'Count the number of w's such that $R(x, w)$'. The function g is #P-*hard* if each $h \in$ #P can be computed in polynomial time by some oracle RAM using an oracle for g. The function g is #P-*complete* if $g \in$ #P and g is #P-hard. It is easy to see that if any #P-hard function g can be computed in polynomial time, then P = NP; for example, being able to count the number of satisfying assignments of a set of clauses is sufficient to tell whether or not the clauses are satisfiable. The #P-complete problems are known to include the counting versions of many NP-complete decision problems such as SAT and HAMILTONIAN CYCLE; this is not surprising.

Valiant [1979] has proved a more interesting #P-completeness result: the problem of counting the number of perfect matchings in a bipartite graph is #P-complete. Here, an instance is a bipartite graph $G = (U, V, E)$ with vertices $U = \{u_1, \ldots, u_m\}$ and $V = \{v_1, \ldots, v_m\}$ and edges $E \subseteq U \times V$. A perfect matching in G is a set of m edges, no two of which are incident on the same vertex. This result is interesting because it does not rely on the difficulty of the existential version of the problem. The existential version, 'Does there exist a perfect matching in G?', can be solved in polynomial time (see Chapter 8 of this volume). Counting perfect matchings is a special case of computing the permanent of a matrix, a problem which arises in certain areas of chemistry and physics. Letting S_m denote the set of all permutations $\pi : \{1, \ldots, m\} \rightarrow \{1, \ldots, m\}$, the *permanent* of an $m \times m$ matrix $A = \{a_{i,j}\}$ is defined by:

$$\mathrm{perm}(A) = \sum_{\pi \in S_m} a_{1,\pi(1)} a_{2,\pi(2)} \cdots a_{m,\pi(m)} \, .$$

Counting the perfect matchings of G is the special case where $a_{i,j}$ is 1 (respectively 0) if there is (respectively is not) an edge between u_i and v_j in G. Despite the similarity of definition between the permanent and the determinant, all known algorithms for the permanent take exponential time, even though the determinant can be computed in polynomial time, e.g., by Gaussian elimination. (It is not obvious that Gaussian elimination runs in polynomial time, due to the possible exponential blow-up in the size of intermediate results. Edmonds [1967] shows that Gaussian elimination, if done properly, can be made to run in polynomial time.) The #P-completeness of the permanent provides an explanation for the apparent difficulty of computing this function.

Some problems in #P do not appear, at first glance, to be counting problems. A problem which arises in network reliability is computing the probability that a network remains connected when edges can independently fail with given probabilities. An instance of this problem is a connected graph $G = (V, E)$ with a rational probability $p(e)$ associated with each edge $e \in E$; the function to be computed is the probability $g(G, p)$ that G remains connected when edge e is removed with probability $p(e)$ independently for each e. To view this as a counting problem, note that computing $g(G, p)$ amounts to counting the connected subgraphs $G' = (V, E')$ of G, where each G' is weighted by the probability that G' is the surviving subgraph. It is not hard to see that there is a function $a(G, p)$ in #P and a function $b(G, p)$ computable in polynomial time such that $g(G, p) = a(G, p)/b(G, p)$. In particular, $g(G, p)$ is #P-*easy*, meaning that $g(G, p)$ can be computed by a polynomial-time oracle machine using some function in #P as the oracle. Provan & Ball [1983] show that $g(G, p)$ is #P-hard, even in the special case that all failure probabilities are identical.

Dyer & Frieze [1988] have studied the complexity of computing the volume of a convex polyhedron. For $x_1, \ldots, x_m \in \mathbb{Q}^n$, let $\mathrm{vol}(x_1, \ldots, x_m)$ be the volume of the convex hull of $x_1, \ldots, x_m$. Dyer and Frieze show that vol is both #P-hard and #P-easy. If the polyhedron is presented by a system of linear inequalities, i.e., as $\{x \mid Ax \leq b\}$, then computing the volume is #P-hard, although it is known to be #P-easy only in special cases.

In order to include #P in Figure 4, we turn it into the class P(#P) of decision problems which are polynomial-time reducible to some function in #P. The inclusion PH $\subseteq$ P(#P) is due to Toda [1991]. This is a surprising result, since it is not clear how a problem defined in terms of alternating quantifiers (such as the problem GAME defined in Section 5.4) can be reduced to a counting problem in #P.

5.6. Polynomial space

The RAM M is of *polynomial space complexity* if there is a polynomial $p(n)$ such that, for each input x, no register r_i with $i > p(|x|)$ is accessed during the computation of M on x, and, for each i with $1 \leq i \leq p(|x|)$, the length of the largest number stored in r_i at any time during the computation is at most $p(|x|)$. A decision problem L is in the class PSPACE if there is a RAM of polynomial space complexity which solves L. Equivalently, PSPACE is the class of decision problems solvable by Turing machines using an amount of tape which is bounded above by some polynomial in the length of the input. Space-bounded machines are not explicitly time-bounded. It is easy to see, however, that a polynomial space bound implies a time bound of the form $2^{q(n)}$ for some polynomial q, assuming that the machine always halts. This is true because, for some polynomial q, there are at most $2^{q(n)}$ different memory states (including the state of the program counter), and if the same memory state is ever repeated in the same computation then the computation must loop forever without halting. It is easy to see that all of the classes considered so far are contained in PSPACE.

A basic PSPACE-complete problem is QBF, which stands for Quantified Boolean Formula. This problem is, in a certain sense, the limit as $k \to \infty$ of the k-move game B_k described in Section 5.4. An instance of QBF is a set of clauses involving a set $\{X_1, \ldots, X_l\}$ of Boolean variables and their negations. Two players take turns setting the truth values of the variables in the order $X_1, X_2, X_3, \ldots, X_l$, so Player I sets X_1, then Player II sets X_2, then Player I sets X_3, and so on. After all variables have been set, Player I wins the game if the chosen assignment satisfies the given set of clauses. The question is whether Player I has a winning strategy. Since this game involves l alternating quantifiers and l is not fixed, it is not known whether QBF is in PH. It is easy to see, however, that QBF $\in$ PSPACE by performing a search of the entire game tree. Even though the size of the game tree is exponential in the number l of variables, the depth of the tree is only l, and the amount of memory needed to perform the search is polynomial in the depth of the tree. Stockmeyer [1977] shows that QBF is PSPACE-complete.

QBF has been used to show that other game-like problems are PSPACE-complete. One example, from Even & Tarjan [1976], is a game played on a graph $G = (V, E)$ with two distinguished vertices s and t. Two players, Red and Blue, take turns placing markers on vertices. At each turn, a player can place one marker on a vertex, other than s and t, which does not already have a marker. When all vertices other than s and t have been marked, Red wins if there is a path of Red-marked vertices from s to t.

Papadimitriou [1985] has considered an interesting variant of QBF where Player II plays randomly: whenever it is Player II's turn to set the truth value of some variable X_i, it is set to *true* with probability $\frac{1}{2}$ or to *false* with probability $\frac{1}{2}$. Given a set of clauses, the question is whether Player I has a strategy under which the clauses are satisfied with probability strictly greater than $\frac{1}{2}$; this problem is denoted SSAT (for stochastic SAT). Papadimitriou calls games of this type *games against nature* since they model situations where one is trying to find a strategy against a randomizing adversary. Papadimitriou [1985] shows that SSAT is PSPACE-complete. He also uses SSAT to show PSPACE-completeness of other more concrete games against nature, such as problems arising in stochastic scheduling and Markov decision processes.

Another general type of PSPACE-complete problem is not related to games, but rather asks whether a system can be moved from one given configuration to another (so these are more like puzzles than games). Indeed, a generic problem in PSPACE asks, for a given RAM M of polynomial space complexity and a given input x, whether the RAM can move from the initial configuration on input x to a halting configuration which gives the answer 'yes'. Orlin [1981] has considered problems in this vein which are 'dynamic' versions of certain NP-complete problems. An example is the dynamic 0–1 knapsack problem: an instance consists of n-vectors a and b of positive integers and an integer d; the question is whether there exists a sequence $\{x^i \mid i \in \mathbb{Z}\}$ of 0–1 n-vectors such that $a \cdot x^{i+1} + b \cdot x^i = d$ for all $i \in \mathbb{Z}$. Orlin shows that this problem is PSPACE-complete.

5.7. Exponential time

A decision problem L is in the class EXPTIME if it can be solved by some RAM of time complexity $O(2^{p(n)})$ for some polynomial p. It is known that $P \neq EXPTIME$. This follows from a general result of Hartmanis & Stearns [1965] which states that if $T_1(n)$ and $T_2(n)$ are two functions such that $T_1(n) \geq n$, $T_2(n) \geq n$, $\lim_{n \to \infty} (T_1(n))^2 / T_2(n) = 0$, and $T_2(n)$ is computable by a Turing machine in time $O(T_2(n))$, then there is a decision problem L which can be solved by a Turing machine of time complexity $O(T_2(n))$ but which cannot be solved by any Turing machine of time complexity $O(T_1(n))$. To obtain $P \neq EXPTIME$, take $T_1(n) = n^{\log n}$ and $T_2(n) = 2^n$.

It follows from Proposition 5.1 that if L is EXPTIME-complete (or even if $EXPTIME \propto L$), then $L \notin P$. More can be said: if $EXPTIME \propto L$, then there is a constant $b > 0$ such that no RAM of time complexity $O(2^{n^b})$ solves L.

Stockmeyer & Chandra [1979] have proved EXPTIME-completeness of certain games played on sets of clauses. One such game is similar to QBF except that there is an initial truth assignment to the variables, and the two players then take turns changing the truth values of the variables, one at a time. For example, Player I can, at each turn, choose any one of the variables $X_1, X_3, X_5, \ldots$, and change its assignment from *true* to *false* or vice versa. A particular variable might be changed many times during play. Player I wins if the clauses are ever satisfied by the current assignment. The problem of determining whether Player I has a winning strategy is EXPTIME-complete. The EXPTIME-completeness of games on clauses has been used to prove EXPTIME-completeness of chess, go, and checkers, when these games are generalized to arbitrarily large boards. For example, Fraenkel & Lichtenstein [1981] show that generalized chess is EXPTIME-complete.

Even higher complexity classes, such as exponential space, double-exponential time (i.e., time 2^{2^n}), etc., can be defined. If a problem is complete or hard for such a class, then a corresponding lower bound on its computational complexity follows. Many decision problems in formal logic have been classified in this way; these results are surveyed by Stockmeyer [1987].

5.8. *Probabilistic classes*

In this section we consider classes defined by algorithms which use random numbers in their computations. These classes are closer to P than the classes considered in Sections 5.1–5.7. A *probabilistic RAM* is a RAM with the additional type of instruction

Random(LABEL1, LABEL2) .

Whenever this is executed, the machine continues execution at the statement labeled LABEL1 with probability $\frac{1}{2}$, or it continues at LABEL2 with probability $\frac{1}{2}$. The *worst-case* (respectively *expected*) *time* of a computation is the maximum (respectively expected) number of instructions executed, taken over all possible outcomes of all the Random instructions executed. The probabilistic RAM M runs in *worst-case* (respectively *expected*) *time* $T(n)$ if, for each x, the worst-case (respectively expected) time of its computation on input x is at most $T(|x|)$. Let $M(x) = b$ denote the event that M produces the output b on input x.

A decision problem L is in the class RP (for random polynomial time) if there is a probabilistic RAM M which runs in polynomial worst-case time and a constant $\varepsilon < 1$ (the error probability) such that:
(1) for all $x \in L$, $\Pr[M(x) = 1] \geqslant 1 - \varepsilon$,
(2) for all $x \notin L$, $\Pr[M(x) = 0] = 1$.
The class RP is sometimes called R in the literature.

The definition of the class BPP is similar, except that the error probability must satisfy $\varepsilon < \frac{1}{2}$, and the second condition becomes:

(2) for all $x \notin L$, $\Pr[M(x) = 0] \geq 1 - \varepsilon$.

In other words, the class RP corresponds to algorithms with *one-sided error*: on instances $x \notin L$, the algorithm is always correct. The class BPP corresponds to *two-sided error*: there can be some nonzero probability of error on any instance. It should be emphasized that there is no notion of averaging over instances as was done in Section 4.3. The time complexity here is worst-case over instances. All the randomization is done within the algorithm itself. The error probability of a probabilistic algorithm can be decreased by running the algorithm several times, using new random choices at each trial. In the case of RP, e.g., the new algorithm should answer 1 if any of the trials answer 1. If there are t trials, the error probability of the new algorithm is at most ε^t. In the case of BPP, the most frequent answer should be taken. Since the error probability decreases exponentially in the number of trials, probabilistic algorithms are potentially useful in practice.

Although there is a long history of using randomization for tasks such as simulation and numerical integration, its use in algorithms for decision problems is relatively recent. An early example was in algorithms for testing primality. It is convenient to state the results in terms of the complementary problem, testing for compositeness.

COMPOSITE
Instance: A positive integer x (encoded in binary notation).
Question: Is x composite? That is, does x have a nontrivial factorization as $x = ab$, where a and b are integers greater than 1?

Since the input x is encoded in binary, the classical algorithm for testing primality, the sieve of Eratosthenes, takes time exponential in $|x|$. Faster algorithms are known, although no polynomial-time algorithm is known. It is obvious that COMPOSITE is in NP, and Pratt [1975] has shown that COMPOSITE is in co-NP. It follows that COMPOSITE is not NP-complete unless NP = co-NP.

Turning to probabilistic algorithms, Solovay & Strassen [1977] and Rabin [1980] show that COMPOSITE is in RP. The algorithms are sufficiently simple to be useful in practice. Although it is natural to use a nontrivial factorization $x = ab$ as a witness of x's compositeness, these probabilistic algorithms do not work by randomly searching for this type of witness, since the error probability is too large. For example, in an extreme case that $x = ab$ where a and b are prime, there is a negligible probability of finding a or b by choosing a random integer in the range from 2 to $\sqrt{x}$; letting $n = |x|$, this probability is $O(2^{-n/2})$. Density of witnesses is the key to showing that a problem L is in RP; if the witnesses are sufficiently dense, then with high probability a witness can be found by searching randomly. Specifically, $L \in$ RP if there is a P-relation R, a polynomial p, and a constant $\varepsilon < 1$ such that (i) for all $x \notin L$, there is no w with $R(x, w) = 1$, and (ii) for all $x \in L$ and $n = |x|$,

$$|\{w \in \{0, 1\}^{p(n)} \mid R(x, w) = 1\}| / 2^{p(n)} \geq 1 - \varepsilon .$$

Adleman & Huang [1987], building on work of Goldwasser & Kilian [1986], give a complicated algorithm showing that COMPOSITE is in co-RP. If a problem L is in RP $\cap$ co-RP, then L can be solved by an *errorless* probabilistic algorithm as follows: alternately run an RP algorithm for L and an RP algorithm for $\bar{L}$ until one of them gives the answer 1. The expected time complexity of this algorithm is polynomial.

Regarding containments, it is easy to see that RP $\subseteq$ NP. Given an RP algorithm for L, we obtain an NP algorithm by replacing every Random instruction with a Split instruction. This works because the RP algorithm *never* answers 1 when given an input $x \notin L$. In general, this transformation does not work in reverse because witnesses might not be sufficiently dense. It is not known whether NP $\subseteq$ RP or whether NP $\subseteq$ BPP. It follows from results of Karp & Lipton [1982] that if either NP $\subseteq$ RP or NP $\subseteq$ BPP, then the polynomial-time hierarchy collapses to the second level. Lautemann [1983], simplifying an earlier proof of Sipser and Gács [see Sipser, 1983], shows that BPP $\subseteq \Sigma_2^P$.

The computational complexity of probabilistic algorithms is formalized by Gill [1977]. Many of the problems which are known to be in RP or BPP, but not known to be in P, are related to number theory. More information can be found in Johnson [1984b].

5.9. *Interactive proof systems*

If $L \in$ NP, then we can imagine a *proof system* by which a *prover P* convinces a *verifier V* that the answer to 'yes' instances of L is indeed 'yes'. If R is a P-relation which defines L, if $x \in L$, and if w is a witness such that $R(x, w) = 1$, then the prover can convince the verifier that $x \in L$ by sending w to the verifier. The verifier checks the proof by computing $R(x, w)$; if $R(x, w) = 1$, then the proof is accepted, if $R(x, w) = 0$, then the proof is rejected. If $x \notin L$, then even if P is replaced by a 'cheating prover' $\hat{P}$, the verifier will reject $\hat{P}$'s 'proof' since $R(x, w) = 0$ for all w. It is sufficient that V be a polynomial-time machine. No bound is placed on the time used by the prover. NP is precisely the class of decision problems having proof systems of this type.

The concept of an interactive proof system, introduced by Babai [see Babai & Moran, 1988] and Goldwasser, Micali & Rackoff [1989], generalizes this type of proof system in two ways. First, there can be two-way communication between P and V, i.e., the proof is interactive. Second, V can be a probabilistic polynomial-time machine, and some small probability of error is allowed. More precisely, (P, V) is an *interactive proof system* for L if there is a constant $\varepsilon < \frac{1}{2}$ such that (i) for all $x \in L$, V accepts P's interactive proof with probability at least $1 - \varepsilon$, and (ii) for all $x \notin L$ and all provers $\hat{P}$, V rejects $\hat{P}$'s interactive proof with probability at least $1 - \varepsilon$. Let IP denote the class of decision problems having interactive proof systems. Clearly NP $\subseteq$ IP, since a one-way proof system is a special case of an interactive proof system.

It is useful to illustrate the definition by an example, the problem of checking whether two given graphs are not isomorphic. This example gives evidence that interactive proof systems are more powerful than one-way (NP) proof systems. Graphs $G_1 = (V_1, E_1)$ and $G_2 = (V_2, E_2)$ are *isomorphic* if $|V_1| = |V_2|$ and there is a permutation $\pi : V_1 \to V_2$ such that, for all $u, v \in V_1$, $[u, v] \in E_1$ iff $[\pi(u), \pi(v)] \in E_2$.

GRAPH ISOMORPHISM (ISO)
Instance: Graphs G_1 and G_2.
Question: Are G_1 and G_2 isomorphic?

Clearly ISO $\in$ NP, although it is not known whether $\overline{\text{ISO}}$ is in NP. Goldreich, Micali & Wigderson [1991] give the following interactive proof system for the complement of ISO. Let G_1 and G_2 be a given instance. The interactive proof proceeds for t rounds, where 2^{-t} is less than the desired error probability ε. At each round, the verifier randomly sets b to either 0 or 1 with probability $\frac{1}{2}$ each. The verifier then constructs H, a random isomorphic copy of G_b, and sends H to the prover. The number b is not sent to the prover. The prover is supposed to respond with a number d such that H is isomorphic to G_d. If $d \neq b$, then the verifier rejects the entire interactive proof. If $d = b$, then the proof continues to the next round. If all rounds are completed without a rejection, the verifier then accepts the proof. If G_1 and G_2 are not isomorphic, then the prover will always be able to respond correctly. If the two graphs are isomorphic, however, the prover can at best guess the correct value $d = b$ with probability $\frac{1}{2}$ at each round, so the probability that the prover guesses correctly at all t rounds is at most 2^{-t}.

This interactive proof system for $\overline{\text{ISO}}$ has implications toward the classification of ISO. It has been a long-standing open question whether ISO is NP-complete. A result of Bopanna, Hastad & Zachos [1987] gives evidence that it is not. They show that if any co-NP-complete problem has an interactive proof system involving a constant number of rounds of interaction, then the polynomial-time hierarchy collapses to the second level. Since $\overline{\text{ISO}}$ has an interactive proof system of this type, it follows that, if ISO were NP-complete, then the hierarchy would collapse to the second level. This result about ISO was obtained independently by Schöning [1987] using different methods.

Goldwasser & Sipser [1989] have shown that if $L \in$ IP then there is an interactive proof system for L in which the prover has complete information of all the random choices of the verifier. Since an interactive proof system of this type is a special case of a game against nature (see Section 5.6), it follows that IP $\subseteq$ PSPACE. Shamir [1990], building on work of Lund, Fortnow, Karloff & Nisan [1990], has shown that interactive proof systems have surprising power: any decision problem in PSPACE has an interactive proof system. Therefore, IP = PSPACE.

More information about interactive proof systems can be found in the survey by Johnson [1988].

6. Approaches to the P vs. NP question

The importance of the P versus NP question is due primarily to the number of important problems which are known to be NP-complete. If it is proved that $P \neq NP$, efforts to find worst-case polynomial-time algorithms for these problems could cease. Methods for coping with NP-complete problems would of course continue to be developed, but it would be done with the knowledge that coping is the only feasible alternative. A proof of $P = NP$ could lead to algorithms of great practical importance. Whichever way the question is finally resolved, new insight into the nature of computation will undoubtedly be gained. In the long run, this insight could be as important as the answer to the question itself.

Although the answer to the P versus NP question is not in sight, results related to this question are known. Research aimed toward an eventual proof that $P \neq NP$ has focused on restricted models of computation. Those who believe that $P = NP$ should be encouraged that deep new methods have been developed to prove the existence of polynomial-time algorithms for various problems. Other results, called relativization results, limit the types of proof methods which could possibly settle the question.

6.1. Restricted computational models

When faced with a difficult open question, it is often useful to first study the question in some special case or in some restricted setting. For questions concerning computational complexity, it is common to study such questions for computational models which are restricted in some way. An interesting result of Razborov [1985a] shows that a certain problem in NP does not have polynomially-bounded complexity in a restricted model which allows only monotone operations. In order to state this result, some new definitions are needed.

A *combinational logic circuit*, or simply *circuit*, is modeled as an acyclic directed graph C. For some n, n nodes of C are labeled with the Boolean variables $x_1, \ldots, x_n$ and have no edges directed into them; these nodes are called *input nodes*. Each of the remaining nodes has two edges directed in and is labeled by some binary Boolean function such as *and*, *or*, *nand*, or *exclusive-or*; these nodes are called *gates*. There is exactly one gate which has no edges directed out; this gate is called the *output node*. Except for the output node, all nodes of C can have any number of edges directed out. If each input node is given a Boolean value, either 0 (*false*) or 1 (*true*), Boolean values are assigned to the gates in the obvious way: if u is a gate labeled by the function g and if there are edges from v to u and from v' to u, then the value of u is g applied to the values of v and v'. For each $x = (x_1, x_2, \ldots, x_n) \in \{0, 1\}^n$, let $C(x)$ be the value of the output node, so $C(x)$ is the function computed by C. A *circuit family* is a sequence $\{C_n \mid n \geq 1\}$ of circuits, such that C_n has n input nodes. Let $L \subseteq \{0, 1\}^*$. The circuit family *solves* L if, for all x, $x \in L$ iff

$C_{|x|}(x) = 1$. The circuit family has *size complexity* $S(n)$ if C_n has $S(n)$ gates for all n.

It is not hard to give a relationship between time complexity and circuit size complexity.

Proposition 6.1. *If $L \in P$ then there is some circuit family of polynomial size complexity which solves L.*

Therefore, to prove $P \neq NP$, it would suffice to show that there is some $L \in NP$ which cannot be solved by any circuit family of polynomial size complexity. It should be mentioned that proving the latter might be harder than proving the former; it is possible, given current knowledge, that $P \neq NP$ and yet every problem in NP can be solved by a polynomial-size circuit family (although Karp & Lipton [1982] show that if this happens, then the polynomial-time hierarchy collapses to the second level). Nevertheless, the circuit model is attractive, since it strips away a lot of the details of RAMs and Turing machines and reduces computation to its combinatorial essence, Boolean operations on bits.

Adleman [1978] has strengthened Proposition 6.1, showing that the hypothesis $L \in P$ can be replaced by $L \in RP$. Bennett & Gill [1981] show further that it can be replaced by $L \in BPP$.

A natural restriction of the circuit model is the restriction to monotone gate operations. A circuit is *monotone* if each gate is labeled by either *and* or *or*. These two functions are called monotone because changing an input from 0 to 1 never causes the output to change from 1 to 0. In general, a *monotone* function $f : \{0, 1\}^n \to \{0, 1\}$ has the property that, if $x_i \leq y_i$ for $1 \leq i \leq n$, then $f(x_1, \ldots, x_n) \leq f(y_1, \ldots, y_n)$. Monotone circuits can compute only monotone functions.

Razborov [1985a] has proved that no polynomial-size monotone circuit family can solve the clique problem. The clique problem is defined as a sequence of monotone functions, one for each number m of vertices. A graph $G = (V, E)$ with vertices $V = \{v_1, \ldots, v_m\}$ is encoded by $\frac{1}{2}m(m - 1)$ Boolean variables $x_{i,j}$ for $1 \leq i < j \leq m$, where $x_{i,j} = 1$ iff $[v_i, v_j] \in E$. For $K : \mathbb{N}^+ \to \mathbb{N}^+$, let $f_{m,K}(x_{1,2}, \ldots, x_{m-1,m}) = 1$ iff the variables encode a graph having a clique of size at least $K(m)$. Since adding an edge cannot destroy a clique, $f_{m,K}$ is monotone for each fixed m and K. By choosing $K(m)$ proportional to $\log m$, Razborov [1985a] shows that any monotone circuit which computes $f_{m,K}$ must have size at least $m^{b \log m}$ for some positive constant b. Using Razborov's techniques, Alon & Boppana [1987] have improved this lower bound to $2^{b(m/\log m)^{1/3}}$, using a larger $K(m)$.

This does not prove that $P \neq NP$, since the circuit families in Proposition 6.1 contain nonmonotone gate operations. One plausible approach to extending the lower bound to general circuits would be to show that there exists a constant d such that, for every circuit C of size S which computes a monotone function $C(x)$ (the circuit itself need not be monotone), there is a monotone circuit C' of size $O(S^d)$ such that $C(x) = C'(x)$ for all x. Unfortunately, this is not true. In a related paper, Razborov [1985b] shows that a certain $L \in P$ cannot be solved by any polynomial-size monotone circuit family. Here, L is the problem of deciding whether a bipartite graph has a perfect matching. Tardos [1988] has shown an exponential gap between monotone and general circuit size complexity.

A result related to P versus NP for a nonmonotone computational model is a result of Paul, Pippenger, Szemerédi & Trotter [1983] showing that there is a decision problem which can be solved by a nondeterministic Turing machine of time complexity $O(n)$ but which cannot be solved by any deterministic Turing machine of time complexity $O(n)$. It is doubtful that their proof technique can be extended to replace '$O(n)$' by 'polynomial'. This result is, nonetheless, important since it is the first to show that nondeterministic Turing machines are more powerful than deterministic ones. The proof uses in an essential way that the memory of a Turing machine consists of tapes. It is still an open question whether a similar result holds for RAMs.

6.2. New techniques for polynomial-time algorithms

In a series of papers, Robertson and Seymour have developed powerful new techniques which prove the existence of polynomial-time algorithms for certain problems. One of their basic results concerns the problem of testing whether one graph is a minor of another. In this section, graphs are undirected but may contain multiple edges and loops. If $e = [u, v]$ is an edge of the graph G, an *edge contraction* on e is performed by removing e from G and identifying the vertices u and v. The graph H is a *minor* of G, written $H \leqslant G$, if a graph isomorphic to H can be obtained from a subgraph of G by a sequence of edge contractions. It is an NP-complete problem to decide, given G and H, whether H is a minor of G. Robertson & Seymour [1986, 1990] show, however, that for every *fixed* H there is a polynomial-time algorithm which, when given G, decides whether $H \leqslant G$. A second basic result of Robertson & Seymour [1988, 1989] is that if $\mathcal{G}$ is any family of graphs which is closed under minors (i.e., $G \in \mathcal{G}$ and $H \leqslant G$ together imply that $H \in \mathcal{G}$), then there is a finite set of graphs $H_1, \ldots, H_k$ such that $G \in \mathcal{G}$ iff there does not exist an H_i with $H_i \leqslant G$. The set $\{H_1, \ldots, H_k\}$ is called an *obstruction set* for $\mathcal{G}$. [A familiar example of an obstruction set is given by Wagner's version of Kuratowski's Theorem which states that a graph is planar iff it does not contain as a minor either K_5 (the complete graph on five vertices) or $K_{3,3}$ (the complete bipartite graph with three vertices on each side).] It follows from the two basic results that if $\mathcal{G}$ is any family of graphs which is closed under minors, then the problem of testing membership in $\mathcal{G}$ can be solved in polynomial time.

As an example, Fellows & Langston [1988] apply the technique to show that the following problem belongs to P: an instance is a graph G, and the question is whether G can be embedded in 3-space so that no two distinct cycles of G are linked (like the links in a chain). Without using the minors approach, it is not even clear that this problem can be solved by any algorithm, regardless of its time complexity.

There are two difficulties with using the Robertson–Seymour results in practice. First, the time complexities of the algorithms involve enormous constant factors. Second, the result proving the existence of an obstruction set does not tell how to construct one. Ongoing work is attempting to improve the running times and to actually construct obstruction sets for various problems; see, e.g., Fellows & Langston [1989]. In spite of the difficulties, these results lend support to the belief that novel methods for designing polynomial-time algorithms have yet to be discovered. The work of Robertson and Seymour and related results are surveyed by Johnson [1987].

6.3. Relativization

Let X be a decision problem. The notion of relativization to X is that machines have access to an oracle for X. For example, the relativization of P, denoted P^X, is the class of decision problems solvable by polynomial-time oracle RAMs using oracle X. Similarly, NP^X is defined in terms of nondeterministic polynomial-time oracle RAMs with oracle X. Other complexity classes, such as the classes discussed in Section 5, are relativized in a similar way. A result involving classes is said to *relativize* if, for any X, the result is true when all classes are relativized to X.

Many results in complexity theory are proved by methods which relativize in a straightforward way to any oracle. For example, most of the containments shown in Figure 4 relativize. The result of Hartmanis and Stearns mentioned in Section 5.7 also relativizes. In contrast, Baker, Gill & Solovay [1975] have shown that, whichever way the P versus NP question is resolved, the result will not relativize: there are decision problems A and B such that $P^A = NP^A$ and $P^B \neq NP^B$. As a consequence of this result, proof methods which relativize should be avoided in trying to settle the P versus NP question. In this regard, it should be noted that certain proof methods are known *not* to relativize. A good example is the method used to prove $PSPACE \subseteq IP$ (see Section 5.9). Fortnow & Sipser [1988] show that there is an oracle A such that co-$NP^A \not\subseteq IP^A$. In the real world, however, co-$NP \subseteq PSPACE \subseteq IP$.

There is a large body of results showing that the answer to various open questions can be forced either way by choosing an appropriate oracle. For example, Baker, Gill and Solovay also show that there are oracles C and D such that $P^C \neq NP^C = $ co-NP^C and $P^D \neq NP^D \neq $ co-NP^D.

7. Parallel computation

As the price of computer hardware decreases, parallel computation is becoming increasingly relevant. Research in parallel computation covers a wide range, including the design of parallel architectures and studies of how parallelism can be used to solve specific problems, and there is a corresponding range of theoretical studies. This section covers a particular theory of parallel computation; the goal of this area is to understand which problems in P can be solved much more quickly in parallel than sequentially. To illustrate what is meant by 'much more quickly', it is useful to look at two simple examples. The first problem is computing the parity of many bits.

PARITY
Instance: $x_1, x_2, \ldots, x_n \in \{0, 1\}$.
Question: Is $\sum_{i=1}^{n} x_i$ odd?

This problem can be solved in time $O(n)$ in the obvious way. It is not difficult to argue that time at least $n - 1$ is required, because the answer depends on all n bits $x_1, \ldots, x_n$ and because at least $n - 1$ binary operations are needed to fan n inputs into one output. Therefore, the sequential, i.e., one-processor, complexity of this problem is n, to within constant factors.

To analyze the parallel complexity of this problem, we use an idealized parallel model where many processors can access the same *common memory* consisting of registers $c_1, c_2, \ldots$. This model, called the parallel RAM, or PRAM, is discussed in more detail below. Initially, the register c_i contains the bit x_i for $1 \le i \le n$. Let $m = \lceil \frac{1}{2}n \rceil$, and assume that we have m processors, $P_1, \ldots, P_m$. For all i in parallel, P_i performs the operation $c_i \leftarrow c_i \oplus c_{i+m}$. Within constant time, the original problem has been reduced to the problem of computing the parity of about $\frac{1}{2}n$ bits. Continuing in this way, we see that parity can be computed in time $O(\log n)$ using $O(n)$ processors. Therefore, the parallel complexity of PARITY is logarithmic in its sequential complexity.

Not all problems in P seem to be amenable to such a logarithmic reduction in complexity. One example is the following problem, of which PARITY is a special case. Recall the definition of a *circuit* given in Section 6.1.

CIRCUIT VALUE PROBLEM (CVP)
Instance: A circuit C and an assignment of Boolean values $x = (x_1, \ldots, x_m)$ to the input nodes of C, where m is the number of input nodes.
Question: Does $C(x) = 1$?

To illustrate the difficulty of obtaining a logarithmic reduction in complexity for this problem, imagine that the nodes of the circuit are divided into *levels* $L_0, L_1, \ldots, L_d$. The input nodes form level L_0, the output node is in level L_d, and an edge can go from a node in level L_i to a node in level L_j only if $i < j$. Suppose, for the sake of example, that there are m levels with at most m nodes in each level. Using m processors, all of the gate operations on the same level L_j can be computed in parallel, provided that the Boolean values of all nodes on levels L_i, $i < j$, have already been computed. Even with m^2 processors, it is not known how to solve CVP significantly faster than computing the values of the nodes in level L_1, then the values in level L_2, and so on. Since the level-by-level parallel algorithm takes time at least m, and since the problem can be solved sequentially in time $O(m^2)$ (by computing the values of the gates one at a time) this parallel algorithm does not achieve logarithmic reduction in complexity.

Just as an NP-complete problem is a hardest problem in NP with regard to sequential complexity, CVP is a hardest problem in P with regard to parallel complexity. The technical machinery needed to make this precise is described next.

7.1. The PRAM – A model of parallel computation

As outlined above, a *parallel RAM* (*PRAM*) consists of a sequence $P_1, P_2, \ldots, P_m$ of RAMs and a common memory with registers $c_1, c_2, \ldots$. Each P_i has its own local memory as well. The RAMs all have the same program, although i is initially written in one of the local registers of P_i, so that different RAMs can operate differently. An (encoded) instance of the problem to be solved is written initially in the common memory. The computation then proceeds synchronously, i.e., at each step, every RAM performs the next step of its program. When all the RAMs have halted, the answer should be written in the common memory. There are several varieties of PRAM, depending on whether different processors are allowed to read from or write into the same common register at the same step. For definiteness, we adopt the conventions used in the paper which introduced in PRAM model [Fortune & Wyllie, 1978]: simultaneous reading is allowed, but simultaneous writing is not. (In the case that simultaneous writing is allowed, a convention for resolving conflicts must also be specified.) In general, the number of processors is allowed to grow as a function of the size of the instance. The complexity of a PRAM algorithm is given by its *time complexity $T(n)$* and its *processor complexity $P(n)$*. On any instance of size n, the PRAM runs for at most $T(n)$ steps and uses at most $P(n)$ processors. So that a PRAM can access a large enough space of registers, the conventions of Section 2.2 concerning register length should be modified to allow registers to contain numbers of length $O(\log(T(n)P(n)))$.

A model of the problems having fast parallel algorithms is the class NC containing those problems which can be solved by a PRAM within time $O(\log^k n)$ using $O(n^b)$ processors, for some constants k and b. This class is very robust to changes in the model of parallel computation, e.g., to changes in the conventions concerning simultaneous reading and writing. It is easy to see that if L is a decision problem in NC, then $L \in P$, since each step of the PRAM can be simulated by a single processor within polynomial time. The question of whether every problem in P can be solved much more quickly in parallel is captured in the following:

Open Question. Is $P \subseteq NC$?

NC abbreviates 'Nick's Class' in honor of the author of Pippenger [1979], the paper which first drew attention to this class and gave evidence for its robustness. Basic computational problems in NC include sorting, and computing the inverse and determinant of a matrix; these results and others are surveyed by Karp & Ramachandran [1990]. Some authors define NC to contain only decision problems.

7.2. P-complete problems

To develop a theory for dealing with the P versus NC question, which is analogous to the theory of NP-completeness, we first need a reducibility under which NC is closed. (NC is not known to be closed under $\propto$.) An obvious choice is the following. If L_1 and L_2 are decision problems, $L_1, L_2 \subseteq \Sigma^*$, then L_1 is *NC-reducible* to L_2, written $L_1 \propto_{NC} L_2$, if there is a function $f : \Sigma^* \to \Sigma^*$ in NC such that $x \in L_1$ iff $f(x) \in L_2$. It is easy to see that NC is closed under $\propto_{NC}$ and that $\propto_{NC}$ is transitive. A decision problem L is *P-complete* (under NC-reducibility) if (i) $L \in P$, and (ii) $L' \propto_{NC} L$ for every $L' \in P$. The analogue of Proposition 2.4 is the following.

Proposition 7.1. *Let L be P-complete. Then $L \in NC$ iff $P \subseteq NC$.*

In the literature on P-complete problems, logspace-reducibility is commonly used in place of NC-reducibility. Logspace-reducibility is defined in terms of Turing machines which have three tapes, an input-tape, a work-tape, and an output-tape. The head scanning the input-tape can read but cannot write. The head scanning the output-tape can write but cannot read, and the movement of this head is restricted to moving right one cell each time a symbol is written. The function f is computable in *logspace* if there is such a three-tape machine such that, for each x, if the machine is started with x written on the input-tape, then the machine will halt with $f(x)$ written on the output-tape, and at most $\log |x|$ tape cells are used on the work-tape during the computation. The decision problem L_1 is *logspace-reducible* to the decision problem L_2, written $L_1 \propto_{\log} L_2$, if there is an f computable in logspace such that $x \in L_1$ iff $f(x) \in L_2$. It is known that if f is computable in logspace, then f can be computed by a PRAM in time $O(\log^2 n)$ using a polynomial number of processors; the proof method can be found, e.g., in Borodin [1977]. It follows that $L_1 \propto_{\log} L_2$ implies $L_1 \propto_{NC} L_2$.

The framework of P-completeness (in terms of logspace-reducibility) and the first P-complete problem were given by Cook [1974]. This paper did not deal with parallel computation, but rather was motivated by the question of whether every problem in P can be solved using space $O(\log^k n)$ for some constant k. The application of P-completeness to the P versus NC question came later.

Ladner [1975b] shows that CVP is P-complete. Goldschlager [1977] proves P-completeness of MONOTONE CVP, the restriction of CVP to instances involving monotone circuits. The decision versions of two classical optimization problems, linear programming and the max-flow problem, are P-complete.

LINEAR PROGRAMMING (LP)

Instance: An $m \times n$ integer matrix A and an integer m-vector b.
Question: Does there exist a rational n-vector $x \geq 0$ such that $Ax \leq b$?

Khachiyan [1979] shows that LP belongs to P, and Dobkin, Lipton & Reiss [1979] give a logspace-reduction from another P-complete problem to LP. To illustrate an NC-reduction, we give a reduction from MONOTONE CVP to LP due to Cook. Let an instance of MONOTONE CVP be the monotone circuit C together with an assignment of Boolean values to its input nodes. We describe an instance I of LP. A variable x_u in I is associated with each node u of C. The constraints will force x_u to be the Boolean value of node u. If u is an input node assigned value 0 (respectively 1), then I contains the constraint $x_u = 0$ (respectively $x_u = 1$). If u is a gate labeled with the function *and*, and if there are edges directed from v to u and from w to u, then I contains the constraints $x_u \leq x_v$, $x_u \leq x_w$, and $x_u \geq x_v + x_w - 1$. If u is labeled with *or*, then I contains the constraints $x_u \geq x_v$, $x_u \geq x_w$, $x_u \leq 1$, and $x_u \leq x_v + x_w$. Finally, if t is the output node, then I contains $x_t = 1$. Ignoring for the moment the constraint $x_t = 1$ associated with the output node, if nonnegative x_u's satisfy the remaining constraints, then each x_u must be the Boolean value of node u. So the constraints can all be met iff the output node has value 1. This transformation can be computed in NC by assigning a different processor P_u to each node u; this processor computes the constraints associated with u.

An instance of the max-flow problem involves a *flow network* which is a directed graph $G = (V, E)$ with two distinguished nodes s and t and a *capacity* $c(e) \in \mathbb{N}^+$ associated with each edge e. A *flow* is a function $f : E \to \mathbb{N}$. For each node u, the *excess* of f at u is the sum of $f(e)$ over all edges e directed into u minus the sum of $f(e')$ over all edges e' directed out of u. A flow is *feasible* if $f(e) \leq c(e)$ for all e, and every node except s and t has excess zero. The *value* of a flow is its excess at t.

MAX FLOW

Instance: A flow network G and a positive integer K.
Question: Does G have a feasible flow of value at least K?

It is known that MAX FLOW can be solved in polynomial time (see Chapter 8 of this volume). Lengauer & Wagner [1990] show that MAX FLOW is P-complete by giving a logspace reduction from MONOTONE CVP to MAX FLOW. This reduction produces instances of MAX FLOW where certain edge capacities are exponential in the size of the instance, so it is crucial that the capacities can be encoded in binary notation.

7.3. Random NC

There are certain problems which are not known to be in NC but which can be solved in time $O(\log^k n)$ using $O(n^b)$ processors if the individual processors are probabilistic RAMs as defined in Section 5.8 and if the parallel algorithm is allowed to produce an incorrect answer with some small probability ε. The class of problems solvable in this way is called RNC (for Random NC). An example of a problem where randomization seems to help is the maximum matching problem. Recall that a *matching* in a graph $G = (V, E)$ is a set of edges, no two of which are incident on the same vertex. A *maximum matching* is a matching containing the largest number of edges. Although it is well known that a maximum matching can be found in polynomial time, known polynomial-time algorithms for this problem are very sequential; they build a maximum matching in iterations where the number of iterations can be as large as $|V|^a$ for some positive constant a. By using a completely different approach, Karp, Upfal & Wigderson [1986] show that the problem of finding a maximum matching is in RNC. A simpler proof of this result is given by Mulmuley, Vazirani & Vazirani [1987]. Karp, Upfal and Wigderson also use the maximum matching algorithm to show that the problem of finding a maximum flow in a network is in RNC when the edge capacities are restricted to be small numbers, i.e., numbers bounded above by a polynomial in the size of the instance. If the maximum flow problem were in RNC with no restriction on edge capacities, then, since MAX FLOW is P-complete, we would have $P \subseteq RNC$. In general, if any P-complete problem is in RNC, then $P \subseteq RNC$. An RNC algorithm for finding a maximum matching in a bipartite graph is covered in Chapter 8 of this volume.

7.4. Other research in the theory of parallel computation

For problems known to be in NC or RNC, much research has been done to seek improved time and processor bounds. Typically, there is a trade-off between time complexity and processor complexity. The ultimate goal of this research is to find PRAM algorithms which make optimal use of parallelism (at least to within a constant factor). It is easy to see that a PRAM algorithm of time complexity $T(n)$ and processor complexity $P(n)$ can be simulated by a single processor within time $O(T(n)P(n))$. A PRAM algorithm of time complexity $T(n)$ and processor complexity $P(n)$ is *optimal* with respect to a particular sequential algorithm of time complexity $T_{SEQ}(n)$ if $T(n)P(n) = O(T_{SEQ}(n))$. A PRAM algorithm for a particular problem is said to be *optimal* if it is optimal with respect to the fastest known sequential algorithm for the problem. The definition of optimal can be made more precise if matching (to within a constant factor) upper and lower bounds on the sequential complexity of the problem are known.

Consider, for example, the parallel algorithm for PARITY described above. Since this algorithm uses $\frac{1}{2}n$ processors and time proportional to $\log n$, it is not optimal since the time-processor product is a factor $\log n$ larger than the sequential complexity of PARITY. There is an optimal parallel algorithm for PARITY, since only $n/\log n$ processors are needed to achieve time $O(\log n)$.

In general, time $O(n/p)$ can be achieved using p processors for any p in the range $1 \le p \le n/\log n$. To see this, note that p processors can, in constant time, reduce a j-bit parity problem to a $(j - p)$-bit parity problem if $j \ge 2p$. Therefore, within time $O(n/p)$, an n-bit parity problem is reduced to an i-bit parity problem for some $i < 2p$, and the i-bit problem can then be solved in time $O(\log p)$. Other problems, such as the maximum matching problem, are not known to have optimal parallel algorithms of time complexity $O(\log^k n)$. It is reasonable to conjecture that there exist problems in NC (or RNC) for which any NC (or RNC) algorithm must be nonoptimal. Karp & Ramachandran [1990] give a survey of research on PRAM algorithms.

Although it is conjectured that P-complete problems do not have parallel algorithms of time complexity $O(\log^k n)$, P-completeness does not mean that parallelism is totally useless for these problems. For example, the P-complete circuit value problem can be solved by the level-by-level parallel algorithm in time proportional to the number of levels in the given circuit. More discussion of parallel algorithms for P-complete problems and additional examples are given by Vitter & Simons [1986].

Another line of research concerns simulations of the PRAM by more realistic models of parallel computation. Although the PRAM is useful for the logical design of parallel algorithms, it is not reasonable to assume that every processor can access an arbitrary register of common memory in unit time. In one type of more realistic model, there is no explicit common memory, but the processors are connected by a communication network. Each processor is directly connected to only a few other processors. In order to simulate a PRAM algorithm on the network model, three problems must be addressed: (i) What should the network of interconnections be?; (ii) How should the PRAM's common memory be spread (possibly redundantly) over the local memories of the processors in the network?; and (iii) When a processor needs to access information held in the local memory of another processor, how should the information be routed through the network? Since all of the processors could be accessing information in parallel, it is important to avoid congestion in the network. The efficiency of a simulation is measured by its *overhead*, which is the time needed by the network model to simulate one step of the PRAM. Simulations fall into two categories, deterministic and probabilistic. Alt, Hagerup, Mehlhorn & Preparata [1987], building on work of Upfal & Wigderson [1987], give a deterministic simulation with overhead $O(\log^2 P)$ where P is the number of processors. Ranade [1987], building on work of Karlin & Upfal [1988], gives a probabilistic simulation with overhead $O(\log P)$.

Acknowledgement

I am grateful to David Shmoys for many helpful comments on this chapter.

References

Adleman, L. (1978). Two theorems on random polynomial time, *Proc. 19th IEEE Symp. on Foundations of Computer Science*, pp. 75–83.

Adleman, L.M., M-D.A. Huang (1987). Recognizing primes in random polynomial time, *Proc. 19th ACM Symp. on Theory of Computing*, pp. 462–469.

Aho, A.V., J.E. Hopcroft, J.D. Ullman (1974). *The Design and Analysis of Computer Algorithms*, Addison-Wesley, Reading, MA.

Alon, N., R.B. Boppana (1987). The monotone circuit complexity of Boolean functions. *Combinatorica* 7, 1–22.

Alt, H., T. Hagerup, K. Mehlhorn, F.P. Preparata (1987). Deterministic simulation of idealized parallel computers on more realistic ones. *SIAM J. Comput.* 16, 808–835.

Angluin, D., L.G. Valiant (1979). Fast probabilistic algorithms for Hamiltonian circuits and matchings. *J. Comput. System Sci.* 18, 155–193.

Arora, S., C. Lund, R. Motwani, M. Sudan, M. Szegedy (1992). On the intractability of approximation problems, manuscript.

Arora, S., S. Safra (1992). Approximating clique is NP-complete, manuscript.

Ausiello, G., A. D'Atri, M. Protasi (1980). Structure preserving reductions among convex optimization problems. *J. Comput. System Sci.* 21, 136–153.

Babai, L., S. Moran (1988). Arthur–Merlin games: A randomized proof system, and a hierarchy of complexity classes. *J. Comput. System Sci.* 36, 254–276.

Baker, T., J. Gill, R. Solovay (1975). Relativizations of the P =? NP question. *SIAM J. Comput.* 4, 431–442.

Bennett, C.H., J. Gill (1981). Relative to a random oracle A, $P^A \neq NP^A \neq co\text{-}NP^A$ with probability 1, *SIAM J. Comput.* 10, 96–113.

Boppana, R.B., J. Hastad, S. Zachos (1987). Does co-NP have short interactive proofs? *Inform. Process Lett.* 25, 127–132.

Borodin, A. (1977). On relating time and space to size and depth. *SIAM J. Comput.* 6, 733–744.

Bruschi, D., D. Joseph, P. Young (1991). A structural overview of NP optimization problems. *Algorithms Rev.* 2, 1–26.

Christofides, N. (1976). Worst-case analysis of a new heuristic for the traveling salesman problem, Technical Report, Graduate School of Industrial Administration, Carnegie-Mellon University, Pittsburgh, PA.

Cobham, A. (1965). The intrinsic computational difficulty of functions, in: Y. Bar-Hillel (ed.), *Proc. 1964 International Congress for Logic, Methodology and Philosophy of Science*, North-Holland, Amsterdam, pp. 24–30.

Cook, S.A. (1971). The complexity of theorem proving procedures, *Proc. 3rd ACM Symp. on Theory of Computing*, pp. 151–158.

Cook, S.A. (1974). An observation on time-storage trade off. *J. Comput. System Sci.* 9, 308–316.

Cook, S.A., R.A. Reckhow (1973). Time bounded random access machines. *J. Comput. System Sci.* 7, 354–375.

Cormen, T.H., C.E. Leiserson, R.L. Rivest (1989). *Introduction to Algorithms*, MIT Press, Cambridge, MA.

Dantzig, G.B. (1960). On the significance of solving linear programming problems with some integer variables. *Econometrica* 28, 30–44.

Dobkin, D., R.J. Lipton, S. Reiss (1979). Linear programming is log-space hard for P. *Inform. Process Lett.* 8, 96–97.

Dyer, M.E., A.M. Frieze (1988). On the complexity of computing the volume of a polyhedron. *SIAM J. Comput.* 17, 967–974.

Edmonds, J. (1965). Paths, trees and flowers. *Canad. J. Math.* 17, 449–467.

Edmonds, J. (1967). Systems of distinct representatives in linear algebra. *J. Res. Nat. Bur. Standards* B71, 241–245.

Even, S., R.E. Tarjan (1976). A combinaorial problem which is complete in polynomial space. *J. Assoc. Comput. Mach.* 23, 710–719.

Feige, U., S. Goldwasser, L. Lovász, S. Safra, M. Szegedy (1991). Approximating clique is almost NP-complete, *Proc. 32nd IEEE Symp. on Foundations of Computer Science*, pp. 2–12.

Fellows, M.R., M.A. Langston (1988). Nonconstructive tools for proving polynomial-time decidability. *J. Assoc. Comput. Mach.* 35, 727–739.

Fellows, M.R., M.A. Langston (1989). On search, decision and the efficiency of polynomial-time algorithms, *Proc. 21st ACM Symp. on Theory of Computing*, pp. 501–512.

Fortnow, L., M. Sipser (1988). Are there interactive protocols for co-NP languages? *Inform. Process Lett.* 28, 249–251.

Fortune, S., J. Wyllie (1978). Parallelism in random access machines, *Proc. 10th ACM Symp. on Theory of Computing*, pp. 114–118.

Fraenkel, A.S., D. Lichtenstein (1981). Computing a perfect strategy for $n \times n$ chess requires time exponential in n. *J. Combin. Theory Ser. A* 31, 199–214.

Garey, M.R., D.S. Johnson (1975). Complexity results for multiprocessor scheduling under resource constraints. *SIAM J. Comput.* 4, 397–411.

Garey, M.R., D.S. Johnson (1977). The rectilinear Steiner tree problem is NP-complete. *SIAM J. Appl. Math.* 32, 826–834.

Garey, M.R., D.S. Johnson (1978). 'Strong' NP-completeness results: Motivation, examples, and implications. *J. Assoc. Comput. Mach.* 25, 499–508.

Garey, M.R., D.S. Johnson (1979). *Computers and Intractability: A Guide to the Theory of NP-Completeness*, Freeman, San Francisco, CA.

Garey, M.R., D.S. Johnson, R.E. Tarjan (1976). The planar Hamiltonian circuit problem is NP-complete. *SIAM J. Comput.* 5, 704–714.

Gill, J. (1977). Computational complexity of probabilistic Turing machines. *SIAM J. Comput.* 6, 675–695.

Goldreich, O., S. Micali, A. Wigderson (1991). Proofs that yield nothing but their validity or all languages in NP have zero-knowledge proof systems. *J. Assoc. Comput. Mach.* 38, 691–729.

Goldschlager, L.M. (1977). The monotone and planar circuit value problems are log space complete for P. *SIGACT News* 9(2), 25–29.

Goldwasser, S., J. Kilian (1986). Almost all primes can be quickly certified, *Proc. 18th ACM Symp. on Theory of Computing*, pp. 316–329.

Goldwasser, S., S. Micali, C. Rackoff (1989). The knowledge complexity of interactive proof systems. *SIAM J. Comput.* 18, 186–208.

Goldwasser, S., M. Sipser (1989). Private coins versus public coins in interactive proof systems, in: S. Micali (ed.), *Advances in Computing Research 5: Randomness and Computation*, JAI Press, Greenwich, CT.

Gurevich, Y. (1991). Average case completeness. *J. Comput. System Sci.* 42, 346–398.

Hartmanis, J., R.E. Stearns (1965). On the computational complexity of algorithms. *Trans. Amer. Math. Soc.* 117, 285–306.

Hochbaum, D.S., D.B. Shmoys (1987). Using dual approximation algorithms for scheduling problems: Theoretical and practical results. *J. Assoc. Comput. Mach.* 34, 144–162.

Hopcroft, J.E. (1987). Computer science: The emergence of a discipline. *Commun. ACM* 30, 198–202.

Ibarra, O.H., C.E. Kim (1975). Fast approximation algorithms for the knapsack and sum of subset problems. *J. Assoc. Comput. Mach.* 22, 463–468.

Jeroslow, R.G. (1983). The polynomial hierarchy and a simple model for competitive analysis, report No. 83272-OR, Institut für Ökonometrie und Operations Research, Rheinische Freidrich-Wilhelms-Universität, Bonn.

Johnson, D.S. (1984a). The NP-completeness column: An ongoing guide (eleventh edition). *J. Algorithms* 5, 284–299.

Johnson, D.S. (1984b). The NP-completeness column: An ongoing guide (twelfth edition). *J. Algorithms* 5, 433–447.

Johnson, D.S. (1985). The NP-completeness column: An ongoing guide (sixteenth edition). *J. Algorithms* 6, 434–451.

Johnson, D.S. (1987). The NP-completeness column: An ongoing guide (nineteenth edition). *J. Algorithms* 8, 285–303.

Johnson, D.S. (1988). The NP-completeness column: An ongoing guide (twenty-first edition). *J. Algorithms* 9, 426–444.

Johnson, D.S. (1990). A catalog of complexity classes, in: J. Van Leeuwen (ed.), *Handbook of Theoretical Computer Science, Vol. A: Algorithms and Complexity*, North-Holland, Amsterdam and MIT Press, Cambridge, MA.

Johnson, D.S., C.H. Papadimitriou, M. Yannakakis (1988). How easy is local search? *J. Comput. System Sci.* 37, 79–100.

Kannan, R. (1987). Minkowski's convex body theorem and integer programming. *Math. Oper. Res.* 12, 415–440.

Karlin, A.R., E. Upfal (1988). Parallel hashing: An efficient implementation of shared memory. *J. Assoc. Comput. Mach.* 35, 876–892.

Karmarkar, N., R.M. Karp (1982). An efficient approximation scheme for the one-dimensional bin-packing problem, *Proc. 23rd IEEE Symp. on Foundations of Computer Science*, pp. 312–320.

Karp, R.M. (1972). Reducibility among combinatorial problems, in: R.E. Miller, J.W. Thatcher (eds.), *Complexity of Computer Computations*, Plenum Press, New York, pp. 85–103.

Karp, R.M., R.J. Lipton (1982). Turing machines that take advice. *Enseign. Math.* 28, 191–209.

Karp, R.M., V. Ramachandran (1990). Parallel algorithms for shared-memory machines, in: J. Van Leeuwen (ed.), *Handbook of Theoretical Computer Science, Vol. A: Algorithms and Complexity*, North-Holland, Amsterdam and MIT Press, Cambridge, MA.

Karp, R.M., E. Upfal, A. Wigderson (1986). Constructing a perfect matching is in Random NC. *Combinatorica* 6, 35–48.

Kernighan, B.W., S. Lin (1970). An efficient heuristic procedure for partitioning graphs. *Bell Syst. Tech. J.* 49, 291–307.

Khachiyan, L.G. (1979). A polynomial algorithm for linear programming. *Dokl. Akad. Nauk SSSR* 244, 1093–1096; English translation, *Soviet Math. Dokl.* 20, 191–194.

Kirkpatrick, D.G., P. Hell (1983). On the complexity of general graph factor problems. *SIAM J. Comput.* 12, 601–609.

Kirkpatrick, S., C. Gelat, M. Vecchi (1983). Optimization by simulated annealing. *Science* 220, 671–680.

Krentel, M.W. (1988). The complexity of optimization problems. *J. Comput. System Sci.* 36, 490–509.

Krentel, M.W. (1989). Structure in locally optimal solutions (extended abstract), *Proc. 30th IEEE Symp. on Foundations of Computer Science*, pp. 216–221.

Ladner, R.E. (1975a). On the structure of polynomial time reducibility. *J. Assoc. Comput. Mach.* 22, 155–171.

Ladner, R.E. (1975b). The circuit value problem is log space complete for P, *SIGACT News* 7(1), 18–20.

Lautemann, C. (1983). BPP and the polynomial hierarchy. *Inform. Process Lett.* 17, 215–217.

Lawler, E.L. (1976). *Combinatorial Optimization: Networks and Matroids*, Holt, Rinehart and Winston, New York.

Leggett, E.W., D.J. Moore (1981). Optimization problems and the polynomial hierarchy. *Theoret. Comput. Sci.* 15, 279–289.

Lengauer, T., K.W. Wagner (1990). The binary network flow problem is logspace complete for P. *Theoret. Comput. Sci.* 75, 357–363.

Lenstra Jr., H.W. (1983). Integer programming with a fixed number of variables. *Math. Oper. Res.* 8, 538–548.

Levin, L.A. (1973). Universal sorting problems. *Problemy Peredachi Informatsii* 9, 115–116; English translation, *Problems Inform. Transmission* 9, 265–266.

Levin, L.A. (1986). Average case complete problems. *SIAM J. Comput.* 15, 285–286.

Lewis, J.M., M. Yannakakis (1980). The node deletion problem for hereditary properties is NP-complete. *J. Comput. System Sci.* 20, 219–230.

Lueker, G.S. (1975). Two NP-complete problems in nonnegative integer programming, Report No. 178, Computer Science Laboratory, Princeton University, Princeton, NJ.

Lund, C., L. Fortnow, H. Karloff, N. Nisan (1990). Algebraic methods for interactive proof systems, *Proc. 31st IEEE Symp. on Foundations of Computer Science*, pp. 2–10.

Megiddo, N., U. Vishkin (1988). On finding a minimum dominating set in a tournament. *Theoret. Comput. Sci.* 61, 307–316.

Meyer, A.R., L.J. Stockmeyer (1972). The equivalence problem for regular expressions with squaring requires exponential space, *Proc. 13th IEEE Symp. on Switching and Automata Theory*, pp. 125–129.

Mulmuley, K., U.V. Vazirani, V.V. Vazirani (1987). Matching is as easy as matrix inversion. *Combinatorica* 7, 105–113.

Nemhauser, G.L., A.H.G. Rinnooy Kan, M.J. Todd (eds.) (1989). *Handbooks in Operations Research and Management Science, Vol. 1: Optimization*, North-Holland, Amsterdam.

Orlin, J.B. (1981). The complexity of dynamic languages and dynamic optimization problems, *Proc. 13th ACM Symp. on Theory of Computing*, pp. 218–227.

Papadimitriou, C.H. (1981). On the complexity of integer programming. *J. Assoc. Comput. Mach.* 28, 765–768.

Papadimitriou, C.H. (1984). On the complexity of unique solutions. *J. Assoc. Comput. Mach.* 31, 392–400.

Papadimitriou, C.H. (1985). Games against nature. *J. Comput. System Sci.* 31, 288–301.

Papadimitriou, C.H., K. Steiglitz (1982). *Combinatorial Optimization: Algorithms and Complexity*, Prentice-Hall, Englewood Cliffs, NJ.

Papadimitriou, C.H., D. Wolfe (1988). The complexity of facets resolved. *J. Comput. System Sci.* 37, 2–13.

Papadimitriou, C.H., M. Yannakakis (1984). The complexity of facets (and some facets of complexity). *J. Comput. System Sci.* 28, 244–259.

Papadimitriou, C.H., M. Yannakakis (1991). Optimization, approximation, and complexity classes. *J. Comput. System Sci.* 43, 425–440.

Paul, W.J., N. Pippenger, E. Szemerédi, W.T. Trotter (1983). On determinism versus nondeterminism and related problems, *Proc. 24th IEEE Symp. on Foundations of Computer Science*, pp. 429–438.

Paz, A., S. Moran (1981). Non deterministic polynomial optimization problems and their approximations. *Theoret. Comput. Sci.* 15, 251–277.

Pippenger, N. (1979). On simultaneous resource bounds, *Proc. 20th IEEE Symp on Foundations of Computer Science*, pp. 307–311.

Pratt, V. (1975). Every prime has a succinct certificate, *SIAM J. Comput.* 4, 214–220.

Provan, J.S., M.O. Ball (1983). The complexity of counting cuts and of computing the probability that a graph is connected. *SIAM J. Comput.* 12, 777–788.

Pulleyblank, W. (1989). Polyhedral combinatorics, in: G.L. Nemhauser, A.H.G. Rinnooy Kan, M.J. Todd (eds.), *Handbooks in Operations Research and Management Science, Vol. 1: Optimization*, North-Holland, Amsterdam, pp. 371–446.

Rabin, M.O. (1980). Probabilistic algorithm for testing primality. *J. Number Theory* 12, 128–138.

Ranade, A. (1987). How to emulate shared memory, *Proc. 28th IEEE Symp. on Foundations of Computer Science*, pp. 185–194.

Razborov, A.A. (1985a). Lower bounds on the monotone complexity of some Boolean functions. *Dokl. Akad. Nauk SSSR* 281, 798–801; English translation, *Soviet Math. Dokl.* 31, 354–357.

Razborov, A.A. (1985b), Lower bounds on monotone network complexity of the logical permanent. *Math. Zametki* 37, 887–900; English Translation, *Math. Notes* 37, 485–493.

Robertson, N., P.D. Seymour (1986). Graph minors XIII. The disjoint paths problem, manuscript (revised, May 1990).

Robertson, N., P.D. Seymour (1988). Graph minors XV. Wagner's conjecture, manuscript.

Robertson, N., P.D. Seymour (1989). Graph minors XVI. Quasi-well-ordering on a surface, manuscript.

Robertson, N., P.D. Seymour (1990). An outline of a disjoint paths algorithm, in: B. Korte, L. Lovász, H.J. Prömel, A. Schrijver (eds.), *Algorithms and Combinatorics, Vol. 9: Paths, Flows, and VLSI-Layout*, Springer, Berlin.

Sahni, S., T. Gonzalez (1976). P-complete approximation problems. *J. Assoc. Comput. Mach.* 23, 555–565.

Schäffer, A.A., M. Yannakakis (1991). Simple local search problems that are hard to solve. *SIAM J. Comput.* 20, 56–87.

Schöning, U. (1987). Graph isomorphism is in the low hierarchy, *Proc. 4th Symp. on Theoretical Aspects of Computing*, Lecture Notes in Computer Science, Vol. 247, Springer, Berlin, pp. 114–124.

Shamir, A. (1990). IP = PSPACE, *Proc. 31st IEEE Symp. on Foundations of Computer Science*, pp. 11–15.

Sipser, M. (1983). A complexity theoretic approach to randomness, *Proc. 15th ACM Symp. on Theory of Computing*, pp. 330–335.

Solovay, R., V. Strassen (1977). A fast Monte-Carlo test for primality. *SIAM J. Comput.* 6, 84–85 (erratum in *SIAM J. Comput.* 7 [1978, p. 118]).

Stockmeyer, L.J. (1977). The polynomial-time hierarchy. *Theoret. Comput. Sci.* 3, 1–22.

Stockmeyer, L.J. (1987). Classifying the computational complexity of problems. *J. Symbolic Logic* 52, 1–43.

Stockmeyer, L.J., A.K. Chandra (1979). Provably difficult combinatorial games. *SIAM J. Comput.* 8, 151–174.

Tardos, É. (1988). The gap between monotone and non-monotone circuit complexity is exponential, *Combinatorica* 8, 141–142.

Tarjan, R.E. (1987). Algorithm design. *Commun. ACM* 30, 205–212.

Toda, S. (1991). PP is as hard as the polynomial-time hierarchy. *SIAM J. Comput.* 20, 865–877.

Upfal, E., A. Wigderson (1987). How to share memory in a distributed system. *J. Assoc. Comput. Mach.* 34, 116–127.

Valiant, L.G. (1979). The complexity of computing the permanent. *Theoret. Comput. Sci.* 8, 189–202.

Van Emde Boas, P. (1990). Machine models and simulations, in: J. Van Leeuwen (ed.), *Handbook of Theoretical Computer Science, Vol. A: Algorithms and Complexity*, North-Holland, Amsterdam and MIT Press, Cambridge, MA.

Venkatesan, R., L.A. Levin (1988). Random instances of a graph coloring problem are hard, *Proc. 20th ACM Symp. on Theory of Computing*, pp. 217–222.

Vitter, J.S., R.A. Simons (1986). New classes for parallel complexity: A study of unification and other complete problems for P. *IEEE Trans. Comput.* C35, 403–418.

Wrathall, C. (1977). Complete sets and the polynomial-time hierarchy. *Theoret. Comput. Sci.* 3, 23–33.

E.G. Coffman et al., Eds., *Handbooks in OR & MS, Vol. 3*

Chapter 10

Computer System Models

Isi Mitrani

Computing Laboratory, University of Newcastle-upon-Tyne, Newcastle-upon-Tyne, NE1 7RU, U.K.

1. Introduction

This chapter is concerned with the application of probabilistic modelling methods to the study of computer systems. The general approach is to replace the real, usually quite complex system, by a mathematical model which captures its essential characteristics. Various processors, I/O devices, communication channels, etc., are treated as abstract servers, while the demands placed upon them are represented by jobs whose arrival patterns and service requirements are characterized by a number of random variables. That model is then analyzed, using the tools of stochastic processes and queueing theory. Inevitably, certain simplifying assumptions have to be made, in order to render the model tractable. However, this does not necessarily diminish the importance of the results that are obtained. The latter provide valuable insights into, and quantitative measures of, different aspects of system performance.

The models that are examined involve sometimes one, sometimes several service nodes, with demands belonging to single or multiple job types. The first objects of interest (Section 2) are the non-preemptive and preemptive priority scheduling strategies. Computer systems have incorporated these strategies, or variants of them, since the early days of batch processing. With the advent of time-sharing systems, and the need to enable several users to access a server in parallel, came the round-robin scheduling strategy and its limiting case, processor-sharing. Two rather different processor-sharing strategies are evaluated in Section 3.

Section 4 is concerned with the characterization of achievable performance in single-server systems with several job types. The related problem of designing scheduling strategies that achieve a pre-specified level of performance is also considered.

The modelling of interactive, virtual memory systems subject to real memory constraints is the subject of Section 5. These models are good examples of a hierarchical approach to performance evaluation, involving closed queueing networks and decomposition approximation. The problem of detection and avoidance of thrashing is examined.

Secondary memory devices, such as disks and drums, can have a considerable effect on the performance of a computer system. The modelling and evaluation of these devices is the subject of Section 6. Special features such as server motion and dependency between successive services are examined.

Throughout this chapter, the emphasis is on presenting results and explaining the ideas behind them, rather than on detailed derivations and proofs. Some familiarity with Markov processes, queues and queueing networks is assumed of the reader.

There is a large and constantly growing literature on computer system modelling and performance evaluation. The list of references at the end of the chapter contains, as well as the entries mentioned in the text, a number of other relevant books and collections of papers. Additional related bibliography can be found in the chapters on queueing theory and queueing networks of Volume 2, see Cooper [1990] and Walrand [1990].

2. Priority scheduling strategies

Consider a system where the demand consists of K job types, numbered $1, 2, \ldots, K$. Their arrival and service requirement characteristics, as well as the relative importance which they have in the eyes of the system administrator, may be different. In these circumstances, reasons of efficiency and profit often indicate that some job types should be treated more favourably, and should be provided with a better quality of service, than others. This is usually achieved by operating some sort of priority scheduling strategy. Our object here is to model such strategies and to evaluate their performance.

Jobs of type i are assumed to arrive into the system in an independent Poisson stream with rate λ_i; their service requirements have some general distribution function, $F_i(x)$, with mean b_i and second moment M_{2i} ($i = 1, 2, \ldots, K$). Service is provided by a single server. These are, in effect, the assumptions of the M/G/1 queueing system [Cooper, 1990]. However, there is now a separate queue for each job type, in which jobs of that type wait in order of arrival (Figure 1).

The job type numbers are used as priority indices: type 1 has top priority, type 2 second top, . . . , type K bottom. Whenever a new service is to be started, the job selected is the one at the head of the highest priority (lowest index) non-empty queue. Thus, a type i job may start service only if there are no jobs in front of it in queue i, and queues $1, 2, \ldots, i-1$ are empty. The server is not allowed to be idle when there are jobs in the system.

Priority scheduling strategies differ in the actions they take when a higher priority job arrives and finds a lower priority one in service. One possibility is simply to place the new arrival in its queue and await the scheduling decision that will be made on completing the current service. In that case, the strategy is

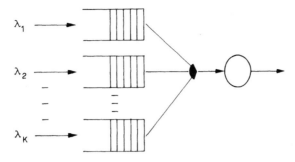

Fig. 1.

said to be 'non-preemptive', or 'head-of-the-line'. Alternatively, the new job may be allowed to interrupt the current service and occupy the server immediately. Such strategies are called 'preemptive'.

Preemptive priority strategies are further distinguished by the way they deal with a job whose service is interrupted. In all cases, that job remains at the head of its queue until the server is again able to attend to it. If, when that happens, the interrupted service is continued from the point of interruption, the strategy is said to be 'preemptive-resume'. If the service is restarted from the beginning, then the strategy is 'preemptive-repeat'. A preemptive-repeat strategy may be 'with resampling', or 'without resampling', depending on whether the restarted service is a new, independent realisation of the corresponding random variable, or whether it is the same realisation as before.

2.1. Non-preemptive priorities

The case where there are no preemptions is in many ways the most straightforward to analyse. Suppose that the performance measures of interest are the steady-state average response time (interval between arrival and departure) for a job of type i, W_i, and the average number of type i jobs in the system, L_i ($i = 1, 2, \ldots, K$). These quantities are of course related (Little's theorem, Cooper [1990]) by $L_i = \lambda_i W_i$, so it is sufficient to determine W_i. Denote by $\rho_i = \lambda_i b_i$ the offered load of type i. This is also equal to the probability that a job of type i is being served. More generally, let $\sigma_i = \rho_1 + \rho_2 + \cdots + \rho_i$ be the total offered load of types $1, 2, \ldots, i$, or the probability that one of those job types is in service. For steady-state to exist, it is necessary (and sufficient) that $\sigma_K < 1$. This is assumed to be the case.

The average response time of an arbitrary type i job (referred to as the 'tagged job'), can be expressed as a sum of four components:

$$W_i = W_0 + W_{qi} + W_{pi} + b_i ,\qquad\qquad (2.1)$$

where W_0 is the average remaining service time of the job, if any, found in service when the tagged job arrives;

W_{qi} is the total average service time of all jobs of types $1, 2, \ldots, i$, found waiting for service when the tagged job arrives;

W_{pi} is the total average service time of all jobs of priority higher than i which arrive after the tagged job but before the latter starts service (this term vanishes if $i = 1$);

b_i is the average service time of the tagged job.

At the moment of arrival of the tagged job (or, rather, just before that moment), there is an average of L_j jobs of type j in the system, $j = 1, 2, \ldots, K$. This follows from the PASTA property of the Poisson stream [Cooper, 1990]. Of those L_j jobs, ρ_j are being served and $L_j - \rho_j$ are waiting. Hence, we can write

$$W_{qi} = \sum_{j=1}^{i} (L_j - \rho_j) b_j = \sum_{j=1}^{i} (W_j - b_j) \rho_j . \tag{2.2}$$

If a job of type j is found in service, then its average remaining service time is the 'forward recurrence time' associated with the distribution $F_j(x)$ [Cooper, 1990]. That quantity is equal to $M_{2j}/(2b_j)$. Therefore,

$$W_0 = \tfrac{1}{2} \sum_{j=1}^{K} \frac{\rho_j M_{2j}}{b_j} = \tfrac{1}{2} \sum_{j=1}^{K} \lambda_j M_{2j} . \tag{2.3}$$

To determine the third component in (2.1), note that the average waiting time of the tagged job is $W_i - b_i$. During that time, an average of $\lambda_j(W_i - b_i)$ jobs of type j arrive and each of them requires an average service time b_j. Consequently,

$$W_{pi} = (W_i - b_i) \sum_{j=1}^{i-1} \rho_j = (W_i - b_i) \sigma_{i-1} , \tag{2.4}$$

where $\sigma_0 = 0$ by definition.

Substituting (2.2) and (2.4) into (2.1) yields a triangular set of simultaneous linear equations for the unknown W_i. Solving those equations one after the other, starting with $i = 1$, produces the following result:

$$W_i = b_i + \frac{W_0}{(1 - \sigma_{i-1})(1 - \sigma_i)} , \quad i = 1, 2, \ldots, K , \tag{2.5}$$

where W_0 is given by (2.3). The above expressions are known as 'Cobham's formulae'.

It is clear both from the definition of the priority scheduling strategy and from the symmetrical nature of Cobham's formulae, that as far as jobs of type i are concerned, all other job types can be grouped into two classes: class a ('above'), containing types $1, 2, \ldots, i - 1$, and class b ('below'), containing types $i + 1, i + 2, \ldots, K$. Either of those classes may of course be empty. The order of service within class a, and that within class b, can be arbitrary, as long as the priority relation between class a, type i and class b is preserved. Class a influences the performance of type i jobs through the offered load, σ_{i-1}, and through the corresponding component of W_0; the influence of class b is only through W_0.

It is possible that steady-state exists with respect to class a and type i, while class b is saturated. This happens if $\sigma_i < 1$, but $\sigma_{i+1} \geq 1$. If that is the case, then the probability that a job of type $i + 1$ is in service is equal to $1 - \sigma_i$, while jobs of types $i + 2, \ldots, K$ are never in service. Cobham's formulae continue to apply up to, and including, type i. However, the expression (2.3) for W_0 should be replaced by

$$W_0 = \tfrac{1}{2} \left[\sum_{j=1}^{i} \lambda_j M_{2j} + (1 - \sigma_i) \frac{M_{2,i+1}}{b_{i+1}} \right]. \tag{2.6}$$

The response times for jobs in the saturated class b are infinite.

When $\sigma_K < 1$, the non-preemptive scheduling strategy that minimises the total average number of jobs in this system, or the overall average response time, is the one that assigns top priority to the job type with the smallest average service time, second top to the next smallest, etc. [Walrand, 1990]. That strategy is referred to as 'shortest-expected-processing-time', or SEPT. The overall average response time, W, under the SEPT strategy is obtained from

$$W = \sum_{i=1}^{K} \frac{\lambda_i}{\lambda} W_i, \tag{2.7}$$

where the job types are numbered so that $b_1 \leq b_2 \leq \cdots \leq b_K$ and $\lambda = \lambda_1 + \lambda_2 + \cdots + \lambda_K$.

If the exact required service time of every job is known on arrival (rather than just the mean), then the optimal non-preemptive scheduling strategy is the one that selects the job requiring least service among those waiting. The performance of that strategy, known as 'shortest-processing-time', or SPT, is the subject of the following section.

2.2. The shortest-processing-time strategy

Consider an M/G/1 system where jobs arrive at rate λ and have service requirements with distribution function $F(x)$, mean b and second moment M_2. Service is given according to the SPT rule: the next job to be served is the one with the smallest required service time; if there is more than one such job, the one that arrived earliest is chosen. Services are not interrupted. The performance measure is the function $W(x)$, representing the steady-state average response time for a job whose service time is x. The condition for existence of steady-state is $\lambda b < 1$.

Suppose first that $F(x)$ is discrete with finite support, i.e., there are K possible service times, $x_1 < x_2 < \cdots < x_K$, which occur with probabilities $f_1, f_2, \ldots, f_K$, respectively. Then, treating these service times as job type identifiers, the SPT strategy becomes a special case of the non-preemptive priority one. Jobs of type x_i arrive at the rate of $f_i\lambda$; the first and second moments of their service times are of course x_i and x_i^2, respectively. The offered load of type x_i is $\lambda f_i x_i$.

Applying Cobham's formulae to this case, we get

$$W(x_i) = x_i + \frac{W_0}{(1 - \lambda \Sigma_{j=1}^{i-1} f_j x_j)(1 - \lambda \Sigma_{j=1}^{i} f_j x_j)}, \quad i = 1, 2, \ldots, K,$$

(2.8)

where $W_0 = \frac{1}{2}\lambda M_2$.

It is easy to see how the above result generalises to an arbitrary distribution function $F(x)$. In general, the offered load for jobs of type (service time) x is $\lambda x \, dF(x)$, and the sums in the denominator in (8) become integrals:

$$W(x) = x + \frac{W_0}{[1 - \lambda \int_0^{x-} y \, dF(y)][1 - \lambda \int_0^{x} y \, dF(y)]}, \quad x \geq 0,$$

(2.9)

where W_0 is again equal to $\frac{1}{2}\lambda M_2$. The notation $x-$ should be interpreted as 'limit from the left at x'. If the function $F(\cdot)$ is continuous at point x, then the denominator in (2.9) becomes

$$\left[1 - \lambda \int_0^{x} y \, dF(y)\right]^2.$$

The overall average response time under the SPT strategy, W, is obtained by integrating (2.9) over all job types:

$$W = \int_0^{\infty} W(x) \, dF(x).$$

(2.10)

This is the lowest average response time achievable by any non-preemptive scheduling strategy.

2.3. Preemptive priorities

Let us return to the assumptions of Section 2.1, and examine the model under the preemptive-resume priority strategy. It is now convenient to decompose the average response time of a tagged job of type i into a sum of two components:

$$W_i = V_i + R_i,$$

(2.11)

where V_i and R_i are the average intervals between the arrival of the tagged job and the start of its service, and between the start and the end of the service, respectively. The latter interval includes all delays caused by service interruptions. The averages V_i and R_i will be referred to as the 'waiting time', and the 'residence time', of the tagged job.

The following observations are helpful in finding V_i and R_i. Since a job of type i can preempt the service of any lower priority job, the job types $i+1, i+2, \ldots, K$ may be ignored in evaluating W_i. On the other hand, while the tagged job is waiting, the fact that the priorities of types $1, 2, \ldots, i-1$ are preemptive, is immaterial. In other words, the average waiting time of the tagged job is the same as it would have been if the priority strategy was non-preemptive, and if job types $i+1, i+2, \ldots, K$ did not exist. Hence, using Cobham's result, we get

$$V_i = \frac{W_{0i}}{(1 - \sigma_{i-1})(1 - \sigma_i)}, \quad i = 1, 2, \ldots, K, \tag{2.12}$$

where W_{0i} is given by an appropriately restricted form of (2.3):

$$W_{0i} = \tfrac{1}{2} \sum_{j=1}^{i} \lambda_j M_{2j}. \tag{2.13}$$

To find R_i, note that the residence time of the tagged job consists of its service time, plus the service times of all higher priority jobs that arrive during the residence time. This implies

$$R_i = b_i + R_i \sum_{j=1}^{i-1} \lambda_j b_j,$$

or,

$$R_i = \frac{b_i}{(1 - \sigma_{i-1})}, \quad i = 1, 2, \ldots, K. \tag{2.14}$$

Substituting (2.12) and (2.14) into (2.11) yields the average response time formulae for the preemptive-resume scheduling strategy:

$$W_i = \left[b_i + \frac{W_{0i}}{(1 - \sigma_i)} \right] \frac{1}{(1 - \sigma_{i-1})}, \quad i = 1, 2, \ldots, K. \tag{2.15}$$

Similar expressions can be obtained for the preemptive-repeat priority strategies, with and without resampling. The analysis of those models is more complicated and need not be reproduced here (an excellent exposition can be found in Conway, Maxwell & Miller [1967]). In order to state the results, some additional notation needs to be introduced.

Let S_i be the random variable representing the total service time used by a job of type i. Under a non-preemptive or a preemptive-resume strategy, this is of course equal to the job's required service time, but under a preemptive-repeat strategy it is generally larger. The following characteristics associated with S_i are obvious analogues of existing quantities:

$$\tilde{b}_i = E(S_i) , \qquad \tilde{\rho}_i = \lambda_i \tilde{b}_i , \qquad \tilde{\sigma}_i = \sum_{j=1}^{i} \tilde{\rho}_j . \tag{2.16}$$

Denote further

$$\xi_i = \tfrac{1}{2}\lambda_i E(S_i^2) , \qquad \Lambda_i = \sum_{j=1}^{i} \lambda_j . \tag{2.17}$$

The Laplace transform, $\tilde{\gamma}_i(s)$, of S_i, can be obtained from the distribution function, $F_i(x)$, and the Laplace transform, $\gamma_i(s)$, of the required service time for type i. The relation depends on whether the repetition of services is with resampling or without resampling. In the case of repetition with resampling, the result is

$$\tilde{\gamma}_i(s) = \frac{(s + \Lambda_{i-1})\gamma_i(s + \Lambda_{i-1})}{s + \Lambda_{i-1}\gamma_i(s + \Lambda_{i-1})} . \tag{2.18}$$

If the repetition is without resampling, then

$$\tilde{\gamma}_i(s) = \int_0^\infty \frac{(s + \Lambda_{i-1}) e^{-(s + \Lambda_{i-1})x}}{s + \Lambda_{i-1} e^{-(s + \Lambda_{i-1})x}} \, dF_i(x) . \tag{2.19}$$

The moments of S_i can be found by differentiating $\tilde{\gamma}_i(s)$ at $s = 0$.

We can now state the results relating to the average waiting time, V_i, and residence time, R_i, under the preemptive-repeat priority strategies. The average residence time has an identical form to (2.14), except that it is given in terms of the S_i characteristics:

$$R_i = \frac{\tilde{b}_i}{(1 - \tilde{\sigma}_{i-1})} , \quad i = 1, 2, \ldots, K . \tag{2.20}$$

Note that, although the form of this expression is the same for repetitions with and without resampling, the actual values obtained are generally different.

The results for the average waiting time are as follows ($i = 1, 2, \ldots, K$):
  (i) if the repetitions are without resampling, then

$$V_i = \frac{\sum_{j=1}^{i} [\xi_j(1 - \tilde{\sigma}_{j-1}) + \lambda_j \tilde{b}_j^2 \tilde{\sigma}_{j-1}]}{(1 - \tilde{\sigma}_{i-1})(1 - \tilde{\sigma}_i)} ; \tag{2.21}$$

(ii) if the repetitions are with resampling, then

$$V_i = \frac{\Sigma_{j=1}^{i} [\xi_j(1 - \tilde{\sigma}_{j-1}) + (\lambda_j/\Lambda_{j-1})\tilde{\sigma}_{j-1} E((e^{\Lambda_{j-1}S_j} - 1)^2)]}{(1 - \tilde{\sigma}_{i-1})(1 - \tilde{\sigma}_i)} . \tag{2.22}$$

Substituting (2.20) and either (2.21) or (2.22) into (2.11), yields the average response time, W_i. It should be pointed out that, in general, preemptive-repeat-without-resampling performs worse than preemptive-repeat-with-resampling, which is in its turn worse than preemptive-resume. This is because the jobs whose services are interrupted tend to be the long ones, and a strategy without resampling remembers those long service times, whereas one with resampling does not. When the required service times are exponentially distributed, there is no difference between the preemptive-resume and preemptive-repeat-with-resampling strategies. This is due to the 'memoriless' property of the exponential distribution [Cooper, 1990]. However, even in this case, the strategy without resampling leads to larger average response times.

Before leaving the topic of priorities, it is worth saying a few words about another well-known preemptive scheduling strategy, called 'shortest-remaining-processing-time', or SRPT. This is not based on fixed priority indices, but we include it in the present discussion because of its optimality property.

2.4. The SRPT scheduling strategy

It has already been mentioned that, without preemptions, the minimal overall average response time, W, is achieved by the SPT strategy. When preemptions are allowed, the scheduling strategy that minimises W is SRPT [Walrand, 1990]. As with SPT, an implementation of SRPT requires that the exact service times of all jobs are known on arrival. At any moment in time, the job (if any) with the smallest remaining service time is being served. If a new arrival has a shorter required service than the remainder of the current service, then the latter is preempted and is eventually resumed from the point of interruption.

Consider an M/G/1 queue with arrival rate λ and distribution function of the required service times $F(x)$, under the SRPT scheduling strategy. Let $W(x)$ be the average response time of a job whose required service time is x. This is given by

$$W(x) = \frac{\lambda}{2} \frac{G_2(x) + x^2[1 - F(x)]}{[1 - \lambda G(x-)][1 - \lambda G(x)]} + \int_0^x \frac{dy}{1 - \lambda G(y)} , \tag{2.23}$$

where

$$G(x) = \int_0^x y \, dF(y) , \qquad G_2(x) = \int_0^x y^2 \, dF(y) .$$

As before, the notation $x-$ means 'limit from the left at point x'. The derivation of this result can be found, for instance, in Coffman and Denning [1973].

The overall average response time, W, is obtained by integrating $W(x)\,dF(x)$, as in Equation (2.10). The resulting value is the smallest that can be achieved for this $M/G/1$ queue, by any scheduling strategy.

3. Processor-sharing strategies

Most multiprogrammed computer systems incorporate some sort of time-sharing facility which allows several active jobs to be processed in parallel. This is often achieved by employing a scheduling strategy called 'round-robin', whereby a single server dispenses service in small quanta of fixed size, Q. The job at the head of the queue occupies the server. It then either completes within the quantum Q and departs, or returns to the end of the queue and awaits its turn for additional quanta. New arrivals join at the end of the queue (Figure 2).

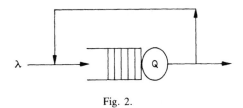

Fig. 2.

Under suitable assumptions, the round-robin scheduling strategy can be analysed in the steady-state by 'tagging' an incoming job and following its progress round the system. That analysis is rather cumbersome because the successive passes of the tagged job through the queue are dependent on each other. However, much of the complexity disappears if the quantum size Q is allowed to shrink to 0. The smaller the quantum, the more frequently each of the jobs in the system visits the server. In the limit $Q \rightarrow 0$, the ever quickening circulation of jobs is smoothed into a number of services proceeding in parallel, all using equal fractions of the available service capacity.

That limiting scheduling strategy will from now on be referred to as 'egalitarian processor-sharing', or EPS. One could define EPS directly, without passing through round-robin, by simply saying that if there are n jobs in the system at time t, then in the infinitesimal interval $(t, t + dt)$, each of those jobs receives an amount of service equal to dt/n. Alternatively, the time necessary for every one of the n jobs to increase its attained service by an infinitesimal amount, dx, is equal to $n\,dx$.

In systems with multiple job types, it may be desirable to introduce a more general form of processor-sharing, one that combines the benefits of parallel service with those of preallocated priorities. Such a scheduling strategy exists and is referred to as 'discriminatory processor-sharing', or DPS. It will be examined in Section 3.3.

The practical motivation for studying the performance of a processor-sharing strategy is that it provides a good approximation to round-robin with a small quantum, and is in general easier to analyse. Those strategies are also of considerable theoretical interest in their own right. We shall start with the EPS strategy, which turns out to have some rather remarkable properties.

3.1. Egalitarian processor-sharing

Consider an $M/G/1$ queue under the EPS scheduling strategy. Jobs arrive at rate λ and their required service times have some general distribution function, $F(x)$, with mean b. The offered load, $\rho = \lambda b$, is assumed to be less than 1, so that steady-state exists. Our first object is to determine the conditional average response time, $W(x)$, of a job whose required service time is x. Clearly, $W(x)$ can also be interpreted as the average amount of time necessary for a job with required service time greater than x to attain service $\dot{x}$. Hence, $dW(x)$ is the average time necessary for such a job to increase its attained service time from x to $x + dx$.

Let us tag a job with a service requirement greater than x, at the moment when it has attained service x. Denote by $L(x)$ the average number of other jobs (excluding the tagged one) that are in the system at that moment. Then, by the definition of EPS, the time necessary for the tagged job to increase its attained service by an infinitesimal amount, dx, is equal to $[1 + L(x)] dx$. Therefore, we can write

$$W'(x) = 1 + L(x) . \tag{3.1}$$

The average $L(x)$ can be expressed as a sum of two components,

$$L(x) = L_1(x) + L_2(x) , \tag{3.2}$$

where $L_1(x)$ is the average number of jobs which were in the system when the tagged job arrived and are still there when it attains service x; $L_2(x)$ is the average number of jobs which arrived after the tagged job and are still present when it attains service x.

To find $L_1(x)$, note that any job which had attained service u when the tagged job arrived, is still in the system when the latter attains service x with probability

$$\frac{1 - F(u + x)}{1 - F(u)} .$$

On the other hand, at a random point in time, the average number of jobs in the system with attained service between u and $u + du$ is equal to

$$\lambda[1 - F(u)] \, dW(u) .$$

This is an immediate consequence of Little's theorem: the jobs with attained service between u and $u + du$ arrive at the rate of $\lambda[1 - F(u)]$ and remain in the system for time $dW(u)$.

Combining the last two expressions and integrating over all values of u, we get

$$L_1(x) = \lambda \int_0^\infty [1 - F(u + x)]W'(u) \, du . \tag{3.3}$$

The derivation of $L_2(x)$ proceeds along similar lines. While the tagged job increases its attained service from u to $u + du$, an average of $\lambda \, dW(u)$ jobs arrive. Each of those jobs is still in the system when the tagged job attains service x with probability $1 - F(x - u)$. Hence,

$$L_2(x) = \lambda \int_0^x [1 - F(x - u)]W'(u) \, du . \tag{3.4}$$

Substituting (3.2), (3.3) and (3.4) into (3.1), yields an integral equation for the derivative $W'(x)$:

$$W'(x) = 1 + \lambda \int_0^\infty [1 - F(u + x)]W'(u) \, du$$

$$+ \lambda \int_0^x [1 - F(x - u)]W'(u) \, du . \tag{3.5}$$

The unique solution of (3.5) is the constant, $W'(x) = 1/(1 - \rho)$, where $\rho = \lambda b$ is the offered load. This, together with the obvious initial condition, $W(0) = 0$, implies that

$$W(x) = \frac{x}{1 - \rho} . \tag{3.6}$$

Thus the average conditional response time of a job is a linear function of its required service time. Short jobs are automatically favoured by EPS at the expense of long ones. This contrasts with the FIFO strategy, where the waiting time is independent of the job length, and with strategies like SPT or SRPT, which require for their operation that the job lengths be known in advance. That is one of the main attractions of EPS (or rather round-robin), as a scheduling strategy for interactive computer systems.

It is notable that $W(x)$ depends only on the mean, and not on the shape of the required service time distribution. That insensitivity is in fact a consequence of the fact that EPS is a 'symmetric' scheduling strategy, in the sense of Kelly. The resulting queueing process is therefore 'quasi-reversible' [see Walrand, 1990]. Two further consequences of this reversibility are the following:

(i) the steady-state probabilities, p_n, that there are n jobs in the system, are geometric with parameter ρ, regardless of the shape of $F(x)$:

$$p_n = (1 - \rho)\rho^n, \quad n = 0, 1, \ldots. \tag{3.7}$$

(ii) the departure process of the EPS M/G/1 queue is Poisson. Moreover, the past of that departure process is independent of the current state of the queue.

A stronger result than (3.7) can be established by considering a more detailed state description. Let $p_n(x_1, x_2, \ldots, x_n)$ be the steady-state probability density that there are n jobs in the system and the remaining required service time of job i is x_i. Then

$$p_n(x_1, x_2, \ldots, x_n) = (1 - \rho)\rho^n \prod_{i=1}^{n} \frac{1 - F(x_i)}{b_i}. \tag{3.8}$$

The overall average response time in the M/G/1 EPS system, W, is obtained from (3.6) by integrating $W(x) \, dF(x)$ over all x. This yields

$$W = \frac{b}{1 - \rho}. \tag{3.9}$$

Expressions (3.6) and (3.9) were first obtained, using a different approach, by Sakata, Noguchi & Oizumi [1971]. The direct derivation based on integral equations is due to O'Donovan [1974].

Comparing expression (3.9) with the corresponding formula for the FIFO M/G/1 queue [Cooper, 1990], we see that for given λ and b, the relative performance of the two strategies depends on the coefficient of variation of the required service time distribution. If $C^2 < 1$, then FIFO has a lower average response time than EPS; when $C^2 = 1$ (e.g., when the service times are distributed exponentially), the two averages are equal; if $C^2 > 1$, then EPS is better than FIFO. Whether a job of a given length, x, is better off under EPS or FIFO, depends both on x and C^2. For instance, if $C^2 = 1$, then the jobs that are shorter than average $(x < b)$ have lower average response times under EPS, while those that are longer than average are better off under FIFO.

So far we have been concerned with the average performance of the EPS strategy. In (3.6) we found the mean of the random variable $V(x)$, representing the steady-state response time of a job of length x. The distribution of that random variable, or rather its Laplace transform, $w(s, x)$, is more difficult to determine. In the case of exponentially distributed required service times, $w(s, x)$ was obtained by Coffman, Muntz & Trotter [1970], and has the following form:

$$w(s, x) = \frac{(1 - \rho)(1 - \rho r^2) e^{-[\lambda(1-r)+s]x}}{(1 - \rho r)^2 - \rho(1 - r)^2 e^{-x(1-\rho r^2)/(rb)}} , \tag{3.10}$$

where r is the smaller of the two positive real roots of the quadratic equation

$$\rho z^2 - (1 + \rho + bs)z + 1 = 0 .$$

Higher moments of the response time can be obtained by differentiating (3.10) with respect to s at $s = 0$. For instance, the variance of $V(x)$ is equal to

$$\text{Var}[V(x)] = \frac{2\rho b}{(1 - \rho)^3} \left[x - \frac{1 - e^{-(1-\rho)x/b}}{1 - \rho} \right]. \tag{3.11}$$

A notable feature of this last expression is that, for large x, the variance of the response time is approximately a linear function of x.

An analogous result for the $M/G/1$ EPS queue was obtained by Yashkov [1983]. The general expression for $w(s, x)$ is considerably more complex than (3.10) and need not be reproduced here. However, the variance of $V(x)$ is again asymptotically linear with x when x is large. The dominant term is a very natural generalisation of the one in (3.11):

$$\text{Var}[V(x)] \approx \frac{2\rho f}{(1 - \rho)^3} x , \tag{3.12}$$

where f is the average residual required service time. That is, $f = M_2/(2b)$, where b and M_2 are the first and second moments of the required service time.

3.2. EPS with multiple job types

Consider now the operation of the EPS strategy in an $M/G/1$ system where the demand consists of K job types. These arrive in independent Poisson streams and have different, generally distributed required service times. Denote, as usual, the arrival rate, average required service time and offered load for type i by λ_i, b_i and $\rho_i = \lambda_i b_i$, respectively. Let $\lambda = \lambda_1 + \lambda_2 + \cdots + \lambda_K$ be the total arrival rate. The total offered load, ρ, and the overall average required service time, b, are given by

$$\rho = \sum_{i=1}^{K} \rho_i , \qquad b = \frac{\rho}{\lambda} . \tag{3.13}$$

Since (3.6), (3.7) and (3.9) are insensitive with respect to the service time distribution, they continue to apply in the present case. The average response time for a job of type i, W_i, is now equal to

$$W_i = \frac{b_i}{1 - \rho} , \qquad i = 1, 2, \ldots, K . \tag{3.14}$$

The joint distribution of the numbers of jobs of different types in the system can be obtained by remarking that a job in the system is of type i with probability ρ_i/ρ. This, together with (3.8), implies that the probability, $p(n_1, n_2, \ldots, n_K)$, that there are n_1 jobs of type 1, n_2 jobs of type 2, ..., n_K jobs of type K in the system, has the form

$$p(n_1, n_2, \ldots, n_K) = (1 - \rho)n! \frac{\rho_1^{n_1} \rho_2^{n_2} \cdots \rho_K^{n_K}}{n_1! n_2! \cdots n_K!}, \tag{3.15}$$

where $n = n_1 + n_2 + \cdots + n_K$.

The marginal distribution of the number of type i jobs in the system, $p(n_i)$, is easily derived from the above result. It turns out to be geometric:

$$p(n_i) = (1 - \sigma_i)\sigma_i^{n_i}, \quad n_i = 0, 1, \ldots, \tag{3.16}$$

where $\sigma_i = \rho_i/(1 - \rho + \rho_i)$.

Note that, although the joint distribution (3.15) has the form of a product, it it not equal to the product of the marginal distributions. In other words, the numbers of jobs of different types in the system are not independent of each other.

3.3. Discriminatory processor-sharing

In interactive computer systems, just as in batch processing ones, it is often desirable to offer higher quality of service to some job types at the expense of others. This can be achieved, without sacrificing the service of jobs in parallel, by employing a processor-sharing strategy which allocates different fractions of the processor capacity to different job types. More precisely a weight g_i is associated with type i ($i = 1, 2, \ldots, K$, where K is the number of job types). If at a time t there are n_i jobs of type i in the system, $i = 1, 2, \ldots, K$, then in the infinitesimal interval $(t, t + dt)$, each job of type i receives an amount of service equal to $r_i \, dt$, where

$$r_i = \frac{g_i}{\sum_{j=1}^{K} g_j n_j}, \quad i = 1, 2, \ldots, K. \tag{3.17}$$

This is the discriminatory processor-sharing, or DPS, strategy. It can also be defined as a limiting case, when the quantum size approaches 0, of a round-robin strategy which allocates g_i quanta of service to a job of type i, whenever the latter visits the server.

Clearly, when all the g_i's are equal, the DPS strategy reduces to EPS. However, there is a large variety of effects that can be achieved through DPS by appropriate choices of those weights. For instance, if g_i is very much larger than g_j, then jobs of type i are effectively given preemptive priority over those of type j. Thus, by choosing some of the g_i's to be close to each other, and others widely different, one can construct a DPS strategy that behaves like EPS with respect to some job types and a priority strategy with respect to others.

Consider an $M/G/1$ system with K job types (same assumptions as in Section 3.2), under the DPS scheduling strategy. Let $W_i(x)$ be the steady-state average response time for a type i job whose required service time is x. These averages (or rather their derivatives) satisfy the following set of integral equations:

$$W_i'(x) = 1 + \sum_{j=1}^{K} \int_0^\infty \lambda_j g_{ji}[1 - F_j(u + g_{ji}x)]W_j'(u)\,\mathrm{d}u$$

$$+ \sum_{j=1}^{K} \int_0^x \lambda_i g_{ji}[1 - F_j(g_{ji}(x - u))]W_i'(u)\,\mathrm{d}u\,, \quad i = 1, 2, \ldots, K\,,$$

$$(3.18)$$

where $g_{ji} = g_j/g_i$. The derivation of (3.18) proceeds along very similar lines to that of (3.5). The main point of difference is that now, while a tagged job of type i increases its attained service by an amount x, any type j job which is together with it in the system increases its attained service by $g_{ji}x$.

Equations (3.18) were solved by Fayolle, Mitrani & Irsnogorodoski [1980]. For general required service time distributions, the solution is given only in terms of Laplace and Fourier transforms, and is of limited applicability. Perhaps its most important aspect is the fact that when x is large, the asymptotic behaviour of $W_i(x)$ is independent of i, the weights g_i and the distributions $F_i(\cdot)$; for the very long jobs, there is no difference between EPS and DPS:

$$W_i(x) \approx \frac{x}{1 - \rho}\,, \quad x \to \infty\,. \tag{3.19}$$

When the required service times are distributed exponentially (with parameter μ_i for type i), the solution of (3.18) has the form

$$W_i(x) = \frac{x}{1 - \rho} + \sum_{j=1}^{m} (g_i c_j + d_j)(1 - e^{-\alpha_j x/g_i})\,, \tag{3.20}$$

where m is the number of distinct elements in the vector $(g_1\mu_1, g_2\mu_2, \ldots, g_K\mu_K)$; $-\alpha_j$ $(\alpha_j > 0)$ are the m negative real roots of the equation

$$\sum_{j=1}^{m} \frac{\lambda_j g_j}{\mu_j g_j + s} = 1\,;$$

the constants c_j and d_j are given by

$$c_j = \frac{\prod_{k=1}^{m}(g_k\mu_k - \alpha_j)}{-\alpha_j^2 \prod_{k \neq j}^{m}(\alpha_k - \alpha_j)}$$

and

$$d_j = \frac{[\Sigma_{k=1}^{K} g_k^2 \lambda_k / (g_k^2 \mu_k^2 - \alpha_j^2)][\Pi_{k=1}^{m}(g_k^2 \mu_k^2 - \alpha_j^2)]}{\alpha_j^2 \Pi_{k \neq j}^{m}(\alpha_k^2 - \alpha_j^2)}.$$

The unconditional average response time of a type i job, W_i, can quite easily be obtained by multiplying (3.20) by $\mu_i \exp(-\mu_i x)$, and integrating over all x. Alternatively, by performing a similar manipulation in (3.18), it can be established that the W_i satisfy the set of linear equations

$$W_i\left[1 - \sum_{j=1}^{K} \frac{g_j \lambda_j}{g_j \mu_j + g_i \mu_i}\right] - \sum_{j=1}^{K} \frac{g_j \lambda_j W_j}{g_j \mu_j + g_i \mu_i} = \frac{1}{\mu_i}, \quad i = 1, 2, \ldots, K.$$

$$(3.21)$$

Equations (3.21) can also be used to solve the following synthesis problem: given the arrival and service parameters λ_i and μ_i, and a desired vector of average response times, $(W_1, W_2, \ldots, W_K)$, what weights $g_1, g_2, \ldots, g_K$ should be used with the DPS strategy in order to achieve that vector? The dimensionality of that problem is $K - 1$, since Equations (3.21) are homogeneous with respect to the g_i's, and therefore one of the latter can be fixed arbitrarily and one of the equations can be discarded.

We shall consider problems of this kind in more detail in Section 4.

4. Achievable performance in single-server systems

Consider a single-server system with K job types. The arrival and required service time characteristics of all types are fixed, but there is freedom in choosing the scheduling strategy. To any given strategy, S, there corresponds a vector of average response times, $W = (W_1, W_2, \ldots, W_K)$, by which the system performance is measured. In other words, the performance achieved by S is W. It is possible, of course, that two or more strategies achieve the same performance.

A question that arises naturally in this connection concerns the characterization of achievable performance: what is the set of vectors W that are achievable by certain 'admissible' scheduling strategies? Ideally, there should be a simple procedure for deciding whether a given vector belongs to that set or not. Moreover, having decided that a vector is achievable, it is desirable to be able to find a scheduling strategy that achieves it. The characterization problem is also related to that of performance optimization: knowing the set of achievable performance vectors is an important step towards finding 'the best' achievable vector according to some criterion.

In addressing these questions, we shall restrict the notion of 'admissible scheduling strategy' by requiring that (a) whenever there are jobs in the system, one of them is being served, and (b) no job departs from the system before completing its service. Strategies that satisfy conditions (a) and (b) are said to be 'work-conserving'. In practice, work-conservation is often violated, due to overheads of switching between jobs, abnormal terminations, etc. The results presented here apply only to systems where such violations are sufficiently minor to be ignored.

Since the server has to deal with all the work that is brought into the system, it is clear that any scheduling strategy that favours one or more job types and thereby decreases their average response times, must necessarily cause the response times of other job types to become larger. The exact nature of these trade-offs is described in the following subsection.

4.1. Conservation laws

It is convenient at this point to introduce the notion of 'virtual load'. For a particular realization of the queueing process under scheduling strategy S, the virtual load at time t, $V(t; S)$, is defined as the sum of the remaining service times of all jobs currently in the system. Since S is work-conserving, $V(t; S)$ decreases linearly with slope -1 whenever it is non-zero. In addition, it jumps up at each job arrival instant by an amount equal to the required service time of the new job. A typical realization of $V(t; S)$ is illustrated in Figure 3.

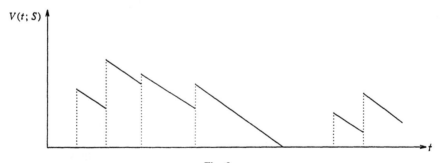

Fig. 3.

It is clear from the above definition that $V(t; S)$ is completely determined by the sequence of job arrival instants and the corresponding required service times. The scheduling strategy has no influence on the virtual load function and may be omitted from the notation: $V(t; S) = V(t)$ for all S. In particular, if the system is in equilibrium, then the expected steady-state virtual load, V, defined as

$$V = \lim_{t \to \infty} E[V(t)],$$

is a constant independent of the scheduling strategy.

Let V_i be the expected steady-state virtual load due to type i ($i = 1, 2, \ldots, K$); that is, the total remaining service time of type i jobs in the system. The vector of these virtual loads, $V = (V_1, V_2, \ldots, V_K)$, does depend on the scheduling strategy: for example, if a certain job type is given higher priority, then its expected virtual load will decrease. However, the dependence of V on S must be such that the sum of its elements remains constant:

$$\sum_{i=1}^{K} V_i = V .$$ (4.1)

This result is referred to as the 'conservation law for virtual load'. Any reduction in the virtual load for one or more job types, achieved by favorable scheduling, is always compensated by an increase in the virtual load of other job types.

The next step is to translate (4.1) into a conservation law for average response times. However, in order to do that, a further mild restriction needs to be imposed on the admissible scheduling strategies. It will be assumed that, when making scheduling decisions, a strategy may use information about the present and the past of the queueing process, but not about its future. In particular, it may not discriminate among jobs on the basis of their total or remaining required service times (such information is not usually available, anyway). Of the scheduling strategies introduced so far in this chapter, only SPT and SRPT fail to satisfy this condition. The reason for the restriction is that with it, the scheduling strategy does not influence the distribution of the required service time of a type i job observed in the system.

Suppose that the required service times of all job types are distributed exponentially, with mean b_i for type i ($i = 1, 2, \ldots, K$). Then, no matter how much service a type i job has received, its average remaining service time is b_i. Hence, the steady-state average virtual load of type i is $V_i = L_i b_i$, where L_i is the average number of type i jobs in the system. Denoting the arrival rate for type i by λ_i (the intervals between consecutive arrivals may have arbitrary distributions, and may even be dependent on each other), and applying Little's theorem, we can write $V_i = \lambda_i W_i b_i = \rho_i W_i$, where ρ_i is the offered load for type i. Then (4.1) becomes

$$\sum_{i=1}^{K} \rho_i W_i = V .$$ (4.2)

Relation (4.2) is known as the 'conservation law for response times in G/M/1 systems' [Kleinrock, 1965]. It states that, while varying with the scheduling strategy, S, the response time vector must always remain on the hyperplane defined by (4.2) (remember that the constant V is independent of S).

A similar result can be obtained in the case of generally distributed required service times, provided that only non-preemptive scheduling strategies are admissible. That is, once started, a job service is allowed to complete without interruptions. Then one can argue as follows (see Section 2.1). Of the expected number, L_i, of type i jobs in the system, an average of $L_i - \rho_i$ are waiting to start their service and one is being served with probability ρ_i. The average remaining service time of a type i job in service is $r_i = M_{2i}/(2b_i)$, where M_{2i} is the second moment of the type i required service time. Therefore, the virtual load due to type i is equal to

$$V_i = (L_i - \rho_i)b_i + \rho_i r_i = \rho_i W_i - \rho_i(b_i - r_i) \,.$$

Then (4.1) can be rewritten as

$$\sum_{i=1}^{K} \rho_i W_i = V + \sum_{i=1}^{K} \rho_i(b_i - r_i) \,. \tag{4.3}$$

Again we find that a linear combination of the average response times, with coefficients equal to the offered loads, is a constant independent of the scheduling strategy. This is the response time conservation law for $G/G/1$ systems [Kleinrock, 1965; Schrage, 1970]. The second term in the right-hand side of (4.3) may be viewed as a correction accounting for the non-exponentiality of the required service time distributions. Of course, in the $G/M/1$ case $b_i = r_i$ and (4.3) reduces to (4.2).

The expected virtual load, V, depends on the arrival processes, as well as on the required service time distributions. In the $M/G/1$ case (Poisson arrivals for all types), the value of V can be shown to be

$$V = \frac{1}{1-\rho} \sum_{i=1}^{K} \rho_i r_i \,, \tag{4.4}$$

where ρ is the total offered load. This expression can be obtained by assuming, for example, that jobs are served in FIFO order, regardless of type. Then the virtual load is also the time a new arrival would have to wait before starting service. Since V is independent of the scheduling strategy, the result is valid for all admissible strategies.

It should be obvious that not all performance vectors that satisfy (4.2) are achievable in a $G/M/1$ system. Similarly, not all performance vectors that satisfy (4.3) are achievable in a $G/G/1$ system by a non-preemptive scheduling strategy. Additional constraints need to be imposed in order to ensure achievability.

4.2. Characterization results

It would be instructive to consider first the case of a $G/M/1$ system with two job types. The performance vectors (W_1, W_2) can now be represented as points on the plane, and the conservation law (4.2) defines a straight line on which all achievable points must lie. However, not all points on that line are achievable. There is clearly a lower bound on the achievable average response times for type 1, W_1^{min}, and that lower bound is reached by a scheduling strategy that gives preemptive-resume priority to type 1 over type 2 (the order of service within type 1 and within type 2 is immaterial). Such a strategy also achieves the largest possible average response time for type 2, W_2^{max}. Similarly, a scheduling strategy that gives preemptive-resume priority to type 2 over type 1 achieves the lowest possible value for W_2, W_2^{min}, and the largest possible value for W_1, W_1^{max}. This situation is illustrated in Figure 4.

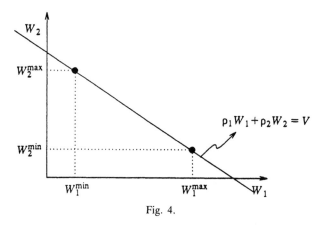

Fig. 4.

Thus we conclude that any point which is outside the line segment between (W_1^{min}, W_2^{max}) and (W_1^{max}, W_2^{min}), is not achievable. On the other hand, it can be shown that every point inside that segment is achievable. To see that, consider the following procedure for 'mixing' two scheduling strategies, S' and S'': at the beginning of every busy period, a random choice is made, selecting S' with probability α $(0 \le \alpha \le 1)$ and S'' with probability $1 - \alpha$; the chosen strategy then operates throughout that busy period. Then, if the performance vectors corresponding to S' and S'' are W' and W'', respectively, that of the mixing strategy is $\alpha W' + (1 - \alpha)W''$. Clearly, by varying α in the interval $(0, 1)$, one can construct a mixing strategy that achieves any performance vector on the line segment between W' and W''.

We now have a characterization of the set of achievable performance vectors in a $G/M/1$ system with two job types: that set is precisely the line segment whose vertices are the performance vectors of the two preemptive priority disciplines using the priority allocations $(1, 2)$ and $(2, 1)$, respectively. Analytically, the necessary and sufficient conditions for a performance vector $W = (W_1, W_2)$ to be achievable are

(a) $\rho_1 W_1 + \rho_2 W_2 = V$ (conservation law);
(b) $W_1 \ge W_1^{min}; W_2 \ge W_2^{min}$ (lower bounds).

The general characterization theorem for $G/M/1$ systems has a similar character [Coffman & Mitrani, 1980; Gelenbe & Mitrani, 1980]. It can be stated as follows:

The set A, of achievable performance vectors in a G/M/1 system with K job types coincides with the convex polytope (a body bounded by planes), whose vertices are the performance vectors of the $K!$ preemptive-resume priority strategies that can be operated by using all permutations of type indices. Analytically, A can be characterized by saying that the elements of an achievable performance vector must satisfy (a) the conservation law

$$\sum_{i=1}^{K} \rho_i W_i = V \; ;$$ (4.5)

and (b) for every proper and non-empty subset of job type indices, $\gamma \subset \{1, 2, \ldots, K\}$, the inequality

$$\sum_{i \in \gamma} \rho_i W_i \geq V_\gamma \, ,$$ (4.6)

where V_γ is the virtual load due to the job types in γ, when those types have preemptive priority over all others, i.e., when the other types do not exist.

Each of the inequalities (4.6) defines a boundary hyperplane of the set A. Therefore, that polytope has $K!$ vertices and $2^K - 2$ facets. The vertex associated with the priority allocation $(i_1, i_2, \ldots, i_K)$ is at the intersection of $K - 1$ boundary hyperplanes, namely those corresponding to $\gamma = \{i_1\}$, $\{i_1, i_2\}, \ldots, \{i_1, i_2, \ldots, i_{K-1}\}$, together with that of the conservation law.

In order to determine the $K!$ vertices, and the $2^K - 2$ constants V_γ, one has to make specific assumptions concerning the job arrival processes and analyze the resulting system under the preemptive-resume priority strategies. For the case when all arrival streams are Poisson, the relevant formulae were obtained in Section 2.

A very similar characterization result is available for the G/G/1 system with K job types, provided that the scheduling strategies do not allow preemptions of service. The role of the $K!$ preemptive-resume priority strategies is now played by the $K!$ non-preemptive priority strategies. In clause (a) the conservation law (4.3) should be used instead of (4.2). The inequalities (4.6) in clause (b) should be replaced by

$$\sum_{i \in \gamma} \rho_i W_i \geq V_\gamma + \sum_{i \in \gamma} \rho_i (b_i - r_i) \, .$$ (4.7)

This conforms with the right-hand side of (4.3). Here, V_γ is the virtual load due to the job types in γ, when those types have non-preemptive priority over all others. Again, the actual determination of the vertices and hyperplanes requires specific assumptions concerning the arrival processes. When the latter are Poisson, Cobham's formulae from Section 2 may be used.

The characterization results have an immediate bearing on certain optimization problems. For example, suppose that one wishes to minimize a linear cost function of the form

$$C = \sum_{i=1}^{K} c_i W_i , \qquad (4.8)$$

where the coefficients c_i reflect the relative weights attached to different job types. Since the set of achievable performance vectors, A, is a polytope, we may assert that the minimum is reached at one of its vertices. In other words, one of the $K!$ priority strategies (preemptive or non-preemptive, depending on the context) is optimal. On the other hand, if the cost function is non-linear, then the minimum may be reached in the interior of A and the optimal scheduling strategy may be more complex.

4.3. Realization of pre-specified performance vectors

Suppose that a performance vector, W, is specified as a target to be achieved, e.g., in an $M/M/1$ system. By checking the conditions of the characterization theorem, it has been established that W is indeed achievable. Note that if W satisfies the inequalities (4.6) but lies above the conservation law hyperplane, then there is at least one achievable vector W' which is dominated by W, i.e., such that $W'_i \leq W_i$ $(i = 1, 2, \ldots, K)$. In that case W' will be the target to be achieved.

The next task is to find a scheduling strategy that achieves the target vector. There may in fact be many such strategies. One possibility is to use a mixing algorithm of the type introduced in Section 4.2. Since the achievable polytope is $(K-1)$-dimensional (because of the conservation law), every point in it can be expressed as a convex combination of at most K vertices. That is, the target vector can be expressed in the form

$$W = \sum_{i=1}^{K} \alpha_i Q_i , \qquad (4.9)$$

where $\alpha_i \geq 0$, $\alpha_1 + \alpha_2 + \cdots + \alpha_K = 1$, and $Q_1, Q_2, \ldots, Q_K$ are performance vectors of preemptive-resume priority strategies. Then a mixing strategy which, at the beginning of each busy period, chooses the ith of those priority strategies with probability α_i, achieves W.

The problem is thus reduced to finding the constituent vectors Q_i and the weights α_i. An equivalent alternative formulation, involving all $K!$ preemptive priority performance vectors $W_1, W_2, \ldots, W_{K!}$, is as follows: find $K!$ non-negative numbers $\alpha_1, \alpha_2, \ldots, \alpha_{K!}$, all but at most K of which are equal to 0, such that their sum is equal to 1 and

$$\sum_{i=1}^{K!} \alpha_i W_i = W .$$

This is the well-known 'initial basis' problem in linear programming. It can be solved by introducing $K+1$ artificial variables, β_0 and $\boldsymbol{\beta} = (\beta_1, \beta_2, \ldots, \beta_K)$, and solving the linear program

$$\max \sum_{i=1}^{K!} \alpha_i \,, \tag{4.10}$$

subject to the constraints

$$\alpha_i \geq 0 \,, \quad i = 1, 2, \ldots, K! \,,$$

$$\beta_j \geq 0 \,, \quad j = 0, 1, \ldots, K \,,$$

$$\beta_0 + \sum_{i=1}^{K!} \alpha_i = 1 \,,$$

$$\boldsymbol{\beta} + \sum_{i=1}^{K!} \alpha_i W_i = W \,.$$

An initial basis for (4.10) is obtained by setting $\alpha_i = 0$ ($i = 1, 2, \ldots, K!$), $\beta_0 = 1$ and $\boldsymbol{\beta} = W$. When an objective value of 1 is reached, the corresponding weights α_i and vectors W_i define a mixing strategy that achieves W.

The case when W is not achievable but dominates an achievable performance vector W', is handled in a similar way. The determination of W' is also reduced to an initial basis problem where the constraints are the conservation law (4.2), the inequalities (4.6) and the inequalities $W' \leq W$.

The above results apply, with straightforward modifications, to an $M/G/1$ system where a target vector is to be achieved by a non-preemptive scheduling strategy. A mixing strategy based on at most K of the $K!$ non-preemptive priority strategies can be found by solving a linear program.

It should be pointed out that, although mixing strategies are quite easy to implement, they have an important disadvantage. The variances of the response times may be unacceptably large, especially at heavy loads. This is because the desired means are achieved by averaging over widely different performance levels. It is desirable, therefore, to try and find families of scheduling strategies which are not only versatile enough to realize any pre-specified performance vector, but also produce acceptable variances of response times.

A family which fulfills these requirements in the context of an $M/M/1$ system is that of discriminatory processor-sharing strategies, introduced in Section 3.3. A DPS strategy is defined by a vector of weights $(g_1, g_2, \ldots, g_K)$, one of which may be fixed arbitrarily. Those weights control the sharing of the processor among the jobs present in the system. It can be shown [see e.g., Gelenbe & Mitrani, 1980], that for every performance vector, W, which is in the interior of the achievable polytope A, there exists a DPS strategy that achieves **W**. The vectors on the boundary of *A* can be approximated as closely as desired with ones achievable by DPS strategies.

The weights g_i that achieve **W** can be determined by solving the set of equations (3.21). These can be written in a slightly shorter form thus:

$$W_i = \frac{1}{\mu_i} + \sum_{j=1}^{K} \frac{g_j \lambda_j}{g_j \mu_j + g_i \mu_i} (W_j + W_i), \quad i = 1, 2, \ldots, K. \tag{4.11}$$

where λ_i and $1/\mu_i$ are the arrival rate and average required service time of type *i* jobs. Being non-linear with respect to the g_i, that set of equations would normally be solved by some iterative method.

One can also conceive of families of non-preemptive scheduling strategies that would realize pre-specified performance vectors in M/G/1 or G/G/1 systems with acceptable variances. For example, after every service completion the strategy could select the next job to be served using fixed probabilities $\alpha_1, \alpha_2, \ldots, \alpha_K$, associated with the different types. Unfortunately, we do not know how to choose the α_i to achieve a given **W**, since that strategy has not been analyzed. However, one could obtain good estimates by simulating the system over a wide range of parameters.

5. Interactive virtual memory systems

A multiprogramming computer system normally contains a number of servers, such as processors and I/O devices, and there is a certain amount of main memory which is shared among the currently executed, or 'active', jobs. The total memory requirement of the active jobs – the sum of their 'virtual memories' – is usually greater than the main memory available. It is therefore necessary to keep portions of those virtual memories on a storage device such as a drum or a disk, and to transfer information to and from main memory according to demand. Moreover, the larger the number of active jobs, the greater the contention for main memory and hence the heavier the input/output traffic resulting from it. In the limit, that traffic becomes the dominant activity in the system. All active jobs spend most of their time waiting at the I/O device and hardly any useful work is done. The throughput approaches 0 and the response time tends to infinity. This phenomenon is known as 'thrashing'.

To avoid thrashing, the degree of multiprogramming should be controlled and prevented from becoming too large. On the other hand, it is undesirable to let it drop too low either, because then the computing resources are underutilized and the throughput is again small. For any system configuration, there is a degree of multiprogramming which is optimal with respect to the average number of job completions per unit time. Our object here is to develop an evaluation procedure that can be used to determine that optimum.

The modelling tool will be a closed queueing network with $N + 1$ nodes, such as the one illustrated in Figure 5.

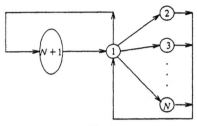

Fig. 5.

Each of the nodes $1, 2, \ldots, N$ has a queue served by a single exponential server according to the FIFO or EPS scheduling strategy. Server 1 represents a central processor, while the others are various input/output devices. Together, these N nodes constitute the 'computational' part of the system and the jobs circulating among them are the active jobs. Node $N + 1$ is a pure delay node representing a collection of K terminals. A job arriving at node $N + 1$ remains there for a 'think period' of average duration τ, regardless of the system state, and then becomes active again.

Thus, at any moment in time, there are K jobs in the system, of which a random number, d, are active and $K - d$ are in 'think state'. The number d is the current degree of multiprogramming. A main memory of size M (pages) is available and is shared among the d active jobs. Assume that the sharing is in equal fractions, so that each active job is allocated M/d pages of main memory.

In the absence of memory contention, the life of an active job would consist of one or more visits to the central processor, alternating with visits to input/output devices. Let the total average service that a job requires from node i during an active phase be S_i $(i = 1, 2, \ldots, N)$. These requirements are given as model parameters and are independent of K, d and M. The competition for main memory causes additional input/output traffic which is state-dependent. From time to time, the node 1 service of a job is interrupted by a page fault, i.e., by a request for a virtual memory page which is not currently in main memory. When that happens, the interrupted job has to leave node 1 and join the appropriate paging device.

The paging behaviour of a job is governed by what is called its 'lifetime function', $h(x)$. Given the amount of main memory, x, available to the job, $h(x)$ specifies the average period of node 1 service between two consecutive page faults. Clearly, $h(x)$ is an increasing function of x, since the more memory a job has, the less frequently it experiences page faults. Two examples of lifetime functions that have been shown to model paging behaviour reasonably well are shown in Figure 6. Both examples display a 'flattening out' of the function for large values of x. This is because, after a certain point, giving more memory to a job ceases to have an appreciable effect on its page fault rate.

With d jobs sharing M pages of main memory, the average amount of

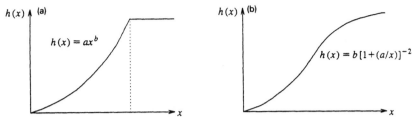

Fig. 6.

processor service that a job receives between consecutive page faults is $h(M/d)$ (that service need not be contiguous; it may be interrupted by other input/output requests). If the total average required processing time for an active job is S_1, then the average number of paging requests that it makes during its lifetime is $S_1/h(M/d)$. Thus the behaviour of jobs in the sub-network consisting of nodes $1, 2, \ldots, N$ depends on the degree of multiprogramming, d. That dependency precludes a product-form solution for the full model in Figure 5 and makes the latter essentially intractable.

The following observation leads to an approximate solution: the average think time, τ is usually much larger than the average service times at nodes $1, 2, \ldots, N$. Consequently, it may be assumed that the computational sub-network reaches steady-state between consecutive changes in the degree of multiprogramming. This suggests a two-step solution procedure. First, nodes $1, 2, \ldots, N$ are treated as a closed network with a fixed number, d, of jobs circulating among them ($d = 1, 2, \ldots, K$). That analysis yields the throughput of those nodes as a function of d: $T(d)$. Then the computational sub-network is replaced by a single state-dependent server which, when dealing with d jobs, has a service rate equal to $T(d)$. The analysis of the resulting model provides system performance measures such as overall throughput, average response time, etc. This two-step procedure is referred to as 'decomposition approximation'.

5.1. Fixed degree of multiprogramming

Imagine that node $N + 1$ is removed from the network in Figure 5 and is replaced by a simple feedback loop from node 1 to node 1. A passage along that feedback loop represents a termination of one active job and an immediate start of another. Thus the degree of multiprogramming in the N-node network remains constant, d.

Suppose that the input/output device used for paging is at node 2, and let b_2 be the average service time (including seek and rotational latency) for a paging request at that device. Then, since the average number of page faults per active job is $S_1/h(M/d)$, the total average amount of paging service, $H(d)$, that such a job requires from node 2 is equal to

$$H(d) = \frac{S_1}{h(M/d)} \, b_2 \,. \tag{5.1}$$

This is of course in addition to the non-paging service requirement from node 2, which has an average S_2. For any other node, i, the total average service requirement of an active job is S_i.

Denote by $L_i(j)$ the average number of jobs at node i ($i = 1, 2, \ldots, N$), when the total number of active jobs is j. Similarly, let $B_i(j)$ be the total average time a job spends at node i, and $T(j)$ be the throughput (number of completions per unit time), when the number of active jobs is j. Then the following relations hold if the network has a product-form solution:

$$B_2(j) = [S_2 + H(d)][1 + L_2(j-1)] \,, \quad j = 1, 2, \ldots, d \,, \tag{5.2a}$$

$$B_i(j) = S_i[1 + L_i(j-1)] \,, \quad i = 1, 3, \ldots, N \,, \ j = 1, 2, \ldots, d \,. \tag{5.2b}$$

The conditions ensuring the validity of (5.2) are that service times at nodes with FIFO scheduling are distributed exponentially (arbitrary distributions are allowed at EPS nodes), and routing of jobs among nodes takes place according to fixed probabilities. The arrival theorem then asserts that the state of a closed network with population j, seen by a job about to join node i, has the same distribution as the state of a network with population $j - 1$, seen by a random observer [Walrand, 1990].

Applying Little's theorem to the whole network we get an expression for the throughput in terms of the quantities $B_i(j)$:

$$T(j) = \frac{j}{\sum_{i=1}^{N} B_i(j)} \,, \quad j = 1, 2, \ldots, d \,. \tag{5.3}$$

Also from Little's theorem, applied to node i, we obtain the relations

$$L_i(j) = T(j)B_i(j) \,, \quad i = 1, 2, \ldots, N \,, \ j = 1, 2, \ldots, d \,. \tag{5.4}$$

Equations (5.2)–(5.4) constitute a set of recurrences which allow $L_i(j)$, $B_i(j)$ and $T(j)$ to be determined for all $j = 1, 2, \ldots, d$. The initial conditions for the computation are $L_i(0) = 0$, $i = 1, 2, \ldots, N$. Note that the value of $H(d)$, appearing in (5.2a), remains constant throughout the execution of the procedure. However, when d changes, $H(d)$ has to be recalculated and the recurrences solved again.

The utilization of node i when the degree of multiprogramming is d, $U_i(d)$, is given by

$$U_2(d) = T(d)[S_2 + H(d)], \tag{5.5a}$$

$$U_i(d) = T(d)S_i, \quad i = 1, 3, \ldots, N. \tag{5.5b}$$

Since $U_i(d) \leq 1$ for all i, this yields a simple upper bound for the throughput in terms of the required service times:

$$T(d) \leq \min\left\{\frac{1}{S_1}, \frac{1}{S_2 + H(d)}, \frac{1}{S_3}, \ldots, \frac{1}{S_N}\right\}. \tag{5.6}$$

It is clear from (5.1), and from the properties of $h(x)$, that $H(d)$ increases without bound when d increases. Therefore, the system throughput approaches 0 when the degree of multiprogramming grows, behaving asymptotically as $T(d) \approx 1/[S_2 + H(d)]$. This provides a quantitative explanation of the thrashing phenomenon, and underlines the need for an admission control policy that would maintain the throughput at a nearly optimal level.

The solution of the recurrence relations (5.2)–(5.4) may be computationally expensive, and prone to numerical problems, when the number of nodes or the degree of multiprogramming is large. On the other hand, it is possible to avoid all recurrences if one is willing to accept an approximate solution instead of an exact one. The idea is to replace the term $L_i(j-1)$, which appears in (5.2), by an expression involving $L_i(j)$ only. One such expression that has been shown to work reasonably well is

$$L_i(j-1) \approx \frac{j-1}{j} L_i(j), \quad i = 1, 2, \ldots, N. \tag{5.7}$$

This relation is of course exact for $j = 1$. It is also asymptotically exact for large values of j.

Substituting (5.7) and (5.4) into (5.2) we get, for $j = d$,

$$B_2(d) = \frac{S_2 + H(d)}{1 - \dfrac{d-1}{d}[S_2 + H(d)]T(d)}, \tag{5.8a}$$

$$B_i(d) = \frac{S_i}{1 - \dfrac{d-1}{d}S_i T(d)}, \quad i = 1, 3, \ldots, N. \tag{5.8b}$$

A further substitution of (5.8) into (5.3) yields a fixed-point equation for $T(d)$, of the form

$$T(d) = f[T(d)]. \tag{5.9}$$

There are several iterative procedures for solving such equations. In the present case, since an upper bound for $T(d)$ is available, the bisection method is convenient.

Before we go on to the second step of the decomposition approximation, it is perhaps worth pointing out that the set of parameters used to specify the computational system model is not unique. For example, instead of the total average service requirement from input/output device i, S_i, one could be given the average service time on each visit to that device, b_i. In addition, the pattern of visits to the input/output devices can be defined by specifying the average node 1 processing interval between consecutive visits to device i, c_i $(i = 2, 3, \ldots, N)$. Then, assuming that all those intervals are distributed exponentially, we can express the average service time on each visit to node 1 as follows:

$$c_1 = \left[\frac{1}{S_1} + \frac{1}{h(M/d)} + \sum_{i=2}^{N} \frac{1}{c_i} \right]^{-1}. \tag{5.10}$$

The probabilities, α_i, that after a node 1 service a job will go to node i $(i = 1, 2, \ldots, N)$, are given by

$$\alpha_1 = \frac{c_1}{S_1}, \qquad \alpha_2 = \frac{c_1}{h(M/d)} + \frac{c_1}{c_2},$$

$$\alpha_i = \frac{c_1}{c_i}, \quad i = 3, 4, \ldots, N. \tag{5.11}$$

Consequently, the total average amount of service that an active job requires from node i (excluding paging requests in the case of node 2), S_i, is equal to

$$S_i = \frac{\alpha_i}{\alpha_1} b_i = \frac{S_1}{c_i} b_i, \quad i = 2, 3, \ldots, N. \tag{5.12}$$

The solution procedure described earlier can now be applied, with $H(d)$ again given by (5.1).

5.2. Variable degree of multiprogramming

Having solved the closed network model representing the computational subsystem we have, for each degree of multiprogramming d, the corresponding rate of job completions, $T(d)$. The system in Figure 5 can now be approximated by the two-node network shown in Figure 7. The first node delays any job that visits it for an average think time τ, regardless of the number present. The distribution of that delay can be arbitrary. The second node contains a single server with a state-dependent service rate. More precisely, if there are j jobs at the computational node, the departure rate from it is $T(j)$. The

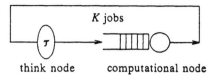

Fig. 7.

intervals between consecutive departures are assumed to be exponentially distributed.

The steady-state probabilities, p_j $(j = 0, 1, \ldots, K)$, that there are j jobs at the computational node, satisfy the following set of balance equations:

$$\frac{K - j + 1}{\tau} p_{j-1} = T(j)p_j , \quad j = 1, 2, \ldots, K . \tag{5.13}$$

These equations, together with the fact that the probabilities sum up to 1, yield

$$p_j = \frac{K!}{(K - j)! \tau^j R(j)} \left[\sum_{j=0}^{K} \frac{K!}{(K - j)! \tau^j R(j)} \right]^{-1} , \quad j = 0, 1, \ldots, K , \tag{5.14}$$

where

$$R(0) = 1 , \quad R(j) = \prod_{i=1}^{j} T(i) , \quad j = 1, 2, \ldots, K .$$

The overall throughput, T_K, of a system with K interactive users is obtained as a weighted average:

$$T_K = \sum_{j=1}^{K} p_j T(j) . \tag{5.15}$$

To find the average response time of an active job, W_K, note that each of the K jobs goes through repeating cycles of being active and in think state. The average length of a cycle is $W_K + \tau$. Therefore, the throughput is equal to $T_k = K/(W_K + \tau)$. Solving this for W_K, we get

$$W_K = \frac{K}{T_K} - \tau . \tag{5.16}$$

A plot of the system throughput, T_K, against the number of users, K, typically has an initial increasing portion, where adding more users helps to utilize the resources better, a maximum, and a decreasing tail corresponding to the onset of thrashing. The object of any admission control policy would be to prevent K from rising to the thrashing level. The main difficulty in devising such a policy is that the lifetime function of the jobs submitted for execution is not usually known in advance. One way of dealing with this is to observe the behaviour of the jobs in the system and maintain an empirical estimate of their lifetime function. Suppose that estimate is $\tilde{h}(x)$. Let also $\tilde{m}$ be the observed average amount of main memory allocated to each active job. That average is of course a function of K. Then the control policy should refuse admission to new users when the value of $\tilde{h}(\tilde{m})$ becomes too small. The ideal operating point is just before the 'flattening-out' portion of the lifetime function (see Figure 6).

Another possibility is to use an indirect control criterion based on some symptom of thrashing. Consider, for example, the activity of the paging device. We have seen that thrashing is accompanied by high page fault rates and hence high demand for paging services. The utilization of the paging device is therefore a good indicator of thrashing. A control policy based on that indicator would monitor the utilization of the paging device and keep a running estimate of the fraction of time that it is busy. When that fraction exceeds a certain threshold – say 60% – new users are denied admission. The threshold should take into account the non-paging demand addressed at the same device.

6. Secondary storage devices

Much of the activity taking place in a computer system has to do with the transfer of information between main memory and various secondary storage devices. It is not surprising, therefore, that the performance of those devices has a considerable influence on the behaviour of the entire system. One aspect of that influence, concerned with demand paging, was examined in Section 5. Other relevant I/O operations involve reading and writing of records from and into user files. In all cases, performance is affected by the physical layout of the data, and by the algorithm used to access it.

The objects of interest in this section are the so-called 'direct access storage devices', or DASD. These devices store and retrieve information on rotating magnetic surfaces by means of read/write heads. The term 'direct access' is intended to emphasise the possibility of addressing records in arbitrary order. This is in contrast with the strict sequential access of records on magnetic tapes.

Two types of DASD will be considered. The first has a set of fixed read/write heads, one of which is associated with each magnetic track. An I/O operation includes, in general, a 'rotational delay', consisting of waiting for the desired record to come under the appropriate head. That type of device will be referred to as a 'drum', regardless of its actual physical shape.

In the second DASD type, there are many more tracks than read/write heads. The latter are attached to a common arm which moves them from one set of tracks to another. An I/O operation is preceded by a 'seek', i.e., an arm movement which positions the head at the appropriate track; then a rotational delay brings the desired record into position for reading or writing. Such a device will be referred to as a 'disk'.

Simplified diagrams of a drum and a disk are shown in Figures 8 and 9, respectively.

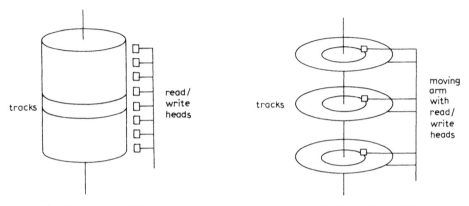

Fig. 8. A drum DASD.   Fig. 9. A disk DASD.

It is clear from the above description that, for both drums and disks, the set of all read/write heads can be modelled as a single server dealing with a stream of jobs, each of which represents an I/O request. The simplest models are obtained by assuming that consecutive services are independent of each other and identically distributed (except, perhaps, for those at the start of busy periods). More realistic, but also more complicated models take into account the dependencies that may exist between consecutive I/O requests, or between the state of the device and the subsequent service time. The results that we shall present can be found in Coffman & Denning [1973], Coffman & Hofri [1986], Neuts [1977] and the references therein. That literature also includes studies of less common devices, such as shift registers and disks with two moving arms.

6.1. The FIFO drum

Let us start with a simple model of a drum where a common queue of requests is served in order of arrival. Information is stored in blocks of fixed size, which we shall call for convenience 'pages'. Suppose that there is room for N pages on a track. Each I/O request involves the transfer, for either reading or writing, of one or more adjoining pages. The time for one drum revolution is T seconds.

Assume that requests arrive in a Poisson stream with rate λ. The starting addresses and required transfer times of consecutive requests are independent and identically distributed random variables. The former are distributed uniformly on the set $\{1, 2, \ldots, N\}$, while the latter take the values $\{T/N, 2T/$

$N, \ldots, T\}$, with arbitrary probabilities. Denote by m and m_2 the mean and second moment, respectively, of the transfer time for a request.

When the value of N is moderately large, the rotational delay for a request, i.e., the time until the drum rotates to its starting address, is approximately uniformly distributed on the interval $(0, T)$. Hence, the mean, b, and second moment, M_2, of the drum's service times are approximately equal to

$$b = \tfrac{1}{2}T + m , \qquad M_2 = \tfrac{1}{3}T^2 + mT + m_2 . \tag{6.1}$$

The offered load, ρ, is given by $\rho = \lambda b$. Since the requests are served by a single-server, the condition for non-saturation is $\rho < 1$. In other words, the arrival rate to the FIFO drum must be less than $2/(T + 2m)$ requests per unit time. When that condition is satisfied, the steady-state average number of requests present, L, is obtained by applying the $M/G/1$ result [Cooper, 1990, Section 7]:

$$L = \rho + \frac{\lambda^2 M_2}{2(1 - \rho)} . \tag{6.2}$$

The average response time for a request, W, is given by Little's theorem: $W = L/\lambda$.

A more interesting and realistic model of the FIFO drum is obtained by relaxing the requirement that the I/O addresses are uniformly distributed. Assume, instead, that page i is requested with probability p_i, $i = 1, 2, \ldots, N$. Consecutive request addresses are independent of each other. Also assume that every request involves the transfer of exactly one page, so that $m = m_2 = 1$. This is known as the 'paging drum' model.

The above assumptions imply that the rotational delay associated with an I/O request, and hence the entire service time, depends on the current position of the read/write head. The latter, in turn, is determined by the address of the previous request. This dependence between consecutive services has to be taken into account in the analysis; the standard $M/G/1$ results no longer apply.

Let us say that a drum service is of type i if it is addressed at page i. Denote by $f_{ij}(x)$ the joint probability density that the service following a type i service is of type j, and its duration is x, given that there is no intervening idle period. Let $\alpha_{ij}(s)$ be the Laplace transform of $f_{ij}(x)$, and $A(s)$ be the matrix of these transforms. The average duration of a service that follows a type i service without an intervening idle period is denoted by α_i and is given by

$$\alpha_i = -\sum_{j=1}^{N} \alpha'_{ij}(0) . \tag{6.3}$$

Similarly, denote by $h_{ij}(x)$ the joint probability density that the service following a type i service is of type j, and its duration is x, given that the drum became idle after the former service (that case has to be considered separately, because the associated rotational delay is different). Let $b_{ij}(s)$ be the Laplace transform of $h_{ij}(x)$, and $B(s)$ be the matrix of these transforms. The average duration of a service that follows a type i service after an intervening idle period is denoted by β_i and is given by

$$\beta_i = -\sum_{j=1}^{N} b'_{ij}(0) . \tag{6.4}$$

Under the paging drum assumptions, it can be shown that

$$a_{ij}(s) = p_j e^{-d_{ij}s} , \tag{6.5}$$

$$b_{ij}(s) = \frac{\lambda p_j}{\lambda - s} \left[e^{-sd_{ij}} - \frac{1 - e^{-sT}}{1 - e^{-\lambda T}} e^{-(s-\lambda)d - \lambda d_{ij}} \right] , \tag{6.6}$$

where $d = T/N$ is the time to transfer one page, and

$$d_{ij} = \begin{cases} (j - i)d & \text{if } i < j , \\ T - (i - j)d & \text{if } i \geqslant j . \end{cases}$$

To evaluate performance characteristics, the queue of requests is considered at consecutive departure instants. The steady-state distribution of the corresponding imbedded Markov chain is specified by the vectors $x_k = (x_{k1}, x_{k2}, \ldots, x_{kN})$, where x_{ki} is the probability that just after a service completion there are k requests in the queue and the type of the departing request is i. The probability generating function of those vectors is denoted by $X(z)$.

By relating the state of the drum at the next departure instant to that at the last one, it can be shown that $X(z)$ satisfies the matrix equation

$$X(z)[zI - A(\lambda - \lambda z)] = x_0[zB(\lambda - \lambda z) - A(\lambda - \lambda z)] . \tag{6.7}$$

The boundary vector x_0, whose ith element is the probability that a departing request is of type i and leaves an empty queue, is obtained by imbedding another Markov chain at consecutive busy period termination instants. The transition probability matrices involved in the analysis of that Markov chain, and hence the vector x_0, have to be calculated numerically. Algorithms for their determination are available.

Performance measures such as average queue length and average response time can be obtained from (6.7). However, the developments are not straightforward. The idea is to introduce the largest (in modulus) eigen-value, $\delta(s)$, of the matrix $A(s)$, and the corresponding right and left eigenvectors, $u(s)$ and $v(s)$:

$$A(s)u(s) = \delta(s)u(s) , \qquad v(s)A(s) = \delta(s)v(s) . \tag{6.8}$$

The vectors u and v are normalised appropriately, so that their derivatives at $s = 0$ can be evaluated from (6.8) to any desired order. A convenient expression for $X(z)$ is obtained by multiplying (6.7) on the right with $u(\lambda - \lambda z)$. This yields

$$X(z)u(\lambda - \lambda z) = x_0 \frac{[zB(\lambda - \lambda z) - I\delta(\lambda - \lambda z)]u(\lambda - \lambda z)}{z - \delta(\lambda - \lambda z)}. \qquad (6.9)$$

The average number of requests at the drum, L, is given by $L = X'(1)e$, where e is a vector of size N whose elements are all equal to 1. By differentiating (6.9) and (6.8) at $z = 1$, it is possible to derive an expression for L. That derivation is by no means trivial. The average response time for a request, W, is equal to $W = L/\lambda$.

6.2. The FIFO disk

All read/write heads of a disk I/O device are attached to a single moving arm. The set of tracks that can be accessed from a given position of the arm is called a 'cylinder'. There are M cylinders on the disk and a request is said to be of type i if it is addressed to cylinder i ($i = 1, 2, \ldots, M$). If a type i request is followed by one of type j, with $j \neq i$, then the arm has to be moved from cylinder i to cylinder j. The time taken by that move, called the 'seek time' t_{ij}, is approximately equal to

$$t_{ij} = \begin{cases} c + d|i - j| & \text{if } i \neq j, \\ 0 & \text{if } i = j, \end{cases} \qquad (6.10)$$

where c and d represent switching overhead and speed of arm movement, respectively. The values of these constants are on the order of 10 msec and 100 μsec/cylinder, respectively.

After the arm is positioned at the desired cylinder, there is typically a rotational delay, followed by the data transmission. As a rough approximation, the last two may be assumed to occupy one disk revolution, T. Then the service time, S_{ij}, of a type j request which follows a type i request without an intervening idle period, can be said to be constant, equal to $S_{ij} = t_{ij} + T$.

There are different ways of handling the disk arm during an idle period. One possibility is to leave it at rest where it was, i.e., at the cylinder addressed by the last request of the previous busy period. Another is to position the arm at some pre-specified, 'central' cylinder. The latter approach aims to reduce the expected seek time of the next request, but has the disadvantage of extra overhead (the next request may arrive while the arm is being moved). The former policy is both simpler and easier to analyse. With it, the dependency between consecutive service times is not at all influenced by an intervening idle period.

The sequence of required cylinder addresses is controlled by a matrix, P, whose element p_{ij} is the conditional probability that the next request is for cylinder j, given that the last one was for cylinder i. In practice, since files are usually stored in contiguous blocks, the address sequence tends to display 'local runs', where the same cylinder is requested several times in succession. To reflect that behaviour, the probabilities p_{ij} may be assumed to have the form

$$
p_{ij} = \begin{cases} p + (1-p)p_i & \text{if } i = j, \\ (1-p)p_j & \text{if } i \neq j, \end{cases} \tag{6.11}
$$

where $(p_1, p_2, \ldots, p_M)$ is some probability distribution over the set of cylinders and p is the probability that a local run continues. Note that if $p = 0$, then (6.11) amounts to assuming independent addressing of cylinder i with probability p_i $(i = 1, 2, \ldots, M)$.

The performance of the FIFO disk is evaluated by applying the analysis of the $M/G/1$ queueing model with correlated service times; an outline of that analysis was presented in Section 6.1 in connection with the FIFO paging drum. The Laplace transforms $a_{ij}(s)$ are now given by

$$
a_{ij}(s) = p_{ij} e^{-s(t_{ij} + T)}. \tag{6.12}
$$

If the arm is left stationary during idle periods, then we have $b_{ij}(s) = a_{ij}(s)$, for all i, j. The average service time, α_i, for a request that follows a request of type i, is equal to

$$
\alpha_i = T + (1-p) \sum_{\substack{j=1 \\ j \neq i}}^{M} p_j(c + d|i - j|). \tag{6.13}
$$

Clearly, the closer the cylinder i is to the middle of the disk, i.e., to $\frac{1}{2}M$, the lower that average service time.

In general, numerical algorithms have to be applied in order to solve the model and obtain the values of performance measures.

6.3. The sector queueing drum

Let us return now to the paging drum model of Section 6.1 and examine a request scheduling strategy which makes a more efficient use of the device characteristics. Suppose that, instead of servicing requests in FIFO order, a separate queue is maintained for each type. In other words, requests directed to page i are placed in queue i $(i = 1, 2, \ldots, N)$. The page frames around the circumference of the drum are referred to as 'sectors' and the associated queues are called 'sector queues'. As the drum rotates and the sectors come in cyclic sequence under the read/write heads, the first request (if any) in each sector queue is served.

Consider the behaviour of sector queue i in isolation. Assuming that an incoming request is for page i with probability p_i, the rate of arrivals into that queue is $\lambda_i = p_i \lambda$. During busy periods, the queue is subject to repetitive service cycles consisting of a service of a request, which takes time T/N, followed by a period of length $(N-1)T/N$ during which the server visits other queues. The latter is called an 'inspection period'. If, at the end of an inspection period the queue is found empty, the server returns to examine it at intervals equal to one drum revolution, T, until eventually a waiting request is found and the service cycles are resumed. Those intervals are referred to as 'server vacations'.

Thus, an isolated sector of the sector queueing drum can be modelled as an M/G/1 queue with inspection periods and server vacations. The service regime described above is illustrated in Figure 10.

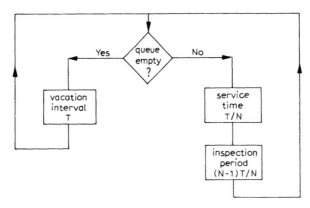

Fig. 10.

Denote the Laplace transforms of the service time, inspection period and vacation interval by $B(s)$, $I(s)$ and $V(s)$, respectively. Then the generating function, $X_i(z)$, of the steady-state number of requests of type i in the system, is given by

$$X_i(z) = \pi_{i0} B(\lambda_i - \lambda_i z) \frac{V(\lambda_i - \lambda_i z) - 1}{z - B(\lambda_i - \lambda_i z)I(\lambda_i - \lambda_i z)}, \qquad (6.14)$$

where π_{i0} is the probability that queue i is empty. In our case, we have

$$B(s) = e^{-sT/N}, \qquad I(s) = e^{-s(N-1)T/N}, \qquad V(s) = e^{-sT}.$$

Also, it is easily seen that $\pi_{i0} = (1 - \lambda_i T)/(\lambda_i T)$. The quantity $\rho_i = \lambda_i T$ represents the offered load of type i. Equation (6.14) now becomes

$$X_i(z) = \frac{1 - \rho_i}{\rho_i} e^{-\rho_i(1-z)/N} \frac{e^{-\rho_i(1-z)} - 1}{z - e^{-\rho_i(1-z)}}. \qquad (6.15)$$

The average number of requests of type i in the system, L_i, is obtained by differentiating (6.15) at $z = 1$. This yields

$$L_i = \rho_i \frac{N+2}{2N} + \frac{\rho_i^2}{2(1-\rho_i)}. \tag{6.16}$$

Let $W_i(s)$, be the Laplace transform of the response time distribution for requests of type i. As in any single-server FIFO system, that Laplace transform is related to the generating function of the queue size as follows: $X_i(z) = W(\lambda_i - \lambda_i z)$. Hence we have

$$W_i(s) = X_i\left(1 - \frac{s}{\lambda_i}\right). \tag{6.17}$$

The average response time, W_i, is of course also given by Little's theorem: $W_i = L_i / \lambda_i$.

In general, the performance of the sector queueing drum is considerably better than that of the FIFO one. This improvement is due to the elimination of long rotational delays. For example, when the request addresses are uniformly distributed and the system is heavily loaded, the FIFO drum manages to serve an average of 2 requests per revolution. Under the same conditions, the sector queueing drum serves N requests per revolution.

6.4. The scanning disk

Abandoning the FIFO servicing of requests in favour of a more regular schedule can bring performance benefits in the operation of a moving arm disk, just as it does in the case of a drum. This objective is achieved by a strategy known as 'SCAN'. Under it, the arm makes repeated sweeps through all cylinders on the surface of the disk, changing direction only when one of the extremes is reached. In other words, the M cylinders are visited in the cyclic order $(1, 2, \ldots, M, M-1, \ldots, 2)$. Incoming requests join different queues, according to their type. If, when the arm reaches a given cylinder, the corresponding queue is empty, then it moves on immediately; otherwise it remains in place and requests are served, until the queue becomes empty.

Thus the scanning disk can be modelled by a circulating server operating an exhaustive service policy. An exact analysis of that model exists, but it is rather complex and the results are not in a form that facilitates the evaluation of performance measures. On the other hand, an approximate solution can be obtained quite simply by treating an isolated cylinder queue as having a server with vacation intervals (like in Figure 10, but without the inspection periods). In this case the vacation intervals consist of the arm movements and busy periods at other cylinders, between two consecutive visits to the same cylinder. Those intervals are of two types, depending on whether the last visit was part of the forward or the reverse sweep of the arm.

Denote the average residence time of the arm at cylinder i on the forward and the reverse sweep by D'_i and D''_i, respectively. The extreme cylinders, $i = 1$ and $i = M$, are visited only once per cycle and so their average residence times need not be primed. Similarly, let C'_i and C''_i be the vacation intervals for queue i in the forward and the reverse sweeps, respectively. Again, no primes are necessary for $i = 1$ and $i = M$.

Clearly, the vacation intervals can be expressed as sums of appropriate subsets of residence times, plus arm movement times. For example, $C'_{M-2} = D'_{M-1} + D_M + D''_{M-1} + 2a$, where a is the time for the arm to move from one cylinder to the next. On the other hand, each residence time can be expressed in terms of the corresponding vacation interval of the opposite direction. If a busy period of queue i starts with k jobs present, then its average duration is $kb_i/(1 - \rho_i)$, where b_i is the average service time and $\rho_i = \lambda_i b_i$ is the offered load. But the number of jobs present at the start of a busy period in the forward direction is equal to the number of arrivals during a vacation interval in the reverse direction. Hence

$$D'_i = \frac{\rho_i}{1 - \rho_i} C''_i, \tag{6.18}$$

and

$$D''_i = \frac{\rho_i}{1 - \rho_i} C'_i. \tag{6.19}$$

We thus have a set of linear equations from which all average residence times and vacation intervals can be determined. It should be pointed out that the sum $C = D'_i + C'_i + D''_i + C''_i$ is independent of i, for $1 < i < M$. This is the total average cycle time of the disk arm. Denoting by $v = (2M - 2)a$ the total arm travelling time, we can write $C = v + \rho C$, where $\rho = \rho_1 + \rho_2 + \cdots + \rho_M$ is the total offered load. Therefore,

$$C = \frac{v}{1 - \rho}. \tag{6.20}$$

Having obtained the quantities C'_i and C''_i, queue i can be approximately modelled as an M/G/1 system with vacation intervals which are equal to C'_i with probability $\frac{1}{2}$ and to C''_i with probability $\frac{1}{2}$. Expression (6.14), with $B(\cdot)$ and $V(\cdot)$ evaluated appropriately and $I(\cdot) \equiv 1$, yields the desired performance estimates.

The above approach, while using the correct value of the average vacation interval, relies on a simplified approximation to the latter's distribution. Other approximations, based on mixtures of known distributions, are also possible.

When the distribution of demand over the different cylinders is reasonably uniform, the scanning disk outperforms the FIFO one. This is due to the reduction of seek delays between consecutive requests. In heavy load, all cylinder queues tend to be non-empty and the seek times are either 0 or a.

References

Aven, O.I., E.G. Coffman Jr., Y.A. Kogan (1987). *Stochastic Analysis of Computer Storage*, Reidel, Dordrecht.

Coffman, E.G., P.J. Denning, (1973). *Operating Systems Theory*, Prentice-Hall, Englewood Cliffs, NJ.

Coffman, E.G., M. Hofri (1986). Queueing models of secondary storage devices. *Queueing Systems Theory Appl.* 2, 129–168.

Coffman, E.G., I. Mitrani (1980). A characterisation of waiting time performance realisable by single-server queues. *Oper. Res.* 28, 810–821.

Coffman, E.G., R.R. Muntz, H. Trotter (1970). Waiting time distributions for Processor-Sharing systems. *J. ACM* 17, 123–130.

Conway, R.W., W.L. Maxwell, L.W. Miller (1967). *Theory of Scheduling*, Addison-Wesley, Reading, MA.

Cooper, R.B. (1990). Queueing theory, in D.P. Heyman, M.J. Sobel (eds.), *Handbooks in OR & MS*, *Vol.* 2: *Stochastic Models*, North-Holland, Amsterdam, pp. 469–518.

Courtois, P.-J. (1977). *Decomposability: Queueing and Computer System Applications*, Academic Press, New York.

Courtois, P.-J., G. Latouche (eds.), (1987). *Performance'87*, North-Holland, Amsterdam.

Disney, R.L., T.J. Ott (eds.), (1981). *Applied Probability – Computer Science: The Interface Vols. 1 & 2*, Birkhauser, Basel.

Fayolle, G., I. Mitrani, R. Iasnogorodski (1980). Sharing a processor among many job classes. *J. ACM.* 27, 519–532.

Gelenbe, E. (ed.), (1984). *Performance'84*, North-Holland, Amsterdam.

Gelenbe, E., I. Mitrani (1980). *Analysis and Synthesis of Computer Systems*, Academic Press, New York.

Iazeolla, G., P.-J. Courtois, A. Hordijk (eds.) (1984). *Mathematical Computer Performance and Reliability*, North-Holland, Amsterdam.

Kleinrock, L. (1965). A conservation law for a wide class of queueing disciplines. *Naval Res. Logist. Quart.* 12, 181–192.

Kleinrock, L. (1975). *Queueing Systems, Vol. 1: Theory*, Wiley, New York.

Kleinrock, L. (1976). *Queueing Systems, Vol. 2: Computer Applications*, Wiley, New York.

Kobayashi, H. (1978). *Modelling and Analysis: An Introduction to System Performance Evaluation Methodology*, Addison-Wesley, Reading, MA.

Lavenberg, S.S. (ed.) (1983). *Computer Performance Modelling Handbook*, Academic Press, New York.

Lazowska, E.D., J. Zahorjan, G.S. Graham, K.C. Srvcik (1984). *Quantitative System Performance*, Prentice-Hall, Englewood Cliffs, NJ.

Mitrani, L. (1987). *Modelling of Computer and Communication Systems*, Cambridge University Press, Cambridge.

Neuts, M.F. (1977). Some explicit formulas for the steady-state behaviour of the queue with semi-Markovian service times. *Adv. in Appl. Probab.* 9, 141–157.

O'Donovan, T.M. (1974). Direct solutions of M/G/1 processor-sharing models. *Oper. Res.* 22, 1232–1235.

Sakata, M., S. Noguchi, J. Oizumi (1971). An analysis of the M/G/1 queue under round-robin scheduling. *Oper. Res.* 19, 371–385.

Sauer, C.H., K.M. Chandy (1981). *Computer Systems Performance Modelling*, Prentice-Hall, Englewood Cliffs, NJ.

Schrage, L. (1981). An alternative proof of a conservation law for the queue G/G/1. *Oper. Res.* 18, 185–187.

Trivedi, K.S. (1982). *Probability and Statistics with Reliability, Queueing and Computer Science Applications*, Prentice-Hall, Englewood Cliffs, NJ.

Walrand, J. (1990). Queueing networks, in: D.P. Heyman, M.J. Sobel (eds.), *Handbooks in OR & MS*, *Vol.* 2: *Stochastic Models*, North-Holland, Amsterdam, pp. 519–603.

Yashkov, S.F. (1983). A derivation of response time distribution for an M/G/1 processor-sharing queue. *Probl. Control Inf. Theory* 12, 133–148.

E.G. Coffman et al., Eds., *Handbooks in OR & MS, Vol. 3*
© 1992 Elsevier Science Publishers B.V. All rights reserved.

Chapter 11

Mathematical Programming Systems

J.A. Tomlin

Department K53, IBM Almaden Research Center, 650 Harry Road, San Jose, CA 95120-6099, U.S.A.

J.S. Welch

Sundown Software Systems, Inc., Silver Spring, MD 20904, U.S.A.

1. Introduction

The pervasiveness of linear programming (LP) in the commercial, applied, operations research community can be largely attributed to one characteristic of LP: if a physical situation can be abstracted to a model that can be expressed in the LP normal form, then there are several algorithms – the simplex is one – and a host of implementations – mathematical programming systems (MPSs) – that can be applied to that normal form to produce an optimal solution to the model. Given the simplicity of the linear programming model:

$$\min_x \ \sum_j c_j x_j \tag{1.1}$$

$$\text{subject to } Ax = b , \tag{1.2}$$

$$L_j \le x_j \le U_j , \tag{1.3}$$

it is surprising how many physical processes are amenable to this abstraction and to LP optimization. Many others are amenable to extensions of LP which allow some or all of the variables to be discrete or nonlinear, and many modern MPSs allow for these extensions.

Mathematical programming systems are much more than just implementations of the algorithms described in textbooks. The practical details of efficient implementation require large suites of computer programs with many options and perhaps many solution strategies which attempt to take advantage of the characteristics of different models. With the increasing size of models being built this power and flexibility is critical. Equally critical is the data management required to handle these models. The deceptively simple form (1.1)–(1.3) is a long way from the kind of data structure which can be successfully used to solve practical problems.

First we must consider the structure of A itself. Fortunately, A is virtually always very sparse, otherwise problems with thousands of rows and columns would involve unmanageable millions of coefficients. In practice there is a relatively small number of nonzeros per column, typically 4 to 7, independent of the number of rows. (Problems with about 10 or more nonzeros per column are considered quite dense and unpleasant). This sparsity has overwhelming consequences for the two areas of mathematical programming with which we shall be concerned – the specification and input of models and their efficient solution. However, it must be remembered that although sparsity may reduce the number of coefficients to be handled from millions to tens of thousands, we are still dealing with large quantities of data. Thus *data management* is a critical aspect, perhaps *the* critical aspect of mathematical programming systems.

MPS development has been a process of evolution [see Orchard-Hays, 1978; Beale, 1985a]. Some of the systems still in use today are developments of, or extensions to systems designed decades ago. Most notable in this respect are the IBM MPS/360 system, built in the sixties, and its modern descendants MPSX/370 [IBM Corp., 1988] and MPSIII [Ketron, 1987b]. The earlier system was an out-of-core design (following in the footsteps of the even earlier LP/90/94) for the rather limited-memory System/360. This greatly influenced the internal data structures and to some extent the algorithmic options available, but even though very much larger memories are available today it is remarkable how much of the algorithmic framework remains appropriate, defining MPS terminology and jargon. Another durable legacy of MPS/360 is its standard method for describing linear programming models, which we discuss at some length below.

The arrival of large, relatively cheap memories, with its enormous simplification of the problem of handling large matrices, as well as other hardware advances, has led to a new wave of mathematical programming products. Many of these are not MPSs in the traditional sense. Some only address model building. Others are simply optimizers with rudimentary standard interfaces. Only a few attempt to provide the full range of capabilities provided by the more traditional mathematical programming *system*, of the type discussed in an earlier survey [Tomlin, 1983]. It is quite impossible to consider all these offerings in this chapter. We shall, however, attempt to indicate several which are particularly comprehensive or provide new and useful capabilities.

2. The standard optimizer interface

The LP normal form (1.1)–(1.3) is a collection of linear constraints and a linear objective function. This normal form is simple in concept and simple in implementation. Further, while discrete and nonlinear algorithms are more complex than their linear cousins, the statement of the model to the MP algorithm remains the expression of the model in a constraint and objective function format. Many MP practitioners prefer to consider their normal form as a detached coefficient representation, i.e., a matrix where the objective function is one row of the matrix. The matrix is a much more concise and economical presentation of an MP model than is a collection of equations where the variable identification has to be repeated for every occurrence of a coefficient.

Presenting the model to the algorithm is, however, only one step of the model management process. A typical medium-sized LP application requires a diverse collection of data. For example, one small lumber industry production planning model of 90 constraints by 180 variables requires 13 different data tables containing over 250 values. Each data table is different from the others in the kind of data it contains. The differences are in terms of both units of measurement and where the data fits into the model. Each of these data values has to be collected from the real-world situation being modeled (measured as it were), verified, edited and placed in the model at the appropriate place. Measured data do not include the coefficients that express the logical relationships that connect parts of the model together into a logical whole; there are at least as many connectors as there are measured data values.

Model management comprises acquiring, storing, editing and processing of measured data, the producing of the MP matrix for the optimizer and the collecting, storing and presenting of the solution values produced by the optimization algorithm. The next section reviews some of the commercial model management tools that perform this process. This section describes the MPS standard model input and output formats in some detail because of their influence on many of these model management tools and their importance in interfacing with most commercial optimizers.

This section provides an overview of the organizational structure of basic mathematical programming system (MPS) data. The operational details appear in most MPS optimizer user manuals. Some understanding of these formats is important for MP system users, particularly those writing programs in a general-purpose programming language to generate the MPS input and report the MPS output. While these files are clumsy to use and inefficient in their consumption of disk space they have the enormous advantage of being widely accepted as the de facto input/output standard.

As indicated in the introduction, the standard MPS input format was inherited from MPS/360. It is a batch mode, sequential input/output concept and has remained so even as it is adapted to minicomputers and desk-top computers. While the MPS input format was conceived as a method for introducing manually prepared LP matrices to LP systems, its traditions affect most other sectors of the modern LP modeling practice:

(1) Home-grown model generators, written in FORTRAN or other general-purpose programming languages, find the MPS format to be a convenient vehicle for communicating the matrix to off-the-shelf MP systems.

(2) The matrix row and column naming conventions of the MPS format have heavily influenced most matrix generation languages. Some of these languages even follow the MPS file organization in the ordering of the major sections of their matrix description.

(3) The limited size, 8 characters, of the matrix row and column names requires that the LP model formulator adopts a consistent and parsimonious method of variable name construction that promotes automated solution retrieval and reporting as well as migration of advanced solution bases.

Three files comprise the standard user interface for LP optimizers. They are:

(1) The matrix input file – describes the model's matrix to the optimizer.

(2) The solution output – presents the solution results of the model.

(3) The advanced basis file – used to restart a model or supply a related model with an advanced starting point.

Most of the widely distributed LP optimizers accept their matrix input in 'MPS' format. They are used for linear, nonlinear and mixed integer models and by both simplex based and interior point optimizers. Similarly, most of the optimizers produce a solution file in a format that is similar to that used by MPSX/370, but their adherence to the strict MPSX format is more casual. The solution file contains the activity levels and shadow costs for the optimal solution identified in the same nomenclature as was used in the matrix input file. The solution file may be printed or written to disk for use by report generation programs. Several high-level matrix generation and solution reporting systems (OMNI and GAMMA are the two most widely distributed) use these standard files as their sole communication media with MP systems.

Many optimizers have their own file formats for saving an advanced basis even though their concepts are similar. The advanced basis is a symbolic representation of some intermediate point along the way to an optimal solution or the optimal solution itself. The advanced basis is used to resume the solution of an existing model or as a starting point for a separate but similar model.

Most MPS optimizers support three other files that are discussed to varying degrees by MPS practitioners:

(1) The problem file is a sequential representation of the MPS matrix that is used for permanent intermediate storage. The problem file format is internal binary and it contains all of the information found in the MPS input file plus some intermediate processing data. The problem file can contain multiple models as well as their solution states. The problem file comes from an era when mainframe computer processing speeds were slower than contemporary desk-top computers. It was then common to solve a model in a succession of computer runs, each run starting where the previous run left off. This approach was more economical when the start-up costs could be minimized and the problem file provided such a starting point. Now such solution strategies are reserved for only the largest models and are not practiced at all in many places.

(2) The 'workfile' is the optimizer's internal representation of the matrix. Older MP systems store the workfile externally on disk. Newer MPS optimizers maintain the workfile in a compressed form in virtual memory. The workfile

format is biased toward optimizer efficiency. The model formulator need not be concerned with the workfile other than to know it exists, since some MP system messages and documentation reference it.

(3) The 'eta' file contains the inverse of the solution's current basis. The eta file is an external disk file for most older optimizers and is stored in virtual memory by the newer generation. Again the eta file is of no concern to the formulator other than to be aware of its existence.

None of these three files will be discussed further as data management topics. The problem file format and usage varies widely between MP systems and does not exist on some, e.g., MINOS [Murtagh & Saunders, 1987] and OSL [IBM Corp., 1991]. The work and eta files are algorithm files and are discussed in other sections of this chapter in that context.

2.1. MPS input file

Data in MPS input format is organized into major sections as shown in Figure 1.

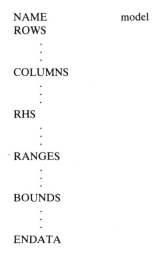

Fig. 1. MPS file structure.

Originally, MPS files were decks of punched cards and the records of MPS input files are still usually (and archaically) referred to as 'cards' because they are in a card equivalent unit record format of 80 columns (where columns 73 through 80 were reserved for deck sequencing). The section headings shown in Figure 1 are records that appear in the MPS input file exactly as shown. The ellipses represent data records.

The file is delineated with beginning (NAME) and ending (ENDATA) records. The model name, that appears in the name record, differentiates models when a sequential MPS input file contains multiple models.

For data management purposes every row in the LP matrix has a unique name. The ROWS section of the matrix defines the names of the matrix rows and indicates the type of constraint that each represents. There is one record per row. The row type is a single character that may take on the values shown in Table 1.

Table 1
Row types

Row type	Constraint type
E	Equality
L	Less than or equal to
G	Greater than or equal to
N	Nonconstraining

The rows are ordered in the MPS internal files in the same order as given in the ROWS section of the MPS input file. There must be at least one nonconstraining row, the objective function. Some systems permit the inclusion of row scales in the row record. A row scale is applied to all coefficients in the row.

The COLUMNS section presents the matrix in column order. Each column is represented by one or more contiguous records. Each record contains the column name and one or two row names and coefficients. Most systems provide only local checking for duplicate column names, i.e., checking is done only for neighboring columns. Duplicate column names will not bother the optimizer but they do affect automated solution retrieval and the processing of an advanced basis. In the interest of space conservation zero coefficients are omitted. A column scale is provided for in some systems. MPSX/370 and some others (e.g., MPSIII [Ketron, 1987b] and SCICONIC/VM [Scicon, 1986b]) recognize various MARKER records that are used to segregate columns into sections. These sections support special solution strategies such as mixed integer programming, generalized upper bounding and separable programming.

The RHS section contains the constant coefficients of the constraints. The RHS format is the same as for COLUMNS. There may be one or more right-hand side columns, each with coefficients in the named rows. A zero coefficient is assumed for rows that are not explicitly specified. Normally, one right-hand side is selected for model solution although some systems permit the creation of a composite right-hand side as a linear function of two columns of the right-hand side section.

The optional RANGES section provides for constraining less than and greater than rows between two limits. The MPS convention is not to specify the upper and lower bounds for a constraint but to specify a limit and the deviation from that limit. The range record contains a row name and the value of the limit. For a less than row the range value allows the row sum to fall below the right-hand side value by only the specified amount. Greater than rows are treated similarly.

The optional BOUNDS section supplies the upper and lower bounds for columns that are other than the default values of 0 for the lower bounds and plus infinity for the upper bounds. Unlike RANGES the upper and lower bounds are explicitly stated. Columns are allowed to go below zero by specifying negative lower bounds. A lower bound of minus infinity makes the column unconstrained below. Each record in the BOUNDS section specifies a single bound. The permitted bound types are shown in Table 2. A column may be mentioned in none, one or two bound records. Some optimizers feature additional bound types to designate integer and semicontinuous variables.

As with any 'standard' format there will be variations between systems. Some have been noted above. The important points to note are the 8-character names, the fixed-field format and the descriptive power and limitations of the semantics. The 8-character name, as noted earlier, is both the corner stone of most model management systems and a modeling limitation. (The 8-character name was also the size of the IBM 360's double precision floating point number, sometimes referred to as a double word. 8 bytes is still the preferred double word size in many modern computers where the architecture is built around 4, 8 and 64 byte packets.) The fixed field format is useful for FORTRAN matrix generation programs because of the nature of the FOR-MAT statement. While the fixed-field format is a nuisance for manual matrix preparation and editing, even with a full screen editor, that sort of activity is almost never performed anymore.

Table 2
MPS bound types

Bound type	Description
LO	Value is the column's lower bound
UP	Value is the column's upper bound
FX	The column is fixed at the given value
FR	The column is unconstrained
MI	The column is unconstrained below (the upper bound is zero unless an upper bound is provided by an accompanying UP record)

2.2. MPS solution file

Most of the MP systems that accept the MPS standard input format also provide a standard output file format that allows the user to write programs to retrieve solution results and prepare tailored reports. The standard solution file is alphanumeric text for some MP systems and a combination of text and binary numeric data for others. The solution file has three major sections:

(1) SOLUTION Section – contains the solution status information ranging from the name of the model to the number of iterations required to reach an optimal or infeasible solution.

(2) RSECTION – contains the row solution values identified by row name and including solution status (basic, at lower bound, at upper bound), activity level, slack level, upper and lower input bounds (from the input file) and the opportunity costs (dual or π values).

(3) CSECTION – contains the column solution values in a format similar to RSECTION and includes for each column the activity level, reduced cost, original cost coefficient and upper and lower bounds.

The solution is a separate physical file, not part of the standard print file.

High-level commercial matrix generators that use the MPS input file as their entry to the MP system use the solution file to retrieve solution values for their report generators.

2.3. Advanced basis file

The status of an MP model, optimal or otherwise, can be preserved in the form of a basis file, sometimes called a PUNCH and INSERT file after the MPSX/370 procedures that process it. This file is fully symbolic with a card equivalent record format. The basis file is a list of the names of the columns active, i.e., nonzero, at the time the basis was saved. Associated with each name is the name of the row it replaces, its activity level and an indication of the status of the displaced row. There is, of course, no row name for a column that is at its upper bound. Columns at their lower bounds and basic rows are not part of the file. Table 3 summarizes the status indicators that appear in file.

Table 3
Basis file status information

Indicator	Meaning
XU	The named column replaces the named row in the basis and the row is set to its upper bound
XL	The named column replaces the named row and the row is set at its lower bound
UL	The named column is at its upper bound

The basis file contains sufficient information to fully restore the solution status of its model. It is a physically separate, fixed-field, sequential file that contains only alphabetic text. The basis file may be read and written by programs implemented in general-purpose languages, although it rarely is. The knowledgeable user may create a basis file as part of the matrix generation process to get the solution of the model off to a flying start. Since the basis file is fully symbolic it may be applied to variations of a given model or transported from one model to another, providing that their naming conventions are identical. These uses of the basis file support the time-honored MP folklore that any starting basis is better than no basis at all.

3. Model description languages

3.1. General purpose programming languages

A popular method of preparing MPS input and reporting MPS output is to write computer programs using a general-purpose language. FORTRAN is normally the language of choice, followed by PL/I, COBOL, C, and, occasionally, SAS. The (perhaps temporary) popularity of this practice stems from:

(1) General-purpose compilers are already available on the user's computer because they are required for projects other than MP modeling. This avoids the cost of buying a high-level special purpose system – an important consideration for privately owned desk-top computers and compilers.

(2) Programmers of considerable expertise in the language of choice are usually available from the central computer center and off-loading the model implementation to them frees the LP analyst for other tasks.

(3) Many central computer centers have a policy of programming in a single language in the interest of uniformity, so special-purpose modeling languages are not welcomed.

(4) The standardized input and output formats described in the previous section provide a simple and intuitively appealing method of interfacing with the MP system. Furthermore, since these formats are accepted by most optimizers, the generator can be used for any of them.

(5) Very large models are efficiently generated by tailored programs written in a general-purpose language.

For convenience we use the term 'FORTRAN' to refer to all of the general-purpose languages used for model management.

In this section we discuss some important practices that have been developed over the years by FORTRAN modelers. Discipline and good modeling practice are a necessity for model maintenance and enhancement, thereby assuring long lived, useful models. Many of the concepts described here apply also to the other model management techniques described later in this section.

The FORTRAN-implemented model system, in its simplest form, comprises two programs that operate in separate job steps independent of the MP system. The first program is the matrix generator that reads its input data from specially formatted input files and produces the MPS input file. The second is the report generator that produces tailored reports from the standard file output after the optimizer has done its work.

The key design consideration is in the handling of the 8-character row and column names. The customary approach is to begin with an overview of the model and observe that the matrix naturally breaks onto row strips and column strips. A row strip represents constraints of similar characteristics. The kinds of row strips customarily seen in an LP model include availability, capacity, balance and demand row strips. For example, an availability row strip contains constraints that limit the amount of raw material that can be purchased. There is one constraint, and one matrix row, for each raw material, source, destination and time-period combination that is possible in the model. It follows that the names of the rows in the available row strip should all have the same name format. That format begins with a one- or two-character row strip identification that distinguishes the strip's rows from rows in other row strips. The remaining characters of the row-name template are a combination of codes from the strip's attributes. For example, the analyst could assign a one-character code to time period, a two-character code to raw material, a two-character code to source and a one-character code to destination. The number of characters required per attribute depends upon how many different members there are in the domain of the attribute and on how these members are identified in the input data.

The matrix can also be visualized as column strips where each strip comprises a homogeneous set of columns of like attributes. For example, an inventory column strip could have the attributes of time period, product and warehouse. Column-name construction follows the concepts of row-name design described above.

There are important reasons to adopt a strict naming convention early in the model formulation process. First, a well-planned naming convention encourages the formulator to take a global view of the model and to be aware of the interaction of row and column strips. Second, a consistent naming convention allows the carrying of an optimal advanced basis from a parent model to its offspring, which are variations on the parent, and to revised versions of the parent. Third, a consistent naming convention permits the use of partial name masks during MP system control to include or exclude sections of the matrix. Finally, a consistent naming convention permits the use of matrix and solution programs, such as PERUSE and ANALYZE [Greenberg, 1983, 1987]. These programs use the row and column name structures to identify discrepancies in large models and to assist in the understanding of optimal solutions.

These remarks on consistent naming also apply to the high-level matrix generation languages described in the next section. The structure of those languages tends to lead the user in the proper direction while the FORTRAN programmer receives no such guidance.

Beyond name construction there are three points that are worth noting, particularly for the first-time model builder. First, 999 999 is not infinity, not even to a computer. Rather than approximate infinite bounds with a large number the MPS input deck uses type symbols in the bound section of the file. The default range for a column is zero below to unbounded above if a column is not mentioned in the bound section that is its range. Some formulators feel it necessary to include explicit bounds for all columns and the default case is approximated with 0–999 999. This bad practice stresses the optimizer, introduces numeric instability and increases run times. Unconstrained columns have the special type of FR, which means the optimizer will let them take on any value, positive or negative. Explicit upper and lower bounds are a useful device for compressing the matrix and improving optimization efficiency, providing the bounds take on realistic values.

The second important point is to observe that the most important statement in general- or special-purpose programming languages is that statement type which permits the conditional execution of a block of statements. 'IF' is the statement in FORTRAN. It has all kinds of uses:

(1) With IF the matrix can be compressed by omitting columns that are fixed at zero or rows that are nonconstraining.

(2) With IF the size of the MPS input file can be kept down by omitting zero coefficients.

(3) With IF numeric stability can be controlled by omitting coefficients that are too small to be significant to the model but large enough to be recognized as usable by the optimizer.

(4) With IF very small ranges in the bound set can be recognized for what they are and the column can be fixed (FX in the MPS bound section) rather than bounded and a source of instability is removed from the solution process.

The third point is to keep control over the FORMAT statements, or whatever device is used to write the MPS file. If the data is meaningful to two decimal places, then two places should be written to the MPS file, i.e., F12.2. If F12.6 is used to write 6 decimal places the optimizer will try to reconcile the model to four more places of illusory accuracy. Putting values into the MPS input file that cannot be measured in the physical world will sometimes cause optimizer breakdown.

These points, and others, are all obvious once they are thought about. They apply not so much to the raw input data, which can be edited during preparation, but to values computed during the generation process, which go unseen.

FORTRAN-implemented interfaces are popular with infrequent model developers who possess programming skills but who are not inclined to learn yet another programming language. However, there are weaknesses in the FORTRAN approach. FORTRAN programs tend to be large and laden with programming details that are not germane to the model itself. They are, therefore, difficult to maintain and enhance, and inaccessible to the non-programmer/analyst. Frequently only the author understands the program well enough to run it, making the system unusable by others. Many a good model has withered and died when its author and caretaker moved on. FORTRAN optimizer interfaces are one man/one model applications.

3.2. Matrix generation languages

Most organizations that are heavy users of mathematical programming have abandoned FORTRAN model management in favor of a high-level, special-purpose model management system. Organizations that do MP recognize that MP applications go through the same life cycles as other computer software systems. In the course of this life cycle the model will be mended, changed, and enhanced under the care of many people with varying skills. A compact and expressive development language that is meaningful to non-programmers reduces the people-cost of modeling and extends the useful life of the model.

Such a model management system has a matrix description language that contains the arithmetic operators of general-purpose languages and is enhanced with special functions that aid in the matrix generation process. These functions are concentrated in the areas of name construction via character concatenation and matrix row and column generation. A high-level model management language automates the housekeeping that the general-purpose language programmer does manually and often with great effort. A high-level language also contains special facilities for retrieving and processing solution values and for breaking row and column names down into their component parts. The assumption is that once the investment of learning a new language is made – and learning a high-level language is usually easier than learning a general-purpose programming language – exchanging CPU costs for skilled analyst time yields big dividends.

Some of the more important matrix generation and report generation systems are listed in Table 4. They were all originally built for mainframe or mini computers, but some have been, or are in the process of being, migrated to desk-top machines [personal computers (PCs)] and engineering work stations. These are the systems that have a proven track record for handling 'industrial strength' matrices. All of them are commercially-supported proprietary software.

Table 4
Main frame model management systems

System	Original hardware platform
CFMS	Honeywell DPS/8
DATAFORM	IBM 30xx
GAMMA	IBM 30xx
MGG	VAX, Prime, IBM 30xx/VM
OMNI	IBM 30xx
PDS/MAGEN	CDC

Absent from the list are smaller systems that began life on the PC and are now being migrated to larger, extended memory, PCs and engineering work stations. We feel that PC-originated systems are not yet fully combat-proven. Llewellyn & Sharda [1990] provide a comprehensive list of all kinds of PC-based math programming tools.

A second dimension along which high-level languages can be viewed is how tightly they are tied into the MPS they are designed to support. CFMS, DATAFORM and MGG are optional components of their host MPS and are not only tightly integrated into their host environment (which is good) but do not possess the flexibility to be used with some other host (which is not so good). Most of the other systems shown in Table 4 are designed to support an MPS marketed by another (usually hardware) vendor. These systems operate as separate job steps and communicate with the host MPS through the standard files described previously. For the most part they are indifferent as to which optimizer is used.

A third dimension for viewing high-level languages is the style used to generate the matrix. GAMMA, OMNI and PDS/MAGEN are activity generation oriented in that the matrix is generated by columns. This means that a column is defined and all its coefficients are generated at one time. These languages serve that part of the formulation world that views an LP model as a collection of alternatives or options, each of which intersects one or more constraints. This approach is also suggested by the standard MPS input file structure. DATAFORM and CFMS are more general in that the matrix may be generated as rows or columns and no row or column has to be generated all at once.

A fourth dimension is the kinds of MP models that can be described by the languages. They all describe models appropriate to their target optimizers, including mixed integer. Since MPSIII includes a generalized upper bounding (GUB) algorithm, DATAFORM contains special constructs for generating GUB sets.

Input to the high-level language systems comes in two parts: the program and the data. The systems provide a procedure language that has a FORTRAN flavor that includes the ability to do arithmetic on data elements along with conditional execution of statements and looping capabilities. The language portion, without any data, is compiled into an execution module of either executable code or interpretative tables. The compiled program represents the structure of the matrix while the data tables provide the coefficients needed to create an instance of the model. The compiled program is reused with different variations on data tables to create many versions of the model. There are individual exceptions to these comments but in general these observations hold.

Users of high-level languages recognize the organization of the LP matrix as row and column strips and segment their programs accordingly. This means that all of the statements relating to a particular row strip or column strip are grouped together and execute all of the functions necessary to complete that strip. These functions include processing data tables, performing computations to make the data ready for the matrix, generating row and column names and inserting those names and the appropriate coefficients into the matrix.

There is also a great deal of similarity in the form in which these systems accept their input data. The consensus is that data is most naturally represented by two-dimensional tables. Each column of a table is identified by a column name and the collection of all column names, in row 0, is called a table's head. Each row of a table is identified by a row name in column 0 which is called the stub. Each element in the table is addressed either by row and column indices, by row and column names or by some combination thereof. In most cases the names that appear in the head or stub are short, i.e., one or two characters, so that they can also be used as an attribute code in the construction of matrix row or column names.

Matrix generator input is a collection of such tables, each identified by a unique name. A multi-dimensional data table is represented by a collection of two-dimensional tables where the codes representing the third and greater dimensions appear in the table name, concatenated to a root that makes each table name unique among its peers. This approach to multi-dimensional data has evolved because it simplifies the logic of the matrix generator and because this is a natural presentation of the data with a full screen text editor. The state of the art in management science representation of model data is explored in detail by Welch [1987b].

An important feature of all systems is the ability to retrieve solution values, i.e., activity levels and reduced costs, from the optimizer and to use these values along with with input data collection to produce tailored reports. Cross case reporting is achieved through multi-solution file access. References to solution values are done in the same manner as a data table and the user need not be concerned with searching sequential input files to get the required solution values. Exxon's PLATOFORM system was one of the earliest (and still active) model management systems that integrated database management, model generation, solution presentation and case management. Exxon sponsored a monograph describing PLATOFORM [Palmer et al. 1984] which includes an incisive discussion of database management in the model management context.

These systems operate on the PC and workstation exactly as they appear on the larger hardware, as batch mode products that accept an input file and produce an output file. Data and programs are prepared with the text editor of the operating system. They require extended memory and a DOS extender, such as PharLap, to be run on a PC.

DATAFORM and OMNI provide an interactive linkage between the PC and mainframe whereby data tables can be created, viewed and edited in a two-dimensional, interactive format on the PC and then uploaded to the mainframe resident model manager. Solution tables can be down-loaded for viewing on the PC screen. OMNI makes use of a conventional spreadsheet for PC-based table manipulation. DATAFORM's interface is tailored to the quick handling of large, multi-dimensional tables. The PC view of the data is in the familiar spreadsheet form and is of any two-dimensional cross section chosen by the user. Both products provide a window into the data portion of production level models that are currently too big for desk-top computers.

All of these products clarify the MPS model and reduce the human cost associated with MPS model description and reporting. The special matrix and solution handling features of these languages make them much more useful than conventional programming languages. However, they are in the end procedural languages with conditional statements and statement ordering.

3.3. Algebraic generation languages

Algebraic, or constraint oriented, languages describe the math programming matrix as a set of equations, a form favored by the academic and engineering communities. The description of the matrix is algebraic in that a statement is an equation (or inequality) comprised of summations of products between model activities and coefficient bearing data tables. A single statement will describe a collection (or strip) of similar constraints and activities. The structure of the language parallels the mathematical summation notation used to formulate the model. The first such language seems to have been Scicon's [1986a] matrix generator generator (MGG) package developed circa 1969.

GAMS [Bisschop & Meeraus, 1982; Brooke, Kendrick & Meeraus, 1988] is the best known, most widely used and most capable of the current algebraic modeling systems. It was originally developed on a CDC mainframe, has been migrated to the IBM 30xx mainframe, UNIX based engineering workstations and can be run on an ordinary PC, under DOS, and in real mode or extended. GAMS shares some of the characteristics of the model management systems just discussed and is a mature system with a proven track record on difficult applications. It uses two-dimensional data tables as its principle input medium, and it is a fully supported commercial software.

GAMS lacks one important feature of the model management systems: it has no database management capability. Data tables and model description both appear in a fixed order in the GAMS symbolic input file (unlike MGG, for example). GAMS does, however, free the user from being concerned with the 8-character matrix row and column name limitation found in the methods discussed earlier. GAMS automates the generation of matrix names while allowing the user to describe data with names of up to 10 characters.

GAMS stands alone in its support of nonlinear programming (other than by separable programming or successive LP). Not only can a nonlinear model be described by the language but GAMS automates the job of providing nonlinear function evaluation support for the optimizer during optimization. When used in tandem with MINOS [Murtagh & Saunders, 1987], GAMS recognizes nonlinear expressions in the model definition and performs all functions necessary to prepare the model for MINOS, and assists MINOS during the solution process by providing MINOS with numeric evaluation of these functions at points along the path to solution. This automates the particularly tedious job of programming the function evaluation procedures in FORTRAN and then linking them with the MINOS library.

GAMS is also a leader in the movement to make the model manager independent of the optimizer and the host hardware and operating system. It is written in PASCAL, which makes it highly transportable to any hardware that supports such a compiler. GAMS interfaces to multiple optimizers via the MPS standard files. Thus, the user is free to mix and match model managers, optimizers, operating systems and hardware platforms.

3.4. Spreadsheets

Personal-computer-based spreadsheet programs are the most significant sociological phenomena to occur in the computing world in the last fifteen years. They have made the desk-top computer approachable and accepted by managers, who tended to be intimidated by anything that said 'computer' on it. Now that spreadsheets are widely accepted, the next step is to equip spread-sheets with more sophisticated computational techniques than simple arith-metic. Spreadsheet LP is one step in that direction.

The spreadsheet uses the two-dimensional screen to take on an interactive two-dimensional view of the model. The matrix is shown as an explicit tableau, i.e., the full LP matrix is presented on the screen. Coefficients are either entered directly at the appropriate matrix row and column intersection or are computed by a function stored at the intersection and using parameters found elsewhere in the spreadsheet or on other spreadsheets. Every LP variable is represented by a cell in the spreadsheet where its activity level will appear when optimization is complete.

Spreadsheet LP seems inadequate for the needs of production level model-ing, for two reasons. First, the limited memory and CPU power of the PC restrict the size of model that can be solved. If a larger computer is available most analysts would rather solve a model in 40 seconds CPU time with 4 minute turnaround rather than tie up his PC for 40 minutes. The spreadsheets now appearing on engineering work stations offer relief to this problem.

Secondly, the text-book nutrition model of 4 columns and 5 rows looks very good as an explicit tableau on the PC screen, but this approach becomes awkward even for small production models of 200 rows and 400 columns. For larger models, the 80 column by 25 row PC screen becomes a peep hole for viewing the Grand Canyon. Abandoning the explicit tableau in favor of a sparse matrix notation, such as the standard MPS file format of Section 2, takes away much of the attraction of the spreadsheet as an optimizer input tool.

Nonetheless, the PC spreadsheet interface to the LP optimizer has found a place in the modeling world because with it the model is stated with an intuitively clear view and because PCs are more accessible than mainframes. For small models and for prototype models the PC is becoming an accepted OR modeling tool. The most widely advertised spreadsheet product is *What's Best!* It is tightly integrated into Lotus 1-2-3 and uses the popular LINDO optimizer [Schrage, 1984]. JANUS [Mylander, 1985] reads a model expressed as an explicit tableau from a Lotus 1-2-3 spreadsheet and prepares an MPS standard input file for the optimizer. Lotus 1-2-3/G comes with a linear programming command built in.

Spreadsheet modeling is like FORTRAN model generation in that a general purpose tool is being applied to a complex, specialized application. Discipline and consistent conventions are the order of the day. Many of the points made earlier about FORTRAN application development apply to spreadsheets.

3.5. Block diagrams

The block diagram appears to be the next generation of matrix description languages because it is a two-dimensional abstraction of the MP matrix that provides an overview of the model within the confines of a PC screen without the detail of the full matrix tableau. An example of this is shown in Figure 2. The block diagram is a two-dimensional display in which the rows and columns represent the row strips and column strips described earlier. The intersections of the diagram are either blank, if there is no interaction between the row and column strip, or occupied by a special iconic symbol. The icons indicate how the matrix is generated. The block diagram developers have observed that a typical MP model contains a limited number of matrix substructures. Each icon represents one identified substructure. One icon references a data table that supplies a block of coefficients, another supplies +1 connectors between rows and columns of the matrix, another is a special symbol indicating an inventory connection, yet another causes the generation of convexity rows and column markers for MIP models. As a row strip represents the generation of several constraints and a column strip represents the generation of several matrix columns so an icon represents the generation of several matrix coefficients at selected row and column intersections. The theory behind the block diagram representation of MP matrices is described by Welch [1987a].

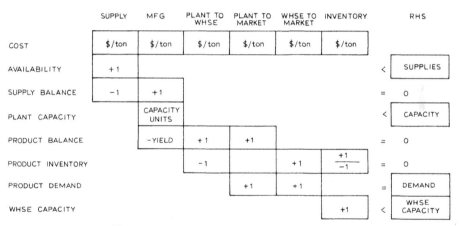

Fig. 2. Labeled block schematic of an LP model.

At present we know of three commercially available block diagram systems:

(1) MIMI/LP is written in C language and runs on a variety of hardware, ranging from IBM mainframes under the CMS operating system to work stations running UNIX. MIMI/LP is part of the MIMI modeling management framework and has an interactive interface in that context [Baker & Biddle, 1986].

(2) PAM is an optional component of MPSIII. PAM is implemented in DATAFORM and therefore restricted to computers that host DATAFORM. PAM uses DATAFORM's PC interactive table handler for its interactive interface.

(3) MathPro has brought an interactive variation of the block diagram approach to PC compatible desk-top computers. MathPro represents the

abstraction of the matrix in familiar spreadsheet style, taking full advantage of the interactive features of the PC in creating and updating the matrix description. The underlying attribute structure of the matrix is displayed by pop-up windows. MathPro runs on IBM PC compatibles in either DOS real mode or PharLap protected mode.

The block diagram approach to describing a matrix has three advantages over the procedural languages described earlier:

(1) MP practitioners have used the block diagram to document their models for many years [Smith, 1968]. Now techniques are being devised to automate the generation of MP matrices from the block diagram.

(2) PC-based interactive programs can make use of spreadsheet techniques and two-dimensional PC displays in the viewing and manipulation of the block diagram which thereby affects the structure of the object LP matrix.

(3) Generation from the block diagram automatically includes a strict matrix naming discipline which can be exploited by the masking features of the various MPS procedures, as discussed in an earlier section.

The block-diagram approach is a developing technology. Future versions will contain new icons representing more complex matrix substructures and they could be the starting point for matrix pre-solution reduction techniques [see Bradley, Brown & Graves, 1983; and Williams, 1985] and solution analyzers based on expert system technology of the kind currently being investigated by Greenberg [1987]. We also note that at least one new MPS, the optimization subroutine library, or OSL [IBM Corp., 1991], is able to make direct use of matrices formulated as an assembly of subblocks, suggesting direct input from model builders of this type, avoiding use of the MPS external interface.

4. MPS modeling concepts

The concepts and language used by veteran MP formulators often reflect the way they think about their models. Basic MP modeling concepts differ from those used in other simulation fields and these differences are worth reviewing.

The intuitively obvious modeling notation has been formalized in the field of discrete event simulation and the languages of that field, e.g., EAS-E, SIMSCRIPT, GASP, etc. Their atomic unit is an entity which represents some concrete or abstract thing in the system being modeled. An entity has attributes. For example, a warehouse in some location could be an entity and its attributes are volume, square footage, construction cost and monthly storage cost. Another attribute of an entity can be its relationship to other entities, called pointers in data base management. Entities are organized into sets, where the members of a set share some characteristic that determines set membership. Finally, a set can be an entity of another set. The network model [Date, 1983] is the most appropriate data model characterization of the entity–attribute–set view of a system description. Markowitz, Malhotra & Pazel [1984] gives a particularly clear description of these concepts.

The entity–attribute–set view of data is awkward for an MP model description because most MP data are about the relationships between entities. MP data relationships are not binary, yes/no, relationships but are relationships of degree. MP data is more likely to be shipping cost from plants to warehouses or product yields for processes and plant combinations. Data concerning one entity is the trivial case and does not even occur in many MP models. A warehouse will have a storage capacity which would be an attribute of that entity, in the entity–attribute–set sense, for a simple LP model. A more realistic model will have different warehouse capacities for different products that vary across time periods.

The Codd [1970] relational model is a useful way of describing MPS data. To the MP practitioner the model has attributes, which are the properties of the system being modeled. Examples of model attributes are warehouses, time periods, octane numbers, plants, etc. Each model attribute has a domain of terms that are descriptive of that attribute. For example, the time-period attribute could have a domain of 52 weeks for a detailed model and quarters for the aggregated version of the model. The data of the model are represented by relations that contain the measure of how terms relate to each other. As noted earlier, mathematical programmers do not speak of domains and relations in conjunction with their models; indices, sets, lists, and tables are their parlance.

A well-formulated MP model is a structure of attributes and relationships between attributes in matrix form. The attributes of the model are warehouses, time periods, shipping costs, capacities, etc. which define the attributes and expected values of the data. The model can be documented and understood without supplying domain terms or numeric values to the data tables. An instance of a model is when the terms and data are supplied.

To illustrate, consider a simplified transportation-type submodel:

$$\min_{x} \ \sum_{j} \sum_{j} \sum_{k} c_{ijk} x_{ijk}$$

$$\text{subject to} \ \sum_{j} x_{ijk} = b_{ik}, \quad \forall i, k,$$

$$\sum_{i} x_{ijk} = d_{jk}, \quad \forall j, k.$$

Mathematically the data of the model, c_{ijk}, b_{ik}, and d_{jk}, are arrays of numbers organized over the indices i, j, and k. The data arrays could be viewed as relations. c_{ijk} is a relation of 4 columns: three key, descriptive columns and a value column containing the costs. When this model is applied to a real-world situation the index i becomes the attribute plant, whose domain is a list of source names, the index j becomes the attribute market, whose domain is a list of destination names, and the index k becomes the domain of products or commodities being shipped. The attributes of the data (plants, markets, and products) are also the attributes of the model.

The definition of the model is independent of the content of the data tables (or relations). A model may represent a detailed system at the plant level on a monthly basis and the domain terms and data values reflect this. An aggregated model will have the same attributes but different terms, i.e., regions instead of plants, years instead of months. A disaggregated model will be at the department level for a weekly time frame. The structure and attributes of the model are the same but the terms of the domains and the scale of the data are different.

Frequently, an MP model is a member of a family of models. Such a family may comprise a raw material purchasing model, a production planning model, a product distribution model and a facilities planning model. The models have different structures and are used for different purposes. By defining the model across the same collection of attributes they are more easily related to one another in the system documentation and they can share domains and data. Thus the attribute 'plants' will have the same meaning and terms for all models in the family.

The formulation process frequently begins with the writing down of a few equations, the constraints of the model. The subscripts of the variables and coefficients represent the attributes of the model. The integer values of the subscripts are positions on the domains, e.g., {plant1, plant2, ...}. These terms relate the values in the data tables to the matrix row and column names.

The notations of modeling and the relational representations of data are different ways of talking about the same thing. Recognizing this indicates how commercial relational database management systems can become part of the modeling process.

5. Practical implementations of the simplex method

There has recently been great emphasis on interior point methods for linear programming, but we begin our discussion of MP algorithms with the simplex method – the oldest successful, and still most widely used, method. Most MP systems continue to be designed round efficient implementations of the simplex method (even very new ones such as CPLEX and OSL). Interestingly, the two approaches tend to complement each other, since the interior methods work best on problems which the simplex method finds difficult for various reasons, while other problems are very amenable to solution by the simplex method without incurring some of the more expensive steps of the interior methods [see Tomlin, 1989].

We should point out that most widely implemented interior methods produce very near-optimal but nonbasic solutions for almost every problem, while the simplex method always produces a basic solution. In many, if not most applications, a basic solution (or at least one with a minimal number of nonzero values) is very important. Reasons for this are:

(1) It is desirable in practice to keep the number of 'active' activities small.

(2) Basic solutions are more 'nearly integer' in many models, e.g., production–distribution models.

(3) It is easier to save and restore model status.

(4) All the standard postoptimality and sensitivity analysis procedures, including ranging and parametrics, assume a basic optimum.

A computational variant of the simplex method called the 'BASIC' technique, for purifying nonbasic solutions, has been a part of MPS for many years. It appears in the early MPS/360 documentation. It may be used to affect a transition from an interior to basic optimal solutions. Megiddo [1991] has described a variant with guaranteed polynomial convergence properties.

Another important feature of the simplex method is that it can accept almost any purported solution of an LP and use it as a starting point. Thus the optimal basis (see below) may be supplied when a problem is slightly modified and allow extremely rapid reoptimization in only a few cheap iterations. This is critical in algorithms which require repeated solution of modified LP problems, such as MIP by branch and bound and SLP (see Sections 8 and 9).

In textbooks the linear programming problem is often stated as in (1.1)–(1.3). In practice the more traditional MP systems often work with the slightly different form:

$$\max \quad x_0 \tag{5.1}$$

$$\text{subject to} \quad x_0 + \sum_j a_{0j} x_j = 0 \,, \tag{5.2}$$

$$\sum_j a_{ij} x_j = b_i \,, \tag{5.3}$$

$$L_j \leqslant x_j \leqslant U_j \,, \tag{5.4}$$

where $L_0 = -\infty$ and $U_0 = +\infty$; to emphasize that the objective function may be treated much like any other row of the problem with a 'free' logical variable [see Beale, 1968; Orchard-Hays, 1968]. It is assumed that the constraints (5.3) include a full set of m unit columns (the 'logical' columns). The coefficient matrix A is assumed to be sparse.

Frequently, the model is preprocessed [see Bradley, Brown & Graves, 1983] in an effort to remove redundancy. In particular, it is easy and worthwhile to remove or ignore variables which are explicitly fixed (i.e., have $L_j = U_j$) and free rows other than the cost row. It is also usually worthwhile to initially identify structurally degenerate rows and columns, i.e., those identifying 'null variables' via constraints of the form:

$$\sum_j a_j x_j \leqslant 0 \,, \quad \text{all } a_j \geqslant 0, \, x_j \geqslant 0 \,,$$

and 'implied free variables' y identified by constraints of the form:

$$\sum_j a_j x_j - ay \le b \,, \quad \text{all } a_j \ge 0,\, x_j \ge 0,\, b \le 0 \,.$$

These are detected and dealt with by a PRESOLVE or REDUCE routine, before 'CRASHing' a starting basis. Formal optimality for the original model may later be enforced by POSTSOLVE [see Tomlin & Welch, 1983].

5.1. Outline of the simplex method

The simplex method works with a basic and nonbasic set of columns B and N. Let x_B and x_N be the vectors of basic and nonbasic variables, respectively, corresponding to this partition of A. Traditionally, the nonbasic variables were assumed to be at either their upper or lower bounds. Now, however, some systems allow them to take values away from their bounds. This is useful in starting from nonbasic solutions and in combatting degeneracy [see Gill, Murray, Saunders & Wright, 1989]. The basic variables are evaluated as

$$x_B = \beta = B^{-1}\left[b - \sum_j N_j x_{Nj}\right]. \tag{5.5}$$

All practical versions of the simplex method work with some factorization of B or its inverse. The original 'product form' [see Dantzig, 1963] maintains the basis inverse as:

$$B^{-1} = E_l E_{l-1} \cdots E_2 E_1 \,, \tag{5.6}$$

where the E_k are elementary column transformations of the form:

$$E_k = \begin{pmatrix} 1 & & & \eta_{1k} & & \\ & \ddots & & \vdots & & \\ & & 1 & & & \\ & & & \eta_{p_k k} & & \\ & & & & 1 & \\ & & & \vdots & & \ddots \\ & & & \eta_{mk} & & 1 \end{pmatrix}. \tag{5.7}$$

These transformations are often referred to as 'column etas' or just 'etas'. Most modern systems use more sophisticated means for computing, maintaining and updating factorizations [see Forrest & Tomlin, 1972; Reid, 1982, and below]. Many of these factorizations employ elementary row transformations of the form:

$$R_k = \begin{pmatrix} 1 & & & & & & \\ & \ddots & & & & & \\ & & 1 & & & & \\ \rho_{p_k 1} & \cdots & & \rho_{p_k k} & \cdots & & \rho_{p_k m} \\ & & & & 1 & & \\ & & & & & \ddots & \\ & & & & & & 1 \end{pmatrix} . \tag{5.8}$$

These are often referred to as 'row etas' and may be intermingled with column etas.

Highly simplified, the steps of a simplex iteration and the terminology associated with them are as follows:

(1) FORMC. Form a 'c vector'. This is usually either the unit vector $\langle 1, 0, \dots, 0 \rangle$ or some more complicated vector expressing the infeasibility function [see Beale, 1970].

(2) BTRAN. Apply the transformations to c in reverse order to form a pricing vector:

$$\pi^{\mathrm{T}} = c^{\mathrm{T}} B^{-1} = c^{\mathrm{T}} E_l \cdots E_2 E_1 .$$

The computation is performed from left to right.

(3) PRICE. Compute the 'reduced cost' (or gradient with respect to the objective) of some or all of the nonbasic variables:

$$d_j = \pi^{\mathrm{T}} a_{.j}, \quad a_{.j} \in N .$$

If $d_j < 0$ and x_j is at its lower bound, or if $d_j > 0$ and x_j is at its upper bound, the variable may profitably be brought into the basis.

(4) FTRAN. Apply the etas in forward order to a profitable vector $a_{.q}$ chosen in PRICE:

$$\alpha = B^{-1} a_{.q} = E_l \cdots E_2 E_1 a_{.q} .$$

The computation is performed from right to left. The α_i are the rates of change of the basic variables as x_q is increased.

(5) CHUZR. Choose a pivot row p, and thus a variable to leave the basis. In its simplest form (assuming that x_q was at its lower bound) this requires finding:

$$\theta = \frac{\beta_p}{\alpha_p} = \min_{\alpha_i > 0} \frac{\beta_i}{\alpha_i} .$$

The θ is the largest value x_q can assume without driving some basic variable infeasible. See Beale [1970] for a more detailed description.

(6) UPDATE. Update the factorization of B^{-1} for the new basis $\bar{B}$. In the simple product form this involves adding a new eta on the left of (5.6):

$$\bar{B}^{-1} = E_{l+1}E_l \cdots E_2 E_1$$

of the form (5.7), where:

$$\eta_{i,l+1} = -\alpha_i/\alpha_p , \quad i \neq p ,$$
$$\eta_{p_{l+1},l+1} = 1/\alpha_p , \quad \quad\quad\quad\quad\quad (5.9)$$
$$p_{l+1} = p .$$

The values of the basic variables are updated in the obvious way:

$$x_{\bar{B}} = \bar{\beta} = E_{l+1}\beta .$$

In practice MP systems use more complicated versions of most of these procedures, but the above outline at least establishes the framework.

No matter what variant of the revised simplex method is used, the BTRAN, PRICE and FTRAN steps consume the bulk of the computational effort. The more advanced factorization methods with complex updates can consume significant time in UPDATE, though this can often be overlapped with the subsequent BTRAN operation [Forrest & Tomlin, 1972]. The MP system developer is therefore primarily (but not exclusively) concerned with the computational procedures and data structures for these steps. Their efficiency, for models with realistic structure, is critical to successful application.

5.2. Pricing

One of the most flexible steps of the simplex method is the choice of entering basis column(s), since all that is required is the choice of one or more profitable d_j's. The original Dantzig criterion is to choose the single column with the most profitable reduced cost d_q, sometimes called 'full pricing'. Most MPSs use some form of 'multiple pricing' and/or 'partial pricing' [see Orchard-Hays, 1968; and Benichou, Gauthier, Hentges & Ribière, 1977]. The idea of these approaches is to choose several potentially profitable columns to bring into the basis, perhaps while examining only part of the matrix. This can save computing many of the inner products for PRICE and is particular appealing if the matrix must be kept out-of-core, but even all-in-core systems can profitably use this technique. For example, the WHIZARD pricing mechanism tries to choose up to five poorly-correlated profitable columns for potential introduction to the basis. This is done by initially partitioning the matrix into sections and PRICE moves to a new section in pseudo-randomly when a good column is found. By choosing the columns in this way one hopes that most of them will lead to profitable 'minor iterations' after the best of them has been pivoted into the basis – a 'major iteration'.

Another powerful technique is the Harris [1973] Devex method, which calls for full pricing, but selects the entering vector on the basis of the best weighted reduced cost d_j/T_j using dynamic weights T_j. This latter technique usually requires a relatively small number of iterations, but the full pricing required often makes it slower than multiple and/or partial pricing in standard mathematical programming systems. However, this method and other full-pricing schemes have gained a new lease of life with the arrival of vector processing. It turns out that, especially for large problems, full pricing can be vectorized more efficiently than any other part of the simplex method [see Forrest & Tomlin, 1990]. It is therefore more efficient to perform the extra arithmetic in PRICE in the expectation of reducing the number of iterations and hence the total work. Both the newer versions of MPSX/370 and the vector version of OSL [see Forrest & Tomlin, 1992a] employ vectorized full and/or Devex pricing.

5.3. Basis factorization

A fundamental step in all simplex implementations is the factorization algorithm (known as INVERT for historical reasons) which periodically produces a representation of the basis B or its inverse B^{-1}. Most modern systems do this via a triangular factorization:

$$B = LU ,$$

which can be in turn written in product form

$$B = L_1 L_2 \cdots L_m U_m \cdots U_2 U_1 ,$$

where

$$L_k = \begin{pmatrix} 1 & & & & & & & \\ & \ddots & & & & & & \\ & & 1 & & & & & \\ & & & l_{kk} & & & & \\ & & & 1 & & & \\ & & & \vdots & & \ddots & \\ & & & l_{mk} & & & 1 \end{pmatrix} ,$$

$$U_k = \begin{pmatrix} 1 & & & u_{1k} & & & \\ & \ddots & & \vdots & & & \\ & & 1 & & & & \\ & & & u_{kk} & & & \\ & & & 1 & & \\ & & & & \ddots & \\ & & & & & 1 \end{pmatrix} .$$

Note that we may then write

$$B^{-1} = U_1^{-1} U_2^{-1} \cdots U_m^{-1} L_m^{-1} \cdots L_2^{-1} L_1^{-1} ,$$

where L_k^{-1} and U_1^{-1} are of the form E_k in (5.7) with $\eta_{p_k k} = 1/l_{kk}$, $\eta_{ik} = -l_{ik}/l_{kk}$ $(i > k)$ and $\eta_{p_k k} = 1/u_{kk}$, $\eta_{ik} = -u_{ik}/u_{kk}$ $(i < k)$, respectively.

Some writers [see Reid, 1982] prefer to express the L and particularly U factors in terms of elementary row transformations of the type (5.8). In that case we could write

$$U = V_m \cdots V_2 V_1 ,$$

where

$$V_k = \begin{pmatrix} 1 & & & & & & & \\ & \ddots & & & & & & \\ & & 1 & & & & & \\ & & & u_{kk} & \cdots & u_{km} & & \\ & & & & 1 & & & \\ & & & & & \ddots & \\ & & & & & & 1 \end{pmatrix} .$$

Although we have expressed B in true triangular factor form, in practice B must be permuted by rows (implicitly) and columns (explicitly) to try and minimize the number of nonzero transformation elements. There are several ways of doing this. The best known are the method of Markowitz [1957] and the partitioned preassigned pivot procedure (P^4) of Hellerman & Rarick [1972]. Both approaches are thoroughly discussed by Duff, Erisman & Reid [1986]. The former is used by Reid [1982] and Murtagh & Saunders [1987]. Some MPSs, e.g., SCICONVIC/VM have used approximations to the Markowitz method, which usually produce more nonzero fill-in, but also generate all column etas. CDC's former MP system, APEX, and MPSIII (including the WHIZARD code) use the P^4 approach. The P^4 method is very fast and efficient on the majority of problems, but can encounter numerical difficulties with larger and denser problems. In such situations it is wiser to fall back on the Markowitz approach.

There are three commonly used methods of updating the basis factorization. Most systems allow use of the standard product form update for 'friendly' (very sparse) problems, and some use only this method, e.g., the very fast CPLEX optimizer. Most of the larger-scale production systems (e.g., MPSX/370, WHIZARD, SCICONIC/VM and OSL) implement the Forrest–Tomlin [1972] method for updating triangular factors of the basis, using row etas. Finally, there is the Bartels–Golub [1969] method using single element etas to maintain triangularity. This has the advantage of a priori numerical stability [Saunders, 1976] and is used in MINOS and by Reid [1982].

6. Interior point methods

The family of interior point methods have been energetically publicized by Karmarkar [1984] and are now beginning to appear in MP systems for general use. We say 'family' of methods because Gill, Murray, Saunders, Tomlin & Wright [1986] have shown that the projective method, as well as the affine scaling methods [Vanderbei, Meketon & Freedman, 1986], are formally special cases of a logarithmic barrier function method. In addition, Megiddo [1989] and Kojima, Mizuno & Yoshise [1989] have developed theory and algorithms for primal–dual methods, based on barrier formulations of the primal and dual LP problems. There now exist MP systems incorporating all these approaches.

The AT&T Korbx™ system [see Cheng, Houck, Liu, Meketon, Slutsman, Vanderbei & Wang, 1989] initially attracted considerable attention. It employs several algorithm variants – primal, dual and primal–dual. Rapid solution of some very large problems, particularly concerned with communications and multicommodity flow, has been reported. However, one of its more striking features is that it was sold as a *turnkey* system with the software bundled in a package with a multi-vector processor 'mini-super' computer. This made it extremely difficult to compare its performance with other systems. See, however, Lustig, Shanno & Gregory [1989] for some comparative figures. More recently, AT&T have moved to unbundle their MP products. The IBM optimization subroutine library (OSL) implements a primal barrier algorithm based on that in Gill, Murray, Saunders, Tomlin & Wright [1986]. The OB1 system [see Lustig, Marsten & Shanno, 1991], Release 2 of OSL [see Forrest & Tomlin, 1992b] and some other codes implement a primal–dual method based on that of Kojima, Mizuno & Yoshise [1989]. The predictor–corrector variant of the primal–dual algorithm developed by Mehrotra [1990] now seems the most generally successful and the current method of choice. We now consider these approaches in turn.

6.1. The primal Newton barrier method

When the LP problem is considered in general bounded form (1.1)–(1.2), the corresponding barrier function problem is:

$$\min_{x} \quad F(x) = \sum_{j} [c_j x_j - \mu \ln(x_j - L_j) - \mu \ln(U_j - x_j)] \tag{6.1}$$

$$\text{subject to} \quad Ax = b , \tag{6.2}$$

where $\mu \to 0$.

Given such a linearly constrained problem, a standard approach is to use a feasible-point descent method [see, e.g., Gill, Murray & Wright, 1981]. Assuming the current iterate x satisfies $Ax = b$, the next iterate $\bar{x}$ is defined as

$$\bar{x} = x + \alpha p , \tag{6.3}$$

where p is the search direction, and α is the steplength. The computation of p and α must be such that $A\bar{x} = b$ and $F(\bar{x}) < F(x)$.

The *Newton search direction* for this problem is defined as the step to the minimum of the quadratic approximation to $F(x)$, subject to retaining feasibility. If $g \equiv \nabla F(x)$, $H \equiv \nabla^2 F(x)$ and π is the vector of Lagrange multipliers for the constraints (6.2), then the search direction satisfies the linear system

$$\begin{pmatrix} H & A^T \\ A & 0 \end{pmatrix} \begin{pmatrix} -p \\ \pi \end{pmatrix} = \begin{pmatrix} g \\ 0 \end{pmatrix}. \tag{6.4}$$

Note that π converges to the Lagrange multipliers for the constraints $Ax = b$ in the original problem.

Now defining:

$$s_j = x_j - L_j, \qquad t_j = U_j - x_j,$$

$$D = \text{diag}\{(1/s_j^2 + 1/t_j^2)^{-1/2}\},$$

$$\hat{D} = \text{diag}\{(1/s_j - 1/t_j)\},$$

the g, H terms in (6.4) are defined by:

$$g(x) = c - \mu \hat{D} e \quad \text{and} \quad H(x) = \mu D^{-2}.$$

It follows from (6.4) that p and π must satisfy the equation

$$\begin{pmatrix} \mu D^{-2} & A^T \\ A & 0 \end{pmatrix} \begin{pmatrix} -p \\ \pi \end{pmatrix} = \begin{pmatrix} c - \mu \hat{D} e \\ 0 \end{pmatrix}. \tag{6.5}$$

Rewriting (6.5) in terms of a vector r defined by $Dr = -\mu p$, we see that r and π then satisfy

$$\begin{pmatrix} I & DA^T \\ AD & 0 \end{pmatrix} \begin{pmatrix} r \\ \pi \end{pmatrix} = \begin{pmatrix} Dc - \mu D \hat{D} e \\ 0 \end{pmatrix}.$$

From this it follows that π is the solution and r the optimal residual of the least-squares problem:

$$\underset{\pi}{\text{minimize}} \quad \| Dc - \mu D \hat{D} e - DA^T \pi \|.$$

The Newton barrier direction projected into the null space of A is then

$$p = -(1/\mu)Dr.$$

The algorithm remains well defined as μ tends to zero.

In practice it is better to work with a correction $\delta\pi$ at each iteration, updating π, d and the reduced gradient r, where the latter two terms are defined as:

$$d = c - A^T\pi ,$$

$$r = Dd - \mu D\hat{D}e .$$

Without going into details on how the barrier parameter μ is controlled the steps of an iteration are:

(1) If μ and $\|r\|$ are sufficiently small, then STOP,
(2) If 'appropriate' reduce μ and recompute r.
(3) Solve a least-squares problem:

$$\min_{\delta\pi} \ \|r - DA^T\delta\pi\| . \tag{6.6}$$

(4) Update the 'pi values' and 'reduced costs':

$$\pi \leftarrow \pi + \delta\pi , \qquad d \leftarrow d - A^T\delta\pi ,$$

and compute the search direction p as:

$$r = Dd - \mu D\hat{D}e , \qquad p = -(1/\mu)Dr .$$

(5) Calculate the steplength α.
(6) Update $x \leftarrow x + \alpha p$. GO TO (1).

The most critical step in each iteration is the gradient projection, i.e., solving the least-squares problem (6.6). This may be done by solving the normal equations, or (as we shall assume) by using a preconditioned conjugate gradient method. Both involve the Cholesky factorization of the normal equation matrix (or its approximation):

$$PLL^TP^T = \bar{A}\bar{D}^2\bar{A}^T := AD^2A^T ,$$

where the permutation matrix P is chosen so that the lower triangular factor L is sparse. We then solve the preconditioned problem

$$\min_{y} \ \|r - DA^TPL^{-T}y\| ,$$

and recover $\delta\pi = PL^{-T}y$.

The essential steps in the conjugate gradient method are calculations of the form:

$$u \leftarrow u + DA^T(PL^{-T}v)$$

and

$$v \leftarrow v + L^{-1}P^{\mathrm{T}}(ADu) \,.$$

There are several nontrivial procedures which must be carried out before the barrier algorithm can even be begun. In particular, the permutation P and the nonzero structure of L must be determined.

To determine P we require the nonzero structure of AA^{T}. This may be obtained by taking the actual logical product of A and A^{T} or by ORing the logical outer products of the columns with themselves. Application of a minimum degree ordering algorithm gives P. This is then followed by a symbolic factorization [see, e.g., George & Liu, 1981]. Once the nonzero structure of L is available, the memory requirements for the algorithm can be computed, and if insufficient space is available the procedure may be halted.

An appropriate data structure is required so that we may compute

$$P^{\mathrm{T}}\bar{A}\bar{D}^2\bar{A}^{\mathrm{T}}P \,,$$

where $\bar{A}$ and $\bar{D}$ are modified to exclude dense columns and those corresponding to x_j's very close to a bound. This requires either the ability to access the matrix A row-wise, or the computation of the outer products of the columns of AD and their addition to the appropriate elements of the data structure which will contain L. The implementation in OSL allows either alternative.

By far the greatest computational effort in most cases now comes in computing the Cholesky factors. Considerable progress has been made in efficient sparse Cholesky factorization and Forrest & Tomlin [1990] discuss vectorization of this step. They also give computational experience comparing primal barrier methods with simplex methods on several models. Those results vary by about a factor of two in either direction, depending on the size and structure of the models.

6.2. The primal–dual barrier method

The primal–dual method as implemented by Lustig, Marsten & Shanno [1991] in the OB1 system (a descendant of Marsten's [1981] XMP code) modifies the formulation (6.1)–(6.2) slightly in that it considers all lower bounds to be normalized to zero. The problem to be solved is then:

$$\min_x \ \sum_j (c_j x_j - \mu \ln x_j - \mu \ln s_j)$$

subject to $Ax = b \,,$

$\qquad\qquad\quad x + s = U \,,$

which has as its Lagrangian:

$$L(x, s, y, w, \mu) = \sum_j (c_j x_j - \mu \ln x_j - \mu \ln s_j) - y^T(Ax - b)$$
$$- w^T(x + s - u) . \tag{6.7}$$

The first-order necessary conditions for (6.7) can be written:

$$Ax = b ,$$

$$x + s = U ,$$

$$A^T y + z - w = c , \tag{6.8}$$

$$XZe = \mu e ,$$

$$SWe = \mu e ,$$

where z is the vector of dual slack variables and $X = \text{diag}\{x_i\}$, $Z = \text{diag}\{z_i\}$, $S = \text{diag}\{s_i\}$, and $W = \text{diag}\{w_i\}$. Assuming, for the sake of simplicity, that the primal and dual variables are currently feasible, a step of Newton's method may be applied to these nonlinear equations to compute a search direction $(\Delta x, \Delta s, \Delta y, \Delta z, \Delta w)$ as follows:

$$\Delta y = (A\Theta A^T)^{-1} A \Theta \rho(\mu) ,$$

$$\Delta x = \Theta(A^T \Delta y - \rho(\mu)) ,$$

$$\Delta z = \mu X^{-1} e - Ze - X^{-1} Z \Delta x , \tag{6.9}$$

$$\Delta w = S^{-1}(\mu e - SWe + W \Delta x) ,$$

$$\Delta s = -\Delta x ,$$

where $\Theta = (S^{-1}W + X^{-1}Z)^{-1}$ and $\rho(\mu) = \mu(S^{-1} - X^{-1})e - (W - Z)e$.

Two step lengths, α_P and α_D, in the primal and dual spaces are chosen to preserve feasibility and the new approximate minimizing solution is determined as:

$$\hat{x} = x + \alpha_P \Delta x , \qquad \hat{s} = s + \alpha_P \Delta s ,$$

$$\hat{y} = y + \alpha_D \Delta y , \qquad \hat{z} = z + \alpha_D \Delta z , \qquad \hat{w} = w + \alpha_D \Delta w .$$

These steps are repeated until the relative gap between the (feasible) primal and dual solution falls below some user specified tolerance.

This extremely terse outline of the primal–dual method is sufficient to point out the relationships with the primal barrier method. Most importantly, the major computational step is seen to be the solution of a linear system, whose matrix $A\Theta A^{\mathrm{T}}$ has the same structure as the matrix AD^2A^{T} whose Cholesky factors we needed in the primal barrier method. Thus the bulk of the work, and the preprocessing, are very similar. The potential advantage of the primal-dual approach is that feasible dual information is available, and the number of steps may be smaller. Lustig, Marsten & Shanno [1991] present impressive computational experience with this method compared with MINOS, and Lustig, Shanno & Gregory [1989] also obtain favorable results comparing OB1 with the Korbx^{TM} system. Other recent computational results for both simplex and interior methods are surveyed by Ho [1989].

6.3. The predictor–corrector method

The predictor–corrector method is a variant, due to Mehrotra [1990], of the primal–dual barrier method. It is now implemented in OB1, Release 2 of OSL, and some other MP codes. It is widely considered the current method of choice for interior point LP. We follow the excellent description given by Lustig, Marsten & Shanno [1990]. The essence of the method is a different approach to solve the first-order necessary conditions (6.8). Instead of routinely appealing to Newton's method for this nonlinear system, Mehrotra asked whether it might not be possible to derive modifications $\Delta x, \Delta s, \Delta y, \Delta x, \Delta w$ of the current trial solution x, s, y, z, w by directly solving for them. Substituting $x + \Delta x$ for x, etc., in (6.8) we obtain the system:

$$A \, \Delta x = b - Ax \, ,$$

$$\Delta x + \Delta s = U - x - s \, ,$$

$$A^{\mathrm{T}}\Delta y + \Delta z - \Delta w = c - A^{\mathrm{T}}y - z + w \, , \qquad\qquad (6.10)$$

$$X \, \Delta z + Z \, \Delta x = \mu e - XZe - \Delta X \, \Delta Ze \, ,$$

$$S \, \Delta w + W \, \Delta s = \mu e - SWe - \Delta S \, \Delta We \, ,$$

where $\Delta X = \mathrm{diag}\{\Delta x_i\}$, etc. Unfortunately this system is also nonlinear, because of the product terms $\Delta X \, \Delta Z$ and $\Delta S \, \Delta W$ in the last two equations. A direct approach is to derive approximations for these product terms, plug them into the right-hand side of (6.10) and then solve the system.

The *predictor* step in the predictor–corrector method solves the *affine* variant of the model, i.e., it omits the μ and Δ-product terms from the last two right-hand sides:

$$A \, \Delta \hat{x} = b - Ax \, ,$$

$$\Delta \hat{x} + \Delta \hat{s} = U - x - s \, ,$$

$$A^T \Delta \hat{y} + \Delta \hat{z} - \Delta \hat{w} = c - A^T y - z + w \, , \tag{6.11}$$

$$X \, \Delta \hat{z} + Z \, \Delta \hat{x} = -XZe \, ,$$

$$S \, \Delta \hat{w} + W \, \Delta \hat{s} = -SWe \, .$$

Just as in the ordinary primal–dual method, the essential step is the solution of a system of the form;

$$A \Theta A^T \Delta \hat{y} = \hat{v}$$

for some right-hand side $\hat{v}$, where Θ is defined as for (6.9).

With $\Delta \hat{x}, \Delta \hat{z}, \Delta \hat{s}$ and $\Delta \hat{w}$ available we are ready to perform the corrector step, which solves the linear system:

$$A \, \Delta x = b - Ax \, ,$$

$$\Delta x + \Delta s = U - x - s \, ,$$

$$A^T \Delta y + \Delta z - \Delta w = c - A^T y - z + w \, , \tag{6.12}$$

$$X \, \Delta z + Z \, \Delta x = \mu e - XZe - \Delta \hat{X} \, \Delta \hat{Z} e \, ,$$

$$S \, \Delta w + W \, \Delta s = \mu e - SWe - \Delta \hat{S} \, \Delta \hat{W} e \, .$$

The essential step is again the solution of a system of the form:

$$A \Theta A^T \Delta y = v \, ,$$

where the right-hand side v is different, but the diagonal Θ is the same. Thus the same factorization of $A \Theta A^T$ is used for both predictor and corrector steps, and only back substitution for Δy, etc. must be done twice. Since the factorization normally dominates the computation, we would expect a net decrease in time if the number of iterations is reduced. Lustig, Marsten & Shanno [1990] report that this is indeed almost always the case (often by a substantial factor), hence the popularity of the method.

7. Special structure linear programs

Despite the prominance of special structure in the MP literature, most MPSs have few facilities for exploiting it. There are some interesting exceptions, however. Several earlier systems incorporated generalized upper bounds (GUBs) [see Beale, 1970]. Some very large problems could indeed be solved in the out-of-core environment using GUB, but for some reason the GUB algorithm seems to have largely fallen out of favor as more powerful in-core systems have developed.

Graves and his disciples have continued to exploit structure on an application by application basis with their XS system [see, e.g., Brown, Graves & Honczarenko, 1987], using primal decomposition and various sub-structures, including network and generalized network structures. More generally, the original work of Glover and Klingman, and of Bradley, Brown & Graves [1977] and Brown & McBride [1984], in developing network simplex methods has led to orders-of-magnitude improvement even over earlier special-purpose algorithms. Gratifyingly, it has also proved that it is possible to integrate much of this network technology into a more traditional, general-purpose MPS rather neatly [Tomlin & Welch, 1985].

Some new opportunities for exploiting special structure are currently being explored. Parallel processing is obviously an attractive option for decomposable models [see, e.g., Ho & Gnanendran, [1989]. The OSL system specifically allows for submodels, and improved solution times using partitioning, and even Dantzig–Wolfe decomposition [see Dantzig, 1963], were reported by Forrest [1991].

8. Nonlinear programming

Most MP systems provide only limited capabilities for nonlinear programming. From quite early on, most of them have provided facilities for separable programming, where the nonlinear functions are restricted to be of the form:

$$F(x) = f_1(x_1) + f_2(x_2) + \cdots + f_r(x_r) ,$$

and each of these functions of a single variable is approximated by a piecewise-linear function:

$$f(z) - \sum_{j=0}^{N} b_j \lambda_j = 0 , \tag{8.1}$$

$$z - \sum_{j=0}^{N} a_j \lambda_j = 0 , \tag{8.2}$$

$$\sum_{j=0}^{N} \lambda_j = 1 , \tag{8.3}$$

where at most two of the variables may be nonzero, and these two must be adjacent [see Beale, 1968]. This latter condition can be enforced by slightly modifying the pivot rules of the simplex method.

Quite sophisticated facilities were provided in some very early systems such as LP/90/94 for automatic interpolation to refine the approximations [again, see Beale, 1968]. Few modern systems support this, and separable programming seems to have fallen out of favor, except for inherently nonconvex piecewise-linear problems.

Many large MP users, particularly in the oil and petrochemical industries, use MP systems to call the simplex method recursively, using successive linear programming (SLP). Griffith & Stewart [1961] introduced this approach, writing the constraints in the form:

$$\sum_j a_{ij} x_j + g_i(z_1, \ldots, z_q) = b_i,$$

entirely segregating the nonlinear variables z_k in every row (whether they appear nonlinearly in it or not). The functions $g_i(z)$ are linearized about the current trial solution in a straightforward way, the resulting LP problem is solved to obtain a new trial solution, etc.

Several variations of the SLP technique have been proposed. A formulation due to Beale [1974] calls for writing what appears to be a linear program, with standard looking constraints:

$$\sum_j a_{ij} x_j = b_i,$$

but allowing the a_{ij} and b_i to be functions of a set of nonlinear variables $y_1, \ldots, y_r$. If all a_{ij} are constant and only the b_i are functions of the y_k, then nothing has really changed. But if some of the nonlinearities can be thrown into the $a_{ij} x_j$ terms the number of nonlinear variables may be dramatically reduced.

By far the most sophisticated system available today for solving general large scale nonlinear programs is the MINOS system [Murtagh & Saunders, 1983], which employs both advanced LP sparse matrix technology and general nonlinear optimization techniques to great effect.

9. Integer programming

In the world of MP systems, integer programming means branch and bound. A great many refinements and extensions have been made to this seemingly pedestrian approach. Computational experience on earlier systems with medium to large scale models is described by Forrest, Hirst & Tomlin [1974] and Benichou, Gauthier, Hentges & Ribière [1977]. Excellent and detailed surveys of branch and bound methodology have been published by Beale [1979, 1985b].

The great improvements in problem solving capability seen in the last two decades can be mainly attributed to three sources. The first is the development of better rules and heuristics for the branch and bound process itself. The second is the development of techniques to deal with complex nonconvexities in the branch and bound framework. Thirdly, there has been the development of 'strong formulations' to reduce the 'gap' between the IP problem we are actually trying to solve and the LP relaxation actually seen by the branch and bound code. We shall not discuss branching heuristics here, but will consider the second and third topics.

The discrete options available in the various MPSs vary, but most of those which offer any capability can handle:

(1) Bivalent variables (usually, but not necessarily zero/one variables).

(2) Semicontinuous variables (which must be zero or lie in some positive interval (L, U)).

(3) General integer variables (which can take on the values 0, 1, 2, 3, etc.)

A great many discrete applications involve either groups of integer variables summing to one, or explicit piecewise-linear nonconvex functions, usually expressing economies of scale. The latter can be handled by various tricks with integer variables [see Dantzig, 1963; and Beale, 1968, but it is much more advantageous to treat them as a special kind of entity in branch and bound algorithms – as *special ordered sets* [Beale & Tomlin, 1970]. Let us consider a model with a concave cost function, expressed as in (8.1)–(8.3) where at most two of the variables may be nonzero, and these two must be adjacent.

When the LP relaxation of such a model is solved we normally obtain an inadmissible solution which interpolates a cost below the actual piecewise-linear curve. Typically (but not necessarily) this involves the first and last variable. Let the LP solution values be λ_j^* and compute the weighted sum of the a_j:

$$w = \sum_j a_j \lambda_j^* . \tag{9.1}$$

Let us suppose this value satisfies

$$a_r \leq w \leq a_{r+1} , \tag{9.2}$$

then (a_r, a_{r+1}) is called the *current interval*. Now we can say that any solution which satisfies the requirements on the λ-variables must be on *either* the $(r+1)$th through last segments of the curve or on the first through rth segments. This is equivalent to saying that:

$$either \quad \lambda_0 = \lambda_1 = \cdots = \lambda_{r-1} = 0 \quad or \quad \lambda_{r+1} = \lambda_{r+2} = \cdots = \lambda_N = 0 . \tag{9.3}$$

One can make a similar statement centered around the right end of the interval:

$$either \quad \lambda_0 = \lambda_1 = \cdots = \lambda_r = 0 \quad or \quad \lambda_{r+2} = \lambda_{r+3} = \cdots = \lambda_N = 0 .$$

$$(9.4)$$

These dichotomies may be used as a basis for branching in a branch and bound scheme in the same way that an integer variable with current value $x = n + f$, where f is fractional, is used to create a dichotomy: *either $x \leq n$ or $x \geq n + 1$*.

A set of zero/one variables summing to one is a *multiple-choice* set. These occur frequently in many contexts [see, e.g., Williams, 1985]. These alternatives can typically be represented exactly as in (8.1)–(8.3), except that now the rule is that at most one of the λ-variables may be nonzero. We shall call this an example of a special ordered set of type 1 (or S1 set). For obvious reasons, when two adjacent members may be nonzero the special ordered sets are of type 2 (or S2 sets).

Let us consider branching individually on the members of a multiple-choice set. The LP relaxation of the model is likely to again produce a solution with two nonzero members (often the first and the last). If we choose to branch on one of these (say λ_0), we are faced with a rather weak choice. The two branches correspond to the decisions to build no plant ($\lambda_0 = 1$) or to build 'something' ($\lambda_0 = 0$). Similarly, with λ_N we have the choice of building the maximum size plant or some indeterminate smaller size (if any). Neither of these branches may take us much closer to a valid solution.

If we compute the weighted solution (9.1), we may once again adopt a 'divide and conquer' approach, considering the dichotomy:

$$either \quad \lambda_0 = \lambda_1 = \cdots = \lambda_r = 0 \quad or \quad \lambda_{r+1} = \lambda_{r+2} = \cdots = \lambda_N = 0 .$$

$$(9.5)$$

The branching procedure generated by such a dichotomy is again obviously analogous to branching on a general integer variable, but likely to require fewer branches to reach a valid solution.

Special ordered sets have proved remarkably amenable to extension. Beale & Forrest [1976] were able to handle smooth nonconvex separable functions and 'linked ordered sets' and 'chains of linked ordered sets' may be used to handle more complex nonconvex nonlinearities [see Beale, 1979, 1985b].

Perhaps the most exciting work in the last decade has been in the development of strong formulations and cutting planes to reduce the 'integer gap' in branch and bound methods. A simple example of this is the disaggregation of constraints. Use of a zero/one variable to force several other variables to zero is quite common. However, a constraint such as:

$$\sum_{j=1}^{K} x_j - K\delta \leq 0 ,$$

can be replaced by multiple individual constraints:

$$x_j - \delta \leq 0, \quad j = 1, \ldots, K,$$

which constrain the LP relaxation more tightly.

Of particular consequence to MPSs has been the development by Crowder, Johnson & Padberg [1983] of the PIPX extension of MPSX for solving large and difficult pure zero/one models. While it is true that pure zero/one models make up a fairly small proportion of the discrete models we see in practice, this shows what can be done by applying powerful mathematical tools in this framework. More recently, Van Roy & Wolsey [1987] have extended many of these ideas to the mixed integer case – a development which potentially has even greater impact.

At present, MPSX/370 (Version 2), SCICONIC/VM and Release 2 of OSL appear to have the most extensive and sophisticated branch and bound facilities.

10. Conclusion

Mathematical programming systems have been under development over most of the history of the electronic computer. They have come to embody many facets of computer science; mathematically, algorithmically and in data management. They remain an exciting field to work in, and we expect them to continue to develop as new mathematical, software and hardware tools continue to be developed, as they most certainly will.

References

Baker, T., D. Biddle (1986). A hierarchical/relational approach to modeling, Presented at the 22nd ORSA/TIMS Joint National Meeting, Miami, FL.

Bartels, R.H., G.H. Golub (1969). The simplex method of linear programming using the LU decomposition. *Comm. ACM* 12, 266–268.

Bausch, D.O., G.G. Brown (1988). A PC environment for large-scale programming. *OR/MS Today* 15 (3), 20–25.

Beale, E.M.L. (1968). *Mathematical Programming in Practice*, Wiley, New York, and Pitman, London.

Beale, E.M.L. (1970). Advanced algorithmic features for general mathematical programming systems, in: J. Abadie (ed.), *Integer and Nonlinear Programming*, North-Holland, Amsterdam, pp. 119–137.

Beale, E.M.L. (1974). A conjugate-gradient method of approximation programming, in: R.W. Cottle, J. Krarup (eds.), *Optimization Methods for Resource Allocation*, English Universities Press, London, pp. 261–277.

Beale, E.M.L. (1979) Branch and bound methods for mathematical programming systems. *Ann. Discrete Math.* 5, 201–219.

Beale, E.M.L. (1985a). The evolution of mathematical programming systems. *J. Oper. Res. Soc.* 36, 357–366.

Beale, E.M.L. (1985b). Integer programming, in: K. Schittkowski (ed.), *Computational Mathematical Programming*, NATO ASI Series F: Computer and System Sciences, Vol. 15, Springer, Berlin, pp. 1–24.

Beale, E.M.L., J.J.H. Forrest (1976). Global optimization using special ordered sets. *Math. Programming* 10, 52–69.

Beale, E.M.L., J.A. Tomlin (1970). Special facilities in a general mathematical programming system for non-convex problems using ordered sets of variables, in: J. Lawrence (ed.), *Proceedings of the Fifth International Conference on Operational Research*, Tavistock, London, pp. 447–454.

Benichou, M., J.M. Gauthier, G. Hentges, G. Ribière (1977). The efficient solution of large-scale linear programming problems – some algorithmic techniques and computational results. *Math. Programming* 13, 280–322.

Bisschop, J., A. Meeraus (1982). On the development of a General Algebraic Modeling System in a strategic planning environment. *Math. Prob. Study* 20, 1–29.

Bradley, G.H., G.G. Brown, G.W. Graves (1977). Design and implementation of large-scale primal transshipment algorithms, *Manage. Sci.* 24, 1–34.

Bradley, G.H., G.G. Brown, G.W. Graves (1983). Structural redundancy in linear programs, in: M. Karwan et al. (eds.), *Redundancy in Mathematical Programming*, Springer, New York, pp. 145–169.

Brooke, A., D. Kendrick, A. Meeraus (1988). *GAMS: A Users Guide*, The Scientific Press, Redwood City, CA.

Brown, G.G., G.W. Graves, M.D. Honczarenko (1987). Design and operation of a multicommodity production/distribution system using primal goal decomposition. *Manage. Sci.* 33, 1469–1480.

Brown, G.G., R.D. McBride (1984). Solving generalized networks. *Manage. Sci.* 30, 1497–1523.

Cheng, Y., D. Houck, J. Liu, M. Meketon, L. Slutsman, R. Vanderbei, P. Wang (1989). The AT&T Korbx system. *AT&T Tech. J.* 68, 7–19.

Codd, E., (1970). A relational model of data for large scale data banks. *Comm. ACM* 13, 631–641.

CPLEX Optimization, Inc. (1990). Using the CPLEX linear optimizer, Version 1.2, Incline Village, NV.

Crowder, H., E.L. Johnson, M.W. Padberg (1983). Solving large-scale zero–one linear programming problems. *Oper. Res.* 31, 803–834.

Dantzig, G.B. (1963). *Linear Programming and Extensions*, Princeton University Press, Princeton, NJ.

Date, C. (1983). *An Introduction to Database Systems, Vol. I and II*, Addison-Wesley, Reading, MA.

Duff, I.S., A.M. Erisman, J.K. Reid (1986). *Direct Methods for Sparse Matrices*, Oxford University Press, London.

Forrest, J.J.H. (1991). Recognition and use of structure in a simplex code, Presented at the 31st ORSA/TIMS Joint National Meeting, Nashville, TN.

Forrest, J.J.H., J.P.H. Hirst, J.A. Tomlin (1974). Practical solution of large mixed integer programming problems with UMPIRE. *Manage. Sci.* 20, 736–773.

Forrest, J.J.H., J.A. Tomlin (1972). Updating triangular factors of the basis to maintain sparsity in the product form simplex method. *Math. Programming* 2, 263–278.

Forrest, J.J.H., J.A. Tomlin (1990). Vector processing in simplex and interior methods for linear programming. *Ann. Oper. Res.* 22, 71–100.

Forrest, J.J.H., J.A. Tomlin (1992a). Implementing the simplex method for the optimization subroutine library. *IBM Systems Journal* 31(1), 11–25.

Forrest, J.J.H., J.A. Tomlin (1992b). Implementing interior point linear programming methods in the optimization subroutine library. *IBM Systems Journal* 31(1), 26–38.

George, J.A., J.W. Liu (1981). *Computer Solution of Large, Sparse Positive Definite Systems*, Prentice-Hall, Englewood Cliffs, NJ.

Gill, P.E., W. Murray, M.A. Saunders, J.A. Tomlin, M.H. Wright (1986). On projected Newton barrier methods for linear programming and an equivalence to Karmarkar's projective method. *Math. Programming* 36, 183–209.

Gill, P.E., W. Murray, M.A. Saunders, M.H. Wright (1989). A practical anti-cycling procedure for linearly constrained optimization. *Math. Programming* 45, 437–474.

Gill, P.E., W. Murray, M.H. Wright (1981). *Practical Optimization*, Academic Press, London and New York.

Greenberg, H.J. (1983). A functional description of ANALYZE: A computer-assisted analysis system for linear programming models. *ACM Trans. Math. Software* 9, 18–56.

Greenberg, H.J. (1987). The development of an intelligent mathematical programming system, presented at the Washington Operations Research/Management Science Chapter (WORMSC) Meeting November 4, 1987.

Griffith, R.E., R.A. Stewart (1961). A nonlinear programming technique for the optimization of continuous processing systems. *Manage. Sci.* 7, 379–392.

Harris, P.M.J. (1973). Pivot selection methods of the Devex LP code. *Math. Programming* 5, 1–28.

Hellerman, E., D.C. Rarick (1972). Reinversion with the partitioned preassigned pivot procedure, in: D.J. Rose, R.A. Willoughby (eds.), *Sparse Matrices and Their Applications*, Plenum Press, New York, pp. 67–76.

Ho, J.K. (1989). A compendium of recent computational results in linear programming, Technical Report, Management Science Program, University of Tennessee, Knoxville, TN.

Ho, J.K., S.K. Gnanendran (1989). Distributed decomposition of block-angular linear programs on a hyper-cube computer, Technical Report, Management Science Program, University of Tennessee, Knoxville, TN.

IBM Corp. (1988). MPSX/370 Version 2 Users Guide, Document number SH19-6552-0.

IBM Corp. (1991). Optimization Subroutine Library Guide and Reference, Release 2, Document number SC23-0519-2.

Karmarkar, N. (1984). A new polynomial-time algorithm for linear programming. *Combinatorica* 4, 373–395.

Ketron Management Science, Inc. (1987a). DATAFORM Users Manual, Arlington, VA.

Ketron Management Science, Inc. (1987b). MPSIII Users Manual, Arlington, VA.

Ketron Management Science, Inc. (1987c). WHIZARD Users Manual, Arlington, VA.

Kojima, M., S. Mizuno, A. Yoshise (1989). A primal–dual interior point algorithm for linear programming, in: N. Megiddo (ed.), *Progress in Mathematical Programming*, Springer, New York, pp. 131–158.

Llewellyn, J., R. Sharda (1990). Linear programming software for personal computers: 1990 survey. *OR/MS Today* 7, 17 (5), 35–46.

Lustig, I.J., R.E. Marsten, D.F. Shanno (1990). On implementing Mehrota's predictor–corrector interior point method for linear programming, Technical Report SOR 90-03, Department of Civil Engineering and Operations Research, Princeton University, Princeton, NJ. To appear in *SIAM J. Optim.*

Lustig, I.J., R.E. Marsten, D.F. Shanno (1991) Computational experience with a primal–dual interior point method for linear programming. *J. Linear Algebra Appl.* 152, 191–222.

Lustig, I.J., D.F. Shanno, J.W. Gregory (1989). The primal–dual interior point method on the Cray Supercomputer, Technical Report SOR 89-21, Princeton University, Princeton, NJ, Presented at the 28th ORSA/TIMS Joint National Meeting, New York.

Markowitz, H.M. (1957). The elimination form of the inverse and its application to linear programming. *Manage Sci.* 3, 255–269.

Markowitz, H.M., A. Malhotra, D.P. Pazel (1984). The EAS-E application development system: Principles and language summary. *Comm. ACM* 27, 785–799.

Marsten, R.E. (1981). The design of the XMP linear programming library. *ACM Trans. Math. Software* 7, 481–497.

MathPro, Inc. (1989). MathPro User Manual, Washington, DC.

Megiddo, N. (1989). Pathways to the optimal set in linear programming, in: N. Megiddo (ed.), *Progress in Mathematical Programming*, Springer, New York, pp. 131–158.

Megiddo, N. (1991). On finding primal- and dual-optimal bases. *ORSA J. Computing* 3, 63–65.

Mehrotra, S. (1990). On the implementation of a (primal–dual) interior point method, Technical Report 90-03, Department of Industrial Engineering and Management Sciences, Northwestern University, Evanston, IL. To appear in *SIAM J. Optim.*

Murtagh, B.A., M.A. Saunders (1987). *MINOS 5.1 User's Guide*, Report SOL 83-20R, Department of Operations Research, Stanford University, CA.

Mylander, W., (1985), *LPS-867 User's Guide*, Applied Automated Engineering Corporation, Pennington, NJ.

Orchard-Hays, Wm. (1968). *Advanced Linear Programming Computing Techniques*, McGraw-Hill, New York.

Orchard-Hays, Wm. (1978). History of mathematical programming systems, in: H.J. Greenberg, (ed.), *Design and Implementation of Optimization Software*, Sijthoff and Noordhoff, Alphen a/d Rijn, pp. 1–26.

Palmer, K. et al. (1984). *A Model Management Framework for Mathematical Programming*. Wiley, New York.

Reid, J.K. (1982). A sparsity exploiting variant of the Bartels–Golub decomposition for linear programming bases. *Math. Programming* 24, 55–69.

Saunders, M.A. (1976). A fast, stable implementation of the simplex method using Bartels–Golub updating, in: J. Bunch, D. Rose (eds.), *Sparse Matrix Computation*, Academic Press, New York, pp. 213–226.

Schrage, L. (1984). *Linear, Integer, and Quadratic Programming with LINDO, 2nd edition*, The Scientific Press, Palo Alto, CA.

Scicon, Ltd. (1986a). MGG users guide, Milton Keynes MK17 8LX, England.

Scicon, Ltd. (1986b). SCICONIC/VM users guide, Milton Keynes MK17 8LX, England.

Smith, D.M. (1968). *Linear Programming, Advanced Model Formulation*, Management Science Systems, Rockville, MD.

Tomlin, J.A. (1983). Large scale mathematical programming systems. *Comput. Chem. Eng.* 7, 575–582.

Tomlin, J.A. (1989). A note on comparing simplex and interior methods for linear programming. in: N. Megiddo (ed.), *Progress in Mathematical Programming*, Springer, New York, pp. 91–103.

Tomlin, J.A., J.S. Welch (1983). Formal optimization of some reduced linear programming problems. *Math. Programming* 27, 232–240.

Tomlin, J.A., J.S. Welch (1985). Integration of a primal simplex network algorithm with a large scale mathematical programming system. *ACM Trans. Math. Software* 11, 1–11.

Van Roy, T.J., L.A. Wolsey (1987). Solving mixed integer programming problems using automatic reformulation. *Oper. Res.* 35, 45–57.

Vanderbei, R.J., M.J. Meketon, B.A. Freedman (1986). A modification of Karmarkar's linear programming algorithm. *Algorithmica* 1, 395–409.

Welch, J.S. (1987a). PAM: A practitioner's approach to modeling. *Manage. Sci.* 33, 610–625.

Welch, J.S. (1987b). The data management needs of mathematical programming applications. *IMA J. Math. Management* 1, 237–250.

Williams, H.P. (1985). *Model Building in Mathematical Programming, 2nd edition*, Wiley, New York.

E.G. Coffman et al., Eds., *Handbooks in OR & MS, Vol. 3*

Chapter 12

User Interfaces

Chris V. Jones

Faculty of Business Administration, Simon Fraser University, Burnaby, BC V5A 1S6, Canada

1. Overview

The field of operations research (OR) has traditionally concentrated on normative techniques for optimizing, simulating, studying – in short – analyzing complex problems to provide better understanding. Yet the analysis techniques do not stand alone. Quite simply, data must be input and reports output and disseminated. The analysis techniques are packaged by a user interface. It is arguable that for many OR projects, the user interface has been primarily an afterthought – a necessary evil, but not given a great deal of attention. Yet different user interfaces for the same task produce significant, measurable differences in user performance [e.g., Card, Moran & Newell, 1980b]. If the techniques are designed to promote maximum understanding of the complexity of the underlying problem, the user interface should be as helpful and sophisticated as the underlying algorithm. Achieving such a helpful user interface is not easy. In this chapter, we present theories, guidelines and techniques to help design and build user interfaces for delivering OR applications.

But how exactly does a user interface contribute to the success or failure of the application of OR? Geoffrion [1976] suggested that the principal benefit of an OR project should be 'insight, not numbers'; to paraphrase, an OR project should contribute insight, not just models. Models are just that, models or approximations of the underlying system. They should not be trusted, at least initially. They must be probed, tested and verified. Model developers frequently have trouble understanding the behavior of their own models: is the strange behavior caused by a programming error? is it caused by an error in the input data? by an error in the model formulation? If model developers experience difficulty understanding the behavior of their own models, why should a manager be expected to accept the model? As Geoffrion [1987] stated, '...MS/OR practitioners and their work often are incomprehensible to non-specialists.'

We assert that understanding model behavior can depend less on the actual models than on how the models are packaged. Developing insight on model behavior is ultimately a process of discovery, of finding trends, surprising behaviors, and comparing the behavior of the model to what is expected or observed in the 'real' system. How well does it match? Where does it differ? Do those changes correspond to what is expected? If yes, why? If not, why not? In one sense developing insight involves recognizing patterns. How does the model respond to changes in parameters? What trends can be detected? How do the trends compare? Pattern recognition can be performed formally with detailed statistical analysis, of course, or on the back of an envelope. Yet pattern recognition is also within the province of packaging of the model, i.e., the user interface. Since the user interface presents the output of the model to the user/modeler/decision maker/manager, it is the primary window onto the actual behavior of the model. Obviously it should be as clear as possible; not so obvious, however, is what is meant by 'as clear as possible'.

Understanding model behavior is only a part of the story, however. The user interface not only presents the output of the model to the user, but also the medium through which the user creates the model. Creating a correct and complete model remains a daunting task. For example, creating a correct linear programming model using MPSX is quite difficult. Matrix generators and modeling languages, by providing a more convenient medium for expressing models, can greatly speed the effective time required to obtain useful results, even though they do not speed the actual execution of a linear programming algorithm in any way. Modeling languages and matrix generators simply provide a more productive interface between the modeler and the OR technique.

This discussion of the importance of user interfaces takes place against a background of increasingly sophisticated hardware and software such as computer graphics, speech generation, mice, light pens, multimedia, and windowing systems. These developments have made possible vastly better user interfaces than those that were possible using punched cards, or paper-fed terminals. As many authors have noted [Bodily, 1986; Vazsonyi, 1982; Papageorgiou, 1983; Wynne, 1984; Geoffrion, 1983], these technologies provide a promising vehicle for delivering OR techniques to a wider audience.

OR technology packaged in a well-designed user interface can be very successful. In a forestry application [Lemberski & Chi, 1984], which won the OR practice prize, a traditional dynamic programming algorithm was developed to determine optimal cutting patterns for logs. Although the dynamic program determined the 'optimal' cutting pattern, Lemberski and Chi stated: 'The challenge in implementing MS/OR is often not in developing a technically sound model and solution algorithm, but in generating credibility in the minds of potential users.' Although the computer was not brought into the forest (as of 1984), operators used the system to hone their decision making skills and to design a revised set of operational procedures for cutting logs. In this and other applications, the packaging of the OR technique proved to be one of the critical factors to the success of the project.

As further evidence of the importance of the user interface, users of interactive modeling and simulation systems that provide animation, when surveyed [Kirkpatrick & Bell, 1989], believe that a more sophisticated user interface improved the understanding of the system modeled, the model itself, statistical relationships, and the options available to solve the problem. Furthermore, the use of the better interfaces, in the opinion of the users, produced a different model and solution than would have been produced through more traditional techniques.

Another example shows that a properly designed user interface can provide better answers more quickly for some problems than the current state of the art algorithm. The work of Ming, Bird & Brodes [1989], Brooks, Ouh-Young, Batter & Kilpatrick [1990] studied the use of a three-dimensional, stereoscopic user interface that includes force feedback for 'molecular docking'. Molecular docking allows a chemist to explore how two molecules, e.g., an enzyme and a substrate, can bond. The problem can be formulated as a non-linear program, with the objective of minimizing potential energy. Employing the user interface, chemists can find 'favorable conformations in minutes . . . when all-day computations can't'. Although this result will certainly provide bait to the OR community to develop better algorithms, it also demonstrates the capability of a supportive user interface to help people solve problems.

Developing easy to use interfaces for OR problems (or any other problem) remains a daunting task. They remain difficult to design, difficult to implement, and difficult to evaluate objectively. Yet, there are design guidelines and theories, implementation aids, and techniques for evaluation that have been developed. In this chapter, we survey the existing theories and technologies of user interfaces as they relate to the research and practice of OR.

We begin by providing a framework describing the lifecycle of an OR project, in order to put the chapter in appropriate context (Section 2). Next, in discussing the theory and design of user interfaces, we delve into cognitive psychology, since one half of the user interface is human (Section 3). That discussion will form the basis for techniques and systems for facilitating the implementation of user interfaces, including current hardware and software technology, concluding with user interface management systems, which are designed to speed the implementation of user interfaces (Sections 4–6). We then discuss disciplines more closely related to OR, including interactive optimization (Section 7), decision support systems (DSS) (Section 8), and modeling languages for mathematical programming (Section 9). Throughout, we relate each of these fields to the framework for OR projects presented in Section 2, identifying successful applications, potential pitfalls and research opportunities. We finally discuss further directions (Section 10).

2. Framework for OR projects

2.1. Introduction

It will prove useful in later sections to have established the following framework to describe the different stages that occur in an OR project. Similar frameworks have been presented by numerous authors including Churchman, Ackoff & Arnoff [1957], Simon [1960], Geoffrion [1987], Bonczek, Holsapple & Whinston [1981a]. We differ from those authors by emphasizing the user interface.

The framework is based on the concept of *representation*. An OR project involves many different representations, from informal problem statement, through formal model, data sets, algorithm output, until final presentation.

2.2. The framework

The tasks that occur in an OR project can be organized in the following, more or less chronological, fashion:

Problem identification. Develop a basic understanding of the interrelationships, goals and decisions to be made in the underlying problem.

Model development. Develop a formal (mathematical) representation of the interrelationships in the underlying problem.

Instance specification. Develop datasets that represent examples of the model developed in the previous step.

Algorithm development. Develop an algorithm, which may involve many interacting algorithms, that is able to optimize, simulate, or otherwise analyze the model instances created in the previous step.

Algorithm invocation. Run the algorithm on the model instances.

Analyze output of algorithm. Determine if the output of the algorithm makes sense.

Present summary to decision maker. The raw output of the algorithm is rarely suitable for formal presentations to management. Multiple runs of the algorithm must be distilled into key results of the analysis.

2.3. Discussion of the framework

2.3.1. Problem identification

When the project starts, the practitioner strives to create an order description of what is initially a distinctly disordered environment. The initial representation created may simply be only a mental model, or perhaps a formal, textual description of the critical issues involved in the problem at hand. The practitioner must attempt to focus on just those ideas that are of critical importance, ignoring extraneous detail, reconciling contradictory information, developing preliminary structures, and identifying areas where more information is required. At least some of the work in decision support systems (DSS), Section 8, addresses this phase of a project; they concentrate on unstructured problems, helping users to identify the critical factors involved in the problem at hand. Frequently, DSS make no use of traditional OR technologies, merely providing a reporting and summarizing capability. As will be seen, DSS also encompasses many of the other functions in the framework.

2.3.2. Model development

In the model development phase, the initial representation of the underlying problem, which most likely is insufficiently precise for OR methodologies to be immediately applicable, is coaxed into a more precise formulation of the problem. The formulation may comprise previously developed models or could be an entirely new model. If the problem might be solved by an optimization technique, such a formulation could be expressed in standard algebraic syntax. The development of a model is the province of modeling languages, which are discussed in Section 9.

2.3.3. Instance specification

We make an explicit distinction between the general description of a model and a particular model instance. A model describes the interrelationships found in a broad class of problems. An instance of a model describes the interrelationships found in one particular problem from the broad class. For example, one form of the knapsack problem has the objective of choosing a subset of given packages of known size to exactly fill a knapsack. An instance of the knapsack problem would specify the exact size of the knapsack and the number and sizes of each package that might be chosen. The representations used for a model and a model instance are quite different. MPSX, e.g., represents only particular model instances, whereas, e.g., structured modeling [Geoffrion, 1987] represents models as well as model instances.

2.3.4. Algorithm development

Given a representation of a model of an underlying problem, developing an algorithm to analyze that model may be trivial. If the model relies on existing technology, e.g., if the model has continuous variables, linear constraints and a linear objective function, then an existing linear programming algorithm should be used. One of the major triumphs of OR has been the development of fast, robust algorithms for many different classes of problems. Most of the ongoing research in OR is directed towards developing fast algorithms for problems that remain difficult to solve. Other researchers are beginning to develop techniques to automatically develop algorithms given a particular problem representation [Lee, 1986; Liang, 1986; Liang & Jones, 1987; Bonczek, Holsapple & Whinston, 1981b; Blanning, 1985, 1986; Desrochers, Jones, Lenstra, Savelsbergh & Stougie, 1989; Desrochers, Lenstra & Savelsbergh, 1990].

2.3.5. Algorithm invocation

We have purposely separated algorithm development and operational use of the algorithm, even though they are frequently indistinguishable. However, if we develop a model independent of a solution technique, and include multiple interacting algorithms to analyze the model, then algorithm invocation can become non-trivial. For example, the production scheduling system MIMI [Chesapeake Decision Sciences, Inc. 1988] combines several heuristics, mathematical programming models, and computer simulation to scheduling factory production lines.

2.3.6. Analysis of output of algorithm

Once the algorithm is run, it produces output. For mathematical programming, output might include the current value of the objective function, a list of primal and dual values, and some simple sensitivity analysis. With the increasing availability of sophisticated OR techniques, understanding the behavior of the underlying system, detecting trends, debugging and validating the model become more challenging. The principal value of presentation graphics packages, which have become widely used (and often abused), is their ability to provide different (perhaps more insightful) representations of the same data. Some researchers have begun to develop new representations for the output of algorithms, in the hopes that they might give better insight, e.g., Jones [1988a,b, 1992]; Jackson, Muckstadt & Jones [1989]; Feiner & Beshers [1990]; Mackinlay, Robertson & Card [1991]. Insight gleaned by the user from the output of an algorithm is sometimes used to guide the algorithm in further analysis. This style of algorithm has been called interactive optimization, e.g., Godin [1978], Fisher [1986].

2.3.7. Presentation of summary results

The representation process comes full circle when a summary of the information gleaned from the model is presented to the decision maker. An OR project repeatedly refines the representation of the problem domain into progressively more structured problem domains, and finally, if successful, the information acquired throughout the process is presented in a format acceptable within the original problem domain.

2.3.8. Limitations of the framework

The framework, of course, greatly oversimplifies the process. The process is highly iterative, with much retreating to previous steps before finally completing. The iterative nature of the process makes it difficult in practice to separate clearly model development, algorithm development, instance specification, analysis of output, and presentation of results. Models are rarely developed without a particular class of algorithms in mind such as mathematical programming, simulation, or queueing networks. In other words, the description of the problem and the solution technique are tightly coupled (by the model developer, not necessarily by the actual problem). Furthermore, to develop algorithms, one must provide some mechanism for allowing instances of the model in question to be input to the prototype algorithm for testing purposes. The algorithm will certainly produce output, if only an error dump, which must be analyzed to understand and perhaps improve the algorithm.

The framework does not explicitly specify the time scale during which the project occurs. With the advent of easier to use OR tools, many projects which previously required a great deal of time can now be accomplished more quickly. In fact, that time scale might be as small as a few hours or minutes or as long as several years. The longer projects would tend to follow the steps listed in a more sequential fashion than those taking less than a day. Increasingly usable tools allow the shorter projects to follow a more evolutionary style of development, where prototype models are quickly built, tested, thrown away or revised.

Moreover, the framework might be viewed as placing the algorithm at the heart of the process. The user interface, in this view, is simply a necessary annoyance. Yet a well-designed user interface significantly changes the entire process. The analysis algorithm can become far less prominent, with more attention paid to the nature of the problem, its expected behavior, and how that behavior should be represented. The analysis algorithm, rather than becoming an end in itself, can become a helpful utility invoked to provide extra insight on the problem at hand. This emphasis on the user interface, although differing significantly from the traditional OR modeling perspective, is the view we adopt throughout this discussion. The idea of placing equal or greater weight on the user interface in comparison to the algorithm has been labelled *visual interactive modeling* (VIM) [Bell, 1985b; Hurrion, 1986], decision simulators [Lemberski & Chi, 1984], and interactive optimization [Fisher, 1986], among others.

In summary, throughout the problem solving process, whether or not the algorithm or the user interface is placed supreme, the computer must not only represent the output of an algorithm to a user, but the user must represent the statement of the problem and a particular instance of the problem to the computer; the computer and user are simply passing representations back and forth, each time hoping that the representation is understood. We seek in this chapter to convey user interface theories, techniques and technologies that can increase the probability that that hope is fulfilled.

We now turn to some general guidelines and theories of the user interface. We begin by discussing some of the limitations of human beings as processors of information.

3. Human information processing capabilities

The information processing capabilities of computers are reasonably well understood, at least when compared to the information processing capabilities of human beings. With computers, the underlying architecture is at least known, and much theory has been developed. With respect to human information processing capabilities, the underlying architecture remains less clearly understood, and the theories that do exist are only provable in the empirical sense. Yet there are nuggets of information about human information processing that are relevant to user interfaces. A general review of cognitive psychology can be obtained from texts such as Lindsay & Norman [1977], Bailey [1982] or Monsell [1981]. Both Allen [1982] and Card, Moran & Newell [1983] give a more thorough discussion of cognitive issues related to user interfaces than can be presented here. One can view the human information-processor [Card, Moran & Newell, 1983] as comprising three different systems:

The perceptual system. External stimuli are detected and transmitted to the cognitive and motor system for further processing or action.

The motor system. Physical actions are produced through the actions of muscles moving parts of the body.

The cognitive system. The perceptual stimuli, stored knowledge, and stored procedures for responding to the stimuli based on the knowledge are processed to produce appropriate actions, either extra stored knowledge or procedures, and physical actions (effected through the motor system).

Each one of these processing systems has particular limitations.

3.1. The perceptual system

Each component of the perceptual system, vision, hearing, taste, smell, and touch, has limitations and strengths. Each of these limitations has a direct effect on the user interface. We consider vision in more detail, since computer terminals and computer graphics are the most widely used output devices for user interfaces. We cannot go into great detail, but present representative results.

For example, the human retina has a certain minimum response time, that is, the time required for a spot on the retina to register a change in the light impinging on it. For human beings, this time is approximately 60–100 ms. This phenomenon, known as persistence of vision, underlies any moving image system such as film and television. To create the appearance of a moving image, the image must be changed at least once every 100 ms, which implies drawing at least 10 frames per second. Although a crude approximation, it does provide an accurate lower bound on commercial television refresh rates (25–30 frames per second) and motion picture refresh rates (24 frames per second).

To consider another example, Cleveland & McGill [1985] studied how well people compare different shapes and colors. They concluded that the human perceptual system compares lengths of vertical or horizontal lines better than it compares the sizes of angles. This result implies that the commonly used pie charts are less effectively used than bar charts. Tufte [1983], in fact, strongly recommends against using pie charts. Mackinlay [1986] used these guidelines to develop an expert system for recommending a particular presentation graphic.

3.2. The motor system

Arms, fingers and legs can move only with limited speed and limited accuracy. The minimum reaction time is approximately 30 ms (ranging to a high of 70 ms) [Card, Moran & Newell, 1983]. This would imply that the fastest typing speed would be approximately 1 keystroke every 140 ms, the down stroke and upstroke each taking 70 ms. This corresponds reasonably well with measured results with actual typists, that are in the range of 100 to 300 ms per keystroke, though there is great variability depending on the type of text being typed and the skill level of the typist.

Another limitation of motor skill has applications to the design of screen layouts. Fitt's law [Card, Moran & Newell, 1983] allows one to estimate the time in ms T required for one's hand to move a distance D to a target located at position of size S:

$$T = K \log_2(2D/S) \, ,$$

where K is a constant approximately in the range of 27 to 122 ms. Examining the equation, movement time increases only as the logarithm of the distance to be traveled, and decreases as the logarithm of the size of the target increases. Or alternatively, movement time depends only on the ratio of the distance to be moved and the size of the target. For example, Card, Moran & Newell [1983] give an example of the improvement in time possible if a gold 'shift' key on a calculator is moved closer to more commonly used keys on the calculator.

3.3. The cognitive system

Many authors organize human memory roughly into short and long-term memory. Using common terms from computer architecture, short-term memory can be thought of as a small set of registers that store readily accessible information. Long-term memory can be roughly thought of as main memory or secondary storage such as disks or tapes and stores much larger quantities of information than short-term memory. Long-term memory takes much longer to access ('to bring to consciousness') than short-term memory. Short-term memory, as proposed by some researchers, may in fact not be distinct from long-term memory, but may be simply a particular view of a piece of long-term memory [e.g., Moray, 1967].

3.3.1. Short-term memory

Much research has been devoted to refining models of the architecture of these memories. Miller [1956], in a classic paper, suggested that the size of short-term memory was seven plus or minus two items (e.g., registers), or chunks of information. Other authors have suggested somewhat smaller sizes for short-term memory, e.g., Simon [1974]. Although capacity in terms of the ill-defined chunk appears small, the concept of a chunk is variable. In other words, although the capacity of short-term memory is limited, the information contained in each chunk expands as people learn. This implies that as users become familiar with a system, they usually want to replace a sequence of commonly used commands or actions by a single command or action. To consider an example related to OR, Orlikowski & Dhar [1986] found that novice LP modelers created models out of chunks such as variables and constraints, whereas expert LP modelers used chunks consisting of standard archetypes.

3.3.2. Long-term memory

Much research has been devoted to the idea that as facts are assimilated, more complicated structures are assembled. These structures facilitate the creation of more detailed chunks, as discussed in the previous section. Yet, the more details stored in the memory, the greater the chance for interference effects. For example, since different computer programs provide different mechanisms for halting (e.g., 'end', 'quit', 'halt'), the more computer programs learned, the more confusion as to which command is appropriate in a particular circumstance. One conclusion to be drawn is that user interfaces should strive for consistency, which is one of the general guidelines for good user interfaces discussed in Section 4.1.

3.3.3. Virtual memory

Models of how humans store and retrieve information from memory are just one aspect of human cognitive processes. When confronted with a problem, humans use different strategies for attacking the problem. Many different models of problem solving have been proposed, as noted by Allen [1982], including those of Greeno [1973], and Thomas & Carroll [1979]. Perhaps the most widely known models are those of Simon [1960], and Newell & Simon [1972]. At a high level of abstraction, Simon and Newell identify three phases in problem solving: intelligence, design and choice. Those three phases can roughly be defined as follows:
Intelligence. What is the problem?
Design. How can we solve it?
Choice. What is the answer?
This framework has obvious parallels to the framework for an OR project presented earlier in Section 2. As will be seen in Section 4, Simon and Newell's model of problem solving parallels many of the models proposed to describe user interfaces.

In short, human beings have limited perceptual, motor and cognitive capabilities, that can have a direct bearing on the design of user interfaces. We now discuss some philosophies and theories of user interface design and implementation.

4. User interface theory, design and implementation

We break down our study into how to design a 'good' user interface, what 'good' means, and how to actually implement a good user interface. With respect to design, we explore further theories and empirical results from the literature on human factors, as well as classification schemes for different styles of user interfaces. Throughout the discussion we use examples based on Lotus 1-2-3 to demonstrate different aspects of user interface design. Lotus 1-2-3 has been recently extended to support multiple windows, e.g., using Microsoft Windows or the Apple Macintosh. We discuss the non-windowed version of Lotus 1-2-3. In discussing implementation (Sections 5 and 6), we discuss the generalizable characteristics of the hardware and software available.

4.1. Theories of user interface design

Many frameworks have been proposed to model the user interface [Norman, 1984; Card, Moran & Newell 1983; Foley and Van Dam 1984; Shneiderman, 1987]. Foley and Van Dam, and Shneiderman, apparently independently, proposed a four-level model:

The conceptual level. Represents the user's mental model of the interactive system, the current talks, and the underlying problem of interest.

The semantic level. Represents the capabilities provided by the interactive system that the user can invoke to accomplish the task at hand.

The syntactic level. Represents the specific sequence of actions the user must perform in order to accomplish the task.

The lexical level. Represents the physical form of the actions necessary to accomplish the task.

This four-level description arose from analogous concepts from computer language design. In particular, one can employ many different languages to write a program to accomplish the same concept, e.g., sorting. Each program would have different syntax, even though each program would sort its input. Furthermore, even individual statements with (essentially) the same syntax would have different semantics. For example, APL and Fortran would interpret the expression $2 + 4 * 3 + 5$ differently (though the proper syntax in APL for that expression is really $2 + 4 \times 3 + 5$). Finally, lower level syntactic details, e.g., the definition of the syntax of a real number, is considered at the lexical level.

This framework for viewing a user interface attempts to separate the look and feel of the interface (lexical issues and syntax) from the tasks it can perform (concept and semantics). For example, consider a user who needs to create a worksheet to help plan expenses for the coming year. The idea for the system would be at the conceptual level. Some of the semantic level functions that the user would need to include would be the ability to enter a new expense, and to prepare a balance sheet. The particular sequence of actions needed to enter the expense (e.g., move the cursor to the appropriate cell, and type the number) would be considered at the syntactic level. The specific keys pressed needed to enter the expense would be considered at the lexical level.

Buxton [1983] proposed a fifth level, the *pragmatic* level, which specifies the particular transducer, i.e., the physical input device such as a mouse or keyboard, used to convey the actual action to the computer. Different input devices, as will be discussed in Section 5.2, can provide vastly different user interface styles at the lexical level. Continuing the example using Lotus, one might use a mouse to point to the cell for the new expense rather than the keyboard.

In contrast to the framework of Shneiderman [1987], and Foley & Van Dam [1984], Norman's four-stage framework concentrates more explicitly on the cognitive processes that occurs as a user tries to perform an individual task. Norman [1984] proposed that users repeatedly engage in the following four actions:

Forming an intention. Deciding what is to be accomplished.

Selecting an action. Deciding how to accomplish the goal.

Executing the action. Performing the needed actions

Evaluating the outcome. Determining if the result corresponds to what was desired.

Norman's framework is similar to the framework for an OR project presented in Section 2. It also parallels Simon's three-stage model of decision making, except that Norman's model adds a step to evaluate the quality of the choice made. For the most part, though, Norman's model is operating at a much smaller time-scale than the framework outlined to describe the stages in an OR project. His framework deals with a single interaction with a computer program, which involves just a few seconds, whereas an OR project will require more time.

In still another model proposed by Card, Moran & Newell [1983], users are motivated by Goals to choose a set of Methods based upon Selection rules: each of the methods is comprised of subsequences of elementary Operations and subgoals (GOMS). The model is closely linked to the production system model of decision making of Newell & Simon [1972] and Newell [1973]. Their model, at first glance, also appears quite similar to those of the other authors. in particular, Norman. Unlike the others, however, Card, Moran & Newell [1983] show how their model can be applied to design problems.

These frameworks are useful because they help to identify many user interface design questions. For example, in Foley and Van Dam's, and Shneiderman's framework, the semantic level identifies the functionality that the system should provide. By successive refinement through the syntactic. lexical, and pragmatic levels, the user interface can be made more precise. Let us consider alternative user interface designs for saving the state of the system. At the syntactic level, instead of selecting the save command from a menu, the user might be required to type in an appropriate command. At the lexical level, the command might be 'SAVE ⟨filename⟩'. An alternative syntactic design would have the user move the mouse to an icon representing the current worksheet, drag the icon across the screen and place the icon on top of a special 'SAVE' icon. The sequence of mouse clicks, the shape of the special icon, would all be questions to be answered at the lexical level.

4.2. Evaluating the user interface

Although the frameworks discussed in the previous section help to frame appropriate questions, they seem less helpful in providing answers to the questions. To design better user interfaces, we need to explore recommended techniques, styles and useful empirical results concerned with the design of good user interfaces. We begin by discussing different measures of user interface quality.

4.2.1. Measures of user interface quality

Much research has been directed to developing methodologies to help build effective user interfaces. Before we explore these methodologies, we must consider what constitutes a 'successful user interface'. In other words, what does 'user-friendly' mean and how can we measure it? Some measurable characteristics of a user interface that help to determine its user-friendliness are [Shneiderman, 1987]:

- Time to learn
- Time to use, once learned
- Error frequency
- User satisfaction
- Retention over time.

Each of these qualities can be measured by conducting carefully designed experiments. Allen [1982] and Shneiderman [1987] discuss factors that complicate the design of a successful experiment to measure the quality of a user interface. Among these are bias due to the environment (e.g., if the lighting conditions are not ideal), and bias due to the experiment (e.g., if instructions given vary significantly among subjects). Controlled experimentation in a laboratory setting may, in some cases, yield inappropriate conclusions [Chapanis, 1967].

4.2.2. User differences

Complicating the application of these measures is the observation that the 'user-friendliness' of a user interface depends a great deal on difficult-to-measure qualities of the user or users and the task required of the user [e.g., Gade, Fields, Maisano, Marshall & Alderman, 1981]. Different users have different training, experience, biases and expectations. User interfaces hailed by one group of users may be condemned by a different group of users. For example, a user interface for airline reservations clerks that uses many abbreviations and special codes to maximize transaction speed would probably not be considered friendly by typical travellers using it to book a flight.

One key difference among users is the difference between expert and novice users. A system that is easy to learn many not be as easy to use once learned, and vice versa. For example, one might label as 'user-friendly' [e.g., Reisner, 1981; Card, Moran & Newell, 1983] systems that minimize the complexity of a user interface (as measured by the expected number of keystrokes, or by the expected time to complete the desired tasks). However, such systems can be difficult to learn; for example, to delete a line using *vi*, a text editor commonly found in Unix, one must type 'dd', which would probably not be initially obvious to a novice user. Furthermore, there is some evidence that for certain users and tasks the fastest possible interface is less desirable than slower interfaces [e.g., Miller, 1968]. The menu system of Lotus 1-2-3, e.g., facilitates both learning and expert use by displaying a traditional menu for novice users, and allowing experts to use quick keystrokes to invoke commands, essentially ignoring the menu.

4.2.3. Models for predicting user performance

Most user interface designs are not subjected to rigorous experimentation, although most authors strongly recommend thorough experimentation to help ensure the success of a user interface [e.g., Baecker & Buxton, 1988]. Most user interfaces are built using the intuition of the programmers, with some input from the intended users. An alternative to empirical testing or seat-of-the-pants development, only for user interfaces intended for expert users, relies on a detailed analysis of the syntax and semantics of the user interface design [Reisner, 1981; Card, Moran & Newell, 1980a,b, 1983; Kieras & Polson, 1985]. Card, Moran and Newell, e.g., proposed the keystroke level model for command oriented interfaces. Essentially, each keystroke required to accomplish a particular task is tallied; this tally then forms the basis for estimating the time required for this task. They showed that their model provided reasonable predictions for expert users, at least in the context of text-editing. Card, Moran & Newell [1980b] extended this model using their GOMS framework. The revised model captured in more detail the mental processes of the users while performing their tasks. The analysis was able to predict with a high degree of accuracy the speed of expert operators in performing text editing tasks. The GOMS model does not explicitly model user error rates, learning, satisfaction or retention, however.

4.3. Guidelines for user interfaces

Given that we have identified some measurable qualities of user interfaces, and discussed predictive models for user interface performance, we now turn to some broad guidelines that have been developed to point towards better user interfaces (see Shneiderman [1987], Helander [1988], Laurel [1990], and Marcus [1991] for more detailed guidelines).

Most sets of guidelines for designing user interfaces begin by emphasizing the importance of knowing and understanding the users and tasks for which the system is intended, which is a consequence of user differences discussed in the previous section. Understanding the users and tasks involved 'cannot be overemphasized', though sometimes it is not possible to identify fully the users or tasks for a particular system. For example, spreadsheets, though initially envisioned for simple financial and accounting applications, have found use in quite different domains. Shneiderman [1987] presents a scheme for categorizing users.

4.3.1. Specific guidelines

Many specific guidelines have been proposed for user interface design. There are guidelines for the design of ergonomic design of input and output devices [Banks, Gertman & Petersen, 1982; Banks, Gilmore, Blackman & Gertman, 1983; Engel & Granda 1975; Card, English & Burr, 1978], for displaying statistical data [Tufte, 1983, 1990], for choosing appropriate colors [Albers, 1975; Barker & Krebs, 1977; Lamberski, 1980; Marcus, 1986], for the design of menu selection systems [Liebelt, McDonald, Stone & Karat, 1982; McDonald, Stone & Liebelt, 1983; Shneiderman, 1987], for specifying error messages [Dwyer, 1981a,b; Shneiderman, 1987], for choosing text-based or graphical representations of data [DeSanctis, 1984; Jarvenpaa & Dickson, 1988], for selecting abbreviation schemes for commands [Ehrenreich & Porcu, 1982], for choosing interaction styles [Shneiderman, 1984, 1987; Gaines 1981; Bullinger & Faehnrich, 1984; Smith & Aucella, 1983; Norman, 1983; Hutchins, Hollan & Norman, 1986], for designing visual languages [Chang, 1990; Graf, 1990; Korphage, 1990; Chang, Ichikawa & Ligomenides, 1986; Fitter & Green, 1979], and for designing icons [Lodding, 1983]. Many of these guidelines are based on extensive experimentation and measurement. Assiduous use of the guidelines will not guarantee the success of a user interface, but, like the models of the user interface, they help to frame the design process.

4.3.2. General guidelines

Shneiderman [1987] proposed a list of general guidelines as good as any:

Strive for consistency. Command syntax, screen design should be as consistent as possible, so that users can legally apply the same rules when faced with new situations. Exceptions include commands that are difficult to reverse, such as deletion of many files.

Enable frequent users to use shortcuts. Expert users, whose principal goal is usually speed, require a different style of interface than novice users, whose principal goal is usually understanding. Shortcuts can be accomplished through the use of, e.g., special keys, and macros.

Offer informative feedback. Any action initiated by a user should have appropriate feedback. Even the simple action of typing in a value should have some form of immediate feedback, especially if the command invoked will require some processing. If a long mathematical programming algorithm will require a great deal of time, e.g., it may be useful to give periodic updates on the progress of the algorithm, e.g., displaying the current upper and lower bounds on the objective function.

Design dialogs to yield closure. User interactions should have a beginning, a middle and an end. In Lotus 1-2-3, in entering a value or formula into a cell, closure is achieved by hitting the return key. Feedback is then provided when the (computed) value is displayed in the cell. One can think of closure like a regeneration point in a discrete event simulation; the user has reached a state where most of the prior history can be put behind and the next transaction begun.

Offer simple error handling. In a perfect system, the user interface would be designed so that errors could simply not occur. For example, in a menu selection system, users cannot make as many errors in invoking commands as with a command language system. When errors do occur, users should be given informative feedback and allowed to correct the error with as little additional effort as necessary.

Permit easy reversal of actions. This might involve the use of an UNDO command, which can be difficult to implement in practice. For potentially catastrophic commands such as quitting the system without saving work, users should be asked to confirm the application of the command. If actions are always reversible, users become less worried about making catastrophic mistakes, anxiety decreases, and acceptance of the system increases.

Support internal locus of control. The user should feel that he or she is in control of the system – not vice versa. The system should not surprise the user with cryptic error messages, or unexpected actions. For example, in Lotus 1-2-3, when a user erases a value in a cell, X, that is referenced by some other cell, Y, perhaps a great distance away from X, upon recalculation, an error indicator ('ERR') will appear in cell Y, with the cause not particularly clear.

Reduce short-term memory load. Users have enough to worry about in using a system without having to remember a mass of details. Inconsistent command languages, cluttered displays, overlong menus all contribute to short-term memory overload.

4.4. User interface styles

As hardware and software capabilities have grown beyond the punched card era, many different user interface styles have been developed:

Question and answer. User responds to questions posed by the computer.

Command oriented. To invoke functionality, the user types in commands according to a particular syntax.

Menu driven. User selects from a displayed list of commands.

Forms oriented. User works enters data into pre-defined templates, i.e., forms.

Natural language. User communicates to computer in his or her native language, with the computer responding in the same native language.

Direct manipulation. User interacts by selecting and moving icons that represent semantically meaningful objects.

Hypertext. User interacts by navigating through a network of interconnected text.

Multi-media. Interface combines sound, moving image, graphics, and user input.

Group support. Interface supports multiple users.

Shneiderman [1987] and Hutchins, Hollan & Norman [1986] compare different interaction styles. Few realized systems rely exclusively on any one style. Since each of the styles has different strengths and weaknesses (in terms of the evaluation criteria of Section 4.2), it is often useful to combine styles, choosing the style appropriate for the task. For example, Lotus uses a forms style interface for entering values and formulas into the worksheet, and a menu driven interface to invoke commands to manipulate the worksheet. One common form of group support, teleconferencing, uses video to link together geographically dispersed individuals to conduct a meeting.

4.4.1. Question and answer style

Question and answer style user interfaces are perhaps the easiest to program; the computer program simply writes the question and reads in the response. The response, of course, should always be checked to see if it is valid, before the course of action prescribed by the response is carried out. Question and answer style interfaces are perhaps best suited for novice users, since they do not place great demands on short-term memory, though they currently assume users are comfortable using a keyboard. Expert users tend to find this style stifling, since expert users are able to specify the operation desired exactly.

4.4.2. Command style interfaces

In a command style interface, the most common of which are probably operating systems, the user specifies the action desired by typing in the appropriate command. This style of interface requires the user to remember the names and syntax of a long list of commands, which places a not insubstantial burden on user's short and long-term memory (e.g., 'I want to delete a line here, but what is the appropriate command and syntax?'), and is therefore better suited to expert users. Command languages, though, once learned, can be extremely efficient. Much work has been directed to developing guidelines for command language interfaces, e.g., Card, Moran & Newell [1980a, 1983]; Reisner [1981]; Ledgard, Whiteside, Singer & Seymour [1980].

4.4.3. Menu selection

In a menu selection style interface users need only choose from a displayed list of allowed commands. Menus can be presented in a variety of ways, e.g., pull-down, pop-up, or drop down. A pull-down menu, such as commonly found on the Apple Macintosh, appears when the user selects an item from a 'main' menu. A pop-up menu appears whenever a user presses a button on a mouse. They can be invoked from the keyboard, or by using a locator device such as a mouse or tablet. The advantage of menu selection over command languages is that users need only recognize the desired command, rather than recall the command name and its appropriate syntax. When there are many commands provided by a system, it is frequently necessary and desirable to organize the menus into a hierarchy, because of limited screen space and the limited short-term memory of users. Especially in hierarchically organized systems, menu selection is best suited to novice or intermittent users rather than to expert users who may find it cumbersome to trace the menu hierarchy.

4.4.4. Forms fill-in

A form style user interface displays a set of labels and fields into which the user can type values. Typical uses for a forms style interface are order entry, where the form displayed on screen is similar to a paper form that could be used to satisfy an order. In fact, Shneiderman [1983] views a forms style interface as a special kind of direct manipulation interface (Section 4.4.6) since the user frequently feels as if they are manipulating directly a computer implementation of a paper form. Spreadsheets are a prime example of a forms fill-in style interface.

4.4.5. Natural language, speech and sound recognition and generation

Natural language understanding. Natural language conversation is inherently appealing; the users of such a system would require little or no training, since they know how to communicate using their native language, if the computer understood the native language. More research has been conducted on computerized natural language understanding than has produced actual applications, though a few commercial natural language systems do exist (e.g., INTELLECT [Harris, 1983]). An ongoing debate has centered around the question of whether or not computers can ever understand 'natural' language [e.g., Winograd, 1980; Hill, 1983; Fitter & Green, 1979; Shneiderman, 1980; Harris, 1983]. For a thorough survey, see Grosz, Jones & Webber [1986] or White [1990].

In OR, a few applications have also been developed. Greenberg demonstrates the use of natural language output (but not input) for analyzing the structure of linear programming problems [Greenberg, 1987, 1988]. Blanning [1984] describes the advantages of a natural language interface to OR models, and some of the difficulties of using natural language style interfaces.

Most detractors of natural language find that computer-based languages can provide a more concise and precise dialogue than can natural languages. Currently, natural language is only practical using a limited vocabulary, limited syntactic constructs in a well-defined problem domain. One environment where these three conditions hold is database query languages, and most commercial applications of natural language are currently in this area. One might expect that limited vocabularies would occur in many modeling situations as well.

Researchers disagree, however, even on the meaning of a natural language discourse, though there have been many attempts to provide a definition [Winograd, 1980; Harris, 1983; Hill, 1983]. The underlying problem with providing a precise definition is that human languages, unlike computer languages, are filled with ambiguities, and assumed knowledge. For example, the statement:

I saw the tree in the forest

could mean that the tree is being cut down or that the speaker simply spied the tree. Much work in natural language understanding has gone to developing mechanisms to resolve such ambiguities and providing background knowledge to the computer about specific problem domains to assist in interpreting such sentences [Rich, 1984].

Speech recognition. The above discussion has not considered the tranducer used to translate human language into machine readable form. One transducer would be the keyboard – easy for the computer, not so easy for the user. Why can the computer not understand spoken language directly? Speech recognition systems are currently available that can understand vocabularies of up to a few thousand words spoken by a single individual. Most such systems further insist that the speaker insert small pauses between individual words. Systems that can understand different speakers have much more limited vocabularies. See Simpson, McCauley, Roland, Ruth & Williges [1985] or Bailey [1982] for a survey. As an example of the difficulty of speech recognition, if a lawyer dictated to a computer the following to be typed [Hill, 1983]: 'With regard to your heirship, . . .' she might be surprised by what is typed (i.e., 'With regard to your airship, . . .'). Several studies have also been conducted where specialized input devices such as mice or tablets are preferred to speech recognition. The results of the studies may have been dominated, though, by the generally low speed and small vocabularies of current speech recognition systems. [Shneiderman, 1987; Bullinger & Faehnrich, 1984]. In short, speech recognition has had limited application because of continuing technical limitations.

Speech and sound generation. Complementing speech recognition [Michaelis & Wiggins, 1982], which use speech and sounds as an input medium, speech and sound generation systems use speech and sound as an output medium. Speech generation cannot be said to be widely used, though it does have applications in particular areas. Generated speech is often useful in situations where a user's visual or motor systems are working at capacity and yet more information must be transmitted to the user. Speech generation is particularly useful in providing warnings, e.g., in a time-critical operation such as air traffic control or nuclear power plant operations.

Much of the literature on novel user interfaces and OR concentrates on exploiting human *visual* pattern recognition skills using graphical representations of models, problem instances, and outputs of analysis algorithms. Sound generation technology can exploit human *aural* pattern recognition skills using sonic representations of models, problem instances, and outputs of analysis algorithms. For example, Yeung [1980] used sonic cues to help identify chemical spectra. The spectrum of an unknown chemical is encoded as sound, and aurally compared to the spectra of known chemicals, and with high accuracy. Gaver [1989] discusses the addition of sounds to the Macintosh User Interface. Blattner, Sumikawa & Greenberg [1989] present design principles for 'earcons', analogous to icons, 'nonverbal audio messages used in the user-computer interface'. Applications of sound generation in an OR context are rate, however. The XCell manufacturing simulation language [Conway, Maxwell & Worona, 1986] allows the user to specify different sounds for different events (e.g., machine breakdowns) as the simulation is running. If the simulation runs for a great deal of time, and machine breakdowns are rare, this feature might prove useful in notifying the modeler that an interesting event has occurred (the modeler can interrupt the simulation at this point, examine the current state, and continue). If the events occur with relative frequency the sonic cues produce a cacophony of questionable value. Gaver, Smith & O'Shea [1991] explore the use of more sophisticated sounds in a simulation of a bottling plant. The simulation required input from two 'operators', who were located in separate rooms, but who could see one another via video monitors. As the simulation ran, bottling machines made 'clanking' sounds, the heater made a 'whooshing' sound and the rhythm of the sounds reflected the speed of the machine. Sounds were apparently added primarily to indicate problems, e.g., when inventory was full, a 'splashing' sound was heard, apparently reflecting the liquid overflowing onto the floor. The authors claim that their use of sounds aided the operators in diagnosing problems in the simulated system.

4.4.6. Direct manipulation

Introduction. With the increasing availability of computer graphics hardware and input devices beyond traditional keyboards, such as mice, lightpens, and tablets, a new style of user interface has emerged that Shneiderman [1983] dubbed 'direct manipulation'. Direct manipulation systems have actually existed since at least the early sixties [e.g., Sutherland, 1963], though they have not been labeled as such. In a direct manipulation user interface [Hutchins, Hollan & Norman, 1986], instead of typing commands to produce actions, using an appropriate input device, the user directly manipulates an appropriate representation of the object of interest. In essence, direct manipulation interfaces bypass the syntactic level of user interfaces. Without an obvious intervening syntax, syntax errors are avoided and the user interface can become so natural as to become transparent. Many authors, e.g., Shneiderman [1983, 1987], claim that direct manipulation interfaces provide significantly more satisfactory user interfaces than other styles, though Hutchins, Hollan & Norman [1986] note that direct manipulation interfaces are not suitable for all applications. For example, they claim that direct manipulation interfaces are unlikely to replace the text-based programming language paradigm.

Direct manipulation interfaces generally require more sophisticated hardware and programming techniques than are required for command languages, menu selection, question and answer, or forms styles of user interaction. Hardware and software to support the development of direct manipulation interfaces are described in Sections 5 and 6. Commonly available examples of direct manipulation interfaces include:

• word processors where users type over and insert into a full screen of text, rather that typing commands to effect changes in the text;

• spreadsheets, where users can directly change values and formulas in cells, and see the resulting calculations;

• Apple Macintosh [Apple Computer, 1985] and similar systems, such as the Xerox Star [Smith, Irby, Kimball, Verplank & Harslem, 1983], Microsoft Windows [Petzold, 1988] and similar interfaces, where users can manipulate icons to copy files and directories, rather than typing commands;

• CAD/CAM systems where users can draw in physical representations of parts, cutting paths, finite element meshes.

In addition to these widely known examples, several other styles of systems that can properly be classified as direct manipulation have been developed including programming by example, hypertext and gestural interfaces.

Programming by example. One class of direct manipulation interfaces has been termed by some authors programming by example (see Myers [1986, 1988] for a survey). It has been primarily directed towards computer programming applications [e.g., Shu, 1988; Gould & Finzer, 1984] or database applications [Zloof, 1977, 1982, 1983] (though Myers [1988] actually believes that Zloof's query by example is actually not an example of programming by example). In this style of interface, users describe an example of what they want (e.g., programs, data) and the system attempts to create general rules based on those examples. In query by example [Zloof, 1977], instead of typing an SQL query [Date, 1984], the system presents a forms style template of the relations currently in the database; the user can then type expressions in any of the domains of each relation to select the records satisfying the expressions. For example, in a database listing names and addresses, if one wished to see the records for people with last name 'JONES', one would simply type JONES in the Last Name field for the appropriate relation. Programming by example has also been used in user interface management systems (Section 6.2), e.g., PERIDOT [Myers & Buxton, 1986; Myers, 1988].

Angehrn [1991] and Angehrn & Lüthi [1990] applied these ideas to OR modeling, calling the idea, modeling by example. In their implementation of the idea, Tolomeo, users can draw a picture illustrating the problem at hand, e.g., facility location on a network, and further suggest a solution, e.g., an initial location of facilities. Based on this input, and relying on expert system rules, the system deduces the type of problem entered, selects a corresponding algorithm to execute, executes the algorithm, and displays the new solution.

Gestural interfaces. A fast emerging technology known as *pen-based computing* replaces the keyboard with an electronic pen. Electronic pens, such as lightpens and digitizing tablets have been available for quite some time. The key to pen-based computing is its handwriting recognition capabilities. Rather than requiring users to type well in order to communicate with a computer, in pen-based computing users need only know how to write. In current educational systems, students spend far more time learning handwriting than typing, so the class of users who can write with a pencil is far larger than the class of users who have a comparable typing proficiency. Each one of the letter forms drawn by the user can be thought of as a *gesture* indicating an action to be taken, hence the term *gestural interfaces.*

One need not use a pen-based system merely to recognize gestures that approximate roman or some other letter forms. Rather, one could use pen-based computing to allow users to make new gestures. Those gestures can then be interpreted by the computer as commands. For example, in a simple drawing example, Buxton [1982] uses a gesture consisting of a left and downward movement of the pen to stand for the command, 'add a circle'. The user need only perform this gesture and the circle is added. Using a typical current drawing program, the user must first select the desired operation from a menu, which could involve a large amount of hand movement, and then position the pointer to the desired location to add the circle. In the gestural interface of Buxton [1982], selection of the command and its execution occur simultaneously.

Direct manipulation and OR. Systems that use direction manipulation within an OR context have been developed in many areas, including production planning and scheduling [Garman, 1970; Jones & Maxwell, 1986; Jackson, Muckstadt & Jones, 1989], vehicle routing [Fisher, Greenfield & Jaikumar, 1982; Babin, Florian, James-Lefebvre & Speiss, 1983; Jarvis, 1983; Mitchell, 1985], facilities location [Brady, Rosenthal & Young, 1984; Bhatanger, 1983], computer simulation (AUTOSIM [AutoSimulations, Inc.], CINEMA [Pegden, Miles & Diaz, 1985; Systems Modeling Corporation, 1988], SEE-WHY [Fiddy, Bright & Hurrion, 1981], TESS [Standridge, 1985], XCELL [Conway, Maxwell & Worona, 1986], IMMS [Engelke, Grotrian, Scheuing, Schmackpfeffer, Schwarz, Solf & Tomann, 1985], Genetik [Insight International, 1988], Witness [ISTEL, 1988]), and queueing networks [Snowdon & Ammons, 1988]. Further discussion of direct manipulation systems can be found in Section 7.

4.4.7. Hypertext

Hypertext (see Conklin [1987] for a survey) attempts to exploit the capabilities of direct manipulation interfaces to create what is claimed to be a new style of presentation of text and other media. Most books and articles present information as a linear sequence of characters arranged hierarchically into words, sentences, paragraphs, sections and chapters. Footnotes, references, tables of contents, and indices allow the content of documents to be accessed in a non-linear fashion, but such devices are limited by the time needed to scan through a book. Hypertext provides quick transitions from one part of a document to any related, but 'geographically' distant, part of a document. For example, while reading a document that cites another article, simply by pressing a key, the cited article could be displayed. References (and other information) from that article could then be displayed, and so on. In fact, an issue of Communications of the ACM that surveys hypertext is available *as* hypertext [Association for Computing Machinery, 1988a]. In essence, hypertext organizes information as a network connecting multiple, interrelated documents and their contents (which need not be only textual) and allows users to traverse the links among the documents quickly.

A hypothetical example of reading a hypertext document about OR might discuss a linear programming model with the model presented in a figure; the user could then point to the model in order to see the optimal values of the decision variables; or the user could point to a value in the model to determine how that value was calculated as input to the model. Bruntz, Clohessy & Daniels [1987] provide such a capability in a prototype system. A limited capability is provided by the cross-reference listings in some traditional mathematical programming languages, e.g., GAMS [Brooke, Kendrick & Meeraus, 1988], structured modeling [Geoffrion, 1987]. However, the listings are static; no facilities are provided to aid the user in navigation through the network described by the cross-reference listing. Kimbrough, Bhargava & Bieber [1988], and Kimbrough, Pritchett, Bieber & Bhargava [1990a,b] explore the use of a hypertext interface for mathematical modeling.

4.4.8. Multimedia

In the 1980s, the most sophisticated human-computer user interfaces made a great deal of use of computer graphics technologies, be they three-dimensional displays, multiple windows, or gestural input using mice and other devices. Such technology, however, does not make use of the full range of human sensation of expression. Multimedia attempts to use other media, particularly sound and moving images (e.g., from film and video), as an integral part of the user interface (see Narasimhalu & Christodoulakis [1991] for a survey). Moreover, most authors now refer not to hypertext, but to *hypermedia*, i.e., the inking of information represented in multiple media.

Multimedia can be seen as part of several trends, with the audio compact disk (CD) perhaps the first artifact of these trends. One of these trends is the movement away from analog to digital representation. Another trend is the integration of computers, communications and home-entertainment systems, i.e., audio and video. That technology, originally developed for home-entertainment audio has been adopted for use by computers. Compact disk read-only memory (CD-ROM), a variation on audio CDs, allows a compact disk to store over 600 MB of digital data and has a manufactured cost of under a dollar [Fox, 1991b]. Moreover, compact disks are being extended to allow the integration of both text, images, as well as sound. Several proposals have been made including compact disk interactive (CD-I), and CD-ROM XA (extended architecture) differing primarily in the quality of sound that they produce.

Compression. The principal current challenge to multimedia involves the huge amount of data needed to store sound and images. A single, uncompressed digital image displayed at 1000 by 1000 resolution, 24 bits per pixel requires 3 megabytes of storage. Full-motion animation requires thirty frames per second, or 90 megabytes per second of animation. One minute of CD quality sound requires 10 megabytes of storage. Such data requirements can easily consume the capacity of most current-day secondary storage media and communications systems.

Some form of compression/decompression scheme is clearly required (see Fox [1991a,b] for a survey). Data compression schemes such as Huffman encoding, run-length encoding, and Lempel–Ziv are currently used to reduce the storage required for standard computer files. Compression schemes specifically tailored to the needs of audio and video are an area of active investigation. Key characteristics of encoding schemes include:

Quality. Some compression schemes are tailored specifically for high quality images and sound, others for lower quality images and sound.

Bandwidth. Bandwidth refers to the rate of data transmission. Some compression schemes are tailored exclusively for low bandwidth transmission media, e.g., 64 Kbit/s, some for medium bandwidth transmission media, e.g., 1.5 Mbit/s, and some for very high bandwidth transmission capability, e.g., 10 Mbit/s and higher.

Scalability. Some compression schemes allow for varying bandwidths (with a corresponding change in quality), others are custom designed for particular bandwidths.

Symmetry. Some encoding schemes are more efficient than their corresponding decoding schemes and vice versa. If a source material need only be encoded once, e.g., a commercial file, then an encoding scheme biased towards speed of decoding would be preferable.

Single/multiple. Some schemes are tailored for single images, others for multiple images.

Synchronization. Some standards explicitly address the need to synchronize sound and image; others ignore this issue.

Loss. Many of the proposed compression schemes for audio and video involve some form of loss, in that the decompressed signal is not identical to the original. Such compression schemes can be acceptable because of some of the limitations of the human perceptual system.

Temporality. Some compression schemes have seen principal application in the compression of a single image, others compress multiple images, in order to facilitate full-motion imagery better.

Many more subtle characteristics of compression/decompression schemes have been identified [see, e.g., Lippman, 1991].

To give an example, a commonly used compression scheme, the *discrete cosine transformation* (see Rao & Yip [1990] for a survey), a variation on the Fourier transform, transforms the input image from the spatial domain into the frequency domain. Since the human vision system perceives low frequencies better than high frequencies, the higher frequency images can be less accurately stored, thereby saving storage space, with some loss. A different encoding scheme proposed by Intel, *digital video interactive* (DVI) (in greatly simplified form), breaks down an image into a sequence of primitives, e.g., a square in the upper left corner, a triangle in the lower left, and merely sends the codes for the primitives. Since the codes for the primitives require much less space than the actual image, a savings can result. Current research attempts to extract even more information about the underlying constructs that constitute a scene. Such *model-based* encoding schemes are more similar to a computer graphics rendering program than a traditional coder [Lippman, 1991]. They generally require specific knowledge about the particular image being encoded, trading more restricted application for greatly increased efficiency.

Standards. Several standards have been proposed for multimedia, both by commercial firms, and international standards setting bodies. The Joint Photographic Experts Group (JPEG) has proposed a standard for single image video [Wallace, 1991]. Based on the discrete cosine transformation, it attempts to provide a variety of different styles of compression, from lossy to lossless modes, to varying levels of scalability. The Moving Picture Experts Group (MPEG) has proposed a standard for compression of video signals [Le Gall, 1991]. Although one could merely use a standard such as JPEG for each individual frame, additional compression can occur by exploiting the similarities among adjacent frames. One challenge faced by the MPEG designers is the ability to provide features similar to those found in a video cassette recorder (VCR) while still supporting compressed video. The MPEG standard has been optimized to work with bandwidths of 1.5 Mbit/s. MPEG has also proposed standards for audio. Another standard, the H.261 or $p * 64$ kbit standard [Liou, 1991], promoted by the International Telegraph and Telephone Consultative Committee (CCITT, abbreviated from the French), arose out of the Integrated Services Digital Network (ISDN) communications standard developed by the telephone industry. ISDN allows communication across one or more 64 kbit/s communications channels, hence the name $p * 64$ (where p is an integer). Given the much more severe restrictions allowed for by $p * 64$ kbit standard, the resulting images can be of poorer quality than those produced using MPEG. The original goal of the $p * 64$ kbit standard was to support visual telephony, since telephone lines generally have low bandwidths. Emerging standards are attempting to integrate more tightly sound, video, and computer data into hypertext and hypermedia environments. Such standards include the Multimedia and Hypermedia Information Coding Expert Group (MHEG) [see Fox, 1991b] and HyTime [Newcomb, Kipp & Newcomb, 1991].

Applications of multimedia. Multimedia systems are becoming more widespread with the advent of hypertext systems such as Hypercard (Apple Computer) and Supercard (Silicon Beach Software). These systems provide built-in capabilities to display compressed video and animation, as well as to play sounds. One can link Hypercard and Supercard to a compact disk read-only memory (CD-ROM) to display video and hear sounds.

Lotus Development's new spreadsheet, Improv [Lotus Development, 1991], provides an example of an application of multimedia to OR. Improv, which currently is only available on a NeXt computer, allows user to annotate any spreadsheet with speech or sound. The spreadsheet can be transmitted via electronic mail to another NeXt computer, and the user of that system can then listen to the speech. Wang Laboratories [1990] developed a similar capability in their Freestyle operating environment. Mathematica [Wolfram, 1991], a system for performing symbolic manipulation of mathematical formulae, e.g., integration, now provides the capability to play mathematical functions as sounds.

4.4.9. Group systems

Work is often not a solitary process. Rather, it can require collaboration among many different individuals, groups and organizations. Yet, until recently most of the work in user interfaces has assumed only a single user at a time. In recent years much attention has been devoted to the area that has come to be known as *computer-supported cooperative work* (CSCW) (see, e.g., Stefik, Bobrow, Foster, Lanning & Tatar [1987] for a survey). A variety of tools and techniques currently exist commercially or in the research community that fall under this moniker including electronic mail, electronic bulletin boards, tele-conferencing, and computer support for scheduling meetings [Beard, Palanlappan, Humm, Banks, Nair & Shan, 1990].

DeSanctis & Gallupe [1987] present a useful framework for classifying different forms of computer-supported cooperative work. The classify such work along two dimensions, the *dispersion* of members, i.e., whether or not they are in close physical proximity or are widely scattered, and the duration of the interaction, e.g., one-time only or ongoing. In other words, group work can be dispersed in either space or time or both. Other possible dimensions include the level of anonymity in the group, the relative amount of parallel communication (for example, some group systems use a 'chauffeur' to guide the group), the cohesiveness among the group members (e.g., friends, enemies or strangers), and the motivation level of the group, among others [Nunamaker, Dennis, Valacich, Vogel & George, 1991]. Different combinations of these dimensions can produce different forms of CSCW. For example, teleconferencing, wherein a meeting is conducted with people widely separated geographically through the use of a live video connection, involves a wide dispersion of individuals, and usually involves a one-time session. Electronic mail supports widely dispersed individuals, but on an ongoing basis.

We discuss here one development that illustrates the nature of group systems work – electronic meeting systems.

Electronic meeting systems. Managers perhaps spend most of their time attending meetings. Tools to increase the productivity of meetings, therefore, could have a high payoff. That is the goal of an electronic meeting system. A typical electronic meeting system, although no typical such system exists, provides each meeting participant with a single-user computer linked by a network, along with appropriate software tools. Many different researchers are exploring electronic meeting systems including Nunamaker, Dennis, Valacich, Vogel & George [1991], Elwart-Keys, Malonen, Morton, Kass & Scott [1990], DeSanctis & Gallupe [1987], and Stefik, Foster, Bobrow, Kahn, Lanning & Suchman [1988]. Gray & Olfman [1989], Pinsonnault & Kraemer [1989], and Dennis, George, Jessup, Nunamaker & Vogel [1989] survey such systems.

In the work of Nunamaker, Dennis, Valacich, Vogel & George [1991], e.g., meeting participants can draw upon the support of a variety of software tools. One such tool is an 'electronic brainstormer', which allows participants to enter their ideas about the topics at hand. Note that ideas can be entered simultaneously and anonymously, which helps prevent some common 'losses' that occur in groups, e.g., from forcing each participant to wait their turn or the reluctance on the part of some to participate. Other tools promote the organization of ideas, perhaps those developed using the electronic brainstorming tools. To further organize the topics, prioritize the ideas, and even help settle disagreements, in order to bring the closer group to consensus, voting tools based on a variety of techniques, include multi-criteria, multi-attribute decision making, are available. Other tools allow participants to frame the topics at hand using various recognized models and ideas, e.g., Michael Porter's value chain [Porter, 1980], among others.

Empirical studies of electronic meeting systems are only beginning to produce clear results. '... we know that electronic meeting systems and non-electronic meeting system groups *are* different, but cannot completely explain *why*' [Nunamaker, Dennis, Valacich, Vogel & George, 1991]. For example, although anonymity can encourage shy individuals to participate, it can also increase the level of critical comments, though whether or not this effect produces a more effective meeting remains undetermined [Nunamaker, Dennis, Valacich, Vogel & George, 1991]. It is generally believed, however, that the anonymity provided by electronic meeting systems allows for a more critical review of the topic at hand. Another result concerns group-size. Although, traditionally, researchers had concluded that small groups (3–5 participants) were optimal for non-electronic meetings, Nunamaker, Dennis, Valacich, Vogel & George [1991] conclude that for some forms of electronic meetings, much larger group sizes are optimal.

Research on electronic meeting systems is still in its infancy. Although the research to date shows promise, the relationship between the characteristics of a task and group and the appropriate electronic support has only been sketched, and is not well understood.

5. Hardware

In the past, the hardware available to provide a user interface consisted almost exclusively of punched cards and line printers. Today, punched cards are quite rare and line printers have been augmented by a wide variety of input and output devices, including paper-based line-at-a-time computer terminals, character-oriented video display terminals, forms-oriented character display terminals, computer graphics terminals, three-dimensional displays, mice, three-dimensional tablets, joysticks, tablets, thumbwheels, video disks, voice recognizers, voice synthesizers, and head-mounted displays. The list of available devices and their capabilities will continue to expand. This section surveys these technologies from the point of view of the constraints they impose on user interfaces. A detailed technical description is beyond the scope of this chapter, but some technical details will be necessary to understand many of the points. More thorough discussions can be found in Foley & Van Dam [1984], Foley, Van Dam, Feiner & Hughes [1990], and Newman & Sproull [1979].

5.1. Output devices

The devices typically used in a computer graphics system can be partitioned into those for display, and those for input. The display device consists of two parts, the physical display, and the display controller. The physical display usually consists of a raster scan cathode ray tube (CRT), or some kind of flat panel display such as a liquid crystal display (LCD), electroluminescent display, or plasma panel, among others. The display controller accepts commands from the host computer and translates them into a physical image. Much greater variety exists in input devices, including such devices as keyboards, mice, joysticks, light-pens, and digitizing tablets.

The principal issues concerned with the physical display concern size and weight, color capability, resolution, brightness, contrast, and power consumption. Many different technologies have been proposed, including (CRTs), LCDs, gas plasma panels, and electroluminescent displays. Each has found use for particular applications. For example, CRTs currently provide superior brightness and contrast but are bulky and require a great deal of power, whereas LCDs are flat and require much less power, but have much worse contrast, though that is improving.

Display controllers exhibit wide differences. Some display controllers almost always provide capabilities to draw a dot or character at a specified location, draw a line between two points, or support simple windowing capabilities. Since communication bandwidths between the host computer and the display controller are typically much less than the processing speed of the host computer, for fast three-dimensional graphics, most of the graphics processing power is offloaded from the host computer to the display controller. Such advanced display controllers provide capabilities to scale, rotate, and translate complicated, smooth shaded three-dimensional objects fast enough continuous motion.

Almost all display controllers contain memories that store the image, in some form, being displayed. The image is usually stored in a frame buffer, a large rectangular array of values, one for each dot or pixel on the screen

[Sproull, 1986]. One common operation provided by the display controller is the 'bit-block transfer' operation or BitBlt (pronounced BitBlit), which transfers large rectangular arrays of pixels between the frame buffer and the host computer's memory. The BitBlt can be used to support interaction styles that use multiple overlapping windows: before a new window overlays another window, a BitBlt can transfer that section to main memory [Thacker, McCreight, Lampson, Sproull & Boggs, 1982]. When the new window is removed, the BitBlt can quickly restore the underlying contents. The BitBlt and its variants also facilitate certain styles of animation. Moving an icon on the screen involves rapidly erasing and moving rectangles of bits from one position to another on the screen. One can also store a sequence of images, and use the BitBlt to rapidly display the images in succession, creating another form of animation. Both of these styles of animation are used not only in video games, but also in simulation animation software.

In addition, some display controllers store the image in a *display list*, as a sequence of primitive commands that can be used to create the image. To create the image, the display controller reads through the display list and makes appropriate changes in the frame buffer. Display lists are useful in overcoming the usually low-bandwidth communication channel connecting the host computer and the graphics display. To rotate a three-dimensional object at interactive rates, the host first sends to the display list the commands needed to display the object; the host need then only send (small) commands to rotate the object. Specialized hardware in the display controller can then create a rotated version of the object quickly enough to give the appearance of smooth motion. Jones [1988a,b], e.g., made extensive use of the display list and rotational capabilities of a graphics workstation to develop a three-dimensional extension of the widely used Gantt Chart. AutoSimulations' three-dimensional factory simulator (AutoSimulations, Inc.) also makes extensive use of sophisticated display list capabilities. How applicable such capabilities will be for interfaces to deliver OR technology remains an open question.

Some emerging computer systems, often called graphics supercomputers, link a high-performance graphics engine with a supercomputer [Diede, Hagenmaier, Miranker, Rubinstein & Worley, 1988; Apgar, Bersack & Mammen, 1988]. Through the use of either a high-speed data channel, or the ability to use computer memory as the frame buffer, they are able to minimize the effects of the communication bottleneck between computer and display. They are able to compute quickly both the application dependent data and display it in complex form.

Other emerging display controllers extend the two-dimensional 'pixel' metaphor into a three-dimensional grid of points, called 'voxels' [Sabella, 1988; Upson & Keeler, 1988; Drebin, Carpenter & Hanrahan, 1988; Kaufman & Bakalash, 1988]. A variety of techniques have been developed to convert a three-dimensional grid of voxels into a two-dimensional matrix of pixels suitable for display. Voxels are proving to be extremely useful in modeling volumetric data, e.g., to show a translucent image of the human body reconstructed from CAT scan data, and their use will surely increase as voxel-processors and accompanying software become more available. Their use in traditional OR applications remains an open question.

5.2. Input devices

The standard input device, the keyboard, takes very little advantage of the expressive power of human beings. In normal conversations, people gesture with their hands and raise their eyebrows and voices. Accelerating a car that is stopped at the top of a steep hill using a manual transmission, involves an intricate synchronization of legs and arms. People using a keyboard, in contrast, can only express themselves with tiny motions of their fingers. The menagerie of other input devices attempts to exploit a fuller range of human expressive power. Key among them are devices such a slightpens, mice, touchscreens, and digitizing tables that allow users to express themselves by drawing and pointing.

These increasingly common input devices have their drawbacks. They are not particularly useful for entering text or precise numbers. They can be partially replaced by using arrow or cursor control keys on the keyboard. Each has its own particular quirks: with light pens, e.g., the user's hand will obscure part of the screen; they also tend to return less accurate positions than tablets or mice [see, e.g., Card, Moran & Newell, 1983; Foley & Van Dam, 1984; Foley, Van Dam, Feiner & Hughes, 1990; Shneiderman, 1987; Buxton, 1983].

Although such input devices can make computers easier to use, they make it more difficult to write a computer program that uses them. This is more of a problem of software than of hardware, and is discussed in Section 6. The principal problem with sophisticated input devices involves synchronization. In an interface that uses a mouse, e.g., the user can click the mouse anywhere on the screen. The application program must be able to interpret that action correctly regardless of when or where it occurs. Most implementations rely on an event-driven approach very similar to that used in computer simulation. In an actual implementation, the application program activates the input device that are available, and then enters a major 'event processing' loop. When an event occurs, the event is dispatched to the appropriate event handler for processing.

Sometimes the event model of a user interface breaks down. For example, the application may need to perform some action while the user moves the mouse so as to drag icons continuously around the screen. The event style of interaction can certainly manage continuous motion: every small movement of the mouse generates a new event. However, tracking the mouse can also be accomplished simply by repeatedly sampling the position of the mouse outside of the event processing loop.

5.2.1. Framework for input devices
The menagerie of input devices inhibits transportability. Some systems rely on tablets, others on mice, and others only on a keyboard. Software trans-

portability requires some general model of input devices, independent of their physical manifestations. Many of the graphics standards, e.g., GKS [ISO, 1985a,b], PHIGS [CBEMA, 1985a,b,c], and CORE [ACM Siggraph, 1979], and many of the commercially available graphics software systems subscribe to a logical model of input devices, proposed with some slight variations by many different authors [Newman, 1968b; Foley, Wallace & Chan, 1984; Foley & Wallace, 1974; Wallace, 1976]. In Wallace's scheme, which many of the graphics standards have adopted in some form, input devices are grouped into the following six categories:

String. Accept a character string, typically typed at a keyboard.

Choice. Input from a finite list of choices, typically a set of function keys.

Locator. Choose a single location in two- or three-dimensional coordinates, typically using a mouse, tablet or lightpen.

Valuator. Choose a floating point number from a continuous range, typically using a dial or sliding potentiometer.

Pick. Select an object on the screen.

Stroke. Draw in a line or a free-hand line segment.

Buxton [1983] pointed out that the model overly isolates the physical input device from the underlying software. For example, the keyboard could be used as a locator device, where the user would be required to type in a pair of coordinates. Even though this type of locator differs significantly from what would be provided by a mouse, tablet or lightpen, in the standard model, they would be viewed as equivalent input devices. Buxton replaces the six-category model of Wallace with a two-axis model of input devices, which identifies nine basic categories of input devices. One of the axes is the number of dimensions the input device returns (e.g., a dial returns one value, a mouse two). The other axis is the property sensed by the device, e.g., position, motion and level of pressure. The category appears to provide a finer distinction among input devices, but no major software development environment has adopted it.

X Window, Microsoft Windows, and the Apple Macintosh provide a much simpler input mechanism. The application program is mainly informed when a mouse button is pressed, released, and when the mouse moves. No higher level interaction models are provided. The simplicity of this scheme allows for a wider variety of user-interaction styles than the previous model, but unfortunately requires more work from the programmer.

6. Software

6.1. Computer graphics standards

Because of the large investment required, an easy to use interactive system should not be tied to a particular computer, interaction device or operating system. Standardized software tools for user interface design promote such application portability. Portability comes at a price, however. Applications developed for computer graphics hardware with special capabilities, such as rotation and scaling of three-dimensional objects at interactive rates, cannot be expected to operate in the same fashion on much less sophisticated hardware. Standards will often allow the interactive system to run without crashing the computer, but the interaction provided may be unusable. When designing an interactive system, though using a graphics standard, one must always take into account the actual environment in which the system will operate.

Standards also tend to institutionalize technology that is rapidly being surpassed. Many of the graphics standards, e.g., GKS [ISO, 1985a,b], PHIGS [CBEMA, 1985a], CORE [ACM Siggraph, 1979], were developed before windowing systems became widespread. These standards usually either assume that they have complete control over the display surface, or that the size of the virtual display surface (a window) remains constant. Standardization efforts are meeting with success for windowing systems (e.g., X Window, Scheifler & Gettys [1987], OSF Motif, Open Software Foundation [1990]). One can expect that technology will move quickly enough to create capabilities and software paradigms that the standardized windowing system will not easily support, e.g., the current X Window standard does not support multimedia, though third-parties have developed multimedia extensions.

Concentrating for now on computer graphics standards, many such standards have been generated both through the marketplace and through international committees, each addressing particular niches (see Bono [1985] for a survey). In the late sixties, the input format required to drive the CalComp plotter because the de facto standard. With the introduction of the direct view storage tube by Tektronix, Tektronix's software package PLOT-10 became the de facto standard. Particular manufacturers typically provide proprietary graphics development tools, some of which conform to many of the standards developed by international committees.

In the late 1970s, the Special Interest Group on Computer Graphics of the ACM (SIGGRAPH) [ACM Siggraph, 1979), developed the first standard not tied to a particular manufacturer, the CORE graphics standard. CORE handles three-dimensional wire-frame objects, but in its original specification did not handle shaded objects well. The graphical kernal system (GKS) [ISO, 1985a], developed by ISO in the early 1980s, had as its goal to provide a graphics standard upon which all applications could be constructed. That goal was never realized as witnessed by the continuing proliferation of graphics standards, but GKS has met with some success. Its limitations include lack of support for three-dimensional objects (though a revised standard, GKS-3D [ISO, 1985b] will address this problem), and limited capability for continuous motion. The programmer's hierarchical interactive graphics standard (PHIGS) [CBEMA, 1985a] supports three-dimensional objects and provides capability for continuous motion; it typically assumes, however, a more powerful graphics display device than is assumed by GKS. It is possible to build PHIGS using GKS, in fact, the standards-making committees are working towards some form of compatibility among the two, but such an implementation would sacrifice the potential speed of PHIGS for compatibility with GKS. The computer graphics interface (CGI), previously known as the virtual device interface (VDI) [CBEMA, 1985c; Vecchiet, 1987], was initially envisioned as a set of lower level routines to support GKS, though can also be used directly by an application program. The computer graphics metafile [CBEMA, 1985b] establishes a standardized file format for interchanging pictures.

Current standardization efforts are emphasizing window-based user interfaces such as found on the Apple Macintosh and Microsoft Windows. The principle non-proprietary standard is the X Window system [Scheifler & Gettys, 1987], which grew out of the academic environment of MIT. MIT wanted to develop instructional software that could run on the menagerie of computer hardware and operating systems that they had. The X Window system has the following goals:

- *Support of a wide variety of operating systems and computers.*
- *Support of* client-server *computing.* Client-server computing allows processing to be divided among several processors connected in a network. In the case of X Window, the application program can run on a computer separate from the computer that runs the graphical interface. The graphical interface is called the *server*; the application program is called the *client*.
- *Independence from a particular look-and-feel.* X Window provides a means to build windowed interfaces, but does not specify how that interface will look and feel, e.g., the design of menus and buttons. Theoretically, one could use X Window to develop user interfaces that follow the style of Microsoft Windows or the Apple Macintosh.

Essentially all the major computer vendors support X Window. Moreover, it is possible to buy software that implements an X Window server for Microsoft Windows and the Apple Macintosh. This allows a PC compatible or an Apple Macintosh to serve as the front-end to an X Window application running on another processor.

Since X Window does not specify the look and feel of the user interface, it is up to others to develop such standards. At least two such standards have been proposed, OSF/Motif [Open Software Foundation, 1990; Hayes & Baran, 1989] and Open Look [Sun Microsystems, 1989]. OSF/Motif has been developed by the Open Software Foundation, which has among its sponsors IBM, DEC, and HP. Open Look has been developed by Sun and AT&T. Note that since both of these standards are based on X Window, a client application running OSF/Motif can theoretically use a server running Open Look (and vice versa).

6.2. User interface management systems (UIMS)

6.2.1. Motivation
Even if one designs a user interface that follows the human factors guidelines, implementing that user interface remains a challenge. Usually, the

most carefully developed user interface must be changed during the implementation process; it is often not possible to identify problems with the design until the interface is actually implemented. So developing a user interface is a highly iterative process, with prototypes created, critiqued and revised, with the user interface perhaps never considered entirely complete [Hewett, 1986].

Developing a sophisticated user interface is not simply a matter of 'getting the format statements correct' after the algorithm has been designed. The images on the screen must be carefully synchronized with the actions a user performs. In a multi-window environment, the user can 'click the mouse' anywhere on the screen, and the user interface must be able to correctly infer the intention of the user. Although desiring an easy-to-use user interface, most application programmers probably either are not trained, or do not want to invest the time to develop such a user interface. *User interface management systems* (UIMS) consist of tools, languages and programming environments to help facilitate the development (and revision) of sophisticated user interfaces.

Analogously to a data base management system (DBMS), which insulates the application from the details of how data is actually stored in the computer, a UIMS attempts to insulate applications from the details of the user interface. Although systems and tools that have since been identified as UIMS have been developed since the late 1960s, e.g., Newmark [1968b], the field has been organized only since 1982 with Kasik's paper [Kasik, 1982] coining the term. Two successive conference proceedings survey research in UIMS [Pfaff, 1985; Olsen, Kasik, Rhyne & Thomas, 1987]. The insulation between a user interface and application program provided by a UIMS is not without cost. From the point of view of the application program, the UIMS somehow displays information to the user, obtains input from the user and then revises the display. To promote such insulation, the application cannot control all possible nuances of how the information is displayed, or how input is obtained. The application programmer will be limited by the default control and display rules provided by the UIMS.

6.2.2. Formal definition of UIMS

There is much debate among UIMS researchers about what constitutes a UIMS, with many different models that have been proposed [e.g., Green, 1983; Tanner & Buxton, 1985; Betts, Burlingame, Fischer, Foley, Green, Kasik, Kerr, Olsen & Thomas, 1987]. To some a UIMS can be simply a graphics package such as PHIGS [CBEMA, 1985a], GKS [ISO, 1985a], or CGI [CBEMA, 1985c]. Such graphics standards provide functionality on the order of 'Draw a set of points', 'Accept input from a string device'. A UIMS generally provides a higher level of functionality, containing already created user interaction techniques (potentiometers, dials, windows). To others, therefore, a set of higher level subroutines that provide features such as graphics, mouse input, and overlapping windows (e.g., the toolkit provided with the Apple Macintosh [Apple Computer, 1985]) constitutes a UIMS. Rosenthal & Yen [1983] called this type of UIMS an *internal control* UIMS, where the application remains in control at all times (Figure 1). Others argue that a UIMS must be supreme in the control hierarchy, invoking application routines only as necessary (Figure 2), which Rosenthal and Yen call an *external control* UIMS. The application is implemented as a modular set of functions that the UIMS invokes as needed. Finally, others argue that neither the UIMS nor the application program should be supreme, but that each should interact as equals. Tanner & Buxton [1985] called such a UIMS a *concurrent* UIMS. They show that concurrency facilitates features such as input devices that can be used simultaneously (e.g., turn a dial to change the size of an object while using the mouse to drag it), as well as multi-user user interfaces.

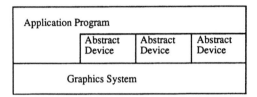

Fig. 1. Internal control UIMS.

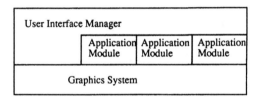

Fig. 2. External control UIMS.

Regardless of the point of view taken, a model of a UIMS developed by Tanner & Buxton [1985] helps identify many of the different components that can be found in a UIMS. In their model (Figure 3), the UIMS consists of two main components, a pre-processor, which provides an environment for developing the user interface, and a run-time component, which supports the finished system while actually in operation. At the heart of the preprocessor component is a 'glue' specification that combines the visual components of the user interface, e.g., icon definitions and screen layouts, with the interactive component of the user interface, e.g., pop-up menus, to produce a complete user interface. Users need not specify brand new icons or individual dialogue components for each new system, of course; they can be borrowed from a library of such tools.

6.2.3. Examples of user interface management systems

Many user interface management systems have been proposed, and many are commercially available. Research systems include SYNGRAPH [Olsen & Dempsey, 1983], the Alberta UIMS [Green, 1985], PERIDOT [Myers &

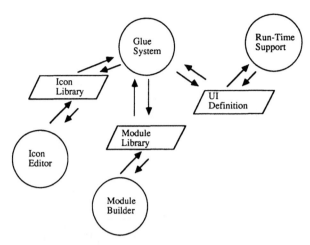

Fig. 3. Tanner & Buxton's [1985] framework for a typical UIMS.

Buxton, 1986; Myers, 1988], MenuLay [Buxton, Lamb, Sherman & Smith, 1983], Cousin [Hayes, Szekely & Lerner, 1985], MIKE [Olsen, 1986], Flair [Wong & Reid, 1982], and Garnet [Myers, Guise, Dannenberg, Vander Zanden, Kosbie, Pervin, Mickish & Marchal, 1990]. Commercial systems include Domain/Dialog [Apollo Computer, 1987], NextStep [Webster, 1989], Prototyper [Smethers–Barnes, 1989], and MacApp [Schmucker, 1986]. External control UIMS would include windowing toolkits such as Macintosh Toolkit [Apple Computer, 1985], Microsoft Windows [Petzold, 1988], Presentation Manager [Southerton, 1989], X Window tools [Scheifler & Gettys, 1987], and the toolkits provided with OSF Motif [Open Software Foundation, 1990; Hayes & Baran, 1989] and Open Look [Sun Microsystems, 1989]. Surveys of work in user interface management can be found in Myers [1989], Hix [1990], and Mannino & Rathnam [1991].

6.2.4. UIMS and simulation languages

Many of the UIMS languages, in concept, are quite similar to computer simulation languages. Event or object-oriented UIMS [Green, 1985; Hill, 1986; Flecchia & Bergeron, 1987; Schmucker, 1986; Webster, 1989] are quite similar to process-oriented simulation languages like Simula. The user specifies events that can occur. Then, for each event, the user specifies the response that should occur, which can involve the triggering of other events. Various transition network-based UIMS [Wasserman, 1985; Jacob, 1983; Newman, 1968a; Parnas, 1969; Kamran & Feldman, 1983; Schulert, Rogers & Hamilton, 1985] are quite similar to network based simulation languages, where control flows from node to node based on the outcome of events occurring at each node. For a user interface, however, the events are not generated by a random number generator, but by the user.

A third style of language for a UIMS does not have any similarity to a particular style of simulation language. It relies on context-free grammars, which have their origins in the linguistic work of Chomsky [1956]. Since grammars are used to describe human language, it would seem natural to use them to describe a user interface. In fact, context-free grammars are widely used to describe the syntax of traditional computer programming languages. A well-known tool in Unix, yet another compiler compiler (YACC) [Kernighan & Pike, 1984], is a good example of such a system. A grammar consists of a set of productions, rules that describe, usually recursively, how to construct complicated objects from simpler objects. As Green [1986] points out, how-ever, context-free grammars work well when used to specify the dialogue sequence in a user interface, but have difficulty altering the display in response, and also providing graceful error detection and recovery. Green provides a thorough comparison of the different language styles that have been used for UIMS, and advocates the use of the event model because of its superior expressive power.

6.2.5. UIMS for OR

The work on UIMS attempts to stay independent of the problem domain, so the topic of this chapter is an oxymoron. However, some systems have been developed that can be labeled UIMS for OR. Although targeted to OR models, they do not address just a single model, but large classes of models.

The SAGE system [Clemons & Greenfield, 1985] concentrates on presenting sensitivity analysis on the output of an analysis algorithm. Similar systems are surveyed in Foley & McMath [1986]. Holsapple, Park & Whinston [1989] proposed a general UIMS framework for problem solving. Jones [1985, 1990, 1991a,b,c; see also Jones & Krishnan, 1990] developed a prototype for building systems for particular classes of models that rely on attributed graphs for representing problem instances. Holsapple, Park & Whinston [1991] proposed the development of a multi-user UIMS based on 'picture grammers'. What distinguishes these examples from systems such as the animation systems that have been grafted onto simulation languages (Section 7.3), is that they are essentially independent of the particular analysis technique used, which is one of the principle tenets of UIMS work.

6.2.6. Other UIMS

ThingLab [Borning 1981; Maloney, Borning & Freeman-Benson, 1989] allows the user to manipulate pre-defined graphical objects to create more complicated objects. The principal construct in ThingLab is called a *constraint*, which is quite similar to the notion of a constraint in mathematical program-ming. In ThingLab, a constraint is simply a relationship between variables associated with particular objects. For example, a constraint defining the midpoint of a line segment would insist that the midpoint appear exactly halfway from both ends of the line. Leler [1988] and Freeman-Benson, Maloney & Borning [1989] survey alternative constraint-based programming languages. Using techniques similar to the automatic recalculation of values found in spreadsheets, as a line segment is lengthened or shortened, the midpoint will automatically move to adjust. Borning illustrates the power of ThingLab by demonstrating the theorem from geometry that states that the polygon formed by connecting the midpoints of adjacent sides of any quadrilateral is a parallelogram.

Recent work has begun to explore UIMS for multi-user systems [Hill, 1990; Patterson, Hill & Rohali, 1990; Holsapple, Park & Whinston, 1991]. Surprisingly, most of that work relies on constraint-based techniques to maintain consistent displays for each of the participants in the multi-user interface.

6.2.7. The user interfaces of UIMS

It is surprising to note that the user interfaces provided for UIMS are often not sophisticated; for example, they rely on standard text-editors. Some UIMS provide direct manipulation user interfaces however, e.g., ThingLab [Borning, 1981], PERIDOT [Myers & Buxton, 1986], MetaMouse [Maulsby, Witten & Kittlitz, 1989], MIKE [Olsen, 1986], and MENULAY [Buxton, Lamb, Sherman & Smith, 1983]. Some commercial systems provide a direct manipulation capability, including Prototyper for Apple Macintosh computers and Interface builder for NeXT computers [Webster, 1989]. Some of these systems rely on the programming by example paradigm. PERIDOT and BASIL, in particular, the direct manipulation interface allows the user to manipulate a physical mouse to manipulate a simulated, on-screen mouse to indicate an example of a user action and then appropriate system response. Using techniques from knowledge-based systems, the UIMS attempts to infer a general description of the desired user interface. An interesting research direction applies these ideas to generating appropriate models, see Angehrn & Lüthi [1990], and Angehrn [1991]. The modeler gives examples of the behavior of the system in question, and the computer program infers a general model of the system.

7. User interfaces and OR

7.1. Introduction

Emerging user interface techniques have been applied in many different disciplines both in the mainstream of OR and closely related to OR. All emphasize slightly different styles of interactivity, though they overlap greatly. *Interactive optimization* (Section 7.2) emphasizes creating a symbiosis between an optimization algorithm and user to produce better solutions; *visual interactive simulation* (Section 7.3) as well as *algorithm animation* (Section 7.4) emphasize animating the execution of simulations or algorithms to help users better understand the simulations or algorithms. *Visual programming languages* (Section 7.5) emphasize using graphical rather than textual representations and user interfaces to specify computer programs. All these techniques can be viewed as special cases of *scientific visualization* (Section 7.6). Scientific visualization within an OR realm has been dubbed *visual interactive modeling* (VIM).

7.2. Interactive optimization

Many researchers and practitioners have adapted optimization algorithms to run in an interactive mode. Fisher [1986] and Bell [1985a,b, 1986] survey many of these systems. Using such a system, a user typically can interactively enter a problem instance, perhaps even a description of the model, invoke the algorithm, and see the result. The uses and advantages of such systems are essentially the same as those described for DSS (Section 8), useful for unstructured problem environments where the objectives, data, or constraints cannot be completely specified, or where it will be difficult to obtain the optimal solution automatically. Bell [1985b] notes that interactive optimization systems generally are costly to develop, so should therefore be used only for projects where possible savings are great. With the continuing improvement in the available development tools, however, one can expect the interactive optimization will become increasingly common.

Among examples of interactive optimization, several subtle characteristics emerge. For example, in LINDO (and its relatives, VINO, GINO, LINGO) [Schrage, 1984, 1986; Liebman, Schrage & Waren, 1986; Cunningham & Schrage, 1989], or IFPS/OPTIMUM [Roy, Lasdon & Lordeman, 1986], the optimization algorithm is basically a *black box*, in the sense that once the user invokes the algorithm, it runs to completion. Certainly many such systems allow step by step execution of the algorithm, but the user does not play an active role in assisting the algorithm to find an optimal solution.

For optimization problems where the objective function is difficult to define or the optimal solution is difficult to find, some systems exploit the user's pattern recognition skills to guide the algorithm. In those systems, the algorithm becomes more of a *grey box*, consisting of a series, or perhaps a network, of black boxes, with user intervention required whenever execution of an internal black box completes. Both black and grey-box systems can provide extensive interaction capabilities for specifying models or model instances, viewing algorithm output, and preparing specialized reports. In fact, proper use will generally require multiple runs to assess the sensitivity of the solution to parameter changes. The key difference lies in the amount of help the user provides in the solution process once the problem instance is specified. Help supplied by the user might include setting of initial parameters, choosing the next algorithm to run, or adjusting the current solution before re-running an algorithm. In these systems, the user must play a much more active role to obtain an optimal or near-optimal solution.

Bell [1986] contrasted the grey and black box approaches to delivering optimization (and other algorithmic) technology. In one view, which he labels *passive*, interactivity is simply viewed as a convention way of delivering, perhaps previously developed, optimization or other analysis technology. In the other view, which he labels *active*, an interactive optimization system is not simply a more or less mechanical addition to an existing algorithm (e.g., 'just getting the format statements right'); rather, when interactivity is included in the design process from the beginning, a new style of problem solving is created. Kaufman & Hanani [1981] noted that adding interactivity to an existing simulation system was much more difficult than including interactivity from the beginning. In Kirkpatrick & Bell's [1989] survey, most users of visual interactive modeling felt that they produced a different model and a different solution than if a more conventional technique had been used. In short, in an active VIM system, the picture becomes the model, with the algorithms supporting the analysis of the pictorial model.

Far more such systems have probably been developed than have been reported in the literature. Among those that have been published include systems related to financial modeling [Jack, 1985; Bell & Parker, 1985], vehicle routing [Fisher, Greenfield & Jaikumar, 1982; Lapalme, Cormier & Mallette, 1983; Shepard, 1983; Belardo, Duchessi & Seagle, 1985; Savelsbergh, 1988], transportation network design [Babin, Florian, James-Lefebvre & Speiss, 1982], water resources planning [Luocks, Taylor & French, 1985], production planning [Garman, 1970; Jones & Maxwell, 1986], the traveling salesman problem [Hurrion 1978], workforce scheduling [Bell, Hay & Liang, 1986], facilities location [Brady, Rosenthal & Young, 1984; Van Nunen & Benders, 1982], facilities layout [Montreuil, 1982], and communication network design [Monma & Shallcross, 1988].

The facilities location system developed by Brady, Rosenthal & Young [1984] is a good example of a 'grey-box' interactive optimization system. They rely on the user's pattern recognition skills to select points located inside the intersection of several circles. The chosen point allows the system to further restrict the size of the region where the facility is to be located; the algorithm terminates when the region contains only a single point, the optimal location of the facility. Fisher [1986] noted that discretizing $\mathcal{R}^2$, as is done in creating the drawings of the circles, could form the basis for a completely automated algorithm, where the system would test each pixel to see if it is located in the intersection region. Essentially Fisher is proposing that image processing techniques could be useful for certain classes of optimization problems. With the trend to implementing graphics and image processing algorithms in high-speed VLSI, research into applying such novel graphics hardware architectures to OR problems could be fruitful.

Experimental proof that interactive optimization helps produce better answers is somewhat sparse. Hurrion [1978, 1980] explored the use of interactive optimization techniques for job-shop scheduling and the travelling salesman problem, with the interactive approach producing better solutions than a batch approach based upon approximation algorithms. However, the experiments were conducted so that the interactive phase of the experiment began with the users trying to improve the best solution generated by the approximation algorithms; one could expect that with enough diligence the users would find a better answer (unless the optimal answer was already discovered by the approximation algorithms). Yet it seems difficult to design an experiment whose results can be widely applied. If an algorithm has not yielded the optimal solution, with enough diligence, even without an interactive implementation, a decision maker might discover a better solution. Another approach would compare different interactive optimization systems for the same problem to identify the best design characteristics for the system and the users; as far as we know this has never been done rigorously in the context of optimization. Bell and Kirkpatrick took a different approach by surveying actual users of interactive optimization and simulation systems [Bell, 1986; Kirkpatrick & Bell, 1989]. They attempted to measure how satisfied such users felt about their use of such systems. One of their main conclusions was that such systems worked as claimed: the system helped identify different options, increase understanding of the system being modeled, and of the model itself. One problem with such systems was the extra time required to develop the interactive system, and the tendency to abandon useful non-graphical techniques such as statistical analysis. One problem with the study, as the authors noted, was its bias towards practitioners who were committed to and had successfully implemented VIM technology.

7.3. Visual interactive simulation

Among the many OR analysis techniques, easy-to-use user interfaces for computer simulation have received the most attention. Hurrion & Secker [1978] coined the term *visual interactive simulation* (VIS) to describe the use of interactive computer graphics systems for the input of simulation models, and animated display of the output of the simulation. Many such systems have been developed which, both as extensions of established general purpose simulation languages, e.g., TESS developed to support SLAM [Standridge, 1985], BLOCKS and CINEMA [Pegden, Miles & Diaz, 1985] to support SIMAN [Pegden, 1985], SIMANIMATION to support SIMSCRIPT (CACI Products Company), and AUTOGRAM to support AUTOMOD (AutoSimulations, Incorporated). New general purpose simulation languages have also been developed explicitly for the interactive computer graphics environment, e.g., SEE-WHY [Fiddy, Bright & Hurrion, 1981], WITNESS [Istel, 1988], Genetik [Insight, International, 1988]. More specialized simulation systems have also been developed, although not capable of all the model expressiveness of the general languages, are generally easier to use for the specialized problem area for which they were intended. Examples or research and commercial systems in the manufacturing area include XCELL+ [Conway, Maxwell, McClain & Worona, 1987], SIMFACTORY [CACI Products Company], GRASS [Jones & Maxwell, 1986], COSMOS [Jackson, Muckstadt & Jones, 1989]. Grant & Weiner [1986] survey such manufacturing simulation systems as of 1986. Bell [1985a,b, 1986] also provides extensive references of examples of VIS.

7.4. Algorithm animation

Bentley & Kernighan [1987], Brown & Sedgewick [1965], Duisberg [1986], and Boyd, Pulleyblank & Cornuejols [1987] have developed systems to facilitate the creation of graphical animations of the operation of computer science algorithms. This is often known as *algorithm animation* or *program visualization*. Examples include sorting a list, determining the minimum spanning tree for a graph, inserting items into and then searching a binary tree. Such systems are intended to support researchers in gaining insights on the behavior of their algorithms, and to support students learning the behavior of particular algorithms. Similar to the systems for interactive optimization, these systems provide different levels of functionality. For example, the system of Brown and Sedgewick allows full interactivity; the animation can be designed so that the algorithm can be stopped at any point, parameters modified, and execution continued. The system of Bentley and Kernighan, heavily borrowing from the Unix tradition of pipes and filters [Kernighan & Pike, 1984], is a postprocessor that can produce animations of an algorithm only after the algorithm has completed. Although the animation can be interrupted while running, one cannot change the execution of the algorithm in midstream. The tradeoff between the two styles is that more computer code is generally required with the interruptible system of Brown and Sedgewick than with the simpler system of Bentley and Kernighan.

A related form of animation called *animated sensitivity analysis* [Jones 1988b, 1989a,b, 1992], animates the *solution* to an analysis algorithm as inputs are changed rather than the steps of the algorithm. In one example, for Euclidean traveling salesman problems, a user can move a city, with the optimal (or near-optimal) tour being recomputed and redisplayed continuously. In another example, users can change an objective coefficient or right-hand side value in a two-variable linear programming problem and simultaneously see its effect on a graphical representation of the problem. Although algorithm animation helps users understand algorithms, animated sensitivity analysis could help users understand the problems being modeled, regardless of the algorithms used to analyze them. Moreover, animated sensitivity analysis can help traditional OR researchers gain insights on problems. In the Euclidean travelling salesman problem, for example, the system of Jones has shown that an optimization algorithm produces a very stable solution, when a city is allowed to change, compare to most any approximation algorithm.

7.5. Visual programming

Visual programming seeks to use pictures rather than text-based representations to represent computer programs [Glinert, 1990]. Graphical representations require a more sophisticated user interface than can be provided by text-editors, the usual tool for creating computer programs. Graphical representations of computer programs and information systems have been widely used for many years; examples include flow-charts, Nassi–Shneiderman diagrams, data-flow diagrams, structure charts, HIPO charts (see Senn [1984] for a survey). Several commercial systems have been developed to allow developers to draw in descriptions of computer systems, e.g., Wasserman [1985]. In addition, many researchers have attempted to create new visual programming languages [e.g., Ichikawa & Hirakawa, 1987; Henderson, 1986; Glinert & Tanimoto, 1984]. Most visual programming systems use more or less complex icons to represent basic units in the programming language. Frequently the icons are then connected by different kinds of arcs to form an attributed graph representation of a computer program. Glinert [1990], Grafton & Ichikawa [1985], and Shu [1988] survey visual programming systems.

Visual programming differs from algorithm animation because it deals more with the input to an algorithm than with the output produced by an algorithm. To confuse the distinction, however, many visual programming languages provide animation of the execution of the program, similar to the algorithm animation systems. Myers [1986, 1988] provides a detailed comparison of visual programming systems and program visualization.

Some of the previously discussed interactive OR systems can be viewed as visual programming systems for a particular problem domain. Many interactive simulation and optimization systems are really visual programming systems for a particular class of problems. For example, the editors for many of the commercial simulation languages allow users to edit the particular attributed graphs underlying the simulation languages.

7.6. Scientific visualization

The computer graphics community coined the term *scientific visualization* to describe computer graphics programs used to help scientists visualize and thereby better understand their research problems [McCormick, DeFanti & Brown, 1987; Nielson, Shriver & Rosenblum, 1990]. This movement has arisen in large part because of the wider availability of supercomputers. Supercomputers can produce large amounts of data quickly. The problem can then become less one of limited calculation speed than one of understanding the data produced by the algorithm. Advocates of scientific visualization argue that computer graphics can greatly help researchers understand the behavior of their models. The promoters of scientific visualization have traditionally concentrated on applications in the physical sciences [e.g., Association for Computing Machinery, 1988b]. For example, in physics, scientific visualization has been applied to problems in fluid dynamics, quantum mechanics, and particle dynamics. In biology, scientific visualization has been applied to the display of complex molecules, and even to the point of animating molecular interactions [e.g., Olson, Tainer & Getzoff, 1988]. Though, really algorithm animation, program visualization, visual interactive modelling are all driving towards the same basic goal: better understanding of problems, models and algorithms.

OR problems often do not have as obvious a representation as the problems tackled by the physical sciences (what is the best way to represent a machine schedule?), yet some work has been done in scientific visualization., Within an OR context, Boyd, Pulleyblank & Cornuejols [1987] present a PC-based system for exploring the behavior of different traveling salesman algorithms. Gay [1987] presents techniques for visualizing the operation of the simplex algorithm in comparison to Karmarkar's algorithm for linear programming. Jones [1988a] discusses the use of three-dimensional computer graphics for visualizing machine scheduling problems. The research on visual interactive modeling [Bell, 1986; Hurrion, 1986] also fits within the scientific visualization paradigm. Yet, with the ever increasing capabilities of computer graphic hardware, heretofore impractical but useful representations of OR problems may become practical. For example, Gay [1987] mentions the possibility of interactively viewing animations of Karmarker's algorithm for linear programming. Jones has explored the use of animation to show how solutions evolve as input parameters are changed [Jones, 1988b, 1989a,b]. Example applications include machine scheduling [1988b], linear programming [1989b], and the traveling salesman problem [1989a].

7.7. Virtual reality

Borrowing from flight simulation [Yan, 1985] and other technologies [Foley, 1987], an artificial or *virtual reality* [Foley, 1987; Meyers, 1985], is a computer generated environment that users find indistinguishable and their real world. Note that the concept of virtual reality has existed for some time – at least since 1965 [Sutherland, 1965]. Foley [1987] gives an example of hypothetical virtual reality where a biologist walking around a three-dimensional image of a pair of proteins, grabbing hold (literally) of both proteins, trying to fit them together like a jig-saw puzzle, and feeling the pull of molecular forces as the proteins change position. Brooks, Ouh-Young, Batter & Kilpatrick [1990] constructed a prototype of such a system where the biologist interacts with a molecule by manipulating a robot arm. As the molecule is moved, the forces felt by the molecule are transmitted through the robot arm to the biologist. Such a force feedback device is known as a *haptic* display, where haptic means 'relating to or based on the sense of touch'. Brooks demonstrated that it produces solutions faster than the best current algorithm. With the development of graphics supercomputers, where powerful graphics and powerful computer capabilities are quite tightly linked [Diede, Hagenmaier, Miranker, Rubinstein & Worley, 1988; Apgar, Bersack & Mammen, 1988], such technology is becoming closer to reality. In an application closer to the OR domain, Feiner & Beshers [1990] discuss the use of stereoscopic display of multi-dimensional financial functions. Users interact with the multiple dimensions using a 'dataglove' [Zimmerman, Lanier, Blanchard, Bryson & Harvill, 1987], which is worn on a user's hands, tracking the position of every finger. Users can essentially grab hold of the functions in order to manipulate them. Another related technology is known as a 'head-mounted display', which consists of a pair of display devices mounted in front of the user's eyes. The display devices display computer-generated, stereoscopic imagery. Furthermore, the position and orientation of the user's head is tracked (using, e.g., the device described in Rabb, Blood, Steiner & Jones, [1979]) so that as the user walks around, tilts his or her head, the image can be updated to reflect the user's new orientation. In this way, the user can be placed into a new virtual world. The cost of devices such as datagloves and head-mounted displays appears to be declining [Pausch, 1991], so research on applications to OR appears, at this point, to be an increasingly intriguing possibility. At least one author [Moran & Anderson, 1990] has proposed a different form of virtual reality that would alter common everyday tools such as blackboards and telephones so that they become more seamlessly integrated. Instead of requiring that users wear exotic clothing, the environment itself would be adaptable. Even though this technology is still in its infancy, it could provide some useful techniques to gain insight on complicated problems and algorithms.

8. Decision support systems

8.1. Definitions

Decision support systems (DSS), as they have come to be known, can be traced to Michael Scott Morton's paper in the early 1970s, 'management decision systems: Computer based support for decision making' [Scott Morton, 1971], which laid out a framework for computer-based systems to augment the decision making machinery of managers. Both the theory [e.g., Keen & Scott Morton, 1978; Bonczek, Holsapple & Whinston, 1981a,b; Alter, 1980; Sprague & Carlson, 1982] and the practice of DSS have expanded greatly since that time. There is now the journal *Decision Support Systems*, a yearly conference, and many widely available commercial tools that can be called DSS.

Much effort is expended in the DSS literature attempting to provide a definition of DSS that distinguishes them from the closely related fields such as electronic data processing (EDP), management information systems (MIS), computer science (CS), behavioral science, as well as OR/MS. In one of Sprague and Carlson's definition of a DSS, they are '*interactive* computer-based systems that *help* decision makers utilize *data* and *models* to solve *unstructured* problems' (italics theirs). They note the conundrum that few systems satisfy all these requirements, and yet if one extends the definition to include any system that 'makes some contribution to decision making', then most any information system can be considered to be a DSS.

8.2. Relationship to OR

What distinguishes DSS from MIS, OR, and other related fields is more a matter of emphasis and style, than actual substance. DSS places particular emphasis on the political, social, organizational environment, in which decisions are made, rather than on the mathematics and computer technology that might be useful in making a decision. Authors that attempt to propose a theory of DSS [e.g., Keen & Scott Morton, 1978; Alter, 1980; Sprague & Carlson, 1982; Bonczek, Holsapple & Whinston 1981a,b] begin by reviewing and expanding theories of decision making, organizational behavior, and cognitive psychology and adapt those theories into the context of a computer-based information system. The theories invariably insist that for a successful DSS, one must understand the problem domain, including the organizational and political issues involved. Only from that base of support can one begin to develop systems that will truly help people make decisions. Their emphasis on understanding the user and problem domain parallels the recommendations for successful OR projects [e.g., Churchman, Ackoff & Arnoff, 1957; Geoffrion, 1987] and successful user interface designs [e.g., Shneiderman, 1987].

The problems attacked using a DSS frequently lack sufficient structure to be readily amenable to the solution techniques provided by OR. Bonczek, Holsapple & Whinston [1981a], define an unstructured decision problem as one where it is difficult to evaluate objectively different possible decisions, or that there is no single method or algorithm that can be used to generate a solution. Labelling a problem as unstructured, as pointed out by Sprague and Carlson, depends upon the individual; novice students of OR would probably label many of their first LP problems to be highly unstructured. In fact, the field of OR, as with all scientific endeavors, can be said to attempt to continue to identify analyzable structures in previously unstructured problem areas. Developments in game theory, probabilistic optimization, multi-criteria optimization have attempted to provide structured ways of analyzing previously unstructured problem domains. Yet, there remain many problems, in fact, the vast majority, where it is difficult to specify all the constraints, specify a single objective exactly, obtain, let alone analyze, all relevant information, or specify the one and only model that could provide useful information for making the decision. In unstructured problem domains, therefore, it is not possible to provide the one true optimal solution. We can only hope to provide a 'good enough' solution, a problem solving strategy Simon [1957] called 'satisficing'. As Keen & Scott Morton [1978] state:

> The *models* for the support of managers' decisions may differ substantially from the optimization algorithms used in the structured area. Small, informal models that get better answers than now exist are required, not elegant and sophisticated examples of the researcher's art (p. 93).

DSS does not particularly shun optimization and other OR techniques, however. Most of the early DSS did essentially ignore optimization, and simply provided mechanisms for accessing and viewing data, and calculating values to perform 'what if' analysis. Recently, however, many established DSS generators [Sprague & Carlson, 1982], have been incorporating mathematical programming (IFPS/Optimum [Roy, Lasdon & Lordeman, 1986]; VINO [Schrage, 1986; Bodily, 1986]). DSS generally views techniques from OR (using a framework from Sprague & Carlson [1982]) as just one class of tools, in addition to databases, presentation graphics, expression evaluation, and spreadsheets.

The willingness to attack unstructured problems generally implies that a DSS requires an easy-to-use user interface. In fact, Sprague and Carlson's definition of a DSS calls for an interactive implementation. One can argue that an easy-to-use interface is a worthy goal for any computer-based system, but in a DSS, it becomes especially important. If the problem at hand has yet to be identified, yet alone one or more suitable objectives, the user interface should not interfere with problem identification, or model development. It is surprising, however, that much of the DSS literature pays little detailed attention to the user interface. Most authors assume an 'English-like' command driven interface. Direct manipulation interfaces are hardly mentioned, though probably because they have only recently become more common.

The willingness to tackle unstructured problems, however, may be the greatest weakness of DSS, because, almost by definition, it will be difficult to evaluate the quality of the derived solution. If one uses a linear programming model, one at least knows that the solution generated is the absolute optimum. That 'optimal' solution, of course, is only as good as the assumptions underlying the mathematical programming model. DSS rejects the notion that such models provide the one true solution. Rather, models provide information that may be useful to a decision maker, but must be evaluated for validity and relevance to the problem at hand. Above all, the models must be packaged in a form that is truly accessible and useful to the decision maker.

Successful practitioners of OR, of course, greatly appreciate the limitations of models and the need to understand the context as well as the content of problem. In fact, those tenets were identified by many of the early authors in OR, e.g., Churchman, Ackoff & Arnoff [1957], who emphasize concentrating on the manager, the problem, and the surrounding environment when constructing a tool to aid decision makers. Advocates of DSS may simply be better promoters of the good problem solving practices that have been advocated by OR since its inception, whereas operations researchers may be better promoters of analytical techniques.

Many researchers have compared DSS to OR with some promoting DSS as an ideal tool for delivering OR technologies [Wagner, 1981; Vazsonyi, 1982; Bodily, 1986], and others worrying that DSS will grow to dominate OR [Geoffrion, 1983; Wynne, 1984]. We believe that the ideas underlying DSS are the same ideas that have permeated this chapter, i.e., OR technology is best delivered in an easy to use interface. OR can offer to DSS better analytical tools to provide supportive help to decision makers. And DSS, with its concentration on the problem domain and the user interface, can offer to OR appropriate delivery vehicles for OR technology. There is no reason why OR cannot develop integrated, flexible, adaptable systems that put the user first and the underlying technology second with the user interface linking the two.

9. Modeling languages for mathematical programming

We discuss work on novel user interfaces for a common OR methodology, mathematical programming. We define a mathematical programming modeling language as a language or system for specifying the general structure of a mathematical programming model that is understandable by a computer, modeler, and decision maker, as it fits within the framework presented in Section 2. They differ from most of the interactive optimization systems discussed in Section 7 because of the broad class of models the languages can capture. Most of the interactive optimization systems have been developed for very specific problems, e.g., vehicle routing problems with time windows. Modeling languages, on the other hand, allow users to specify particular models from a very broad problem class, such as mathematical programming, queueing network analysis or simulation.

Although modeling languages for mathematical programming have been discussed in Chapter 11, in this section we concentrate on the user interface aspects of those languages. We attempt to provide several criteria for classifying the languages:

(1) Model paradigms supported.

(2) Emphasis on problem, model or model instance.

(3) User interface sophistication (batch, conversational, direct manipulation).

(4) Level of procedurality.

Geoffrion [1987, 1989], Fourer [1983], and Welch [1987] provide other, somewhat similar, criteria for categorizing modeling languages for mathematical programming.

9.1. Model paradigms supported

Many modeling languages are associated with a particular solution paradigm (criterion 1). For example, Fourer [1983] defines a modeling language as 'a declarative language that expresses the modeler's form of a linear program in a notation that a computer system can interpret.' That definition does not encompass, e.g., more general mathematical programming techniques, languages for stochastic analysis, and simulation modeling. Most matrix generators allow a modeler to specify linear, non-linear, integer, and network optimization algorithms [Fourer, 1983], but do not provide algorithms from outside the mathematical programming paradigm. Structured Modeling can capture models from many different modeling paradigms, including mathematical programming, stochastic analysis, simulation, and also from fields outside traditional OR, such as relational databases. MIMI [Chesapeake Decision

Sciences, Inc., 1988] is also not limited to particular modeling paradigms, currently supporting mathematical programming, as well as production planning scheduling.

Increasing the ability of a modeling language to capture problems in different problem domains must be balanced against the added burden required of the user interface to support the added expressiveness. LINDO [Schrage, 1984], e.g., since it concentrates only on linear programming (continuous and integer), is able to provide functions specifically tied to linear programming, such adding and deleting a column. GINO [Liebman, Lasdon, Schrage & Warren, 1986], which can handle non-linear as well as linear models, does not provide any facility for manipulating columns, since there is no easy analog to a column in a general non-linear programming problem. Sensitivity analysis on the allowable ranges of the right-hand side and objective function coefficients, as commonly found in linear programming is also not provided by GINO, since it relies on a more general constrained non-linear optimization algorithm. Developing a modeling language that can capture models from many different paradigms and remain easy to use is non-trivial.

9.2. Problem, model, or model instance specification capabilities

Many modeling languages actually do not allow a user to specify the general structure of a model, only particular instances. The widely used MPS input format is the prime example of such a language. Another example is LINDO, although its interactive interface makes it easier to use than MPS.

In contrast, languages like GAMS [Brooke, Kendrick & Meeraus, 1988] AMPL [Fourer, Gay & Kernighan, 1987], LINGO [Cunningham and Schrage, 1989] and Structured Modeling [Geoffrion, 1987] cleanly separate specification of the model and specification of the underlying data, though the distinction in GAMS can easily be blurred. In Structured Modeling, e.g., generic structure captures the description of the model; the elemental detail captures the particular problem instance. Separation of model and data has been advocated by numerous authors [Geoffrion, 1987; Fourer, Gay & Kernighan, 1987]. In GAMS, the user specifies a model using a computer-readable algebraic syntax; the data for a particular problem is embedded as part of the same input file. One can argue, however, that reproducing the results of the model are enhanced when the data and model are tightly coupled; if they are not, if the data is changed, which may occur frequently, the results will change independent of any change to the model.

Advocates of particular modeling languages make the implicit or explicit claim that their language makes is easier for modelers to use the underlying tools. However, whether the language is appropriate for a decision maker not trained in OR techniques is another matter. One style of interface, found in both GAMS and AMPL adapts widely used algebraic syntax for specifying mathematical programs to computers. Non-technically trained managers may not feel tremendously comfortable with double and triple summation signs, however. Structured Modeling provides explicit facilities for presenting models to non-technically trained users. In Structured Modeling, the modular structure, which organizes the generic structure, and the ability to extract different views of the modular structure (and hence, the model) provide a rigorous but only mildly 'technical' representation that seems better suited for presentation to non-technical decision makers than traditional algebraic syntax. Such an emphasis could, of course, be added to an existing modeling language by enforcing conventions for the content and style of the comments of the model.

Perhaps what is required are multiple, simultaneously viewable and editable representations of the same model. Different people will prefer different representations. Different tasks may be better performed with different representations. By allowing for many representations of the same underlying model, one can hope to support different tasks and users. Structured Modeling provides several different representations of the same model. Greenberg & Murphy [1991] provide a survey of representations that might be useful in a modeling environment.

9.3. Style of user interface

It is interesting to note how little explicit attention is given to the user interface by most modeling languages, with several notable exceptions to be discussed. Most modeling languages only support a 'batch' mode of operation similar to traditional computer programming: a file containing a syntactically correct specification of the model is created using a standard text-editor, fed into the modeling system, and solution results printed. This style of interface has two distinct advantages: it is easily adapted to any computer system, from personal computer to super-computer, and it provides a simple interface to other programs such as databases and spreadsheets. For a more thorough survey of user interfaces for mathematical programming, see Greenberg [1988] and Greenberg & Murphy [1991].

Many authors from within computer science have attempted to provide specialized user interfaces for existing computer programming languages [e.g., Reps & Teitelbaum, 1981; Reps. 1986; Nagl, 1987]. The interfaces typically provide special commands to help the user create only syntactically correct computer programs; syntax errors are detected while the program is being created, rather than at compile time. Holsapple, Park & Whinston [1989] have used the work of Reps and Teitelbaum to develop syntax directed (textual) editors for linear programming and suggest its application to a commercial language such as GAMS. Holsapple, Park & Whinston [1991] propose extensions to support graphical editors. Jones [1990, 1991a,b,c; see also Jones & Krishnan, 1990] discusses the development and an actual implementation of a graphical syntax directed editor to support OR modeling.

Notable exceptions to the batch style of user interface are LINDO [Schrage, 1984], which uses a command style user interface, and VINO [Schrange, 1986], which relies on a spreadsheet style of interface. Here, the user enters commands to create an instance of a linear programming problem, then asks for a solution, and performs sensitivity analysis. For large mathematical programs, however, it may be more useful to create the linear programming instance using a text editor and then use the TAKE command to read the instance into LINDO. Many of the interactive financial planning systems, e.g., IFPS, which have been extended to include optimization capabilities [Roy, Lasdon & Lordeman, 1986], also rely on a command oriented interface.

With the development of spreadsheets and other forms style direct manipulation interfaces, modeling languages have begun to take advantage of that style of interface. VINO [Schrage, 1986] relies on LOTUS 1-2-3 for creating simplex tableaus for input to a linear programming solver, which can report the results in a format acceptable to LOTUS for further analysis. MIMI and Structured Modeling also rely on a forms style direct manipulation interface. A mathematical programming language based on interactive computer graphics under development is LPSPEC [Ma, Murphy & Stohr, 1987, 1989; Murphy & Stohr, 1986]. In this system, a linear program is represented as a hierarchical attributed graph, which can be edited by the user. Glover & Greenberg [1988] propose the use of 'Netform' graphs to represent both the abstract structure and detail of network flow models, though they do not discuss an implementation. Bruntz, Clohessy & Daniels [1987] report on the use of iconic (network) representation for linear programming, combined with natural language output based on Greenberg's work on linear programming analysis [Greenberg, 1987]. Structured Modeling, since it relies on many underlying graphs as part of its specification, is also envisioned to benefit from an interactive computer graphics interface. Such an interface is also under consideration for MIMI [Chesapeake Decision Sciences, Inc., 1988]. Jones [1985, 1990, 1991a,b,c; see also Jones & Krishnan, 1990] uses an attributed graph framework for representing not only mathematical programming models, but any class of models usefully represented as an attributed graph.

It is interesting to note, however, that most of the modeling systems that provide a sophisticated user interface also provide some kind of batch interface. For example, the TAKE command of LINDO and GINO reads a file and executes the enclosed commands. A batch facility appears essential for allowing the modeling system to interface to other systems.

9.4. Procedural or non-procedural

Fourer discussed the advantages and disadvantages of procedural and non-procedural modeling languages for mathematical programming [Fourer, 1983]. A procedural specification of a model gives an algorithm for translating input data into the representation required by the solution algorithm. Procedural modeling languages are analogous to procedural computer programming languages, with their accompanying burdens of validation, maintainability, and documentability. Non-procedural modeling languages on the other hand do not require an explicit algorithm for performing the translation from input data into the representation required by the solution algorithm. Rather, the model is specified as a set of declarative statements. Non-procedural modeling languages are generally considered to be easier to use because they are closer to the conceptual representation of models used by actual modelers.

Unfortunately, several forms of non-procedural modeling languages have been proposed, even within mathematical programming. For linear or more general mathematical programming, one common form is the algebraic form exemplified by GAMS [Brooke, Kendrick & Meeraus, 1988], AMPL [Fourer, Gay & Kernighan, 1987], LINGO [Cunningham & Schrage, 1989]. These systems specify the mathematical programming in a row-wise fashion.

Another style of non-procedural language for linear programming (PAM [Welch, 1987], MIMI [Chesapeake Decision Sciences, 1988]) represents the simplex tableau as a set of symbolic blocks, each block having a similar underlying structure. The appropriate places are determined by a translation scheme (using the COLUMNS, ROWS and DATA tables) that loops through the rows and columns to identify the non-zero locations for the particular block. Welch compares some of the advantages of the algebraic and block-wise approaches, claiming that many experienced mathematical programmers prefer the block-structured approach.

9.5. Further considerations

With some modeling languages attempting to provide an appropriate representation or representations for the decision maker, modeler, and computer, it would seem just as important to provide a representation for algorithm invocation. Many modeling languages provide a single command (e.g., GO, for LINDO), to invoke the appropriate analysis algorithm. However, for developing specialized algorithms, e.g., integer programming techniques such as branch and bound, Lagrangean relaxation, etc., modelers probably require a programming language, i.e., conditional execution, looping, and perhaps recursion. Certainly that could be provided by an existing programming language, with appropriate procedures or subroutines provided to access the model definition and problem instance. Another alternative would be to provide a separate language, more closely integrated with the data. Matrix generators generally provide such a language, frequently known as program control language (PCL). Many of the non-procedural modeling languages, such as GAMS and AMPL, provide limited such capabilities. Grafting a procedural language onto a non-procedural language may be heretical to the theology of non-procedurality. Two interesting research topics could address this issue: one would extend one of the non-procedural languages for mathematical programming to allow creation of specialized algorithms such as Lagrangian relaxation. The other would attempt to identify automatically a suitable analysis algorithm for the model as specified. Some work has begun on automatically developing solution techniques for formulated problems, e.g., Lee [1986]. Bradley & Clemence [1988], and Bhargava, Kimbrough & Krishnan [1991] discuss the use of knowledge about the dimensions of parameters and decision variables to facilitate semi-automatic integration of different mathematical programming models.

With the variety of representations possible for a mathematical program, perhaps it would be best to allow users to view their problems in multiple forms, with the user making the choice as to the best representation. If a change is made in one representation, all related representations would be simultaneously updated. Several authors advocate this approach including Kendrick [1990] and Greenberg & Murphy [1991].

10. Future directions for user interfaces

Predicting the future is always a dangerous prospect, because one is usually more often wrong than right. Predicting the future in the computer business is probably even more dangerous because of its historically rapid rate of change. Certain trends in user interfaces, however, seem likely to continue in at least the near future, and, based on the predictions of Marcus & van Dam [1991], we attempt here to predict the impact those trends will have on OR.

Almost certainly, the capabilities of the user interface hardware will become more powerful, and become less and less expensive. Displays will be able to display more colors, with finer spatial resolution. Display processors will be significantly faster, able, e.g., to draw realistic three-dimensional images fast enough for purposes of animation. More sophisticated input devices will become less expensive, allowing a fuller range of expression by human users. Integration of multiple media, i.e., graphics, sound, and full-motion video, will become a reality.

Whatever the hardware trends, the quality of user interfaces to deliver OR technology will continue to improve through the use of spreadsheets, user interface management systems, better modeling languages, and other tools discussed in this chapter. Command driven interfaces will probably never die, but direct-manipulation, multi-media, multi-user interfaces will become more and more the norm. Multi-media and virtual reality based systems show promise to provide a richer set of tools for delivering OR technology.

This increase in the quality of the user interface will allow users both to make greater use of OR technology, while insulating them more and more from that very technology. We may give seductively powerful tools to people not well-trained in the technology. Blindly applying OR technology without understanding the underlying assumptions and limitations can and frequently does lead to disaster. Perhaps the research in artificial intelligence will create tools that will help prevent such disasters. One can argue, however, that the requirement for an intelligent appreciation of the tools will not disappear.

Furthermore, packaging OR technology in an easy to use interface may make OR a less prominent field even as it allows traditional OR techniques to be more widely used. For example, linear and non-linear solvers are now commonly packaged with leading spreadsheet packages. With OR tools so easy to use, anyone can use the tools without need for an OR analyst. Although OR practitioners might worry about job security, this is immaterial to the people who have the problems to be solved, as long as their problems are solved. Of course, those users may misapply the tools, with grievous results. Furthermore, no shortage of intractable problems currently exists. In short, there will remain sufficiently difficult problems to provide continued demand for OR skills.

Finally, as user interfaces improve, user expectations of their user interfaces will rise. OR modelers will be expected by their clients to provide easy to use interfaces delivering sophisticated tools.

We ignore at our peril the importance of user interfaces for delivering OR solutions.

References

ACM Siggraph (1979). General methodology and the proposed core system. *Comput. Graphics* 13(3), 1–179.

Albers, J. (1975). *Interaction of Color*, Yale University Press, New Haven, CT.

Allen, R.B. (1982). Cognitive factors in human interaction with computers, in: A. Badre, B. Shneiderman (eds.), *Directions in Human/Computer Interaction*, Ablex, Norwood, NJ.

Alter, S.L. (1980). *Decision Support Systems: Current Practice and Continuing Challenges*, Addison-Wesley, Reading, MA.

Angehrn, A.A. (1991). Modeling by example: A link between users, models and methods in DSS. *European J. Oper. Res.* 55(3), 296–308.

Angehrn, A.A., H.-J. Lüthi (1990). Intelligent decision support systems: A visual interactive approach. *Interfaces* 20(6), 17–28.

Apgar, B., B. Bersack, A. Mammen (1988). A display system for the stellar graphics supercomputer model GS1000. *Comput. Graphics* 22(4), 255–262.

Apollo Computer (1987). *The DOMAIN Dialogue User's Guide*, Apollo Computer Inc, 330 Billerica Road, Chelmsford, MA.

Apple Computer (1985). *Inside Macintosh, Volumes 1, 2, 3*, Addison-Wesley, Reading, MA.

Apple Computer, Hypercard, Palo Alto, California.

Association for Computing Machinery (1988a). *Hypertext on Hypertext* (Software), ACM Press: Database and Electronic Products Series.

Association for Computing Machinery (1988b). *Visualization: State of the Art* (Video), ACM Press, P.O. Box 64145, Baltimore, MD.

AutoSimulations, Inc., PO Box 307, 522 West 100 North, Bountiful, Utah 84010.

Babin, A., M. Florian, James-Lefebvre, H. Speiss (1982). EMME/2: An interactive graphic method for road and transit planning, Publication No. 204, Centre de Recherche sur les Transports, Université de Montreal, Quebec.

Baecker, R.M., W.S. Buxton (1988). The design of a voice messaging system, in: R.M. Baecker, W.S. Buxton (eds.), *Readings in Human-Computer Interaction*, Morgan Kaufman, Los Altos, CA, pp. 5–7.

Bailey, R.W. (1982). *Human Performance Engineering: A Guide for System Designers*, Prentice-Hall, Englewood Cliffs, NJ.

Banks, W.W., D.I. Gertman, R.J. Petersen (1982). *Human Engineering Design Considerations for Cathode Ray Tube-Generated Displays*, NUREG/CR-2496, U.S. Nuclear Regulatory Commission, Washington, D.C.

Banks, W.W., W.E. Gilmore, H.S. Blackman, D.I. Gertman (1983). *Human Engineering Design*

Considerations for Cathode Ray Tube-Generated Displays: Volume II, NUREG/CR-3003, U.S. Nuclear Regulatory Commission, Washington, DC.

Barker, E., M.J. Krebs (1977). Color coding effects on human performance, an annotated bibliography, Office of Naval Research, Code 212, Arlington, Va.

Beard, D., M. Palanlappan, A. Humm, D. Banks, A. Nair, Y.-P. Shan (1990). A visual calendar for scheduling meetings, *Proceedings of the Conference on Computer-Supported Cooperative Work*, New York: Association for Computing Machinery, pp. 279–290.

Belardo, S., P. Duchessi, J.P. Seagle (1985). Microcomputer graphics in support of vehicle fleet routing. *Interfaces* 15(6), 84–92.

Bell, P.C. (1985a). Visual interactive modeling as an OR technique. *Interfaces* 15, 26–33.

Bell, P.C. (1985b). Visual interactive modeling in operational research: Successes and opportunities. *J. Oper. Res. Soc. Am.* 36, 975–982.

Bell, P.C. (1986). Visual interactive modeling in 1986, in: V. Belton, R. O'Keefe (eds.), *Recent Developments in Operational Research*, Pergamon Press, Oxford, pp. 1–12.

Bell, P.C., G. Hay, Y. Liang (1986). A visual interactive decision support system for workforce (nurse) scheduling. *INFOR* 24(2), 134–145.

Bell, P.C., D.C. Parker (1985). Developing a visual interactive model for corporate cash management. *J. Oper. Res. Soc. Am.* 36, 779–786.

Bentley, J.L., B.W. Kernighan (1987). A system for algorithm animation: Tutorial and user manual, Computer Science Technical Report No. 132, AT&T Bell Laboratories, Murray Hill, NJ.

Betts, B., D. Burlingame, G. Fischer, J. Foley, M. Green, D. Kasik, S.T. Kerr, D. Olsen, J. Thomas (1987). Goals and objectives for user interface software. *Comput. Graphics* 21(2), 73–78.

Bhargava, H.K., S.O. Kimbrough, R. Krishnan (1991). Unique names violations, a problem for model integration or you say tomato, I say tomahto. *ORSA J. Comput.* 3(2), 107–121.

Bhatnager, S.C. (1983). Locating social service centres using interactive graphics. *Omega* 11, 201–205.

Blanning, R.W. (1984). Conversing with management information systems in natural language. *Commun. ACM* 24(3), 201–207.

Blanning, R.W. (1985). A relational framework for join implementation in model management systems. *Decision Support Systems* 1, 69–82.

Blanning, R.W. (1986). An entity-relationship approach to model management. *Decision Support Systems* 2, 65–72.

Blattner, M.M., D.A. Sumikawa, R.M. Greenberg (1989). Earcons and icons: Their structure and common design principles. *Hum.–Comput. Interaction* 4(1), 11–44.

Bodily, S.E. (1986). Spreadsheet modeling as a stepping stone. *Interfaces* 16(5), 34–52.

Bonczek, R.H., C.W. Holsapple, A.B. Whinston (1981a). *Foundations of Decision Support Systems*, Academic Press, Orlando, FL.

Bonczek, R.H., C.W. Holsapple, A.B. Whinston (1981b). A generalized decision support system using predicate calculus and network data base management. *Oper. Res.* 29(2), 263–281.

Bono, P.R. (1985). A survey of graphics standards and their role in information interchange. *IEEE Computer*, 63–75.

Borning, A. (1981). ThingLab – A constraint-oriented simulation laboratory. *ACM Trans. Program. Lang. Syst.* 6(4), 353–387.

Boyd, S.C., W.R. Pulleyblank, G. Cornuejols (1987). Travel – An interactive travelling salesman problem package for the IBM personal computer. *OR Letters* 6(3), 141–143.

Bradley, G.H., R.D. Clemence Jr. (1988). Model integration with a typed executable modeling language, *Proceedings of the 21st Hawaii International Conference on System Sciences*, Kailu-Kona, Hawaii, January 5–8, 1988, 403–410.

Brady, S.D., R.E. Rosenthal, D. Young (1984). Interactive graphical minimax location of multiple facilities with general constraints. *AIIE Trans.* 15(3), 242–254.

Brooke, A., D. Kendrick, A. Meeraus (1988). *GAMS: A User's Guide*, Scientific Press, Palo Alto, CA.

Brooks, F.P., M. Ouh-Young, J.J. Batter, P.J. Kilpatrick (1990). Project GROPE – haptic displays for scientific visualization. *Comput. Graphics* 24(4), 177–185.

Brown, M.H., R. Sedgewick (1985). Techniques for algorithm animation. *IEEE Software* 2(1), 28–39.

Bruntz, M., J. Clohessy, P. Daniels (1987). A system of text-supported iconic representation, Technical Report, Department of Mathematics, University of Colorado, Denver, CO.

Bullinger, H.-J., K.-P. Faehnrich (1984). Symbiotic man–computer interfaces and the user assistant concept, in: G. Salvendy (ed.), *Human-Computer Interaction*, Elsevier, Amserdam, pp. 17–26.

Buxton, W. (1982). An informal study of selection-position tasks, *Proceedings of Graphics Interface '82*, pp. 323–328.

Buxton, W. (1983). Lexical and pragmatic considerations of input structures. *Comput. Graphics*, 31–37.

Buxton, W., M.R. Lamb, D. Sherman, K.C. Smith (1983). Towards a comprehensive user interface management system. *Comput. Graphics* 17(3), 35–42.

CACI Products Company, 3344 North Tory Pines Court, La Jolla, CA 92037.

Card, S., W. English, B.Burr (1978). Evaluation mouse, rate-controlled isometric joystick, step keys, and text keys for text selection on a CRT. *Ergonomics* 21(8), 601–613.

Card, S.K., T.P. Moran, A. Newell (1980a). The keystroke-level model for user performance time with interactive systems. *Commun. ACM* 23(7), 396–410.

Card, S.K., T.P. Moran, A. Newell (1980b). Computer text-editing: An information-processing analysis of a routine cognitive skill. *Cognitive Psychology* 12, 32–74.

Card, S., T.P. Moran, A. Newell (1983). *The Psychology of Human–Computer Interaction*, Lawrence Erlbaum, London.

CBEMA (1985a). Programmers hierarchical interactive graphics system (PHIGS), Document X3H3/85-21, X3 Secretariat, CBEMA, 311 First St. NW, Suite 500, Washington, DC.

CBEMA (1985b). Computer graphics metafile (CGM), dpANS X3.122-198x, X3 Secretariat, CBEMA, 311 First St. NW, Suite 500, Washington, DC 20001.

CBEMA (1985c). Computer graphics virtual device interface, Document X3H3/85-47, X3 Secretariat, CBEMA, 311 First St. NW, Suite 500, Washington, DC 10001.

Chang, S.K. (Ed.) (1990). *Principles of Visual Language Systems*, Prentice-Hall, Englewood Cliffs, NJ.

Chang, S.K., T. Ichikawa, P.A. Ligomenides (1986). *Visual Languages*, Plenum Press, New York.

Chapanis, A. (1967). The relevance of laboratory studies to practical situations. *Ergonomics* 5, 557–577.

Chesapeake Decision Sciences, Inc. (1988). *Manager for Interactive Modeling Interfaces, User's Manual*, Chesapeake Decision Sciences, Inc., 200 South St, New Providence, NJ.

Chomsky, N. (1956). Three models for the description of language. *IRE Trans. Inf. Theory* 2(3), 113–124.

Churchman, C.W., R.L. Ackoff, E.L. Arnoff (1957). *Introduction to OR*, Wiley, New York.

Clemons, E., A. Greenfield (1985). The SAGE system architecture: A system for the rapid development of graphics interfaces for decision support. *IEEE Comput. Graph. and Appl.* 5(11), 38–50.

Cleveland, W.S., R. McGill (1985). Graphical perception and graphical methods for analyzing scientific data. *Science* 229, 828–833.

Conklin, J. (1987). Hypertext: An introduction and survey. *IEEE Computer* 20, 17–41.

Conway, R., W.L. Maxwell, J.O. McClain, S.L. Worona (1987). *User's Guide to XCELL+ Factory Modeling System*, The Scientific Press, Redwood City, CA.

Conway, R., W.L. Maxwell, S.L. Worona (1986). *User's Guide to XCELL Factory Modeling System*, Scientific Press, Palo Alto, CA.

Cunningham, K., L. Schrage (1989). The LINGO modeling language, Technical Report, University of Chicago.

Date, C.J. (1984). *A Guide to DB2*, Addison-Wesley, Reading, MA.

Dennis, A.R., J.F. George, L.M. Jessup, J.F. Nunamaker Jr., D.R. Vogel (1988). Information technology to support electronic meetings. *MIS Quarterly* 12(4), 591–624.

Desrochers, M., C. Jones, J.K. Lenstra, M.W.P. Savelsbergh, L. Stougie (1989). A model and algorithm management system for vehicle routing and scheduling, Tech. report, Department of Decision Sciences, the Wharton School, The University of Pennsylvania.

Desrochers, M., J.K. Lenstra, M.W.P. Savelsbergh (1990). A classification scheme for vehicle routing and scheduling problems. *European J. Oper. Res.* 46, 322–332.

DeSanctis, G. (1984). Computer graphics as decision aids: Directions for research. *Decision Sciences*, 15, 463–487.

DeSanctis, G., B. Gallupe (1987). A foundation for the study of group decision support systems. *Manage. Sci.* 33(5), 589–609.

Diede, T., C.F. Hagenmaier, G.S. Miranker, J.J. Rubinstein, W.S. Worley Jr (1988). The Titan graphics supercomputer architecture. *IEEE Computer* 21(9), 13–31.

Drebin, R.A., L. Carpenter, P. Hanrahan (1988). Volume rendering. *Comput. Graphics* 22(4), 65–74.

Duisberg, R.A. (1986). Animated graphic interfaces using temporal constraints, *Proceedings SIGCHI'86: Human Factors in Computing Systems*, Boston, MA, pp. 131–136.

Dwyer, B. (1981a). Programming for users: A bit of psychology. *Comput. People* 30(1, 2), 11–14, 26.

Dwyer, B. (1981b). A user friendly algorithm. *Commun. ACM* 24(9), 556–561.

Ehrenreich, S.L., Porcu, T. (1982). Abbreviations for automated systems: Teaching operators and rules, in: A. Badre, B. Shneiderman (eds.), *Directions in Human–Computer Interaction*, Ablex, Norwood, NJ, pp. 111–136.

Elwart-Keys, M., D. Halonen, M. Horton, R. Kass, P. Scott (1990). User interface requirements for face to face groupware, *Human Factors in Computing Systems: Proceedings of CHI'90*, Association for Computing Machinery, New York, pp. 295–301.

Engel, S.E., R.E. Granda (1975). *Guidelines for man/display interfaces*, Technical Report TR 00.2720, IBM, Poughkeepsie, New York.

Engelke, H., J. Grotrian, C. Scheuing, A. Schmackpfeffer, W. Schwarz, B. Solf, J. Tomann (1985). Integrated manufacturing modeling system. *IBM J. Res. Develop.* 29, 343–355.

Feiner, S., C. Beshers (1990). Worlds within worlds: Metaphors for exploring *n*-dimensional virtual worlds, *Proceedings of the ACM SIGGRAPH Symposium on User Interface Software and Technology*, October 3–5, Snowbird Utah, pp. 76–83.

Fiddy, E., J.G. Bright, R.D. Hurrion (1981). See-why: Interactive simulation on the screen, *Proceedings of the Institute of Mechanical Engineers*, c293/81, pp. 167–172.

Fisher, M.L. (1986). Interactive optimization. *Ann. Oper. Res.* 5, 541–556.

Fisher, M.L., A. Greenfield, R. Jaikumar (1982). VERGIN: A decision support system for vehicle scheduling, Working Paper 82-06-02, Department of Decision Sciences, The Wharton School, University of Pennsylvania, Philadelphia, PA.

Fitter, M., T.R.G. Green (1979). When do diagrams make good computer languages? *Int. J. Man–Mach. Stud.* 11, 235–261.

Flecchia, M.A., R.D. Bergeron (1987). Specifying complex dialogues in algea, *Proceedings of CHI and Graphics Interface '87*, Toronto, Canada.

Foley, J.D. (1987). Interfaces for advanced computing. *Scientific American* 257(4), 127–135.

Foley, J.D., C.F. McMath (1986). Dynamic process visualization. *IEEE Comput. Graph. Appl.* 6(3), 16–25.

Foley, J.D., A. Van Dam (1984). *Fundamentals of Interactive Computer Graphics, 1st edition*, Addison-Wesley, Reading, MA.

Foley, J.D., A. Van Dam, S.K. Feiner, J.F. Hughes (1990). *Computer Graphics: Principles and Practice, 2nd edition*, Addison-Wesley, Reading, MA.

Foley, J.D., V.L. Wallace (1974). The art of man–machine conversation. *Proc. IEEE*, pp. 462–471.

Foley, J.D., V.L. Wallace, P. Chan (1984). The human factors of computer graphics interaction techniques. *IEEE Comput. Graph. Appl.* 4, 13–48.

Fox, E.A. (1991a). Standards and the emergence of digital multimedia systems. *Commun. ACM* 35, 26–29.

Fox, E.A. (1991b). Advances in digital multimedia systems. *IEEE Computer* 24(10), 9–22.

Fourer, R. (1983). Modeling languages versus matrix generators for linear programming. *ACM Trans. Math. Software* 9, 143–183.

Fourer, R., D.M. Gay, B.W. Kernighan (1987). AMPL: A mathematical programming language, Computer Science Technical Report No. 133, AT&T Bell Laboratories, Murray Hill, NJ 07974.

Freeman-Benson, B.N., J. Maloney, A. Borning (1989). An incremental constraint solver. *Commun. ACM* 33(1), 54–63.

Gade, P.A., A.F. Fields, R.E. Maisano, C.F. Marshall, I.N. Alderman (1981). Data entry performance as a function of method and instructional strategy. *Hum. Factors* 23, 199–210.

Gaines, B.R. (1981). The technology of interaction – Dialogue programming rules. *Int. J. of Man-Mach. Stud.* 14, 133–150.

Garman, M. (1970). Solving combinatorial decision problems via interactive computer graphics, with applications to job-shop scheduling, Unpublished PhD dissertation, Carnegie-Mellon University, Pittsburgh, Pennsylvania.

Gaver, W.W. (1989). The SonicFinder: An interface that uses auditory icons. *Hum.–Comput. Interaction* 4(1), 67–94.

Gaver, W.W., R.B. Smith, T. O'Shea (1991). Effective sounds in complex systems: The arkola simulation, *Reaching Through Technology: Human Factors in Computing Systems; ACM SIGCHI '91 Conference Proceedings*, pp. 85–90.

Gay, D.M. (1987). Pictures of Karmarkar's linear programming algorithm, Computer Science Technical Report No. 136, AT&T Bell Laboratories, Murray Hill, NJ 07974.

Geoffrion, A.M. (1976). The purpose of mathematical programming is insight, not numbers. *Interfaces* 7(1), 81–92.

Geoffrion, A.M. (1983). Can MS/OR evolve fast enoguh. *Interfaces* 13(1), 10–25.

Geoffrion, A.M. (1987). Introduction to structured modeling. *Manage. Sci.* 33(5), 547–588.

Geoffrion, A.M. (1989). Indexing in modeling languages for mathematical programming, Technical Report, Anderson Graduate School of Management, UCLA, Los Angeles, CA.

Glinert, E.P. (1990). *Visual Programming Environments, Applications and Issues*, IEEE Computer Soc. Press, Silver Spring, MD.

Glinert, E.P., S.L. Tanimoto (1984). Pict: An interactive graphical programming environment. *IEEE Computer* 17(11), 7–25.

Glover, F., H. Greenberg (1988). Netforms provide powerful tools for enhancing the operations of expert systems, Center for Applied Artifical Intelligence, Technical Report, University of Colorado, Boulder, CO.

Godin, V. (1978). Interactive scheduling – Historical survey and state of the art. *AIIE Trans.* 10, 331–337.

Gould, L., W. Finzer (1984). Programming by rehearsal, Tech. Report SCL-84-1, Xerox Corporation, Palo Alto Research Center.

Graf, M. (1990). Visual programming and visual languages: Lessons learned in the trenches, in: E. Glinert (ed.), *Visual Programming Environments: Applciations and Issues*, IEEE Press, New York, pp. 452–454.

Grafton, R.B., T. Ichikawa (1985). Visual programming. *IEEE Computer* 18(8), 6–9.

Grant, J.W., S.A. Weiner (1986). Factors to consider in choosing a graphically animated simulation system. *Ind. Eng. (NY)* 18, 37ff.

Gray, P., L. Olfman (1989). The user interface in group decision support systems. *Decision Support Systems* 5, 119–137.

Green, M. (1983). Report on dialogue specification tools, in: G.E. Pfaff (ed.), *User Interface Management Systems*, Springer, Berlin, pp. 9–20.

Green, M. (1985). The University of Alberta user interface management system. *Comput. Graphics* 19(3), 205–213.

Green, M. (1986). A survey of three dialogue models. *ACM Trans. Graph.* 5(3), 244–275.

Greenberg, H.J. (1987). ANALYZE: A computer-assisted analysis system for linear programming models. *OR Letters* 6(5), 249–259.

Greenberg, H.J. (1988). *Intelligent User Interfaces for Mathematical Programming*, Unpublished monograph, Mathematics Department, University of Colorado, Denver, CO.

Greenberg, H.J., F.H. Murphy (1991). Views of mathematical programming models and their instances, Technical Report, University of Colorado at Denver, Denver, CO.

Greeno, J.G. (1973). The structure of memory and the process of solving problems, in: R. Solso (ed.), *Contemporary Issues in Cognitive Psychology: The Loyala Symposium*, Academic Press, London.

Grosz, B.J., K.S. Jones, B.L. Webber (1986). *Readings in Natural Language Processing*, Morgan Kaufmann, Los Altos, CA.

Harris, L.R. (1983). The advantage of natural language programming, in: M.E. Sime, M.J. Coombs (eds.), *Designing for Human–Computer Communication*, Academic Press, New York, pp. 73–86.

Hayes, F., N. Baran (1989). A guide to GUIs. *Byte* 14, 250ff.

Hayes, P.J., P.A. Szekely, R.A. Lerner (1985). Design alternatives for user interface management systems based on experience with COUSIN, *Proceedings SIGCHI'85: Human Factors in Computing Systems*, San Francisco, CA, April 14–18, pp. 169–175.

Henderson, D.A. (1986). The Trillium user interface design environment, *ACM SIGCHI'86 Conference Proceedings, Human Factors in Computing Systems*, pp. 221–227.

Hewett, T.T. (1986). The role of iterative evaluation, in: M. Harrison, A. Monk (eds.), *Designing Systems for Usability*, Cambridge University Press, Cambridge, pp. 196–214.

Hill, I.D. (1983). Natural language versus computer language, in: M.E. Sime, M.J. Coombs (eds.), *Designing for Human–Computer Communication*, Academic Press, New York, pp. 55–72.

Hill, R.D. (1986). Supporting concurrency, communications and synchronization in human–computer interaction – The Sassafras user interface management systems, *ACM Trans. Graph.* 5(3), 179–210.

Hill, R.D. (1990). A 2-D graphics system for multi-user interactive graphics based on objects and constraints, in: E. Blake, P. Wisskirchen (eds.), *Advances in Object Oriented Graphics*, Springer, Berlin.

Hix, D. (1990). Generations of user-interface management systems. *IEEE Software* 7(5), 77–87.

Holsapple, C.W., S. Park, A.B. Whinston (1989). Generating structure editor interfaces for OR procedures, Technical report, Center for Robotics and Manufacturing Systems, University of Kentucky, Lexington, KY.

Holsapple, C.W., S. Park, A.B. Whinston (1991). Framework for DSS interface development, Technical report, Center for Robotics and Manufacturing Systems, University of Kentucky, Lexington, KY.

Hurrion, R.D. (1978). An investigation of visual interactive simulation methods using the job-shop scheduling problem. *J. Oper. Res. Soc. Am.* 29, 1085–1093.

Hurrion, R.D. (1980). Visual interactive (computer) solutions for the traveling salesman problem. *J. Oper. Res. Soc. Am.* 31, 537–539.

Hurrion, R.D. (1986), Visual interactive modeling. *European J. Oper. Res.* 23, 281–287.

Hurrion, R.D., R.J.R. Secker (1978). Visual interactive simulation: An aid to decision making. *Omega* 6, 419–426.

Hutchins, E.L., J.D. Hollan, D.A. Norman (1986). Direct manipulation interfaces, in: D.A. Norman, S.W. Draper (eds.), *User Centered System Design: New Perspectives on Human–Computer Interaction*, Lawrence Erlbaum, Hillsdale, NJ, pp. 87–124.

Ichikawa, T., M. Hirakawa (1987). Visual programming – Toward realization of user-friendly programming environments, *Proceedings 2nd Fall Joint Computer Conference*, pp. 129–137.

Insight International, Ltd. (1988). 21 Oxford Street, Woodstock, OX7 1TH, United Kingdom.

ISO (1985a). Graphical kernal system (GKS) functional description, ISO 7942 and ANS X3.124-1985, ANSI, 1430 Broadway, New York, NY 10018.

ISO (1985b). Graphical kernal system for three dimensions (GKS-3D), ISO DP 8805, ANSI, 1430 Broadway, New York, NY 10018.

ISTEL Visual Interactive Systems, Ltd. (1988). Highfield House, Headless Cross Drive, Redditch, Worcs., United Kingdom.

Jack, W. (1985). An interactive graphical approach to linear financial models. *J. Oper. Res. Soc. Am.* 36(5), 367–382.

Jackson, P.L., J.A. Muckstadt, C.V. Jones (1989). COSMOS: A framework for a computer-aided logistics system. *J. Mfg. Oper. Manage.* 2, 222–248.

Jacob, R.J.K. (1983). Executable specifications for a human–computer interface, *Proceedings of the CHI'83 Human Factors in Computing Systems* (Boston, MA), ACM, New York, pp. 28–34.

Jarvenpaa, S.L., G.W. Dickson (1988). Graphics and managerial decision making: Research based guidelines. *Commun. ACM* 31(6), 764–774.

Jarvis, J. (1983). IRG – Interactive route generator: A narrative description, International Dairy Federation, Computerized Bulk Milk Collection Systems, Workshop Proceedings, Toronto.

Jones, C.V. (1985). Graph based models, Unpublished PhD thesis, Cornell University, Ithaca, New York, 14853.

Jones, C.V. (1988a). The three-dimensional Gantt chart. *Oper. Res.* 36(6), 891–903.

Jones, C.V. (1988b). Animated sensitivity analysis of production planning, *Proceedings of the 1988 International Conference on Computer Integrated Manufacturing*, IEEE, Los Angeles, CA, pp. 171–180.

Jones, C.V. (1989a). The stability of algorithms for the Euclidean travelling salesman problem, Technical Report 89-07-02, Department of Decision Sciences, The Wharton School, The University of Pennsylvania, Philadelphia, PA.

Jones, C.V. (1989b). Anima-LP: A system for illustrating the behavior of linear programming problems, Technical Report 89-08-04, Department of Decision Sciences, The Wharton School, The University of Pennsylvania, Philadelphia, PA.

Jones, C.V. (1990). An introduction to graph-based modeling systems, Part I: Overview. *ORSA J. Computing* 2(2), 136–151.

Jones, C.V. (1991a). An introduction to graph-based modeling systems, Part II: Graph-grammars and the implementation. *ORSA J. Computing* 3(3), 180–207.

Jones, C.V. (1991b). An integrated modeling environment based on attributed graphs and graph-grammars, Tech. Report, Faculty of Business Administration, Simon Fraser University, Burnaby, BC.

Jones, C.V. (1991c). Attributed graphs, graph-grammars, and structured modeling, Tech. Report, Faculty of Business Administration, Simon Fraser University, Burnaby, BC.

Jones, C.V. (1992). Animated sensitivity analysis, Presented at ORSA Computer Science Technical Section Conference, Williamsburg, VA.

Jones, C.V., R. Krishnan (1990). A visual, syntax-directed environment for automated model development, Technical Report, Faculty of Business Administration, Simon Fraser University, Burnaby, BC, Canada.

Jones, C.V., W.L. Maxwell (1986). A system for scheduling with interactive computer graphics. *IIE Trans.* 18, 298–303.

Kamran, A., M.B. Feldman (1983). Graphics programming independent of interaction techniques and styles. *Comput. Graph.* 17(1), 58–66.

Kasik, D.J. (1982). A user interface management system. *Comput. Graph.* 16(3), 99–106.

Kaufman, A., R. Bakalash (1988). Memory and processing architecture for 3D voxel-based imagery. *IEEE Comput. Graph. Appl.* 8(6), 10–23.

Kaufman, A., M.Z. Hanani (1981). Converting a batch simulation program to an interactive program with graphics. *Simulation* 37, 125–131.

Keen, P.G.W., M.S. Scott Morton (1978). *Decision Support Systems: An Organizational Perspective*, Addison-Wesley, Reading, MA.

Kendrick, D.A. (1990). Parallel model representations. *Expert Systems with Applications* 1, 383–389.

Kernighan, B.W., R. Pike (1984). *The UNIX Programming Environment*, Prentice-Hall, Englewood Cliffs, NJ.

Kieras, D., P.G. Polson (1985). An approach to the formal analysis of user complexity. *Int. J. Man–Mach. Stud.* 22, 365–394.

Kimbrough, S.O., H. Bhargava, M. Bieber (1988). Oona, Max and the WYWWYI Principle: Generalized hypertext and model management in a symbolic programming environment, Tech. Report 88-03-09, Department of Decision Sciences, The Wharton School, University of Pennsylvania, Philadelphia, PA, 19104.

Kimbrough, S.O., C.W. Pritchett, M.P. Bieber, H.K. Bhargava (1990a). The coast guards KSS Project. *Interfaces* 20(6), 5–16.

Kimbrough, S.O., C.W. Pritchett, M.P. Bieber, H.K. Bhargava (1990b). An overview of the coast guards KSS project: DSS concepts and technology, *Transactions of DSS-90: Information Technology for Executives and Managers, Tenth International Conference on Decision Support Systems*, Cambridge, May, 1990, pp. 63–77.

Kirkpatrick, P., P.C. Bell (1989). Visual interactive modelling in industry: Results from a survey of visual interactive model builders. *Interfaces* 19(5), 71–79.

Korphage, R. (ed.) (1990). *Visual Programming and Visual Languages*, Plenum Press, New York.

Lamberski, R.J. (1980). A comprehensive and critical review of the methodology and findings in color investigations, *Proc. Annual Convention of the Association for Educational Communications and Technology*, Denver, CO, ERIC Doc. No. ED-194063/IR008916, pp. 338–379.

Lapalme, G., M. Cormier, C. Mallette (1983). A colour graphic system for interactive routing, Paper Presented at the ORSA/TIMS Joint National Meeting, Orlando.

Ledgard, H., J.A. Whiteside, A. Singer, W. Seymour (1980). *Commun. ACM* 23(10), 556–563.

Lee, J.S. (1986). A model base for identifying mathematical programming structures, Working paper 86-06-05, The Wharton School, University of Pennsylvania, Philadelphia, PA.

Le Gall, D. (1991). MPEG: A video compression standard for multimedia applications. *Commun. ACM* 34(4), 46–58.

Leler, W. (1988). *Constraint Programming Languages*, Addison-Wesley, Reading, MA.

Lemberski, M.R., U.H. Chi (1984). 'Decision simulators' speed implementation and improve operations. *Interfaces* 14(4), 1–15.

Liang, T.P. (1986). A graph-based approach to model management, *Proceedings of the Seventh International Conference on Information Systems*, San Diego, pp. 136–151.

Liang, T.P., C.V. Jones (1987). Meta-design considerations in developing model management systems. *Decision Sciences* 19(1), 72–92.

Liebelt, L.S., J.E. McDonald, J.D. Stone, J. Karat (1982). The effect of organization on learning menu access, *Proc. Human Factors Society*, 26th Annual Meeting, pp. 546–550.

Liebman, J., L. Lasdon, L. Schrage, A. Warren (1986). *Modeling and Optimization with GINO*, The Scientific Press, Redwood City, CA.

Lindsay, P., D.A. Norman (1977). *Human Information Processing*, Academic Press, New York.

Liou, M. (1991). Overview of the px64 kbit/s video coding standard. *Commun. ACM* 34(4), 59–63.

Lippman, A. (1991). Feature sets for interactive images. *Commun. ACM* 34(4), 92–102.

Lodding, K.N. (1983). Iconic interfacing. *IEEE Comput. Graph. Appl.* 3(2), 11–20.

Lotus Development (1991). Improv, Cambridge, Massachusetts.

Loucks, D.P., M.R. Taylor, P.N. French (1985). Interactive data management for resource planning and analysis. *Water Resources Research* 21(2), 131–142.

Ma, P., F.H. Murphy, E.A. Stohr (1987). Computer-assisted formulation of linear programs. *IMA J. Math. Manage.* 1(3), 147–162.

Ma, P., F.H. Murphy, E.A. Stohr (1989). A graphics interface for linear programming. *Commun. ACM* 32(8), 996–1012.

Mackinlay, J. (1986). Automating the design of graphical presentations of relational information. *ACM Trans. Graph.* 5(2), 110–141.

Mackinlay, J., G.G. Robertson, S.K. Card (1991). The perspective wall: Detail and context smoothly integrated, *Human Factors in Computing Systems: ACM SIGGCHI' 1991 Proceedings*, pp. 177–180.

Maloney, J., A. Borning, B. Freeman-Benson (1989). Constraint technology for user-interface construction in ThingLab II, *Proceedings of the 1989 ACM Conference on Object-Oriented Programming Systems, Languages and Applications*, New Orleans, Oct. 1989, pp. 381–388.

Marcus, A. (1986). Computer graphics today, tutorial 14: The ten commandments of color. *Comput. Graph. Today* 3(10), 7ff.

Marcus, A., A. Van Dam (1991). User-interface developments for the nineties. *IEEE Computer* 24(9), 49–57.

Maulsby, D.L., I.H. Witten, K.A. Kittlitz (1989). Metamouse: Specifying graphical procedures by example. *Comput. Graphics* 23(3), 127–136.

McCormick, B.H., T.A. DeFanti, M.D. Brown (1987). Visualization in scientific computing. *Comput. Graphics* 21(6), entire issue.

McDonald, J.E., J.D. Stone, L.S. Liebelt (1983). Searching for items in menus: The effects of organization and type of target, *Proc. Human Factors Society*, 27th Annual Meeting, pp. 834–837.

Meyers, W. (1985). Computer graphics: The next 20 years. *IEEE Comput. Graph. Appl.* 5(8), 69–76.

Michaelis, P.R., R.H. Wiggins (1982). A human factors engineer's introduction to speech synthesizers, in: A. Badre, B. Shneiderman (eds.), *Human/Computer Interaction*, Ablex, Norwood, NJ.

Miller, G.A. (1956). The magic number seven, plus or minus two: Some limits on our capacity for processing information. *Psychol. Rev.* 63, 81–97.

Miller, R.B. (1968). Response time in man–computer conversational transactions, *Proceedings Spring Joint Computer Conference 1968* 33, AFIPS Press, Montvale, NJ, pp. 267–277.

Ming, O., D.V. Beard, F.P. Brooks Jr. (1989). Force display performs better than visual display in a simple 6-D docking task, *Proceedings of the IEEE Robotics and Automation Conference*, May, 1989, pp. 1–5.

Mitchell, K. (1985). How much vehicle routing can you do on a microcomputer?, Presented at CORS/SCRO National Conference, Halifax.

Monma, C.L., D.F. Shallcross (1988). A PC-based interactive network design system for fiber optic communication networks, Technical Report, Bell Communications Research, Morristown, NJ.

Monsell, S. (1981). Representation, processes, memory mechanisms: The basic components of cognition. *J. Am. Soc. Inf. Sci.* 32, 378–390.

Montreuil, B. (1982). Interactive optimization based facilities layout, Unpublished PhD Dissertation, Georgia Institute of Technology, Atlanta, Georgia.

Moran, T.P., R.J. Anderson (1990). The workaday world as a paradigm for CSCW design, *Proceedings of the Conference on Computer-Supported Cooperative Work*, Association for Computing Machinery, New York, pp. 381–393.

Moray, N. (1967). Where is capacity limited? A survey and a model. *Acta Psychologica* 27, 84–92.

Murphy, F.H., E.A. Stohr (1986). An intelligent system for formulating linear programs. *Decision Support Systems* 2, 39–47.

Myers, B.A. (1986). Visual programming, programming by example and program visualization; A taxonomy, *Proceedings SIGCHI'86: Human Factors in Computing Systems*, Boston, MA, April, pp. 13–17.

Myers, B.A. (1988). *Creating User Interfaces by Demonstration*, Academic Press, Boston, MA.

Myers, B.A. (1989). User interface tools: Introduction and survey. *IEEE Software* 6(1), 15–23.

Myers, B.A., W. Buxton (1986). Creating highly-interactive and graphical user interfaces by demonstration, *Comput. Graphics* 20(4), 249–257.

Myers, B.A., D.A. Guise, R.B. Dannenberg, B. Vander Zanden, D.S. Kosbie, E. Pervin, A. Mickish, P. Marchal (1990). Garnet: Comprehensive support for graphical, highly interactive user interfaces. *IEEE Computer* 23(11), 71–85.

Nagl, M. (1987). A software development environment based on graph technology, in: H. Ehrig, M. Nagl, G. Rozenberg, A. Rosenfeld (eds.), *Graph Grammars and their Application to Computer Science*, Springer, Berlin.

Narasimhalu, A.D., S. Christodoulakis (1991). Multimedia information systems: The unfolding of a reality. *IEEE Computer* 24(10), 6–8.

Newcomb, S.R., N.A. Kipp, V.T. Newcomb (1991). The 'HyTime' hypermedia/time-based document structuring language. *Commun. ACM* 34(11), 52–66.

Newell, A. (1973). Production systems: Models of control structures, in: W.G. Chase (ed.), *Visual Information Processing*, Academic Press, New York, pp. 283–308.

Newell, A., H.A. Simon (1972). *Human Problem Solving*, Prentice-Hall, Englewood Cliffs, NJ.

Newman, W.M. (1968a). A system for interactive graphical programming. *Proceedings of the Spring Joint Computer Conference, Atlantic City, NJ*, Thompson, Washington, DC, 1968, pp. 47–54.

Newman, W.M. (1968b). A graphical technique for numerical input. *Computing J.* 11, 63–64.

Newman, W.M., R.F. Sproull (1979). *Principles of Interactive Computer Graphics*, McGraw-Hill, New York.

Nielson, G.M., B. Shriver, L.J. Rosenblum (1990). *Visualization in Scientific Computing*, IEEE Computer Soc. Press, Silver Spring, MD.

Norman, D.A. (1983). Design rules based on analysis of human error. *Commun. ACM* 23(10), 556–563.

Norman, D.A. (1984). Stages and levels in human-machine interaction. *Int. J. Man–Mach. Stud.* 21, 365–375.

Nunamaker, J.F., A.R. Dennis, J.S. Valacich, D.R. Vogel, J.F. George (1991). Electronic meeting systems to support group work. *Commun. ACM* 34(7), 40–61.

Olsen, D.R. (1986). MIKE: The menu interaction kontrol environment, *ACM Trans. Graph.* 5(4), 318–344.

Olsen Jr., D.R., E.P. Dempsey (1983). SYNGRAPH: A graphical user interface generator. *Comput. Graphics* 17(3), 43–50.

Olsen, D.R., D. Kasik, J. Rhyne, J. Thomas, (1987). ACM SIGGRAPH workshop on software tools for user interface management. *Comput. Graphics* 21(2), 71–72.

Olson, A.J., J.A. Tainer, E.D. Getzoff (1988). Computer graphics in the study of macromolecular interactions, Research Institute of Scripps Clinic, Molecular Biology Department, La Jolla, CA 92037.

Open Software Foundation (1990). *OSF Motif Style Guide Revision 1.0*, Open Software Foundation, Cambridge, MA.

Orlikowski, W., V. Dhar (1986). Imposing structure on linear programming problems: An empirical analysis of expert and novice models, *Proceedings of the National Conference on Artificial Intelligence*, Philadelphia, PA (August).

Pagageorgiou, J.C. (1983). Devision making in the year 2000. *Interfaces* 13(2), 77–86.

Parnas, D.L. (1969). On the use of transition diagrams in the design of a user interface for an interactive computer system, *Proceedings of the 14th National ACM Conference*, San Francisco, CA, Aug. 26–28, ACM, New York, pp. 379–385.

Patterson, J.F., R.D. Hill, S.L. Rohali (1990). Rendezvous: An architecure for synchronous multi-user applications, *Proceedings of the Conference on Computer-Supported Cooperative Work*, Association for Computing Machinery, New York, pp. 317–328.

Pausch, R. (1991). Virtual reality on five dollars a day. *Human Factors in Computing Systems. SIGCHI Proceedings*, New Orleans, LA, pp. 265–270.

Pegden, C.D. (1985). *Introduction to SIMAN*, Systems Modeling Corporation, Calder Square, P.O. Box 10074, State College, Pennsylvania.

Pegden, L.A., T.I. Miles, G.A. Diaz (1985). Graphical interpretation of output illustrated by a SIMAN manufacturing simulation model, Gantz, Blais, Soloman (eds.), *Proceedings of the 1985 Winter Simulation Conference*, The Society for Computer Simulation, pp. 244–251.

Petzold, C. (1988). *Programming Windows*, Microsoft Press, Redmond, Washington, DC.

Pfaff, G.E. (ed.) (1985). *User Interface Management Systems*, Springer, Berlin.

Pinsonnault, A., K.L. Kraemer (1989). The impact of technological support on groups: An assessment of the empirical research. *Decision Support Systems* 5(2), 197–216.

Porter, M. (1980). *Competitive Strategy: Techniques for Analyzing Industries and Competitors*, Free Press, New York.

Rabb, F., E. Blood, R. Steiner, H. Jones (1979). Magnetic position and orientation tracking system. *IEEE Trans. Aerospace Electron. Systems* 15(5), 709–718.

Rao, K., P. Yip (1990). *Discrete Cosine Transform – Algorithms, Advantages, Applications*, Academic Press, London.

Rathnam, S., M.V. Mannino (1991). User interface management systems: Themes and variations – A review of the literature, *Proceedings of the 24th Annual Hawaii International Conference on the System Sciences*, pp. 489–498.

Reisner, P. (1981). Formal grammar and human factors design of an interactive graphics system. *IEEE Trans. Software Engrg.* SE-7(2), 229–240.

Reps, T.W. (1986). *Generating Language-Based Environments*, MIT Press, Cambridge, MA.

Reps, T., T. Teitelbaum (1981). The Cornell program synthesizer: A syntax-directed programming environment. *Commun. ACM* 24(9), 563–573.

Rich, E. (1984). Natural language interfaces. *IEEE Computer* 7, 39–47.

Rosenthal, D.S.H., A. Yen (1983). User interface models summary, in: J.J. Thomas, G. Hamlin (eds.), *Graphical Input Interaction Technique Workshop Summary*, Comput. Graphics 17(1), pp. 16–20.

Roy, A., L.S. Lasdon, J. Lordeman (1986). Extending planning languages to include optimization capabilities. *Manage. Sci.* 32(3), 360–373.

Sabella, P. (1988). A rendering algorithm for visualizing 3D scalar fields. *Comput. Graphics* 22(4), 51–58.

Savelsbergh, M.W.P. (1988). *Computer Aided Routing*, Centrum voor Wiskunde en Informatica, Amsterdam.

Scheifler, R.W., J. Gettys (1987). The X Window System, *ACM Trans. Graph.* 5(2), 79–109.

Schmucker, K.J. (1986). MacApp: An application framework. *Byte* 11, 189–193.

Schrage, L. (1984). *Linear, Integer and Quadratic Programming with LINDO*, The Scientific Press, Palo Alto, CA.

Schrage, L. (1986). *VINO: Visual Interactive Optimizer*, The Scientific Press, Palo Alto, CA.

Schulert A.J., G.T. Rogers, J.A. Hamilton (1985). ADM – A dialogue manager, *Proceedings of the CHI'85 Human Factors in Computer Systems, San Francisco, California*, ACM, New York, pp. 177–183.

Scott Morton, M.S. (1971). *Management Decision Systems: Support for Decision Making*, Harvard University Graduate School of Business Administration, Cambridge, MA.

Senn, J.A. (1984). *Analysis and Design of Information Systems*, McGraw-Hill, Englewood Cliffs, NJ.

Shepard, S.W. (1983). DISPATCH: Downsized interactive system for planning assignments to trucks using combinational heuristics Exxon, Corporation CCS Department, P.O. Box 153, Florham Park, NJ.

Shneiderman, B. (1980). *Software Psychology: Human Factors in Computer and Information Systems*, Little, Brown and Col, Boston, MA.

Shneiderman, B. (1983). Direct manipulation: A step beyond programming languages. *IEEE Computer* 16(8), 57–69.

Shneiderman, B. (1984). Correct, complete operations and other principles of interaction, in: G. Salvendy (ed.), *Human-Computer Interaction*, Elsevier, Amsterdam, pp. 135–146.

Shneiderman, B. (1987). *Designing the User Interface: Strategies for Effective Human-Computer Interaction*, Addison-Wesley, Reading, MA.

Shu, N.C. (1988). *Visual Programming*, Van Nostrand Reinhold, New York.

Silicon Beach Software, SuperCard, San Diego, CA.

Simon, H.A. (1957). A behavioral model of rational choice, in: H.A. Simon (ed.), *Models of Man*, Wiley, New York, pp. 241–260.

Simon, H.A. (1960). *The New Science of Management Decision*, Harper and Row, New York.

Simon, H.A. (1974). How big is a chunk? *Science* 183, 482–488.

Simpson, C.A., M.E. McCauley, E.F. Roland, J.C. Ruth, B.H. Williges (1985). System design for speech recognition and generation. *Hum. Factors* 27(2), 115–141.

Smethers–Barnes, Inc. (1989). *Prototyper V2.0*, 520 SW Harrison Ste 435, Portland, OR.

Smith, S.L., A.F. Aucella, (1983). *Design Guidelines for the User Interface for Computer-Based Information Systems*, The MITRE Corporation, Bedford MA 01730, Electronic Systems Division (March 1983), 279 pp. Available from the National Technical Information Service, Springfield, MA.

Smith, D.C., C. Irby, R. Kimball, B. Verplank, E. Harslem (1983). Designing the star user interface, in: P. Degano, E. Sandwell (eds.), *Integrated Interactive Computing Systems*, North-Holland, Amsterdam, pp. 297–313.

Snowdon, J.L., J.C. Ammons (1988). A survey of queueing network packages for the analysis of manufacturing systems. *Manuf. Rev.* 1(1), 14–25.

Southerton, A. (1989). *Programmer's Guide to Presentation Manager*, Addison-Wesley, Reading, MA.

Sprague Jr., R.H., E.D. Carlson (1982). *Building Effective Decision Support Systems*, Prentice-Hall, Englewood Cliffs, NJ.

Sproull, R.F. (1986). Frame-buffer display architectures, in: *Annual Review of Computer Science*, Annual Reviews, Inc., pp. 19–46.

Standridge, C.R. (1985). Performing simulation projects with the extended simulation system (TESS). *Simulation* 45(6), 283–291.

Stefik, M., D.G. Bobrow, G. Foster, S. Lanning, D. Tatar (1987). WYSIWIS revised: Early experiences with multiuser interfaces. *ACM Trans. Office Inf. Syst.* 5(2), 147–167.

Stefik, M., G. Foster, D.G. Bobrow, K. Kahn, S. Lanning, L. Suchman (1988). Beyond the chalkboard: Computer supported collaboration and problem solving in meetings, in: I. Greif (ed.), *Computer-Supported Cooperative Work: A Book of Readings*, Morgan Kaufmann, Los Altos, CA, pp. 335–366.

Sun Microsystems, Inc. (1989). *Open Look Graphical User Interface Functional Specification*, Addison-Wesley, Reading, MA.

Sutherland, I.E. (1963). *SKETCHPAD: A Man–Machine Graphical Communication System*, SJCC Spartan Books, Baltimore, MD, p. 329.

Sutherland, I.E. (1965). The ultimate display. *Information Processing 1965, Proc. IFIP Congress 65*, pp. 506–508.

Systems Modeling Corporation (1988). *Cinema User's Manual*, Systems Modeling Corporation, The Park Building, 504 Beaver St, Sewickley, PA 15143.

Tanner, P.P., W. Buxton (1985). Some issues in future user interface management system (UIMS) development, in: G. Pfaff (ed.), *User Interface Management Systems*, Springer, Berlin, pp. 67–79.

Thacker, C.P., E.M. McCreight, B.W. Lampson, R.F. Sproull, D.R. Boggs (1982). Alto: A personal computer, in: D. Siewiorek, C. Bell, A. Newell (eds.), *Computer Structures: Principles and Examples*, McGraw-Hill, New York.

Thomas, J.C., J.M. Carroll (1979). The psychological study of design. *Design Studies* 1, 5–11.

Tufte, E.R. (1983). *The Visual Display of Quantitative Information*, Graphics Press, Cheshire, CT.

Tufte, E.R. (1990). *Envisioning Information*, Graphics Press, Cheshire, CT.

Upson, C., M. Keeler (1988). V-buffer: Visible volume rendering. *Comput. Graphics* 22(4), 59–64.

Van Nunen, J., J. Benders (1982). A decision support system for location and allocation problems within a brewery, in: *OR Processings*, Springer, pp. 96–105.

Vazsonyi, A. (1982). Decision support systems, computer literacy, and electronic models. *Interfaces* 12(1), 74–78.

Vecchiet, K.S. (1987). The computer graphics interface: The latest developments. *Comput. Graphics* 21(2), 172–174.

Wagner, G.R. (1981). Decision support systems: The real substance. *Interfaces* 14(2), 77–86.

Wallace, G.K. (1991). The JPEG still picture compression standard. *Commun. ACM* 24(4), 30–44.

Wallace, V.L. (1976). The semantics of graphic input devices, *Proc. Siggraph/Sigplan Symp. Graphics Languages*, pp. 61–65.

Wang Laboratories (1990). Freestyle, Cambridge, MA.

Wasserman, A. (1985). Extending state transition diagrams for the specification of human-computer interaction. *IEEE Trans. Software Engrg.* 11(8), 699–713.

Webster, B.F. (1989). *The NeXT Book*, Addison-Wesley, Reading, MA.

Welch, J.S. (1987). PAM – A practitioner's approach to modeling. *Manage. Sci.* 33(5), 610–625.

White, G.M. (1990). Natural language understanding and speech recognition. *Commun. ACM* 33(8), 72–82.

Winograd, T. (1980). What does it mean to understand language? *Cognitive Sci.* 4, 209–241.

Wolfram, S. (1991). *Mathematica, a System for Doing Mathematics by Computer*, Addison-Wesley, Reading, MA.

Wong, P.C.S., E.R. Reid (1982). Flair – User interface dialog design tool. *Comput. Graphics* 16(3), 87–98.

Wynne, B.E. (1984). A domination sequence – MS/OR; DSS; and the fifth generation. *Interfaces* 14(3), 51–58.

Yan, J.K. (1985). Advances in computer-generated imagery for flight simulation. *IEEE Comput. Graph. Appl.* 5(8), 37–51.

Yeung, E. (1980). Pattern recognition by audio representation of multivariate analytical data. *Anal. Chem.* 52(7), 1120–1123.

Zimmerman, T., J. Lanier, C. Blanchard, S. Bryson, Y. Harvill (1987). A hand gesture input device, *Proceedings of ACM SIGCHI and GI 1987*, Toronto, Ontario, April 5–7, 1987, pp. 189–192.

Zloof, M. (1977). Query by example: A data base language. *IBM Syst. J.* 16(4), 324–343.

Zloof, M. (1982). Office-by-example: A business language that unifies data and word processing and electronic mail. *IBM Syst. J.* 31(3), 272–304.

Zloof, M.M. (1983). The query-by-example concept for user-oriented business systems, in: M.E. Sime, M.J. Coombs (eds.), *Designing for Human–Computer Communication*, Academic Press, New York, pp. 285–309.

Surveys on user interfaces

Baecker, R.M., W.A.S. Buxton (eds.) (1987). *Readings In Human–Computer Interaction*, Morgan Kaufmann, Los Altos, CA.

Bibliography of software tools for user interface development (1987). *Comput. Graphics* 21(2), 145–147.

Card, S., T.P. Moran, A. Newell (1983). *The Psychology of Human–Computer Interaction*, Lawrence Erlbaum, London.

Foley, J.D., A. Van Dam, S.K. Feiner, J.F. Hughes (1990). *Computer Graphics: Principles and Practice, 2nd edition*, Addison-Wesley, Reading, MA.

Helander, M. (ed.) (1988). *Handbook of Human–Computer Interaction*, North-Holland, Amsterdam.

Laurel, B. (ed.) (1990). *The Art of Human–Computer Interface Design*, Addison-Wesley, Reading MA.

Marcus, A. (1991). *Graphic Design for Electronic Documents and User Interface Design*, Addison-Wesley, Reading, MA.

Martin, J. (1973). *Design of Man–Computer Dialogues*, Prentice-Hall, Englewood Cliffs, NJ.

Newman, W.M., R.F. Sproull (1979). *Principles of Interactive Computer Graphics*, McGraw-Hill, New York.

Norman, D.A., S.W. Draper (1986). *User Centered System Design: New Perspectives on Human–Computer Interaction*, Lawrence Erlbaum, Hillsdale, NJ.

Shneiderman, B. (1987). *Designing the User Interface: Strategies for Effective Human–Computer Interaction*, Addison-Wesley, Reading, MA.

Subject Index

Handbooks in Operations Research and Management Science
Contents of the Previous Volumes

Printed and bound by CPI Group (UK) Ltd, Croydon, CR0 4YY
08/05/2025
01865023-0001